Date Due

THE ONTARIO HISTORICAL STUDIES SERIES

The Ontario Historical Studies Series is a comprehensive history of Ontario from 1791 to the present, which will include several biographies of former premiers, numerous volumes on the economic, social, political, and cultural development of the province, and a general history incorporating the insights and conclusions of the other works in the series. The purpose of the series is to enable general readers and scholars to understand better the distinctive features of Ontario as one of the principal regions within Canada.

The Biographies of the Premiers

J.M.S. Careless (ed.), THE PRE-CONFEDERATION PREMIERS
A. Margaret Evans, SIR OLIVER MOWAT (Premier, 1872-1896)
Robert J.D. Page, SIR GEORGE W. ROSS (Premier, 1899-1905)
Charles M. Humphries, SIR JAMES P. WHITNEY (Premier, 1905-1914)
Charles M. Johnston, HON. E.C. DRURY (Premier, 1919-1923)
Peter N. Oliver, HON. G. HOWARD FERGUSON (Premier, 1923-1930)
John T. Saywell, HON. MITCHELL F. HEPBURN (Premier, 1934-1942)
J.L. Granatstein, HON. GEORGE A. DREW (Premier, 1943-1948)
Roger Graham, HON. LESLIE M. FROST (Premier, 1949-1961)
A.K. McDougall, HON. JOHN P. ROBARTS (Premier, 1961-1971)

PETER OLIVER

G. Howard Ferguson:
Ontario Tory

Published by University of Toronto Press
Toronto and Buffalo
for The Ontario Historical Studies Series

Canadian Cataloguing in Publication Data

Oliver, Peter N., 1939-
  G. Howard Ferguson

  (Ontario historical studies series ISSN 0380-9188)

  Bibliography: p.
  Includes index.
  ISBN 0-8020-3346-6

  1. Ferguson, George Howard, 1870-1946. 2. Ontario —
Politics and government — 1923-1943.* 3. Prime
ministers — Ontario — Biography. I. Title.
II. Series.

FC3074.1.F47045   971.3'03'0924   C77-001173-X
F1058.F47045

This book has been published during the
Sesquicentennial year of the University of Toronto

For Heather

Contents

The Ontario Historical Studies Series

The Ontario Historical Studies Series originated with the suggestion some years ago by Floyd S. Chalmers that there should be biographies of the recently retired Premier Leslie M. Frost and of some of his predecessors in office. The suggestion was approved with enthusiasm by the then Premier, John P. Robarts, his deputy minister, J.K. Reynolds, and the Minister of Education, William G. Davis, and planning for the series was soon under way.

It shortly became apparent that very little work had been done on the history of Ontario. Ontario has many fine historians, but much of their work has been focused on national themes, despite the fact that the locus of many of the important developments in the history of Canada – as recent events remind us – was, and is, in the provinces. While other provinces have recognized this reality and have recorded their histories in permanent form, Ontario is singularly lacking in definitive works about its own distinctive history.

Thus, when the Ontario Historical Studies Series was established by Order-in-Council on 14 April 1971, the Board of Trustees was instructed not only to produce authoritative and readable biographies of Ontario premiers but also 'to ensure that a comprehensive program of research and writing in Ontario history is carried out.'

From the outset the Board has included both professional historians and interested and knowledgeable citizens. The present members are: Margaret Angus, Kingston; J.M.S. Careless, Toronto; Floyd S. Chalmers, Toronto; R.E.G. Davis, Toronto; D.F. McOuat, Toronto; Jacqueline Neatby, Ottawa; J. Keith Reynolds, Toronto; John F. Stephenson, Thunder Bay; and J.J. Talman, London. E.E. Stewart and Raymond Labarge served as valued members of the Board in its formative period. The combination of varied interests and skills of Board members has proven useful. A consensus was soon reached on the need for research in neglected areas of Ontario history and for scholarly and well-written works that would be of interest and value to the people of Ontario. We trust our work will satisfy these criteria.

After much careful deliberation the Board settled on six major areas in which to pursue its objectives: biographies of premiers; a bibliography; a historical atlas; a group of theme studies on major developments (social, economic, and cultural as well as political) in the province; the recording on tape of the attitudes, opinions and memories of many important leaders in Ontario; and, as a culmination of these studies, a definitive history of Ontario.

The first edition of the bibliography was published in 1974. As it was well received, the Board has sponsored the preparation of a second, comprehensive edition which will appear in 1979. Our first major publication is the present detailed and scholarly study of the life and times of G. Howard Ferguson by Peter N. Oliver. We hope it will find a large and interested reading audience and that it will be followed each year by one or more equally interesting books, the total of which will inform and illuminate Ontario history in a new and lasting way.

The Board has been heavily dependent upon its two editors, Goldwin S. French, Editor-in-Chief, and Peter N. Oliver, Associate Editor. Both men have served the Board with diligence and devotion and we are greatly indebted to them for the refinement of topics and the selection of authors for the many projects we have undertaken.

Murray G. Ross
Chairman, Board of Trustees
Ontario Historical Studies Series

15 April 1977

For many years the principal theme in English-Canadian historical writing has been the emergence and the consolidation of the Canadian nation. This theme has been developed in uneasy awareness of the persistence and importance of regional interests and identities, but because of the central role of Ontario in the growth of Canada, Ontario has not been seen as a region. Almost unconsciously, historians have equated the history of the province with that of the nation and have depicted the interests of other regions as obstacles to the unity and welfare of Canada.

The creation of the province of Ontario in 1867 was the visible embodiment of a formidable reality, the existence at the core of the new nation of a powerful if disjointed society whose traditions and characteristics differed in many respects from those of the other British North American colonies. The intervening century has not witnessed the assimilation of Ontario to the other regions in Canada; on the contrary it has become a more clearly articulated entity. Within the formal geographical and institutional framework defined so assiduously by Ontario's political leaders, an increasingly intricate web of economic and social interests has been woven and shaped by the dynamic interplay between Toronto and its hinterland. The character of this regional community has been formed in the tension between a rapid adaptation to the processes of modernization and industrialization in modern Western society and a reluctance to modify or discard traditional attitudes and values. Not surprisingly, the Ontario outlook is a compound of aggressiveness, conservatism, and the conviction that its values should be the model for the rest of Canada.

The purpose of the Ontario Historical Studies Series is to describe and analyse the historical development of Ontario as a distinct region within Canada. The series as planned will include approximately fifty volumes covering many aspects of the life and work of the province from its original establishment in 1791 as Upper Canada to our own time. Among these will be biographies of several prominent political figures, a three-volume economic history, numerous works on such topics as social structure, education, minority groups, labour, political and administrative institutions, literature, theatre, and the arts, and a comprehensive synthesis of the history of Ontario, based upon the detailed contributions of the biographies and thematic studies.

In planning this project, the Editors have endeavoured to maintain a reasonable balance between different kinds and areas of historical research, and to appoint authors ready to ask new kinds of questions about the past and to answer them in accordance with the canons of contemporary scholarship. Ten biographical studies have been included, if only because through biography the past comes alive most readily for the general reader as well as the historian. The historian must be sensitive to today's concerns and standards as he engages in the imaginative recreation of the interplay between human beings and circumstances in time. He should seek to be the mediator between all the dead and the living, but in the end the humanity and the artistry of his account will determine the extent of its usefulness.

The biography of the Honourable G. Howard Ferguson is the first volume in the series to be published. It depicts the life and times of a major political figure whose opinions and values epitomized the cross-currents of stability and change in the Ontario of his generation and who exerted a substantial influence on its economic and social development. We hope that this study will illuminate the character and circumstances of Howard Ferguson and thereby deepen the understanding of twentieth-century Ontario.

Goldwin French
Editor-in-Chief
Peter Oliver
Associate Editor

Toronto
15 April 1977

Preface

The purpose of this biography is to tell the story of the life of Howard Ferguson in relation to his times. My emphasis has been on the broad goals of Ferguson's political life and on the techniques of political management by which he sought to attain his ends. While attempting to avoid the stifling detail which episodic treatments sometimes offer, I have tried to give a sense of the times and a feel for the circumstances of the day. The issues Ferguson faced and the role he played can be understood only by reference to the rich events of the period and to the society in which he was a principal actor, and throughout I have examined his career in this context.

A principal difficulty has been the state of Ontario historiography. Ideally a biographer is able to draw on a substantial body of material relating to 'the times' of his subject, but unfortunately there has been little scholarly examination of the development of Ontario since Confederation. What does exist aided me immeasurably and I owe a substantial debt to the work of Christopher Armstrong, Charles Humphries, Jean MacLeod, H.V. Nelles, Robert Stamp, E.E. Stewart, and others. Nonetheless my understanding of 'the times' as well as of 'the life' of Howard Ferguson has perforce been gained largely from research in primary sources. Because so little has been written in the field, I have been forced to pay considerable attention to the background of many of the issues Ferguson confronted. Even so, space limitations prevented my dealing with many matters I deem of importance to Ferguson's career. Some of these may be followed in my book, *Public & Private Persons*, Clarke, Irwin, 1975. I do not pretend to offer the last word with respect to the developments discussed herein. Of the deficiencies of this account, no one is more aware than myself.

In the course of this work I have incurred many debts. Ramsay Cook directed the thesis, on which the first part is based, with much compassion and a sharp pencil and he also read the entire book in manuscript and made many valuable suggestions. Goldwin S. French, my colleague on the Ontario Historical Studies Series, has offered encouragement and support throughout. My colleagues in the

Department of History at York University, particularly Robert Cuff, P.D. Stevens, J.L. Granatstein, and J.T. Saywell, gave criticism and advice, as have Jean (MacLeod) James, Paul Axelrod, Norman Hillmer, and Robert Stamp. Two readers for the Ontario Historical Studies Series provided careful and constructive criticism. At the University of Toronto Press, Jean Houston and Jean Wilson gave the manuscript painstaking editorial attention.

The following assisted through interviews and/or correspondence: Judge J.C. Anderson, Lord Avon (Anthony Eden), Dr James Band, Elmer Bell, Mrs Gordon Conant, W.E. Elliott, Hon. Leslie M. Frost, Arthur Ford, H. Vernon Hearst, Patrick Henry, Margaret Higginson, Mrs Aemilius Jarvis, R.N. Johnston, H.T. Johnston, T.A. Kidd, Leopold Macaulay, W.M. Nickle, Senator Paul Martin, Hon. J.C. McRuer, Farquhar Oliver, Douglas Oliver, Rt Hon. Lester B. Pearson, Hon. J.W. Pickersgill, Kelso Roberts, Earl Rowe, Leslie Saunders, Miss M.E. Saunderson, Mrs John Stephenson, H.R. Stevenson, Margaret Storey, Alice Turner, Senator David Walker, Charlotte Whitton, Judge F.W. Wilson, Mme Georges P. Vanier, E.J. Zavitz.

I also thank Fred M. Cass for providing me with correspondence of W.H. Casselman; C.A. Morrison for correspondence of J.J. Morrison; Henry Borden and Professor Craig Brown for permission to use the Borden Diaries; Mrs R.H. McGimpsey and Miss Margaret Hindman for correspondence of Dr Forbes Godfrey; Senator David Walker for access to his diaries; Hon. J.W. Pickersgill for permission to use the King diaries for the closed period; Mme Vanier for permission to use the Georges P. and Pauline Vanier papers; and Leslie M. Frost, who allowed me to see papers then kept in his home in Lindsay.

Throughout my work I received courteous co-operation from libraries and archives and I wish to thank in particular the York University Library, the Public Archives of Ontario and of Canada, and Robert Potvin of the Centre de Recherche en Civilization Canadienne-Française, Université d'Ottawa.

Two research assistants, Joseph Weisberg and John Witham, gave able support and I also received help from graduate assistants provided by the history department of York University. The students in my Ontario history seminar offered stimulation and challenge. Research costs were met by the Canada Council and the York University Minor Research Committee. The Canada Council provided a Research Fellowship and York University generously granted leave which permitted a year of (almost) uninterrupted research and writing.

The bulk of the photographs were made available by Miss Margaret Storey and Mrs John Stephenson of Kemptville and Miss Margaret Higginson and Miss Isabelle Higginson of Toronto. The photographs they supplied were reproduced with the assistance of the Ontario Archives and York University's audio-visual services. I also thank the Ontario Hydro for the photograph of Charles Magrath, Margaret Van Every of the Ontario Archives for various photographs, particularly of members of the legislature, and Mrs M.A. Cox for providing a photograph of her father, W.N. Tilley.

Mrs Jo-Anne Degabriele and her staff in secretarial services at York University worked on an untidy manuscript with unfailing courtesy and skill. I wish particularly to thank Leleith Smith, Patricia Humenyk, and Norma Tarnofsky.

My family, and particularly my wife, Heather, have lived with this book for more years than I care to mention. For them, no thanks can be adequate.

PO

Abbreviations

ACFEO   French Canadian Educational Association of Ontario
AR   Annual Report
BP   Bennett Papers
CAR   *Canadian Annual Review*
CHAAR Canadian Historical Association Annual Report
CHR   *Canadian Historical Review*
DCER *Documents on Canadian External Relations*
DLF   Department of Lands and Forests
DO   Dominions Office
FO   Foreign Office
FP   Ferguson Papers
HEPC   Hydro-Electric Power Commission
HP   Henry Papers
KP   King Papers
MP   Meighen Papers
OH   *Ontario History*
OHSS   Ontario Historical Studies Series
PRO   Public Record Office

Howard's boyhood home in Kemptville

Dr Charles F. Ferguson,
Howard's father

Elizabeth Ferguson, Howard's mother

Howard's sister, Marion, age 10

Howard's brother, Jack, age 6 (left) and Howard, age 8 (right)

Mrs G. Howard Ferguson (Ella)   Howard, age 17

Howard, age about 32

Howard and Ella's Kemptville home

Mr Justice William N. 'Pat' Ferguson, a lifelong friend of Howard, Mr Justice
Ferguson's sister, Mrs Ferguson-Burke, and Ella and Howard

With Premier Taschereau

The residence on Avenue Road in Toronto which was the party's gift to Premier Ferguson

Canon Cody, Howard and W.L. Mackenzie King

On the Fall Fair Circuit

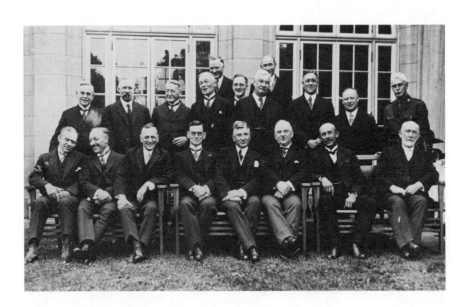

The Ferguson Cabinet

The Orator

Howard and Ella

Sir William Hearst

T.W. McGarry

H.H. Dewart

George S. Henry

E.C. Drury

W.E.N. Sinclair

W.E. Raney

W.H. Price

W.F. Nickle

Lincoln Goldie

Forbes E. Godfrey

Charles McCrea

W. Norman Tilley

Charles A. Magrath

Selling Canada Abroad

The Fergusons with Stanley Bruce of Australia

With R.B. Bennett

Signing on behalf of Canada. J.H. Thomas is standing third from the left.

G. HOWARD FERGUSON: A BIOGRAPHY

1

The Fergusons of Kemptville

Family tragedy has changed many lives. In 1894 when Howard Ferguson received the news of his brother's death, he was beginning a promising law career in Toronto. The Fergusons were a close-knit family and Howard was now the only surviving son. Leaving behind the bustling provincial capital with whatever it might have held for him, he returned to Kemptville, the little eastern Ontario town in which he had grown up. Probably it took little family persuasion to convince him to remain home on a permanent basis. Of the seven children born to his parents, Dr and Mrs Ferguson, two had died in infancy; nineteen-year-old Charles, a medical student, had succumbed to a kidney ailment; and now Jack, a year younger than Howard and in his third year of medicine at McGill, was dead from a head injury suffered in a football game. Howard's return brought great comfort to his parents and his sisters, Marion and Irene. With Dr Ferguson still deeply involved in his political career, they may have suggested to him that he was needed at home more than ever. Howard's father, the long-time member of Parliament for North Leeds and Grenville, was often absent at Ottawa and when he was home his large medical practice drew deeply on his resources and his time. As for Howard's own future, Kemptville of course could not offer the excitement and challenge of Toronto. Yet it presented opportunities of its own.

For, by any measure, the Fergusons were one of Grenville County's first families. Although they had missed by almost half a century that sure imprimatur of eastern Ontario approval, a Loyalist heritage, they fitted well into their adopted home. Howard's grandparents, as so many other immigrants of the 1830s, were Scotch-Irish. Originally from Drumgunnion, Leitrim, Ireland, the Robert F. Fergusons had settled in Kitley Township, Leeds County, in the years prior to the Rebellion of 1837. Howard's father, Charles, was born in 1834 at the family homestead in Kitley. Robert Ferguson must have attained a degree of prosperity. In spite of the cost, which denied the opportunity to many another Upper Canadian farm boy, he was able to send his son to the District Grammar School at Smiths Falls. Charles Ferguson was a boy of ambition and intelligence.

After grammar school he studied medicine at Queen's the little university founded at Kingston the previous decade. When he received his degree in 1859 he encountered no shortage of opportunities for doctors in Upper Canada. He had only to decide where he wanted to hang out his shingle. He chose Kemptville.[1]

Its proximity to his old home was one consideration. Grenville and Leeds were neighbouring counties, a fact destined to have an important influence on his subsequent political career. But mostly, it was the village itself, nestled comfortably in the valley of the South Rideau River, which attracted him. By 1850 the area's dense forest covering had yielded before a growing community which proudly boasted several churches, three public schools, and a grammar school. With its inevitable saw mill, grist mill, and tannery evidencing its dependence on the surrounding farm and lumber development, it seemed a typical eastern Ontario settlement.[2] However, there were those who, for a time, believed that a great future was in store for Kemptville. Its Rideau situation made it a part of the great Ottawa Valley, then in the midst of its timber-born prosperity, while south and west it looked to the St Lawrence, to the 'River of Canada' and the wealthy heartland it served. Kemptville thus felt the competing pulls of two great river systems. Its economic dreams were never to be fulfilled; its merchants proved unable to master the promise of their geography. For some of its citizens the same geography offered not economic potential but a richly diverse social and political experience, a heritage waiting to be won. Yet first, briefly, the hopes of economic power seemed almost realizable. In the 1850s Kemptville caught railway fever.

The man who brought the railway to Kemptville was Howard Ferguson's uncle, Robert Bell, a remarkable combination of dynamic business promoter and shrewd politician. Born in Ireland, he migrated with his parents to the United States and later to Canada. Settling some four miles south of Kemptville, the Bells prospered. Robert Bell became a land surveyor and civil engineer and it was with his keen surveyor's eye that he first envisaged the possibilities of a rail link between the St Lawrence River and the Rideau Canal. A man of action, he set about organizing a combination of Ottawa, Prescott, and Kemptville businessmen and soon became the first president of the Prescott & Bytown Railway. Many of the citizens of Kemptville demonstrated their faith in him and in their town by buying stock to make the railway a reality. Kemptville's great day came in 1854. The 'populace was thrilled to see and hear the great wood-burner engine puff into the village station, after going at the dizzy speed of twenty-five miles an hour.'[3] Robert Bell went on to become one of Bytown's great men and to sit in the pre-Confederation Canadian Assembly for Russell. But he was always a frequent visitor to Kemptville, his old home, where his sister and other members of his family remained.

At first Kemptville seemed about to grasp the railway's promise of growth. New markets opened for the area's timber and farm products. In 1855 the village's first newspaper was founded. By Confederation 'the thriving community had many businessmen, general stores, blacksmith shops, milliners, tailors, cabinet makers, coopers, tanneries, shoemakers' shops, a wheelwright, three hotels, a chemist, several doctors and barristers and Francis Jones, Member of Parliament for North Leeds and Grenville.'[4] But the prosperity of the 1850s and 60s endured only in attenuated form and the expansionist dreams of the merchants were never realized. Its ambitions denied, Kemptville remained a pleasant little eastern Ontario village. It was the kind of place in which Charles Ferguson would be quite content to practise his profession and raise his family.

Not long after his arrival in town the young bachelor had met Elizabeth Bell, sister of the famous railway promoter and politician. She was, by all accounts, a charming and intelligent person. Charles Ferguson soon brought her as his wife to the large stone house on the corner of North Main and Rideau Streets, their home for the rest of their lives. For Elizabeth Bell Ferguson, the move was really a return. Not so many years earlier she had attended in the same building the private day school where the young ladies of Kemptville 'learned the gentle arts of painting, sewing and penmanship.'[5] It was a source of quiet amusement to the staunchly Tory Fergusons that their home had originally been built with funds raised by the notorious 'Hunters' Lodges.' A few sympathizers with the rebels of 1837 had raised funds in the inhospitable climate of Kemptville to help overthrow British rule in Canada. Their schemes betrayed, they fled for their lives to the United States. When feelings subsided, the treasurer of the Kemptville Lodge returned home and used its funds for the more sensible purpose of erecting the building on Main and Rideau where he kept hotel until his death. The next owner used it as a store and school as well as a residence. When the Fergusons acquired it, renovations turned it into a beautiful and spacious home. In it the Ferguson children were born and from it Dr Charles carried on his medical practice.

Charles Ferguson was the very prototype of the legendary family doctor. Usually seen in a Prince Albert coat and a high hat, he was a trusted friend as well as physician to the families of the area.[6] The relationship, a very special one, deepened further during the almost quarter century that he represented North Leeds and Grenville in the House of Commons. Charles Ferguson's active interest in public affairs dated from the 1860s. As did many a contemporary, he deplored the country's apparent inability to cope with the serious economic and sectional problems it was facing. Attracted to the bold solution of a union of British North America, he became known as a strong advocate of Confederation.[7] In these years too Charles Ferguson lost his political heart, completely and forever, to the irresistible charm of John A. Macdonald. He believed intensely in the nation-building policies of Macdonald Conservatism and was first elected to the Commons in 1874 as a supporter of Macdonald's proposed transcontinental railway. He retained the constituency until his retirement in 1896.

Although eastern Ontario was good Tory territory, a member could not expect to hold his seat on this basis alone. North Leeds and Grenville expected its representative to ensure that it received its share of the political spoils and a politician who proved unable to perform this essential function could not expect to spend much time in Ottawa. Dr Ferguson's political longevity is proof that he did his duty. He regarded it as one of his more important accomplishments that he was instrumental in having the bed of the south branch of the Rideau River deepened to permit navigation to proceed to Kemptville. With such achievements to his credit, his supporters could more easily bear the disappointment that he never secured a place in the ministry.

Perhaps the exigencies of geographical representation or perhaps his continued commitment to his medical practice determined that he would not join John A. as a cabinet colleague. Nonetheless, while he remained a backbencher, he was of that breed that Macdonald proclaimed he admired most – a man who supported him when he was right but, more important by far, on whom he could rely when he was wrong. 'One of the staunchest of the old guard' was how Macdonald described Charles Ferguson, and their friendship was as much personal as political. With the single exception of the 1891 election, Dr Ferguson adhered staunchly to party orthodoxy. In the home in which Howard Ferguson grew up, it was assumed that the Holy Trinity was God, Queen Victoria, and John A. Macdonald, though not necessarily in that order.[8] Charles Ferguson believed Macdonald's National Policy to be forging a great nation. He and his fellow Tories scoffed at the narrow pessimism of those men of little faith, Blake, Mackenzie, and Cartwright, the leaders of Ontario Liberalism. Though the Grits might claim that Macdonald's policies would bankrupt the nation, Dr Ferguson agreed with his leader that the Pacific railway had to be built. Built it was and Charles Ferguson at once went himself to Manitoba and saw the sights of the west in an open carriage.[9] On his return he made a stirring three-hour report to Parliament of the wonders he had seen. His speech created such interest that thousands of copies were distributed abroad as immigrant propaganda.

Kindly country doctors are not wholly immune from political troubles. Dr Ferguson's came in 1891 and sorely tried a lifetime of political orthodoxy. With an embattled Conservative party rallying for its last campaign under the Old Chieftain, Charles Ferguson experienced his first major political reverse. For reasons which are none too clear, Dr Ferguson was not renominated. In his place a rebellious convention selected the scion of a powerful Ottawa Valley family. Charles Ferguson regarded his defeat as a deliverance. Approaching sixty years of age, he was pleased at the prospect of having more time to devote to his family and to his large medical practice.

However, he had not reckoned with the fighting spirit of his Irish-born wife. Elizabeth Ferguson, furious at the ungrateful convention, now performed the feat which accounts for some of the many stories about this remarkable woman.[10] A combative and intensely political person, she refused to accept the convention's rebuff. At her insistence the name of Ferguson once more was presented to the electors, this time as an independent Conservative candidate. At first her ploy seemed to no avail. Party loyalty in eastern Ontario was not taken lightly; one suspects that Dr Ferguson himself had qualms about running as an independent.

At this stage, a fine feminine hand intervened decisively. When the electors trooped to the polling booths on election day, they encountered an unusual notice pinned near the entrance to each booth. It read:

To the Conservatives of North Leeds and Grenville. I respectfully request your support for my old friend Dr Charles Ferguson.

(signed) John A. Macdonald

Nothing else was necessary. Dr Ferguson was re-elected with a margin of 146 votes over both his opponents. The outraged official candidate hastened to Ottawa and was soon venting his feelings upon a flabbergasted Macdonald. The old man heatedly denied having written any such message and promised punishment for the authors of the apparent forgery.

Elizabeth Ferguson was ready. She too journeyed to Ottawa, taking with her the original copy of the message which had so raised John A.'s ire and which she forthwith presented to him.

'Who signed this letter?' asked the party leader.

'John A. Macdonald,' answered an unrepentant Elizabeth Ferguson.

'I never wrote that signature,' thundered Sir John.

'Of course not. That is the signature of John A. Macdonald, our blacksmith in Kemptville and a very old friend of ours.'

Fortunately for the Fergusons, old age had not dulled the Macdonald sense of humour. He dissolved in laughter and the official candidate never did get any satisfaction. Dr Ferguson was at his accustomed place in the Commons when the first session of the new Parliament met. Exploits such as this made Elizabeth Ferguson something of a legend in Grenville and caused it to be said, with justice, that although Dr Ferguson was the MP, it was his wife who won the elections.

Howard Ferguson was born in 1870, four years before his father entered the Commons. As a boy he must have missed his father deeply during his absences but the trip to Ottawa was a short one and Dr Ferguson was able to spend more time with his family than was possible for most MPs. And the Ferguson home was always far from empty. Its great halls rang with the sounds of the Ferguson children and, as often as not, aunts, uncles, or political friends occupied the three extra bedrooms. In 1874 a star of the Queen's football team of that year also became a member of the Ferguson household when Dr Charles, busy with politics, formed a partnership with young Dr J.A. Jones. 'There were guests to dinner nearly every night,' Howard's younger sister Marion recalled later, 'and politics was the talk at table.'

Never in robust health, young Howard encountered more than his share of the usual childhood diseases. Most serious, a severe attack of measles at age five or six resulted in the almost total loss of the sight of one eye. Howard's poor health prompted his father to send him to live for a time on a nearby farm. Although he did become more sturdy, his impaired vision made it difficult to participate in athletic activities. Yet he was hardly transformed into a retiring or bookish figure. When Howard Ferguson became an important political person-age, enquiring reporters found that his home town bristled with stories of his pugnacious and extroverted youth. According to one neighbour, 'he started hitting out with his fists as soon as his nurse took him and by the time he was ten years old he was juvenile champion of Oxford Township and Kemptville village.' Jim Hagen, a schoolmate, recalled the fights in Harding's flour mill when old man Harding would throw coppers onto the big bare mill floor, and after school the boys would pair off and scrap for the stakes. In these contests, Howard was 'top boy' and Jim Hagen told of his taking ten fights in succession, often against boys bigger than himself. Marion, to whom Howard was close, remembered him as forever in mischief and coming home with black eyes and other wounds, 'which only endeared him to me the more. Fred Napp, of roller boat fame, wore two gold teeth in front, as a result of a shinny argument with Howard.'[11]

A boyhood spent in the pleasant surroundings of late nineteenth-century Kemptville almost had to be a happy one. Although the Fergusons were better off than many of their neighbours, they were far from wealthy. There were few rich families in Grenville County and little real poverty. These were happy and serene years for Ontario. What mattered most were the events of village life. Not that people failed to keep a close eye on Ottawa and far-off London. But the local farming and merchant communities had cause to be satisfied with their lot. And of course these were the years of the Pax Britannica. It was good to be British. A sense of security and pride was created by membership in the world's greatest Empire. It was even better to be Canadian and, fortunately, these were years in which Queen Victoria's Empire made few demands on its Canadian subjects.

Kemptville, Canada, the British Empire, in that order — these were important to the boy growing up in the 1880s. In spite of his exuberant spirits, there was a serious side to young Howard Ferguson. His quick mind served him well in school. Although he had nothing of the bookworm in him, he was undeniably bright and at age eleven easily passed his 'entrance examinations' — that fearsome hurdle still remembered with awe by members of an older Ontario generation. That same year, as he later liked to recall, Howard first met Sir John A. himself.[12] Not foreseeing the possibility of a night session, Dr Ferguson had taken his son on a visit to the Parliament buildings. When he was forced to remain, the Prime Minister took the young boy to his office, helped him off with his boots, collar, and tie, and, covering him with his greatcoat, put him to bed on his sofa. In local legend at least, there was many a subsequent meeting between the old man and the boy, a fact frequently remarked upon in later years when the boy himself had become a mighty Tory sachem. Sir John, it is said, became a frequent visitor to the Ferguson home and Howard overheard many a discussion of high policy and political gossip by the leaders of the young nation. Such stories of his boyhood later became part of the Ferguson legend and Tory organizers seldom hesitated to point out that Howard Ferguson came rightly by 'the Macdonald touch.'

Howard was not a success at high school. Forbes Godfrey, later a political and personal intimate, related that he had the reputation of being able to fight anybody, 'until he tackled his teacher twice his size and met his Waterloo.'[13] Although he was bright and alert, his masters must have wondered whether he was worth the trouble he brought them. Once he caused consternation by dropping gunpowder in the school stove and blowing off the lid. Another time he fixed the school bell so it would not ring. And on one occasion, the day the inspector was to visit, he unscrewed all the seats and desks from the floor, creating 'vast hullaballoo and confusion when the pupils came in and sat down with a crashing and smashing under the grave inspector's outraged eye ...' Howard was suspended, 'no questions asked, but just the teacher saying weakly, "Howard! Leave the room!" ...' At home he was banished to the woodshed as his father and mother debated his fate. Erratic grades and frequent suspensions were disquieting to his mother in particular, left alone so often to raise her young family while Dr Charles was off in Ottawa. Howard on this occasion received a stern upbraiding from his father and was sent off to work for a while in the shanties, hauling railway ties. Yet the good doctor admired his son's spirit and assured his wife that 'if we can only control him until the serious affairs of life begin to interest him, I am certain Howard will be a success, for he is filled with vigor and ardor.'[14]

Howard's style appealed to his youthful cohorts and he became the recognized leader of his group. One pastime he enjoyed was to go to the gypsy camp to play cards with the gypsies. According to Marion, 'one of his favorite games was to attend auction sales in the town and when any well-known town skinflint began to bid for something, Howard would bid too, running bids up to much more than the other had hoped to pay, and when Howard felt he had gone as far as was safe, he would drop out.' Once his instinct deserted him, and he ended up paying $8.35 for a pile of junk. Or at least Dr Charles paid the cash and Howard paid by getting one of the two switchings Marion could remember being administered to him by their father. Other events had happier conclusions. One of the Kemptville landmarks treasured by the boys of the 1870s and 1880s was an old cannon symbolically guarding the river from American incursions. On special holidays, this artillery piece was put to good use by the younger generation. Geography divided Kemptville into two camps, separated by the river. The Fergusons lived on the north side and Howard often led 'the norths' in the 24th of May activities. In this particular year, he and his cohorts seized the cannon and loaded it with gunpowder ready to fire when the 'souths' swept across the bridge. In the midst of the fray, the powder went off too soon and Howard, face blackened and wavy locks singed, stood gallantly by his men until the enemy was in full retreat.[15]

Once these mischievous propensities landed him in serious trouble. By custom, the boys coming into high school were given a good hazing by their elders, a process known locally as 'bumping.' In a year in which Howard played a prominent role, one boy was hurt and an irate parent took the 'bumpers' to court. Howard was fined $8 and then and there decided 'there was a good deal about the law worth knowing.' The law, he told his chums, would be his profession.[16]

In all these activities, young Howard seldom lost his temper and he was always prepared to 'own up' and take his punishment. Mischievous but not malicious, he was liked and looked up to by his peers and regarded indulgently by his elders. His escapades, however, were not only amusing but also significant because the character traits they revealed he retained for the rest of his life. Competitive, scrappy, utterly unwilling to take the affairs of the world with the solemnity some thought they deserved, Howard from the beginning was an individualist. Perhaps it was his poor eyesight or some other physical trait which accounted for these characteristics; perhaps it was simply Howard. There were other influences which had a greater impact. Politics was in his blood, the politics of the small town and the rural county.

'The practical side of politics, the manual labor of the game,' Marion related,

has been familiar to him since childhood. By the time he was ten years of age, he was out driving through the country distributing campaign literature, posting up notices, and accompanying his father on canvassing trips, learning the art of political discussion and of soliciting a vote. These things were not chores to him. They were manly stuff, and he took the most ardent interest in the whole game. I recall him coming home to dinner with the latest political gossip that he had picked up sitting around the stores with the men of the town. And I remember his goings and comings on winter nights near election time when he was driving through the country in a cutter, going messages for his father, delivering literature, or arranging the practical details of meetings.[17]

Politics and medicine were practised by Charles Ferguson almost as part of the same trade. Although Howard Ferguson's intimate understanding of the underside of political life left him with few illusions and in later years created the impression of cynicism, he inherited from his father an idealism and a sense that politics meant service on behalf of those who needed it most. This redeeming quality went far to nullify the label of machine politician by which his enemies would one day characterize him. Indeed, Charles Ferguson, MP, in many ways was a less significant influence on the impressionable youngster than was Charles Ferguson, MD. Kindhearted and tireless, he lacked few of the qualities of the proverbial Good Samaritan. Occasionally Howard accompanied 'the Governor,' as he came to call him, on his calls over some of Grenville County's roughest roads, watched him operate under the crudest of conditions, did what he could when called upon to assist in some small way.

Dr Ferguson's contribution was not limited to his politics and his practice for he opened his home too as a place of refuge for anyone down on his luck. 'Above the big, homely kitchen ... was a commodious attic. The doctor had some beds placed there, and any tramps or unfortunates who knocked at the Ferguson door found a haven where they could remain as long as they liked.' A few stayed the whole winter. The 'tramp' who had the greatest influence on the family stayed thirteen years. He was a former Oxford student named Keane who had gone wrong and who turned to the small-town Ontario doctor for assistance. Keane eventually became one of the most useful members of the community, an outstanding preacher and author of much good in the area.[18]

Here lay the source of much of Howard Ferguson's later appeal. Although a driving ambition and elements of shrewd calculation came much to the fore in his character, they never submerged the warm humanity and concern for people which had been so much a part of his early environment. Elizabeth Ferguson's tender sensibilities and concern for all about her and the constant example of his father created a home life which left a deep imprint. And somewhere along the line Howard became a proud wearer of the badge of the Sons of Temperance. Perhaps this commitment may be attributed to Marion's influence, for they signed the pledge together. Or perhaps it was an inspiration received at a revival meeting. Howard Ferguson's own later habit of speaking with only the briefest of notes before him he attributed in part to his 'attendance at revivals in the good old days when people spoke as the spirit moved them.' Later, in 1888, a post of the Salvation Army was established in Kemptville and Howard became a frequent visitor at its meetings.[19]

It was fitting that Dr Ferguson should live to a ripe old age to see his family grow up around him and his son a member of the Ontario legislature. He practised medicine for thirteen years after his 1896 retirement from the Commons and during that time served again on the Kemptville Board of Education and in other municipal affairs. He died after a night call in 1909 which another doctor had turned down because the family was too poor to pay a fee.

But this is to look ahead a good deal and anticipate much. To return to the 1880s, young Howard stayed firm with his early resolve to become a lawyer. Perhaps it was the presence of the law school in Toronto that accounted for his decision to do his university work there rather than at his father's alma mater, nearby Queen's. When he did go to Toronto 'it was not on the strength of a scholarship – he was not even a matriculant – but on the candid advice of the headmaster at home to "ship him off".'[20] That worthy pedagogue had endured all he could of G. Howard Ferguson. As a result, Howard was forced to try matriculation examinations at the university before being accepted for classes. Sitting in a little bedroom in a rooming house at 191 McCaul Street, he was lonely and despondent. No one had bothered to speak to him at registration and, for an instant, with his carpet bag unopened on the floor, he was strongly tempted to throw it all up and head west for a life of adventure. At that moment, an older boy, Jack Ferguson by name, but no relation, knocked at his door, introduced himself, and took him under his wing. Gregarious Howard took naturally to the city and the university. He passed his matriculation exams with ease and for seven years, first as an arts undergraduate, then as a law student, he continued his happy-go-lucky ways in the Queen City.

In fact his parents were soon alarmed at the zest with which Howard took to his new life. On their first trip to Toronto after Howard had registered, he introduced them to his new roommate. They were thoroughly disturbed. No long acquaintance with young Stephen Leacock was necessary for them to know that it would never do for Howard to be paired with him. Someone would have to be found who was less like Howard himself.[21] So the future humorist was replaced by a future university president, Harry Cody from Galt. Harry, a more senior student, was a quiet, studious boy. Since he graduated in 1889 with the most brilliant record of his generation at Toronto, one may assume that Dr Charles could have had no complaint about Cody's influence on his son. In later years the two men were frequently and intimately associated. But at college Howard continued to be much closer to Stephen Leacock.

The two were very much a pair, although Leacock was incomparably the superior student. From an academic standpoint Howard Ferguson's university career was less than brilliant. At one point he once again found himself counting his money with a view to taking off for the west.[22] That particular crisis passed and Howard learned to apply himself to his books long enough at least to get by. In the 1889-90 session, for example, he achieved a first in English constitutional law, a second in economics, a second in general jurisprudence, but only a pass in history and was 'below the line' in the history of English law. In his fourth year, the 1890-1 session, he concentrated more on political science, in which he achieved a second-class standing.[23] An occasional low grade could not dampen his spirits for long. The important thing, he knew, was to get his year. He had no desire to emulate a record such as Harry Cody's.

On occasion even that measure of achievement seemed in jeopardy for Howard Ferguson was a popular young man. To a boy from small-town Ontario, Toronto, its high Victorian virtues notwithstanding, was an exciting place, while university itself brought a new and sometimes intoxicating freedom. Howard enjoyed this life to the full. Evidently his contemporaries were attracted to his genial personality. At the same time they recognized that a good deal of ability lay behind his easygoing manner. Thus after a year in which the student newspaper, *The Varsity*, hovered dangerously close to bankruptcy, Howard was pressed into service as its business manager. That same year Stephen Leacock served as associate editor and columnist. Further recognition of Howard's position on campus came when he was elected vice-president and then president of the class of '91 while Stephen served as class poet.[24]

Toronto itself possessed attractions, and again there were pranks and high jinks. One story, possibly apocryphal, has it that walking along the tracks one day Howard and Stephen happened upon an idling locomotive. On an impulse, the two boys hopped into the cab and sped off, leaving in their wake much shaking of fists and blue air.

During his years at University College, Howard was an active member of the Literary Society and served on many of its committees. In the fall of 1890 he represented the Arts undergraduates at a McGill dinner but unfortunately overdid the festive aspects of the occasion. When it came time to report to the Lit on what had transpired in Montreal, he was in a fluster, not knowing what to do. Harry Cody came to his rescue. 'Tell them you forget,' he suggested. Howard did so and brought down the house. 'Mr Ferguson reports having had a most delightful trip,' noted the *Varsity*, and he 'advocated a similar festivity for his Alma Mater. The Society agreed with Mr Ferguson.'[25] One of the highlights of 1891 came when Howard heard an old friend deliver his final speech of a great career. He was as moved as the rest of Sir John A. Macdonald's audience at the emotional appeal, 'A British subject I will die.'[26] During these years of growth and development, Howard Ferguson's experiences outside the classroom were as important as those within.

Perhaps inevitably, then, an occasional academic crisis had to be met. Such a crisis occurred a few short weeks before graduation when Howard faced an examination in mathematics. Here was a weakness he shared with language major Stephen Leacock, who was again his roommate.[27] The facile Leacock suggested a solution. After much scanning of the catalogue, he decided that a credit in ethnology would serve equally well to get them their degrees and was more to their taste. Howard was always willing to defer to Leacock's judgment in matters academic, although the necessary exam would have to be written the following day. 'Leacock hurried to the library and discovered that Sir Daniel Wilson, principal of the university, had written two books on the subject.' He brought the books back to their room and they spent the night reading aloud to each other. Each was content to graduate with a third in ethnology.[28]

Howard Ferguson's university years were happy, well-rounded, and successful. In an ode to the University of Toronto written in 1916, Stephen Leacock looked back, nostalgically, to the friendships of those days:

And, yes, perhaps the most important one
Friend of my youth, good Howard Ferguson
The kindest man that ever failed to pass
In First Year Trigonometry, Alas: —
This man of place and power, has he forgot
His boyhood friend? Oh, surely, he has not
When next some well-paid sinecure you see
Oh, Howard, pass it, pass it on to me.[29]

Despite the problems posed by Toronto high life and first year trigonometry, Howard Ferguson was awarded his BA in 1891. The following year he attended law school in Toronto and took his LLB. After reading law in the offices of the provincial Conservative leader, William Meredith and then, perhaps for a change of pace, with the firm of Mowat and Smyth, he was called to the bar in 1894. The young man had every intention of making Toronto his home and practising his profession there. But fate intervened with the news of his brother's tragic death. Howard Ferguson returned home to Kemptville to his family and his friends.

2

'The Cheeky Shall Get There'

As a home-town boy and the son of Dr Ferguson, Howard Ferguson was in a better position than are many lawyers when they hang out their first shingle. In short order, however, he won a good deal of respect by dint of his own professional abilities. The practice of law came easily to him, and soon he acquired a reputation as a thorough defender of his clients' interests. The great majority of his cases were not, to be sure, of vital significance. The records of a probably typical morning in Division Court reveal that Howard Ferguson acted, sometimes for the plaintiff, sometimes for the defendant, in cases involving a balance due on some hay, the price of some salt, a suit to recover a sewing machine, a disputed store bill.[1] Occasional business trips to Prescott, Ottawa, and Toronto brought some variety to such a routine. Living at home, surrounded by his family, these too were happy years. Howard remained close to his sister Marion and he also enjoyed playing the role of the sought-after and popular bachelor. It was probably in this period too that he joined the Orange Order. That body was at the height of its strength and in eastern Ontario communities was an integral part of the social and political order.

Then, in April 1896, his second year in Kemptville, he took a predictable step, marrying a childhood sweetheart, Ella Cumming. The daughter of Alexander Cumming, a substantial local merchant who served two terms as reeve in the 1870s, Ella was small, quiet, and possessed a lively intelligence. Her friendship with Howard survived her family's move to Buckingham, Quebec, and Howard's years in Toronto. The young couple could see each other summers and holidays, though for a while even this was difficult. Ella was sent to a Montreal school, Bute House, and after finishing there she went abroad with a small party of girls, chaperoned by a teacher. Her tour so fascinated her that she remained in England for a further year at a school at Highgate. There she took the Cambridge extension courses. Ella must have been an unusual girl for her time, for on her return, still anxious to travel, she journeyed to California, as far as Mexico, then back through the Canadian Rockies. Later she visited the Maritime provinces. In spite of these long absences, Ella and Howard early arrived at an understanding. Ella was in England while Howard was studying law and even then their romance was general knowledge.[2]

Now Ella returned as a bride to the very house in which she had lived as a child.[3] It was the beginning of a perfect comradeship of half a century. Ella Ferguson was adept in all the housewifely arts. More unusual, perhaps, was the extent of her commitment to her husband's career. Despite the long hours which Howard devoted to law and then politics, Ella gave him every encouragement. When Howard was pleading a case in the local court house, Ella frequently was an interested spectator. When he turned to politics in 1897 it was with her full approval. Howard for his part adored her always and completely. In 1898, when a son was born, he was named Charles, after his grandfather.

That Howard Ferguson would turn his hand to politics was as inevitable as the four seasons of the Canadian year. It surprised no one when late in 1897 Howard announced his candidacy for the town council. It was only to be expected that he would do well at the polls, easily winning his election. Political success was another family tradition. The Kemptville *Advance* took note of his arrival by remarking that, at twenty-seven, he 'breaks the record as regards youthful councillors.'[4]

The new councillor soon served notice that, in politics at least, youth even in 1898 was no respecter of age. By a series of acts characteristic of his early years in both municipal and later in provincial politics, Howard refused to play the role expected of a political apprentice. To the annoyance of his seniors, this self-confident young man began to talk as though he knew as much about the affairs of the town as did they, with the wisdom gained from years of experience. Howard Ferguson would have to be put in his place.

No doubt, too, political rivalry was one of the sources of the conflict which divided the Town Council of 1898 into two bitterly warring factions. Angus Buchanan, Kemptville's veteran reeve and a gentleman of substance and character, had twice in the past been the Liberal standard-bearer in provincial campaigns. The electors of Grenville had declined to send him to Queen's Park but he was undeniably an able, popular man. Now in his sixth term as reeve, there was little about the town's affairs with which he was not intimately familiar. The early debates in Council in 1898 were not unaffected by the knowledge that Angus Buchanan was again planning to offer himself as a candidate in the March provincial election.[5] Few people failed to notice that Howard Ferguson and his close friend Jim MacGregor, the leaders of the anti-Buchanan insurgency, were ambitious young Tories.

But more than political partisanship was involved. When the two new members, Ferguson and MacGregor, a local businessman, had some chance to observe how the Council conducted affairs, they liked little of what they saw. Councillors were slow, conservative, married to traditional procedures, uninterested in new initiatives. As eager young men everywhere, Ferguson and MacGregor knew that they could do much better. Soon their brashness and activism stirred up the resentment of the rest of the council. According to the *Advance*, the doings of the Council became 'the talk of the Town.' Through stormy sessions and long debates, Ferguson and MacGregor pressed forward with a concerted campaign of local improvements. And for a while in February, Howard got his first real taste of a provincial election campaign. He was in the chair at a packed meeting of Kemptville Conservatives when their candidate, Robert Joynt, and the federal member, Dr Reid, exhorted the local faithful.[6] The bickering on Council did not abate after Reeve Buchanan's defeat at the polls at the hands of Joynt.

It was not that the older councillors were against progress. They simply disliked its cost. The plans of Ferguson and MacGregor, it was predicted, could only end in financial disaster for Kemptville. It was wise, to be sure, to replace the old board sidewalks with paving, but why try to do so much in one year? Finally a crisis of sorts was reached when Ferguson and MacGregor, who was chairman of the streets committee, had the audacity to extend a new walk a trifle further than had been agreed to by the whole council. Two of the exasperated old members decided to take advantage of this opportunity to put the upstarts in their place. By threatening to resign, they expected that fear of Kemptville's thrifty voters would give Ferguson and MacGregor little choice but to back down. To their indignation, Howard Ferguson reacted by presenting a motion that their resignations be accepted. Outmanoeuvred, the embarrassed councillors had no choice but to go through with their announced intentions. This left Ferguson and MacGregor in temporary control of the Council. The subsequent by-elections confirmed Ferguson's political judgment; he and MacGregor, jubilant at the defeat of their opponents, were now able to forge ahead with their program. In particular, they were finally able to do something constructive about the disgraceful old bridge across the South Rideau near Clothier's Mill.

On this issue Ferguson and MacGregor discovered to what lengths their opponents would go. Clothier's Bridge was a tottering ancient structure in such bad shape that Jim MacGregor had often warned the town that it might soon find itself on the wrong end of a damages suit. The Council now tore the old bridge down and accepted a tender of $2,410 for a new structure. Early in December a staff of eight or ten men started work.[7] Suddenly, with the annual elections fast approaching, the opposition struck back. The gang of workmen had been making substantial progress with the excavation work when the bailiff appeared on the scene. All activity ceased at once when he served the contractor with an injunction. The stop-work order had been obtained by several local merchants and residents including, of course, the former councillors. Their complaints were two: the bridge could not be built because funds had not been voted to pay for the work; one of the new councillors who had voted for the bridge had not been legally elected.

The squabble was soon presented to the electors. The town hall was packed for the nomination meeting. Howard Ferguson was singled out for personal attack and falsely accused of acting as solicitor for the corporation while a member of the Council. His response was a ringing justification of his policies. In spite of its program of improvements, by careful management the Council had actually lowered taxes and he was sure that the oldest resident present 'would scarcely remember when the rate of taxation was lower than this year.' Confidently, he recounted the Council's program and boasted that 'according to several experts Kemptville has granolithic sidewalks second to none in Canada.' Finally, he turned to the great issue of the day. The bridge had been an eyesore for years. It was so dangerous that none would 'drive over it with two or three tons but such dare-devils as Jack Dillon or Sam Patterson.' 'By us building it, we simply loan the Government the amount it takes to build it. That bridge can be built at $4,000 and not raise the taxes over 20 mills on the dollar.'

His opponents were noticeably shaken. Former Reeve Buchanan could only counter by an attack on Howard's father who, he argued, had failed to get financial assistance from the former Conservative government in Ottawa. W.H. Anderson, a prominent merchant, next took up the cudgels and warned his fellow citizens to beware of youthful ambition. He knew Messrs Ferguson and MacGregor all too well, he claimed. 'In their bibles at home there is a passage which says, "the meek shall inherit the earth," but they read it "the cheeky shall get there".'[8] Such notes of disapproval carried little weight with the voters. When the ballots were marked early in January 1899, Howard Ferguson could hardly have received a stronger vote of confidence. With eight candidates running for Council, he headed the polls. But, curiously, Angus Buchanan was again returned as reeve. Perhaps the voters believed the two men would balance each other; or perhaps they had enjoyed the spectacle of a lively Council so much that they had opted for a return performance. That is exactly what they got.

The new year, the last of the old century, saw many a heated battle between the two groups; it also saw a good deal of solid achievement. Howard was more than ever a force for reform. At his suggestion, a committee was set up to gather information regarding 'arc and incandescent electric lighting' to see if street lights were feasible. He also worked successfully to have the town lend financial support to improving the road from Beckett's bridge to Kemptville. And late in the fall of 1899, in response to a campaign led by such interested citizens as Dr Ferguson and the Reverend C.P. Emery, he took the lead in Council in an effort to obtain a library. On his motion, the town clerk was instructed to prepare a by-law to establish a public library and reading room to take advantage of the Public Libraries Act of 1895. In 1900 the library came into existence with Howard as its first chairman.[9] On the old issue of the bridge, however, the Council remained divided and for months nothing was done.

Although Howard had become a storm centre in local affairs, his political opponents found it hard not to like the young man who played politics with such zest. His fellow townsmen continued to demonstrate their confidence in his legal abilities and his practice prospered. Of course, practising law in Kemptville was no way to get rich but this failed to worry Howard Ferguson. He was always ready to find time for relaxation and enjoyment. In September 1899, he took a late summer trip which was becoming increasingly common for residents of Ontario and journeyed to Toronto to attend the Exhibition. Then, suddenly, shortly after his return from Toronto, tragedy struck the Ferguson household. Little Charles, not yet a year old, died of encephalitis.[10] His death was an enormous blow. Ella reacted by immersing herself even more deeply in her husband's career. Perhaps the demands of business and politics upon his time helped Howard to bear his sorrow a little more easily.

Municipal elections were fast approaching once again and at the same time Grenville Conservatives were starting to prepare for the federal elections, which were expected at any time. In November 1899, some fifty Kemptville Tories together with the town band boarded a train for Prescott to hear Sir Charles Tupper and the provincial leader, James P. Whitney, address a mass rally. But first Sir Charles spoke to a gathering at the Kemptville railway station and, in turn, was presented with an address read by Howard Ferguson.[11] The municipal campaign followed shortly. This time Howard stood for the office of reeve. In a quiet campaign the voters recognized his ability by returning him with a twenty-six vote majority.

The new century thus started auspiciously for the young eastern Ontario lawyer. As one of his first duties, Howard Ferguson faced a solemn task. The British Empire was at war. Young Canadian volunteers were facing death and dismemberment in far-off South Africa fighting the Boers. Surely it was his responsibility to see that those who went from Kemptville received the support they deserved from the reeve and citizens of their home town. The call went out and early in January a public meeting was held in the town hall to recommend means of accomplishing this. The plan adopted was a grand patriotic concert. Held on 31 January with Reeve Ferguson presiding, only those wearing patriotic badges were admitted. As the *Advance* noted proudly, 'the entire programme was given without a hitch. ... The brief addresses by all the clergymen were brimful of patriotism. ... The receipts totalled up the magnificent sum of $150' for the Canadian patriotic fund.[12] So great was the success of the first concert that a repeat was staged the next evening and once again Howard and the clergymen were 'brimful of patriotism.' At both gatherings, 'Soldiers of the Queen' was sung with unprecedented gusto.

Almost a year later, to the strains of the same melody, Reeve Ferguson welcomed home 'A Returned Hero,' Sergeant Thomas Griffin, Kemptville's representative in the Boer War. The proud citizens had lost none of their military ardour. Braving a fierce snow storm, they turned out in force at the station.

Howard Ferguson never better expressed the feelings of the townspeople than when he told Sergeant Griffin, 'During the past year you and your brothers in arms have done heroic service for the good old British Empire and have covered yourselves with honour and glory. ... Those who have had the good fortune to escape the bullet of the treacherous Boer have reason to thank God...' Once more the band played 'British Grenadiers' and 'Soldiers of the Queen.' Within days of the little celebration, 22 January 1901, the Queen for whom Sergeant Griffin had fought was dead. A Canadian village, like hundreds of others across the immense snow-covered land, mourned with a sense that never again could things be the same. The Boer War, rightly regarded with disgust by later generations, fulfilled, in much of English Canada at least, some of the purposes of Joseph Chamberlain and his imperialist friends. The British Empire had experienced its 'blooding.' In little Kemptville the citizens had gathered together to do homage to their warriors and to sing the Empire's patriotic hymns. Events such as these nurtured in Howard Ferguson and his generation in Ontario the spirit of British patriotism that remained characteristic of many of them.

For three years, 1900 to 1902, Ferguson was reeve of Kemptville. Now in his early thirties, he found the demands on his time of small-town office were slight. By conscientious attention to the interests of his clients, he continued to gain in reputation and frequently filled in as judge at Division Court in Prescott. However, it was not his law practice but his political career which generated most of the excitement in his life, for the old divisions in Council remained. And what could be more appropriate as the bone of contention than that old perennial, Clothier's Bridge?

Defending his first year as reeve at the town's December 1900 nomination meeting, Howard Ferguson told his audience how on every issue, the Council had divided into two warring camps, Angus Buchanan, Dr Holmes, and Patterson against MacGregor and Ferguson.[13] A committee of Buchanan, Holmes, and MacGregor had been appointed to correspond with a contractor and obtain plans; but once this was accomplished, two of the committee, Buchanan and Holmes, worked covertly to seize control of the whole operation. The result was apparent to everybody. The new bridge was a shoddy, imperfect structure; Howard Ferguson finally prevailed on the Council to pay neither the engineer nor the contractor until the work was completed properly. Howard's opponent for reeve withdrew and the return of the Council by acclamation was an impressive vote of confidence in Ferguson's leadership.

The following year Howard fulfilled every politician's dream and became part owner of his own newspaper. The little *Kemptville Telegram* at least gave him a ready forum for his ideas and policies. A series of editorials soon appeared attacking the Liberal government at Queen's Park for corruption, machine politics, and other iniquities. Although unsigned, one may assume that the man who had by this time become the recognized leader of Kemptville Conservatism played no small role in their composition. And an occasional article began to appear under the Ferguson signature.[14]

Of particular interest was a piece entitled 'Growth of the Pulp Industry.'[15] Waxing enthusiastic about Canada's industrial development, the neophyte journalist noted that 'our mineral wealth has excited the interest of the world. Our agricultural products bear an enviable reputation in the world's markets.' After a tedious sketch of the history of papermaking from ninth-century China on, the young writer finally got to the point and vividly described the impressive strides of the Canadian industry. 'Today we have thirty-five mills in operation with a capacity of 1200 tons a day,' with unlimited amounts of capital being attracted to Canada. Somehow, the small-town lawyer had developed a keen awareness of the potential of Canada's vast resources. Perhaps it was from his uncle, Robert Bell, the railway promoter, that he inherited an appreciation of the need for an aggressive approach to the development of those resources. Howard admired the dynamic businessmen and entrepreneurs who were opening the Canadian west, building new railways, and harnessing natural resources. He himself, as soon as he had the money to spare, invested all he could in that vast area of his own province referred to as 'New Ontario.' Howard Ferguson, with his chunky eyeglasses and conservative suits, would have looked perfectly at home behind the local banker's wicket or at a counting-house desk.

Although Howard's last two years as reeve were quiet, a good deal was achieved for Kemptville. Substantial sums were spent on a system of electric lights. In 1902 a site was purchased for the agricultural fairgrounds. Largely as a result of Howard's conviction that the economic future of Kemptville depended on its links with the rest of the county, the town paid two-fifths of the cost of the model road to the junction. There was one unsuccessful effort on which Kemptville's progressive reeve expended a good deal of time in the summer of 1901. This was his attempt to induce an important new industry to locate in the town. After much correspondence, the proprietor of a Montreal cigar factory came to see what Ferguson and Kemptville had to offer. The employer of fifty or sixty men, he made it clear that what attracted him to Kemptville was the prospect of cheap labour. Perhaps it was as well that the town refused to meet his demands for tax concessions and a $15,000 bonus. The project collapsed.[16]

Despite this failure, Ferguson overwhelmed his only opponent, a mill owner and prominent Grit, in the January 1902 elections. The following year he was opposed once again by the same man but this time a new issue appeared. The reeve, it was pointed out, had recently been an aspirant for higher office and apparently had not abandoned such ambitions. This was quite true. In May 1902 Howard Ferguson had boldly challenged the provincial member for Grenville, Robert Joynt, at a Tory nominating convention. He had narrowly failed to unhorse Joynt and it was an open secret that he intended to try again at the earliest opportunity. Perhaps for this reason, Ferguson withdrew from the election.

Howard Ferguson retired from local office with no regrets. Local politics had taught him much. The brash and inexperienced young man first elected in 1897 had proved himself a constructive innovator, bold enough to press his own views against those with far wider experience, able enough to have those views translated into realistic policies. If he was pushy, he was pushing for improvements: for new roads, paved sidewalks, electric lighting, a library, a park, an improved bridge, and new industry. Howard Ferguson of Kemptville had become part of an important municipal reform movement which was changing for the better many aspects of Ontario's urban landscape. Clearly he was alert to the spirit of this movement and acted effectively to implement much of its detail in his little eastern Ontario village. He recognized too that such concerns had a universal application. These were the issues which touched voters most closely; what Howard learned in Kemptville stood him in good stead for the rest of his life.

Kemptville also had offered the opportunity to develop traits and practise techniques which in truth were almost instinctive to him. He was discovering how to handle himself in public life, the importance of mastering the issues, seizing the initiative, and pressing ahead. Always he would prepare his ground and throw himself into the fray. Kemptville liked his aggressive, confident manner, the way he planted himself squarely on the platform and seemed to confide in his audience as though they were his friends and neighbours. Of course they were precisely that and the platform manner developed in little Kemptville would one day serve him well in Toronto, in London, England, and even in far-off Geneva. Never in his life would Howard orate at an audience. Friendly, warm, witty, by turns ingratiating and forceful, by no means a great speaker, he was often devastatingly effective. Direct and to the point, above all sensitive to the mood and interests of those he was addressing, he sold himself and his ideas in about equal parts. Those who heard him understood him, felt they knew him, knew they could approach him without fear of rebuff or misunderstanding.

This was the effect he had on people. He never lost these attributes. In Ontario in his day and for many years thereafter, the small-town folksiness and earthy shrewdness he expressed so perfectly were political gold. His own appeal, backed, of course, by solid talents, would prove irresistible. In five municipal elections, Kemptville had demonstrated its faith in him and in later years it would be said that the mere act of filing nomination papers was notice to all that Howard would be sitting again for Grenville. Yet as he retired from local affairs to claim his heritage, he found the road blocked and as a consequence learned another lesson which, no less than his municipal experience, profoundly influenced his attitudes and helped shape his political methods.

Many a young man of ambition and promise has found his way up the political ladder blocked by the unavailability of a constituency. Challenges to sitting members at party nominating conventions are infrequently made and rarely successful for the advantages are held by the person in possession of the seat. When Howard Ferguson first went after a place at Queen's Park he engaged in a battle not with the Grits but with a fellow Tory, which split the Conservative party in Grenville for the best part of a decade. The circumstances of his entry into the Ontario legislature provide a fascinating study of patterns of political rivalry within one constituency in turn-of-the-century Ontario.

Ambition is an urgent thing which permits no indefinite postponement. A politician's working lifetime is usually brief. In eastern Ontario the ambitious Tory who waits for the Liberals to defeat his party rival and thereby open the constituency must be a man of unusual patience. Ambition deferred would probably become a career denied. Unless some arrangement can be worked out within the party, there is no easy alternative. At some point he must challenge the sitting member, openly and aggressively. Howard Ferguson may have entered upon this course reluctantly, knowing its dangers, but he did so with a realization that it was a legitimate and necessary part of political life. Unfortunately, the factional fight waged at a series of Tory conventions affected the party's fortunes in Grenville in no fewer than three provincial elections. Ambition, political revenge, the relationship within a constituency of federal and provincial elements, the depth of sectional or at least local feeling even within a county unit, these were some of the elements involved.

While the welter of charges and counter-charges has obscured some of the details of the dispute, others are clear. Howard Ferguson had his eye on Grenville's provincial seat from at least 1901. Although his interests had always centred on the federal arena, his father's old seat was now firmly held by Dr Jack Reid of Prescott, an influential and vigorous figure. The provincial situation presented a different aspect. The sitting Conservative member, Robert Joynt, a middle-aged merchant from Augusta Township in the southern part of the riding, was a man of moderate abilities. It may have seemed to Ferguson that he was ripe for the plucking. Joynt, however, fought desperately for his job. The result was the kind of struggle which in other times and places has ruined a party locally for years. Not the least important consequence of the affair was that Howard Ferguson was thereby stamped as the man who had entered the House by defeating a fellow Tory. Years later, when he was fighting for the premiership in 1923, his enemies would attack him for his role in the Joynt affair.

Howard's retirement from Kemptville politics advertised his provincial ambitions throughout the constituency. His intentions were the subject of local gossip as early as May 1901 when the North Augusta *Citizen* noted rumours that he intended to be the Conservative candidate in the next election, although the paper also observed that the sitting member, Robert Joynt, had given no indication of an intention to retire. To this the *Kemptville Telegram* replied rather testily, 'there is no reason why any man should not aspire to the honour but as for Mr Ferguson it will rest entirely with the convention what course he takes.'[17] Ferguson's name, it was thus suggested, would be put before the constituency's next nominating convention.

Ferguson's intention did not seem to do him any damage in Tory circles, where his star continued to rise. At the annual meeting of the North Leeds and Grenville Conservative Association, he and Jim MacGregor were elected to the executive. Yet rumours of a fight among Grenville factions were beginning to reach as far as the provincial capital. In July 1901, the ardently Tory Toronto *Telegram* for the first time took note of the eager young Grenville politician who was causing all the trouble:

Howard Ferguson, who comes rightfully by his taste for public life, being the son of a former MP for North Leeds and Grenville, is bound to be a candidate at the provincial election. He is a Conservative, but failure to capture the party nomination will not frighten him away from his ambitions, as his friends declare he will run as an independent. He is a young man, but is not as popular as R.L. Joynt, the present Tory MPP, who is almost certain to be renominated. Meanwhile the Liberals are on the scene with delight, trusting that two Tories will be in the field on election day...[18]

The *Kemptville Telegram* quickly declared that its Toronto namesake 'is very wide of the mark and has really not learned anything about the case. Mr Ferguson has never expressed any desire to run the independent course but on the contrary says he will abide by the convention ... and as to his popularity it has never been tested beyond the village of Kemptville. ... One thing is certain and that is that Mr Ferguson is not dividing the Conservative Party.'

On 7 May 1902, Grenville Conservatives held their annual meeting. Since this was an election year it was the task of the convention to select a candidate.[19] The vote, 36 for Ferguson, 54 for Joynt, showed that the Kemptville lawyer had overstepped himself. In the subsequent campaign Howard did his duty as the leading Kemptville Conservative. Appearing with Joynt on a Kemptville platform, he assured him that the town would provide a good Conservative majority. And it did. Joynt's majority in Grenville as a whole was 860, the largest in the constituency's history.[20]

Provincially, the Liberals clung to office by the narrowest of margins. All Premier Ross's vaunted energy and oratorical power had been required to withstand the determined assault of the Whitney Conservatives. Jubilant yet also disappointed with the final count of 51 Liberals to 46 Conservatives, the Whitney men were determined that next time the whole prize would be theirs. The Grits were on the run. Their days of power were numbered and their whole edifice could collapse at any moment. In Tory eyes the next election could not come too soon. As for Joynt, he seems never to have fully recovered from the shock of Howard Ferguson's convention challenge. Throughout his second term in the legislature he remained nervously preoccupied by events back home in Grenville. Since a quick election and a new convention were distinct possibilities, Joynt's fears were justified. Indeed, it may well have been less some overt act on Ferguson's part than Joynt's apprehensions that accounted for the accusations which now blew the whole affair into the open.

It happened at a meeting of the Grenville Conservative Association held at Spencerville in October 1903. Joynt, emboldened by Ferguson's absence, made accusations which he believed would assuredly end any challenge for his seat.[21] The charges were startling and unequivocal. According to Joynt, Howard Ferguson, unscrupulously ignoring all his promises to support the Tory nominee, early in the 1902 election campaign had gone on a secret mission to Toronto. There he had sought out Alex Smith, the long-time organizer of the provincial Liberal party. Ferguson had actually solicited Liberal support for himself as a candidate in the election. This information, Joynt assured the startled Tories, had been given him by Albert Whitney, a Prescott lawyer, and by John Mundle, also of Prescott, who in turn had been so informed by Alex Smith himself.[22]

Such treachery was unpardonable. If Joynt's accusations had spread unchallenged, Howard Ferguson's hopes for a political career would probably have been wrecked. Even if promptly denied, charges of such a nature had the potential to do irreparable damage. Incredibly, however, if notarized statements are to be trusted, there was not a word of truth in them. Howard Ferguson certainly wasted not a moment in giving them the lie direct. Within two days, Alex Smith himself had signed a notarized document declaring: '...I have never been interviewed by G. Howard Ferguson on such a subject either in Toronto or anywhere else.' Similar affidavits were issued on 19 October and 21 October by Albert Whitney and John Mundle. Both men swore they had said nothing to Joynt to indicate that they had ever had such a conversation. Mundle swore that 'such a statement if made by Joynt is absolutely false and is without the slightest foundation.'[23] According to Ferguson's own account, he had worked loyally and energetically on Joynt's behalf in the 1902 campaign.

When Joynt could offer no proof for his reckless accusations, it became clear that he had engaged in an exercise of self-destruction. Ferguson could now act openly against the man who had tried to destroy him. The power of the Ferguson forces was soon demonstrated. Hardly a year and a half after Joynt's triumphant re-election to Queen's Park, they were able to force another nominating convention.

Held at Spencerville on 8 December 1903, its purpose was to pick both federal and provincial candidates.[24] The occasion or perhaps excuse for such a convention was federal more than provincial. The constituency had been divided by the Laurier government and it was now necessary to select a new federal candidate for Grenville. To some members of the Grenville Association, this presented a golden opportunity. The Ferguson forces would use the occasion to nominate a provincial candidate as well. As Joynt later complained in an open letter, 'a certain clique, contrary to all ideas of fair play, took advantage of my temporary absence in the West and forced Mr Reid, the candidate for the Dominion House, to enter into an agreement or combination by which he, Mr Reid, would receive the nomination for the Dominion House and Mr Ferguson for the Local.' Since Joynt might, in the normal course of affairs, expect to have two sessions still to serve in the legislature, he protested bitterly to the Grenville association executive that there was no reason for such a convention. But his protests had no effect for, in his words, 'the combination was too strong to be broken.'[25] The constituency executive refused either to postpone or change the purpose of the proposed convention.

Robert Joynt's concern is understandable, for Dr Reid had in fact entered the lists on behalf of Howard Ferguson. A shrewd political practitioner and notorious manipulator, Jack Reid in later days became one of the most powerful figures in the Borden cabinet. Against a combination of Reid and Ferguson, Joynt's cause was hopeless. When Grenville Tories met on 8 December, Reid was the unanimous choice for federal candidate of the 89 delegates. Next the provincial nominations were called for and Joynt made his move. Since no provincial election was expected for three years, there could be, he charged, no justification for a nominating convention. At this point, however, the delegates determined on an immediate nomination, with 54 voting in favour and only 34 against. Robert Joynt now refused to stand. Ferguson was the convention's unanimous choice.[26]

Although in subsequent months Howard was often introduced at public functions as Grenville's next representative in the Ontario legislature, his position was difficult and uncertain. A furious Robert Joynt went about telling everyone who would listen that Ferguson was a pettifogging young scoundrel who had unscrupulously manipulated a rigged convention to get a better job. Association president Carmichael reported to James Whitney that several newspapers contained 'letters from our representative Mr Joynt, and also interviews with newspapers and also an Editorial in the World.'[27] Indeed Joynt seemed to be having a good deal of success for undeniably, an appearance of unfairness surrounded the whole business. Colonel Carmichael, however, warned Whitney against accepting Joynt's account, assuring him that 'at all our organization meetings, and other meetings up to and including the Convention, Mr Joynt was present, although the interviews would lead the public to believe otherwise.' Carmichael offered a different explanation. 'Never at any meetings or even at the Convention was there any fight between Joynt and Ferguson. It was entirely a fight from the North end of this riding, owing to the Redistribution, that they should have either one of the representatives, and nothing we could do could prevent giving them one.' Furthermore he pointed out to Whitney that 'it was honestly believed a local election would be brought on immediately after the Dominion Election ... Now that a Session of the Local has been called, I have not the slightest doubt that a new Convention will be called when the House dissolves, and Mr Joynt and Mr Ferguson and anyone else can test their strength. ... In justice to Mr Ferguson, he has expressed his willingness to do this at any time the party may wish it.' In fact, Carmichael told the Conservative leader, at the convention Howard Ferguson had not insisted on pressing the issue. He had 'expressed himself as willing to agree to an adjournment, but it seemed impossible to control the delegates to agree to any other decision than they did.'[28]

This may not be entirely convincing, but it does lend a different complexion to the affair. Not Ferguson's ambition so much as an expectation of a quick provincial election and a deep-seated sectionalism within the constituency had contributed to Joynt's discomfiture. One may perhaps doubt that Howard Ferguson was quite as forebearing as Carmichael would have had Whitney believe. During the 1904 federal campaign, Ferguson and Joynt had little choice but to appear together in Kemptville on the same platform to assist Dr Reid's campaign for re-election. No one was surprised when Howard's platform effort completely outshone Joynt's undistinguished oratory. The Ross administration, he asserted, had been guilty of acts of the most disgraceful kind and in this regard the Laurier government was no different. 'They ought to be hurried from power.' But Ferguson's announcement to his Kemptville audience that he was going to talk about public morality was too much for them. They knew full well what was going on in their own constituency and with Reid and Joynt sitting on the platform behind Ferguson, this served to underline the fact. Howard heard the tittering from the audience and saw the broad smile on its face. Equal to the occasion, he told them, 'When I come to speak of public morality, you think I am joking. Well, don't do as I do, do as I say.'[29] Jack Reid was returned with an easy majority of some six hundred and continued to be a source of support to Ferguson.

The Ferguson supporters now changed their strategy. Joynt was winning sympathy so they announced they would consent to another convention. Even Joynt agreed that this would be a fair means of settling the issue. With the provincial election to be held a few weeks later, on 25 January 1905, he could hardly have objected. At 10:30 on a cold morning early in January the leading Grenville Tories, ninety in all, gathered in the village of Spencerville.[30] The notoriety of the protracted Ferguson-Joynt contest had attracted a large number of expectant observers. Colonel Carmichael took the chair, the credentials of the constituency members were examined with more care than usual, and nominations were called for. Ferguson offered himself as the man of reason, pleading for party harmony and promising to support the choice of the convention if defeated himself. Again he made the sectional argument, suggesting that since the federal member came from the southern part of the riding, the provincial nominee should be chosen from the north. For his part, Joynt attacked the idea of regional representation and appealed for fair play for a man who had served his constituents well and whose political appeal had been proven by the size of his majority in the last election, the largest in the history of the constituency. Pointing to the division in party ranks, he mocked Howard Ferguson's claim to be a loyal party man uninfluenced by personal ambitions.

But it was to no avail. On the first ballot Ferguson received 45 votes to 40 for Joynt and five for a third candidate. On a second ballot, Howard took the constituency by a slim eight votes. The race had been close and the critical moment was less the voting than the aftermath. Although Howard at once delivered a ringing appeal for unity in the face of the impending contest with the Grits, an embittered Joynt insisted the convention had been packed. A few days later he issued a circular letter containing specific charges of irregularities concerning the election of delegates to the convention from Edwardsburg, Burritt's Rapids, and elsewhere.

...I feel that it would be an act of cowardice on my part and that I would be treating the electors of Grenville very shabbily if I allowed these men to profit by their unfairly obtained victory without a protest, and have determined to appeal from the decision of the so-called convention to the people of the whole riding, and therefore announce myself as a candidate for your suffrages at the approaching election on the 25th of January. I have no doubt the electors have a choice between a lawyer whose first efforts were a series of tricks to get to Parliament, and a straightforward businessman, with whom there was no complaint...[31]

It promised to be an interesting campaign. Howard Ferguson began at once to distribute election posters and arrange speaking engagements throughout the riding. At this point things looked promising for the Liberals. The disruption in the Conservative ranks was noticed as far away as Toronto and Montreal and was a major disquieting factor in their generally smoothly functioning eastern Ontario campaign. When Ferguson read the charges against him in Joynt's circular letter, he offered his accuser time at any of his meetings to make his charges, but apparently no such confrontation took place.[32] The Liberals put Joynt's disaffection to every possible use and Joynt himself did not hesitate to use whatever means came to hand. He even sought out the office of the Brockville *Recorder,* the newspaper of prominent Liberal politician George P. Graham, a recent addition to the Ross cabinet.[33] Graham found Joynt's information invaluable and on many a public platform he trumpeted that Howard Ferguson had purchased his victory in the Grenville convention by buying delegate votes at ten dollars a head. The Tories were corrupt, their whole campaign was the purest hypocrisy. Since James Whitney's well-documented charges of corruption against the Liberal government were at the heart of Tory strategy, Graham's counterattack was a shrewd and dangerous threat to the Conservatives.[34]

Whitney must have regarded this situation with grave displeasure. On the eve of overturning the entrenched Liberal régime, he could not permit such mudslinging to continue. No evidence seems to remain as to what pressures may have been applied from party headquarters but less than a week before the 25 January election, Robert Joynt retired from the contest. The reason given was that a Liberal had finally entered the Grenville contest and Joynt had decided not to risk losing the seat to the Grits. More likely, Whitney had spoken.

The Tory bickering did the Liberals little good in Grenville. With Joynt eliminated, Ferguson disposed of the Liberal candidate by a 548-vote majority. He had chosen a great year to enter the Ontario legislature. After a drought of thirty-five years, Conservatism in Ontario swept the boards in an unprecedented victory. The province had rid itself of the Grits with a vengeance. Despite the heroic exertions of George Ross, suddenly a rather tragic figure, the Liberals returned only 29 members to 69 for the Tories. There is no indication of Ferguson's feelings about the means of his accession to the Ontario legislature, yet he probably had few qualms of conscience. A measure of notoriety attached itself to him but he had never really broken the rules of the political game. He had gone after what he wanted but his ambitions were legitimate. Ferguson had every right to compete for the nomination and his victory over the rather ineffectual Joynt considerably strengthened the party in eastern Ontario. The episode thus had a happy ending for both Ferguson and the party. In such circumstances Whitney, who admired a fighter, could afford to adopt a generous attitude towards whatever indiscretions his new supporter from Grenville may have committed.

As he took his place in the legislature, Ferguson may well have reflected that his ouster of Joynt, while it had given him some anxious moments, had done him little permanent harm. He knew that as the member for Grenville, he could mend his fences at his leisure. With pleasure and anticipation, he turned his attention to Queen's Park, where the Tories with aplomb and assurance were taking over the places of power which had eluded them for so long.

3

'Ontario Must Take the Lead'

For a decade, Howard Ferguson served as a backbench supporter of James P. Whitney. His political outlook was immeasurably broadened by his presence during one of the more creative periods of Ontario's political history. Educational and electoral reforms, developmental programs for the north, the dextrous and courageous management of the dangerous liquor issue, and the creation of a great publicly owned Hydro system were the policies which formed the vital structure of Ontario Conservatism in the new century. They would be the stuff of politics years later when he himself would occupy the place then held so masterfully by Whitney. Ferguson's own policies and approach would owe much to the lessons learned under the tutelage of the great Tory leader.

Although his political skills developed rapidly in these years and his abilities did not go unrecognized, Ferguson never attained a place in the Whitney cabinet. Perhaps his independent ways and his aggressive thrusts to the fore served him less well at Queen's Park than they had in Kemptville. Although there could never be any doubt about the depths of his Toryism or the strength of his party loyalty, Ferguson was too strong-minded and impatient to accept unquestioningly the lead of others or to do mute service on the backbenches. Instead, from the beginning, he asserted his opinions forcefully and showed little deference to the party's hierarchy. He gained thereby an early reputation as an individualist, someone who would play the party game but play it according to rules not readily recognizable to his political fellows. 'When he came into the House,' a former Tory member recalled in 1923, 'he was a continual thorn in the flesh of Sir James Whitney, and those of us who were in caucus in the early days of the Whitney administration well remember the exasperation of the grand old man when he threatened to read the present leader out of the party and debar him from caucus.'[1]

One can readily conjure up an image of the formidable Whitney barking out his indignation at the young pup who presumed to offer frequent advice on what the government should do in this situation or that. Yet many of the stories about friction with Whitney originated later with Ferguson's political enemies and contemporary evidence makes it clear that the Premier fully appreciated and frequently drew upon Howard Ferguson's political talents. No doubt Whitney was irritated from time to time by Howard's bumptiousness but if a split between the two did develop, it seems likely that it was brought about not by personality clashes but by the role the younger man assumed as the champion of English-language instruction and opponent of bilingualism in the schools of Ontario. There was no more emotionally charged issue in pre-war Ontario. When Howard Ferguson donned the robes of a crusader and campaigned across the province on behalf of his particular vision of the Canadian destiny, he was appealing to emotions which no party leader, provincial or national, henceforth would be able to ignore.

The Ontario legislature opened on 22 March 1905 'amid a blaze of electricity and the roar of cannon.'[2] For the first time since Confederation, the proceedings were directed by a Conservative government. Ferguson took his place along with numerous other freshman members in the obscurity of the long Tory backbenches. The Premier, meanwhile, had formed a cabinet which bespoke the kind of leadership he would give the province. J.J. Foy, Attorney-General and chief lieutenant, a Roman Catholic of Irish origins, symbolized by his presence the demise of the ultra-Protestantism which had once been rampant in Tory circles while Arthur Reaume, Commissioner of Public Works, was the first French Canadian to hold a portfolio in an Ontario administration. Dr R.A. Pyne in Education, A.J. Matheson as Provincial Treasurer, and S.N. Monteith in Agriculture were solid but unspectacular members. More significant was the appointment of W.J. Hanna of East Lambton as Provincial Secretary. A formidable figure whose powerful oratory and executive abilities raised him to the first rank but whose reputed friendship with the liquor interests and long connection with the Standard Oil Company made him a source of much controversy, he brought reassurance to elements which had been disturbed by Whitney's anti-corporation speeches. So too did John S. Hendrie, a former mayor of Hamilton with close connections with the business community who served, along with W.A. Willoughby, a veteran member from eastern Ontario, and Adam Beck of London, as ministers without portfolio. Beck, intrepid ideologue and empire-builder, would soon achieve power which rivalled even the Premier's. A little later the initial group was joined by Frank Cochrane, the tough, resilient Sudbury hardware merchant who headed the newly named Department of Lands, Forests and Mines. In him, Whitney had found his man for New Ontario, someone who understood the north and who possessed as well rare talents as a political organizer.

Whitney had wrought well. It was an impressive cabinet, perhaps the strongest in the province's history. Its program evolved in reaction to the predominantly rural outlook of the old Liberal régime and to that régime's close ties to Ontario's corporate élite. The Whitney men, unfettered by old alliances and anxious to bring change to a province ruled for too long by politicians whose methods and ideas were rooted in an earlier, simpler age, boldly seized the promise of the new day. Theirs was a program called forth by the needs of a rapidly urbanizing, increasingly industrialized province. Nowhere was this better illustrated than in the contrast between the financial restrictions and petty political interferences to which the University of Toronto had been subjected by the Liberal ministers and the generous policy of the new administration. Financial support was immediately increased while a royal commission was appointed whose recommendations resulted in a new form of university government under which the institution would be managed by a Board of Governors with academic issues being left to the Senate; security of tenure and higher salaries were achieved for faculty; and the School of Practical Science and the Faculty of Medicine were integrated into the University. Political interference was to be negated largely through the appointment of a new and vigorous president who could breathe life into the whole structure.

The man for the job, Howard Ferguson informed Whitney in June 1906, was the Rev. H.J. Cody. 'I attended college with Cody and have known him intimatly [sic] for a number of years. He possesses the brains, cultural and executive capacity to do the position great credit.' Whitney demurred. Although he professed great respect for Cody, he felt that the difficulties of the position demanded someone who could be something of an 'intellectual tyrant.' Whitney did not think Cody 'would be "ugly" enough for the place. I am sure you will understand what I mean...' Ferguson, however, did not let the matter rest and told his leader that '...I feel sure when occasion required (he) would show sufficient of the "tyrant. ... "' Furthermore I think I need scarcely tell you that already the University has suffered from too much tyrrany [sic] and not enough individuality.'[3] Ferguson expanded at some length on Cody's qualifications. If this lecture from a new member irked Whitney, he betrayed no sign in his reply, in which he pointed out that his reference had been to the dealings of the new president with the Board of Governors. Finally, the appointment went to Robert Falconer, a Nova Scotian who had served as principal of a Presbyterian college in Halifax.

In short order, principally in the first few years of the new government's tenure of office, Whitney progressivism took shape. W.J. Hanna took hold with a firm hand of the province's social institutions and effected long-needed changes in penal administration and other forms of institutional care. Dr Pyne, with the assistance of John Seath and a new breed of professional educators, overhauled a dated structure and looked towards new methods and machinery fitted to the educational needs of an industrial state. Whitney's crusade against electoral corruption reached partial fruition when the numbered ballot was abolished, while Foy's radical Elections Act of 1908 attempted with mixed success to eliminate all possible types of corrupt behaviour. Whitney himself, playing the traditional role of defender of provincial rights, presented what he described as 'drastic' legislation aimed at checking the alarming effort of many companies operating in Ontario to avoid provincial regulation by acquiring only federal charters.

From the perspective of Ferguson's later career, Whitney's adept treatment of the prohibition question was particularly significant. With the dry cause on the march across North America, the Premier refused to succumb to the excited rhetoric of extremists of either side but handled a truly difficult problem with caution and moderation. His Liquor License Act of 1906, which increased license fees, established stricter regulation of the trade and adopted a local option procedure based on a three-fifths clause, succeeded politically because it was a reasonable approach which appealed to moderate opinion. Prohibition was an issue which gave Ferguson, a member for a largely rural district, much cause for thought. At first he believed that the three-fifths clause was 'un-British and contrary to the genius of responsible government,' but after discussing the matter with temperance men and others he concluded that 'the new Legislation makes for permanency of the temperance cause.' In 1907 he was present when several hundred members of the Dominion Alliance vociferously presented their views to Whitney, but he was unmoved and still held that 'the question should not be how many votes should be required to carry a by-law but how can the movement best be made permanent.'

Many of his constituents remained unsatisfied, however, so in March 1908 he presented his position at great length in a letter to the Rev. J.B. Robinson. 'I want to express my entire sympathy,' he told Robinson 'towards the temperance movement. I yield to no man in my dislike to [sic] the evils of intemperance.' Yet he insisted, as did Whitney, that the growth of temperance must be 'a steady progress based on public opinion' and he doubted that many of the towns were yet ready for complete prohibition. He argued too that the mass of opinion 'is not nearly so advanced as some over-enthusiastic temperance lecturers would have us believe. I sympathize with these men, but very often ... I think that they are wilfully or ignorantly mistaken.' A man's rights, Ferguson insisted, must not be lightly taken away. 'Am I wrong in premising that any great moral question directly affecting the public must be approached with the utmost care...?'[4] In his view, Whitney's policy, sensible and courageous, was admirable in every way.

Most important perhaps, certainly most controversial, was the Tory policy of public ownership of the province's incredibly rich hydro-electric resources and the accompanying production and distribution systems. Although the full program unfolded only gradually, private interest groups from the beginning opposed the Hydro as revolutionary, socialistic, confiscatory, and unjust. It took all the demoniac energies and often unscrupulous tactics of Hydro's first great chairman, Adam Beck, to launch successfully the amazing new venture in government ownership, but it required as well the wise guidance and occasionally the swift exercise of awesome political power by Whitney himself, who held back the anti-Hydro sentiments of such members of his own cabinet as Hendrie, Cochrane, and Hanna. While Hydro undeniably became the keystone of the structure of Ontario progressive conservatism, Whitney's support was based less on ideological zeal than on pragmatic considerations. If he restrained Beck's enemies in Tory ranks, he also managed to keep in check some of the Hydro czar's own wilder enthusiasms. As had Whitney, Ferguson in his day would support Hydro and Beck while subjecting both the man and his vision to much-needed control and discipline.

Equally important to the future career of the Grenville member were the reforms effected by Frank Cochrane in New Ontario. Ferguson had first demonstrated his interest in the north in articles written for his Kemptville newspaper, and in subsequent years he made investments as substantial as the profits from a small-town law practice allowed in northern Ontario mining stock. During this period, the younger man became a protégé and admirer of the masterful Cochrane. Howard was a close observer as the minister and his deputy, Aubrey White, overhauled the timber regulations and put the province's relations with the big lumber concerns on a more businesslike basis. He appreciated the developmental significance of Cochrane's efforts to promote the refining of ores within Ontario and admired the strong hand with which the minister overrode the protests which greeted new mining tax legislation. From Cochrane, too, the political boss of the north, he learned how northern development could serve the needs of both the province and the party.

It was an impressive performance. The Tory hold on power was confirmed and strengthened as Whitney led his party to three more great election victories and the Liberals became reduced to what seemed at times to be permanent minority status. As for Ferguson, he was hardly likely to go unnoticed even in a party which possessed no shortage of talented members. In 1907, in a gesture which meant more then than it does now, he was chosen to move the address and delivered the customary panegyric in praise of government operations. He was grateful when George Graham, newly chosen Liberal leader, complimented him by remarking that he could hardly have performed other than well, having inherited his political talents. Later that session, Ferguson drew on his experience in municipal affairs and his new role as a member of the legislature's Committee on Municipal Law to present an amendment to the Municipal Act. At Hanna's request, he withdrew his proposal but a little later brought forward significant amendments to the Ditches and Watercourses Act and the Municipal Drainage Act. Speaking at length, he argued that the province should undertake a sweeping survey of eastern Ontario's drainage problems and for his efforts won praise not only from regional newspapers such as the Brockville *Times*, but from Whitney himself, who as an eastern Ontario man was well aware of the area's special problems.[5] When the amendments passed, Ferguson had won his spurs as a spokesman for his region and his constituency. He never lost sight of the fact that eastern Ontarians, living in a part of the province which had never fully shared in the prosperity of the western peninsula, expected their politicians to work hard on behalf of their material interests. Whether this involved a fair share of patronage, new roads, or government buildings, Ferguson as backbencher and Premier understood perfectly this fundamental reality of eastern Ontario political life.

In 1908 he was entrusted with the chairmanship of some of the legislature's most important committees. By this time he was speaking frequently and effectively in the House and addressing Conservative meetings about the province. In March, for example, he explained the Whitney record to Hamilton Conservatives and attacked the Laurier Liberals for 'graft and corruption.' Demonstrating a deft political touch, he supported the cause of technical education by declaiming, 'if a school is to be built, why not in the Birmingham of Canada?' An impressed Hamilton *Spectator* prophesied that the young Tory would hold a responsible position in the cabinet 'in the not distant future.'[6]

That June the province faced an election. In reality it was a triumphal procession. George Graham took refuge in the Laurier cabinet and the new Liberal leader, Alexander MacKay, salvaged only 19 seats, compared to 86 for the Conservatives, with one going to a labour member. In the province at large, the campaign was dull. In Grenville, however, Howard Ferguson faced a desperate fight. Robert Joynt had refused to take his enforced retirement gracefully and had occupied himself by spreading the word that Ferguson and Jack Reid were scoundrels who had stolen his seat. Worse still, Ferguson had been unable to restore harmony to constituency factions. Not only had the southern part of the riding, with the intense loyalty of a rural area, remained firmly behind Joynt, but in the north many Conservatives were supporting the man from Augusta. There was no more influential Conservative family in the riding than the Kidds of Burritt's Rapids, for example, and T.A. Kidd himself was backing Joynt.[7]

Despite this, the Joynt forces were not strong enough to challenge Ferguson at the official convention and he was nominated by acclamation. This time Joynt went the independent route and the Liberals, anxious to co-operate, did not nominate a candidate. At the all-party nomination meeting, Joynt launched an impassioned attack on Ferguson, claiming again that the convention at which Ferguson had first won the nomination had been rigged and that Jack Reid had been 'taken by the throat by either Howard Ferguson or his father' and forced into line. Not only that, but Ferguson had played a corrupt role at Toronto and spent his time 'lobbying' and 'holding his hand behind his back.'

At this point the split in Tory ranks seemed so deep that Joynt with Liberal support stood an excellent chance of taking the seat. It was Reid, furious at Joynt's manoeuvres, who spoke on his friend's behalf. Joynt, he charged, was lying about his own role at the convention and the stories he was now spreading about Ferguson's 'corruption' were utterly unfounded. Evidently they were based on Ferguson's vote in a matter relating to the Ottawa Valley Power Company and Reid insisted that in it he had merely followed the course desired by the mayor of Ottawa.[8] It would take more than words, however, to dispel the ugly rumours and insinuations.

This was a situation to which Ferguson would grow accustomed. In his future career he would frequently face similar charges and be forced to defend himself against aspersions on his honour and integrity. In each case, he would flail out against his traducers, fight back vigorously, and emerge stronger than ever. Whether his propensity for such episodes demonstrated a kind of ineptness or something worse, he seemed to revel at the confrontations he faced and he became, at the very least, the province's most adept practitioner of the politics of crisis and survival.

In this case, however, Howard was under no illusions about the dangers which confronted him. Before the campaign started, he considered eliminating Joynt by a time-honoured method. Someone, perhaps Joynt himself, intimated that the rift could be healed and Joynt would retire if some sinecure could be made available. Although the details are obscure, Ferguson later reminded Whitney that 'I might have had my election by acclamation.' This would have suited Ferguson well; in his opinion the weapons in the government's armoury were to be used, not dissipated. But when he discussed the matter with Whitney, the Premier 'expressed a preference to have him disposed of at the polls rather than at the Parliament Buildings. It was largely for this reason that I undertook a task which I know I could have made much easier and less expensive...'[9]

Still, there was satisfaction in running Joynt to the ground. During the weeks ahead, Reid was seldom absent from his friend's side and the Whitney government offered its aid, partly in the form of a speech by Provincial Treasurer Matheson, delivered at Merrickville, deep in Joynt territory. Matheson declared himself the envoy of Whitney, prevented from being present on account of illness, and he praised Ferguson in fulsome terms, promising that he would soon be in the cabinet. Reid said the same thing.[10] Joynt's efforts clearly had the Tories worried.

Nevertheless Whitney did not hesitate to ask Ferguson to help out in other eastern constituencies. When Stormont became a trouble spot and a leading Cornwall barrister appealed to Whitney, the Premier told him to get Ferguson. 'I mentioned this subject to him here a few minutes ago ... and you may rely upon it that he will do good service. ... Ferguson is one of our best men.'[11] High praise, indeed, from the gruff Whitney. 'One of our best men,' the Premier had proclaimed, but despite such faith in his talents as a stump orator, Ferguson could afford few absences from Grenville. At his committee rooms, cheering on his workers, keeping in touch by phone with all parts of the constituency, travelling about by horse and buggy on the abysmal roads of the day, he was working day and night. Joynt meanwhile remained abusive while Ferguson kept to the issues and avoided meeting Joynt's attack in kind. That, it had been decided, would be his best strategy, plus the continued emphasis that Ferguson was Whitney's man. When Joynt scoffed at the possibility of Ferguson joining the cabinet, the *Telegram* insisted that Matheson's words represented a solemn pledge, and that 'Hon. J.P. Whitney is not a man to talk at random.'[12]

Despite all this support, Ferguson sneaked in by a mere twenty-three votes. The south side had declared strongly for Joynt, the north for Ferguson, but Prescott, traditionally Liberal and in Joynt's territory, had failed to deliver as large a majority for the Augusta man as anticipated. Here Reid's machine deserved the credit. With the lead bouncing back and forth for most of the evening, excitement mounted and when it was all over the boisterous Kemptville crowd knew no restraint. A band appeared, a torchlight procession formed, the newly returned member was hoisted on eager shoulders and paraded around town. For hours on that June evening in 1908, Howard's friends marched through the streets, celebrating their victory. A monster bonfire in Riverside Park capped it all and not until morning did the townspeople finally wend their way home, tired but happy.

Henceforth, Grenville belonged to Howard Ferguson. As he put it himself, the fight in the riding was over and he was at peace with all men. For the rest of his career the announcement of his candidacy was enough to ensure his election. On the provincial level, however, the creativity of the first Whitney term was not repeated. Although Whitney retained his hold on the affections of the electorate, his government, with a few significant exceptions, slipped gently into a routine of administrative competence and legislative inactivity. This proved equally true with regard to the cabinet in which in the years ahead the Premier made few changes. The most serious loss was Cochrane, who in 1911 joined the new Borden administration in Ottawa, but his departure was somewhat compensated for by the accession to his old position of William Hearst, another New Ontario man.

For Ferguson there was no cabinet appointment. Although he remained an ambitious man, there is no evidence to suggest grievous disappointment or any measure of bitterness. Whitney liked the familiar faces of his old comrades and in any case there were no vacancies from eastern Ontario. During his second term Howard settled comfortably into the routine of a member's life. Now in his late thirties, he had not yet been overtaken by the portliness of later years, and with his full head of hair, his stylish moustache, and eyes peering out from behind thick glasses, he was set apart from other members by a certain boyish quality, a kind of zest and enthusiasm that he never lost. By this time the friendships first formed in 1905 were deepening. The victory of 1905 had been repeated and after 1908 members sensed that they were building a new Tory era which could be as enduring as the Mowat age from which the province had emerged. In these circumstances, there was a sorting out process at work among the newer Tory members.

One observer has recalled that in those days the old Grand Union Hotel in Ottawa was a frequent meeting place for many of the younger provincial and federal Conservatives. The Grand Union was 'noted for its large dining room, good food and for its long bar and its good liquor. ... I remember that the older Conservatives like Sam Hughes and Frank Cochrane would speak of these young Conservatives as "Young Howard Ferguson," "Young Tom McGarry," "Young Tom Wallace," "Young Eddie Dunlop," and so on.'[13] It was there, in the long bar or in the lounge, and in similar establishments in Toronto and elsewhere that Ferguson, McGarry, Herb Lennox, Forbes Godfrey, and an occasional congenial Liberal would be found. Whiskey, cigars, great leather chairs, political cronies, political talk. The hours would pass, friendships ripen, business would be done. Howard Ferguson, like Macdonald in earlier days, placed a high value on friendship and on the time spent in this way. Most of his knowledge came from people, from their foibles and their wisdom, not from books or study.

Howard's closest political friend was Tom McGarry, the hard-drinking, good-humoured Irish Catholic member from Renfrew. Both were first elected in 1905 and both had politics in their blood. From the beginning, each saw the other as a kindred spirit. Their close friendship became one of the best known political and personal associations of pre-war Ontario politics. Early in the 1909 session Whitney received a request from the party whip asking that Ferguson and McGarry be permitted to change their places in the House and sit together.[14] Few opposition members could keep their composure during a speech when subjected to the loud heckling and sharp taunts of the Ottawa valley pair.

In 1910, for example, when a Liberal member made a strongly personal attack on Cochrane and Whitney for their administration of northern Ontario, Whitney replied with a typically curt dismissal, but Ferguson would not let the matter rest. He rose to make a slashing defence of Whitney and Cochrane. A moment later when Liberal frontbencher J.C. Elliott had harsh words for the Hydro Commission it was McGarry's turn and Elliott received a sound verbal trouncing. Whitney enjoyed the exchange. 'I cannot allow the occasion to go by without repeating how thoroughly I appreciate[d] your performance the other day,' he wrote Ferguson. 'Everybody saw and understood that between you and McGarry there was nothing left of those gentlemen across the floor and in all probability they were kicking themselves for not having held their tongues.'[15]

On the whole, however, the occasional flurry of excitement could not conceal the dreary routine into which public life had fallen in the later Whitney years.

Although Whitney claimed that he had fulfilled the promises made when he came into power and asserted that his purpose had become sound administration, others believed that the government had run out of ideas. In such circumstances the short legislative sessions of the day permitted private members to spend most of their year at home. Howard Ferguson did so, diligently tending his law practice and his business and newspaper interests. Of course a small-town practice would not make him rich, but acting in an endless variety of small disputes he continued to deepen his understanding of people and their motivations. Practising law, meeting friends, having coffee in the main street restaurant and home for lunch with Ella, he savoured the pleasures of small-town life. A good deal of time was spent in Bill Hyland's shoe repair shop, known locally as the 'Board of Trade.' Howard had his own chair at the back, near the window, where he and his friends, the local businessmen and retired farmers, would sit and smoke and mull over the problems of the world and of Kemptville. Occasionally he would attend meetings of the local Orange Lodge; on Sundays he and Ella worshipped in St James Anglican church. Although Howard liked to enjoy himself, he worked hard; there were no trips, for example, to visit the England he loved so well but had never seen. Law and politics remained his dominating passions and his future would be determined by the fortunes of political life. As he settled gradually into middle age, he had become, finally and irrevocably, a professional politician.

'That in the opinion of this House no language other than the English language should be used as a medium of instruction in the schools of this Province.' So read the blunt, infelicitous words of the motion of which Ferguson gave notice in the first days of the 1911 session. The hostility it expressed towards the French language Ferguson shared with many of his fellow Ontarians. Later that year 73 of 86 Ontario constituencies would reject Laurier Liberalism and bring to an end an era in Canadian history. 1911. The date recalls the anti-reciprocity crusade, the Borden-Bourassa alliance, the confrontation which moved Rudyard Kipling to cry, 'it is her own soul that Canada risks today.' Laurier himself believed the election had not been lost by the anti-reciprocity cry. Rather, Protestant Ontario had rejected a prime minister who was French and Catholic. All Laurier's fears had been realized. Never again, he was convinced, should one of his race attempt to be Prime Minister of Canada.

It was no coincidence that this year of religious and racial antagonisms and political upheavals should also see Howard Ferguson's 'English only' resolution. He was merely giving expression to emotions many felt. He did so in typically forthright fashion and apparently without reference to the views of his party leaders. He became thereby a figure of notoriety in the eyes of French Canadians. They knew his sort only too well: a small-town Ontario Protestant, an Orange bigot, narrow, fanatical, and anti-French. His motives seemed a typical mix of politics and prejudice. No less a person than Laurier himself later expressed the belief that Ferguson had calculatingly grasped for himself the leadership of the extreme Orange element and was opposing bilingual schools for the sake of party advantage. For years this was the image his name evoked for French Canadians.

Soon, however, after the provincial government promulgated educational regulations along the lines desired by Ferguson, the dispute broadened, and since both provincial political parties supported the new policy, popularly known as Regulation 17, the leaders of each were attacked and denounced. Strong words were used on both sides as French Canadians engaged in determined resistance to what they believed was a deliberate effort to destroy the language rights which were the very fount of their struggle for national survival. In retrospect it is clear that the passions engendered by Regulation 17 arose not as a result of some political intrigue or plot but from the brutal clash of French-Canadian nationalism at its most aggressive with all the pride and strength embodied in the Ontario psyche. Howard Ferguson was thus a central figure in a recurring tragedy which has faced each generation of Canadians.

In late nineteenth-century Ontario, the rapid growth of French-Canadian numbers in several eastern counties had excited an excessive fear in some quarters. The Toronto *Mail*, for example, had warned its readers that 'if it be allowed to continue, the Eastern part of Ontario ... is doomed before many years to be as dark a spot, on the map of intelligence, as any portion of Quebec.'[16] Unlike neighbouring Prescott, Russell, and Carleton counties, Howard Ferguson's Grenville did not experience a large French influx. Yet it seemed next in line and young Howard could not have been uninfluenced by what was happening in other eastern counties. The Mowat government in 1890 responded with new regulations which made it clear that English was to be the language of instruction in the schools except where this was clearly impracticable. The Department of Education, however, did not apply the new policy harshly and for a while the schools issue largely dropped from sight.[17]

It returned with a vengeance early in the new century. By this time the 'new imperialism' developed in English Canada during the Boer War years had clashed with the 'new nationalism' propounded in French Canada with such force by Henri Bourassa and his friends. Few English Canadians at this time were able to understand much less accept the Bourassian notion of a bilingual, bicultural Canada and they reacted as they had to, in terms of their beliefs, their values, and the state of their culture. French-Canadian nationalism appeared to many Ontarians as an outrageous attempt to subvert the value system and destroy the institutions of Canada as they knew it.

Against this background of renewed cultural strife, there occurred a demographic phenomenon which was perhaps its most fundamental cause. In the

1880s when Mowat had maintained generous concessions to French schools, only five per cent of the province was French-speaking; by 1909 this had risen to approximately ten per cent. It was the Irish-Catholic community which was most immediately affected, for competition between Irish and French mounted both in the church and in the separate schools which the two groups shared. The struggle was waged most fiercely in Ottawa, where Irish influence in the schools waned as French numbers grew. Unsettled conditions led the province in 1908 to undertake an investigation of bilingual teaching in the schools of the Ottawa Valley. The work was carried out by a commission headed by F.W. Merchant, the province's chief inspector. The commission discovered that bilingual schools in the Valley were generally inefficient, their teaching inadequate, and the great majority of their students without facility in English. To help rectify the situation, the province established a new bilingual training school for teachers at Sturgeon Falls.[18]

Unfortunately, by this time the situation was attracting the attention of Protestant extremists. In the midst of this delicate balance, members of the province's Franco-Ontarian community decided to take matters into their own hands. In January 1910, amid the glare of national publicity, a great assemblage of Franco-Ontarian leaders gathered in Ottawa. Laurier, members of his cabinet, Borden, Cochrane, Beck, and various ecclesiastical dignitaries were among the invited guests at a gathering whose purpose was to bring together and organize the French community in Ontario. The congress gave birth to an organization destined to play a vital role in Ontario history. The new body was called L'Association Canadienne-Française d'Education d'Ontario (ACFEO). The distinguished Ottawa lawyer, Senator Napoléon A. Belcourt, became its first president and in short order a list of requests dealing principally with bilingual schools was submitted to the Ontario cabinet for consideration.[19]

It is unclear why leaders of the French community presented their case in so public a fashion. ACFEO's requests, which included the dubious assertion that French was a legal and official language in Ontario, were certain to excite a hostile reaction in many quarters. At once the demands of ACFEO were viewed by some as evidence of a growing campaign by French-Canadian leaders to extend their language and cultural rights across Canada, to expand their political influence, and perhaps even to cut all ties with the British Empire. 'This spread of our race and our language,' wrote one young Quebec nationalist in 1910, 'is going on also beyond the bounds of our Province. Witness the great congress which has just been held at Ottawa...' In a struggle for survival between two ways of life, the article continued, 'we have at present a preponderant voice in about fifteen counties of Ontario ... in a century, this province ... will itself be gallicized by the logic of events.'[20]

One immediate result of the Ottawa congress was to awaken the fears of Orangemen across the province. At a meeting of the lodge of Ontario West, the

Grand Master warned that 'this shows that the object of the French Canadians is to put their language upon equality with English ... and is the first step in a campaign which aims at driving English-speaking electors out of the eastern counties...'[21] Of course some Irish Catholics were already in arms against the Franco-Ontarians. The anti-French campaign was led by Bishop Michael Fallon of London, who harboured personal grievances against French Catholic leaders. Thus ACFEO had thrust itself into a situation of great ferment and danger. Already in March 1910 Whitney had written Archbishop F.P. McEvay of Toronto that the government would not be able to give proper consideration to the needs of the financially hard-pressed separate schools because 'the memorandum submitted to us on behalf of a Congress of French Canadians, held at Ottawa, has so complicated matters that we find it quite out of the question to deal with the subjects thoroughly...'[22] Not unnaturally, English-speaking Catholic leaders, desperately seeking concessions from the Whitney government for the separate schools, blamed the French demands for the collapse of their hopes.

Despite the aggressiveness with which ACFEO presented its case, it would be wrong to conclude that Franco-Ontarian leaders, conscious of the growing power of their numbers, were recklessly engaged in a campaign to win new privileges and conquer new worlds. To be sure, racial pride was at the very heart of ACFEO and certainly it expressed a full measure of conscious and ambitious nationalism. Nonetheless the tactics of 1910 were a reflection more of desperation than of aggression. Numbers alone had not brought any assurance of cultural survival to the scattered Franco-Ontarian communities. Most often the Franco-Ontarians were poor farmers and workers, close to the bottom of the economic ladder, facing what seemed like inevitable assimilation into the larger, richer, and better educated society which surrounded them. Even in communities where a numerical majority had been able to win a French school, the level of educational achievement was abysmally low and the handicaps all but overwhelming. Most French-speaking children dropped out of school well before they faced the almost insuperable barriers of English-only entrance examinations and English-language high schools.

As a result, young Franco-Ontarians were losing their language and culture at an alarming rate. Even so, community leaders remained largely ignorant of the rate of assimilation and one purpose of the 1910 congress had been to gather precise information. Congress organizers soon had their fears confirmed and the committee on statistics learned that the situation they faced was 'grave, sinon intolérable.' There existed among Franco-Ontarians, the committee reported, 'l'apathie et la négligence, le manque de confiance en eux-mêmes et dans leurs compatriotes, le manque d'entente, d'union et les jalousies personnelles.'[23] It would be overstating the case to conclude that the congress of 1910 and the strategy laid down at that time represented the last chance for the French community of Ontario. Still, undeniably, the situation was desperate; and bold, even extreme measures seemed called for.

All this was beyond the ken of most members of the majority culture. Howard Ferguson was typical in his reaction to what he viewed as aggressive French demands. A frequent speaker at Orange gatherings, in 1908, for example, he had talked in innocuous terms to his Orange brethren in Grenville, telling them of the Orange contribution to Christian standards. Now, in the summer of 1910, a harsh, strident note appeared. To some five thousand eastern Ontario Orangemen gathered to celebrate the anniversary of the Battle of the Boyne, Ferguson related that great pressure was being put on the Premier to establish a system of bilingual schools. Whitney, however, had refused to surrender to the demands of the bilingualists and Orangemen could rest assured that so long as he remained in power, there would be no bilingual school system in Ontario.

Why had Ferguson chosen to speak out so strongly? Why in the months and years ahead did he place himself in the forefront of a determined campaign to prevent any extension of French-language rights in Ontario? To such queries there is only the unsatisfying response that he was behaving as did many other small-town eastern Ontario Orangemen. Of course he was not uninfluenced by political ambition, but given the depths of his imperialist passion and the proximity of his constituency to counties which had experienced the heaviest influx of French numbers, his sentiments were anything but surprising. And his message to his brethren that Whitney would stand firm would shortly prove correct.

On 12 August Whitney returned his long-awaited reply to the requests presented at the January congress. There could be no question, he announced, of creating a new category of school founded on 'a racial instead of upon a religious basis...' Yet Whitney's letter was friendly in tone. It admitted that there were difficulties in the elementary schools 'where French is now one of the languages of instruction,' but argued that with the one exception noted all the matters urged in the memorial could be dealt with by the law as it then stood.[24] Although this was disappointing to ACFEO, it offered no hint that the future would bring not concessions but new restrictions. The question, however, was far from closed by Whitney's August letter and in November Whitney ordered F.W. Merchant to investigate the schools situation and make recommendations.

By this time, tragically, racial emotions were inflamed. Whatever Dr Merchant might recommend, it would be impossible to find common ground between Franco-Ontarian desires and the Irish-Orange alliance which was beginning to take shape. In 1910 the Orangemen had no stronger spokesman than Howard Ferguson. Bilingual schools had been an unfortunate concession from the beginning, Ferguson told the Grenville Conservative Association in December. The Germans in western Ontario and the Poles in Renfrew had not asked for such schools while the large French population in New England knew better than to hint that any language other than English be used in their schools.[25] Clearly, to Ferguson the French in Ontario were simply another group of immigrants and must expect to be assimilated.

Then, in January 1911, months before the Merchant Commission had completed its work, Ferguson gave notice in the House of his 'English only motion.' Was he trying to force Whitney's hand? Later that year Colonel J.J. Craig, a Tory member, declared that when the Ferguson motion came up in caucus it was opposed by members of the cabinet.[26] According to another report, Ferguson had great difficulty finding someone to second it.[27] Certainly it was drastically amended before finally being presented to the legislature with party backing. The new wording suggested that Ferguson had beat a hasty retreat:

The English language shall be the language of instruction and of all communication ... except where in the opinion of the Department of Education it is impracticable by reason of the pupils not understanding English.

According to the *Globe*, this 'went little further than to declare that the English language should be used wherever practicable' while the francophobe Toronto *Telegram* described it as a 'gold brick of the yellowest variety.'[28]

Had Ferguson, then, stepped out of line in an effort to gain a little glory by exploiting what gave promise of becoming the issue of the day and been unceremoniously slapped back by the Premier? Ferguson's motion, as the Kemptville *Advance* noted, 'has made the member for Grenville the most conspicuous figure in the Provincial Legislature for the time being. Whether it will serve to increase his popularity with the Whitney Administration, or otherwise, remains to be seen.' The evidence that has survived, fragmentary as it is, leaves little doubt that Ferguson was playing a lonely and dangerous role. Some years later David Jamieson, a member of Whitney's caucus, confided in P.M. Dewan, a prominent Hepburn Liberal, that Premier Whitney lashed out viciously at Ferguson over the Kemptville man's too-free tongue at Orange picnics. Jamieson had never seen any man get such a dressing down as Whitney gave Ferguson and the presumably chastened member had tears in his eyes when he emerged from caucus.[29] Yet when Ferguson at the beginning of the session gave notice of his motion, under the rules of the House this prevented all further debate on the matter, something the Tory leaders might well have appreciated. Had there been some strategy to this effect from the beginning?

In any case, Ferguson refused to admit that his amended motion signified a retreat. On introducing it, he denied that it represented any desire to revolutionize the existing situation 'at one fell swoop.' Emphasizing that he did not wish 'to say anything derogatory of any class or creed of people,' he insisted that 'abuses have crept in, and can be got rid of without disadvantage to anybody.' It was admitted on all hands, he continued, 'that it is to the advantage of all peoples in this country to understand the English language thoroughly ... and we can only hope to do that through the medium of our public schools.' In terms reminiscent of D'Alton McCarthy and the one-language crusaders of the 1890s, he proclaimed it 'a disadvantage to have a division of races if we hope to build up a strong citizenship, and I have had that in view entirely.' Since the new resolution 'goes further than my resolution in some respects,' it had his full support. Whitney expressed similar views, saying that the use of the words 'in the opinion of the Department of Education' gave the Department power it had hitherto lacked to ensure that English was the language of instruction. And in words which again emphasized how foreign to some Ontarians was the concept of a bilingual Canada with two co-equal official languages, he added that the clause allowing children to continue to use their native tongue until they understood English applied equally to 'the French or German language, or whatever language it may be...'[30]

Thus with the Merchant Commission in the midst of its investigation, the Ferguson resolution had elicited from the Premier a statement which made it clear that there would be one dominant language in the province's schools and provided new legal authority for the Department of Education to support that policy. Remarkably, too, the resolution received the unanimous support of all members. Clearly the Franco-Ontarian deputies did not yet suspect that more restrictive changes would be forthcoming and they chose, apparently, to interpret the resolution much along the lines of the *Globe* and the *Telegram*. Interestingly, in Ferguson's home town the Kemptville *Advance* responded to the original resolution by warning members not to 'raise the devil of racio-religious warfare.' While a problem did exist, 'let us remember that Canada was originally a French country and that in future the Canadian people will become more and more mixed as to racial origins.' Now, however, the *Advance* proclaimed that the resolution contained 'one change which is well worth all the fighting done by Mr Ferguson, Bishop Fallon and other enemies of the Bilingual System. ... Heretofore French could be introduced as a medium of instruction in any public or separate school at the option of the trustees. ... Under the amended law ... the Provincial Government takes the responsibility of law enforcement.'[31]

From this distance it is impossible to disentangle in Ferguson's motives firmly held conviction from political ambition. For Ferguson and millions of other English Canadians in 1911, the British Empire and its values were part of their daily experience. The Empire gave meaning to their Canadian nationality, it provided assurance that their country would resist the pull of the great but threatening Republic to the south, and it brought a sense of identity which the people of Kemptville and hundreds of other towns and cities across the Dominion took for granted. To such people, Bourassian ideals of dualism were utterly foreign, while Bourassa's opposition to imperialism could only be regarded as an attack on much of what they held dear. There was as yet nothing in the Ontario experience which could render comprehensible to its people the idea of bilingualism or of a compact of Confederation under which French and English had equal rights from sea to sea. By most it was assumed that the Confederation settlement had determined that Canada would be an English-Canadian country with one bilingual province. Many in Ontario remembered the struggle between French and English in the west and believed the decision taken there had been the only possible one if some kind of polyglot nation were to be avoided. And for all their dislike of American habits and character, Ontarians shared with the Republic democratic and cultural traditions which made them disinclined to grant to French Canadians what they viewed as privileges which must be denied to other ethnic minorities. The constitution, it was believed, did not grant such privileges and in fact the French even more than other groups had to be held to a strict interpretation of their rights – if only because experience had demonstrated that they were more aggressive in demanding cultural privileges and possessed the political power to back up some of those demands. These were the beliefs that found expression in the newspapers of the day, in private correspondence, on street corners, and in a variety of legislative bodies. Recent events had caused Howard Ferguson and many others to give a good deal of thought to matters which previously had been taken for granted. Over the next few years Ferguson would speak out often about the kind of Canada he wanted.

In so doing his sincerity and the urgency of his convictions are hardly open to question. But politics creates an urgency of its own. Ferguson's stand attracted enormous public attention. For the first time he became a figure of provincial importance, his name blazoned in headlines alongside that of Bishop Fallon as a leader in one of the great questions of the day. There was coming once more to the fore in the Ontario of 1911 the old tradition that the French of Quebec backed by the international power of the Roman Catholic church, aided by racial pride and shrewd political cohesiveness, had unfairly dominated Canadian politics in their own interest. A few months before Howard Ferguson took his stand, the Kingston *Standard* asserted that 'the leader who makes as the principal plank of his platform the abolition of Bilingual Schools will sweep the Province of Ontario.'[32] With his resolution now party and provincial policy, the member for Grenville did not rest but proceeded to travel about Ontario as a crusader against bilingualism.

This remained his theme during the 1911 federal election campaign. According to Jack Reid, Ferguson was the first man Frank Cochrane asked for when he agreed to take charge of the organization of Ontario for Robert Borden.[33] The full explanation of the enormous majority Ontario gave to Borden that year cannot be found only by reference to the rising tide of racial and religious resentment. But undoubtedly a general sense that somehow the Laurier government did not reflect British, Ontario, and imperial interests to a sufficient degree was an important part of the mood of that election. On the 'glorious twelfth' of July, Ferguson told 7000 Orangemen in Prescott that 'dyed-in-the-wool Tory as I am, I'd rather see Reciprocity carried and Laurier remain in power till doomsday, than see this Nationalist campaign a success.' Ontario, however, was safe with Whitney, who was pledged to a gradual elimination of bilingualism. 'We have his promise and it will be done.'[34] Ferguson was also taking advantage of his close association with Cochrane during the election to learn more of the fine points of political organization from the old master. But in the public eye he was known primarily for his opposition to bilingual schools. At a Tory victory celebration following the overthrow of Laurier, the mayor of Prescott introduced him as 'Eastern Ontario's silver tongued orator.'[35] As he moved about the province, his political base continued to grow. In scores of constituencies Orangemen and their friends occupied positions of power. Ferguson had become their spokesman.

He continued his efforts with redoubled energy in the 1911 provincial election called by Whitney to take advantage of favourable political conditions. The election was another romp. Seventeen Tories, including Ferguson, were returned by acclamation. Not only did the Liberals have a relatively unknown new leader, the young Methodist lawyer Newton Wesley Rowell, but they had, according to Mackenzie King, 'no money, no anything, the outlook was hopeless.'[36] Again there were rumours that Ferguson would be appointed to the cabinet, this time as Provincial Treasurer, but the reports proved false. Perhaps Ferguson's new notoriety made Whitney hesitate to elevate him. His acclamation did give him freedom to move about and at Erin, in Toronto, in Prescott, and elsewhere, he preached against 'the bilingual evil.' There was nothing original about his views, which were notable primarily for the frankness and vigour with which he presented them. Similar opinions could be found in almost every issue of such extremist journals as the Toronto *Telegram* and the Orange *Sentinel* but they appeared as well in most small town weeklies and in the daily journals of practically every city in the province. More experienced politicians, men with finer sensibilities, who knew the awesome responsibility of power or, like Whitney, remembered from first-hand experience the terrible cultural strife of the 1890s, would not talk in such terms. Ferguson, unburdened by responsibilities, eager and forthright, quick to anger at the nationalist rhetoric of the Bourassas and Lavergnes, would regard his words as bold and patriotic but wiser heads knew how narrow, self-defeating and, finally, dangerous such talk could be.

Still, Ferguson was expressing what thousands felt. To a country which had just experienced the greatest immigration in its history and was still reeling at its impact on established habits and customs, he warned that future newcomers must be 'carefully selected from nationalities of the north temperate zone whose habits, instincts and ideals are similar to our own. In short we want the Anglo-Saxon type.' But immigrants from a variety of countries had come and would come to Canada and in this situation Ontario had a duty and mission. 'Ontario must take the lead in the work of assimilation of races that must take place. We want British traditions and British ideals to be instilled into the minds of the rising generation...' As young Ontarians sought new homes in the great west 'and mingle with the foreigners there,' they must 'put the impress of their character and personality upon the community in which they live. ... This is the great work that Ontario must do for Canada.' If this noble purpose were to be achieved, Ontarians must insist upon the adoption of one language in their own educational institutions. The Frenchman, the German, would be welcomed, but 'they must be given to understand that in the great work of building up a virile, healthy, vigorous citizenship, the strain of the Anglo-Saxon must dominate.'

In his concern with virile, loyal, and healthy citizens, Howard Ferguson was no different from many others of his day, including Germans, Americans – and French Canadians; only the content of that citizenship was different in each case. Turning to the American example as an ideal, one in which a national school system recognized but one language, he insisted that the American experience amply proved the wisdom of such a system. There was no hyphenated citizenship there, no bilingualism. 'The bilingual system encourages the isolation of the races. It impresses the mind of the youth with the idea of race distinction and militates against the fusion of the various elements that make up our population.' 'That is why I am opposed to bilingual schools...,' Ferguson continued. 'This is a British country and we must maintain it as such if we are to maintain the high destiny that Providence intended for Canada.' Not only had educators the world over condemned the bilingual system as retarding the development of the child, but Canada's own experience in the west showed what could happen with mixture but not assimilation of races. In Manitoba, with French, Ruthenians, and others, 'the very atmosphere is foreign.'

Apparently, then, it was up to Ontario to save the Dominion. 'Ontario is the leader of the nine Provinces of the Dominion. ... If Ontario can demonstrate that the bilingual system is unnecessary she has won a great victory for British citizenship...'[37] At times, the Bourassas and the Fergusons could sound remarkably alike. Although Bourassa and his colleagues were demanding an extension of bilingualism across the country while Ferguson and the Orangemen were insisting that only in Quebec did French and English have co-equal rights, both men were shrill and outspoken proponents of ideas which in the context of 1911 could only be destructive of Canadian unity. Ultimately, of course, the Bourassian vision of dualism triumphed over the pan-Britannic nationalism of Ferguson, and Regulation 17 became one of the unlamented casualties of the clash of ideas.

In his speeches during the 1911 election, Ferguson expressed the belief that when Dr Merchant finally reported, the whole bilingual system would be swept away. Doubtless Whitney was deliberately delaying the report until after the election but this did not prevent the bilingual question being debated more widely than ever before or since in the province's history. Several Toronto newspapers, including the *Star* and the *Globe*, conducted their own investigations and their reports emphasized that in a number of schools in the east and north little English was being used at any level. As passions mounted, other Tory members such as Forbes Godfrey, W.K. McNaught, Thomas Crawford, and W.D. McPherson became as outspoken on the issue as Ferguson, while Rowell for the Liberal party remained ambiguous and Whitney stated he was awaiting the Merchant Report. Despite this official stance, Attorney-General Foy handed the press a statement saying that there could not 'lawfully be any bilingual schools in the Province of Ontario, and if they are found, they must cease to exist.' Foy's cabinet colleague, Dr Reaume, immediately declared that these views did not represent government policy.[38] As the debate raged, Ferguson remained firm in his belief that it was necessary to educate public opinion to ensure that the government would make no mistake when it finally decided to act. And the faithfully extreme Toronto *Telegram* declared that Ontario's hope for the maintenance of Anglo-Saxon institutions lay 'neither in the politics of Sir James Whitney nor in the purposes of N.W. Rowell but in the election to the legislature of such men as Howard Ferguson.'[39]

As Whitney swept back into power, many Franco-Ontarians switched their support to the Liberals. Their loss cost the Conservatives two, perhaps three, seats. To party strategists the defections must have seemed insignificant. The Tories took 83 seats, the Liberals 22. Two months later, the Merchant Report appeared. Dr Merchant found that on the whole the bilingual schools were 'lacking in efficiency' and that 'a large portion of the children ... leave school to meet the demands of life with an inadequate equipment in education.' So staunch a friend of the French language as C.B. Sissons of Victoria College believed the report 'only served to substantiate the spectacular statement of Bishop Fallon.'[40] In the vast majority of so-called bilingual schools in eastern and northern Ontario, French alone was the language of instruction and in many of these schools the teachers were unqualified and had slight command of the English language. To remedy this, Dr Merchant recommended that French be gradually replaced by English in the upper grades of the primary schools during Form II. But when Whitney announced his policy, popularly known as Regulation 17, it went much further than Merchant had recommended or than John Seath, Ontario's Superintendent of Education, believed wise. The use of French as the language of instruction was not to be continued past Form I, except for one more year in the case of previously defective training. Other sections of the new regulation proved equally controversial. At once ACFEO and the Franco-Ontarians were up in arms.

'...I, personally, was largely responsible for the establishment of Regulation 17.'[41] So Ferguson informed a supporter years later. In fact the influences which shaped its precise nature and wording remain obscure. Ferguson may have meant his remark only in the general sense that he had spoken and worked on behalf of a policy which would restrict bilingual teaching. Whatever its source, the new regulation as formulated was a serious error in judgment. For a decade and more, Regulation 17 would remain a great barrier separating French from English Canadians. Most tragically of all, perhaps, the outbreak of World War I meant that the schools crisis had to be dealt with in a period in which emotions were strained beyond the breaking point. Surely it was a supreme irony that during the Great War it fell to Howard Ferguson as Acting Minister of Education to deal with the crisis that he, as much as any individual, had been instrumental in creating.

Tory Hatchet Man

From the beginning, Howard Ferguson had found the life of a provincial member much to his liking. He particularly savoured the cut-and-thrust of legislative debate. In those days the Ontario House in some ways approximated more closely the style and manner of an over-sized county council than it did the federal House of Commons. Quick-witted and thick-skinned, Ferguson enjoyed the informality and banter and was well suited to the rough exchanges and partisan manoeuvres which characterized the politics of pre-war Ontario. Before long he was performing an essential function for his party and performing it superbly. The role of political hatchet man has always been as necessary as that of political diplomat. It was the path which Howard Ferguson followed to the inner councils of Ontario Conservatism.

It is unlikely that it was ever assigned to him or even that he assumed it consciously. However, it suited him well and his party leaders doubtless encouraged him in it. On at least four separate occasions, the Trent Canal investigation and its stormy aftermath, the Evanturel affair, the Proudfoot charges, and in a confrontation with Adam Beck, Howard Ferguson was the centre of a political storm. Soon there was added a new dimension to the fame or notoriety which he had gained during the bilingual schools question and which stuck with him for the rest of his career. Although he failed in these years to achieve cabinet status, his name was becoming better known than that of many of the ministers. A pattern was emerging from these incidents and from his day-to-day activities in the legislature. A picture was being fixed indelibly in Ontario's political consciousness of a skilled political infighter, a talented partisan. Howard Ferguson had become his party's political policeman.

Well equipped to function in this way, he thrived on controversy and galloped to the political wars with incredible zest. Brash and ambitious, a dangerous man on his feet, he commanded all the tools of his trade and used them often. His many scraps in municipal politics in Kemptville and his drawn-out donnybrook with Robert Joynt had turned him into a political pugilist at an early stage in his career. In private Howard was warm, friendly, even folksy, but during his first years in the House quick repartee and personal allusion became his trademarks. The elder statesmen in the Whitney cabinet – Hanna, Pyne, Jim Foy, and Whitney himself – soon learned that here was someone who could be relied on to descend to the arena to fight their battles and, when necessary, to do their dirty work. Yet Ferguson was not irremediably wedded to the methods of those days – though he found them useful for a good number of years. When he became Premier he would realize that a different touch was needed. Although the old fire sometimes still struck an opponent who was becoming bothersome, Ferguson was usually content to let others perform the function that had been his when he had served his apprenticeship on the Whitney backbenches.

The closing years of the Whitney era, from the 1911 election to the Premier's death in 1914, saw few innovations in provincial policies. The Workmen's Compensation Act of 1914 caused a stir and was attacked by some as 'socialism of the worst kind' but for the most part this was a time of quiet reform and administrative competence. It was also a period of political aging for the Whitney administration and, with much of its reform zeal exhausted, slipshod methods and occasional abuses began to sully the government's record. In these circumstances, Whitney's supporters often had their work cut out for them and the scrappy Kemptville lawyer found that his services were called on frequently. Yet the political storm which almost cost Ferguson his seat in the House and saw a concerted attack on him by furious Liberals determined to make him pay the price of his partisanship originated in a federal royal commission.

In 1912 the Borden Conservatives decided to investigate the construction and administration of the Trent Valley Canal. Borden and his colleagues had long been convinced that the Laurier Liberals had participated in a series of shady and questionable operations. The parliamentary sessions of 1906, 1907, and 1908 had been 'largely scandal sessions, and the general election that followed was a scandals election.'[1] While in opposition the Conservatives, despite scattered successes, had failed to drive their accusations home with solid proofs. Now, after 1911, with all the resources of the government at their beck and call, eager Tories were certain they would be able to uncover the evidence which had previously proved so elusive.

One major area in which the Liberals had been unable to hide their dirt, so much of it indeed existed, was in the often unbelievable sphere of the Laurier railway policies. Here the Tories started their search at once and soon the results of their investigation were made public. The report of the Transcontinental Railway Commission Investigation appeared in February 1914. Jubilant Conservatives claimed it vindicated all their charges. *The Mail and Empire*, beside itself with joy, announced in its banner headline of 16 February: 'STAGGERING BLOW TO THE LIBERALS.' According to the Toronto Tory mouthpiece, 'the grave scandal now brought to light is the most staggering blow ever dealt to a political party at any time in the history of Canada.'[2] Knowledgeable

Conservatives were even then aware that Howard Ferguson was almost ready to present his own report on the Trent Canal investigation. Still more ammunition seemed in prospect.

The appointment in 1912 of Ferguson as a one-man royal commission to investigate the smouldering Trent Canal situation had paralleled the investigation of Liberal railway policies. The very name of the man who had directed the Trent project for the Liberals was enough to make sensitive Tory ears prick up. The Hon. J.R. Stratton was none other than the former Liberal member for Peterborough who had been so discredited by the notorious Gamey revelations of 1903. Better still, George P. Graham, one of the few former Laurier ministers from Ontario with much fight left in him, would be the man held responsible for any improprieties that were uncovered. Graham of course was an old eastern Ontario antagonist of Howard Ferguson and a former provincial Liberal leader to boot. Even so, although he must have been sorely tempted, Ferguson at first declined when Borden's Minister of Railways and Canals, Frank Cochrane, asked him to undertake the task.[3]

The very idea of Howard Ferguson as a royal commissioner seemed preposterous to many. Ferguson knew he was too closely involved in the political scene to accept what was essentially a judicial function. Years later when he himself was being investigated by a royal commission he effectively destroyed its credibility by attacking its heads as partisan Liberals. He may have anticipated precisely this in 1912 and for that reason was reluctant to accept the offer. Yet Frank Cochrane was a hard man to refuse. He pointed out to Ferguson that already three men had been sent to investigate Liberal activities on the Trent and that all had drawn a blank. Ferguson, Cochrane doubtless suggested, would not be put off the track as easily. In any case, everyone understood the purpose of this particular royal commission. Ferguson would not have to make the painful effort to attain a semblance of impartiality. The only requirement was that when he 'got the goods' on the Grits, he have the evidence to support it.

When Frank Cochrane put it to him as a personal favour, Ferguson cast aside his doubts and accepted. He had always shared Whitney's belief that the Liberals were corrupt and deceitful. Most Tories who had participated in the fight against the Ross government held this opinion. In his speeches Ferguson had often denounced the 'carnival of graft and corruption' which existed among Liberal henchmen. Probably Whitney, to whom Grit corruption was almost a lifetime fixation, fully approved of his follower acting for Ottawa. A good deal of Ferguson's time for the next year and a half was spent in the work of the Trent Commission and in preparing the report of some seven hundred pages, which he presented to the Borden government in February 1914.

Meanwhile, during the rather humdrum 1913 session, Ferguson's political abilities received a challenge of a different sort. Shortly before the House was to be prorogued, William Proudfoot, the Goderich lawyer who was Rowell's closest confidant in the Liberal party, caught Ontario – and the Conservatives – by surprise. On a mild day in April the Public Accounts Committee chaired by Ferguson was droning through the usual dull detail of its work. Proudfoot seemed to be going through a long but entirely routine examination of a witness when suddenly his voice rose to an excited pitch as he snapped out an unexpected question: 'While you had contracts with the Government did you make a contribution to the Government or any member of it for political purposes?' Thus originated the famous Proudfoot charges. They were the most dangerous accusations ever levied against an administration which valued, above all else, its reputation for probity. Involved was the touchy issue of the corrupt acceptance of campaign funds and the reputation of one of the dominant figures of Ontario Conservatism, Provincial Secretary W.J. Hanna.

Thomas McGarry, veteran of a hundred courtroom victories, first realized what was happening. Reacting instinctively, he shouted, 'You cannot put that question on the record.' Now Ferguson acted. Knowing that his party had been taken by surprise and thinking perhaps of the afternoon's newspaper headlines, he used his chairman's power to sustain McGarry's opinion and force an immediate vote before Proudfoot could do more damage. Next he ordered all the objectionable remarks stricken from the record and turned a cold face to the outraged cries of Rowell and Proudfoot. 'If you have any charges to make against anybody,' he insisted, 'the place to do it is on the floor of the House.'[4] Finally Proudfoot capitulated. Between them, Ferguson and McGarry had stemmed the tide. They had bought time for the government and given it a chance to prepare a defence.

The respite was brief. That afternoon Liberal members took their fight to the House and in addition attacked Ferguson's conduct of the Committee. In reply Ferguson insisted he had given Proudfoot great latitude until the Liberal member had begun to make 'insinuations and innuendoes that should not be made before the Committee but on the floor of the House.' But still the attack continued and an irascible Whitney all but ordered the Speaker to keep the opposition members strictly to the point. Finally he promised to consider the whole matter over the weekend and make a statement on Monday. At that time the Premier informed a quiet House that Hanna had indeed accepted a campaign contribution from the source in question in 1908 but if anybody believed a wrong had been done the Public Accounts Committee was not the place to discuss it. He promised the members that either the Committee on Privileges and Elections or a special committee would deal with the question. The following day Ferguson and McGarry again blocked Liberal attempts to use the Public Accounts Committee as their forum. When Proudfoot subsequently read his list of charges in the legislature, an apparently rattled Premier labelled them 'absolutely false' and gave the members a glimpse of the famous Whitney temper: 'in this world one meets some good people and one meets abandoned wretches of the worst type, without all sense of decency, fair play and self-respect.' The Proudfoot charges, Whitney announced, would be referred to the Committee on Privileges and Elections. Liberal demands for a royal commission he dismissed out of hand.

The Committee met the next day. Apparently Whitney had approved of Ferguson's resourcefulness when Proudfoot first levelled his charges, for the Conservatives on the Committee elected him as chairman. With representation on the Committee proportional to standing in the House, it was easily dominated by the government. But the situation remained touchy; numbers alone might not prevail against the Liberal frontbenchers. The eyes of the province were on the Committee. The government's reputation was at stake. The House stood adjourned while the committee proceeded with its investigation.

The game began at once. The Liberal press denounced the new Committee and the *Globe* editorialized:

Does any sane man believe that a committee of political partisans, every man of them bound by party allegiance, would be unbiased in its attitude? Worse than that. Members of this Committee are already committed in their opinions by their conduct as members of the Public Accounts Committee, the new Chairman notoriously so.[5]

When the Committee met, and the Liberals came face to face with the stubborn Ferguson and his quick gavel, Hartley Dewart, the shrewd Toronto lawyer who acted as Proudfoot's counsel, refused to proceed. Instead he attacked the Committee before which he was appearing.[6] Not that Dewart lacked provocation. Over Liberal objections Ferguson excluded item after item from testimony. When Hanna admitted receiving a $500 campaign contribution Ferguson proceeded to exclude all further evidence regarding it. Liberal supporters were furious. In an editorial the next day entitled 'The Gagged Investigation,' the *Globe* declared that 'the Chairman made himself ridiculous by ruling that the committee must decide whether the payment was corrupt or not and excluding all evidence on which such a decision could be made.'[7] But Ferguson, no shrinking violet, reacted to Dewart's harangue by administering a severe scolding. 'You will stop there. If you want to withdraw you must do it in a gentlemanly way, and cast no reflections on this committee.' Ferguson was visibly taken aback when one by one the Liberal members rose, attacked the Committee and its chairman, and withdrew. He hesitated only a moment, however, before proceeding to call the next witness.

Only in the House were the Liberals able to confront the government directly. Their opportunity came on 7 May when Ferguson presented his Committee's report and moved its adoption. As expected, the Committee concluded that 'there was not one tittle of evidence from any source that the money was used improperly or that the contribution in any way ... influenced

either Sir James Whitney or the Hon. W.J. Hanna...' Ferguson's presentation was
not conducive to a calm examination of the case. After defending his position as
Chairman of the Public Accounts and Privileges and Elections committees, he
launched an unexpected attack not on Proudfoot but on Rowell. The Liberal
leader, he charged, had not had the courage to make the charges himself but had
referred them to an underling. Proudfoot 'had tried to shield Mr Rowell because
he [Rowell] wanted to be in a position to dodge the odour and venom brought
on the shoulders of the man who made the charges. Mr Rowell had not the
courage to take the position he should have taken...' An outraged Rowell
declared the charge 'absolutely and unqualifiedly false' and Ferguson serenely
withdrew it. The majority report having been moved, the Liberals presented a
minority statement condemning the government. Tom McGarry then moved his
own amendment censuring William Proudfoot for the alleged irresponsibility of
his charges and his conduct. Then came the inevitable. The majority report and
McGarry's amendment were adopted on a party vote.

Undeniably, Ferguson, Whitney, and the Tories had handled the Grits roughly
and unceremoniously. By force of numbers the government had repulsed the
Liberal attempt to win political yardage on an issue that, for all its potential, was
never brought home in an effective manner. Yet the degree of Liberal success
could only be gauged at the polls. The Proudfoot charges became the dominant
issue of the ensuing North Grey by-election, during which Hanna and Proudfoot
met head-on in debate.[8] The government victory in a traditionally Grit riding
was a stunning disappointment to the Rowellites. By the end of 1913 there was
virtually no public discussion of the case and Rowell was forced to search for
another issue to loosen Whitney's firm grip on power. From the Tory point of
view, Howard Ferguson had contributed his share to the highly satisfactory
outcome of a dangerous situation. By his tactical abilities and by his tactical
excesses which diverted attention from the question originally at issue, he had
effectively performed the function of political policeman for the Whitney
ministers.

An exhausted Whitney prorogued the legislature shortly after Ferguson's
majority report had been accepted. The Conservative leader was aging rapidly.
Later that year he suffered a heart attack and was unable to take his place for
the 1914 session. Attorney-General James Foy was Acting Premier when a
totally unexpected incident threw the House into turmoil.

By this time an election was in the offing. The Liberal party under Rowell
had developed a progressive program of social and economic reform. But
Rowell's zeal did not stop there. Howard Ferguson once described the Liberal
leader aptly: 'I am sorry for him. ... He was brought from the pure atmosphere
of the Layman's Missionary Movement and plunged into the slimy pool of
Liberal politics.'[9] At the very centre of his reform program Rowell was
determined to place the fervently held temperance views that meant so much to

him and to hundreds of thousands of other Canadians in 1914. Under Rowell the Liberals were increasingly critical of Whitney's liquor policies, attacking them as insincere and hypocritical palliatives. By 1913 Rowell had converted his party to a much more advanced position than it had taken in the 1911 election; the Liberals adopted as the most prominent plank in their platform the policy of 'abolish-the-bar.'

With an election approaching, the temperance issue was being debated with considerable heat. Here at least Rowell had mapped out for his party a policy significantly different from the Conservatives, one he was able to promote in many areas of the province to good effect. Or so at least many apprehensive Conservatives believed. Convinced that under the wise moderation of local option and strict enforcement the province had become progressively more temperate, they regarded the element of fanaticism in Rowell's policy with distaste and found the Liberal tone of moral superiority hard to take. Above all, they feared its effect on their rural support.

This was the situation then when on 25 February the government was subjected to yet another attack for its allegedly improper connection with the liquor interests. Most members were surprised, however, when Gustave Evanturel, the Liberal representative for Prescott, rose to speak. Evanturel had always avoided voting on temperance divisions and was known to be out of sympathy with Rowell's liquor policies. Now, to desk-thumping applause from his colleagues, he referred to Rowell as 'our beloved leader' and delivered a sweeping attack on the connection between the Tories and the liquor interests in his own riding. Among other things, he charged that the licence inspector was a Tory hack and that the vice-president of the Conservative association, who was a saloon keeper, violated the province's liquor laws with impunity. Dramatically, he promised to resign if he failed to prove his allegations.

Evanturel's awakening was rude and rapid. Howard Ferguson rose. A few of the members noticed he had a letter in his hand as he spoke. In an angry voice, he announced to the House that he would show, over Evanturel's own signature, that he was the servant of the very liquor interests he had just attacked and which he claimed were allied with the Tories. When a man comes into the legislature, Ferguson insisted, 'and attempts to attack either a person or the administration of a department, he must come in with clean skirts.'

A graveyard silence had seized the legislature. Ferguson paused for breath. Nobody stirred. The members sensed what was about to happen. When Ferguson began again it was to challenge Evanturel to admit that he himself had been negotiating with the liquor interests. Twice came the challenge, twice the denial. Then Ferguson told the members that Eventural had thereby forced him 'to do what I am sorry to do, read this letter to the House.' Dated 4 September 1913, it was addressed to the secretary of the Ontario Licensed Trade Association:

Dear Sir: — I have written a long letter to the Secretary of the Hotelkeepers' Association for Ontario, asking him to submit my letter to the Directors of the Association at their first meeting. In that letter I pledged myself as a true friend of this Association and prepared to fight in the House and vote against my Leader on that question of abolishing the bars, etc. ... I am and I have always been a true friend to the Liquor interests. ... I am a poor man ... and in my letter to the Board I ask at least $10,000 payable $3,000 now and the balance per installments in order to support me. I am prepared for that salary to be the defender of the Association, and introduce before the Legislature any amendments to the Government measures to restrict the liquor traffic, etc. I am the only MPP in the Ontario House who will place himself openly against that policy of Rowell and the restrictions to the trade brought from time to time by the Government. I believe it would be useful to your Association to have an MPP who would be there in the House...[10]

When Ferguson read the words 'always been a true friend to the Liquor interests' an anguished Evanturel cried out that it was unfair to bring these things out in the House at that time. Unmoved, Ferguson continued, making barbed comments along the way, noting too that the letter was written on official legislature paper.

I regret that I had to make this statement on the floor of the House. I was so amazed, so dumbfounded, when he stood up on his feet to-day and attempted to deal with this question in the way he did, knowing that he had attempted to hide behind his leader's skirts while all the time he was playing his own miserable, mean, selfish game of stabbing his leader and that policy in the back.

To a deafening roar of applause for his effort and of derision directed at the unfortunate Evanturel, Ferguson concluded his remarks.

When Evanturel tried to make a personal explanation that evening, Ferguson pointed out that he was out of order. The Speaker a little later permitted Rowell to make a statement. The shaken Liberal leader was brutal to his erring member. To all intents and purposes he read him out of the party then and there. Rowell might better have stopped when he disclaimed all responsibility for Evanturel's actions. Instead he pressed on. Evanturel had 'brought attention to certain grave abuses. ... It is absolutely no answer to that to make a charge or attack upon the member himself...'[11] The very fact that Howard Ferguson had such a letter in his hands, Rowell asserted, was evidence of an intention on the part of the hotel keeper to whom it was written to injure the Liberal party. There the debate ended for the day. Its repercussions would affect the prospects of both parties in the approaching elections.

The manoeuvring was apparent the next day in the party press. The *Globe* demanded Evanturel's immediate resignation. The *Mail and Empire* directed its fire at the self-proclaimed champion of the temperance movement: 'Quite evidently in his letter writing this supporter of Mr Rowell regarded the Whitney Government ... as the dread enemy of the liquor interests.' In the legislature that afternoon the Ferguson-led Conservative effort to use the revelations to discredit Rowell began in earnest. When Rowell informed the House that Evanturel had been expelled from the Liberal caucus, Ferguson jumped to his feet. It would be surprising indeed, he pointed out, for Rowell not to attempt to repudiate his former follower. But by doing this could he really dissociate his party from Evanturel's conduct? Until publicly exposed, Evanturel had been a valued member of the Liberal party:

I remember only yesterday the enthusiastic applause with which the Leader of the Opposition received the remark of the hon. gentleman from Prescott when he referred to him as "my beloved leader, whom I am proud to follow." He went arm in arm with his leader in advocating the policy of abolish-the-bar, and all the time he had expressed a desire to make an official connection of the liquor interests with the Liberal party, to get a large contribution from the liquor party, no doubt to be made use of in the interest of the Liberal party.

'Oh, that is rotten,' several Liberals responded from across the floor. 'You are about the only man in the House who would say such a thing,' shouted one Grit. When the rattled Rowell denied travelling about Ontario with Evanturel on an abolish-the-bar platform, Ferguson explained that he was speaking figuratively. And when Evanturel spoke in his own defence on 4 March, apologizing to the legislature for his 'indiscretion,' Ferguson ignored him to deliver another onslaught against Rowell. Rowell replied in kind, engaging in the fruitless activity of blasting the House's most partisan Tory for his partisanship.

Yet the encounter had not ended in a draw. No one expected Ferguson to be the voice of rectitude; Rowell's reputation was of a different type and somehow it left the Evanturel affair a little tarnished. Not that very many people actually believed Ferguson's veiled suggestions about Rowell's complicity; still, the Liberal leader had been willing to accept support from a member whose opposition to the party's basic moral policy was notorious. The Evanturel affair aired this fact throughout Ontario. A good deal of the pristine vigour with which the Grits had advocated their temperance crusade had been dissipated in a few days. To this extent the Evanturel affair was a minor turning point in Ontario politics.

Near the end of April Rowell dredged up another set of liquor charges, the so-called Snider case, in which Provincial Secretary Hanna was alleged to be implicated. Once again Ferguson refused to permit Rowell to discuss such a case in the Public Accounts Committee and Hanna dismissed the latest Grit effort as charges trumped up 'to serve miserable petty campaign ends.'[12] The Snider charges failed to compensate the Liberals for the Evanturel affair. The events of the session, as the 1914 election demonstrated, had in a minor way impaired Rowell's credibility as a moral reformer. More significant, they had restored Tory morale and self-confidence in the acceptability of their own liquor policies.

As for the loose ends of the Evanturel affair, the Prescott member, repudiated by his constituency association and threatened with action by the Attorney-General's Department, finally announced his resignation. But Rowell's troubles with Evanturel had not ended. Not only did he insist on running in the 1914 election as an independent Liberal but his Prescott constituents administered an embarrassing rebuke to Rowell by electing him over the official Liberal.

One question remained. How had Ferguson gained possession of the Evanturel letter? Grits suggested again that it had been given to him by liquor men anxious to damage the Rowell Liberals; Ferguson claimed he had received it from a personal friend. Perhaps. The most amazing feature of the affair was that Ferguson had received the letter six months previously and when he sat in the House with it in his pocket on the day of Evanturel's speech, 'not a soul knew that I had this letter, except the man from whom I got it last fall.'[13]

Thus in the two most charged episodes since the 1911 election, a private member had borne the burden of the Tory case. Ferguson's name had no chance to disappear from the front pages. On 10 March 1914, the very day the Speaker accepted Evanturel's resignation, the report of his investigation into Trent Canal irregularities was made public. As everyone had anticipated, it followed in the spirit of the earlier railway investigation. Commissioner Ferguson had found what he had been looking for and the *Mail and Empire* screamed triumphantly:

MONEY FOR TRENT CANAL WENT INTO CAMPAIGN FUND
DECEPTION AND DISHONESTY IN ITS MANAGEMENT UNDER LIBERAL REGIME

Surveying the construction and early management of the Trent Canal project, Ferguson charged that 'over a number of years devious and sometimes corrupt methods had been used, with padded payrolls, incompetent management and a deplorable lack of system...' As well, in 1910 certain money had found its way into Liberal campaign funds. The Commissioner was particularly critical of the canal superintendent, a defeated Liberal candidate for the House of Commons:

McClellan seems to have engaged himself largely with matters of political patronage and pleasure jaunts at the public expense, and the bills for liquor and other refreshments and meals on the canal boat speak eloquently of his popularity as an entertainer. The last bill for liquor and cigars to regale the guests aboard the Bessie Butler was paid in October, 1911, when the carnival of corrupt padding of pay lists came to an end, but so far as control and management are concerned there has been no improvement and cannot be under the present incumbent. ... He [McClellan] says that when he went on the canal he was told by Hon. J.R. Stratton that there should be an election fund of from five to seven thousand a year from the canal office, and that he proceeded on that basis.[14]

Commissioner Ferguson also criticized auditor Nethersell of Ottawa. Evidently he and McClellan were close friends. In one case Nethersell returned an irregular voucher and warned McClellan that 'there may be some persons on the lookout for any such irregularity.' As Ferguson put it in the report:

To my mind these are most remarkable letters to go from an auditor to the man whose accounts he audited. They throw some light on the reprehensible departmental methods that have obtained.

The Conservative press was jubilant. Of course the revelations could not compare with those of the railway investigation in February; but Ferguson had uncovered quite enough. The *Mail and Empire* pressed home its advantage in an editorial entitled 'Isolating Corruption.'

Wrong cannot be made right by vehement denial in behalf of the guilty or by abuse of the accuser...

The Commissioners appointed to investigate the construction of the National Transcontinental have reported that the cost was needlessly swollen by the immense sum of $40,000,000. ... No amount of scurrilous treatment to which the investigators may be subject will lessen by the weight of a hair whatever burden of wrong lies at the door of the late government.

Similarly, the report of graft in the use of money paid out on the Trent Valley Canal account cannot be dispelled by language of irritation against the present Government or its investigators.[15]

The Conservative paper had correctly anticipated a sustained Liberal campaign to discredit Tory muckraking activities. In Ontario it began with a determined attempt by the Rowell Liberals to pry into various old provincial accounts, including Guelph prison expenditures and disbursements on the new asylum at Whitby. Ferguson, still Chairman of the Public Accounts Committee, prepared to help stem the Liberal counter-attack. But instead, unexpectedly, it came not in the Committee but in the legislature itself.

Somehow, incredibly, a terrible blunder had been made. To their shame, Ontario Conservatives read about it over their coffee in the *Globe* of 16 March. 'Ferguson,' announced the Grit journal, 'has according to the revised statutes of Ontario forfeited his seat in the Legislature and becomes liable to a penalty of

$2,000 per day for every day on which he had occupied his legislature seat since his acceptance of the Trent Valley Canal Investigation Commission from the Dominion Government.' The *Globe* account continued:

Mr Ferguson, in apparent defiance of the statutes, accepted for the Dominion Government the commission. ... Under the statutes, the conception of which was evidently to prevent a politician in one Legislature accepting commissions of emolument from politicians in another Legislative body, the large penalty to which he has become liable can be collected from him by process of law by any citizen who desires to take action.

The *Globe* referred its readers to the Revised Statutes of Ontario for 1914, Chapter II, section 10. That day the legislature saw its most sensational scene since the Gamey revelations of a decade earlier.

There was frantic activity at Queen's Park that morning. When the legislature opened, Acting Prime Minister Foy was ready with a bill to amend the Legislative Assembly Act to relieve any member who was liable under the amendment which had trapped Howard Ferguson. But with Ferguson in imminent danger, the government's difficulty was clear. To help Ferguson, Foy's bill had to be passed that day. To avoid giving the required two day's notice for his bill, Foy accompanied it with a motion to suspend the rule requiring notice. Rowell reacted as Foy doubtless anticipated. The motion to suspend the rules could not be made without notice except by unanimous consent, he pointed out. In reply Foy pleaded the urgency of the case. He reminded members that there were innumerable instances of bills receiving three readings in one day. His real argument lay in an appeal to a Liberal precedent. In 1903 the Legislative Assembly Act had been amended by the Ross government to protect a member who had accepted temporary employment with the Laurier government.

That was a reasonable law ... most fair, most proper. There was nothing morally wrong in it, and nothing legally wrong from 1903 until recently, when the clause seems to have been dropped in revision without any special attention having been directed to it. The object of this Bill is to return to that law. And the reason for putting this Bill through so quickly is that the case is urgent. A member of this House will forfeit his seat if this law is not promptly enacted.

Because the passage of time would be fatal for Ferguson, the Liberal strategy was to delay. The opposition needed to give serious consideration to 'an amendment of such great importance and affecting the rights of all the members who sit in this House.' Rowell would not budge from his position that unanimous consent was needed to set aside the rules of the House without a prior motion. Otherwise the government could at any time sweep away all the rights of the minority in the House. So the battle was on. Tempers were lost on both sides as point of order followed point of order. With Proudfoot, Rowell, and J.C. Elliott all speaking at once for the Liberals, the Speaker was losing control of the House. But the government by brute force continued to push its bill through the House. The turmoil increased. On occasions the uproar became so intense that members, casting aside argument, stood shouting at each other from across the House or pounded desks to drown out opposing arguments. On two occasions members were 'named' by the Speaker. As disorder mounted, it seemed that for the first time since Confederation the Sergeant-at-Arms would be forced to interfere.

All afternoon, all evening, and into the morning the struggle continued. At last Rowell adopted a new tack, maintaining that he would support the bill provided it was not phrased in general terms but applied only to Howard Ferguson. Tom McGarry was not far from the mark when he declared that this proved that personal animus lay behind Rowell's position. 'If I understand the spirit of the members of this side of the House, we are prepared to stay here all night and all day tomorrow and the next night to see that this goes through.' That proved unnecessary. Shortly before five in the morning to thunderous applause from the government benches the bill received third reading. Later that morning when Queen's Park formally opened its doors, the Lieutenant-Governor gave his assent. Ferguson, released from his briefly enforced silence, was at his place at the head of the Public Accounts Committee.

The Liberal press tried valiantly to extract all possible political mileage from the affair. The *Globe* editorial writer called forth his most righteous indignation when he claimed that 'no more barefaced outrage ... had ever been seen in a British Parliament.' The next day under the heading 'Political Slaves' it outdid itself with its absurd exaggerations:

A great and lamentable blow has been struck at provincial autonomy and the independence of members of the Legislature ... the Dominion Government when it gets into a dispute with the Province will be quite within the law in buying up the representatives of the people of Ontario. ... No more odious measure for the promotion of political corruption ... has been presented to a Canadian Legislature since Confederation.

Interestingly, the *Globe* praised Howard Ferguson's Trent Canal report: 'He has found much evidence of impropriety and of actual dishonesty. ... Mr Ferguson's report will do good, because it lets daylight into an ugly mess. But Mr Ferguson, in his search for lawbreakers, himself broke the law...'[16] What the *Globe* in its fulminations did not note was that all the bill did was to restore what had in fact been the statute law of the province until it had been inadvertently dropped in 1908. Nor did it mention what many knew to be the case and what Howard

Ferguson himself pointed out, that 'there are a great number of members of the House in Toronto who have made valuations, searched titles and done other work for the Dominion Government who are all in exactly the same position as myself.'[17]

Still smarting over the Trent Valley Canal report, the Grits took after Howard Ferguson once again that year, this time in the House of Commons. Not by coincidence, their attack came shortly before the provincial election as two of the leading Liberal lights in Ontario, Hugh Guthrie and George P. Graham, declared Ferguson's conclusions the partisan report of a partisan commission. But Jack Reid, Borden's Minister of Customs, had little trouble in defending his old friend's report. Finally even the Liberals admitted that Ferguson's investigation had disclosed some highly irregular and improper practices.[18]

Ferguson's talents were used by Whitney in one final way in the months before his death. Unlike some members, Ferguson from the beginning paid close attention to the affairs of the Ontario Hydro. Because of Hydro's focus on Niagara he feared, and rightly, that eastern Ontario would receive the short end of the stick from the public utility system and would fall even further behind the rest of the province in prosperity and growth. He kept after Beck not to neglect the east, telling him, for example, in a January 1912 letter that he should put up 'a vigorous campaign in Eastern Ontario' and that 'more attention should be devoted to the district between Cornwall and Kingston...' Ferguson himself preached the virtues of the Hydro but found that many people knew almost nothing about it. Emphasizing to Beck that attention should be paid to the smaller communities and the farms as well as to large towns, he believed that the advantages of the Hydro would 'put them on a par with the larger towns so far as power and light advantages are concerned which means rapid development and prosperity.' He promised Beck to push the scheme 'through the East if I can only get loaded up with all the facts and figures...' Beck responded that he was 'glad that you are taking such an interest in the matter. I find a lack of interest and energy on the part of most of the members of the House, even in their own localities.'[19]

The day would come, and soon, when Beck would no longer appreciate Ferguson's interest in Hydro matters. The member for Grenville continued to press Beck and his lieutenants for action, telling chief engineer Fred Gaby in December 1913 that 'I am constantly being interrogated about Hydro power all through the eastern district.' Perhaps because of this concern, it was to Ferguson that Whitney entrusted a delicate mission. The story is told briefly in W.R. Plewman's biography of Beck. The Hydro chief, a man of imperious temperament and towering rages, exercised enormous power in pre-war Ontario and apparently Whitney had become more worried than usual about one of his empire-building projects. He sent Ferguson to apply the brakes and Plewman's biography graphically describes what was the first of many confrontations between two strong personalities:

"What can Whitney do?" Adam Beck inquired scornfully. "This is what he can do – he can break Beck," replied G. Howard Ferguson. "He can repudiate you; and his majority in the Legislature will back him up, and that will be your finish."[20]

Beck was not used to being spoken to like that. He and Ferguson for many years remained bitter enemies.

By this time, the province was in the midst of another election. Held in late June a few weeks before the outbreak of the world holocaust, the outcome again was never in doubt. Whitney, as he put it, 'back ... from the shadow of the dark valley,' made only one major campaign appearance but, as long as he lived, Ontario was his. The only issue that seemed to mean much was Rowell's ban-the-bar crusade but even that failed to catch fire. The schools controversy was seldom discussed and, curiously, Ferguson did not seem inclined to raise it. When promulgated in 1912, Regulation 17 had elicited outraged cries of persecution from French Canadians and in 1913, in an effort to meet the wishes of the Franco-Ontarian community part way and to clear up ambiguities in the original regulation, an amended version had been issued. Under it, teaching in French was permitted, with the approval of the chief inspector, 'in the case of pupils beyond Form I who are unable to speak and understand the English language.' There were other concessions as well and all in all the changes represented a fair-minded effort to meet the wishes of French leaders without granting a full bilingual system.[21] If administered liberally, the new policy was at least as generous as that followed by Mowat in the 1880s and 1890s. ACFEO, however, regarded the 1913 changes as more odious and unjust than ever and continued its campaign of resistance. The relative absence of the issue from the 1914 election suggests either that ACFEO's efforts were having limited success or that emotions were not yet raised to a fever pitch. With the war, all that would change. Still, the campaign did see additional erosion of the Tory party's erstwhile support in Franco-Ontarian areas. The Liberals made gains in east and west Ottawa, Cochrane and North Essex, where Reaume's failure to win renomination eliminated French representation from the cabinet.

Ferguson had no difficulty in gaining re-election in Grenville. His only opponent, the mayor of Prescott, was a long-time Conservative whose political ambitions caused him to run as an independent. During his campaign Ferguson inevitably made reference to his recent role in the House, remarking that he had accepted the Trent Commission with the greatest reluctance and only at Cochrane's insistence. And he seemed more than a little embarrassed by the Evanturel affair.[22] No very active campaign was necessary in this his fourth provincial election. Within weeks, his tenure as a private member would end. Soon, as he struggled with the burden of administering two great departments and attempted to cope with the endless problems of wartime politics, he may have looked back, nostalgically, to those carefree days when he was learning his trade and playing his part so well on the Whitney backbenches.

5

The Hearst Administration

James Whitney's death shortly after the outbreak of World War I was a grievous blow to the Conservative party. Whitney's unrivalled popularity had disguised party weaknesses during the 1914 election but there were growing signs even then that the coalition of interest groups which had kept the party in power was starting to disintegrate. The new premier, William Hearst, a lawyer from Sault Ste Marie, had served since 1911 as Minister of Lands and Forests but his record suggested little more than gray competence. Although Whitney himself had regarded Hearst as having strong claims for the succession, his selection occasioned a struggle that left factions which favoured Adam Beck or W.J. Hanna angry and disillusioned. Beck refused to serve in the Hearst cabinet and an aging administration was further weakened.

Within weeks Hearst placed his own nominees in key positions. Ferguson and Tom McGarry, the Siamese twins of the House as the *Globe* called them, received the portfolios of Lands, Forests and Mines and Treasury, respectively.[1] The new men moved quickly to the fore and before long were exercising a disproportionate influence on Hearst. Ferguson served in the Hearst administration for almost five years. He shared its fortunes and, to an extent surpassed only by Hearst himself, controlled its destinies. During most of that period, the Great War was the lurid, pervasive reality around which most issues revolved. Prohibition, votes for women, educational affairs, social problems, and even many of the concerns of Ferguson's own Lands, Forests and Mines Department were shaped in various ways by war conditions. In Ferguson's Department, for example, the enlistment of large numbers of experienced personnel could not help but impair efficiency, while the demand for war matériel and planning for post-war reconstruction were important policy considerations.

Ferguson embarked on his new duties with his usual enthusiasm. Although from eastern Ontario, he proved himself in spirit as much a man of the north as Cochrane and Hearst had ever been. In the early twentieth century, many viewed New Ontario as an Eldorado, the province's last great frontier whose vast resources would make Ontario the envy of the continent. The wedding of the wealth of the Laurentian frontier with the urban and industrial skills of the southern heartland would create a mighty new civilization and Ontario would be not only the workshop of Canada but a dominant partner in the whole British Empire. All would be achieved through industry, enterprise, in a word, development. Although a simple faith and one not without defects, it was founded on more than dreams; the future would bring disappointments, particularly to the northern regions themselves, but also an ample measure of fulfilment. Howard Ferguson became the leading prophet of this new faith. Over the course of his long career, he exemplified better than any other Ontarian the vision of northern development.

First he had to master his own department. This task was formidable. Mines and Lands and Forests were in reality two separate bodies linked by the minister himself. Both units, with far-flung field forces and administrative practices more suited to a simpler day, sorely needed to be tamed and modernized. Some insight into the administrative nightmare posed by a Department staffed largely by field personnel living in the most inaccessible parts of Ontario can be gained from the fact that in 1917 Lands and Forests employed no fewer than 1500 cullers with responsibility for protecting the province's interest during timber cutting operations. When the Tories came into office in 1905, Frank Cochrane and Deputy Minister Aubrey White had attempted to reform and reorganize provincial timber administration. The shift of the centre of the lumbering industry from the Ottawa Valley and Georgian Bay areas to the northwest had led to diminished government control and during the 1905 election the Tories had charged that New Ontario was being 'ruthlessly exploited by timber barons aided and abetted by a revenue-hungry government.'[2] In power they established a system based on a trained field staff which would allow the province to charge dues and bonus on every foot of timber cut.

Unfortunately the new method placed too much responsibility on a field force all too lacking in training and supervision. Well before Ferguson assumed office, it became clear that the White-Cochrane reforms had broken down in execution.[3] To some extent this reflected the failure of the Department to utilize the pool of talent available through the University of Toronto's Faculty of Forestry, which was founded in 1907. Its Dean, the redoubtable B.E. Fernow, a leader of the scientific forest management movement in North America, had alienated both White and Cochrane by the tactless manner in which he made it clear that the policies of the province did not measure up to his standards. As a result, 'in the Faculty's first few years none of its graduates entered the Ontario service.' Of fifty-one graduates between 1909 and 1915, only one joined the Ontario department.[4]

Ferguson, confronted by this situation of paper reforms and dubious practices when he assumed office, soon learned that the war years were not the time to attempt to rectify matters. Because so many employees enlisted, a substantial number of senior personnel had to be kept on past the retirement age.[5] The Department suffered a serious blow in 1915 with the death of Aubrey White. His successor as Deputy Minister, Albert Grigg, a former Tory member, had little talent for or even interest in his new position. For this appointment Ferguson must assume responsibility, but he soon realized Grigg's deficiencies and by-passed him by relying on his personal secretary, Carroll Hele, who was also appointed secretary to the Department, and on Dr E.J. Zavitz, the head of the Forestry Branch and one of the pioneers of the forestry movement in Canada. The Branch's duties included reforestation and forest fire protection.

This arrangement led to clashes between Grigg and Zavitz, with the parsimonious deputy minister often objecting to the more imaginative Forestry head's policies. In these circumstances, Zavitz learned he could count on Ferguson to support new methods and innovative programs and he became an unabashed admirer of his minister.[6] But if this made for fairly satisfactory conditions in Forestry, it did nothing to help the Lands Branch, the other major unit into which Lands and Forests was divided. The Lands Branch was responsible for sales, land grants, surveys, patents, and relations with the forest industries. It was here that the lack of new blood in the Department was felt most severely and the busy minister assumed many responsibilities he should have delegated to others.

Staffing deficiencies may not have been the only reason for Ferguson's decision to play a major personal role in this area. For one thing, relations with the lumber barons were sensitive and often difficult; as well, there were political reasons for the minister himself to assume a degree of control. Furthermore, Ferguson at some stage had developed firm views about the policies necessary to stimulate the development of the north and found in Ontario a great and firmly based forest industry. His primary responsibility, he believed, was to further the economic growth of the province and in pursuit of this objective the regulations of the department were there to guide but not restrict him. After all, the minister, in his view, was politically responsible and the province stood to benefit from imaginative policies flexibly developed which could contribute to the establishment of an expanded industry and the creation of new wealth.

Some insight into Ferguson's methods was offered in 1919 by George Meade, the president of the Spanish River Pulp and Paper Co., who related that he had received assurances from the minister that 'if the company desired to increase production at the Espanola, or at any other plant, and if there was any question of us not having enough wood to operate the plant, perpetually or for a number of years, then the Government would at all times endeavor to find us the wood.' In pursuit of these goals, Ferguson played fast and loose with regulations and even the requirement of competition and tender sometimes went by the board. Thus in his last days as minister, he set aside some 5700 square miles of pulpwood without competition for Spanish River, informing them that 'there can be no doubt that industries such as yours can be more economically and efficiently conducted on the basis of large units, and it is to the best interests of the Province as a whole that a reasonable number of large mills should be maintained...' His hopes were further revealed when he granted 1500 square miles of pulpwood to the Abitibi Co. in April 1919, again without competition, informing the Company that 'my ambition has been to see the largest paper industry in the world established in this Province, and my attitude toward the pulp and paper industry has been directed toward assisting in bringing this about...'[7]

Such disregard for statutory regulations involved Ferguson as the central figure in one of the most sensational political scandals in Ontario's history. It almost destroyed his career and certainly forever blackened his reputation in the minds of some. Yet that came at a later date when the Tories had ceased to rule and for the moment Ferguson pursued his course unchecked and certainly unchastened. As minister he believed that in practical terms the regulations providing for tender and competition often had little relation to business and geographic realities. Large companies had, or must have, clearly defined spheres of influence. If capital was to be invested, plants built and operations maintained, a supply of wood had to be permanently available. The pulpwood contracts between government and companies were careful, intricate documents and Ferguson seems to have considered it more realistic for the Crown to protect its rights through such agreements than by often meaningless competitions. Of course the procedures he adopted were open to political abuse and there is no doubt that he acted arbitrarily and high-handedly.

Most of these issues, however, were raised only during the 1919 election and after. For the moment the Department, despite personnel and organizational problems, seemed to be functioning well enough. As minister, Ferguson demonstrated an enormous capacity for hard work and an ability to make decisions quickly and effectively. Regulations were passed allowing enlisted men to retain their interest in Crown land and changes in the Mining Act exempted military personnel who held unpatented claims from statutory requirements. When the Colonization Branch in 1916 was shifted from Agriculture to Lands and Forests, responsibility for immigration and settlement devolved upon Ferguson. Given the growing shortage of manpower and the virtual ending of all immigration from Europe, it became a challenge of some significance to attract immigrants from the United States. At a February 1916 meeting between Agriculture and Lands and Forests officials, it was decided to send immigration agents south. The Department report later noted that 'we experienced great difficulty in convincing favourable applicants that Canada was not under military conscription,' yet in 1916 and 1917 several hundred farm labourers were attracted through these efforts.

The most pronounced effect of the war on Ferguson's Department was to slow the pace of northern settlement. 'Owing to a great number of our best settlers having enlisted,' the 1916 report stated, 'it was difficult to get sufficient labour to carry on the work in certain sections.' Costs of labour and supplies forced the department to defer much road construction and Ferguson noted that 'settlement in Northern Ontario has been almost completely arrested by the War...'[8] The appointment of a special 'Commissioner for Northern Development,' J.F. Whitson, who was given responsibility for administering the funds provided by the Northern Development Act of 1912, helped somewhat and the 1917 report boasted that 'there were 728 people who took up land in Northern Ontario last year as compared with 641 the year before. This is wonderful, considering the retarding influence of the war...' One cause of the increase was the booming production of the province's mines and forest industries. The war machine voraciously consumed the products of the north and the production of pulpwood increased from '173,903 tons in 1912 worth $1,235,343, to an estimated 500,000 tons in 1916 worth $4,200,000.' The Bureau of Mines report of 1918 revealed a total production of over $80,000,000 compared with $53,000,000 in the last year before the war.[9]

The most ambitious and in some ways the most revealing war-related project was the Kapuskasing Veterans Colony. As early as 1915 Ferguson and Hearst represented Ontario at a dominion-provincial conference on the care and treatment of wounded soldiers and the training of returned men. As the war progressed, more thought was given to such matters and Ottawa formulated a soldiers' land project on the prairies. Ontario's own plan was designed not only to assist veterans but to check the drain of farmers to the west which had started in the pre-war years. Another social objective was to mitigate the tendency for farmers' sons to desert their fathers' way of life for the attractions of city life. Of course the province was not so naïve as to place its major hopes for reconstruction on a 'back-to-the-land' movement and even the Kapuskasing project was planned along lines which would place the returned man 'on the land in communities having a common centre, avoiding in large measure the isolation which unfortunately has prevailed in many of the northern districts.'[10] Still, a sense of nostalgia for the province's rural past and a hard-headed fear of the consequences of rural depopulation created considerable enthusiasm in the urban press for efforts such as Kapuskasing. The *Globe* spoke of drawing 'thousands who are doing badly in the cities back to the independent life of the agricultural producer.'[11] Although the Kapuskasing project was finally a disappointment, it was a product of its time and received widespread support in diverse circles.

Nor was it based on idle enthusiasm. The Great Clay Belt some 450 miles north of Toronto offered substantial possibilities for agricultural settlement and the construction of the National Transcontinental through northern Ontario and Quebec in the years prior to the war first revealed the area's potential. Soon the

T&NO RR was completed to Cochrane, the junction point of the two lines. In 1914 the annual departmental report predicted that when the new trans-continental was in regular operation, 'people will move into the country in large numbers. ... The land, of course, is intended for actual settlers.'[12] By the spring of 1917, detailed plans were ready and by the Returned Soldiers and Sailors Settlement Act of that year, five townships were reserved for the farm colony. The townships were surveyed into hundred-acre lots, ten acres of each was cleared in advance of settlement and the colonist paid nothing for his land. Colonization roads were constructed, a sawmill erected, and initially the province even provided stock, heavy farm machinery, and $500 loans. A $150 grant assisted the veteran in the construction of a home. Applicants were carefully screened and those selected underwent a training course in northern farming techniques. In all a million dollars was appropriated for a project regarded by contemporaries such as J. Castell Hopkins as 'a new departure in colonization work in Canada.'[13] Its failure may have owed something to lack of foresight in planning but was attributable far more to the unrestrained enthusiasm about the future of the north which had been prevalent in Ontario for more than a decade. Its collapse was a minor tragedy of reconstruction.

A different kind of tragedy occurred in July 1916. Until then, according to E.J. Zavitz, 'there was no permanent fire protection service. ... The details in the north were taken care of by the Crown Timber agents.'[14] That year, after an intensely hot July, 'a great number of small fires, fanned by a violent wind, united in "one seething cauldron of flame" that ... burned clean an area equal to twenty townships or some thirteen hundred and twenty square miles, and during its course destroyed seven towns and villages...'[15] Two hundred and twenty-four lives were lost in the catastrophic Matheson conflagration. Ferguson ordered Zavitz to reorganize the whole service and the result was the Forest Fires Prevention Act of 1917. This measure established the post of Provincial Forester – Ferguson immediately named Zavitz to the job – and created a more effective organization for the Forestry Branch. By the Act, the Provincial Forester received extensive new powers to enforce fire prevention measures. Wooden look-out towers were erected across the north and fire rangers, paid for by a tax on timber licences, gave the province the means to enforce its regulations on both public and private property. The measure owed a good deal to the close relationship between Zavitz and his minister. 'For the first time,' the official departmental history concluded, 'the Province now had a Fire Protection Act "with teeth in it"; and, more important, professional foresters were to be brought into the service of the Department, to carry it into effect.'[16]

As Minister of Lands, Forests and Mines, Howard Ferguson took charge with a will, mastered the details of his Department, earned the respect of his ablest assistants, and laid down broad policy lines which profoundly affected the economic development of Ontario. For much of this same period, he was also heading another department and was at the centre of a dispute which rocked the country and threatened to open an irreparable gulf between French and English Canadians at a critical moment in history. With Dr Pyne serving overseas as a military hospital administrator, Ferguson between 1915 and 1917 assumed responsibility for the Department of Education. By this time war tensions had exacerbated the old dispute over Regulation 17 and the French Canadian Educational Association had organized a loud and determined resistance. The Ottawa separate school board remained at the centre of the storm and when provincial inspectors entered the classrooms, Franco-Ontarian youngsters led by their teachers usually filed out of the schools. In April 1915 the government, supported by Rowell, established a special commission to run the Ottawa schools. In July a Supreme Court judge dismissed an appeal against a court order to reopen the schools and commented that he was 'unable to find anything which supports the contention that the right to use the French language in the Separate Schools of the Province was guaranteed by treaty or otherwise...' The following month Ferguson became Acting Minister of Education.

In many ways his appointment was inauspicious. His record on this issue was not likely to lessen an emotional crisis which was all but out of control, while his abrasive tongue could do much damage. And in 1916 the crisis escalated. Several teachers physically resisted efforts by the special commission to eject them from their schools, thousands of children marched in protest through the streets of Ottawa, and violent language became commonplace on both sides. 'Of what use is it,' asked *Le Droit*, the newspaper of French-speaking Ottawa, 'for us to fight against Prussianism and barbarity ... when the same condition exists at home?' English Canadians were moved to fury when many French Canadians announced they could not support the war effort while French civilization was threatened 'on the banks of the Ottawa River.'[17]

Into the midst of this national crisis marched Orangeman and imperialist Howard Ferguson. The Acting Minister soon made it clear he had not changed his mind about the justice of Ontario's position and he acted energetically to counter the most formidable challenge ever mounted to provincial authority in the schools. Yet power and responsibility seemed to have moderated his opinions and perhaps too he now grasped the dangers the question presented to Canada's future. In his speeches and correspondence, as well as in his actions as minister, he argued that Ontario's attitude towards French in the schools was not 'an unreasonable one or an ungenerous one.' Every request which reached the Department, he told the House, 'has been granted the fullest latitude, widest discussion and most generous treatment that I was capable of meting out.' Everything possible was being done 'to give the Franco-Ontarians teachers of their own race' and to 'encourage the training of teachers of the French tongue.' Although there were four English-French training schools, there remained a serious shortage of such teachers and therefore the Department, he pointed out, accepted teacher training candidates whose qualifications did not come up to provincial standards and provided board and expense money for anyone wishing to attend one of the four schools. 'This year we have set apart a special fund of $15,000. ... We will say in a poor section ... if the teacher demands five or six hundred dollars a year salary and you can only raise $200 we will give you the other $300.' As for the use of the French language, Ferguson argued that Regulation 17 extended privileges which did not exist in the Canadian constitution and to support this he referred to Senator Belcourt's statement in June 1912 that 'the use of the French language ... in the Province of Ontario is not sanctioned by the constitution of Canada nor by the Ontario laws.'

The Department has long thought that. We believe that today, but we have not assumed the attitude of hewing to the line and demanding our strict legal rights because it is obvious the French people would be denied the use of their language in the schools. We recognized we had a exceptional condition here. There were many people of French origin who were entitled to have some means of educating their children. Some method had to be devised of giving them a proper education, so the regulation, instead of being something that would restrict the use of the French language in the Province, was really a privilege extended to them and according to the opinion of their best legal advisers ... it does not exist as a matter of law.[18]

To those who remembered the Howard Ferguson of 1911 and 1912, the fire-eating Orangeman of the 'English-only' resolution, such reassurances were deeply suspect. 'Merely a lawyer's brief' was the reaction of one Ottawa priest who pointed to Ferguson's 'scornful and sarcastic' insistence that 'all the machinery of the law will be used to put down this agitation stirred up by a few irresponsible and interested persons'; Ferguson, he asserted, remained the vindictive partisan he had always been.[19] Understandably, it was hard for French Canadians not to believe that Regulation 17 was part of a plot to annihilate the French language outside of Quebec.

Yet Ontario's case was not entirely unconvincing. Regulation 17, Ferguson insisted, was a policy recommended by educational experts and based on the report of one of the most broad-minded and able educators in Canada. It was designed to correct abuses pointed out over many years by a series of government commissions and was an effort to ensure that every child in the province would receive an education which would fit him or her for life in the urbanized and industrialized English-speaking province of Ontario. When complaint had been made against the original regulation the government, Ferguson noted, amended it to permit as much teaching in French as was possible with this end still in view.

Certainly Department of Education officials believed that their policy was right and proper and did not represent a veiled effort to proscribe the French language. A 1915 departmental document argued persuasively that in certain parts of the province where French was the language of the home and the community it was only through the school that a reasonable facility in English could be gained.

As to attempting to take away the French language, such a thing is simply nonsense. It would be as unwise as it would be unjust and impossible. The French people have a perfect right to their mother tongue and no one should, for a moment, desire to deprive them of it. That the Department has no such desire or intention is fully proven by the liberal and just way in which the English-French schools have always been treated ... the kindness and care ever extended to these schools in the endeavour to increase their efficiency, and the special help to meet special needs, should convince any reasonable person...[20]

A similar argument appeared in *Memorandum re regulation 17*, prepared for Ferguson in March 1916. Its thesis was that Regulation 17 'affords the child equal opportunities for the learning of both languages.'

When it is considered that the school day in Ontario calls for five hours of study, that one of these hours is devoted to the teaching of French in the French language, that half an hour a day is devoted to Religious Instruction, which may be given and usually is, in the French language, it leaves only 3½ out of 16 hours of the child's waking life in which he has an opportunity to speak or be spoken to in the English language. When it is further considered that even this small proportion of time, 20%, is effective only for the last two-thirds at most of the pupil's life in the elementary schools, it should be apparent that the objection to the use of English as the language of communication and instruction is really an objection to the study of English at all; to say that this minimum should be reduced, is to say in effect that one does not desire the pupils to learn English.[21]

This was the case Ferguson made in the legislature and in statements to the press. He also argued it in memoranda presented to Robert Borden in February and April 1916. On the first occasion Borden told him that a petition for disallowance of the legislation creating the special Ottawa school commission was to be presented to the Commons and requested 'a memorandum ... in which the exact position will be clearly expressed.'[22] Then in early April, with the Liberals proposing to raise the issue of Regulation 17 in the federal Parliament through a formal motion, Ferguson and Borden conferred at length. The Prime Minister noted in his diary that Ferguson had told him that 'feeling in Ontario is intense and that Liberals are as strong as Conservatives; that Government would not live an hour if it made slightest concession.'[23] Ferguson assured Borden that about 25 per cent of the English-French schools of the province were using Regulation 17 'with apparent satisfaction,' but half of the bilingual schools were in the Ottawa area and these schools had defied the Department from the start. 'To say that the regulation is an impracticable one, without even attempting to try it out, is surely an unreasonable and untenable position...'[24]

Ferguson repeatedly advanced the dubious thesis that most of the trouble could be traced to racial agitators. To an Irish-Catholic ex-school trustee from Plantagenet who complained that everything had been harmonious throughout his twenty-two years as a trustee until the French won a majority, he replied that it was not the French people themselves who were to blame but their leaders 'who wilfully distort the facts.'[25] To Borden he complained that 'I have never known any public question upon which there has been so much gross misstatement. ... Even a casual investigation of the law and the facts will convince anyone of the utter absurdity and falsity of the allegation that the Ontario Government are endeavouring to annihilate the French language.'[26] In a major statement released on 11 March, he insisted that 'there have been so many misstatements ... that I feel the time has come to explain...' and he proceeded to do so at length. In the legislature on 14 April he angrily charged that many French Canadians did not understand the actual state of affairs because they were 'being told day after day that we are trying ... to annihilate the French tongue ... There was never a more dishonest statement.'[27] In September he informed E.L. Patenaude, one of Borden's Quebec ministers, that 'there is not a shade of doubt in my mind that the agitation of interested parties has so befogged the real situation that the reasonable people have been misled...'[28] The province, Ferguson made clear, would enforce its will even if the Ottawa school commission were struck down.

Robert Borden never showed much sympathy for the Franco-Ontarian cause. He was unmoved by a cabinet crisis and an ultimatum from his Quebec colleagues and when the Liberals in May presented the Lapointe Resolution to the effect that the House of Commons should respectfully suggest to the Ontario legislature 'the wisdom of making it clear that the privilege of the children of French parentage of being taught in their mother tongue be not interfered with,' Borden took his stand on provincial rights and against federal intervention. Laurier, on the other hand, with Bourassa and the Nationalists demanding justice for the Franco-Ontarians, put great pressure on federal and provincial Liberals from Ontario. Although most of the federal Ontario members supported the Lapointe Resolution, Rowell refused to co-operate. When Stewart Lyon of the *Globe* explained that 'Howard Ferguson and the extreme Orange element feel that there is party advantage for them in insisting upon greater restrictions in the teaching of French,' Laurier responded angrily that, 'we, French Liberals of Quebec, are fighting Bourassa and Lavergne; will the English Liberals in Ontario fight Howard Ferguson and the extreme Orange element?'[29]

But Rowell and his friends were in essential agreement with the Ontario government's position and when the Liberal leader in partial deference to Laurier's wishes suggested another commission of investigation, he was subjected to a devastating attack from Ferguson. Rowell, Ferguson charged, was playing the game as directed by Laurier and his advisers who were 'trying to get the English-speaking Liberals of Ontario to line up behind the French-speaking Liberals to support Sir Wilfrid Laurier in bringing in a resolution making demands upon this Province which they have no right to make.'[30] Rowell reported to Laurier that public opinion in Ontario was never more sensitive and 'judged by Ferguson's position and attitude yesterday, the Government intends to make all the political capital it can out of the matter by falsely charging that there is a Liberal plot to try to make political capital out of the issue...'[31] Yet there was a measure of truth to Ferguson's charges. Borden himself warned Laurier that the Lapointe Resolution 'could do no good and might do great harm,' but Laurier, Borden confided to his diary, responded that 'he was alarmed at conditions in Quebec and that he must have some sheet anchor with which to fight Nationalists...'[32]

At the same time, Howard Ferguson's insistence that the controversy was the product of the work of agitators revealed an enormous capacity for self-delusion and a large degree of ignorance of French Canada. Although ACFEO was the spearhead of the resistance, there were few members of French Canada's élite who did not regard opposition to Regulation 17 as a vital question of national survival. Not only Laurier and nationalist spokesmen such as Bourassa and Lavergne but almost the entire French-speaking hierarchy of the Roman Catholic church and the political leaders of the province of Quebec were determined to defend the rights of the Ontario minority. French-language journals habitually referred to 'les blessés d'Ontario' and feeling was further inflamed when Quebec passed a bill to permit local school commissions to contribute money to the Franco-Ontarian cause.

Yet if the Ontario Tories were not unmindful of the effect of their policies on the Orange vote and if Laurier was looking over his shoulder at Bourassa, the motives of ACFEO itself are open to question. Were Franco-Ontarian leaders sincerely interested in a settlement which would restore conditions as they had been prior to Regulation 17 or were they bent on putting the emotional crisis which had won to their cause great support in the mother province of Quebec to political use? In the period before Regulation 17, the French community remained unorganized and weak; assimilation had proceeded apace. The campaign against Regulation 17 brought a new spirit and pride to the French in Ontario. To return to the past would be to restore the period of indifference and anglicization. Thus the previous year when Archbishop Bruchési of Montreal intervened in the dispute as a mediator and meetings took place with Chief Inspector Waugh and McGregor Young, the province's lawyer, his efforts were viewed by ACFEO and French-speaking members of the old Ottawa School Board with less than enthusiasm. Nonetheless, negotiations continued and McGregor Young in a letter addressed to an intermediary but meant for Bruchési assured him that Hearst was well disposed and that Ferguson, 'orangiste lui-même, aurait déclaré qu'il voyait les choses différement depuis son entrée dans le cabinet et qu'il sympathisait beaucoup avec les Canadiens-français.'[33]

This was interesting. More interesting was that when Bruchési informed his Ontario friends, the proposals were greeted with suspicion and hostility. Bruchési replied that he believed the province sincerely desired to arrive at an understanding. When it was put to him that under the proposed compromise the hated system of the double inspectorate by which an English-speaking and a French-speaking inspector would visit each English-French school would remain in existence, he answered that he failed to see that such an inspector could do much damage in a half hour. The archbishop said that unless the proposals were accepted, the Franco-Ontarians would be accused 'de vouloir continuer la lutte pour la lutte.'[34] A few weeks later Bruchési returned to Ottawa and told the priests of the French-speaking parishes 'que s'ils s'obstinent à refuser les propositions du gouvernement, ils perdront toutes les sympathies qu'ils ont dans Québec.'[35] If this and all other attempts at settlement failed, it is clear that the blame for that fact did not rest entirely with the province.

Of course the extremist rhetoric used by both sides increasingly precluded any possibility of compromise. Thus during the summer of 1916 Ferguson again charged the Liberals with fomenting religious and racial prejudice to win votes in Quebec. 'I want to say this to Sir Wilfrid Laurier, that no man in public life today was ever guilty of a greater crime against the well-being of Canada. I say deliberately, knowing whereof I speak, that Sir Wilfrid Laurier and the other leaders of the Liberal party ... connived and planned to make the Ontario school question an issue in Dominion politics so as to solidify the province of Quebec, and to do that in the midst of this awful war for no other purpose than party advantage.' The same month Bourassa exhorted French Canadians to resist with all their might the threat to their rights being mounted by the 'Yankees of Toronto' and declared that while the constitution 'guarantees us in Quebec against any invasion on the part of the barbarians of Ontario,' yet the main army of French Canadians in Quebec must not lose touch with their brothers in 'the outposts.' That same day a young nationalist spokesman, Paul Emile Lamarche, declared that 'Canada is a bilingual country. ... The flow of immigration would not swamp French Canadians,' who within a century would number one hundred million and thus overcome 'the vermin' who had been brought to Canada at $5 per head. In the same tone was Howard Ferguson's insistence that August to a meeting of Toronto Orangemen that the agitation did not come from French Canadians but from French priests expelled from the mother country who had infiltrated the schools and were 'instilling into the hearts of the

French people here the idea of a new France – of segregating themselves in this new continent and building up here a greater France than ever existed in Europe.' If he pretended to believe such charges, retorted Sam Genest, the fiery chairman of the Ottawa Separate School Board, Ferguson was 'a fool, ignoramus and malicious scoundrel.' An anonymous letter told him that 'people of your mentality are the worst enemies of our Canada. ... Men of your stamp deserve the gallows, I hope that you will get them.'[36]

Undaunted, Ferguson achieved new heights of irresponsibility when he opened the Tory campaign in a by-election in Southwest Toronto.

"This bilingual question is the greatest of the issues before us," exclaimed Mr Ferguson. "It entirely overshadows nickel and booze and every other question. It touches the vitals of our province and our Dominion. If it is not dealt with the whole national fabric will be destroyed. The government I represent upholds British traditions, British institutions and one flag and one language for this Dominion. Unless something is done to meet this French-speaking invasion, this national outrage, this Dominion will be stricken to its foundation as this war has not stricken it. George P. Graham, Sir Wilfrid Laurier, Senator Dandurand and our own 'Little Rowell' are urging the French to fight for their rights, and Hartley Dewart is asking you to support him in that kind of thing."

Again Ferguson repeated his charges about the influence of French priests. Schools in which the French Canadians were left alone were obeying Regulation 17. There were sixty such schools and they were getting good results. But there were over two hundred more which remained defiant and the trouble was that 'the rest of the schools were under the control of some French-speaking father, an Oblate or Franciscan or some other kind of father.'

Those controlling church influence in the Province of Quebec and among the French-speaking people had, declared Mr Ferguson, no gratitude or affection toward old France. "That isn't the doctrine the people are being taught. The French priests in Quebec and Ontario are decrying enlistment; they are encouraging French-Canadian young manhood to stay at home and fight the battles of language. ... Well, we don't propose to stand for that kind of thing."[37]

Once again Ferguson was the extremist of 1911. He may have believed the equally abusive language to which the province of Ontario was being subjected justified such behaviour; he may even have believed the essence of what he was saying. War emotions provide an explanation but not a justification for such appeals. But how could ACFEO ever believe in the good faith of a man who could simultaneously voice such extremism to win a few Orange votes in Toronto and offer reassurances to the Franco-Ontarians that their language was not under attack?

Fortunately two external decisions now served to calm passions which seemed all but out of control. Not even Orangemen and nationalists could ignore the Empire's highest court and the Pope when they spoke virtually in unison. On 26 October a letter was published from His Holiness Benedict XV addressed to Cardinal Bégin and the Archbishops and Bishops of Canada. Benedict stated that 'nobody can deny that the Civil Government of Ontario has the right to exact that children should learn English in the schools. ... Nor on the other hand is there any reason to contest the right of French Canadians, living in the Province, to claim, in a suitable way, that French should be taught in schools attended by a certain number of their children...' The Pope asked that 'counsels of moderation prevail.' Early in November the Judicial Committee of the Privy Council stated that Regulation 17 was *intra vires* and the legislation establishing the special commission *ultra vires.*[38] Of course nothing was finally settled but for the rest of the war period, the participants in the schools controversy, as if horrified by what had been happening to Canada, conducted themselves with more restraint.

Yet neither side really altered its views. The Hearst government passed legislation appointing a new Ottawa school commission similar to that which the Privy Council had struck down; while in another hard-line move, Franco-Ontarians petitioning for land in northern Ontario were required to submit signed pledges that they would obey the school laws. Senator Belcourt was infuriated by the new school commission measure, which he described as 'in flagrant defiance of the decision of the Privy Council. The French Canadian people of Ontario have been told ad nauseam to obey the law,' he informed Hartley Dewart. 'One would think that the Provincial Executive would not need to have to be told to obey the law...'[39] The legislation was never proclaimed. Ferguson and Hearst apparently expected that timely concessions to boards willing to implement the province's school laws and the withholding of grants from others would wear down resistance. Senator Belcourt, who remained one of the driving forces behind ACFEO, believed that the Hearst government 'did not try at any time to settle the question, that it did not want the question to be settled, that it looked upon the difficulties caused by Regulation 17 as its best ground for retaining power.'[40] The decision of the JCPC that the province's school commission legislation was unconstitutional did not relieve the Ottawa Board from the MacKell injunction of 1914 which prevented the Board from borrowing or from paying the salaries of teachers so long as it refused to obey the regulations of the Department of Education. Although chairman Genest risked jail to pay the salaries of his teachers, often there were no funds to do so and the Board hovered on the brink of bankruptcy. In other parts of the province, those French Canadians who rejected Regulation 17 sometimes resorted to the costly expedient of founding private schools for their children. Thus deadlock had ensued. When the Hearst government went down to defeat, neither side had been able to win a clear victory.

As for Howard Ferguson's role, undeniably he had played to the passions of the Orange mob in several speeches and had attempted, with little success, to exploit the issue in by-elections. He had also, however, endeavoured to reach a compromise solution and, more importantly, he had argued on many occasions, in different forums, on behalf of the rights of the French language in the schools of Ontario. Should his insistence that the purpose of Regulation 17 was 'not to obliterate the French language but to promote the teaching of the English language' be regarded merely an elaborate piece of casuistry? Much of the evidence for the view that Regulation 17 was a fair and workable solution for the problems pointed to by Dr Merchant's two commissions, one which would have benefitted the French language in Ontario and promoted a better education for Franco-Ontarians, came from Ferguson and his officials and was hardly disinterested.

Yet Ferguson's oft-repeated claim that Regulation 17 permitted enormous amounts of French-language teaching in the schools could win him few votes in Ontario, and he maintained this position in the face of unrestrained denunciation from those who questioned his motives and his integrity. At the same time, the ACFEO position is entirely understandable. How could Belcourt and Genest ever trust the government which had attempted to seize control of the Ottawa separate school board and which cut off grants to all schools which refused to conform to what from their perspective at least appeared to be an iniquitous regulation? There was, in short, little trust on either side and the war years were the least propitious time of all to attempt to settle a problem of the kind which had bedevilled the country since its foundation. After the war was over and passions had subsided, it might be possible for men of good will to attempt the delicate task of restoring a measure of trust and harmony. Otherwise the country could not endure.

Ferguson's wartime responsibilities were not restricted to the administration of his own department and Education. With Hearst ill early in 1916, he assumed part of the Premier's load. Already he was being regarded in some circles as the man of the future and Borden in August noted in his diary that John Willison of the Toronto *News* 'considers Ferguson and Beck only available leaders to succeed Hearst.'[41] Certainly Grenville in 1916 reaped considerable benefit from being represented by Ferguson. In September it was he and not the Minister of Agriculture who announced that Kemptville had been chosen as the location of a new agricultural school. At one point the plum was about to be awarded to Lennox and Addington and construction equipment was actually out on a site in Napanee but finally Ferguson prevailed. An agricultural college was much needed in eastern Ontario and immediately it had a substantial impact on the economy of Kemptville and the surrounding area.

Increasingly Hearst drew on his talents as a political strategist and more often than not it was Ferguson who took the government's case to the voters. One responsibility which led to some stormy moments developed when the Premier deputed his two cabinet firebrands, Ferguson and McGarry, to ride herd over Sir Adam Beck. In 1916 the provincial Auditor reported that it had been impossible to audit Hydro accounts for several years because Beck refused to co-operate. Since Beck at this time was pressing the cabinet to support a vast scheme to blanket Ontario with electric radial railways and since the government was also giving serious consideration to the proposed giant generating station at Chippawa, it was vital that the Hydro chairman be brought under control. But when McGarry presented legislation to make an annual audit compulsory, Beck waged a furious campaign and exacted a number of concessions.[42] He was less successful in a confrontation with Ferguson, who forced through over his head the purchase of the extensive Seymour power interests in central Ontario. Ferguson had long campaigned for power at cost for east as well as west and now as part of an effort to redress Hydro priorities he promised to 'make the whole of the power on the Trent available to the people at actual cost and put them in the same position as the western portion of the Province is with the Niagara Power...' According to his biographer, Beck was 'seething with rage' that Ferguson rammed the purchase through and when Hydro's chief engineer, Fred Gaby, ordered an operating engineer to check out the newly purchased plants, he intervened:

"Gaby told me to go," replied the operating chief. "Let Gaby mind his own blankety blank business," said Adam Beck. "That blankety blank of a blankety blank Ferguson bought the system. Let the blankety blank operate it."[43]

But Beck had met his match and Hydro assumed the new system Ferguson had thrust on it. It was disturbing, however, that disputes between Beck and members of the cabinet should cause such discord and Hearst, unlike Whitney, seemed at a loss to know how to cope. When Beck's massive newspaper and municipal support rallied to his cause, few could take seriously Ferguson's claim that reports that the government was not co-operating with Beck were 'utter preposterous rot.' More accurate was Joseph Atkinson's judgment that Beck was 'playing an effective role in pulling down the Cabinet with which he has been in more or less rivalry since the beginning.'[44]

More serious even than friction with Beck was the division in cabinet and party over prohibition. Hearst, an active Methodist with known dry opinions, gave active support to the prohibitionists while the war itself provided an enormous boost to their cause. Manpower shortages and scarcities of grain and other foodstuffs allowed the drys to argue convincingly that the war effort demanded total prohibition, while few could resist the thesis that restraint on the part of those enjoying life at home was as nothing to the sacrifice made by thousands overseas. During the 1915 session Hearst responded by creating a Liquor License Board under J.D. Flavelle with broad regulatory powers. The drys under the able leadership of George Warburton and the 'Committee of One Hundred' pressed for total victory.

The cabinet, however, was divided. In September Hearst admitted that it had been grappling with the issue for over six months. In October, the Toronto *Star* reported that 'a right royal battle' was being fought between two factions, with Hearst and several other ministers favouring an earlier closing of the bars and Hanna, McGarry, and Ferguson resisting stubbornly. The *Globe* saw the issue as the critical point of Hearst's career. 'The masterful McGarry believes the war can be won without closing the bars at 7 o'clock. The worldly wise Ferguson, with his finger on the party pulse, fears the effect of early closing when the Government goes to the country. ... He [Hearst] stands at the crossroads. Should he take the wrong road the eloquence of McGarry and the political cunning of Ferguson will not avail...'[45] This time the views of Ferguson and McGarry did prevail and the drys, dissatisfied with the earlier closing time decided upon, redoubled their efforts. In 1916 ten thousand marchers from all parts of the province presented a huge petition bearing the signatures of 825,572 drys. The total vote in the last Ontario election had been 462,450. There was no mistaking the mood of the province.

Howard Ferguson played a central role in the unfolding drama. On no one was the wet label more strongly pinned than on him. Press reports described him as the leader of the cabinet wets, Rowell singled him out for criticism and years later, as party leader himself, he faced the charge that he had fought prohibition with all his strength and after losing had stabbed his leader in the back in the 1919 election. There was no truth to this canard and Hearst promptly asserted that 'no man ever fought a harder or more unselfish fight for a leader than Mr Ferguson did for me in 1919.' Nor was it true that Ferguson opposed prohibition to the last ditch. With Hearst ill in the period before the 1916 session, it was Ferguson who drafted much of the Ontario Temperance Act and, in Hearst's words, 'was busy ... laying plans to ensure its enactment.'[46]

Nonetheless Ferguson did approach the issue from a perspective entirely different than Hearst's. It was no secret that the man from Grenville had long since fallen away from the temperance pledge made with his sister so many years ago, and that he was out of sympathy with the crusading fervour of many drys. Ferguson never viewed it as a function of government to regulate private morality or to campaign on behalf of great moral causes. His conversion must be explained by reference to the war and to the depth of his imperialist convictions. Obviously, too, a man with his finger on the party pulse would recognize the extent of the shift in public opinion. The OTA was finally introduced on 22 March by another erstwhile wet, W.J. Hanna. According to the press, last-ditch opposition in the Tory caucus delayed the opening of the House by several hours that day. Probably the opposition was not to the measure itself but to the failure to provide any compensation to licence holders. Nor was there any provision for a plebiscite, although the throne speech had suggested such a move and several western provinces had held votes on the issue. The party, however, was whipped into line and the measure carried unanimously in the House. Soon the OTA was supplemented by federal orders-in-council and total prohibition, a state of affairs the provincial Tories may not have anticipated, came into effect in Ontario. Ultimately the OTA would contribute largely to the collapse of the Hearst government.

Ferguson was even more deeply involved in another war-related issue which proved damaging to the government's reputation. Ontario was by far the world's greatest supplier of nickel. Before the war Germany had stockpiled Canadian nickel but now its supply of this vital war matériel was running out and small amounts obtained elsewhere could not satisfy the demands of German war industries. From these facts it was deduced by some that Germany was still obtaining the Canadian product and that this was possible because International Nickel Co. was American-owned and the German munition manufacturers, the Krupps, held stock in it. Before the war, Ontario had tried to have Inco establish a Canadian refinery, but the Company had bluntly refused. Thus vast quantities of raw ore continued to be shipped to the neutral United States and sensational charges appeared in the press that much of this made its way to Germany.

Although both federal and provincial politicians categorically denied the charges, the suspicions lingered and the press campaign reached hysterical proportions. In September 1915, Ferguson moved to forestall criticism, and also to further Ontario's old ambition to gain a refinery, by appointing the Royal Ontario Nickel Commission with instructions to subject all facets of the question to the closest scrutiny. He hoped that a comprehensive study by expert advisers would not only provide a blueprint for government action but by impressing Inco might achieve another end. 'This question,' he informed Robert Borden, '...has been a live one with this Government for a number of years.' The war added new urgency and the cabinet had decided 'it was not only important from a commercial standpoint, but essential from an Imperial standpoint, that steps should be taken to bring about the refining of our nickel ore in Canada, and preferably in this province.'[47]

When the Liberals during the 1916 session moved a motion on the nickel issue, with Rowell arguing that 'the nation which controls the supply of nickel controls the future of naval armaments...' and another member grandiloquently demanding that 'if it costs a billion dollars the Empire should be made safe,' Ferguson retorted that it would be folly to act before the Nickel Commission could report.[48] That summer, however, the shrill headlines returned when the U-boat *Deutschland*, loaded, it was charged, with 240 tons of Canadian nickel, sailed from the United States. In the Southwest Toronto by-election, Hartley Dewart exploited the issue for the Liberals and although Ferguson stated that every ounce of nickel shipped from Ontario went under Dominion licence and was watched in the United States by 'an army of secret service men,' Dewart was elected with a resounding majority.[49]

With the entry of the United States into the war in 1917, the issue lost most of its impact. Yet there had been one highly beneficial result. Inco, which under peace conditions had refused to budge, in January 1916 announced that it would build a Canadian refinery. Pressure from Borden on Inco president Ambrose Monell had contributed to this decision but so too had the provincial stance. The Nickel Commission, Ferguson told Borden, 'had some influence. ... In fact my interview with Mr Monell and his associates convinced me it had had a good deal to do with it.'[50] Monell knew that Ontario was working hard to develop its own refining process and since Inco's monopoly to some extent was based on its exclusive technological knowledge, this was important. In July 1916 Ferguson proudly announced that Ontario had secured patents for at least two refining methods, one of which utilized electricity. 'It is my idea,' the minister told the press, 'that if the processes should prove commercially successful, the government should provide that all nickel should be refined in Ontario, and by these processes for which the refining companies should pay the government royalties.'[51]

Ferguson was wielding the big stick. He knew from interviews with Monell that Inco executives had not taken kindly to his presentation of the province's position. Monell's January announcement that his company would build a Canadian refinery had not resulted in action and now, four days after Ferguson's press conference, the Company informed Borden it would locate in Ontario only if it received the full co-operation of the Ontario government. Inco's terms followed in a 20 July letter to Borden. They included Ontario aid in securing land at 'reasonable prices'; assistance in developing electric power; legislation granting relief from harassing injunctions and damage suits arising out of refinery fumes; and, in a direct reference to Ferguson's announcement, freedom to use whatever refining process it chose.[52]

Ferguson was not the man to surrender to blackmail. The existence of a rival entrepreneur, the British-American Nickel Co., a joint Canadian-British venture, strengthened Ontario's already strong position. In such a situation, Inco's demands could safely be ignored. Possibly private assurances smoothed matters over to some extent and on 25 July, the International Nickel Co. of Canada Ltd. was incorporated. A month later steps were taken to purchase land at Port Colborne and in 1918 the refinery became operational. In the meantime, in March 1917, the Royal Ontario Nickel Commission issued a masterful report.

Shortly thereafter Ferguson amended the Mining Tax Act to establish a progressive but far from onerous rate graduated according to profit level. With considerable satisfaction he noted that 'in the future every bit of Crown land leased or sold would be subject to a requirement that the mineral be refined in Ontario.'[53] Thus the war emergency and the nationalist outcry had helped the province achieve goals which had eluded it in peacetime. And Inco, its cries of outrage at Ferguson's 1917 Mining Tax Act notwithstanding, did not fail to make enormous profits in the 1920s.

Despite his heavy administrative load, Ferguson by 1916 was paying increasing attention to the whole range of political considerations. This was largely by choice, partly from necessity. For much of his premiership, William Hearst maintained a degree of detachment from what he may have considered the seamier side of the political process and often it became the lot of the Fergusons and the McGarrys to tend to such matters. The growing unpopularity of the government made this no easy chore. In the middle of 1916 with the nickel issue at its height there was much evidence that the government's record on prohibition was causing massive defections from Tory support in urban Ontario. In the vital 1916 by-election held to fill Jim Foy's seat in Southwest Toronto, the Tories had not scrupled to run a wet candidate against Hartley Dewart. Many good citizens were shocked when Howard Ferguson and Provincial Treasurer I.B. Lucas went into the riding and let it be known that the OTA, so recently proclaimed a military necessity and a great moral achievement, might well be amended in a wet direction.[54] Joseph Atkinson, in company with many others, considered this shameless behaviour and when Dewart won his overwhelming victory Atkinson gloated that Tory efforts had 'presented a manifestation of almost inconceivable weakness and duplicity on the part of the government.'[55] Hypocritically, he said nothing about the propriety of Dewart, whose outlook on the liquor question he detested, running under the Rowell banner. Equally strange to some ears was Ferguson's complaint that Dewart's election represented 'a revengeful victory of the liquor interests.'[56] For the first time in a quarter of a century, a Liberal candidate had won a Toronto seat. Did Dewart's success herald a political revolution?

Certainly in 1916 provincial Liberals were more exuberant than they had been for many years, and with cause. In Peel the Conservative member resigned amidst charges of war profiteering and when he ran again without official support he was soundly defeated. North Perth also fell to the Liberals despite active campaigning by a number of cabinet ministers. Taken together with Southwest Toronto, these results caused speculation that the Tory administration was collapsing. In 1917 the Tories managed to hold on to the constituencies of Northwest Toronto and West Simcoe but Liberal hopes remained high. Howard Ferguson's attempt to rally the Conservative forces by presenting his party as the champion of the English language failed in both North Perth and

Southwest Toronto and Atkinson commented privately that the minister's attempt to exploit the issue 'fell flat.'[57] The early months of 1917 showed no improvement and O.D. Skelton of Queen's University believed that 'the provincial Government is steadily losing ground. ... The squabbles in the Cabinet between Hanna and Beck and Ferguson have weakened it and the vulgar abuse to which Ferguson and McGarry have sunk in some recent by-elections have further discredited them.' Skelton noted that 'Rowell has gained very appreciably in public favour.'[58]

Now, however, the war situation intervened to alter radically the Ontario political landscape. Newton Wesley Rowell was a sincere patriot who gave strong support to the war activities of the Hearst government. After the January 1917 by-elections, the two parties agreed there would be no more by-elections until after the war ended and no general election until a session had passed after that. This gave the Tories a chance to regroup their forces. At this point too the great campaign for Union Government in Canada was underway and as early as January Rowell was pressing it on Sir Wilfrid Laurier. Not surprisingly, Hearst and his ministers during these difficult days gave vocal support to the cause of Union Government and conscription. It was Ferguson who did his best to size up the Ontario situation for the federal Tories. During the early weeks of manoeuvring he was in the south on an enforced holiday. 'Mr Ferguson's health broke down during the session,' Hearst informed his son, '...I hope he soon recovers his usual vigour as he is a specially valuable assistant...'[59]

Returning to Canada in early June, Ferguson spent as much time as possible travelling about the province, testing the political winds. In July he reported to Borden that 'in the interests of the Empire, and to save Canada's good name and prestige before the eyes of the world, it is absolutely essential that conscription should be put into force...' Although he had at first believed that the Tories should pass conscription 'and a proper franchise bill' and go to the country, he now warned that a combination of a large foreign vote in the west, the French influence in Ontario, which controlled about eight seats, and in the Maritimes, and 'the big army of slackers' might lead to the defeat of conscription or at best a small majority in its favour. This, he stated, 'would be disastrous' and he recommended that every effort be made to establish a coalition government. George Graham, F.F. Pardee, and Rowell, he suggested, should be included as Liberals from Ontario. Once this was done, there would be no need for an election and an extension bill could be put through.[60]

As time passed, however, and the Military Service Act and the War Time Election Act became law without Union Government being achieved, Ferguson became suspicious of the purposes of some Liberals. In a meeting with Borden he warned that Graham and Pardee had been playing politics and were discredited. The following day he wrote the Prime Minister that the Liberals were deliberately dragging their heels over Union Government as part of an effort to discredit him. Rowell would still be a useful acquisition but if four Ontario Liberals were given cabinet posts it would cause dissatisfaction in Tory circles. In any case, Ontario by this time was so strongly behind him that 'you can drop all this crowd now if you feel like doing so and the public will strongly endorse the course you have followed...'[61]

Soon Union Government was a reality. Rowell's decision to join and the emotional circumstances surrounding that decision ruined the Ontario Liberal party. Thousands of Laurier Liberals flocked to the anti-conscriptionist banner of Hartley Dewart, while Rowell's successor in the Ontario leadership, William Proudfoot, was not a strong man. The Hearst government had been given a chance to regroup and to develop a program for the post-war period. The challenge was there and it was up to the ministry to meet it as best it could.

On 20 October 1919, the Hearst administration suffered a stunning defeat at the hands of an assortment of Liberal, Labour, and Farmer candidates. The result had been anticipated by few. The government had to its credit a substantial amount of progressive legislation and Hearst did not believe the rebuff could be attributed to the failings of his administration. Certainly there was much evidence that the times were out of joint and that Hearst had succumbed to the abnormal conditions of the day. Runaway inflation, a serious housing shortage, and growing labour unrest presented a challenge to all governments and gave new strength to labour activists in the cities. The farmers were furious over what they regarded as the betrayal of the promise not to conscript farmers while the continuing drift from farm to city made many feel that the government was failing to protect rural interests. Co-operation between rural and urban dissidents was close during the campaign and in addition to 64 candidates running under the banner of the United Farmers of Ontario and 20 Independent Labour party candidates, there were 10 who ran as Farmer-Labour supporters.[62] As for the Liberals, they remained sorely split. In a June 1919 convention, Hartley Dewart grasped the Liberal leadership from a humiliated William Proudfoot, only to be denounced by the party's erstwhile leader, Newton Rowell, as the 'rising hope' of the liquor interests.[63]

Yet the Tories themselves had never recovered from internal differences over prohibition and Hydro policy. Adam Beck remained disaffected and finally ran as an independent while the legislation Hearst introduced providing for a liquor referendum reopened many old wounds. The decision to hold the referendum on the same day as the general election did not help the Tories. As well, many party members objected to Hearst's support of such reforms as women's suffrage and denounced their leader as an undisciplined theorist. Thus the party went into the campaign suffering from deep and long-standing divisions which refused to heal.

Howard Ferguson managed the Conservative campaign. Shortly before the election was announced, one Tory dissident informed J.J. Morrison of the UFO that Ferguson had opened an office on Yonge St. 'Do you know what that means?' he enquired of Morrison. 'That means that Mr Ferguson is distributing the election funds.'[64] On most questions of strategy and tactics, the Premier continued to defer to his active minister. 'I was wondering,' he asked Ferguson in late September, 'if we could get a little Committee capable of turning out good campaign material that would be used by the press. ... You know better than I do whether we could get material of this kind utilized and I am dropping the thought for your consideration.'[65] Although Ferguson was better equipped than any other Tory to take charge, the machine did not function smoothly. In previous contests he had worked closely with Frank Cochrane but Cochrane had died weeks earlier and his guidance was missed. Frank Keefer, an experienced Lakehead politician, reported to Borden that 'things were not well managed.' In his own district, for example, the party 'lost two seats by bad decisions...' in which weak candidates were needlessly run against sympathetic labour men.[66] Even in Grenville, the Tories had been ill-informed of the extent of rural unrest. 'I can only say the result was a surprise to everyone...,' Jack Reid told Borden. 'In my own constituency we believed Ferguson would have been elected with about fifteen hundred majority. He had a weak man against him and he was elected by sixty-two.'[67]

One possible cause of Ferguson's relative ineffectiveness may have been the growing crescendo of charges that he was corrupt and had raised the Tory campaign fund by exploiting his position as Minister of Lands, Forests and Mines. That September Joseph Marks of the ILP claimed that the government was giving away the province's nickel and timber resources to the great corporations.[68] Hartley Dewart was more specific. 'Hon. Howard Ferguson is the most corrupt influence in the Government,' he announced, '...Is there a department which he has administered honestly?' Mining licences, Dewart claimed, had been exploited by the hundred by those who stripped them of their timber and exported it to the United States, while the lumbermen were forced to pay tribute to the Tory campaign fund.[69] When the press took up Dewart's charges Ferguson attempted to make light of them. 'It is more of Hartley's bluff. ... just election stuff,' he claimed, but the rumours persisted, and one of the agrarian leaders, E.C. Drury, even came to Grenville to promise that if the Farmers came to power they would launch an investigation of Ferguson's activities.

Election day was a slaughter. Tory numbers dropped from 78 to 25, the Liberals retained 29 seats compared to their former 30, the ILP went from nothing to 11, and the UFO, with a previous representation of two, elected 45. Hearst himself lost to a Labour candidate. It was a sad day for a once proud party. There were, of course, many lessons to be drawn and Ferguson learned almost as much from the failures of the Hearst years as he had from the successes of Whitney. Although he angrily attacked the drys for deserting the party that had done so much for them, he was too shrewd to believe his own party blameless in the circumstances of its rejection.

Nonetheless he was not chastened. He emerged from the wreck of the Hearst administration shaken, perhaps, yet hardened to his task. Soon he would assume the burden of leadership and utilize in his own and his party's behalf that vast repertoire of political knowledge gained while serving under Whitney and Hearst. For Ferguson, however, the first priority became less the reconstruction of Toryism than his own political survival. The months ahead were a personal and political nightmare, the blackest period of his life.

6

'Hides on the Fence'

When a tense cabinet met two days after its defeat, Howard Ferguson was pointed to by press and pundits as 'the mainspring of the remaining Conservative forces.' According to the Toronto *Star*, Ferguson arrived, 'hat askew and smiling, as Queen's Park has known him since his first day in the Legislature.' A little later, after the Farmers were asked by the Lieutenant-Governor to form an administration, the Tories met in caucus. Harsh things were said about the Hearst régime, with many blaming the party's misfortunes on the radical changes of policy imposed by Hearst. Since the old leader had no intention of clinging to his position, the major business of the meeting was to discuss the choice of a successor. The *Star* speculated that 'the old guard wants Ferguson as leader, but the younger bloods would prefer a man more in keeping with the spirit of the times...' Ferguson, however, was pre-eminently the ablest man in the party and it seems unlikely that there was much if any opposition. William Hearst himself pressed hard for him to accept. But Ferguson was unwilling. He later related that he 'emphatically refused' the offer because he had made up his mind to retire. He had carried exhausting burdens during the war and had considered stepping down even in 1917. Now he looked forward to a measure of relief. During this period he received more than one lucrative proposal from private business. Fifty years old, he had served as Hearst's right-hand man and perhaps he agreed that the difficult task of rebuilding the party should go to someone who could draw on fresh reserves of energy, someone who had not been a member of what was now known as 'the old gang.'

Yet he did agree to become temporary leader. This expedient may have been adopted in the hope that Ferguson would later change his mind or possibly the intention was that at an appropriate date a leadership convention would choose a different leader. The federal Liberals that August had used such an instrument to select Mackenzie King and the Tories may have calculated that a convention could serve as a source of party rejuvenation. When the House opened for the 1920 session, Ferguson was in the place once occupied by Whitney and Hearst.

But the attention of the province was not on the vanquished Tories. The result of the election had presented the spectacular possibility that Ontario might be governed by a farmer-labour coalition and the Farmers with by far the largest group of members were forced at once to clarify their political goals. The extent of their success had been anticipated by no one and they lacked even a leader. J.J. Morrison, who served as secretary both of the UFO and of the United Farmers' Cooperative Company, was of the opinion that the new Farmer members had been elected to represent the economic and class interests of Ontario agriculture and that they must resist all efforts to transform them into a traditional political party. Behind the agrarian uprising had been the conviction of many farmers that the party system with its trappings of party discipline, party whips, the caucus, cabinet secrecy, and cabinet solidarity had served to shackle the representatives of the people to the service of the plutocracy. According to the critique of party government propounded by Morrison and other UFO leaders, political parties were the class tool of powerful business interests and in the past had prevented fair consideration being given the views of the agricultural group. Believing this, agrarian leaders demanded reforms to create a structure more democratic and more responsive to the needs of the people. They were attracted not only by such devices as the recall, the initiative, and referendum, the transferable vote and proportional representation, all the stock in trade of a generation of populist debate in the United States, but also by a more radical proposal which became known as group government. Under such a system, each economic group would have representation in the legislature according to its numbers. There would be no party whip or cabinet secrecy but policy would be debated openly among the different occupational groups and decisions would thereby be more apt to reflect legitimate economic concerns. No longer would a single interest be able to manipulate the system so as to dominate the others. Although group government found its theoretical justification largely in the work of the Albertan, Henry Wise Wood, the philosophy as developed by J.J. Morrison and his friends probably owed more to their own experience of the working of county councils, in which decisions were arrived at in open debate without benefit of the apparatus of party government.

J.J. Morrison was greatly disturbed when he learned that Farmer success in the election had been so great that his group might be called on to form a government.[1] He had hoped that the agrarians would have the independence and numerical strength to force the government to pass measures in the interests of agriculture and he even believed they might hold the balance of power. Morrison recognized that there would be enormous pressure to enter a coalition with the Labour members, with whom the Farmers had co-operated during the campaign, but he feared that in any such arrangement differences would come to the fore and 'the result might be disastrous. Finally he knew that in the Farmer group itself there was not a man who had sat a full term in the legislature and no one with executive experience beyond the level of municipal government. In many ways the election of forty-five UFO members had been the result of a spontaneous burst of agrarian protest and the major UFO leaders had not even sought election. To form a coalition government in circumstances in which the old-line parties would desperately resist any effort in the direction of occupational representation would be to set in motion forces which would pull both farmers and labour toward the very kind of traditional party government against which so much of the UFO effort had been directed. In fact the precarious position of the Farmers in the House would tempt the cabinet to impose a party discipline more rigid even than that which had existed under Grit or Tory rule.[2] The involvement of the farmers in politics according to rules designed by and for the urban business community might not only wreck their newly vigorous political movement but could also destroy the laboriously constructed United Farmers' Cooperative Company. Recognizing these pitfalls, Morrison opposed accepting the call to form a government.

Morrison's views did not prevail. Instead the UFO members formally agreed to enter a coalition with the eleven ILP representatives and to accept an invitation from the Lieutenant-Governor. This necessitated the selection of a leader. After J.J. Morrison declined to serve and also blocked an ill-advised overture to Sir Adam Beck who would only have manipulated the agrarian movement to serve his own ends, the offer went, at Morrison's suggestion, to E.C. Drury. A graduate of the Ontario Agricultural College, the son of a former Liberal Minister of Agriculture, E.C. Drury at forty-one, although himself a successful farmer, had spent much of his life playing an active political role as a former Master of the Dominion Grange, the first secretary of the Canadian Council of Agriculture, a founder of the UFO, and a defeated Liberal candidate in the 1917 federal election. Ambitious, able, a strong orator, Drury like his fellows lacked parliamentary experience and he clearly recognized how difficult and perilous his task would be. He believed, however, that the Farmers would be subject to ridicule if they declined to take the responsibility which had fallen to them and he was confident enough in his own talents to believe that much could be achieved. 'May we not hope,' he asked, 'that this political movement, which has begun as a class movement, representing farmers and labour, may expand and broaden out until it embraces citizens of all classes and occupations and becomes indeed a People's Party.'[3]

The next day Drury set about his difficult task of cabinet selection. Not surprisingly, the man from Crown Hill proved an uncertain leader. He made many mistakes and his administration from the beginning was besieged both from within and without. At the next election it was resoundingly rejected by the voters of Ontario. Given his inexperience, his political naïveté, and a measure of arrogance which grew, no doubt, out of a rigid sense of his own moral superiority, he achieved as much as could have been expected and lasted longer than most had anticipated. Certainly his cabinet provided little support. Drury himself described Harry Nixon as lazy, Beniah Bowman as indolent and indifferent, and Peter Smith as 'disastrously ... the weakest link in the Cabinet chain.' These three occupied the key portfolios of Provincial Secretary, Lands and Forests, and Treasurer. The new positions of Minister of Labour and Minister of Mines were filled fairly competently by ILP representatives Walter Rollo and Harry Mills. Highways Minister Frank Biggs demonstrated an alarming weakness for patronage and a proclivity towards heavy expenditures which gave the province some excellent additions to its roads system, clearly in contravention of the Farmer pledge of economical administration. Manning Doherty proved to be an active and able Minister of Agriculture but again his activities were not in line with those desired by the United Farmers and his political insensitivity brought the anger of rural Ontario down on his head.

Finally, with no lawyers elected on the Farmer side of the House the selection of an Attorney-General from outside would be crucial to the administration's success. Drury and Morrison discussed the matter closely and agreed on W.F. Nickle, a highly regarded Kingston Conservative who had served in both provincial and federal Houses and was known for his adherence to principle and his independence of thought. When Morrison left for a trip to the west, he understood that Nickle's acceptance was assured and was shocked to learn that W.E. Raney of Toronto had been appointed in his place.[4] Drury had sounded Morrison on Raney and had received the reply that 'he would not be a wise choice under the circumstances; that he was not considered to be an able lawyer, that his practice professionally had not led him to the forefront; that he was generally considered to be a single track man, following certain lines of thought almost fanatically...'[5] In Morrison's estimate, the choice of Raney would not add any prestige to the government but would turn many moderates against it. Many others agreed. Raney had served as counsel to the Moral and Social Reform Council of Canada, a prominent group composed largely of churchmen who campaigned on behalf of prohibition, anti-gambling legislation, and a wide variety of other 'uplift' measures. The truth was, however, that Drury, W.C. Good, and a few of the other agrarian leaders had over the years played a role of some significance in the moral reform movement and they were infused with the social gospel spirit. Raney was attractive to Drury because he was a kindred spirit.

Nonetheless Raney soon justified the views of Morrison and the others. Retrospectively, E.C. Drury liked to regard his administration as dedicated primarily to the cause of social reform and he even claimed that it 'enacted such a programme of social legislation as Ontario and indeed all Canada and North America had never seen or perhaps thought possible.'[6] In reality the Drury administration's record in the social field was not strikingly dissimilar to that of preceding Conservative administrations. Since the days of Oliver Mowat, the province had followed cautiously progressive social policies which often placed it somewhat ahead of other provinces. In the pre-war and war years, however, the reform movement in the western provinces had to its credit a number of major achievements and Ontario in this period sometimes was following behind the western example in many of its programs. In any case, much of the Drury legislation had been prepared by career civil servants such as Dr W.A. Riddell and brought into final form during the Hearst years. Such widely heralded Drury achievements as the Mothers' Allowance Act and the Minimum Wage Act for Women fall into this category and so too perhaps did the increase in the rate of the Workmen's Compensation Act. Even so, some of the government's labour supporters complained it had been like pulling teeth to get the government to place these measures on the books. George Halcrow, the ILP House leader, bluntly said as much.[7] And it was no accident that after the first and second sessions, there was little more by way of significant legislation. The measures prepared by Hearst had been passed and the Druryites had few ideas of their own. As well, the agrarian philosophy was fundamentally antagonistic to such programs and when Drury in 1920 put through a superannuation scheme for provincial civil servants, it excited enormous opposition from Morrison and the United Farmers. When the administration's labour supporters attempted to get an eight-hour day put into effect on government works and have fair wage provisions written into government contracts, they found the government unsympathetic.[8]

That a government placed in power by a farmer movement devoted to individualism, economy, and honest administration should fail to initiate significant new social policies is hardly surprising. E.C. Drury notwithstanding, what distinguished the Farmer-Labour government most sharply from other Ontario administrations was its commitment to moral reform. For this two men were responsible: Drury and Raney Of course they were not the only cabinet members who believed in prohibition and other uplift causes and rural Ontario in general remained strongly dry. Still, the rest of the administration, except perhaps for Nixon, probably felt no more strongly about such questions than members of other parties and the labour wing was known to be not entirely sympathetic. In the UFO itself, Secretary Morrison had largely ceased to believe in the efficacy of sumptuary legislation and he clearly feared Raney's proclivities in this direction.[9] Like his Attorney-General, Drury could not see that there were two sides to moral questions and throughout his administration he zealously supported the dry cause. Yet undeniably it was Raney who set the tone of the administration. Each year, for example, he brought in amendments designed to tighten up the OTA. In 1921 he and Drury together put their prestige behind the dry position in the plebiscite of that year which resulted in importation from other provinces being forbidden and totally dried up the supply of legal alcohol, except for native wines and medical prescriptions. Faced with bootlegging and open defiance of the law, Raney reorganized the OPP to give it the added duty of enforcing temperance legislation, he put pressure on provincial magistrates to ensure strict enforcement, and he created a special liquor squad which acted independently of local officials.

Howard Ferguson cleverly took advantage of this and never lost a chance to characterize Raney as 'this little Napoleon who persecutes everybody.' Any departure on the government's part from the strictest standards provided an occasion to mock the moralizers with the charge of hypocrisy. Thus when a convivial gathering replete with women and liquor was held in 1921 in the Queen's Park office of the Provincial Treasurer, it immediately became a major political issue. J.J. Morrison thundered against 'that awful last night party' and the Tories gleefully added their own chorus of outraged virtue; Raney was being hoist by his own party's petard.

This line of attack developed only gradually. For the first year and perhaps two of the Farmer administration, the government, despite its lack of a comfortable numerical superiority over the combined Liberal and Tory oppositions, had little need to fear defeat in the House. Both parties wanted to avoid giving Drury any excuse to call an early election; they preferred to wait him out, confident that Farmer inexperience would lead to major errors and swift disillusionment. It was very well for Drury to strike a high moral note as in his maiden speech in the House when he explained that the people were 'tired of the old game of politics. They want to see the creation in some way of a new order of things...'[10] But when he tried to implement the new order and told the members that he intended to 'loosen up a whole lot of these unreasonable parliamentary rules' by giving greater responsibilities for legislation to the backbenchers of all parties and, where the rules permitted, allowing bills to be introduced by private members, he found his way blocked and learned that he could achieve little.[11]

Soon Ferguson read the Premier a lecture in responsible government, pointing out in school-masterish fashion that under the British system of cabinet administration there were good reasons for the constitutional principle that only ministers of the Crown could introduce legislation directly affecting the revenues of the province. A few weeks later Drury, somewhat chastened about his efforts to loosen party discipline, admitted he was 'unable to say just how that can be done ... because as soon as it is attempted a cry will be raised that we are attempting to evade responsibility.'[12] Drury also failed in the 1920 session to move on the proposals for direct legislation and proportional representation but instead set up a study committee. And he surrendered to House opposition and withdrew a clause in a new election act which would have limited the Premier's right to call an election before the end of a four-year term to circumstances in which his government had been defeated by a vote in the House.

Although the old-line parties thus resisted substantive changes in the rules of the game, they were walking a narrow line. At a Tory meeting in early February, Ferguson warned that 'to unduly harass the new Government before they have had an opportunity of really getting into office, familiarizing themselves with procedure, elaborating and enunciating their policies ... would be unfair, unsportsmanlike...' and, most important of all, 'might mean another appeal to the electors...'[13] If Ferguson was content to bide his time, convinced that 'the hysteria could not last,' the Druryites were determined to press their advantage. Motivated by precisely that combination of high-minded idealism and heavy-handed opportunism that left the Tories so enraged, the Farmers now moved to cleanse the province and fortify their own position by destroying the political career of the man whose skills and experience presented the greatest challenge to their movement.

They attacked on three fronts. In February the government appointed a three-man commission chaired by W.F. Nickle to inquire into the Kapuskasing Farm Colony. The Conservatives believed the investigation was undertaken for political reasons and their suspicions were soon confirmed. Everyone knew that the settlement had had its problems, but the report, which appeared on 16 March and was formally approved by the government, could find little of value in the whole effort. In response, Sudbury Conservative Charles McCrea charged that the investigation had 'been staged with the express purpose of baiting the ex-minister of Lands, Forests and Mines' and Ferguson turned the tables on his critics in a masterful two-and-a-half hour speech in the House. Pointing out that the commissioners had not bothered to swear in a single witness or even to make a transcript of their hearings, he charged that they had talked to all the malcontents and to none of those who were satisfied. Ferguson read letters from settlers expressing satisfaction with the colony and pointed out that although these had all been available in the files of the Department, the commissioners had ignored them and spent only two hours there. The House broke into roars of laughter as the Tory leader skilfully ridiculed Nickle and his colleagues. 'These commissioners were accustomed to living lives of comfort or of luxury. Take them out of Kingston or Hamilton, put them up in the north where the snow is deep and there is no carpet on the floor – do this, and then ask them if they like it, and they shake themselves, shimmy-like, and say "No".'

Ferguson's most telling tactic, one he would use often and with devastating effect on his Farmer tormentors, was to counterattack. A good deal had been accomplished in agricultural work at Hearst, some seventy miles west of Kapuskasing, and Ferguson remained confident in the future of the Clay Belt. Now he told the House that 'what I chiefly object to is that there is not a single word, from end to end, of commendation, for the country. The Commission has struck a blow at Northern Ontario and its agricultural possibilities from which it will take us a long time to recover.' Even political novices realized not only that their effort had failed but that they themselves had been skilfully impaled by Ferguson's response. Atkinson's *Star*, which regarded Ferguson as the political devil incarnate, admitted that 'his defence ... won the admiration even of those who thought he had a poor case.'[14]

Soon Drury and Raney tried again. When Arthur Payne, the defeated UFO candidate for Grenville, placed in their hands documents which suggested that Ferguson had used dubious and perhaps corrupt means to achieve his re-election, they seized eagerly on the opportunity to unseat him. Although UFO lawyer Gordon Waldron, not a man to be shocked by prevailing electoral practices, advised caution and warned that 'G. Howard Ferguson was a shrewd lawyer and no doubt there would be counter charges laid against the UFO members...,' they ignored his advice.[15] Nor were they deterred by the fact that they had not the slightest knowledge of how to go about an election trial or by the lack of the small sum of money which would be required to proceed. The Premier introduced a rustic note, promising to sell some lambs to raise the funds. If such an exchange would give him Ferguson's hide, it would be a small sacrifice to make. Again the effort misfired. When Ferguson learned what was afoot, he went to see Drury and several of his ministers. J.J. Morrison described the incident in his *Memoirs*. According to his account, Drury emerged a thoroughly frightened man and told the UFO secretary that the charges would have to be dropped. The affair degenerated into a comedy of errors, a furious Payne wrongly blamed Morrison for the Premier's reluctance to go ahead; Morrison was enraged when Drury tried to get UFO money to pay some of the expenses and when the trial did take place, Ferguson and his lawyers, W.H. Price and W.N. Tilley, made the government look foolish. The case of the botched election trial demonstrated again that Drury and Raney were utterly beyond their depth.

Yet sure of their own integrity and convinced of the rottenness of the old system and of the man who symbolized and embodied its ugliest features, they proceeded on a third front. E.C. Drury had not forgotten the charges of corruption levied against the Minister of Lands, Forests and Mines during the 1919 campaign. On 9 March 1920, a Timber Commission was appointed and ordered to investigate, among other matters, the 'accuracy or otherwise of all returns made pursuant to The Crown Timber Act, section 14, by any holder of a timber license.' The Commissioners, two former Liberals, justices W.R. Riddell and F.R. Latchford of the Supreme Court, were also to look into any activity of the lumber companies or the Department which they thought affected the public interest.

Thus originated one of the most sensational episodes of Ontario's political history. The Drury government hoped to utilize the Commission to prove the Conservative party guilty of gross corruption in its relations with the lumber companies of the north; and E.C. Drury believed the revelations of the Commission would drive Howard Ferguson from public life. For a time it seemed that he was right and Commission counsel R.T. Harding gloated to Mackenzie King that 'the disclosures will be of such a nature that, in my opinion, there will be no Conservative Party in this country for many years.'[16] From March 1920 to January 1922, the Timber Commission carried on its work, always in the glare of enormous publicity. The testimony of such lumber barons as E.W. Backus of Backus-Brooks and Jim Mathieu of Shevlin, Clarke, a friend of Ferguson and MPP for Rainy River, showed how flagrantly the lumbermen of the far northwest had ignored Crown land regulations when they conflicted with their selfish interests. Early in the hearings it became evident that it had been totally unrealistic to expect the White-Cochrane reforms of an earlier day, predicated as they were on close administrative control over an enormous and far-flung field force, to function effectively, particularly in the war period, which had so depleted the ranks of the provincial service.

Yet even Riddell and Latchford seemed amazed to discover how extensively the minister himself had ignored the statutory regulations of tender and public competition. In the last year of Tory rule at least 1200 square miles of cutting rights had been disposed of in this fashion. The enormous list of individuals and companies who had received timber without tendering was given province-wide publicity; the Commissioners hardly needed to spell out the implication that the exigencies of the Tory campaign fund had become more important than the regulations of the Department. 'Why were so many of these grants made about October?' Riddell asked a Lands and Forests official. 'They seem to have given away most of the north country not already disposed of,' commented Harding.[17]

During these long months, Ferguson knew moments of the deepest despair. According to an old and dear friend, Justice Ferguson of the Ontario Supreme Court, Howard 'was almost without faith and hope.'[18] What sustained him was the stubborn loyalty of a small band of personal and political friends. Most of all he leaned on Harry Cody. 'That you believed and stood by him,' Justice Ferguson later told Cody, 'gave him at that trial the heart and courage that enabled [him] to fight the good fight and retain and strengthen his faith in God and man.'[19]

He was helped too, however, by more than his share of luck. Rumours which did not lack foundation began to appear in the press to the effect that Commission counsel Harding was on the payroll of E.W. Backus and Drury's statement that Harding had severed this connection when he accepted his appointment did not prevent a growing distrust of the Commission and its activities. Then, at the end of September 1920, the confrontation everyone had been anticipating took place as Ferguson himself appeared before the Commissioners. His performance was masterful, one of the high points of his public career. Using the debating skills honed during fifteen years in the legislature, and displaying an amazing knowledge of the details as well as of the general principles of the department he had administered for five years, he immediately seized the initiative and soon completely turned the tables on his inquisitors. He began as though he were seeking to enlighten laymen who could, after all, not be expected to understand all the manifold details of the functioning of a highly complex government department. Patiently he explained why the tender system was an improvement over sale by public auction which Justice Latchford seemed to favour. And when Latchford questioned Ferguson about the existence of 'dishonest cullers under careless Crown Lands agents...,' Ferguson, instead of admitting some of the inadequacies of the field force, insisted that 'my experience in this Department is that there have been very few exceptions to honesty...' Surprisingly, this vital question was dropped and Ferguson proceeded to lecture the commissioners that 'if the Crown assumes the attitude of a Crown prosecutor seeking to get all the evidence of condemnation that is possible, and not seeking to get a single word of justification of anything, the Crown can get anything at all.'[20]

The following day began the same way, with Ferguson intimating that the commissioners in discussing some of the technical practices of the Department had moved beyond their depths. When this elicited the angry comment from Justice Riddell, 'Please do not imagine we are a parcel of old women. We do know something about business,' Ferguson sensed that the time had come to mount a full-scale attack. For the first time he let his indignation overflow as he took heated objection to the way the commission had treated claims that large numbers of documents had been removed from the Department's files. In fact, Ferguson pointed out, there had been only three such allegations and of these two were utterly insignificant while a third file had been mislaid somehow. Ferguson told the commissioners that over a million letters had gone through the Department while he was Minister and that although men had been delving through files for nine months 'pulling the files apart and looking for information that would be detrimental to the Minister of the Crown of that day, you have succeeded in learning that one little file of two or three letters cannot be discovered. ... So that out of that infinitesimally small matter, a tremendous ... furore has been raised all over the province, that Ferguson dishonestly extracted documents from the files of the Department. I say again that it is absolutely unfair; it is unwarranted, and it is untrue. ... I want that cleared up for all time.'[21]

Furthermore this was only one of the many rumours and insinuations that had been 'disseminated all over the Province of Ontario that closely touches my personal integrity.' The fact was that as a minister he had 'never had one cent invested in either mines, timber, pulp or anything else in the Province of Ontario, never have bought or sold stock, never had advised a man with respect to stock of any character in all that country.' And yet government counsel Harding had gone to great pains to create the impression that Howard Ferguson was personally corrupt. Why else had he asked one witness, Colonel J.A. Little, such questions as, 'Did you give him [the Minister] three one thousand dollar bills?' Little's denial could not lessen the effect left by such insinuations.

So much for Howard Ferguson's reputation. What about the commissioners'? This, said Ferguson, was a delicate matter, but in justice to himself he had to refer to it.

If this matter was being laid before a jury I would certainly feel that I should challenge your Lordships' qualifications as jurors ... the work of your Commission has limited itself to possibly a period of ten years; at any rate, a period that is entirely within the life and administration of the Liberal-Conservative Government. As your Lordships have both indicated, you have both had long service in public life.

Frank Latchford in particular, as Attorney General in the Liberal cabinet of George Ross, had shared in the collective responsibility for the policies of the Department he was now expected to judge. Perhaps, Ferguson intimated, this was why 'this has developed into a persecution. What began as an Inquiry in the public interest has developed into an attack upon the man who was the head of the administration of this Department.' Skilfully Ferguson had manoeuvred the two judges into a misguided attempt to justify themselves to the man they were examining. Riddell even assured Ferguson that while he had 'nothing whatever to withdraw' later events 'will modify, or may modify my judgment...' But Ferguson, his voice pulsing with emotion, launched into a final denunciation of the methods of the commission and warned the judges that they would not have the final say in the matter.

the great Jury of the Public is the one that has to deal with these questions, and I am quite prepared to submit my case to the Public. ... I say the conduct of the Crown Counsel from the beginning leaves in the mind of nobody any doubt as to what his purpose and attitude was. And knowing, as I do, that amongst the men who instructed him has been made the declaration that, "We are going to get Ferguson," he has been carrying out his duty to the letter ... but he is going to fail in getting Ferguson, because Ferguson has done nothing that won't stand the light of day, and upon which he won't be delighted to have you turn on the spotlight. ... I don't propose to allow myself to be improperly represented before the people of this Province after the faithful service I have given to the Province either by Commissioner, lawyer, or anybody else.[22]

It had been a stellar performance, angry and sincere, one that Ferguson could hardly have improved upon. But was it enough? Could anything be enough? Many of Ferguson's points had been well taken, but was there really any answer to the testimony that had been elicited from Albert Grigg, Jim Mathieu, Colonel Little, and the others? Could the province ever put its trust in such a man as Howard Ferguson? Would the events of the timber investigation mean that henceforth he was stamped as a clever but unscrupulous politician of the old breed? And what about the Conservative party? The deterioration it had experienced in the later Hearst years necessitated a major rebuilding effort. Surely, it would be all but suicidal for a party in such a tenuous position as were the Tories to attempt to carry such a burden.

It was several years before all these questions were answered. In 1923 the province as a whole would demonstrate that it sympathized with the colourful politician who had been singled out for destruction; perhaps it had been impressed at least by the vigour of his defence. Assuredly it admired his courage. Likely too, puritan Ontario was revealing once again one of the stranger components of its character; it still preferred 'John A. drunk to George Brown sober.' As for the party, its attitude was revealed more immediately but no less decisively. The Conservative leadership convention had been planned for many months but, perhaps because of the timber hearings, it was not finally held until early December. As the delegates assembled in Toronto to choose a new Tory chieftain, the timber probe remained the great issue of Ontario politics.

In fact little else was talked about. In the weeks before the convention met, the Timber Commissioners had issued two interim reports, one of which condemned the terms on which Ferguson granted timber berths to Shevlin, Clarke and recommended that the province sue that firm. Ferguson responded that the regulations the commissioners alleged had been violated had originated not with William Hearst, as the report suggested, but sometime shortly after Confederation, 'and while they are for the general guidance of the Minister, no Minister has ever hesitated to put aside a regulation where the public interest required it.' Again, Ferguson charged, the commissioners had 'clearly indicated their partisan feeling, and their active interest in the welfare of the old party.'[23] Yet despite Ferguson's bold front, the prospects could hardly have looked darker. On 26 November the ultra-Tory Toronto *Evening Telegram* ran an editorial entitled 'Getting Rid of Jonah,' which argued that 'a leader must be sought who can go into the fight with unquestionably clean hands. ... The Conservative party can save itself only by saving the province. It has small chance of doing either unless it is resolutely ready to jettison all the political Jonahs of yesteryear.' And on 1 December, the day the convention opened, the same journal insisted that the future of the Conservative party was 'More Important than Vindication of Hon. G.H. Ferguson.'[24]

And yet, as the delegates assembled for their party's first leadership convention, there was no denying the sympathy many felt for their acting leader. To this was added a shrewd belief that it would be bad politics to abandon the man from Kemptville at such a moment. Of course the party regulars deeply admired Ferguson as a skilled practitioner of the political arts. The members of the caucus recognized the ability with which he had been directing the party in the legislature and they admired the spunk he had shown before the Timber Commission. They liked him too as a person. Howard Ferguson had been in politics since before the turn of the century. He was on a first-name basis with hundreds of delegates who knew him to be a warm and friendly individual. Such long-established personal and political ties would not easily be broken in a time of crisis. At the same time many delegates proved able to distinguish between a man's personal honesty and the code of political life.

They were not likely to be shocked by a minister who was said to have collected campaign funds from companies with which his Department did business. In 1920 this was practical politics; by these standards Ferguson was the best practical politician on the horizon.

By the same token, because they were politicians, many of the delegates must have had second thoughts. There were those who felt as did Thomas Crawford, the veteran member for Northwest Toronto and a well-known Methodist layman. Shortly before the convention opened, Crawford lamented to a Toronto audience that while no charge could be laid against Ferguson personally and there was certainly no question as to his ability, the party's position was not as satisfactory or as promising as it might be.[25] The implication was clear and was expressed by other delegates as well. In spite of Ferguson's enormous following in the party and the almost solid support of the caucus, there remained important elements which found the ebullient, free-wheeling veteran not safe enough or respectable enough for their taste. It seemed unlikely, however, that they would have sufficient strength to stop him.

For one thing, they lacked a viable alternative. To many, W.F. Nickle appeared as the man best suited to rebuild the party. An outstanding lawyer and an experienced politician who had sat in both the House of Commons and the Ontario legislature, he was also a morally imposing person who possessed the very sort of respectability which Ferguson lacked. But over the years Nickle had earned a reputation as a somewhat prickly character, while his dickering with the UFO over the position of Attorney-General and his role in the Kapuskasing investigation had won him few supporters in the Tory camp. On the opening day of the convention his friends received a telegram announcing his decision not to stand. It seems likely that Nickle had been playing a waiting game for Howard Ferguson, despite his spirited defence before the commissioners, had never finally abandoned his intention to retire. According to one source, he had actually accepted a $30,000 a year position in the corporate world, with duties which would have given him and Ella the opportunity they had always wanted to travel about the world. The Fergusons made great plans and looked forward every day to their new life. But from Queen's Park and from Ottawa, the Tories came, asking him to reconsider, telling him that to leave while under attack would never do, either for the party or himself. Still he had held out and, as one account has it, he paced the floor for most of the night before the convention, trying to decide. Finally it was Ella who spoke and who made the decision he wanted to hear. 'We will stay.'[26] There followed Nickle's withdrawal and the two other candidates, the stolid, safe party regulars, A.E. Ross and George Henry, presented only token opposition. A third possibility, Adam Beck, would have been political dynamite, but, like Nickle, he too decided that discretion was the better part of valour.

Before the convention's love feast with Howard Ferguson could begin, there were other important matters to attend to. The convention had been carefully organized. It was designed to perform several vital functions for the party. As well as choosing a leader, the delegates had to find new policies and make plans for a comprehensive reorganization of the party machinery which in 1919 had proven so disastrously inadequate. Perhaps the most striking evidence of change in party thinking was the decision that the polling division was to be the basis of representation at the convention. Of course not every poll in the province was expected to send a representative, but even so the crush of some 2500 delegates demonstrated a new spirit in the old Tory party. So too did the boisterously independent attitude which the delegates exhibited. When chairman Joseph Thompson, the party whip, started to read from a prepared list the names of members who were being proposed as a nominating committee to strike the other committees, he was greeted by shouts from the floor that the names should be put forward by the convention as a whole. Thompson adroitly suggested that more names could be added to his list, but that was not good enough either. The chairman surrendered and to loud cheers agreed to start all over again with floor nominations. Soon committees had been struck, introductory speeches made, and the day's session was over. The morrow would see the convention's highlight, the selection of a new leader.

By this time few were expecting any surprises. As the Toronto *Globe* put it, Ferguson would 'undoubtedly make a tremendous and clever effort to re-establish himself...'[27] Doubtless by prearrangement, Ross and Henry spoke first. They delivered two of the strangest speeches ever uttered by leadership candidates. Ross proclaimed that he wanted it clearly understood that his candidacy was not an expression of criticism of Ferguson but that 'I am a candidate today because this great assembly is gathered and you wish the voice of the rank and file to prevail. And if we were all to retire, some portion of this meeting would go home and say a plant had been made.' George Henry followed with more of the same. He was not standing because he desired the leadership but because he thought it his duty to allow the delegates to express their preference. 'Be they many or few makes no difference to me. I am ... as happy as a lieutenant as I would be as a leader.' Then, to the surprise of the delegates, Henry sang a lengthy hymn of praise for his old friend, Howard Ferguson. 'I have been associated with him from day to day for some time and I want to say that of the men we have developed in this Province there are few who measure up to the calibre of Hon. G. Howard Ferguson.' In the midst of a sentence came a rude inquiry from the floor which dissolved the convention in laughter: 'Who are you voting for?' Undaunted, Henry continued to laud his 'rival' amid frequent calls that he 'Talk about Henry.' He finished on another sour note when a brief reference to William Hearst brought the curt demand that he 'cut his name out.'

Then, conveniently, the convention adjourned for lunch and the delegates primed themselves for the performance they knew would follow. With the leadership already assured, Ferguson directed his speech as much to the province as to the delegates. All along, he told the delegates, he had refused to accept the permanent leadership of the party, intending to retire from public life. But the campaign of vilification to which he had been subjected, including the Kapuskasing inquiry, the disputed election, and the timber probe, had forced him to change his mind. Cleverly he emphasized that 'this running fire of attack on Ferguson, these demands to "Get Ferguson" are not on account of Ferguson personally ... they hope the attack on him will reflect on the party, destroy its future and affect its fortunes.' After the Kapuskasing matter had been disposed of, Ferguson related, 'I got another shot from the same source. ... It was a protest against me sitting in the Legislature for the County of Grenville, and I was charged with all kinds of iniquities and crime.' And shortly thereafter he discovered that 'secretly without the knowledge of anybody ... a commission of Supreme Court judges was appointed to investigate, to muck-rake all through the Department to see if there was not some smell, smudge or smoke they could raise about Ferguson.' For almost a month not even the legislature knew about the commission. During that time 'my friend Bob Harding, guided by that other never-to-be-forgotten public benefactor, Hartley Dewart, with J.M. McEvoy and a staff of accountants and lawyers, were at work smelling in that Department. ... And day after day they came running to the Commission, asking, "Will this make a scandal, will this make a stink about Ferguson?"' It was only in November, after 'this smelling organization that snuffed around the baseboards and floors of the Department' had issued an interim report deliberately (but unsuccessfully) designed to influence the outcome of a by-election in Northeast Toronto, that he began to reconsider his decision not to run. He did this, he explained to the convention, after prominent party members told him that his retirement would be interpreted as an admission of the guilt of the Hearst government.

By this time Ferguson in full voice had moved to the offensive. He assured the delegates that his record in Lands and Forests was an honourable one which would in no way limit the type of campaign he intended to wage throughout the province. 'I know that it is not possible to point the finger of shame at one single act in which I was guilty of any impropriety or dishonesty of any kind.' To the now cheering delegates he promised that if they selected him he would wage 'not any war of defence' but 'the most vigorous, active, energetic offensive campaign that ever was carried on in the Province of Ontario, and let me tell you right here that I have the ammunition now.' Turning to Hartley Dewart, his adversary of many a battle, Ferguson administered a tongue-lashing that must have made even that facile politician wince. Nor did he let their judicial robes protect the timber commissioners. Only a year before, he maintained, Justice Riddell had been Hartley Dewart's candidate as federal Liberal leader. As for Frank Latchford, what a man 'to investigate fairly and honestly the integrity of the Government that licked the head off him a few years ago, the Government that put him down

and out with the rest of the barnacles that were sucking the life out of Ontario.'
And now Latchford had returned to play his part in the destruction of the
Conservative party. Latchford, Riddell, and the Liberals, Ferguson announced,
had entered a conspiracy with the leader of the Farmer government which would
shock and startle the electorate. 'When I get through,' Ferguson promised, 'some
of these fellows' hides will be on the fence.' As for Bob Harding, he had claimed
that 55 timber permits had been granted just before the 1919 election when in
fact those permits had been issued over a five-year period. And of those who
received cutting permits whose politics were known, 19 were Liberals and only
15 Conservatives. Never before in the history of the province had 'the honour of
the Crown ... been entrusted to a man who had so prostituted that position for
party purposes as had Mr Harding.' To loud applause Ferguson promised, 'I am
going to take the hide off him before I am through with him.'

With that remarkable address, Conservatism in Ontario found again the spirit
it had lost sometime during the Hearst régime. The Conservative party had
recovered its soul and regained its nerve. It was once again a fighting
organization. Now it was cheering wildly for the man it knew would put it back
in power. It had been a partisan speech for a partisan audience. The voting began
at once and Ferguson easily took an absolute majority on the first ballot.
Pandemonium broke out anew. In a simple acceptance speech Ferguson's voice
broke as he promised to discharge his responsibilities to the best of his ability
and to follow policies based on Conservative principles 'too well known ... to
need any discussion by me at this time.'

The rest was anticlimax. The perfunctory proposals of the resolutions
committee were accepted by the delegates practically without comment. They
endorsed Arthur Meighen, the protective tariff, and the Hydro. They condemned
the Timber Commission and various policies of the Farmer government. As for
the platform committee, its chairman merely declared that it had had
insufficient time to prepare a considered platform so it endorsed the work of the
resolutions committee. More appropriately it declared that 'our platform is our
leader and our leader is our platform.' That, after all, was what the convention
had been all about. More serious work was done by J.R. MacNicol and the
organization committee. Howard Ferguson might be indifferent to party
platforms; organization was an entirely different matter. MacNicol's committee
recommended the immediate establishment of a provincial Liberal-Conservative
association organized across the province in six districts. In effect this would
mean the separating of federal and provincial organizations, a move that
thoroughly alarmed federal leader Arthur Meighen. The following day Meighen
wrote to Sir John Willison about the dangers of a schism in the party. 'I
understand Mr Ferguson thinks this will evolve satisfactorily in due time. I
sincerely hope so as duplicate organizations are going to be not only
cumbersome but chaotic.'[28] But even before the convention had adjourned the

new provincial organization was launched and officers elected. As Arthur Meighen had feared, relations between the two organizations were sometimes unsatisfactory, but the move proved a good one from the standpoint of the provincial party, one that Ferguson never had cause to regret.

One other matter dealt with by the convention was also heavy with significance for the future. On the last afternoon the convention hall became the scene of an uproar between two camps which expressed opposite views on the merits of the Ontario Temperance Act. But the party managers moved swiftly and stifled the controversy with a harmless resolution condemning the Drury government's ineffective enforcement of the temperance legislation. Of more immediate concern were indications that as Ferguson began his formal leadership he would be faced with the disaffection of influential elements in the party. In particular these included not so much the regular politicians who had a first-hand appreciation of Ferguson's skills, but businessmen and others not at the centre of politics whose support was vital to the reconstruction of the party. These groups were not only sceptical as to Conservative chances under Ferguson but had grave reservations about entrusting either the party or the province to a man with his reputation.[29] Over the years the sceptics remained ready to pounce if Ferguson should falter and not even his great victory in 1923 won him the trust of certain circles.

The Toronto *Evening Telegram*, for example, wondered whether 'Mr Ferguson's ambition has not blinded him to the fact that in accepting leadership ... he has jeopardized the prospects of the party...' *Saturday Night* was more brutal. In an editorial entitled 'The Ontario Conservative Fiasco,' it concluded that 'If Premier Drury had been asked to select a leader for the Conservative party ... and had scanned the field for the man least likely to embarrass his party in the event of a general election, he would undoubtedly have chosen Mr G. Howard Ferguson.' After attacking Ferguson for his 'cheap, infamous, Bolshevik' diatribes on justices Riddell and Latchford, the journal concluded that the Tories had 'deliberately followed a course which, in the judgment of all thinking party supporters, means certain humiliation and defeat.'[30] The loudest cries of outraged virtue came from the opposition parties and the opposition press. Typical were Clifford Sifton's remarks to J.W. Dafoe that the Conservative convention had been dominated by the baser element of office seekers and party heelers and that Ferguson's selection would likely put the Ontario party in opposition for the next twenty years and seriously injure Meighen in the federal arena. 'The proceedings of the Convention would reduce politics in the Province to the level of a barroom fight. There has never been such an exposure of systematic, long-continued corruption and pilfering. ... Ferguson admittedly broke the law corruptly, deliberately, and frequently. His attitude is that of a thief who is caught with the goods and starts to make charges against the character of the officer who arrested him. It would appear as though the Conservative party had got into the hands of blackguards.'[31]

Whatever his enemies might say and the press might conclude, Ferguson's task, formidable as it was, was a good deal less bleak than it appeared to outsiders. For one thing the Conservative convention had an immediate epilogue. The day after it adjourned the Ferguson leadership received a sensational boost and Harding's hide, sooner perhaps than even Ferguson could have anticipated, was hanging high on the political fence. On 4 December the press carried the dramatic news that Harding had resigned from the probe under the most peculiar circumstances. A few days earlier Riddell and Latchford had been informed that while acting on behalf of the government Harding had also kept a retainer from E.W. Backus and was collecting evidence on his behalf to use against Shevlin, Clarke. No wonder the Commission had spent so much time investigating the activities of Jim Mathieu; no wonder it had for the most part steered clear of the affairs of E.W. Backus who, coincidentally, had also just concluded a major deal with the Farmer government itself. This was too much for Supreme Court judges to tolerate. On 2 December they had sent their resignations to Attorney-General Raney. The Attorney-General, with the Timber Commission tumbling down around him and political disaster staring him in the face, had at once obtained Harding's resignation and somehow prevailed upon Riddell and Latchford to continue. The press was on to some of the sordid story at once; the rest of it leaked out in the months ahead.[32]

The timber hearings continued but the Farmers could no longer appear before the public in their guise of pristine purity. Their own reputation had been tainted, their motives challenged, and their relationship with the Backus interests subjected to constant public scrutiny. Ferguson himself had nothing but contempt for the devious role he believed Drury was playing. When the *Telegram* in May 1921 published additional correspondence between Harding and the government, he told C.A.C. Jennings of the *Mail and Empire* that:

Drury failed entirely in his duty when with a great show of integrity he told Harding that he must sever his connection with Backus. ... If he was in earnest in desiring to keep his skirts clean from suspicion he should have discharged Harding from acting for the Government. This correspondence shows very clearly how ineffective his reprimand to Harding was because Harding continued to act for Backus notwithstanding what Drury said. The result is that all the evidence placed before the Commission has been prepared by a man who has shown himself entirely unscrupulous. ... Of what use from a public point of view can a finding by any Commission be that is based upon a foundation of that character. I told the Commission that Harding was distorting evidence and supressing [sic] evidence. Subsequent developments have proven this to be true. A properly conducted inquiry might show where improvement could be made in the system of administration, but all this large expenditure is to be wasted because the inquiry was inspired and instituted with partisan motives, and has been continued with utter disregard for honesty or fairness.

It struck me that you could well take that high ground in dealing with the Commission and do a real public service.[33]

The Tories still had much to fear from the report of the Timber Commission but in the months ahead they were armed, as Howard Ferguson had promised, with ammunition at least as potent as their enemies possessed.

Of course it was the Farmers not the Conservatives who had promised a new order and it was they and their followers who experienced the pangs of disillusionment. Ontarians held a different image of Howard Ferguson. The Tory leader, they knew, was a cynical jaunty professional who revelled in the joys of political battle. Ferguson contemptuously refused to confuse the slogans and sounds of the political struggle with some crusade on behalf of a new society. Soon after the Massey Hall convention, he was the subject of a sketch by a reporter who put his own words in the Tory leader's mouth but managed to catch the quintessential Ferguson as he appeared to his fellow Ontarians. Asked about his political prospects, Ferguson, in the reporter's version, replied with his usual banter:

Oh, I'm all right. The bread and butter of a Conservative leader are sure, and there's some satisfaction in furnishing sport. Next season we're going to have sport, all right, and then some. I'd hate to tell you what I'm going to do to the Queen's Park...

The Farmers had opened several constituencies to find seats for Drury, Raney, and Doherty and in at least one instance awarded a job to one of the members who had surrendered his seat. 'Doherty has dashed their political piety by promising Clark a job,' Ferguson related.

I met Hartley on the street a couple of days ago, and we had a good laugh over it. ... When Drury begins to play the regular game, why shouldn't we sharpen the old tools? This idea that there are to be no rewards for political service is all buncombe. We want the old-time political religion. ... I'm not running a Sunday school class or a standard hotel. I've got to take the Conservative harps off the willows and give the boys some political jazz. They've had about enough moping by the waters of Babylon. ... Doesn't a lot of the uplift stuff that's talked nowadays make you tired? ... Politics is politics. Do you expect men to work for the party and then see somebody else get the offices...

Certainly the Howard Fergusons and the Hartley Dewarts approached political life with expectations and assumptions that had nothing in common with those of Drury and Raney. They knew as fully as did the Farmer leaders that within the political arena a deadly serious struggle for power was being waged and they recognized as well that competition existed among different social classes and economic groups. But perhaps because so many of the positions of power and leadership had traditionally been controlled by the class or group to which they belonged, the city lawyers and business interests, they insensitively viewed this state of affairs as natural if not inevitable. To them the moral fervour of the ILP and the UFO was almost incomprehensible and was regarded as an aberration which could not endure.

Politics to Ferguson was not a crusade but a craft. A true conservative, he believed the party system had evolved over the centuries and whatever its faults was vastly superior to the nostrums advocated by its critics. Within each party and within the cabinet itself, the interests of economic classes and of different cultural, religious, and regional groups were represented and protected. Of course there were imperfections and the system required much by way of compromise, timely concessions, and shrewd management. To Ferguson 'politics was politics' and those who believed they were working on behalf of some new order were 'neophytes' who would 'disappear with the noon-day sun.'

The interviewer's version of Howard Ferguson reciting the articles of his political faith read like a parody of all the UFO attacks on the machine politician:

Get office by promising the people what they want. Try to give it to them if you can. Make friends. Hold on to office. The more you are open to attack the more you attack the other fellow. ... there are different codes for politics and business and very different codes for politics and home life. In elections you say anything that occurs to you about your opponents. Of course they are grafters and nincompoops, ready to sell the province or the country for their own selfish ends. The other side has all the vices of political crookedness. Your side has all the virtues of public devotion. They have all the politicians. You have all the statesmen. There's no trick they won't play. There's no self-sacrifice you won't make. You view with alarm all they have done, and point with pride to every-thing your own side is going to do.

When the elections are over you forget it, if you lose, and if you win you do your best to make everybody else forget it. Having won one election your chief business is to win the next. To that end the policies of the Government generally, and the management of the departments in particular, must be directed.[34]

In the mood of 1919, a politician with such an image might be expected to be assigned to the political ashcan. But as the 1920s progressed and the province experienced the reality of Drury-Raney rule, it grew bored and disdainful. The unrest of 1919 and the memory of the failings of the Hearst administration faded into the background. A growing distaste for prohibition and uplift and a conviction that the province had fallen by accident into the hands of men who lacked political legitimacy and possessed little talent for government made the leaders of the traditional parties seem attractive by comparison.

There remained, however, the timber scandal. Even with Druryism on the wane, the Tories still lived in dread of new revelations. The government position was further eroded, however, when Peter White, Conservative counsel on the Commission, resigned after a disagreement with Raney and the correspondence between the two men was made public. When White had complained that the investigation was being restricted entirely to the period of Conservative administration, Raney replied that 'the onus is on you to bring before the commission any matter ... prior to the coming into power of the Conservative government in 1905, or subsequent to the Conservative regime.' White pointed out that a large staff of accountants, lawyers, and clerks had been employed for weeks before the existence of the probe had been made public and he argued that because the Drury government had prosecuted the inquiry in its own way for almost a year it could not escape its 'responsibility by attempting to shift the burden to the Liberal-Conservative party...' Raney's only response was that 'your retainer was amply sufficient to justify you in taking any steps you or the Conservative Opposition thought proper in bringing to the attention of the commissioners any irregularities ... prior to 1905 or under the regime of this government...'[35] In other words, the government of Ontario was interested only in Tory crimes and misdemeanours!

Yet in many ways the 1921 hearings were no better from the Conservative standpoint than those of the previous year. Ferguson, Hearst, Hele, Grigg, company officials and experts of various kinds again appeared and the deficiencies of the Department under Ferguson were delineated anew. Again Grigg's testimony was damaging as he described the Department's bookkeeping procedures as 'a disgrace to a country grocery store.' But Riddell and Latchford were no longer the sole inquisitors. Howard Ferguson conducted searching examinations of Harding and others before the Public Accounts Committee of the legislature and the Tory members did their share. Early in the 1922 session Forbes Godfrey unleashed a typically blustering attack on the Timber Commission and a well-researched effort by Charles McCrea also attracted wide attention. More also emerged about the disreputable activities of Harding and when the Toronto *Telegram* published some astounding correspondence between Harding and members of the Backus firm, the Conservatives seized the initiative by demanding the House adjourn to allow a special debate.

Most damaging of all to Drury's reputation was his own concession in 1920 of the English River limits to the Backus firm. The Tories brought all their newspaper and other resources to bear on the English River deal. Privately

Clifford Sifton was convinced that the Backus deal would do more to destroy public confidence in the Farmers 'than all the attacks, arguments and policies of their opponents.'[36] From London, Tory political manager and *Free Press* editor Arthur Ford reported that in western Ontario 'the Farmers' Government is losing ground. I have been pounding very hard on Drury's deal with Backus.'[37] Howard Ferguson leaped eagerly to tar Drury with the brush of corruption with which he himself had been blackened. 'What a farce to call such a transaction a public sale,' he announced, 'what hyprocrisy to say there was any competition! This Backus deal will ... stand as a lasting monument to Mr Drury's public life.'[38]

Despite Ferguson's charges, the Backus deal was similar in most of its features to the practices he himself had pursued as minister. Although the Farmers seem to have honoured the formal requirements of the regulations, the matter had been handled so as to ensure that only Backus was in a position to benefit. The briefest of periods had been allowed for inspection, and possible competitors were given little opportunity to cruise the limit to estimate the value of the timber. In any case, all available power resources, the Tories charged, had been handed over to Backus, thus effectively shutting out everyone else. None of this was surprising. The Kenora area was dominated by the Backus operations, which were now proposing to construct giant new facilities which would have a major impact on the region's depressed economy. Backus had the backing of municipal politicians from Kenora and apparently the enthusiastic support of most people from the area. In such circumstances, as Ferguson well knew, the formal statutory requirements of public tender and competition had little meaning. But since the Farmers were attacking him with such vigour for practices which they now in effect had adopted themselves, it was natural that he should make the most of his opportunity. Sonorously, he thundered against the deal, emphasizing that 'Backus secured from the Government this vast empire of forest wealth for ... about one-third of a cent per cord at a time when pulp wood was selling as high as $6.00 per cord.'

It seems incredible, given the activities of the Timber Commission, that the Farmers should condone such procedures and fall into such a trap. Clifford Sifton's final assessment, delivered after the 1923 election, was that 'Drury's dealings with Backus did more to destroy the Farmers Party than anything else. It knocked their whole set of principles on the head and destroyed public confidence completely.'[39] Sifton might have added that it was Ferguson's sure political instinct which had seized upon this aspect of Farmer administration. From hundreds of political platforms across the province, the Tory leader taunted the Druryites with their fall from a state of grace.

All this time he was also lashing out at Riddell and Latchford as 'this nefarious outfit' and 'the minions of Mr Drury.' Frank Latchford returned the compliment, describing the Tory leader in private correspondence as 'a malignant liar.' The Timber Commission, however, had become so suspect that

Drury was taking the line that not it but the courts would finally justify or condemn Ferguson's administration of his department. In August 1921 he remained confident enough to assure Mackenzie King that 'evidence of Timber probe in courts would leave the Conservative party without a following in Ontario.'[40] Drury promised the province that he would recover as much as possible of the millions of dollars out of which, he alleged, it had been defrauded. In the resulting action, Newton Rowell acted for the Crown against Shevlin, Clarke. By a decision of Justice Logie in 1922, the province was awarded $169,991.29 for pine trees already cut and the Company was ordered to pay $17.60 per thousand feet log scale, Doyle rule, on all remaining timber. Logie declared the licences for two notorious berths, 45 and 39, invalid because Crown regulations had not been followed. He dismissed Ferguson's claim that the limits had been granted for purposes of conducting a brush-burning experiment by noting that 'methods of brush destruction ... were ... well known and easily ascertainable...' The agreement was 'nothing more than license to cut timber on ungranted public lands; and being made in the teeth of the regulations, was, and is, null and void *ab initio* on the short ground that the acts of the ministers, no less than the acts of the subordinates, are subject to the laws.'[41]

Although Logie had stated there was no fraud involved and Ferguson claimed the judgment was 'not a condemnation of myself or my administration,' the decision was a stunning blow. Probably only the earlier revelations about the Backus deal and the Commission's own difficulties allowed the Tory leader to carry on. Nonetheless Shevlin, Clarke might have had a good case if it had been in a position to appeal against Logie's judgment but the government had put a gun to its head and held up other timber supplies. It recognized, therefore, that for the time being Drury held all the cards and it agreed to pay a new price on the original sale. Wellington Hay, who by this time had replaced Dewart in the Liberal leadership, offered strong support to Ferguson when he told the House that experienced lumbermen who were competitors of Shevlin, Clarke had told him that the former minister had probably obtained a fair price when he had disposed of berths 45 and 49 in the first place and Charles McCrea rightly pointed out that when the Drury government called tenders for timber in the area it had received no bids which were higher than the amount which Ferguson had extracted from Shevlin, Clarke. It was with some justice, then, that the Tories criticized the Logie decision and the strong-arm methods which the Drury administration had used to exact a higher price from the company. Wellington Hay added that he had no doubt that Ferguson had gained nothing personally from the transaction and that what he had done had been in the best interests of the province.[42] Hay's comments no doubt were bad politics but the Liberal leader, a fair and decent man, felt it his duty to speak his mind.

Then, on 29 June 1922, after two and a half years of activity and having heard some three and a half million words of testimony, the Timber commissioners issued their final report.[43] Incredibly, they had failed to bring their suspicions home to rest. They discovered no evidence of improper contributions to campaign funds and on the whole they were amazingly reticent in their remarks about the former minister. Of course they recommended many changes in departmental procedures but, surprisingly, it was less Ferguson's administration than the reforms effected by White and Cochrane which were blamed for the state of affairs in the department. 'Before the year 1906' the report asserted, 'there were officers of the Department whose duty it was to check the work of the cullers ... but in that year the system was changed and ... the Department had no check by its own officers upon the honesty and capacity of the cullers.' In many cases, they found, there was no check upon work done in the woods while in some local Crown Timber Offices little attention was paid to the accuracy of returns and they were not subjected to proper examination in the department itself. The continued use of the outdated Doyle rule as a measuring technique and the practice of allowing cullers to seek employment with the lumber companies were strongly criticized. Much was said of the administrative problems posed by the White-Cochrane system and the former method in effect under the Liberals whereby the purchaser paid the bulk of the price at the time of purchase plus a small amount per thousand feet of cut was commended. This, the report concluded, gave the province greater lump sums of money, meant that the interest of the lumber men in preserving the limit from fire was enhanced and reduced the temptation to dishonesty in measuring logs.

As for Ferguson's role, the commissioners after giving the matter full consideration agreed that the arrangement he had made with Shevlin, Clarke to burn the brush on limits 45 and 49 of Quetico might yield 'some useful information...' It cited the 1919 report of the Commission of Conservation that over twenty times as many trees had been burnt as were cut by lumbermen. Ferguson's Forest Fires Prevention Act of 1917 was praised and Jim Mathieu was cited as having estimated 'the loss by fire in the Rainy River District at from 400,000,000 to 600,000,000 feet ... one billion, eight hundred million dollars.' In fact fire would remain a terrifying threat not only to Ontario's forest wealth but to the lives of the settlers and it was sheer ignorance to argue, as had Justice Logie, that because experiments had been conducted elsewhere further efforts along similar lines might not yield invaluable results for Ontario.

Equally important, Riddell and Latchford, who had lived with the problem for over two years and who by this time must have understood the practices and problems of Lands and Forests administration, did not condemn, as bluntly as had Logie, the former minister's attitude to departmental regulations. Not that they failed to challenge Ferguson's claim that the regulations existed only for the minister's general guidance and that he possessed the right to set them aside when in his judgment they conflicted with the interests of the province; yet they may have realized that Ferguson had accurately described a situation which existed with some frequency and with some justification in provincial departments and had merely followed procedures which prevailed all too often in governmental affairs. Perhaps for this reason, then, the commissioners merely pointed out that Ferguson had 'not respected' the regulation requiring public competition on all major sales and they expressed the 'opinion' that no officer, minister or otherwise, 'should have the power to grant rights over large areas of the public domain at will without regard to regulation...' Except for a few minor suggestions, however, such as improved bookkeeping and filing systems, and the general recommendation that the Department needed a 'cleaning-up' and administration 'on business principles,' that was all. The report was amazingly brief. The commissioners had resisted the temptation to reply in kind to Ferguson's many attacks on their integrity. They had been scrupulously fair to the former minister, perhaps fairer than he had deserved.

For the first time in years, the Conservatives could breathe easily. The feared timber report was a dud. Ferguson jauntily proclaimed that there was nothing wrong with Ontario's timber policy, past or present. The commissioners after two years of study had been 'unable to make any concrete suggestions of improvement.' This, rebutted the Toronto *Star*, was nonsense to be explained only by the fact that 'Mr Ferguson may have been so relieved by finding no words of castigation directed at him...' Drury, who surely recognized the extent of his defeat, admitted grudgingly that 'the commissioners found ... there was inefficiency, to put it mildly. We cannot go further and say there was corruption.'[44] For Ferguson, the days of doubt and depression were over. Now he could face the coming electoral confrontation with confidence, even joy; now, for the first time, he knew that soon he would succeed Drury as premier of Ontario.

7

The Old-Time Political Religion

From its first days in power, the Drury régime carried within itself the seeds of its own destruction. Before many months had passed, organized labour, notorious for its political ineptness and internecine strife, reverted to its customary role, and its relationship with the Drury government became stormy and uncertain. As well, the strength of old-party ties and a continuing commitment to the two-party system even by voters who had cast protest ballots in 1919 emerged as a perhaps insuperable barrier in the way of Drury's efforts to create a 'People's Progressive Party.' Most of all, the bitter differences between the majority of the legislative group who supported Drury and the UFO led by Morrison tore at the vitals of the new administration.

Perhaps it could have been different. The Tories would not easily recover from the rebuke the province had administered in 1919 and they were further handicapped by the leadership of an old guard politician whose own behaviour as a cabinet minister was regarded by many as a permanent monument to political corruption. Drury, on the other hand, with the resources of the provincial government at his command and supported not only by elements of organized labour but by many of the more liberal-minded forces in the wider community, might well have been able to consolidate his hold on power. Ferguson's fear of an early election ensured that the Druryites would have an opportunity to put some of their programs into practice. With the support of traditionally liberal journals such as the *Globe* and the *Star* and assured of the friendship of Mackenzie King and of· such provincial Liberals as Major Tolmie of Windsor, R.L. Brackin of Kent West, Thomas Marshall of Lincoln, and J.W. Curry of Toronto, their prospects seemed favourable. Of course Drury had other friends as well including Colonel J.B. Maclean, whose powerful *Financial Post* was enthusiastic about the rule of what it regarded as the economy-conscious, small property-owning members of society. In particular, the *Financial Post* looked to Drury to put a halt to the big spending and reckless socialism of Adam Beck and the Ontario Hydro. Here, surely, were all the elements for a fundamental recasting of party lines. From the beginning Drury had argued that the farmers' political movement could succeed only through formal alliance with other political groups and he determined to achieve a 'broadening out' of his group which if successful could have left the Conservatives in the political wilderness for years.

But Drury's strategy posed enormous problems. Most obviously, those such as the UFO and Colonel Maclean, who regarded the government as the province's best hope for a return to individualism and conservatism, had little in common with some of Drury's ILP supporters or with leftist Liberals such as Curry, who believed his party should give 'a generous support to the UFO ... to show not only the farmers, but the labour element that the ideals of all three are very closely allied.' Curry told Mackenzie King that the only hope he could see for the Liberal party lay in the advocacy of such measures as public ownership of utilities such as railways, telegraph and telephone lines, and in a program of advanced reforms 'at the earliest possible moment.'[1] This was not a stance which appealed to Curry's leader, Hartley Dewart, who preferred to fight the UFO at every opportunity. Although Curry, Tolmie, and others were refusing to follow Dewart in the House on a variety of questions, his continued leadership of Liberalism served to block the road to any alliance with the Druryites.

The unchallenged hegemony of J.J. Morrison in the UFO was an equally formidable barrier to Liberal-Farmer co-operation. On most policy matters Morrison remained a more legitimate representative of rural opinion than Drury. For example, he and his supporters vigorously opposed as 'class legislation' the premier's 1920 proposal to establish a superannuation plan for the civil service. Morrison's control of the UFO organization did not give him sufficient leverage to dictate government policy, yet Drury for his part was always constrained by the knowledge that any move away from the traditional rural goals would renew the struggle with the UFO. The superannuation issue reinforced Morrison's determination that the Farmer cause remain undefiled by entangling alliances.

In these circumstances, it required astute and forceful leadership by Drury to take advantage of the fluidity of party lines and create a new organization. He and his colleagues were unable to measure up and instead it was the Fergusons and the Dewarts who seized the initiative. By the 1921 session, the facade of co-operation with a fledgling administration was gone completely and Ferguson 'sharpened the old tools' in earnest. For the next two and a half years, in the House and across the province, he pursued the government without mercy, relentlessly bringing to bear all his resources of bluster and guile until Drury, enraged and confounded, called an early election which resulted in a landslide Tory victory. Ferguson's performance as an opposition leader was masterful. Having inherited a shattered party, he restored its confidence, healed its internal divisions, provided it with a sense of purpose, and constructed an organization of formidable strength. Fighting his way out of the timber scandal morass, refusing to be daunted even when many Conservatives continued to believe he should step aside for the good of the party, he restored the Tories to power and there, except for the Depression interlude of Hepburn rule, they have remained ever since. Conservatism in Ontario owes Ferguson a debt it has never fully acknowledged.

'I have felt from the beginning,' he informed Arthur Meighen late in 1922, 'and have directed all efforts towards keeping the Drury government on the defensive and creating a critical attitude in the minds of its own friends. I think we have fairly well succeeded...'[2] At party meetings and from platforms in every part of the province, Ferguson campaigned tirelessly throughout 1921 and 1922. In small northern mining towns, in quiet eastern Ontario villages, in the rich farming country west of Toronto, in Beeton and Brampton and Pine Grove and Sarnia, Ferguson sold himself and his party. His message changed little over the years of Drury rule. 'The present administration has indulged in a perfect orgy of expenditure,' he charged over and over again. 'This administration will go down in history as the most reckless spendthrifts the province has ever known.' 'Patronage is rampant in its most vicious form all over the province.' Drury and Raney obligingly provided the Tory leader with all the ammunition he needed. Constantly he proclaimed that the government was incompetent, that it had failed to live up to its ideals, that it had cynically abandoned its promises of economy. By attempting to avoid cabinet responsibility and by appointing a host of commissions at great cost to the province, the government, he suggested, was guilty of political cowardice. In 1921 the Conservatives drove this home by a motion in the House which accused the administration of abandoning the principles of responsible government won at such great cost. Nor did Ferguson ignore the running battle within the government group over 'broadening out.' Tauntingly, he told Drury that his movement could not continue to live as a class organization, yet by broadening out 'you relinquish the claim upon the class distinctive basis of your whole organization. Morrison is right, if you want to keep the United Farmers together...'[3]

This was work Ferguson enjoyed immensely. As he crossed and re-crossed the province, accompanied in the north by Charles McCrea and joined frequently by other members of his party's small legislative band, he was able to renew contact with hundreds of party members who welcomed him to their homes and offered support and friendship. Still the effective stump speaker Whitney had remarked upon so long ago, Ferguson could effortlessly expound upon the sins of government and inspire the local faithful. In May 1921, for example, although he had hoped to deliver a serious analysis of the weaknesses and dangers of group government to an eastern Ontario audience, he found that 'our Ottawa friends ... desired me to make more of a fighting campaign speech that might awaken enthusiasm amongst our party friends there.'[4] Why waste Ferguson on scholarly analysis when his forte was thumping the opposition, especially when the

Farmers were such tempting targets. These efforts received wide publicity, but their most important purpose, as Ferguson implied, was to carry the message to Conservatives outside Queen's Park and to ensure that local supporters had no cause to feel neglected.

Howard Ferguson had no airs or pretensions. A son of Main Street, he understood because he shared the emotions and interests of the average Ontarian. Because his experience had been so broad, he could talk with the local farmers about his own orchard or about the pigs he was raising on his Kemptville farm as easily as he could discourse with the bankers and businessmen of the cities. Apparently, he was blessed as well with a near flawless memory for names; one young Tory recalls a first meeting which lasted a moment followed over a year later by another chance encounter at which Ferguson addressed him by name.[5] Ferguson had few of the attributes of the great political orators yet there were few who could address a meeting with such effect. Usually brief, always informal and witty, he would make his case deftly and unpretentiously. 'I never prepare more than a few notes for a speech of that kind,' he told Jennings of the *Mail and Empire*, 'preferring to feel the pulse of my audience and act accordingly as I go along.'[6]

It was in the House itself, however, that his ascendency was demonstrated most forcefully. Day after day he and Dewart (who often was coached by the Tory leader) delighted to torment the almost defenceless cabinet. Although Drury never forgave Ferguson for his political sins, Ferguson and Dewart took each other less seriously. It had been Dewart who had cried loudest in the period prior to the fall of Hearst that Ferguson was corrupt and he had, as Ferguson put it, 'times without number called down vengeance on my political head.' Yet personally the two could hardly have been closer and on Dewart's death in 1924, his old rival insisted on providing legal assistance without fee on behalf of the estate. In the House, Dewart was at his best in the evening sessions, having wined and dined in appropriate style, and on such occasions the old Ontario House was a raucous, lively arena. He and Ferguson, aided and abetted by a few other hit-and-run debaters such as Herb Lennox and Forbes Godfrey, gave the government no rest. Word spread about Toronto that Queen's Park was the best show in town and the galleries filled. Slouched in his seat, feet on the desk, slouch hat pulled over his forehead to protect his eyes, Ferguson would appear to be asleep until an opportunity arose and suddenly he was on his feet, sometimes in a slashing attack, more often pointing to ill-conceived legislative proposals or raising questions about dubious government programs. Crowded galleries watched as the ministers shrank before brutal heckling. For Ferguson the most satisfying confrontations were those with the Attorney-General and he developed great skill in goading him until he was able to provoke him almost at will. Raney's response was no match for the seasoned invective of Ferguson.

House rules dictated that Ferguson's choicest epithets could be used only outside its walls and it was at a Toronto ward meeting in May 1922 that he described the government members as 'intellectual and political freaks who were projected into prominence by accident and who grew out of the garbage.'[7] In his major address during the 1923 session and in a subsequent campaign pamphlet entitled 'The Government and Its Chief Critic,' Raney paid the Tory leader the compliment of complaining endlessly about his language and his tactics and castigating him for 'common bar-room black-guardism.' 'They were not cases of hot debate in which ... the honourable member lost his temper ... it was repeated again and again with variations on scores of occasions before scores of audiences from Cornwall to Windsor, and from Niagara to Cochrane.'[8] The province indulgently accustomed itself to such performances from the colourful Tory leader, and complaints from the administration and its friends, however justified, had little impact. 'Ferguson and the outlaw Dewart, have I think overdone the business of obstructing the Drury Government,' Gordon Waldron suggested hopefully. 'I hear on all sides evidence that the public realizes the unfairness of these attacks and there is suddenly a growing realization that the public business has been prejudiced seriously because it has been impossible for the Ministers to disengage themselves from the wrangles promoted in the House...'[9] W.C. Good sympathized with Drury that he was 'having all kinds of trouble in the Legislature with a few obstructors.'[10] The 'few obstructors,' however, remained unrepentant until finally it was not the premier but Ferguson who controlled the House and set the pace.

Even hostile observers were impressed by the Tory leader's performance. The *Star* quoted one critic that 'disagree with him as non-Tory observers must, Ferguson is fulfilling the conditions of leadership, which demand that a leader shall make the pace. ... Quick perception, swiftness of attack, resourcefulness in retort; raillery and contempt, the incision of a scalpel, the bruise of the bludgeon – these things are at his command.'[11] Raney himself paused for a moment to describe the Tory leader as a brilliant lawyer and critic of legislation. 'When he has so willed he has given excellent constructive criticism. I don't know anyone who can do it better.'[12] Ferguson and his caucus were equally effective in committee work. When the Public Accounts Committee discussed Chippawa, he somehow ensured that Fred Gaby, Beck's principal assistant, appeared fully armed with documentation and received ample opportunity to put his material to good use. 'Who do you think is running this committee?' asked Raney in frustration.[13]

Ferguson's knowledge of the work of government departments seemed so intimate that Wellington Hay pondered publicly that the civil service might be feeding the Tories with confidential information. Undeniably, many members of the bureaucracy regarded Ferguson with sympathy and when the deputy minister of agriculture spoke at the official opening of the Agricultural College at Kemptville he raised some eyebrows by his description of the local member as a man whose 'long and honorable career sheds lustre on the name of Kemptville.' But Drury himself had no complaints about the loyalty of the civil service and

Ferguson's virtuoso performances in the House owed more to his quick mind and his intimate familiarity with the workings of provincial government than to any illegitimate relationship with the bureaucrats.

Ferguson's task was eased by the effectiveness of the small Tory contingent in the House. Lennox and Godfrey were tough, experienced members who had served since the early days of the Whitney administration; together with Colonel John A. Currie, the victor of a by-election in Southeast Toronto in 1922, they were vociferous proponents of more liberal liquor legislation and succeeded, despite their leader's politic silence, in making the party attractive to the anti-prohibitionists. The presence of Jim Mathieu and General Don Hogarth assured the support of the mining and lumbering interests, although that was never in doubt. But those who along with Ferguson bore the brunt of the burden were George Henry, hard-working and sincere, with a knowledge of departmental business which rivalled that of his leader; Colonel W.H. Price, a sharp-nosed veteran with a reputation for political shrewdness who had practised law with W.J. Hanna and supervised election trials for the Tory opposition in the days of the Ross régime; and Charles McCrea, an intelligent, hard-working Sudbury lawyer whose popularity and political instincts ensured that in any Ferguson ministry he would be the spokesman for New Ontario.[14]

The greatest accretion of strength to the Tories caught the province by surprise; if engineered by Ferguson it was a master stroke. In a Kingston by-election in 1922, W.F. Nickle re-entered the provincial House after an absence of almost a decade. Nickle, of course, had almost joined the Farmer government in 1919 and at the time of the Kapuskasing investigation Ferguson understandably had described him as 'not a good Tory.' He must have known that many Conservatives had been disappointed when Nickle had declined to contest the leadership in 1920 and this element in the party still regarded the Kingston man as a possible alternative to Ferguson. But he recognized that Nickle's reputation for unbending integrity and his support for prohibition would add to the appeal of the party in rural Ontario while his great abilities would increase its hitting strength in the House. Ferguson immediately entrusted him with key assignments in the House and in 1923 would award him the most prestigious portfolio at his disposal.

If Ferguson had reason to be satisfied with the performance of his party in the House, he was under no illusions that the strength demonstrated there would necessarily be translated into votes at election time. Unlike some political leaders who rely on personal popularity or the attractiveness of the party platform to carry the day, Ferguson, perhaps because he had been trained in the school of Reid and Cochrane, believed that assiduous cultivation of the party organization was essential for even the strongest of political organisms. For a party in opposition, there were special difficulties and, again in contrast to many politicians who considered that their role was to think great thoughts and make fine speeches, Ferguson was convinced that the leader himself was in the best position to sustain interest and inspire the local workers. Not that he hesitated to delegate as much as possible and in W.H. Price he possessed a lieutenant who performed all the tasks required of a ward politician with quiet efficiency. As behind-the-scenes manager and political wire-puller, Price carried much of the load and while many of his activities remain as obscure now as they necessarily were then, the party machinery in the 1920s functioned with an effectiveness which inspired vitriolic denunciations from the Grits, who muttered periodically of Tammany methods and machine rule.

Yet in 1923, the occasion of the first and in many ways the greatest of the Ferguson landslides, the Tories were in no position to act as dispensers of patronage and purveyors of power; in that campaign, victory was achieved by hard work and astute management. Price in turn was assisted by two paid organizers, William Clysdale and Garrett Tyrrell, who served the party throughout the decade and later. Tyrrell was a loyal, efficient worker who tended the affairs of the Tory organization in Toronto; Clysdale, described by one who knew him well as 'a ruthless Tammany type politician,' was an astute and fastidious professional on whom Ferguson never hesitated to rely.[15] For more than a decade he looked after the hard-grinding work of organization for the Ontario Tories, by preference a back-room figure deliberately avoiding all limelight. Together, Ferguson, Clysdale, and Price were a formidable team; under their direction the party never suffered from organizational weaknesses.

Bill Clysdale was employed by both the provincial and the federal parties and the relationship between the two was of significance. Ferguson worked hard to establish close liaison and co-operation between the two wings. One early difficulty was the continuing existence of Union Government in Ottawa. Arthur Meighen may not have appreciated Ferguson's outspoken opposition to a concept he was attempting to maintain; he may even have linked Ferguson to that other proponent of a return to traditional party lines, his old Manitoba enemy Bob Rogers, for the two were known to be friends. When the anticipated collapse of the Meighen government occurred and the federal Tories in the 1921 election were reduced to a rump of fifty seats, Ferguson found solace in the fact that the farmer movement had failed to gain the 'village vote.' He was sure that 'taken as a whole the result in Ontario points with no uncertainty to the collapse of the class movement. Ontario refuses to accept the doctrine that we can be better governed by groups founded upon occupational distinction.'[16]

The federal defeat drew Meighen and Ferguson closer together. Both were now opposition leaders attempting to rebuild their parties and Meighen was convinced that his own future success would depend in large measure on the reconstruction of Conservatism in Ontario. Many federal men believed that the first step was to restore the party to power in its old bastion of Ontario. Party veteran Edmund Bristol reflected this attitude when he called on his fellow

Tories to 'get to work in every constituency in Ontario' and make a determined effort to 'bring back to full life and vigour the old time Conservative Party of Ontario as it existed under Sir James Whitney.'[17]

The first evidence of the new co-operation was the assistance Ferguson provided to Meighen, who needed a seat in the Commons after his personal defeat in Manitoba. The federal member for Ferguson's own constituency of Grenville agreed to step aside and Howard personally looked after the arrangements, which ensured Meighen's success in the subsequent by-election. 'I need not say how much I am indebted to you,' Meighen assured his provincial counterpart, who had even handled expenses and had looked after relations with the local people right down to the chairmen of polling subdivisions. 'I think I told you,' Ferguson wrote Meighen, 'that I had already written explaining your hurried departure for the South ... but, a letter coming direct from you would be greatly appreciated.' After the campaign, Meighen continued to solicit advice from Ferguson and was told in detail what the local member was expected to contribute to fall fairs, women's institutes, and the like.[18]

For some reason, however, there were soon rumours in party circles of friction between the two men. Possibly the contrast in approach between the worldly, easy-going Ferguson and the intense and somewhat remote Meighen contributed to the stories, but more was at issue than style. When Meighen arrived very late for a political picnic in eastern Ontario in September 1922, he was surprised to learn subsequently, as he informed Ferguson, 'that some of the local members, strong friends of yours, quite resented my absence and seem to have an idea that I meant some slight to you...' Although Meighen told Ferguson that 'I have a determined ambition to be true to men who have been true to me, and there are few, if any, to which that applies more than to you,' the federal leader had not grasped the meaning of the incident. Ferguson assured Meighen there was no basis for suggestions 'of personal friction' yet he confirmed that there did exist a good deal of 'complaint and dissatisfaction,' all of which he had done his best to smooth over. Ferguson's letter was friendly enough but its tone suggested that he shared the feelings he attributed to others. 'Statements have come to me frequently,' he told Meighen, 'which indicate that there has been a feeling that the provincial party and the provincial campaign is being relegated to second place at these joint gatherings. My people, of course, point out that the rehabilitation of the party at Ottawa must be brought about by· success in the provincial election. ... Our members ... think for that reason that provincial issues and provincial interests should be kept in the foreground.' Meighen responded, as Ferguson hoped, that 'practically our whole force should be settled on winning provincially...'[19]

More important than precedence at meetings was the responsibility of each section of the party to pull its weight in paying organizational expenses. Meighen had little interest in or aptitude for organization and his strategy was to draw on the strength of the provincial parties. In Ontario he had found disconcerting the decision of the Massey Hall convention to develop a strictly provincial organization, and the two sections had continued to act together to a considerable extent, sharing, for example, the services of Bill Clysdale. But the provincial group had proceeded to establish the Ontario Liberal-Conservative Association and at a party meeting in September 1921, officers were selected for each of the six districts into which the province had been divided. The Toronto District was put into the hands of the long-established 'Central' Association and Eastern, East Central, Western, West Central, and Northern districts were established. An executive committee with two representatives from each of the hundred and eleven provincial ridings reinforced the provincial nature of the new body. Early in November the Association met and an organizer was appointed for each of the six districts. Many of the delegates to the November meeting were at pains to point out that the conference was a purely provincial gathering.[20]

While the framework thus erected was elaborate, it is unclear whether the new district bodies were immediately effective or even whether the regional approach was a viable principle of party organization in Ontario. A year later Ferguson lamented to Meighen that there were 'a great many ridings where there is no organization at present' and he was urging the local associations to meet and elect officers. Where conditions were favourable he also advocated the selection of candidates. 'All this,' he told Meighen, 'will do a good deal to rouse party activity.'[21] Ferguson still gave much thought to means of developing enthusiasm among party workers. When Meighen advocated a general party gathering for late 1922, he favoured holding off until early 1923 because 'the fall and early winter is the time to hold local meetings particularly in the rural ridings and in the process of organization we would be able to get the best men selected to attend the function.'[22] With Ferguson still regarded in many circles with disapproval, money for the party was not readily forthcoming. At the end of 1922 he complained to Meighen that 'the task is rather a slow and somewhat difficult one when we have no funds at our disposal to take care of the incidental expenses that are inevitable in such work.'[23]

Western Ontario was particularly difficult. R.K. Anderson, the federal member for Halton, informed Meighen in 1922 that 'our stumbling block in the local is Mr Ferguson. He is not regarded with much confidence in this part of the province...'[24] Arthur Ford told Meighen he was 'not enthusiastic over a continuance of Howard Ferguson as leader. ... I like Howard personally and if he remains as leader we will give him every possible support provided he does not advocate a wet platform and unfortunately there is a growing impression in these parts this is what is in the air. ... We will not have the chance of a snow-ball in hell in staid old Western Ontario with such a policy.'[25] Organizationally as well, the west in Ford's view was 'the part of the province most neglected' and he pointed out to Sir John Willison that 'the Conservatives must not depend upon

[sic] their majority upon Western Ontario.'[26] Apparently the western district unit created in 1921 had failed to provide the necessary leadership.

Within a week of Ford's letter, Ferguson advised Meighen that he had 'arranged with the London fellows to open an office and put a permanent man there to give special attention to organization matters in Western Ontario...'[27] Gordon Reid was the organizer appointed although the office was directed by Ford himself. Whatever the reason for the delay in establishing an effective Western Ontario Association, Ford was delighted with the progress that was now made. He had long been convinced that if southwestern Ontario constituencies were to be redeemed, 'it must be done by direction from London and with a Western Ontario organization rather than from Toronto. There is great jealousy,' he told Meighen 'between Toronto and the rest of Ontario, while the Toronto viewpoint is in many ways entirely different.'[28] The development of a strong Western Association with its own organizer would prove to be a significant factor in the area during the election. Ford later noted with great satisfaction that 'we ... largely directed our own campaign, of course, in close cooperation with Toronto.'[29]

That Meighen and Ferguson could co-operate in the common cause was demonstrated in the course of several 1922 by-elections. In the fall of that year Ferguson was counting on an easy victory in the constituency of Southeast Toronto but he feared the good effect of that victory would be dissipated if the Drury government was able to retain Russell. At this time Drury was actively promoting co-operation with the new Liberal leader, Wellington Hay, and since Russell contained many Liberal voters Ferguson believed it was essential that this effort be nipped in the bud. If co-operation succeeded in Russell, Hay and Drury might find it easier to work together along more general lines in the future. Ferguson told Meighen that his strategy, therefore, would be to offer Tory support to the Liberals and he intended to tell 'all our friends who believe in the party system ... to vote for the Liberal candidate. To achieve this, how-ever, the Hay-Drury scheme must be circumvented and Ferguson asked Meighen to speak to Charles Murphy, a member of the King cabinet who exercised great influence in the constituency: 'talk the matter over with him confidentially. ... From what I have heard from the south end of that county the United Farmers are very optimistic. If we have a straight Liberal in the field I am satisfied that I can swing a lot of votes to him down through Osgoode township where I know the situation pretty well.'[30] Meighen did as requested. The strategy worked. The Liberals won Russell, the Tories took Southeast Toronto, and the Drury government had experienced a major setback.

For his part, Ferguson was always willing to do his best for the federal party. Thus when Lanark was opened by the death of the sitting member, Ferguson went to work on the day of the funeral trying, as he told Meighen, 'to get a line on the general situation.' He warned the federal leader that there was likely to be a plethora of candidates, but 'none of those aspiring look to me like safe winners.' Dr Preston of Carleton Place seemed the likeliest choice but he had assured Ferguson that he 'won't touch it'; failing Preston, W. Thorburn, a former member, was the best bet, partly because 'he is the only man in sight that has any money.' Preston did agree to stand but the riding remained doubtful and Meighen asked Ferguson to take another run through because 'you can size these things up better than I can, and I would feel a lot safer if I had your advice after a look over the ground.'[31] Finally, Preston won an impressive victory, doing no better than expected in the towns but making significant gains in the country vote. Clearly, both federally and provincially, prospects were good for the Tories. The close co-operation between Ferguson and Meighen had contributed much to this result.

Thus by election year the Ontario party was in fighting trim. It was also equipped with a program which distinguished it from the other political groups, one designed both for its political appeal and as an expression of Tory philosophy. Under Ferguson, the party moved further to the right than it had under either Whitney or Hearst. In part this was the result of circumstances. Ontario Hydro, for example, by the 1920s was no longer a crusade able to inspire the progressive spirit. As well, other social and political realities of the decade, particularly the predominance of the liquor issue, which in a sense served as the opiate of the politically conscious masses, contributed to an upsurge in traditional conservative values. Undeniably, however, Ferguson himself, with his enormous distaste for the impractical idealism he believed characterized the Farmer movement, his almost religious faith that the solution to the province's problems lay in growth and development, and his conviction that Ontario needed less legislation and better administration, contributed to the resurgence of a free enterprise, self-help mystique.

In this connection the timber hearings did a curious service for the Tories. They proclaimed to everyone that the Conservatives, in contrast to the party of Raney and Drury, were the friends of the lumbermen and mining promoters, the entrepreneurs and the businessmen. Repeatedly and loudly, the Farmer-Labour coalition had attacked the 'special privileges' businessmen allegedly received and just as loudly and certainly as often, the Ferguson Conservatives rose to the defence of the so-called 'practical men.' When the Timber probe ran into trouble, the *Mail and Empire* noted with satisfaction that the mining industry was 'quietly smiling over the setback of the Drury government; for mining men remember and resent keenly the Premier's implication some months ago when he said that after he had investigated the "crooks and grafters" in the lumber business, the mining industry was "next." '[32]

From the beginning, mining and lumber interests were fearful that the Drury administration would establish a new scale of taxation. A 10 April 1920 editorial in the *Northern Miner*, the newspaper published in Cobalt which faithfully reflected the views of such concerns, attacked Drury and his ministers for their frequent hints that 'the mining industry was to be the source of revenue for this or that reform.' The *Northern Miner* waged a virulent campaign against Drury, charging him with a vicious imperialism whose purpose was to exploit the north country on behalf of the farming interests of the south. Northerners reacted with outrage to suggestions late in 1919 that the Drury government might sell the T&NO RR to the Dominion government and they were even angrier the following year when the government administered the Acreage Tax Act in a way that, according to the *Northern Miner*, 'suddenly and with but feeble warning deprived thousands of owners of their patented mining claims on the excuse that pitifully small sums were in arrears...'[33]

The fiercest fight came when the government proceeded with its mining tax legislation. Predictably, the industry waged a furious struggle. Given the widespread unemployment in many of the mining camps and the economic difficulties of some mining concerns, the government's timing played into the hands of those determined to fight to the last ditch. Great public meetings were organized, and the *Northern Miner* published lists of companies forced by economic conditions to close down, including even the numbers of men thrown out of work. 'Only one silver company is able to pay a dividend,' complained the *Northern Miner*, 'yet the Minister of Mines, who should know something about mining, but who apparently doesn't, wants to squeeze the mines for more taxes...'[34] Of course the Tories were delighted to be able to do simultaneous battle for the unemployed men and the mine owners. Ferguson charged that the Drury government had recklessly 'wiped out' going concerns because of arrears of taxes. Ferguson, McCrea, and Price, joined later by Dewart and a few Liberals, kept up a sustained opposition to the government proposal. McCrea stressed the hazardous nature of mining investment and development, pointing out that most shafts although sunk at great expense provided no return while even the successful mines averaged only eight to ten years of life. A higher mining tax would have a depressing effect on the economy of the entire province. Already, he pointed out, the Anglo-Canadian nickel mines had closed and there was a practical suspension of work at Mond and International.[35] The government drew back and postponed its measure. When it was reintroduced later in the session, Ferguson fought again to make it more to the liking of the mining companies.

A similar stance was adopted with regard to the lumbering companies. When the government in 1921 held up the cutting rights of Shevlin, Clarke on five berths pending the financial settlement arising out of the Logie judgment, Ferguson denounced this as 'the most scandalous proposition I've ever heard in my life. ... You'll ruin a firm with a ten or fifteen million dollar investment in this Province.'[36] When the Timber inquiry probed the relationship between Ferguson and George Meade of the Spanish River Pulp and Paper Co., the Great War Veterans of Sault Ste Marie petitioned on behalf of the Company and requested that it receive still more timber. 'This Company,' the veterans' association argued, 'has been very prominent in building up this district and at Espanola and Sturgeon Falls...'[37] Needless to say, their petition was supported by the Tories.

The Farmers were alienating an entire section of Ontario. Ferguson devoted the major portion of his address during the throne speech debate of 1923 to the affairs of the north country. Business interests throughout that great territory were uneasy, he claimed. The lumberman carried on his business by receiving credit on the title and licence he held and if that title were questioned on technicalities, the banks would no longer regard it as sufficient security. In Ontario, Ferguson asserted, seventy-seven lumber companies had been organized; fifty-six had gone to the wall. Only half a dozen others had been able to pay dividends, 'and yet lumbermen throughout Ontario are charged with being timber pirates, and that attitude is encouraged and abetted by the present administration...'[38]

The Tory leader's views were identical with those of the mining and lumbering industries. The *Northern Miner* was not satisfied when Drury dropped his 1921 tax legislation and it pointed constantly to what was alleged to be the government's neglect of the north and its failure to pursue an active developmental policy. Finally and bitterly, in the weeks before the 1923 election, the same journal announced that 'Druryism has been a curse to the north' and asserted that it would do its best to drive the Druryites from power.[39] W.H. Casselman, a UFO member, complained of the 'inattention, and neglect and broken promises' which characterized the government's attitude towards the north, noting, for example, that such great mines as the Hollinger, the Dome, and the McIntyre were isolated because the roads leading to them were practically impassable at certain periods, 'due to the Government's neglect.'[40] During the campaign Ferguson had only to announce that 'the greatest problem in Ontario today is the handling of Northern Ontario affairs' and to promise roads, railway extensions, and other job-creating programs. That was the talk the north wanted to hear.

This approach in 1923 was as appealing to southern communities as to New Ontario. In the early 1920s, and indeed throughout the decade, prosperity was intermixed with spotty unemployment. People wanted desperately to put their problems behind them, to experience the economic benefits and savour the technological advances of the bold new age that was opening up. In a post-war community anxious to blot out even the memory of deprivations and sacrifice, the politician who could appeal to the spirit of development and work with the business community to harness the wealth locked in the forbidding reaches of the Canadian Shield would garner a rich harvest of votes. Howard Ferguson personified the spirit of development. Only yesterday he had seemed a man of the past, discredited and expendable, but the future had been tried and it did not work. Suddenly it was Drury and Raney who stood in the way of progress. Ferguson was still not an entirely respectable person but in his reckless air and jaunty self-confidence, he became the embodiment of the new spirit which demanded development, condoned speculation, and encouraged every man to hope for a brighter economic future with a full share of the consumer goods trumpeted by the new advertising industry and made possible by mass production.

This was a natural stance for a Conservative party. During these years the Tories hewed out a readily identifiable position on the right of the political spectrum. Here was an attractive policy, one whose appeal was to a far wider constituency than its business orientation might suggest. In the 1920s there were few even among the farming and labour communities that had led the uprising of 1919 who were not impressed by the argument that the whole province would benefit from policies designed to promote the welfare of the investor and the entrepreneur. If a few lumbermen and mine owners accrued vast fortunes, so much the better, for they were providing a vital service of entrepreneurial leadership and their success would attract even more risk capital to Ontario. This was what Ontario needed and demanded; it was what Ferguson would provide.

Although Ferguson's appeal was directed first to the entrepreneurs of the north with whom he was on terms of intimacy, the Tory message would be heard and understood by the larger business community of the south, many of whom, of course, were the self-same figures who operated in New Ontario. Thus when Raney in 1923 introduced a bill to provide stricter securities legislation to protect the investor, popularly known as 'Blue Sky' legislation, the Tories could be depended upon to take the appropriate position. Ferguson used the since well-worn argument that the very fact that a company had been examined by a governmental body would lull the public into a false sense of security and create a belief that the issues had received the stamp of official approval. Ferguson's doubts about the constitutional validity of the Raney proposal and his conviction that the same end could be attained by an improved Companies Act without extending the bureaucracy did not lack merit. Nonetheless his position on the issue reinforced the image of the Tories as the party of free enterprise. Again he was strongly backed by McCrea, the *Northern Miner*, and the mining interests to whom untrammelled speculation was a way of life.

Far more than under Whitney, who had stayed at arm's length from some at least of the great corporations, the Ferguson Conservatives had the support of the whole spectrum of business and financial interests, from the industrial giants to the speculators and promoters and including as well the small, local businessmen whose psychology the Tories understood so well. Perhaps because the province itself remained so strongly committed to the Protestant ethic and because the majority of its enterprises remained small, the party's business orientation did not set it against other sections of society. Here was proof that the upheavals of 1919 were more an aberration based on fear, Red Scares, and post-war psychology than a symptom of a permanently polarized society. Class feeling existed in Ontario in quantity, and always had, but only in special circumstances did it become transformed into class conflict of any durability or intensity. By becoming the truest spokesman for the business ethic, the Tories were addressing themselves to the self-image of Ontarians in the 1920s.

What was taking place between 1919 and 1923 under Ferguson's deft management was the restructuring of the Whitney coalition in a form appropriate to the changed circumstances of the day. Ferguson understood instinctively the essential thrust of the province's identity and proved able to orchestrate the variations so as to restore the old Tory party in its traditional form of an alliance of interest groups. Constantly he was searching for policies and adopting positions which would appeal to all the social and economic groupings which conceivably could be brought together under the banner of Conservatism. As well he was using his political instinct to avoid policies, many of which the hapless Farmers stumbled into, which would alienate potential supporters. Cautious about welfare programs because he was imbued with the ethic of his day, which regarded governmental economy as the greatest blessing any administration could bestow on a people, he was also Tory enough to doubt that great quantities of legislative enactments would improve the lot of anyone. Yet ultimately he was a pragmatist who would support spending programs and sponsor legislation which politics, in the broadest sense of the term, demanded. Thus he seized the opportunity when Drury in 1921 presented a tax bill which charged two mills on the dollar on all property transfers. Virtuously he argued that this would work a hardship on the poorer sections of the community and he proposed that homes below the value of $4000 be exempted.[41] There is no reason to doubt his sincerity but he could not restrain his delight when Rollo and Mills, the Labour representatives in the cabinet, were forced to swallow their principles and for the sake of cabinet solidarity support the new tax.

Ferguson's efforts reinforced what was happening in any case to the ILP-UFO coalition. In September 1920, J.J. Morrison had informed western agrarian leader T.A. Crerar that 'the Labour Party in Ontario is quite as socialistic as in Manitoba, and I am quite sure that their views are just as objectionable to the farmers here as to the farmers in the West.' No stable union between the two elements was possible, Morrison asserted, 'because we believe in lessening the cost of production. ... Labour men generally believe in increasing the cost of production by increased wages and shorter hours.'[42] The years of Drury rule confirmed the truth of Morrison's judgment. Although Tom Moore, the president of the Trades and Labour Congress, had been distinctly friendly to the ILP in 1919, soon he and other Congress officials were harshly critical of the failure to establish fair wage provisions on government contracts, particularly on the Chippawa, and they were equally antagonistic to Drury's apparent opposition to the principle of public ownership as embodied in Hydro. Drury had boldly challenged Adam Beck's pet Hydro radial scheme by appointing the Sutherland Royal Commission to investigate the need for such a project and he had followed this up by appointing W.D. Gregory to carry out a general investigation into the Hydro. In some ways these two Commissions performed a signal public service but Drury paid a high political price. The enraged Hydro chairman hastened to make his peace with the Conservative party and in 1923 Beck ran again as a Conservative. The Tories had become once more the party of Hydro and the support Beck possessed in labour and other circles was marshalled behind the Ferguson cause. In particular, the T&LC denounced Drury for blocking the Hydro radials which some labour men believed would have put a comfortable home in the suburbs within the reach of every worker.

But the malaise was far deeper than discontent over specific Drury policies. Tom Moore and his colleagues believed that Drury hoped to bring 'city conditions ... to the level of labour conditions in the backlot farms' as part of a deliberate plan of 'degrading the city worker until he will return to the farm to avoid starvation.'[43] Although the opposition to the Farmer-Labour government came principally from the ranks of the trade unionists, it existed even within the ILP and its legislative group. M.M. MacBride of Brantford almost from the beginning supported the Conservatives in the House and crossed the floor to sit apart from his colleagues. Although the majority of the ILP members did not approve of MacBride, they hesitated also to put themselves too completely into the hands of the governmental coalition and in an effort to maintain some independence chose as their House leader neither Rollo nor Mills but George Halcrow of Hamilton. Halcrow and others of the Hamilton group were deeply offended by Drury's effort to broaden out, believing that any new 'People's Progressive Party' would reflect Drury's free trade views while they themselves were strongly protectionist.[44] Halcrow seems to have shared Tom Moore's opinion that the Drury government was strongly anti-Labour and when he deplored the lack of significant labour legislation after the 1920 session and suggested that the legislation which had been passed had been granted only with great reluctance, he was deposed from the ILP House leadership.

Normalcy had returned to the ranks of the labour movement. Enthusiasm had disappeared and internal bickering prevailed. When the ILP's 1922 convention was held in Hamilton, only twenty-eight delegates were in attendance.[45] Like the UFO itself, organized labour had been totally unprepared for the success of 1919. It proved a relatively simple matter for the protectionist Tories with their urban appeal and their renewed alliance with Beck to win back the labour vote. Since both Drury and the Liberals remained strongly prohibitionist, many workingmen had yet another reason to support the Conservatives, who were offering broad hints in the direction of a wetter Ontario. In 1923 labour would vote for Howard Ferguson.

A similar process was at work in rural Ontario. The government's ineptness served to alienate farm voters and Ferguson's astuteness ensured that the Tories would capitalize on every mistake the Druryites made. This was the supreme irony of the whole period. Manning Doherty, probably the ablest man in the cabinet, set out to improve the lot of the farmer by enforcing standards of quality control, developing new grading procedures, and establishing an efficient marketing system. As one student of Ontario's agricultural history has noted, 'he was convinced that the salvation of agriculture lay not in attacking business but in adopting its methods' but in doing so he ran afoul of the inherent conservatism of the Ontario farming community.[46] Despite stubborn resistance, Doherty tried to reform and centralize the marketing of dairy products by passing legislation to incorporate the Co-operative Dairy Products Co. Ltd, a body which would compete with a private dairy 'co-op' already in the field.[47] But his worst political mistake came when he ignored vigorous protests from the farming community to pass a much-needed Dairy Standards Act. This was another piece of warmed-over legislation put on the books by the Hearst administration, which had been astute enough not to proclaim it.[48] Ferguson took the politic stance that the legislation was good but premature. Thus the Department of Agriculture under Manning Doherty was as deeply resented by the agricultural community as ever it had been in the days of the Hearst régime; Doherty must have been relieved when his political career ended a few years later and he switched his field of operations to the Toronto Stock Exchange.

As if bent on self-destruction, the Druryites pursued other policies which were equally unpopular in rural areas. Their 'good roads' policy which greatly increased the province's expenditures did much to give Ontario a better highways system but flew in the face of the UFO economy plank and of the farmer position that a good rural road system should take precedence over provincial highways. Ferguson denounced Frank Biggs for spending money like a drunken fool and proclaimed him 'the greatest highwayman in Ontario.' In educational policy, the farmers had hoped for a system designed less exclusively as an academic procession through high school to university but one which would reflect more of the practical concerns of the farming community. But when W.H. Casselman, the UFO member for Dundas, presented a bill to amend the Adolescent School Attendance Act along lines desired by many farm communities, the Premier offended Casselman by stating publicly that his bill would be 'consigned to a death chamber designed for the purpose of killing such undesirable measures.'[49]

Finally, in the field of hydroelectric policy, many farmers had long believed that their taxes were used to develop energy for urban consumers and to drive the wheels of industry and that those who controlled the system had done little to bring electricity to the countryside. Drury was expected to rectify this and during the first session of the legislature a House committee chaired by

J.G. Lethbridge was appointed to investigate the possibility of a more equitable distribution of electricity across the province. The committee presented proposals to achieve this and believed it had the sympathetic support of the Premier. When Drury failed to act on any of the committee's recommendations, Ferguson in 1921 claimed the farmer was being ' "goldbricked" and the small centres ... cut out of consideration'; he demanded 'that Agriculture should get more than what he termed one per cent of Hydro-Electric distribution.'[50] Finally, on the last day of the session, a bill prepared by the Minister of Public Works and satisfactory to the committee members was presented for first reading but at the very last minute Beck talked Drury into replacing it with an effort he had prepared himself. Casselman, Lethbridge, and some of the other Farmer members were outraged and Casselman described the bill as practically useless to rural Ontario.[51]

On such occasions, Ferguson sought out the views of Casselman, Lethbridge, and other UFO backbenchers and did what he could to meet their wishes. As a result, the Tory position was often more reflective of rural opinion than was the government's. Finally Casselman read himself out of the Drury party and some others who remained were almost equally disenchanted. With no organization in the cities of Ontario, Drury was cutting himself off from the countryside which had nurtured him. 'It is a long road that has no turn,' Morrison advised Casselman in August 1921. 'With regard to the platform and the way it has been smashed at the Parliament Buildings, I fully agree with all you say. Prohibition is the only plank that has been upheld. Everything else has gone by the board.'[52]

Thus during four years of political warfare, the Tories emerged with a program and an image. Assiduously and cleverly, they courted the farm and labour votes they had lost in 1919. Consistently, they presented themselves as defenders of 'responsible government' upholding traditional values against Drury's half-hearted efforts to effect changes in the political system. Ferguson, disdaining even verbal conformity to Drury's confused idealism, uttered a ringing defence of political patronage. 'I have never believed in the spoils system,' he announced, 'but a minister ... must have some voice in selecting the subordinates with whom he is to surround himself in his department. A civil service commission only helps the ministers to evade responsibility.'[53] And of course the Tories kept both hands on the flag. When Raney presented an abortive bill to abolish appeals to the British Privy Council, Ferguson rang all the tested and true imperialist themes.[54]

Most of all, the Conservatives offered themselves as 'practical men' who would rescue the province from the incompetent rule of fanatics and fumblers. Ferguson's Tories were friendly to businessmen. They would know how to tend to the welfare of the economy, then in a none too certain state, and to the development of the province's resources. Gone was the equivocal image and ideological confusion which in the days of Hearst had caused tried and true party members to desert the ship. The Tories, it seemed, were knowledgeable men of the world; the Farmers, they hoped Ontarians would recognize, were ineffectual theorists. Ferguson Conservatism harkened back to the days of Whitney yet was finely tuned to the needs and spirit of the 1920s. It offered as well the stability the province had known under Whitney and the restoration of the traditional party structure. The Conservatives felt no urge to save the morals of Ontarians; they promised no social experiments or legislative adventures. They were not reformers. To a people tired of uplift and longing for conditions as they imagined they had once existed, Ferguson was preaching the old-time political religion.

The 1923 election came sooner than anticipated. Throughout his period of office, E.C. Drury with grim determination pursued his impossible dream of a 'People's Progressive Party.' As early as January 1920, Morrison had issued a public statement that Drury's efforts represented 'a betrayal of the farmers.'[55] Drury's viewpoint failed to receive a hearing at the 1920 and 1921 UFO conventions and at the 1922 meeting the Premier's policy was unequivocally condemned. It was hopeless. The UFO executive felt ignored and betrayed by the government and Drury for his part had similar feelings towards those who controlled the UFO. But since the ILP had disintegrated and the trade unionists were calling for the Premier's blood, the alternatives were complete surrender to Morrison, which would probably mean the government's defeat in any case, or an alliance with the Liberals. Morrison and his friends, many of whom came from Conservative backgrounds, seem to have been suspicious that this was what broadening out meant from the beginning. After all, the man from Crown Hill had stood as a Liberal in the 1917 federal election and his sympathies were no secret. Morrison himself by 1922 was convinced that Drury had no place else to go. 'Our Ontario fellows have lost prestige terribly,' he told Norman Lambert in December 1922, 'Drury's chance to be Premier again is lessening every day unless he forms a Grit alliance...'[56] But according to Drury, three of his own ministers, Doherty, Grant, and Nixon, 'who had been brought up in the Conservative faith, voiced the strongest possible opposition to the idea of coalition.'[57]

Desperation, however, demanded an arrangement with the Liberals. The return to vigour of the Tories under Ferguson made the Liberal situation almost as dark as the government's and many of that party's supporters continued to advocate some kind of alliance with the Farmers. Although Mackenzie King was suspicious of any coalition which might cause the Liberals to lose their identity, his 1921 offer to Drury of a place in his cabinet placed him squarely in the ranks of those who desired co-operation. Dewart, who had always preferred to do battle with the Farmers, found his position impossible and in October 1921 he resigned from the leadership, complaining of 'the open attacks and the more veiled but equally appreciable disloyalty of others...'[58] In December 1921, Drury sent for Wellington Hay, the Listowel grain merchant who had become acting Liberal leader, and proposed co-operation in by-elections and in the House, possibly for two sessions, followed by a cabinet reorganization and an election.[59] But even with Dewart gone, co-operation proved impossible to attain. Quite apart from opposition from within the UFO and ILP, there remained many Liberals who thought as did W.E.N. Sinclair, the member from Oshawa who would soon contest his party's leadership with Hay. 'I am prepared to do my share of work,' Sinclair assured Howard Ferguson, 'in getting rid of the bunch in charge of the government. ... I am anxious that there should be as much harmony as possible between our two parties...'[60]

Sinclair even believed that if Hay continued to lead the Liberals there would be 'every chance for reasonable cooperation' with the Tories and he told Ferguson how delighted he was at Arthur Meighen's election in Grenville. 'It is the only way to eliminate the UFO.'[61] However, when the Liberal leadership convention was held in March 1922, Wellington Hay called for co-operation both federally and provincially with the Farmers. Although Hay won a clear victory, the convention's first resolution declared unswerving loyalty to 'the identity, solidarity and permanence of the Liberal party in the pending contest.'[62] Not yet recovered from the wartime split over conscription and Union Government, buffeted still by the ideological division between its Rowell and Dewart wings, unable to fight on its own yet equally attracted and repelled by the prospect of an alliance with Drury, the Ontario Liberals lacked scarcely one of the classic symptoms of a political party in trouble. Now they were led by a nice but inept man; 'too much Hay and not enough Wellington' went the devastating quip. During the 1922 session the party was ineffectual in the House and invisible out of it.

As election year began, the Tories had reason to feel confident. The opposition groups lay in tatters and unless they could pull themselves together, they would be ravaged in the pending contest. In January, Mackenzie King confided to his diary that 'the Ontario Liberals are deserting the ship like rats all seeking cover in the Senate – Hartley Dewart, Sinclair, Wilkie, Spence, etc. etc. etc. They will be badly beaten.'[63] A little later one of his Ontario ministers informed him that 'Wellington Hay has fallen down. ... There is no Liberal organization for Ontario – no candidates and apparently no effort to obtain them. ... We will have a Conservative Government in Ontario – No coalition under a new name will succeed...'[64] Undoubtedly Ferguson was fortunate in his opponents; they were not worthy of his mettle. Yet the bedraggled condition of the other groups was no fortuitous accident; power did not fall from the skies into the hands of a grateful but passive Tory chief. The political process is characterized by interaction and Ferguson's successful reconstruction of the Conservative party contributed largely to the demoralization of his opponents and exacerbated their internal disorders.

The broadening-out mess ended sordidly in mid-April of the 1923 session. It was an appropriate climax to four years of Farmer rule when Andrew Hicks, the party's former whip, launched a vicious attack on his leader, accusing Drury of 'inordinate lust for power' and denouncing him for engaging in negotiations for fusion with the Liberals 'without the consent or knowledge of his followers.'[65] Hicks was supported by Casselman and Leslie Oke (UFO, East Lambton) and Casselman moved a resolution which condemned the government for failing 'to live up to the ideals which brought the Farmer movement into being and placed this Government in power.' Of course the Tories made the most of this opportunity. Nickle proclaimed that Casselman's resolution was a want of confidence motion and demanded that the government go to the country at once. Ferguson insisted that Drury reply immediately to the 'charges' levied against him. 'Not in my time ... have we had quite so grave a situation arise. ... I think no member in this House ... has ever before heard hurled across the floor of the House at one of the leading public men of the province the words "betrayer," "traitor" and other severe epithets that indicated a course of conduct on his part that I would be sorry to think he would be guilty of.' Rattled, Drury lied to the House, claiming there had been no bargaining with the Liberals; then he adjourned the debate. The Morrison wing had laid down the gauge of battle on the floor of the House and had humiliated the premier. The next morning, in what he later described as a 'fit of temper,' Drury announced that the House would be dissolved within three weeks and an election held in late June.

At once Drury introduced in blank three bills providing for proportional representation, the single transferable vote and redistribution. Although in 1921 the majority report of a committee of the legislature had recommended that proportional representation be tried in select areas of the province and that the transferable vote be used elsewhere, a majority of the Farmer group had opposed legislation to this effect and Drury previously had refused to act.[66] There can be little doubt that the failure of broadening out now stimulated Drury's interest in electoral reform. As W.C. Good warned Raney, 'if the election is held now with three cornered contests in most constituencies ... the Conservative Party will secure an altogether undue proportion of representatives.'[67] The problem, as Good had pointed out to Morrison, was that if Drury brought in a measure in a pre-election session which provided for PR in a few of the large cities, 'the Conservatives will make capital ... because it will undoubtedly be represented as an effort to take an unfair advantage of the Conservative party. ... Ferguson is ready to strike a body blow if the opening is given him...'[68] Most of all, however, the Druryites wanted to avoid a general redistribution which would favour the urban population. Thus as early as 20 February, M.H. Staples, the UFO educational secretary, warned W.C. Good that the opposition were intending 'to ignore P.R. and to press for redistribution.' He added that T.H. Lennox was threatening that 'if the Government attempted to put through P.R. and the transferable vote farm members would do no farming this year...'[69]

Now, with Drury's three bills before the House, the battle was on. With an election already announced, the Tories would never submit to a hasty and radical restructuring of the electoral system. They were furious too over a speech Drury had just made in Milton in which he referred to the Conservative members as 'the dregs and leavings of the Conservative party.' As a result they were itching for a showdown and when Drury introduced bills which differentiated sharply between the kind of representation provided for rural, urban, and northern Ontario and even treated Toronto differently than other cities, Howard Ferguson warned him that the Tories would fight such 'vicious and erroneous' legislation to the last ditch. For four days the filibuster lasted and in the absence of closure procedures, Drury could not win. As Drury weakened, Ferguson exacted total surrender:

Hon. Mr Ferguson: Then you undertake to move that the orders be discharged and these bills be withdrawn?
Hon. Mr Drury: Yes.
Ferguson: Then withdraw them tonight.
Drury: No. I will withdraw them tomorrow when the orders are called.
Ferguson: No. The House is in session tonight; we are discussing these bills. Let us have them withdrawn now and have the matter settled definitely.
Drury: All right, then, I will withdraw them now.

The Toronto *Telegram* described the unforgettable scene. 'The Government broke; Drury waved the white flag and Ferguson snapped the whip of victory over Drury's head.' Instead of savouring his victory, Ferguson pressed for more, demanding that Drury 'definitely inform this House of his plans for dissolution and election...'

'Now the hon. member for Grenville is asking too much,' Drury whimpered. 'He has no right to dictate to me when I shall appeal to the Lieutenant-Governor...'

Again the whip snapped. 'This situation is not of our seeking,' Ferguson insisted brutally, 'and we are prepared to continue the discussion, if need be, until the snow flies next fall...' Drury collapsed. The election, he promised, would be in the last week of June. Ferguson had asserted his control of the Ontario legislature; the election would soon confirm his dominance.

Now it all came together. The years of back-breaking labour. The smoke-filled rooms. The slurs from friend and foe alike. All seemed worthwhile. The

Conservatives entered the campaign not, to be sure, as a totally united party but driven by an irresistible determination to seize power from the usurpers of 1919 and restore legitimacy to the government of Ontario. As the campaign began, Ferguson braced himself for the attacks he knew would follow. 'Ontario's search for an ideal successor to Howard Ferguson is a detail which can be postponed,' proclaimed the Toronto *Telegram*, 'Ontario's delivery from Druryism is a duty which must not be postponed.' Instinctively, however, all the opponents of Conservatism concentrated their attacks on Ferguson. 'Mr Ferguson's record tends to repel non-partisans and even members of his own party,' asserted the *Globe*. The Ottawa *Citizen* found it difficult 'to see how anyone can support Mr Howard Ferguson ... after reading the reports of the Timber Investigation Commission.'[70] W.C. Good privately assured the editor of the *Farmers' Sun* that 'it would be a catastrophe of the worst kind if a certain group of men should come into power in Ontario, not because they are called by a certain party name, but because so far as I can see they are personally disreputable and unreliable, and are allied with some of the worst forces in the country.'[71]

Within the party, doubts remained. In March 1923 Arthur Ford lamented to Willison that 'if the Conservatives had a strong, outstanding leader, they would sweep the country. The election of Mr Ferguson was a handicap.' According to press reports, Ferguson had been forced into the filibuster tactics in the House by a group of wet Tories who, the *Globe* asserted, had 'temporarily assumed leadership' and the same journal claimed that Ferguson's appointment of the astute but not very popular Edmund Bristol as campaign manager had caused another rebellion. 'Ferguson has been practically told to keep his hands off Toronto. The big Tory machine in this city is going to run things...'[72] And in June, R.C. Matthews, a Tory financier from the city, told Arthur Meighen that he had worked terribly hard at his club to create 'sentiment in favour of Mr Ferguson,' whose reputation still created distrust in the 'best circles.'[73] Colonel Pratt, the renegade Tory who had caused so much trouble in 1919, claimed that 'every third Conservative that you meet on the street is most outspoken in his disapproval' of Howard Ferguson.[74] Ferguson was hurt personally by the stories and was determined to minimize the damage. To rehabilitate his image he conscripted into the campaign such ultra-respectable figures as Sir John Willison and Canon Cody of St Paul's, who spoke at the major rally in Toronto.

One result of these lingering doubts was that despite the Tory pro-business stance, campaign funds did not flow generously into the hands of the party managers. Arthur Ford, who was in a position to know, has related that 'few elections were ever fought with less money. ... The Conservative Party, provincially and federally, was never at a lower ebb, and the wealthy men of the party had still little confidence in Mr Ferguson.'[75] One likely source of funds were the breweries and distilleries, who sensed they had a friend in Ferguson and were repelled by the Liberals and Farmers who remained bone-dry. During and after the campaign it was charged that Toryism was being floated on great waves of liquor money and the Toronto *Star* later claimed that in return for specific commitments the Conservatives accepted 'campaign funds totalling about $300,000...'[76] Ferguson of course replied that 'so far as my own knowledge goes and that of any member of the government ... no liquor organization, either distiller or brewer, ever contributed one dollar...' Indeed there was little evidence during the campaign that the party had received any $300,000 windfall. To raise money Ferguson mortgaged both his farm and his home and 'owed the bank $27,000 for which I had pledged every security I had in the world.'[77]

Still, it would be naïve to conclude that so practical a politician as Ferguson would not be counting in one way or another on support from the liquor interests and there is little doubt it was forthcoming. The liquor issue was the one pitfall which in 1923 might have prevented a Tory sweep. The Farmers did their best to paint Ferguson as a conspirator against prohibition. Throughout the whole period of Farmer rule, there were hints that Ferguson would come out on a wet platform. Ford periodically issued warnings against such a course and Meighen told Ferguson that 'the "Free Press" intends to stand by you subject only to one condition, i.e. that no wet plank is adopted. If that is done, he [Ford] says the Free Press will oppose.'[78] Ford was convinced that rural Ontario, particularly western Ontario, which he knew intimately, would rise up against any party that betrayed prohibition. Ford had reason to be alarmed. A variety of incidents suggested that the party's wet wing was gaining strength. When the government in December 1921 took away the right to dispense liquor from 311 doctors who had been abusing the privilege, the Conservatives, according to the *Star*, had mailed sympathetic propaganda to every doctor in the province.[79] In 1922 Herb Lennox levied sensational charges against Raney's administration of the OTA, claiming prosecutions were achieved through the employment of 'thugs and criminals' who corrupted youths and served as *agents provocateurs* in order to attain convictions. The Tories used the committee of the House which was appointed to examine the Lennox charges as a forum in which to expose what they described as Raney's fanaticism; as a result, press speculation that they were about to adopt a wet platform increased dramatically.[80]

In this contest, the advantages belonged to Ferguson. The Farmers approached prohibition as a moral issue; to Ferguson it was purely political. In May 1922 he infuriated his opponents by a much-quoted statement that he would announce his stand on the question, 'when the proper time comes' and that it would 'appeal to every reasonable man in the Province.'[81] In July he flew a trial balloon, stating that his policy would be 'more generous' than the OTA and the reaction convinced him that he should lie low for a little longer.[82] In the months ahead he said little but Tory members such as Godfrey, Currie, and Lennox and, with the campaign on, such candidates as James McCausland in Toronto and Frank Wilson in Windsor, captured the headlines with their wet addresses.

Ferguson remained noncommittal. 'We have no platform regarding liquor,' he announced, 'Do you think it safe for a party in opposition to have a platform? Don't you think it best to let the other fellow show his hand first and then play your cards?'[83] Such tactics could backfire. In March, Ford complained to Sir John Willison that 'Ferguson is taking no stand and Drury will make the most of this,' and as late as 11 May he reported to Meighen that the Tory leader 'so far has not stated where he stands. ... I have been assured for about two months that Mr Ferguson was going to make a statement...' Meighen told the worried Ford he would urge Ferguson to comply with Ford's wishes.[84]

That very day in a speech at Huntsville, Ferguson made the long-awaited pronouncement. 'When the OTA is changed it must be in the way it was enacted,' he promised, presumably after a referendum in which the people themselves decided.[85] Any Conservative government would enforce the OTA but, he asserted in the same breath, 'not in the spirit of fanaticism.' For the rest of the campaign, he added little to this vague statement, but he had said enough to allow Tory propagandists to claim that Howard Ferguson, a principal author of prohibition in Ontario, stood firm by his handiwork. Of course he did nothing to silence the Tory wets and there was no doubt where the 'smart vote' of the cities would go. 'Since Mr Ferguson has at last declared himself on the Temperance Question,' M.H. Staples lamented to W.C. Good, 'it may not be quite so easy for the Drury forces to make capital ... those who want to make him out to be a staunch supporter of Temperance will not have any great difficulty in doing so. ... There are still so many people who are hide-bound politicians that anything which gives them an excuse for rallying around the party flag is heartily welcome.'[86] Ferguson had never forgotten how the liquor question had all but destroyed Hearst. His clever manipulation of the issue which enabled him to play both sides of the fence was the major tactical coup of the 1923 campaign.

Furthermore, despite the grumbles and the lack of enthusiasm in some quarters, the Tory leadership difficulties were manageable, indeed negligible, in comparison with those of the other parties. In W.H. Price's opinion, the charges against Ferguson were old stuff and their impact was minimal when set against popular interest in the Backus 'steal.' 'The attacks on Mr Ferguson personally have fallen very flat,' he assured C.A.C. Jennings.[87] That party morale was high was demonstrated by the excellent group of candidates the Tories assembled. On no aspect of political management did Ferguson lavish more attention than on the choice of candidates. In Norfolk, John S. Martin, a wealthy and well-educated poultry farmer, was an excellent choice. In Perth Dr J.D. Monteith, a member of Stratford's premier political family, would run strongly against Wellington Hay. In West Elgin, Finlay MacDiarmid, who had served in the Hearst ministry, agreed to stand. Adam Beck's candidacy in London announced the restoration of the Hydro alliance. Lincoln Goldie in Wellington South, a successful businessman and pillar of his community, was the type of candidate arduously sought in many constituencies. Arthur Meighen gave his blessing when Frank Keefer, a former federal member still active in national politics, agreed to stand in Port Arthur. In Toronto, Ferguson worked hard to get R.C. Matthews, tempting him with the post of Provincial Treasurer. 'They are surrounding me,' Matthews told Meighen, but he finally declined to run out of distaste for a convention fight for one of the much sought-after Toronto nominations.[88] And all the Tory regulars, except Lennox who retired for business reasons, were eager to stand again.

The carefully nurtured alliance with Arthur Meighen also paid dividends. Early in 1923 Meighen suggested that Ferguson and one or two of his lieutenants could help establish closer relations with the federal members by attending a caucus in Ottawa. 'The interest of our fifty men in the coming provincial contest is very great, and good work would be done by attendance...' Ferguson considered this an excellent idea and it may have added to the already close rapport between the two sections. Meighen kept his eye on Ottawa area constituencies for Ferguson and could not have been more accommodating. 'I have been urging our men all to take every possible part in the provincial contest, and to make attendance on the House here a secondary matter. ... On any phase of the contest ... I am at your service.'[89] By contrast, Mackenzie King refused all requests to participate in any way, even ignoring his own North York constituency and Senator Arthur Hardy, a key figure in Ontario Liberalism, pointed to the 'extraordinary state of apathy and discontent ... on account of our Ontario Federal Ministers so totally holding aloof ... not one word even of sympathy seems to have come from Ottawa...'[90]

The Farmers for their part feuded among themselves almost to the end and finally only papered over their differences. Morrison kept the UFO out of the contest and Drury has estimated that his group's entire election fund 'was less than $1,500,' most of which he apparently contributed himself.[91] The campaign itself rose to no heights and occasionally plumbed the depths. Its highlight was a debate in Fergus between Raney and Ferguson. Farmer incompetence, extravagance which resulted in an increase in ordinary expenditure from under $21.5 million in 1919 to over $37.5 million in 1922 and in direct liabilities from under $98 million to almost $241 million, and a multitude of new taxes were the points the Tories drove home most frequently. During the last session, W.F. Nickle delivered a monumental attack on Farmer spending and budget practices, charging the government with fraudulent manipulation of the accounts as part of an attempt to disguise the true state of the finances. Now the Conservatives published his remarks as a campaign pamphlet, 'Financial Squandering And Bogus Deficit,' and Peter Smith responded, prophetically it turned out, that if even a portion of the Tory claims were true, he as Treasurer would belong behind prison walls. Across the province, the Tory speakers hit the same theme. In Victoria-Haliburton, for example, young Leslie Frost, although not himself a candidate, warned of Farmer extravagance and called for a return to economy and sound management.[92]

Ferguson campaigning was at his best. At such times his broad humanity and his ability to translate the great events of government into simple, human terms served him well. In a witticism not lost on the rural community, he asked the voters to provide relief from 'stable government.' Seeking to dramatize the contrast between the government's vaunted virtue and the real facts of Ontario life, he mocked the Farmers by frequent reference to 'that awful last night party.' And, most effectively of all, he took up the story of how Drury had refurnished the Premier's office with a 'hundred dollar coal scuttle' and none too scrupulously he turned the coal scuttle into a vivid symbol of broken Farmer promises of economy.

Finally, with the Tory coalition restored almost to the vigour of the Whitney period, there remained one last element to complete the image of the risen phoenix. In the early 1920s the Roman Catholic community began a major campaign to win tax and other concessions for the separate school system. At the same time, the French Canadian Education Association received repeated assurances from Drury that early action would be taken to provide relief from the hated Regulation 17. Drury did not live up to his promises and ACFEO officials were utterly disillusioned with the Farmer administration. And by failing to provide relief for separate schools, or even to offer assurances of future consideration, Drury had alienated the English-speaking Catholics as well. As a result, on 15 May, at a meeting of the Bishops of Ontario held at the residence of Archbishop Neil McNeil of Toronto, it was decided, as the Bishop of Alexandria put it, 'that pastors, or at least some of them, should be informed *in confidence* that word should go round quietly advising Catholics not to support the Farmers' Government at the coming elections...' Thus Bishop Scollard of Sault Ste Marie made it clear to some of the priests in his diocese that:

The highest Ecclesiastical authority in the province of Ontario has decided that the Drury Government is the bitter enemy of Catholic Schools...

Catholic electors then must vote against all candidates of the Drury Government on June 25th, be the candidate UFO or labor man, attached to Drury.

If there is any Drury candidate in the field in your territory, you will make known to the Catholic Electors the above direction of their Church authorities.

If there is no Drury candidate running, you can be silent about the above, as the electors are perfectly free to vote liberal or conservative.[93]

Ironically, the Farmer government's failure to aid either the French- or the English-language separate school systems won little support for Drury in the Protestant community. Immobilized by his fear that any action on the schools question would excite an Orange backlash, Drury had not recognized that foolish equivocations and drawn-out negotiations could have the same effect. After it was all over, C.B. Sissons reported to Senator Belcourt that 'the Orangemen were practically a unit against the Farmer candidates generally.'[94] Faced with a choice between Ferguson and Drury, few Orangemen hesitated. By election day there remained hardly any significant social, cultural, or economic group in Ontario that the Farmer government had failed to alienate. For the Druryites, it had been a remarkable performance.

When election day arrived, Ferguson was in a state approaching complete exhaustion. Ella had collapsed a few days earlier with an illness which kept her in poor health for months. But Ferguson was content; he had left nothing undone and was predicting that his party would be returned with sixty-five seats. Others, like Joseph Flavelle, misled perhaps by the fact that there were 53 three-cornered contests and more candidates than in any previous election, could find 'no one sure as to what will happen ... I cannot see how Ferguson, even if he had the largest group, can assure his Excellency that he could carry on Government.'[95] The large number of three-cornered contests, however, worked to the Tory advantage. In 1919 Dewart, viewing Hearst as his principal enemy, in many constituencies had not run Liberals against the Farmers; now, ironically, although Hay and Drury were not unsympathetic to each other, the circumstances which had prevented formal co-operation forced Liberals and Farmers into mutual opposition. The resulting split in the anti-Tory vote aided Ferguson immeasurably.

June 1923 was a month of extraordinary heat which broke at about 7 PM on the 25th, election day. A great electrical storm and winds of hurricane proportion swept over Toronto and much of western Ontario. The natural conditions were a complement to a man-made gale. When Howard Ferguson arrived at Union Station from Kemptville about 9:45 that evening, he was told that already the Conservatives had elected forty-three, the Liberals and UFO only one each. He could hardly believe his ears. Everyone was as thunderstruck by the extent of the Tory sweep in 1923 as they had been in 1919 by the dimensions of the same party's failure. Flavelle pointed out that 'the significant feature is the size of the majorities – hundreds where one would expect tens, and thousands where one would expect hundreds.'[96] Given the number of candidates, the Conservative total of fifty per cent of the votes was truly impressive, up almost twenty per cent over 1919. Of the 944,933 votes cast, they received 472,796, the UFO 207,691, Liberals 198,563, Labour 42,532, and Independents 23,551. While the Tory total of 75 seats was spread fairly evenly across the province, western Ontario exceeded Arthur Ford's fondest dreams and the Conservatives were particularly strong in the cities, winning, for example, all eleven seats in Toronto and the Yorks. The UFO returned 17, the ILP 4, and the Liberals 14, less than half their 1919 total. The cabinet was decimated, only Raney, Biggs, Doherty, and Bowman surviving; and the Liberal frontbench fared no better. Hay lost in North Perth to Dr Monteith while Major Tolmie in Windsor fell before Frank Wilson, an outspoken wet.

One key to the cause of it all was provided by the experience of Hartley Dewart in Southwest Toronto, where his enormous majority of 1919 melted away before an undistinguished Conservative candidate. Dewart lost by almost five thousand in a total ballot of fourteen thousand, clearly a stunning drop in a total vote which in 1919 had exceeded twenty-five thousand. The pattern was province-wide, with an almost twenty per cent drop in the popular vote from 1919. Post-war unrest had lost its urgency, and there was no liquor referendum to bring out the electors. Voting had reverted to its more or less normal patterns in Ontario. The Tories reaped the advantages.

Howard Ferguson's victory brought to power the only Conservative government in Canada. The elation of the crowds election night belied the smallness of the total vote. In an era before television and with radio in its infancy, the returns were greeted in the committee rooms and on the main streets of Ontario. On this night, torrential rains notwithstanding, the crowds were huge and elated. In Toronto, seat of government and capital of post-Victorian virtues, waves of enthusiasm swept the assembled throngs. Anticipation filled the air. Few doubted the meaning of Ferguson's victory. Torontonians had grown weary of humorless uplift and believed that under 'Fergie' the days of the OTA were numbered. Here was election fever at its most virulent, something more than normal gratification over a party victory. Vast throngs jammed the streets, downtown traffic was at a standstill, street cars had to search out new routes. To responsive roars from thousands of throats, the bands blared forth such ditties as 'How Dry I Am' and 'A Wee Deoch and Doris.' A flushed Howard Ferguson, leaning far over the *Telegram* balcony, responded to the mood. 'God bless you Ferguson,' came a voice from the crowd. 'The reign of tyranny is over,' promised the Tory deliverer. Then, exhausted, he returned to Front St and his Toronto home in the old Queen's hotel.

8

The Return of the Old Order

Back in business in Queen's Park, the Tories could afford to regard the Drury years as an aberration. In 1919 social unrest and political mismanagement had momentarily shattered the provincial consensus, but from the beginning Ontarians were uneasy with their unanticipated adventure. Ontario, like Howard Ferguson himself, was conservative to the core and across the province, in the north and on the farms, in the homes of the workers and the mansions of the rich, the rejection of Druryism now was greeted with satisfaction and more. Although Drury's departure from the customary Ontario norms was more apparent than real and his radicalism was no more threatening than that of Mackenzie King, many thought otherwise. John Willison, for example, professed himself 'deeply convinced of the tyranny of the UFO group and the undesirability of class government.'[1] By four years of clever politics, Ferguson had helped create a mood in which his victory could be regarded in some circles as a timely deliverance from political thraldom.

Now, an enormous majority at his back and facing demoralized opponents, he was in a position of almost unexampled authority. Ontario, Mackenzie King lamented, was his to rule 'for possibly an indefinite period.'[2] But first, he and Ella returned to Kemptville, to the rambling old Victorian home which stood in the shadow of the Agricultural College, and to the friends and neighbours they knew so well. Throughout his years in office, Howard would make the trip as frequently as circumstances permitted. Once there he loved to walk about his farm, always well tended by Alf Moore, the hired man, to stroll through his prize orchard, and to inspect with a critical eye the state of the livestock. Usually too he would drive about the countryside in a cutter pulled by 'Old Fred,' the devoted nag whose fame the press people soon spread about the province. His elevation to high office changed little in his relations with the friends of a lifetime. One local character still made it a practice to hit him for money 'to get a set of teeth' and Howard would always laugh and tell his sister, 'I guess Jim hasn't got his teeth yet.' To the children he remained simply Howard, or sometimes 'Uncle' Howard and they knew he was always good for a treat at the local confectioner's. Kemptville refused to hold its most famous son in awe; they knew him too well for that. Shortly after his elevation, Howard asked one old crony what people around town thought of his becoming Premier and the reply, which took him aback for a moment, was that 'the boys are still laughing.'

These were the people from whom he derived whatever he possessed by way of political philosophy. 'Howard Ferguson always knew what was going on in the barbershop in Kemptville,' became the boast of his colleagues. But he drew far more than a sense of public opinion from his trips home and from the time he spent talking and making friends with hundreds of people about Ontario. Of course he was learning what people were thinking; he was also recharging his own batteries, for this was what nourished him. To him Kemptville was more than a place, it was a point of view. The highlight of each visit home was usually Saturday morning when Howard would 'mainstreet.' His sister Marion, now the wife of Dr Storey, lived in the old family home on the other side of town. Sometime during the morning he would set out and it would be many hours before he would reach his destination. One obstacle was the barbershop; still more formidable was the 'Board of Trade,' the establishment of shoemaker Bill Hyland. In the back of his store, erect as a ramrod, surrounded by footwear of all kinds, staunch Tory Hyland held court. There Howard would sit, resting on one of the blocks of wood that served as chairs, always neatly dressed, for he never tried to be one of the boys, and the hours passed happily. Many were the stories he swapped with the 'Board of Trade' regulars, often retired farmers who had moved into town. Then, usually, he would amble across the street to the old Macpherson House for more of the same.

One trip, made days after the election, was unlike any other. On that 28th of June 1923, the chilly air and threat of thundershowers savoured more of fall than early summer, but this did not dampen the ardour with which the townsfolk and people for miles around greeted their old friend who had become premier. On election night, Howard had left for Toronto before the returns had come in; now he was coming home.

Five thousand strong they turned out, the greatest crowd the village had ever seen. As he stepped from the train, a roar went up and hundreds rushed forward. He shook scores of hands before stepping into the flower-decked car which was to lead the procession. Slowly and noisily, hundreds of cars, their horns honking, wound their way through a Kemptville gay with Union Jacks, bunting, and streamers. Five bands played along a route lined with war veterans and cadets in full panoply. Before long, the procession had looped the town until its front end met its tail. Now, standing in the tonneau, bareheaded to the rain and wearing a huge grin, Howard returned the shouted greetings. Finally, Riverdale Park was reached. Someone counted 504 cars passing the park gate.

146 G. Howard Ferguson

By this time, the rain was falling more heavily. There, in the middle of the park on a hastily erected platform, were his brother-in-law Mayor Storey, Arthur Meighen, Charles McCrea, federal and provincial members, and delegations of town councillors, reeves, and other dignitaries from miles around. Scores of reporters crowded the platform area. Amidst giant firecrackers, children throwing streamers, and rockets flying through the rainstrewn skies, the inevitable speeches began. Arthur Meighen, who privately had expressed the opinion that the Ontario result had been the personal victory of Howard Ferguson, who had shown 'astonishing pluck,' now elicited a cheer when he told the crowd that Ferguson's triumph was the greatest he had ever witnessed. Ferguson won a louder cheer still when standing on a table on the platform, he invited everyone to visit Kemptville's ice cream parlours and refreshment stands at his expense.

But the speeches were brief. Few could hear. The sirens of the autos continued to send out their message of triumph while the bands were eagerly anticipating the dancing to follow. For once the politicians surrendered the stage and after a while they retired happily to the rambling Ferguson home across town. There they could savour for the moment the sweet taste of victory before turning, quickly and eagerly, to lay their plans for the new efforts which would soon be upon them.

Ferguson's first task was cabinet-making. The key appointment was Attorney-General. His prickly character and political unorthodoxy had always made W.F. Nickle a man apart. Undoubtedly his reputation was greater with some sections of the public than with his fellow members, who often found him difficult to work with, yet he was a man of brilliant parts. Despite profound differences in style and character, Ferguson and Nickle genuinely liked each other and from time to time the two families visited back and forth.[3] Nickle, however, recognized that his administration as Attorney-General of the OTA would not be unaffected by his personal temperance opinions and he knew that he would find himself in an impossible position if the province continued to move away from prohibition. Ferguson may have had reservations on these grounds and he had also heard the whispers that the Kingston man would be suitable as an early successor to the Premier's chair. Others as well perceived the potential for a party split but a correspondent of Liberal politician Charles Murphy gauged things accurately enough when he wrote that 'Howard is pretty slick. I said soon as he got Nickle for Attorney-General he would trim that gent...'[4] Eventually, although it gave Ferguson no pleasure, that was what happened.

In the meantime, Nickle was a source of strength to the government. Not only did the drys applaud the appointment but those who remembered Nickle's long feud with Mackenzie and Mann believed that here was the man who would keep 'the interests' in their place. At least one element in the community was disappointed. One of Nickle's first moves was to announce that the controversial bill Raney had presented to prohibit the publication of race track betting information would be strictly administered. More important, there would be no laxity in the administration of the OTA and the new Attorney-General promised early reforms to improve and tighten enforcement.

McCrea, Henry, and Price were the other senior appointments. During the campaign Ferguson had promised that McCrea would receive Mines; in the years ahead the Sudbury lawyer would prove a sound and progressive minister able to retain the confidence of both owners and operators. He was also the sole representative in cabinet of the Roman Catholic community. And George Henry, loyal lieutenant and close friend, was ideal for Public Works and Highways. Earnest, hard-working, and able, as one of the pioneers of the good roads movement in Ontario he maintained in the Department the enthusiasm Biggs had created but added as well the careful management that had been lacking under the Farmers. Of course 'Billy' Price was slated for a cabinet post but those who viewed the member for Parkdale primarily as a wily ward politician were surprised when Ferguson gave him the Treasury. Still, in opposition his role on the Public Accounts Committee had made him a Treasury watchdog and earned him the sobriquet, 'Price the prober.' Now he would have a chance to show what he could do in the portfolio which had drawn so much Tory fire over the past four years.

The second rank of ministers was led by Dr Forbes Godfrey, who became Minister of Labour, to which he added, following legislation in 1924, the new portfolio of Health. An old crony of Ferguson, noted as much for bluster as for ability, his appointment pleased the wets; but Dr Godfrey had waged a long campaign on behalf of public health improvements and was known as an advocate of a provincial sanitarium system, so in that respect his appointment as Health minister did not lack logic. In Agriculture, John Martin of Norfolk was ideal. A poultry farmer on a large scale, he had won numerous international competitions and was known as 'the Wyandotte King.' But he was also an experienced municipal politician and brought to bear on the portfolio the quiet intelligence of a former high school classics teacher. Lincoln Goldie, the Guelph miller who had served on the Canadian Wheat Board and had been boomed during the campaign as a businessman of stature, became Provincial Secretary. James Lyons, who operated his own fuel supply business and who as mayor of Sault Ste Marie had demonstrated real ability, was the second New Ontario man in the cabinet, receiving the traditionally northern portfolio of Lands and Forests. There were also four ministers without portfolio: Adam Beck, back after an absence of almost a decade; Thomas Crawford, the dean of the House; J.R. Cooke, who was appointed to the Hydro commission; and Dr Leeming Carr of Hamilton. A notable absentee was Finlay MacDiarmid, a former colleague in the Hearst administration. Ferguson, remembering his performance under Hearst, doubted that he would show the energy expected of a minister.

Ferguson retained Education himself. His interest in the portfolio had never subsided and he knew that he could lean heavily on A.H.U. Colquhoun, the Deputy Minister, whose political sense and intimate knowledge of the ways and wiles of Queen's Park could be relied on to keep the minister out of trouble. As well, the professional expertise of F.W. Merchant would carry much of the daily weight of administration. Ferguson was particularly alert to the political dimension of Education and later confided to a colleague that 'there is an army of people in the province who occupy a position more or less unique – teachers, supervisors and inspectors are closely in touch with community and family life.' Serving as Minister would help a busy Premier keep in contact with opinion leaders from across the province. He knew as well that 'there are constantly delicate questions to be handled, many of which can be set aflame and create dissatisfaction and political difficulty if not tactfully handled.'[5]

One such question, of course, was Regulation 17, and with that matter still unsettled, Ferguson may have hesitated to include in his cabinet a Franco-Ontarian. Yet from Quebec, Rodolphe Monty, a former Borden minister, urged such an appointment and Arthur Meighen, believing it of perhaps vital significance to the federal party, pressed it upon him on several occasions. Although Ferguson had urged Dr Casgrain of Windsor to stand during the election, intending to appoint him to the ministry, Casgrain decided not to run and Ferguson believed that the only Franco-Ontarian elected as a Conservative was unsuitable.[6] Now there was some talk of opening a constituency for the right man but, to Meighen's disappointment, nothing was done.

On the whole it was a satisfactory cabinet. Its Tory identity was attested to by the inclusion of five Anglicans and four lawyers out of 13 members but it contained as well three farmers, two doctors, and a cattle merchant. It was not, perhaps, up to the standards of Whitney's first ministry but certainly Nickle, Price, McCrea, Henry, and Beck far outshone any of the opposition members. As Ferguson had gone about his task, there had been a good deal of concern over the kind of men to whom he might turn. R.C. Matthews, for example, told Meighen he was 'a little apprehensive on account of old associations' and Mark Irish hoped 'that Ferguson will remember that much of Whitney's greatness was attributable to those he had the sagacity to gather around him...' But now the press reacted favourably; Willison described it as 'a really good Cabinet'; and in Ottawa that crusty old Tory Sir George Foster told his diary that Ferguson 'has avoided some objectionable appointments...' From the inner circle, Price confided to Willison that Ferguson 'under considerable difficulty, has chosen a cabinet that at least starts well.'[7]

It was also a cabinet which knew its master. Apart from some initial difficulty with that most difficult of men, Adam Beck, and the later split with Nickle on a matter of principle, Ferguson's authority and judgement over the years remained unchallenged to a perhaps unfortunate degree. The personal and ideological battles that had wracked the Whitney administration and bedevilled Hearst were conspicuously absent. Doubtless the conventional conservatism of a prosperous age was primarily responsible for such apparently sweeping agreement on political fundamentals, but the iron will of the leader contributed significantly to the new aura of harmony. Ferguson had learned a lesson from the internal feuds of the pre-war and war years and he had benefitted too from the hungry time in opposition to construct a taut, cohesive team. Now the overflowing backbenches by all the rules of politics should have brought internal trouble but did not. By careful management and assisted by his shrewd understanding of men, he exerted such an unchallenged control over back-benchers and cabinet colleagues that the opposition would soon raise the cry of dictatorship. Not even the tiresome prohibition question − by far the most serious threat to Tory unity − was allowed to damage more than momentarily the party fabric. Even when his power in Ontario approached the absolute, Ferguson continued to recognize how completely it depended on the health and vigour of the party; with the opposition groups all but eliminated from the House, he remained ever the sensitive politician, tending his party as a living organism, lavishing it with constant attention and care.

With the cabinet selected and his government well launched, he struck out for the north, accompanied by Harry Cody and W.F. Cockshutt, the Lieutenant-Governor. For months after the election, his movements were restricted by the illness of Ella, who remained bedridden and in need of constant attention. But this brief respite was a holiday he sorely needed; it was an arduous but, according to unofficial reports, high-spirited and rollicking expedition. The objective was Moose Factory, the first time a Premier had been to Ontario's tidewater. From the end of steel at Oil Can, which lay 45 miles north of Cochrane, to the Bay was about 130 miles by foot and canoe and each of the distinguished travellers hoisted a pack of some sixty pounds. The way out was simpler, thanks to Roy Maxwell, one of Ontario's great bush pilots.

For Ferguson it was the elixir he needed and he came back bubbling with enthusiasm. Still, his first pronouncements were unrelentingly conventional. Almost half a year would pass before he would face the House and during that period he left the province in no doubt as to the character of his administration. At every opportunity, he made it clear that 'our first duty will be to pare to the very bone every unnecessary expenditure and to reorganize every branch of the Government, so that it will be founded on a sound administrative basis.' Clearly, his campaign attacks on Farmer extravagance had been in earnest; he was a man of his times in his belief that 'the people of Ontario are today groaning under a burden of taxation and a provincial debt such as has never been dreamed of before.' There would be 'no new expenditures of any account,' he promised, 'until we have taken full care of our present obligations.'[8]

It all sounded terribly dull. Gradually over the years he would admit that the growing demands on provincial governments required a loosening of the purse strings; in time he would justify the spiralling expenditures which were anathema to most politicians of his generation by arguing that for Ontario to prosper and grow, the province must spend more. Clearly, however, this was a circumstance to which few politicians of the 1920s, federal or provincial, ever reconciled themselves; they had no inkling of the massive growth of government functions and costs which the future would bring. In this sense the Fergusons, the Kings, and their kind had more in common with the men of the nineteenth century than with their successors of a more indulgent age.

His emphasis on 'sound administration' was another commonplace of the day and it aptly expressed his belief that weak leaders had allowed the machinery of government to deteriorate, causing inefficiency and extravagance. The new administration was not in office for long, however, before it realized that something more fundamental was wrong with the provincial bureaucracy. Evidence of administrative laxity and sheer corruption began to surface in several of the most important departments and Ferguson was appalled at the state of affairs he encountered. If honest with himself, he must have recognized that responsibility did not lie entirely with the Drury administration. Undoubtedly the weakness and inexperience of the Farmer government had contributed to conditions which now came to light, but during the war, and before, the provincial government had reached into previously untouched areas of social concern and placed new demands on its civil service. In the early 1920s the Drury men did not realize the need for radical repair and in any case the agrarian philosophy was inimical to the expansion of the government service. With weak ministers at the head of weakly staffed departments and a service generally lacking in organizational skills and professional training, the potential for disaster was large.

The extent of malfeasance and inefficiency came fully to light over the next couple of years. From the beginning, however, enough was apparent to cause the new administration to place a high priority on efforts to reform and modernize the machinery of government. 'We have in view,' Ferguson told W.H. Price in January 1924, 'a comprehensive reorganization of the service...' The Treasury was the department most radically affected and one of Ferguson's first moves was to appoint an experienced accountant to the new position of financial comptroller. He also instituted an audit of all government receipts, something which, incredibly, had not previously been done. In fact the affairs of all departments came under scrutiny as accountants began a widespread study of operating procedures and administrative practices. To some extent, no doubt, Ferguson's motivation was political and he had good reason to suspect that investigation would uncover Farmer irregularities; more positively, the Tories were motivated by a desire to reform the outdated governmental machinery and to justify their self-proclaimed image as tough-minded administrators.

They were also bringing to bear some old-time political techniques. The first head to be chopped was that of J.G. Ramsden, a Liberal appointed to the Hydro

Commission by Drury. Ramsden did not go quietly. 'Was it Sir Adam, or you Mr Premier,' he asked in a public letter, 'that turned four or five provincial police and detectives loose on my office and broke open my desk? ... Did you want to remove my copies of the minutes so that I would have no evidence of the transactions which took place during my tenure of office? I removed nothing but my personal letters. ... You were a bit of an expert at it when you left the Crown Lands Office, or what was left of the Crown Lands.'[9] There were other efforts in the same direction, including the cancellation of a contract Biggs had entered into for auto markers.

But fears of a general purge went unrealized. In contrast to what would happen in 1934, there was no dramatic turnover of civil service personnel in either 1919 or 1923. Civil Service Commission personnel statistics reveal 306, 272, 492, and 426 resignations in 1919, 1920, 1921, and 1922 respectively; the figures for 1923 to 1925 were 631, 487, and 348, indicating that changes were above average in 1923 but not greatly out of line. In 1934, there were 1168 resignations. The slightly larger figure for 1923 was attributable in part to Ferguson's conviction that a fat and over-staffed service would benefit by judicious trimming. Yet despite his determination to cut back, an irresistible if moderate expansion in the total number of civil servants soon set in. The bureaucracy (including permanent inside and temporary outside personnel) grew from 5655 in 1919 to 6491 in 1923 and reached 7427 in 1930.[10]

One change of significance was in the relationship between the government and the Hydro Commission. For years Adam Beck had been a law unto himself and with the help of his formidable political machine had resisted all efforts to bring the Hydro under proper statutory and political control. 'Hands off the Hydro' and 'Keep the Hydro out of politics' were his slogans and when Hearst and, more effectively, Drury, had challenged these axioms, he had worked towards their destruction. Ferguson did not intend to let himself be coerced or ignored by Sir Adam. In November he was embarrassed when a visitor to his office reported that Beck, according to the press, had plans underway to acquire the Kaministiquia Power Company. This was news to Ferguson and occasioned a curt reprimand.

'I dare say you have been wrongly reported. ... Indeed I hope so,' he began, 'because I certainly would not expect you to make such a statement without having discussed it with me in advance. ... I have said to you a number of times, I only intend to proceed after I have thoroughly considered each step and have been able to exercise my own judgement and approval. I expect to have the closest cooperation with you in the matter, and when you have suggestions or plans in mind ... I feel sure you will realize the necessity of giving me an opportunity of considering it before your views are made public.'[11] Under Ferguson the Hydro remained by statute a body with wide powers of independent action but no longer was it allowed to ride roughshod over the elected representatives of the people. Henceforth the government's statutory powers of audit and supervision took on real meaning as Hydro's responsibility to the cabinet, and through it to the House, began to be effectively enforced by a determined Premier.

Yet those who recalled Ferguson's previous clashes with Beck and hoped that these portended a general effort to put the damper on Ontario's great experiment in public ownership were disappointed. Ferguson's attitude to the Hydro was essentially that he had learned from Whitney. 'My own view,' he later related privately, 'is that the success of the Ontario Hydro ... is due to the fact that power is a natural monopoly and it is possible to control the whole situation. In ordinary commercial or industrial enterprises that cannot be done, and you jeopardize the investment of public money by subjecting it to private competition. ... With the development of democratic institutions ... there naturally arises a demand to democratize business enterprises ... on the basis of public ownership. I do not believe that view could be adopted as a general principle ... Of course the mere phrase "public ownership" has a tremendous appeal with the average citizen. If you were looking for votes only, you could paint a picture that would be most attractive.' But a general extension of public ownership was not, in Ferguson's opinion, an effective way to promote resource development and create new jobs. He was willing to admit, however, that 'each situation must be dealt with upon its merits,' and his knowledge of Ontario conditions and needs led him to an abiding commitment to the Hydro as an instrument which served Ontario well both internally and in its external affairs.[12]

There were political considerations as well which now influenced his attitude to the Drury-appointed Gregory Commission. The Farmers, he claimed, had attempted to destroy the Hydro and he announced that he was putting an end to its 'persecution.' He ordered the Gregory Commission to wrap up its work and passed an order-in-council telling it to restrict its remaining efforts to the Chippawa project. Yet when its report and supporting documents, an enormous bulk of one hundred and three volumes, were delivered to Queen's Park in March 1924, it almost seemed, as Beck's biographer suggests, as though Ferguson had 'winked' at the commissioners when he told them to wind down their activities. Gregory and his colleagues had carried out a painstaking examination of Hydro's activities and it seems likely that Ferguson realized that their evidence and recommendations would strengthen his own hand in future dealings with the Hydro and its chairman.

The report praised Hydro's engineering operations but criticized many of its procedures and pointed to instances in which funds had been used without proper authorization. It looked askance at Hydro's notorious political activities, including the provision of funds for the OMEA, which had served as its private pressure group, and it found as well, in substantiation of the earlier Sutherland Commission, that Hydro had made a great mistake in entering the radial railway field. 'In performing its functions as administrator of a great public trust,' the commissioners concluded in words which facilitated Ferguson's task, 'the Commission ever should bear in mind that it was created by the Legislature, is financed by the Province and its powers and authority are defined by statutes.'[13]

However much he agreed with this, the Premier chose to ignore in public the critical note. 'It must be a great gratification to the members of the Hydro Commission,' he told the House, that a two-year probe by an antagonistic Commission should result in a report 'which completely vindicates the Hydro project...' Ferguson knew that the Gregory Commission report contained much wisdom; it strengthened his refusal to have anything to do with Hydro radials, for example, while generally it coincided with and contributed to a turning point in the Hydro's relationship with government and province.[14] The days of the great crusade were over; the age of administration had dawned. In the years ahead, the province would implement many of the recommendations of the Commission Ferguson appeared to have dismissed so disdainfully.

If his first months in office helped set a new pattern in relations with the Hydro, Ferguson and his colleagues also set out to convey a message to businessmen and investors. The new premier believed one of the government's most important functions was to help create a mood of confidence which would develop stability, attract investors, and encourage development. He was aided in this aim by the province's sense that the Tory victory had ended the era of political adventuring. Ferguson in 1923 had made few promises but 'business as usual' was the conclusion to be drawn from his return to power. This assumed added significance because well into 1924 the economy remained sluggish, agricultural prices were depressed, unemployment still existed, and northern dissatisfaction endured. 'The public,' Ferguson told Flavelle on 3 January 1924, 'are restless, irritable and unreasonable. Our efforts are directed chiefly to establishing public confidence. If we can do anything towards stabilizing financial conditions and carry on persistent propaganda of optimism, I am hopeful that our people might be aroused from a sort of lethargic depression...'[15]

Typical of the views the new administration was conveying to the business community was Charles McCrea's statement a few days after taking office. 'The thing of initial importance,' he asserted 'is to give confidence to the practical mining man and the investor. Legal questions are continually arising that must be dealt with in a spirit of equity. ... A sympathetic government policy will encourage capital to enter our mining field. It makes fright at the slightest suspicion of government hostility...'[16] McCrea promised an aggressive policy of assistance and support to the industry.

Ferguson's early announcement that he would not proclaim Raney's Blue Sky securities legislation at first blush was an appeal to the same interests; the wildcat promoters appeared to have won. The province, the *Globe* declared, had the knowledge, 'that a Conservative government, really conservative, is in power.'[17] Still, the government's decision reflected the fact that similar legislation in

Saskatchewan had already been held *ultra vires* and Ferguson and Nickle did promise to find a more effective way to protect the investing public. In 1924 they passed a weak bill of restricted scope, perhaps in anticipation of judicial criticism. Yet the government had risked a good deal to go as far as it did in the face of opposition from the backbenchers. J.C. McRuer, an assistant Crown Attorney who had assisted in the bill's preparation, was called by Nickle to explain some of its provisions to the Tory caucus. The members grumbled but Nickle told them it was going through whether they liked it or not. Passed but not proclaimed, it was evidence that the Ferguson government had not abandoned its responsibilities in the area of securities regulation.[18] Constitutional doubts remained and the government continued to search for a better solution to what it recognized as a pressing problem.

A new premier encountering a mild but nonetheless real economic recession and not yet having faced the legislature for the first time might normally have been expected to tend rather closely to the press of business at home. Ferguson, however, soon demonstrated that he held no narrow conception of the political responsibilities of a Tory Premier of Ontario. His close working relationship with Arthur Meighen continued and in December 1923 in response to pressure from federal and prairie Conservatives, he accompanied Meighen on a western tour. 'I think I addressed about 12 meetings,' he reported to Jack Reid, 'so that there was not much holiday about it. ... Besides being in Edmonton and Saskatoon I was at Battleford, Regina, Winnipeg and Portage La Prairie. Everywhere I found the same sentiment, a sudden trend toward the Conservative Party.'[19] In the years ahead, the country became accustomed to the Ontario Premier's roving political eye. Although always jealous of his provincial party's prerogatives, he also regarded himself as one of the leaders of a great national organization and never shirked the consequent responsibilities. Now he assured Reid that political conditions in the Maritimes were improving wonderfully and that he found 'entirely a new atmosphere in Montreal. Eddie Beatty says that Quebec will split up and that the Conservative Party will get a substantial support...' Always a bustling figure with many irons in the fire, Ferguson over the next few years greatly extended an already wide acquaintanceship with businessmen and politicians across the country.

But his politicking did nothing to counter the 'lethargic depression' he had described to Flavelle. Nor did he plan to improve conditions by a program of legislative reforms. With the first session of the sixteenth legislature about to begin, he confided to Reid that 'I hope to get through in a couple of months. We will not have any very important legislative programme...'[20] That a new administration led by a man of fertile imagination should take such an attitude seemed surprising. But it was something the province came to expect of him. Although he would place some legislation of first-rate importance on the statute books, he seemed to hate to admit as much. Each time the opposition berated the government for the vacuity of its throne speech, he responded that it gave him 'great satisfaction, if not pride, that there is a lack of a long legislative programme...' In 1926 he claimed that most voters believed 'we have been legislated to death ... that what our people need is education. ... I think it was Voltaire who said that a great multitude of laws in a community was like a great multitude of doctors – it indicated weakness and malady...' What was desirable was as little legislation as possible and even then the best laws were merely 'the crystallization of public sentiment and thought.' The purpose of every government, he asserted, should be to conduct the business of the state so that 'the very minimum of legislation' was required. Legislation created an irresistible tendency for citizens to look to government rather than their own initiative to solve problems.[21]

What then, Ferguson asked, was the function of government if not to legislate? Its role, he responded, was complex. Its first duty was 'to encourage the development of a sound, healthy, intelligent public sentiment upon all questions of material and moral welfare in the community...' Ferguson believed the Premier's office provided the best pulpit in the land and that the power which went with the position was as much moral as physical. Perhaps his own more restrained behaviour shows best how greatly he felt the responsibility of his new office. Although the roistering 'Fergie' of political legend would never disappear entirely, there was a new dignity to his public utterances; although his opponents would still feel the sharpness of his tongue, his general demeanour became one of courtesy and tact. More and more, his discourses took on the aspect of the wise and benevolent school-master; standing at his desk in the House, hands spread before him, patiently enunciating his policies, he had become the voice of sweet reason. Similarly in his addresses to the province at large, he usually took the lofty course and at times sounded almost like the uplifters he professed to detest. No doubt too his new stance of non-partisanship was deliberately assumed and used to excellent political effect. His opponents must have found it infuriating when he exploited the prestige of his office to preach what they regarded as an unabashedly political message. To Ferguson, politics was in large measure applied psychology, a matter of understanding the drift of opinion, and of knowing when and how to intervene to guide it in a particular direction.

Secondly, he asserted, 'a government ... should give leadership and general activity to all that tends to the general advantage of the province...' This seemed even vaguer than the duty to encourage a sound and intelligent public sentiment but in the years ahead what he meant by it became clear enough. Ferguson's attitude towards state intervention was essentially that of the nineteenth century. Governments, he believed, could and should intervene in the life of the province and lend encouragement in a variety of ways to the social and economic activities of society. On the economic side, this could mean the kinds of assistance Charles McCrea held out to the mining community, including free assays, government exploration and surveys, and a degree of regulation in the interest of the health and welfare of the operators. In the field of social policy, it could mean financial assistance to the underprivileged members of society, aid to those who could not help themselves, and even minimum wage legislation for women and children. But with the exception of Hydro, which Ferguson made clear was a special case, provincial support was severely limited. If certain economic enterprises received assistance, it was because they were expected to generate employment and contribute to development which would benefit the province many times over for its limited contribution. Such regulatory legislation as existed was to protect the weak and the helpless. Provincial support in the health and welfare field was directed, with few exceptions, at the destitute members of society and even then it was usually niggardly and offered only as a supplement to private charity and municipal aid. There was little in all this of the tradition of the positive state.

Since Ferguson was above all a practical politician who moved with the currents of the day, one whose understanding of prevailing social arrangements and political attitudes was unexcelled by any other Ontarian, his commitment to the status quo is a commentary on the spirit of the age. Yet with urbanization and industrialization proceeding apace, much in Ontario was changing and as each day passed traditional responses seemed less adequate. In a very real sense, Ferguson was a transitional figure whose career reflected the ironies and ambiguities of a man trapped by time and circumstances. A Tory confronted with upheavals on every side, an enthusiast who placed himself in the van of the demands for progress and development, he loved as well what was familiar and stable in the province's past and worked to carry much of the heritage of the past forward to another day. Most amazing is the extent to which the older, largely nineteenth-century, institutional and ideological structures to which Ferguson was committed remained in place throughout the 1920s. Despite cracks in the edifice, and despite the democratic thrusts which Ferguson partially understood and to some extent embodied, the ideological framework continued to limit purely provincial initiatives and to emphasize individual efforts and local responsibilities. Only the Depression and another world war would sweep away old ideas and practices.

In this spirit, then, the operative word in Ferguson's second credo of government was 'leadership.' The province might initiate certain activities and even provide supervision and a degree of financial assistance. In all normal cases, however, the principal responsibility lay elsewhere. It rested upon the citizenry to be exercised through either self-reliance or, if necessary, private philanthropy, and upon the municipal governments which Ferguson regarded as more closely in touch with the social needs of the local communities than was Queen's Park. The provincial government, he believed, should direct much of its energy to external relations and ensure that provincial rights and, more broadly, Ontario's conception of the national interest, were treated with due respect and proper deference in Ottawa and elsewhere.

'Lastly,' he asserted, 'a government should give efficient administration to the public business of the province.' In the 1920s, as the efficiency expert achieved the status of folk hero, the conviction that modern management techniques and the application of business principles of administration could work miracles affected the public sector almost to the same extent that it held sway in the corporate world. There is some irony in the fact that it was the old politico of the timber scandal who now propounded the gospel of honesty and efficiency but it was also appropriate. Ferguson had always been impressed by the 'captains of industry' who tamed the new technology and applied innovative techniques of management to the administration of vast and far-flung enterprises. Why should not government do the same? Never in awe of the businessmen and always too much the politician ever to think that Queen's Park could be run as just another big business, he believed nonetheless that government had much to learn from the corporate moguls. In this tradition were new audit procedures and other administrative changes while the creation of key positions of supervision and control in the bureaucracy, such as a financial comptroller and a supervisor of settlement, brought the age of the expert to Queen's Park. The application of technology to the provincial services through the expansion of the Motion Picture Bureau, the founding of a Provincial Air Service, and experimental techniques in the Department of Education would extend governmental influence to new areas of the province. Most of all, the emphasis on administration rather than legislation reflected a faith in the abilities of bureaucrats and professionals to recognize and meet the needs of the province better than the elected member. It was no accident that this process was started so firmly and carried so far by Howard Ferguson. He viewed the Tories as the governmental party and, appropriately, when he appealed for a new mandate in 1926, his party's principal piece of campaign propaganda bore the title, 'Business Methods in Public Administration.'

Such an approach downgraded the role of the private member and of the House. So too did the size and docile nature of the Ferguson majorities. With so much power concentrated in the Premier, the structure assumed elements of a presidential system. Drury tried in his day to expand the role of the back-bencher and to take some of the load of responsibility off the cabinet; Ferguson did the opposite. The seven sessions of the House held under his premiership averaged only 44 days and he rushed business through with despatch to try to wrap things up each year by Easter.[22] Controversial matters, such as a redistribution of seats in 1925, would be dealt with in the final few days. Important policy decisions which did not need legislative approval would almost always be made when the House was not in session. There was an obvious and calculated political purpose in all of this. Ferguson was determined to give controversial business as low a political profile as possible; opposition to some of his educational and liquor policies could come as easily from his back-benchers as from the opposition groups. With the House in session, there was always a focus for agitation and so, to limit dissent, he deprived it of a forum.

Just as the role of the private member was restricted, similarly few of his ministers would make an important move without consulting him. This does not seem to have caused friction; he was tactful and most ministers were happy to draw on his wide experience. In any case, they had little choice. A friendly reporter present when James Lyons was about to announce the establishment of the Provincial Air Service recalls that everything was ready but it was five o'clock and the press release had not been prepared. Lyons was about to send his secretary home when Ferguson intervened. 'Keep her,' he said, 'it goes out tonight.'[23] The ministers grew accustomed to working with a premier who often seemed to know more about their departments than they did.

Despite his new image of statesman and his effort to speak to the province above the din of party politics, he was still, finally, the high-handed partisan alert to the main chance, willing to kick an opponent when he was down if political advantage could be gained. Personally he remained the most affable of men; when young Farquhar Oliver stumbled badly during his maiden speech, it was Ferguson who restrained the hecklers and prompted the novice member.[24] Such courtesies were not extended to the opposition parties as such. Although the UFO after the 1923 election had elected more members than the Liberals, Ferguson arbitrarily refused to accept them as the official opposition and stated that W.E.N. Sinclair, whom the Liberals had just selected as their temporary and House leader, would be recognized as leader of the opposition. There was not a shred of justification for such a move; facetiously and cynically, he claimed he was merely recognizing the official statement of the UFO that it was out of politics. Manning Doherty, the new leader of the parliamentary group, was outraged but Ferguson turned a deaf ear to his protests. Finally the Speaker ruled that Doherty was entitled to the $1500 specified by statute for the leader of a group of 15 or more members. The Liberals under Sinclair, who disliked third parties as much as Ferguson, readily agreed to the outrageous manoeuvre. If there had ever been any doubt, it was now certain that the old order had returned with a vengeance to the political life of Ontario.

Normalcy was restored to Ontario but it did not necessarily mean reaction. Undeniably Conservatism in the 1920s under Ferguson's guiding genius would not be 'progressive' as it had been in Whitney's days. Circumstances had altered, needs were different, old issues had matured and new appeared. The 1920s had a tempo all their own; under Ferguson the Tories would march to the beat of the day. Their style would be aggressively political; their thrust would be towards free enterprise and economic development; their social program would depend largely on circumstances as they unfolded. Most of all, it would be the needs of the province and the demands of the whole spectrum of regional, class, and economic interests which would determine government policy. Ferguson undeniably was a strong-minded leader with a full complement of theories and prejudices, but finally he was a professional whose decisions were a response to the realities of brokerage politics as they emerged through the sieve of Tory ideology. Because he was that kind of politician, the Tory program in the 1920s embodied in a very real way the political wisdom of the province as a whole.

The storm centre of Ferguson's first administration was the liquor issue. The elation of the wets with the return of the Tories to power proved premature. The new Premier seemed content to remain an observer of the struggle between the prohibitionists and the liquor trade while Attorney-General Nickle vigorously enforced the OTA and presented amendments to improve and tighten the province's dry legislation. In an effort to suppress bootleg drug stores, pharmacists filling liquor prescriptions were required to obtain a permit from the License Board; the Board began to keep a record of the number of six-ounce prescriptions issued by doctors; the Board of Health was empowered to analyze patent medicines, which were enjoying a remarkable popularity; the provincial police were given authority to arrest without warrant those suspected of liquor offences; and vehicles engaged in bootlegging were made subject to confiscation.[25] This was not the policy which some of the more vocal supporters of the new administration had anticipated and the letters of thanks which Nickle received came from the ranks of the drys.

'If there was any reason under the sun why this government succeeded at the last election,' muttered Jim McCausland, the Tory member for Southwest Toronto, 'it was because the people wanted a change in the OTA.' Lawlessness and hypocrisy were spreading and local option and government control were the only answers. Surely, McCausland insisted, the rules of democracy decreed that the small towns should not be allowed to dictate to Toronto.[26]

Such arguments had become the stock-in-trade of the wets. With Quebec and British Columbia enriching themselves with new tax revenues and an opulent traffic in American tourists and with Manitoba and Alberta in 1923 also abandoning the dry camp, the pressure on Ontario mounted. The government control solution possessed a remarkable appeal and Ferguson's agents were keeping a close watch on western developments. The problem, in Ferguson's mind, remained primarily political. With wet strength waxing across the country and with city members like F.W. Wilson, McCausland, and, within his own cabinet, Godfrey, McCrea, and Leeming Carr increasingly impatient, Ferguson realized that the possibility of a split in Tory ranks was growing. Those like Earl Rowe and T.L. Kennedy who represented rural constituencies remained insistent that any move away from prohibition would court disaster in their part of the province. Of course the fact that the division was by no means entirely along rural-urban lines complicated matters and Ferguson also knew that if he moved in a wet direction both the Farmers and Liberals would be in an excellent position to appeal to a host of dry Tories. He was still haunted by what had happened to William Hearst. If anything was certain, it was that he would take every precaution and would move only when all the risks had been carefully weighed and assessed. In the meantime, his task was to manage the unruly element within his own ranks. When a confrontation seemed in the making at the party's November 1923 annual meeting, he defused it by repeating with new emphasis his pledge that a plebiscite would be held as soon as it was desired by a sufficient body of opinion. This of course hardly put the quietus to public agitation.

The 1924 throne speech revealed the lengths to which he was prepared to go to keep his options open. A bill, the Lieutenant-Governor announced, would be presented to the House to authorize the cabinet to hold a liquor plebiscite and to determine both date and questions as it saw fit. Infuriated temperance men immediately charged that Ferguson was about to pay off his election debts to the liquor interests. When the OTA Plebiscite Enabling Bill was presented, it even gave the cabinet blanket power to decide whether more than one vote should be necessary. Nothing else that session caused such a stir. The eyes of the province were on the House, galleries were packed, and hundreds turned away. Although Tory ranks held, the Liberals presented their usual sorry spectacle with the Franco-Ontarian members refusing to follow the party line. A frustrated Raney asked 'when do we come to the end of referenda and plebiscites and settle down to a fixed condition of things?' Bill Sinclair commented that he counted thirty-two alleys up which the government might go in a single subsection. 'Outrageous and unprecedented' spluttered Raney. Certainly Ferguson was allowing for all possible contingencies. Unmoved by broadsides from the pulpits of the province, he used his majority to 'steamroller' through what Raney aptly described as 'a blank and irrevocable power of attorney for the government to do what it pleases.'[27] Ferguson countered that it was a return to responsible government and intimated that a vote would be taken within a year and it would be a plebiscite, not a referendum. Again this increased his own latitude but the event would also prove that, unwittingly, he was setting a trap for himself.

Still, he could now act when and as he wanted and if the House was not in session the drys in all parties, including his own, would be at a considerable disadvantage. Then, on 17 July, forty-five of sixty provincial constituencies in Saskatchewan opted for government control and the wets won convincingly even in rural parts of the province. The following day, Ferguson announced that there would be a plebiscite in Ontario on 23 October.

As these events unfolded, there can be little doubt that Ferguson expected that his own task would be facilitated by a resounding wet victory. With his ear to the ground, he knew that the great dry machine which once had swept all before it was in a state of imposing disarray. The committee under the Reverend A.S. Grant which had waged the 1919 referendum campaign instead of disbanding had set itself up in opposition to the Ontario Branch of the Dominion Alliance. Charging that the extremism of Alliance secretary Ben Spence was damaging the dry cause, the Grant group refused to co-operate with the Alliance and the result had been duplication of effort in the 1921 importation campaign and subsequent financial problems. Thus when the Alliance, deeply in debt, launched a 'special Relief Fund' in 1922, it was rebuffed by one of its most reliable supporters, Sir Joseph Flavelle, who refused to provide funds for two groups which could not act in harmony.[28]

Yet financial problems and internal feuds were less the cause than the consequence of the dry malaise. Once they had attained their objective, and particularly after the 1921 plebiscite had resulted in ending importation from outside the province, the drys had been placed on the defensive. Although there were still many loopholes in Ontario's sumptuary legislation, after 1921 it had become annoyingly difficult for the great middle class to get its alcohol. Many who supported prohibition because it would close the public bars were those who could afford to order in quantity, stock their cellars, and drink in the comfort of their homes. These people had not really counted on being unable to keep a good supply on hand for themselves. Typical was that examplar of middle-class values, Mackenzie King, who on 18 April 1921 told his diary, 'this morning I voted against the importation of Liquor ... learned tonight the referendum had been carried ... but Ottawa and several other cities were opposed. The agricultural population is the saving of the nation. By a coincidence the two boxes of whiskey I had asked Lemieux to purchase for me in Montreal came today.' Few Ontarians could aspire to the levels of hypocrisy achieved by Mackenzie King, but in increasing numbers they grumbled about the amount of bootlegging and evasion of the law which existed on every hand.

As important as the shifting mood of the province was the failure of the drys to capitalize on their victory. Although brilliant organization and unceasing propaganda had been major elements in the dry success, the attitude now seemed to be that the millennium had arrived and was meant to be enjoyed. Prohibition had come to stay, E.C. Drury proclaimed in 1921, and there was no danger of backsliding. In 1924 T.A. Moore of the Methodist Church lamented that the drys had abandoned their propaganda effort just when the other side had started to work harder than ever and 'now we have to overcome our former neglect and to defeat three years of propaganda in about three weeks.' A colleague complained to Moore that 'too many of our leaders are old war horses who are taking things for granted.'[29]

Shortly before the 1923 provincial election, dry leaders had attempted to mend fences. Ben Spence was removed from his post of secretary of the Alliance and the reunification of the temperance forces was heralded by the foundation of a new organization which at a January 1924 meeting was given the name Ontario Prohibition Union. It was some time, however, before the new body could function effectively and as late as 20 July George Warburton, still one of the ablest of dry leaders, was struggling to have it 'recognized as the one unifying organization in the province.'[30] By this time, the ill-prepared Prohibition Union was plunged into the most desperate encounter in the history of the movement, the 1924 plebiscite. Although this was a do-or-die effort, the drys were unable to reach any agreement on strategy, with Warburton arguing that 'the key to the situation this time is the cities' while others wanted to expend their energies in an effort to buttress their rural fortresses.[31] Nor were they able to surmount organizational weaknesses. Only in September, after several others had declined the job, did George Nicholson of Cochrane agree to serve as campaign chairman and Nicholson allowed his business activities to keep him out of the province during much of the critical month before the vote. The extent of dry confusion was highlighted by the fact that the man who was named campaign treasurer learned of his appointment only by a press account in late September and then declined to accept the position. T.A. Moore was pressed into service as campaign director and much of the work fell on his overburdened shoulders. Members of the campaign committee estimated their costs at $125,000, a figure Moore described as 'many thousands less than any previous campaign' yet, even so, only $100,000 was raised and of this some $15,000 remained unspent.[32]

In contrast the wets were highly organized and well financed. The prohibitionists were aware of efforts on the part of the so-called Moderation League to reach the foreign-born population of the cities and the substantial Franco-Ontario vote, but they seemed unable to do anything to counter this. As well, the banishment of Ben Spence from a position of influence had not weeded out the extremists, who continued to damage the temperance cause. Most of all, there was W.E. Raney, whose frequent outbursts and charges that Ferguson was a puppet of the liquor interests threatened to alienate thousands of sincere temperance Conservatives. 'The Ferguson organization,' Raney announced 'will be the liquor organization for propaganda purposes and for getting out the vote and if the OTA is not destroyed it will be because the Ferguson influence is not strong enough.'[33] George Warburton feared that Raney's 'ill-timed, unwise and partisan' pronouncements might, if not repudiated, 'drive conservatism into the moderation camp. ... It is not the facts which Mr Raney states as to political debts but the unwisdom of stating them.'[34] Warburton took some comfort from private assurances from Ferguson that the Tory organization would take no part in the campaign and the Premier added that he had also asked cabinet ministers and Tory members to abstain in order to ensure 'an untrammelled opinion from the electorate.'[35]

This did not prevent an incident over what questions were to be put to the voters. Dry spokesmen were unhappy that to the simple question 'Are you in favour of the continuance of the Ontario Temperance Act?' there had been added a second question, 'Are you in favour of the sale as a beverage of beer and spirituous liquor in sealed packages under Government control?' Then, when T.A. Moore privately asked the Attorney-General for a legal opinion on the status of other liquor legislation should the OTA be repealed, Ferguson insisted on answering himself. In a press release he emphasized that under government control there would be 'no return to the bar or sale by glass in any form.' Furious dry leaders believed that Ferguson had attempted to sabotage their cause, but short of an open fight with the Tories, they had no recourse.[36]

There is little doubt that Ferguson was counting on the electorate to take the liquor problem out of his hands. On voting night, a carnival atmosphere existed in cities across Ontario. In Toronto huge crowds thronged the downtown streets. 'The flapper was there in a thousand degrees and a thousand glories, the shopgirl, the home miss, the university student ... and whenever news on the screen was particularly wet, it seemed they all shouted in all keys and clefs together.'[37] By nine o'clock, the wets had pulled into a 60,000 vote lead, five-sixths of that from Toronto, but then, inexorably, old Ontario was heard and the country districts swept back the tide. The final results showed 585,676 in favour of the OTA with 551,645 opposed. Although the narrow majority had been won on the farms and in the small towns of Ontario, such urban communities as Belleville, Brantford, Kingston, Oshawa, Owen Sound, Peterborough, St Thomas, and Woodstock also remained in the dry column. Toronto, Ottawa, and Hamilton, dry in 1919, now went resoundingly wet, as did fourteen other cities.[38] The Ontario Tories were in deep trouble.

Although he stated at once that the government intended to use its best efforts to enforce the OTA, Ferguson knew that the closeness of the vote and the frustration of urban wets would occasion a redoubled agitation. The cry was now for local option. Ferguson had been warned, McCausland told the press, 'to put a local option clause on the ticket. If after this vote local option is not given the people, it will mean political suicide for the Ferguson government.'[39] The day of local option, countered the *Farmers' Sun*, was gone forever.[40] 'Today, with the possibility of ten thousand cars leaving Toronto in the morning and being in Kingston, Lindsay, Collingwood, Owen Sound or Goderich by noon, an intolerable condition would be created.' One dry assured the Premier that he should disregard the large city wet vote because it was 'largely made up by Jews, Foreigners and Roman Catholics,' while in Guelph a disgruntled hotel keeper announced that farm folk were no longer welcome at his establishment.[41] At a ward meeting in Toronto in November, McCausland declared that if Ferguson decided to play the Hearst game, he was headed for a political hearse and other speakers pointed out that every ward of every Toronto constituency had voted wet; unless Ferguson came up with a local option policy, Tory Toronto would be no more.[42] Rumours swept Queen's Park that Leeming Carr was about to resign from the cabinet and that other defections would follow.

For Ferguson the test came at the party's annual meeting in November. Two members, W.G. Weichel of North Waterloo and Frank Wilson of Windsor, presented a government control and local option motion which at once transformed an orderly meeting into a state of turmoil. The premier met the challenge head on. 'There is no office in the gift of the people,' he proclaimed, 'that has sufficient attraction for me to cause me to violate an obligation...' This carried the day and on a standup vote the resolution found only three supporters, with Weichel and Wilson not among them. At once suspicious drys suspected that assurances had been given under the table. This seemed confirmed when Leeming Carr told reporters he was confident that satisfactory steps would be taken at the next session.[43]

For Ferguson, it remained a problem in political management. He analyzed the plebiscite results, compared them to previous ballots, and came to the only possible conclusion: prohibition was irreversibly on the way out. The 1924 majority for the OTA was about a tenth what it had been in 1919 and even on the farm the drys had lost ground. In all but three constituencies throughout the province, the dry vote had dropped. Obviously, many of the same people who voted to banish booze in 1919 had now opted for its return. It is with this fact that the several theories about the causes of prohibition in Ontario must reckon. If large numbers of Ontarians had originally been moved to deny liquor to others because of nativist fears or as part of an effort to reassert their status in a rapidly changing society, they must have reassessed their position in a remarkably short span of years. More likely what was taking place was a change of mood as people realized that all the millennium had achieved was the creation of a new class of criminals and a growing contempt for the law. Ferguson was increasingly concerned about these aspects of the noble experiment which he believed to be seriously damaging to the social fabric of the province.

Still, all his efforts at management seemed to have backfired. The drys, angry at being put through another plebiscite, loudly proclaimed that they had won and that was that. They would denounce the slightest weakening in prohibitory legislation as a betrayal by Ferguson of his pledge to abide by the result. As for the wets, sensing that victory was near, they became more boisterous and demanding than ever. Virtuously insisting that by all the canons of democracy, the rural folk – who, it was said, frequently resorted to stills and home-brew even as they cast their dry ballots – must not be allowed to impose their will on the great cities of Ontario, the urban wets were in no mood meekly to accept such dictation. In the middle, in imminent danger of being crushed, was the clever author of the clever plebiscite legislation which had failed so utterly.

Ever resourceful, Ferguson now employed another ruse. He would keep his pledge to the drys and satisfy some of the wets for a time at least by offering a new brew, non-alcoholic yet thirst-quenching. The throne speech of 1925 announced that legislation would be introduced 'enacting that liquor with an absolute alcoholic content by volume, of more than two and a half per cent, shall be conclusively deemed to be intoxicating...' This was equivalent to 4.4 per cent proof spirits, as opposed to 2.5 per cent currently allowed. Ferguson claimed that experiments, 'laboratorical and otherwise,' had led to the conclusion that 4.4 was non-intoxicating.

How he had convinced his intractable attorney-general to agree to the new policy must remain one of the minor mysteries of Ontario politics. Like many other prohibitionists, Nickle owed his ardour to a tragic experience in his own family. Now he became the most formidable advocate of the new beer, which was promptly dubbed 'Fergie's Foam.' Even Jim McCausland allowed that it would mean 'a palatable glass of beer' and Tom Moore of the T&LC pronounced it what the working man ordered. To Raney, of course, it represented a betrayal which he described as 'the most astounding thing in the history of Canadian politics.' Ben Spence, hewing to the argument that alcohol was a deadly poison, told Ferguson privately that even moderate drinking which did not eventuate in drunkenness would destroy the body and the mind and publicly he proclaimed it 'a booze proposition from beginning to end.' To the *Christian Guardian*, it was 'one of the most barefaced and unpardonable pieces of political apostasy that the history of Canada has yet revealed.' Dissatisfied wets were less vehement but the Moderation League did not disguise its disappointment and Frank Wilson vowed to continue to press for government control.[44]

Ferguson was the target for most of the abuse. Bill Sinclair moved that the legislature 'views with disapproval the direct violation of the pledged word of the Prime Minister...' while the Toronto *Star* held that 'in twenty-four hours Mr Ferguson, who had been represented before his rise to power as a shifty and not too scrupulous politician, lost all the gain in prestige that he had made as a result of a fairly creditable two years as Prime Minister. Hereafter he will be thought of as "the faithless Premier".'[45] During the 4.4 debate, Raney complained to a packed House that Ferguson had been 'four times on the beer wagon, three on the water wagon.'

Nickle led the government defence.[46] Stressing that the plebiscite proved that urban Ontario had lost faith in the OTA, he pointed to the folly of attempting to impose on people something in which they had no faith. In many areas OTA infractions were not taken seriously and enforcement had become a nightmare with convictions virtually impossible to secure. 'In the city of Windsor I think I failed to secure convictions in some fifty odd cases in four or five days.' Another result was the escalating number of prescriptions issued for dispensary liquor. In 1920-1, for example, there were 588,000 prescriptions; in 1923-4, 810,000. On 15 December 1924, the dispensaries did $22,000 worth of business, on 23 December, $55,000, but 'on December 26, the ... epidemic had so subsided that only $11,000 was sold.' The House laughed; Nickle responded that the OTA was debasing the medical profession and the druggists. 'Not one doctor but a score of doctors have come to me and said, "Cannot something be done to lift from our shoulders the iniquity of being the bartenders for the Province of Ontario?" ' Pointing also to native wines, which reached in 1924 a production of 1,912,000 gallons and the existence of 30,000 home brew permits, which could be had for the asking, to say nothing of bush stills and other illegitimate sources, he concluded that prohibition had failed to prohibit. 'The pendulum is swinging against the OTA...,' he asserted, 'and as a temperance man, I am satisfied that unless something is done to relieve the stress, the OTA is doomed to be destroyed.' To assuage the sensibilities of those who remained unconvinced, the 4.4 bill was accompanied by additional legislation tightening enforcement procedures.

As had Nickle, Ferguson presented 4.4 as a prohibition drink; its purpose was to save the temperance movement from itself. Although 4.4 would be sold in a variety of outlets, he assured the House that permission to sell would have to be secured from the Attorney-General's Department, which would insist that vendors be persons of respectable character with suitable premises.[47] He answered his private correspondence with some asperity; the constant attacks on his character and intentions were beginning to nettle. To Irwin Hilliard, a dry Conservative from Morrisburg, he wrote that practically all scientists believed 4.4 to be non-intoxicating. 'I cannot understand,' he told Hilliard, 'why people cannot give the Government credit for having the well-being of the people at heart...' But the vituperation continued. 'Here lies G. Howard Ferguson. The man who gave the people 4.4 beer' was the epitaph suggested by a Toronto Conservative. Many told him he was setting back the cause of human progress. 'You ought to be horsewhipped,' an anonymous writer assured him.[48]

Soon Ferguson's reputation for integrity was in some measure restored. The great day was 21 May. There was excitement across the province and border communities in particular steeled themselves for invasion by hordes of thirsty Americans. But the enthusiasm of early morning had become 'mild interest by sundown and apathy and dejection by closing time.'[49] The Premier had been right; the stuff really was non-intoxicating. At the end of the day, a $100 prize offered by a brewer to the first person to get drunk on 4.4 remained unclaimed. A few days later one Morris Kelly, well known in Toronto police court circles, won newspaper plaudits as the first to achieve intoxication on Fergie's Foam. Six quarts gave him a glow and nine did the trick, but he admitted to having consumed one drink as a starter. 'That stuff? It's suds boy! Just slops! Never again.'[50]

Most Ontarians concurred. Many others objected to the price, usually ten cents a glass compared to five for the old temperance beer. Restaurant and store owners who had gone to considerable expense to renovate in order to be eligible to sell 4.4 watched with dismay as sales fell off. When the government at the beginning of September relaxed its licensing policy, those who had spent large sums unnecessarily were even angrier. Yet from the beginning there was a suspicion that 4.4 was an interim measure to prepare the ground for government control. This view was reinforced when the beer legislation was followed by a major redistribution of legislative seats. Although a committee of the legislature was appointed to consider redistribution, effective control was placed by Ferguson in the reliable hands of George Henry. '...I have been given the rather thankless task,' Henry informed the mayor of Goderich, 'of finding some seven or eight seats in the rural sections of the Province, so that extra representation may be given to the centres which are growing very rapidly.'[51] Redistribution was long overdue and, as Henry pointed out, there were constituencies such as his own with a population of 120,000 while many rural ridings contained only 12,000 or so. Deciding not to disturb northern ridings or to insist on absolute equality between rural and urban seats, he later reported that 'we considered for rural representation a unit of 15,000 or over, and for the cities and suburban centres varying quotas would be found ranging from 30,000 to 40,000...'[52]

Even so, the drys screamed. The bill, presented on the last day of the session, eliminated nine dry seats and added ten wet. 'It is rotten,' declared Ben Spence; 'very undesirable' added J.J. Morrison, 'it is putting power into the hands of people in the congested centres of population, many of whom have no stake in the country,'[53] For the Liberals, Malcolm Lang charged that it was the worst gerrymander the province had ever known and Bill Sinclair promised to challenge it from every stump in Ontario.[54] Yet apart from the way in which the Tories had provided little information to the House Committee which was supposed to be handling redistribution and the fact that it had been jammed through on the last day of the session, there seems to have been little justification for the criticism. Although the opposition complained about the five new seats for 'Hogtown,' the population increases in Toronto and the Yorks, Ottawa, Hamilton, and Windsor justified the changes. Ferguson pointed out that the city of Toronto and county of York with a quarter of Ontario's population still had only a sixth of the total representation. More legitimate were charges that in several cases semi-rural suburbs had been tacked onto city constituencies. The government, E.C. Drury predicted, intended to go to the country on a government control platform and trust to the 'Fergymander' to get them through.[55]

With government revenues from the sale of 4.4 falling off and dissatisfaction again increasing in both dry and wet camps, Ferguson must have been desperately canvassing the possibilities of yet another shift. But with Nickle as Attorney-General, any move to government control would split the cabinet and have incalculable repercussions on the members and in the constituencies. To do nothing was equally unsatisfactory; with the opposition pressing for by-elections to fill several vacancies, the situation seemed impossible. 'If ever a government got into difficulties through lack of courage and straightforwardness,' sermonized the *Star*, 'it is the Ferguson government in connection with the liquor problem. The Premier's policy that was to please everybody has satisfied nobody.'[56]

The year 1926 was ushered in with widespread gestures of disrespect for the OTA. Liquor flowed freely at Toronto hotels, newspapers carried rumours of 'orgies,' and Ben Spence pronounced it all 'an act of treason to the state.' A weary Attorney-General's Department began a new round of investigations. One straw in the wind was the bull market which developed for hotel and club properties. Yet the throne speech said nothing. At a Tory caucus on 23 February, Ferguson apparently directed his ministers to stay in the background and let the back-benchers fight it out among themselves. Almost daily the press printed rumours that a plebiscite would be held on government control, that the government intended to present legislation, or that Ferguson would call a snap election. The *Star* charged that the brewers and distillers had made massive contributions to the Tory campaign fund in 1923 and were threatening to cut the party off without a penny unless government control was brought in. Raney chose this moment to introduce a private bill to prohibit campaign contributions from brewers, distillers, hotel keepers, public contractors, and public lessees. Ferguson warmly denied that a penny of liquor money had gone to his 1923 campaign. And, as usual, private members of all parties tried their hand and presented a variety of bills sufficient to float the biggest cocktail party in town.

During these efforts all parties suffered breakdowns in party solidarity; the Liberals fared worst. When J.C. Brackin, the brilliant Liberal lawyer from West Kent, introduced a government control bill, the Liberals split up the middle, five for, six against, while four Tories also supported it. Ferguson was usually able to handle such efforts easily enough, managing, for example, to have a similar bill introduced by Toronto Conservative J.A. Currie declared out of order. But he also found it useful to listen to the ongoing debate in the House and out of it. On the Currie bill, for example, wet speakers emphasized that every province with government control had a balanced budget and had experienced an influx of tourists. The point was made with equal emphasis that government control did not mean a return to the open bar but was a more effective means of coping with the liquor problem. The more such arguments were aired, the easier it would be for Ferguson when he finally decided to move. When the 1925 budget appeared with a $5 million dollar deficit, the province's seventh in a row, speculation increased that government control would be presented as the only means by which Ontario could achieve solvency. Liberal financial critic Harold Fisher suggested the Tories might be deliberately piling up deficits to give Ferguson an excuse to call a 'booze or bankruptcy' election.[57]

Close observers would have noticed that Tory wets were becoming less vociferous than they had been for some time. In late March, for example, when Frank Wilson presented a wet motion at the annual association meeting, he failed even to find a seconder. Colonel Currie, who had acquired a recent interest in a distillery, actually urged Wilson to withdraw his motion in order to avoid embarrassing the Premier. Obviously, assurances had been given yet publicly

Ferguson said not a word. In April the new Progressive party, formed out of some of the remnants of the UFO, held its first annual meeting and prohibition emerged as its distinguishing feature. On 14 May, the new United Church vowed it would support only drys in a provincial election and some of the other Protestant churches felt as strongly.[58]

For a while, the dry forces seemed to be rallying and there were reports that Ferguson had reassessed the situation and was about to throw off his party's wet wing. Others said he had decided to appoint a royal commission which would report after an election. No rumour seemed too wild to believe. By the summer and early fall of 1926, prohibition had crowded out all other issues from the Ontario political stage.

9

Power to the Provinces

In the panorama of Canadian history, the 1920s is viewed as the decade in which the balance of power in the Canadian Confederation shifted dramatically in favour of the provinces. The story, a familiar one, is told to best effect in the 1940 report of the Royal Commission on Dominion-Provincial Relations. 'The national integration (achieved through wheat), which tied the country together by East-West bonds of trade and opportunity was weakened,' the Rowell-Sirois Commissioners asserted, 'as Central Canada and British Columbia felt the direct and competing tug of export demand on their regional resources. New economic frontiers, the exploitation of which was of primary interest to Ontario and Quebec, developed on the pre-Cambrian Shield, – where water power, base metals and pulp and paper came into their own...' Thus, the Commissioners argued, the importance of a national economic integration for some regions declined. With the opening of the west fully accomplished and the railway lines built and overbuilt, 'no obvious and pressing challenge to action presented itself in the federal sphere in this period.'[1] As well, the burden of war debt, the cost of railway nationalization, and the regional splintering of the national political system as reflected in the 1921 election were further barriers to new federal initiatives. In any case, burgeoning urbanization and the onrush of the automobile age created demands for expensive new programs which had to be met primarily by the provinces. Finally, even if the national government had determined on a program of social and economic action, the Judicial Committee of the Privy Council in a series of decisions, most notably the Board of Commerce case of 1922 and Toronto Electric Commissioners v Snider, 1925, blocked the way and in continuance of the historical trend further narrowed the sphere of federal jurisdiction. All this placed new burdens on the hard-pressed provincial fiscal systems. The total revenues of the provinces in 1930, the Rowell-Sirois *Report* noted, were nearly double those of 1921, but more than two-thirds of this increase came from three new taxes, motor vehicle licences, gasoline, and liquor.[2] Thus the events of the decade not only exacerbated an often harmful regionalism but left the provinces dependent on an uncertain and inadequate tax base.

In the Rowell-Sirois scenario, the villains of the piece were the powerful provincial premiers, particularly Howard Ferguson and Alexandre Taschereau, whose determined provincialism had contributed largely to the erosion of federal powers. Leading members of the Commission, and none more than J.W. Dafoe, seemed to regard the Ontario and Quebec premiers as virtual wreckers of Confederation. Yet the extension of provincial authority can hardly be attributed merely to the belligerence of the Fergusons and the Taschereaus or even to the socio-economic circumstances of the day, as the Commissioners also hinted. Nor was it true that the federal government under Mackenzie King's cautious leadership, obsessed by the burden of the national debt, had simply abdicated its responsibilities and left the field to the provinces by default.

Ontario's experience demonstrated that this was anything but the case. In a multitude of matters, some of which he deemed of vital significance to Ontario, Ferguson found his way blocked by a federal administration determined to have its own way. The national government fought stubbornly for its constitutional primacy on economic issues ranging from the regulation of business activity to the ownership of electrical power in navigable streams. By contrast, in the field of social policy the game was shaped by different imperatives and there the very absence of new federal programs was a reflection of deliberate federal decisions. The King administration's withdrawal from many of the shared-cost programs initiated by the Union Government was greatly regretted by the Ontario government. Ferguson often invited federal initiatives in the social policy field and when Ottawa did little to assist the unemployed, alleging that this was not a federal responsibility, he pointedly remarked that 'Parliament surely is supreme and can vote public moneys for any purpose it may deem proper.'[3] Although the spending power and the taxing power remained potent instruments of national policy, the King Liberals for the most part refused to act. Usually willing to do battle for abstract constitutional rights, Mackenzie King in the 1920s seldom followed through with constructive social reforms. Yet while King was more ready to fight for principles than for programs, some of the federal departments were less reticent; there is no doubt that if the courts had been more accommodating or the provinces less vigilant, the Dominion even under King's hesitant leadership would have cut a far more positive figure on the Canadian stage.

There was, after all, another side to the coin. Undeniably Howard Ferguson was an aggressive defender of provincial rights. In this role he developed a strategy which drew to some extent on the work of his predecessors but which under him hardened into a fighting credo. When federal politicians, stymied by judicial decisions, talked of new procedures for constitutional amendment, Ferguson sprang forward to defend the status quo; when the same politicians suggested that the Supreme Court of Canada replace the Privy Council as the final court of appeal, Ferguson muttered of veiled treason to the Empire. Most of all, there was the compact theory. Of course the concept that Confederation was a compact among the provinces whose terms could be altered only with provincial consent was 'old hat'; it had been used by Blake, Mowat, and many others. In Ferguson's hands it developed into rigid dogma backed by all the political power at his command. Despite the extent of that power, all these efforts would succeed only if Ferguson was able to rally behind him the support of other powerful provincial groups. It was to Quebec that he turned most frequently and it was in Taschereau that he found his staunchest ally.

Despite the vigour with which these two promoted the provincial cause, neither Ontario nor Quebec in the 1920s aggressively demanded major new rights – in striking contrast to that other period of expansive provincialism, the 1960s. And Ferguson's only truly belligerent effort was blocked by none other than the JCPC. In 1924 Attorney-General Nickle sponsored a Judicature Act which reorganized the High Court of Ontario in an effort to increase efficiency by giving the province the right to make changes in the responsibilities of the judges and to name the chiefs of the several divisions. One immediate effect was the elimination of the position of Chief Justice of Second Divisional Court, a post occupied by Frank Latchford. The opposition charged that this was Ferguson's revenge on one of the Timber Commissioners, and in a letter asking Justice Minister Ernest Lapointe to exercise the power of disallowance, Liberal member Harold Fisher insisted that Ferguson was 'not asserting any important provincial right. All he is doing is grasping at patronage...' Latchford himself described the bill as Ferguson's attempt to 'revenge himself as he threatened more than once, upon me for having ... exposed some of his nefarious dealings...'[4] In March 1925 Ontario's effort to fish in troubled waters was held by the JCPC to be *ultra vires*.

There were few other instances of such blatant Ontario aggression. More typical was a clash which occurred in 1924 when Ernest Lapointe brought forward to the House of Commons a resolution addressed to the Imperial Parliament requesting an amendment to the BNA Act regarding Canadian extra-territorial rights. Deputy Attorney-General E.W. Bayly at once warned Nickle that this move was 'apt to be the basis of encroachment upon matters of legislation unquestionably given to the Provinces' and he pointed to 'the recent "antics" of Dominion Departments in general and of the Department of Insurance in particular, in matters of legislation trenching upon provincial fields of jurisdiction.' Ottawa, Bayly recognized, did possess 'the initiative for securing amendments' to the BNA Act, but since that Act had originally been a product of the provinces, Parliament 'should not in fairness act without the sanction of the Provinces...'[5] Nickle needed little urging and he hastened to ask Lapointe to amend the resolution to include the words, 'otherwise within its competence' after 'Canada.'[6] To make certain that no one missed the point, Ferguson in a speech at Prescott described the extraterritorial resolution as 'a breach of faith with the provinces.' Confederation, he reiterated, 'was the result of certain compromises between the provinces entering into it' and amendments should not be made 'without the consent of the provinces ... any amendment which would extend the authority of the Dominion might easily be a serious menace to our national unity.'[7] In the event, Lapointe quietly agreed to the change suggested by Nickle.

This incident had a speedy resolution. More typical was the exhausting struggle over regulation of insurance companies. It was this discreditable dispute which Bayly had in mind when he referred to the 'antics' of some Dominion departments. From the 1870s, Dominion and provincial governments had both legislated in the field but the conflict between the two jurisdictions reached its peak only in the 1920s. When the Privy Council in the Reciprocal Insurers' case, 1924, struck down what it interpreted as the federal effort to make use of its jurisdiction over the criminal law to regulate the insurance business, the Dominion presented new legislation and the struggle continued. At last a furious Howard Ferguson told Mackenzie King that his government's manoeuvres constituted 'a third attempt on the part of the Dominion to assert its jurisdiction to regulate the business of insurance' and that 'Dominion legislation on this subject-matter has each time been declared *ultra vires* by the Privy Council...'[8] Ferguson's angry exchanges with King continued for some time and finally he warned the Prime Minister that 'this is an issue which transcends politics ... its settlement should not turn on the advice or viewpoint of one Deputy Minister or another Deputy Minister...'[9] When one disputed section of federal legislation was proclaimed despite assurances Ontario had received to the contrary, Nickle reacted with indignation to King's suggestion of a meeting, rightly pointing out that the highhanded federal move 'augurs ill' for the utility of such a gathering. The Ontario government, Nickle told George Graham of the federal cabinet, 'resents the affront which it has suffered at the hands of your government' and would 'take all necessary steps in the future, as in the past, to enforce and strengthen its jurisdiction over the business of insurance in the Province.'[10]

The dispute continued. In a decision reported in 1926 under the title *Re Insurance Contracts*, the provincial Supreme Court upheld the Ferguson government's position. The provinces continued to work together through such organizations as the Association of Superintendents of Insurance of the Provinces of Canada in order to achieve common goals. Ottawa, however, all but ignored the court decision and the following year presented new insurance act amendments as though the reference had never taken place. In fact this was typical of federal attitudes and methods. The Ottawa mandarins had little regard for their provincial cousins; undoubtedly too they felt a national responsibility which they believed the provinces could never share or comprehend. And, not least, the jobs of federal bureaucrats were at stake. Ferguson and his colleagues through long and disagreeable experience learned to take such imperialistic attitudes for granted. It was the federal officials who never ceased to be surprised and resentful at what they viewed as the presumptuousness of lower orders of government. The disagreement over the insurance business remained to embitter federal-provincial relations for the rest of the decade and longer.

Most important by far among the provincial rights controversies of the 1920s was the question of the ownership of water power on navigable streams. By the early 1920s it was clear that not even the vast Chippawa project would be able to supply the power needs of Ontario. The two major untapped sources were the Ottawa and St Lawrence rivers; thus, in one of his first official pronouncements, Ferguson voiced the cry, 'On to the St Lawrence.' Ontario, he told an audience of Toronto Tories, faced a power famine so serious that if demand continued to expand at the rate of recent years, there would soon not be a horsepower for sale. 'This government,' he asserted, 'must see to it that if we are in the power business we have power to sell.' Waterpower, he insisted, belonged to the provinces and the Dominion could reserve only what was needed for navigational purposes. If Ottawa was not prepared to embark on the St Lawrence project, it should 'stand aside and let someone else go in.' Ferguson promised that he would press Ontario's case 'until our rights on the St Lawrence are recognized.'[11]

Ferguson's speech brought the issue fully into the public arena. Even the Liberal *Star* warned the federal government against challenging the provincial position by 'taking the untenable position held by Sir John Macdonald...' in his various battles with Mowat.[12] Ferguson's threat was no mere political posturing. At this time the press was reporting with some alarm that the development of northern Ontario was being seriously retarded by power deficiencies while eastern Ontarians were made irritable by high prices and frequent shortages. In a province which lacked coal, industrial development was dependent on a reliable source of hydroelectric energy. Ontario officials, aware of the abundance of electrical power in Quebec, feared that in the 'keen competition in these two adjoining provinces for new industries ... if Ontario has to switch over to steam for primary power ... that Quebec will have a decided advantage with those seeking an industrial location in Central Canada.'[13] Ferguson had to ensure that Ontario possessed a supply of electrical energy adequate to the needs of her people and her industry.

Before the war, Adam Beck had regarded the St Lawrence as the answer to Ontario's future power needs. In 1918 he had submitted a detailed report on the river's power possibilities to the International Joint Commission recommending development in the international section between Morrisburg and Cornwall. The all-Canadian section, of course, would not serve Ontario's purpose since it was entirely within Quebec. When Ferguson came to office, he and Beck conferred over a strategy for St Lawrence development and on 9 January 1924, the Hydro chairman submitted a detailed proposal to the province.[14] There was, however, one hitch. The Beck plan, calling for construction of a dam to the American side, could only be undertaken with the co-operation of the federal government and the American authorities. Two days later, Beck, leading a delegation representing some 350 Ontario municipalities, appeared before Prime Minister King to urge early acceptance of Hydro's proposal. That June, Ferguson passed an order-in-council which permitted Beck to file a formal application for the Morrisburg project with the Department of Railways and Canals. He was determined, he told one correspondent, to secure federal recognition of Ontario's right to develop power on the St Lawrence 'so long as the province does not interfere with the paramount use for navigation purposes' and he intended 'to place the province in a position where its claim is on file and its right in the matter recognized.'[15]

Ferguson probably recognized that he could not hope for speedy approval. He must have suspected that Ottawa would not regard the Morrisburg proposal as separate from the larger question of the St Lawrence Seaway. Just prior to the outbreak of war, the United States had approached Canada about the Seaway and although the war had made such a development impossible, the question was again to the fore. Early in 1919, the United States asked whether the Canadian government was 'now ready' to direct the IJC to investigate and report on the Seaway project; when Borden concurred, a Joint Engineering Board was created to collect data while the IJC held hearings. Despite some opposition, most Americans strongly favoured the project but the IJC reported that, as for Canada, only in Ontario was there general support while there was strong opposition from Quebec interests. Nonetheless, in December 1921 the IJC recommended that the governments of Canada and the United States proceed with the St Lawrence project. The IJC also recommended that power works 'be built, installed, and operated by and at the expense of the country in which they are located.'[16] Most private utility companies, assuming that the Hydro would control power development in the Ontario section, opposed the seaway.

The official American response was to favour the negotiation of a treaty based on the IJC report. Mackenzie King replied that 'having regard to the magnitude of the project and the large outlay of public money involved' it was not 'expedient to deal with this matter at the present time.'[17] Considering the Canadian debt burden, the staggering cost of the project to a country of nine million, and the opposition of powerful interests, particularly in Quebec, on which the Liberals depended to stay in office, King's caution was understandable. When Arthur Meighen, who favoured the seaway, presented the project to the Tory caucus in the summer of 1923, he was amazed to discover that a majority of the Conservative members, apparently alarmed at the country's financial condition, were anything but favourable.[18] But with the Ontario Hydro pressing for action and Ferguson making threatening political noises about Ontario's power shortage, Mackenzie King may have decided that politically it would be expedient to renew negotiations with the United States. In 1924 the US was advised that Canada was prepared to have the Joint Engineering Board reconstituted to conduct further investigations and King also appointed a National Advisory Committee to make recommendations to his government. If King's purpose was delay, he succeeded admirably; the Joint Engineering Board did not report until 1926 and the National Advisory Committee seems to have done virtually nothing for several years.

Unfortunately for Ontario, the federal government appeared unwilling to investigate the Morrisburg proposal in isolation and insisted as well on studying the implications of a power development on future canalization. The several studies by Hydro engineers seem to have shown that from a technical standpoint the use of the water for electrical purposes at Morrisburg would in no way interfere with navigation; much of the delay in approving the provincial application was attributable to the federal government's unwillingness to admit a clear separation between the power and navigational aspects of the question.[19] If Canada should decide at some future date to proceed with the St Lawrence project, the control and sale of the electrical energy generated might well be used to pay for a substantial part of the costs of canalization.

For Ontario this was ominous. If the federal Liberals, possibly in alliance with the private power interests, were able to make power production dependent on navigational improvements, Ontario energy users would be paying an enormous tribute which would do incalculable damage to the province's economy. And it would mean disaster at the polls for any Ontario government which permitted it to happen. If Ottawa was able to use its authority over navigation to assert a claim over whatever electrical energy might be generated on the Ottawa and the St Lawrence, and if it chose to grant power leases to private companies, it might even mean the end of Ontario's great experiment in public ownership. Two such leases had already been granted for development on the Ottawa and if these were acted upon and other grants made, Ontario would no longer control how and when its power resources would be developed and distributed. What was at stake was an empire of unimagined wealth. According to one federal estimate, the installed horsepower in Ontario and Quebec would increase from about four million to eight million in 1945 and capital expenditures on this development would average over $68 million per year. The energy potential on the Ottawa alone was estimated at over one million horsepower. The future not only of Hydro but of Ontario itself was bound up in the outcome of this dispute.[20]

What did the BNA Act say about ownership of water power? By section 108 'the public works and property of each province, enumerated in the third schedule to this Act, shall be the property of Canada.' Among the items so conveyed were 'canals, with lands and water power connected therewith.' As well section 91 gave the federal government control of navigation and shipping. On the other hand, property and civil rights were vested in the provinces and judicial decisions, notably in the case of the Ontario Rivers and Streams Act, made it clear that riparian ownership belonged to the provinces. By the 1920s the conveyance mentioned in section 108 had become the basis for the federal claim that it owned the water power 'available from all the surplus water flowing adjacent to or in the vicinity of' the Carillon, Welland, Trent, and Rideau Canals. It was agreed on all sides that because of these several federal rights, there could be no power development on any navigable stream until a licence was issued by the Department of Railways and Canals. From the Ontario point of view, this was a formality to protect navigation and once federal engineers could stipulate that navigational rights were being safeguarded, approval should follow automatically. Ontario also argued against Ottawa's being allowed to generate and sell additional amounts of water power from these canals, insisting that all the federal government had a right to use was the amount necessary for the functioning of the canals. In fact Ottawa was unwilling to step aside and allow the provinces to control completely such a rich resource yet at the same time it hesitated to challenge the provincial position by a frank statement of the precise extent of the federal claim to power rights on navigable streams.[21]

International complications relating to the broader question of the St Lawrence Seaway gave Ottawa an excuse to postpone indefinitely any decision on Hydro's Morrisburg proposal. Naturally, therefore, Ontario turned to the Ottawa River as an alternative source of the electrical energy it needed so desperately. But here too there were difficulties and again the question of federal and provincial rights to the waterpower on navigable streams stood in the way. In 1894, before waterpower rights had assumed great significance, the Georgian Bay Canal Company, now controlled by the sons of Sir Clifford Sifton, had received a charter from the federal government and although no development had taken place this had been renewed no fewer than fourteen times. More recent rights had been granted to another company for development in the Carillon area where a federally owned dam already existed.

When Howard Ferguson learned that the Quebec-New England Corporation, which claimed to have acquired the holdings at the Carillon of the National Hydro Electric Company, had applied to develop additional power, he wrote Mackenzie King in September 1923 arguing that his would result in the flooding of lands in Ontario and would utilize all the power in that section of the river. Protesting against any federal action being taken before Ontario 'has ample opportunity to look carefully into the situation,' he made a claim of enormous importance. 'Ontario,' he told King, 'does not concede that the Dominion lease on which the present application is founded conveys to the lessees any right to use the surplus waters of the Ottawa River. So far as the waterpower is situated within the boundaries of this Province we claim the right to apply such conditions and rentals to the development as may be deemed to be in the interests of the people of Ontario.'[22]

In reply, James Robb, Acting Minister of Railways and Canals, stated merely that no advance had been made towards granting the application. No argument was made on the great principles involved.[23] Then, in April 1925, Ferguson learned that the same company had received a lease for power rights at Carillon from Quebec and had applied to Ottawa for an export permit. 'I again desire,' Ferguson told King, '...to make protest against the issuance by the Department of Railways and Canals of the above or any further leases or permits without first securing the consent of the Province of Ontario...'[24] King referred Ferguson's letter to Justice Minister Lapointe, who took the view that any power production at Carillon would result from works erected for the improvement of navigation and that 'any interest which the Province may have in the matter is of a limited character, dependent possibly upon the ownership of lands in the bed of the river or within the area to be flooded.' King therefore replied to Ferguson that any power production would be incidental to navigational improvements and while he would welcome representations from Ontario, 'it is impossible for the Government of Canada to recognize any right on the part of the Province to control its action in the exercise of its recognized constitutional powers.'[25]

This was disturbing. It caused the Ontario lawyers much anguish. What was Ottawa claiming? What were the intentions of the federal government? Was Ottawa seriously considering the possibility of using its undoubted authority over navigation to lay claim to all the power that might be developed on the Ottawa and the St Lawrence? Was Mackenzie King a prisoner of the Quebec bloc and the private power interests? No one in Ontario really knew. The National Advisory Committee was a model of inactivity while the private interests at the Carillon and the Siftons with their Georgian Bay Canal charter continued to play the game close to the vest. Probably they wished to avoid a direct legal challenge to their rights by the Ontario Hydro or a political counter-offensive by Ferguson – yet in these circumstances, with rival interests and hostile governments manoeuvering for position, the game became intensely political. Ferguson, Taschereau, King, and the private power barons were playing for the highest of stakes.

In the meantime, while hoping that Ontario's urgent need for power might force King to make an early decision on the province's Morrisburg application, Ferguson and the Hydro looked for other sources of power. In February 1925, Ferguson told Minister of the Interior Charles Stewart that Ontario was considering diverting an estimated 3000 cfs of Albany River water from Hudson Bay into the Great Lakes system and he requested some assurance that this water would 'be treated as being exclusively the property of the Province...' After taking the matter to cabinet, Stewart assured Ferguson that in any international negotiations, the

Albany water would be regarded as exclusively Canadian. Yet 'the project itself will necessarily have to be submitted to this Government for consideration under the Navigable Waters Protection Act...'[26]

Temporarily aground on the Albany, Ferguson turned to the Niagara. This time much of the negotiating for Ontario was done by Charles Magrath, the distinguished chairman of the Canadian section of the IJC. Adam Beck had died in 1925 and after much persuasion the able and experienced Magrath agreed to be his successor. Ferguson always demonstrated a knack for getting the right man to agree to serve the province; he could have found no one more knowledgeable on water power matters than Magrath. Now in a series of meetings with Stewart and with George Graham, the Minister of Railways and Canals, Magrath drove home the seriousness of Ontario's power problems, emphasizing too that a proposed arrangement by which Ontario and New York state would divide an additional 20,000 cfs from the Niagara would largely satisfy Ontario needs for another three years. Ferguson persisted as well, telling Stewart that conditions in the industrial area of southern Ontario had 'reached an acute stage' which demanded immediate action.[27] He outlined in detail the kind of agreement he hoped Ottawa would sign with the United States as an interim arrangement pending fuller investigation and new treaty arrangements. Stewart proved receptive as was Graham who advised King that giving Ontario what it wanted at Niagara would 'in a large measure, protect us from the political attack Premier Ferguson is making, on account of his inability to procure from the Dominion Government the right to proceed with the development of the St Lawrence.'[28] Reeling from their October 1925 election losses in Ontario, the King Liberals proved more willing to recognize the urgency of the province's power needs. Unfortunately, negotiations with the United States dragged on; finally, years later, the American Senate rejected the Niagara treaty. Ontario's search for new power sources continued.

So too did the province's effort to protect its legal and constitutional position. For Ferguson this held true whether it was King Liberals or federal Tories who were threatening provincial rights. In the early 1920s the Meighen government had passed legislation regulating Lake of the Woods waters. In 1925 Ferguson pressed for repeal of this legislation and an embarrassed Arthur Meighen asked him to desist because Mackenzie King 'will be turning somersaults if he is enabled to announce that the Ontario Government agrees with him and is against my views.' Ferguson replied bluntly that the rights of the province were involved and 'the Government here feels that we should not be placed in the position of having to contend for the Provincial sovereignty against legislation passed by our friends at Ottawa.'[29]

While the province's hands were not entirely tied in the search for new energy sources and streams totally within the province such as the Nipigon River in northern Ontario could be exploited more fully, such palliatives did not address themselves to the massive needs of the province's industrial and urban heartland. At the same time, there were other dangers. When Ferguson learned that the Dominion Power and Transmission Company which served Hamilton was hoping to receive more power from the Welland Canal, he urged that the province be given ample opportunity to make representations. Again he reminded King of 'the well-established rights of the Province to the surplus waters on navigable streams' and was pleased to hear from King that the federal government had no plans to enlarge the right which the Company had to divert water.[30]

A few weeks later in a show of force, the Ontario legislature passed a motion, presented by Ferguson in an address the Toronto *Star* described as 'most warlike,' and seconded by the Liberal leader, protesting against the large quantities of water the Sanitary District of Chicago was abstracting from the Great Lakes system and diverting to the Gulf of Mexico. The Chicago water steal, as it was known in the 1920s, moved many Canadians to fury and was a fertile source of anti-American feeling. Ontarians had long believed that the federal government had not been vigorous enough in protesting to the American government against what they regarded as an arrogant disregard of international treaty obligations. Now, unanimously, to loud thumping of desks, the Ontario legislators made known their displeasure and urged Ottawa to action.[31]

This was all very well but in truth little progress was being made by the Hydro on either the Ottawa or the St Lawrence and time was running out. Adam Beck had talked boldly of building steam plants but this was an expensive expedient and at Beck's death virtually nothing had been done. Ferguson knew enough of Mackenzie King's methods to be suspicious of the Liberal leader's delaying tactics. Because the political pitfalls involved in any major St Lawrence development were so substantial, King was unlikely to move until the pressures became compelling and then he would be entirely capable of attempting to make power users pay the cost of the navigation project. In July 1926 Ferguson told Frank Keefer, the Port Arthur MPP who acted as a watchdog for the province on St Lawrence matters, that anti-Hydro interests were 'pressing to have power and navigation linked together in the consideration of the power scheme, because they realize it means delay.'[32] He believed it would be years before a proper ship channel would be constructed to the sea and 'for this reason I am pushing the power project, and I do not propose, if I can help it, to allow it to be hitched up with the navigation so the waterways development will become a condition of the power development.'

These were bold words but there were powerful forces to be contended with. If Ferguson and Hydro were to achieve their purposes, they would need help. It was to Quebec that Ferguson turned. The sister province was equally interested in challenging any federal claim to control the water power on navigable streams. The two existing federal grants on the Ottawa represented as much a threat to Quebec interests as they did to those of Ontario. Likely too,

Taschereau feared that Ottawa might negotiate a St Lawrence treaty with the United States which would involve the construction of federal power plants and the use of energy generated thereby to pay part of the cost of canalization.

Tragically, standing in the way of Quebec-Ontario co-operation was the old grievance of Regulation 17. Quebecers felt as strongly as ever that Ontario was trampling on the rights of the French language and from their very first meetings Taschereau pressed Ferguson to grant concessions to Ontario's French minority.[33] Until Ontario took some action on the schools question, it would be difficult to achieve co-operation on other matters.

In any case, the position of the two provinces on electrical energy matters for a while seemed so far apart as to all but preclude an alliance. Quebec remained the bastion of the private power companies against which the Ontario Hydro had campaigned for so long. As well, Montreal business interests constituted a powerful lobby against the St Lawrence Seaway. Most important of all, perhaps, Quebec was well supplied with electrical energy largely through streams flowing into the St Lawrence and felt no immediate need to tap either the St Lawrence itself or the Ottawa. Such rivers as the Gatineau remained largely untouched and the province could hardly have been enthusiastic about new developments, on the Ottawa for example, which would provide power which was not needed in Quebec but would serve to increase Ontario's ability to compete for new industries.

Far from an alliance being in existence, Ferguson was long suspicious of the Quebec influence on the energy situation. In March 1924 he heard rumours of a new federal charter being requested by an American group to build a canal though a portion of the St Lawrence and up the Ottawa River, with the power development entirely in Quebec. He promised Meighen that if this went ahead, 'there will be the devil of a row in Ontario over it.' Ferguson believed that 'there is an avowed purpose on the part of the Province of Quebec, through its Prime Minister and some of his political associates,' to prevent the approval of the Morrisburg development which was so vital to Ontario. Their opposition, he considered, was 'actuated by purely political motives. If it is their determination to prevent Ontario getting the benefit of the power entirely within our own Province on the St Lawrence, I intend to have something to say about the activities of the Quebec Government at Ottawa.'[34]

Ferguson's resentment may have been fuelled by the failure of Hydro's efforts to tap for Ontario's benefit the power surplus which existed in Quebec. As early as November 1923 Adam Beck had concluded that 'a friendly arrangement with Quebec to take all its surplus power...' would be vastly preferable to the construction of steam plants.[35] In December 1924, Hydro met with the Hull Power Company but no agreement was reached. There were other efforts at negotiation that year between Beck and private companies in Quebec but all broke down over price.[36]

The portents did not improve when Howard Ferguson during a January 1925 'bonne entente' visit to Quebec launched a defence of Regulation 17 and was warmly attacked by some of the French-language press for his effort. His remarks seemed so contrary to the spirit of the occasion that there were derisive suggestions that he must have partaken too freely of Quebec wines, to which he was 'unaccustomed.' Yet the two premiers used the meeting for a frank exchange of views and Taschereau later assured Ferguson that 'we have too many interests in common ... not to become closely united in community of ideas and unity of action.'[37] A few weeks later Ferguson announced the appointment of a commission to investigate the problem of the French language in the schools of Ontario; presumably a private understanding existed with the Quebec premier. Indeed Taschereau later hinted that he had insisted on such assurances before negotiations on the power question were allowed to proceed.[38] And Liberal organizer Andrew Haydon assured Mackenzie King that the Regulation 17 settlement was undoubtedly a quid pro quo.[39]

If a Ferguson-Taschereau axis became a reality in 1925, the promise of an accommodation on Regulation 17 was only one factor. Quebec, after all, did possess surplus power and Taschereau, fearful of King's intentions on the St Lawrence, had taken a position unalterably opposed to export of electrical energy to the United States. That left Ontario as a possible market. With Quebec interests still violently opposed to the St Lawrence Seaway, it would be useful to find some way to divert the Ontario government from continuing to press for its development. If Quebec agreed to supply Ontario with cheap power, there would be less enthusiasm in Ontario for the Seaway. Ferguson, always suspicious that his province would be victimized in any Seaway agreement agreed to for Canada by the King Liberals, on general principles was unenthusiastic about negotiating a treaty with the United States. He distrusted the Americans and suspected that they would get the best of any bargain struck with Mackenzie King. Anti-American emotions were running high because of the Chicago water steal. Taschereau must have calculated that an agreement to sell power to Ontario would serve the interests of Quebec in a number of ways.

The negotiations were long and arduous. More was involved than the mere sale of power. One advance came in May 1925 when both premiers made pronouncements opposing the granting of an export permit to the private interests which held the Carillon lease. Ferguson believed that 'since power has become such an important factor in industrial development, and we have the advantage of our friends to the south in that respect, our proper course is to require them to spend their capital on this side of the line. Unless we are to make the best use of our natural resources, we might as well make up our minds to be hewers of wood for our neighbours.'[40] He remained apprehensive that notwithstanding his protest and that of Taschereau Ottawa might 'grant the lease in question and with an export permit.' If that happened he was determined to take his cause to the people. When *La Presse* questioned his sincerity, pointing out that Ontario itself allowed substantial amounts of power to be exported, he noted that this was done unwillingly under contracts made by a private company before it was taken over by Hydro. This was the very sort of thing, he continued, that Ontario was determined to avoid in the future:

Any contract to export power necessarily alienates for a long time a great natural resource which is becoming more and more necessary to Canada. The project now under consideration at Ottawa would bind this country to permit exportation for 43 years. In the struggle for industrial supremacy, electricity is figuring every year to a greater extent. It follows that the country which has an abundant supply of electrical energy will possess an immense advantage over its competitors, and may eventually be able to drive their products from the market. Would it not be a deplorable situation if the electrical power by which this country has been endowed by Providence were sent abroad to maintain industries that would take employment from our own people, and deprive them of their means of livelihood?

This is the danger which those of us who are earnestly opposing the sale of electrical power are trying to avert. The situation of this Province regarding exportation of power illustrates better than anything I can picture what will take place if we do not, as Canadians, profit by the experience of the past to safeguard the interests of the future.

If our enterprising neighbours want Canadian electrical power, which is a great natural resource, let them come to the source of supply and use it in Canada. Let them bring along their capital, employ Canadian labour and raw materials, and thereby contribute to the prosperity and development of this country. ... We will not sell our birthright for a mess of pottage.

Turning to Ontario-Quebec relations, he argued that 'our interests are alike, and ... I am confident that, if we will stand firmly together for the preservation of our Canadian heritage, we will accomplish what will be of great service to this generation and to those who come after.'[41]

Yet if the two premiers could stand together against federal policies, it proved more difficult to achieve positive co-operation. Ferguson, whose needs were more pressing, was the initiator. In response to his wish for an early meeting to discuss power matters, the Quebec Premier wrote in December 1925 that he was 'sure we can come to an understanding. ... We are decidedly against allowing power to be exported to the United States but favourable ... to supplying the sister provinces.'[42] One obstacle was the payment of an export tax which together with long-distance transmission costs threatened to price Quebec power out of the Ontario market. Another Ontario objective was to reach agreement on a means of developing the Ottawa. In January 1926, Magrath told Ferguson that certain rights were up for sale on the Quebec side of the Ottawa at the Chats but that apparently any power to be exported to Ontario from that development 'must be available for use in Quebec at any time by giving one year's notice which practically prohibits its being used in this Province.'

Apart from the Chats development, Hydro was negotiating with other interests having rights on the Ottawa within Quebec but it seemed to Magrath that 'we may have difficulty in agreeing on a price that will justify Hydro taking any of that power.'[43] High transmission costs meant that no deal could be made unless the Quebec government was willing to allow the power to be sold for a price below that for which it was available on the Quebec market, and unless the power could be granted in a long-term contract. In a memorandum prepared for Ferguson's use at a meeting with Taschereau scheduled for 18 January, it was pointed out that in the absence of such concessions, 'at the very best delivery cost in Ontario would be $5.00 per HP greater than in Quebec.'[44] On the other hand, if Taschereau agreed to Ontario's terms, he would be vulnerable to political attack in Quebec. Because of these difficulties, Magrath still believed that 'we must in some way bring the development of the St Lawrence River to a head without any further loss of time.'[45]

Despite this view, some joint form of development or at least a division of power rights on the Ottawa seemed a more probable solution. One barrier was the determination of the boundary between the two provinces; another was the two existing federal charters. For a while Ontario remained uncertain about its attitude to the National Hydro-Electric Company, which hoped to generate power on the authority of its federal charter and was willing to sell some of that power to Ontario. 'I personally think we should take the power from the Carillon,' Magrath told Ferguson on 1 March. 'If we do not do so that power, before long, will be carried eastward to Montreal.'[46] Magrath at this time was meeting with Amos of the Quebec Streams Commission, attempting to reach an agreement by which Ottawa power would be divided on a fifty-fifty basis.

By this time A.R. Graustein, the aggressive head of the International Paper Company, was negotiating with Hydro for the sale of power to be generated on the Gatineau and, for once, negotiations did not break down over price. Graustein in a meeting in Toronto agreed to accept the figure which Hydro was insisting on – $15.00 per HP.[47] And the deal was made. There can be little doubt that Graustein would not have gone ahead unless he knew the arrangement would have Taschereau's approval. Magrath hastened to inform the Quebec leader of all the details of the contract.

Ferguson was fairly bubbling in mid-April when he announced the signing. 'It will be a matter of great satisfaction,' read his statement, 'that Hydro have succeeded in securing a very substantial block of power to augment our present supply and take care of our power requirements for the next five or six years.' He was particularly gratified that there would be no export tax levied by

Quebec. The agreement provided for delivery of 230,000 to 260,000 HP by the Gatineau Power Company at the boundary near Ottawa. The province would build a transmission line of some 230 miles in length at a cost of ten to fifteen million dollars to connect with the Niagara system. The cost was estimated at seven or eight dollars per HP less than power produced by steam plants. It was guaranteed for a thirty-year period.[48]

As it turned out, this was the first of several contracts made with Quebec companies. Ferguson regarded it as about the best piece of business he had ever done for the province. Years later Mitchell Hepburn and his attorney-general Arthur Roebuck would bitterly attack the Quebec power purchases, suggesting improvidence, bad planning, fraud, and political corruption. Their position was based on political venom and ignorance. Given the province's rising consumption curve and its vital energy needs, there could be no doubt at all of the enormous value to Ontario of the Quebec purchases.

Politically, too, it was a brilliant stroke. From Taschereau's point of view, it meant that Ontario would no longer need to press urgently for action on the St Lawrence Seaway and soon Ferguson would publicly and dramatically alter his position on that question. Andrew Haydon was convinced that Ferguson had carried off the laurels. 'This contract,' he told King, 'is one of Mr Ferguson's most far-reaching power achievements – he succeeds in securing in perpetuity a huge block of Quebec power. The serious crisis that faced the Hydro ... has been automatically postponed for six or seven years. This postponement affords the Ontario Premier ample time to attempt jockeying the Dominion Government into a position where it will be made to appear that the Federal Government is deliberately pursuing a course ... which violates Provincial rights.' Haydon believed that Ferguson had pulled the wool over Taschereau's eyes and he told King that the Quebec premier 'is in a vulnerable position with his own people,' having 'permitted the exportation into industrial Ontario' of a huge block of cheap power 'all of which could and would be absorbed in the much nearer Montreal areas and just as quickly.' In Haydon's view, 'Taschereau's alliance with Mr Ferguson rests on certain misconceptions,' including his apprehensions about federal intentions on the St Lawrence. He urged that 'all these fears and misunderstandings' be removed and 'Ferguson's political manoeuvering countered...'[49]

There were signs that Ottawa was attempting precisely that. Possibly its delicate political circumstances following the 1925 election had led the federal government to soften its anti-provincial stance. In any case in the House of Commons on 7 April 1926, Charles Stewart made it clear that in any St Lawrence development, power and navigation would be kept absolutely separate. He stated too that 'there is no dispute so far as this government is concerned with respect to the ownership of the water-powers. ... Nor does this government raise any question as to the right of Ontario to develop this particular power. ... The situation in that respect is identical with the situation at Niagara...' The only hold-up, he asserted, was an engineering disagreement and as soon as the Joint Board of Engineers made its report, 'there will be no hesitancy in dealing at once' with Hydro's application. The fears of Ontario members were further allayed when the Commons then unanimously resolved that the Ontario Hydro 'should be given leave at the earliest possible date to develop and generate power on the St Lawrence river at what is known as the Morrisburg dam, and should also be given power to use an increased flow of water from the Niagara river to relieve the acute shortage of power in Ontario.'[50] Although this seemed definite enough, later events would prove that a resolution of the House of Commons meant no more to the King government than the decisions of the JCPC meant to some federal departments.

Indeed continued apprehension about Ottawa's intentions ensured that the Taschereau-Ferguson axis not only remained in effect but was strengthened. Interviewed in Montreal at the end of April following another conference with the Quebec leader, Howard Ferguson asserted that Ontario and Quebec would stand shoulder to shoulder to protect their rights and that they regarded the banks and beds of streams and the water as theirs, Ottawa having 'an easement for navigation purposes only.'[51] Despite Stewart's assertions, the issue between Ottawa and the central provinces was unresolved and interprovincial co-operation would remain a powerful influence in the years of manoeuvre and confrontation that lay ahead.

Andrew Haydon had been right on one count. The Gatineau contract gave Ontario the time it needed to defend its position in all its implications and removed the need for early compromise. Now Ferguson made it clear to Magrath that he and Taschereau would not buy power from the Carillon interests because this would suggest tacit acceptance of the validity of their federal charter.[52] In September he was ready with a full-scale proposal for development on the Ottawa. By this time he was less worried about the Carillon group, now controlled by Shawinigan Power Company and presumably susceptible to Taschereau's influence, than about the Georgian Bay charter held by the Siftons, whom he regarded as buccaneers determined to put the power users of Ontario to ransom. 'My understanding,' he told Taschereau, 'is that we are both deter-mined to resist to the very utmost any movement of that kind.'[53]

It was a measure of the strength of the ties between the two premiers that Ferguson now urged division of the Ottawa according to the equal rights principle adopted in international practice and even argued that, though it would be a departure from the usual Quebec practice, the two provinces should develop the power at all unallotted Ottawa sites themselves. Amazingly, he also suggested that 'with some reasonable cooperation' from Ottawa the provinces might play a substantial role in improving Ottawa River navigation.[54] The change in tone may be attributed in part to the advent to power in late June of the

Meighen government but if Ferguson thought that with his friends now in office he would have it all his own way, he was rudely awakened. On 20 August, during the federal election campaign, Meighen, then in Edmonton, wired Sir Henry Drayton that he was 'entirely convinced' a short extension of the Shawinigan company's rights at the Carillon was 'abundantly justified. Montreal friend is asking me telegraph you instructions to have such extension made now as immediate action very necessary.'[55] Poor Sir Henry, alone in Ottawa, would face the wrath of Howard Ferguson if he took any such steps.

Still, Meighen's exigencies, related perhaps to the needs of Tory fund raisers, took precedence. On 24 August Drayton wrote Ferguson that 'such extension is entirely without prejudice to any rights, whatsoever, of the Province of Ontario, including the right to contend that the lease in question and any extension thereof are beyond the powers of the Dominion...' Anxious not to anger the Ontario premier, he even added that 'this government will not approve of any detailed plans so as to enable the National-Hydro Electric Company Limited to proceed with actual construction until it is assured that the company has entered into an agreement with the Hydro-Electric Power Commission of Ontario satisfactory to your government to sell power to it to an amount and on terms satisfactory to the commission and enabling the commission to acquire the ownership of one-half share and interest in the Carillon development, including one-half of the stream flow on terms to be agreed on.'[56]

Although all the evidence is not available, Arthur Meighen's 'immediate action very necessary' telegram perhaps merits as much notoriety as John A.'s 'Must Have Another $10,000' in an earlier election. Meighen, however, was luckier and more discreet. Nonetheless, once back in office, Mackenzie King cancelled the settlement Meighen and Drayton had made with National-Hydro on the grounds that the Company had contributed to Tory campaign funds.[57]

On 25 September, King returned to power. Negotiations were now underway to allow power to be harnessed at the Carillon but the complex interests of three governments and the Shawinigan organization proved impossible to reconcile. With Taschereau about to depart for England, Ferguson hastened to Quebec City on 4 October and on his way back to Toronto fired off a telegram urging his friend to protest in writing 'against the invasion of Provincial rights.'[58] Apparently Ottawa was still determined to play a role at the Carillon and Taschereau responded that he would take the matter up with the federals personally. Meanwhile the practical burden of the Quebec-Ontario alliance was carried by Magrath and by Amos of the Quebec Steams Commission, but despite frequent meetings a positive program for Ottawa River development seemed as far off as ever.

At the same time Ontario started to talk directly with New York State in the hope of getting matters underway on the St Lawrence. Just when a common front was developing, the New Yorkers had a change of heart, perhaps caused by premature publicity, and withdrew from the negotiations.[59]

All in all, however, as polling day approached, the Ferguson administration politically was in a satisfactory position. A few nonsensical editorials in the Toronto *Telegram* and other pro-Beck journals complained that by buying power from private Quebec corporations, Ferguson and Magrath were abandoning the public ownership principles of the Hydro founder, but such absurdities were easily countered. Clearly it was Ottawa which was hurting on the power question. As Andrew Haydon pointed out a little later to King, there was enormous apprehension in Ontario about the course of federal power policy; between Ferguson's manoeuvres and the lack of any clear-cut policy statement on the part of Ottawa, 'the public have been led to believe anything...'[60] On an issue of vital concern not only to businessmen and farmers but to the population at large, most Ontarians believed that Ferguson had proven himself a vigorous defender of the province's interests against the obscurantism of Mackenzie King. Most important, he had provided the energy Ontario needed to ensure its industrial future.

The power question overshadowed other important dominion-provincial issues. Yet long-standing jurisdictional conflicts on such matters as the regulation of insurance companies, the provincial right to regulate the sale of shares and other securities of companies incorporated under federal charters, and the Dominion's right to incorporate companies whose operations were purely provincial all remained outstanding. As well, differences among the provinces themselves in legislation affecting succession duties were increasingly bothersome and Ferguson was bombarded with demands that the annoying disharmonies be eliminated. But more than anything, it was the desire of some of the poorer provinces for higher federal subsidies which occasioned the calling together in Ottawa in June 1926 of the first interprovincial conference since 1902.

It was Ferguson who issued the call for the conference. At the request of Premier Stewart of PEI, he had tried to arrange such a gathering as early as 1924. At once federal officials were suspicious. 'It is, of course, in the interest of the Federal Government that such a conference should be delayed as long as possible,'[61] read a memorandum prepared for Mackenzie King. King himself advised Taschereau that because of 'the tremendous war burdens incurred since the last adjustment of subsidies,' no good case for an increase could be made.[62] Federal officials were also concerned about 'the tendency of various provinces to invade the field of direct taxation in more or less camouflaged forms, eg, the recent gasoline taxes.' Finally, with four Tory administrations now in power, King cautioned Taschereau that a campaign by unfriendly provincial governments 'might involve a good deal of embarrassment.'[63]

Yet the Conference exhibited little of the bellicose spirit of the more famous gathering called together by Honoré Mercier in 1887.[64] In the prosperity of

1926, a sense of urgency was lacking, and the premiers met almost as directors of a successful corporation gathered to iron out minor annoyances. The assembled leaders showed general sympathy for the financial situation of the Maritime provinces; the Dominion was asked to adopt such measures 'as will enable Canadian coals to be marketed in the central parts of Canada...'; it was resolved that all provinces should take steps to avoid multiple taxation in the succession duty field, that the incorporation of companies for purely provincial purposes should not be undertaken by the Dominion, that the Dominion should repeal its legislation regulating contracts of insurance or should at least appeal the decision of the Ontario courts to the JCPC, and that the provinces should work together to achieve uniform approaches in the field of corporation tax law. Since constitutional limitations had hitherto frustrated provincial efforts to regulate the sale of securities by companies incorporated federally, Ferguson as chairman was asked to present a draft bill on the subject to Ottawa.

Although it was all very businesslike and moderate, many of the matters dealt with had long been the source of considerable disagreement between Ottawa and the provinces. In this respect, the results were substantially the same as in 1887. Ottawa, of course, was unrepresented and took little official notice of what was going on. When Ferguson communicated with King regarding the securities regulation measure, he was told merely that 'at this stage of the session it is difficult to add to our programme of legislation.'[65] Equally, the struggle over regulation of insurance continued unabated and there was no general increase in subsidies.

Of course Ontario itself could have little interest in achieving such an increase. For Ferguson, as Mackenzie King had suspected, the gathering had provided an opportunity to form alliances and lay the groundwork for future action. In short, it was a 'warm-up' for the full dominion-provincial conference which would meet in the near future. Chairing the meeting could only strengthen Ferguson's political image. Just as he approached the 1926 election in an unassailable position on the electrical power issue, so too by presiding over the interprovincial conference he had added to his stature in Ontario and perhaps in the country at large.

10

'On the Tide of Prosperity'

'Ontario,' asserted the Diamond Jubilee booklet *On The Tide of Prosperity*, 'is an Empire in size and a treasure-house of natural resources.' Describing the province as 'the land of opportunity,' it asked rhetorically, 'can the world do without Ontario?'[1] Without question, the prosperous twenties gave birth to a pride of accomplishment and self-conscious sense of the rich potential of the province's natural resources which was almost belligerent in some of its expressions. And Howard Ferguson, of course, was the grand panjandrum presiding over this golden age of enterprise and achievement.

Undoubtedly the Ferguson government's most characteristic contribution lay in the field of economic policy and management. Yet, surprisingly perhaps, most of its efforts in this area were unrelentingly conventional. Its budget policy, for example, which emphasized economy and cautious management, echoed the approach of the federal Liberals and reflected the orthodoxy of the day. Although Ferguson put his own vigorous stamp on the administration's several development programs, there was little about them that Hearst, Whitney, or even Mowat would have found surprising. More than anything else, it was the new administration's style, self-assured, intensely political, reflecting the leader's own personality and carefully attuned to the optimism of the day, which provided an approach which was distinctively and undeniably its own. Certain lines of endeavour were pushed ahead with imagination and determination and the atmosphere of confidence and stability which Ferguson invariably exuded contributed much to the material achievements of the day.

Taken individually, provincial policies were unremarkable. Even by its own criteria, the financial performance of the first Ferguson administration was far from outstanding. Expenditures, which had grown so rapidly during the Drury period, were contained somewhat; yet notwithstanding the improvement in economic conditions, Treasurer Price announced a deficit in each of his three budgets. With a deft political touch, Price manipulated this spotty record until it appeared to many that the Tory ministers were stern economizers struggling to rescue Ontario from the financial morass bequeathed by four years of Drury rule. At the same time the administration won the applause of the business community in its guise as the adept manager of Ontario's natural resources and aggressive proponent of development. The tone was set by Ferguson, both by his actions and by several major policy pronouncements delivered during his early months of office. A superb publicist, he used his office as a platform to announce grandiose schemes and draw enchanting pictures of the province's future.

There was, of course, his ringing challenge, 'On to the St Lawrence,' in which he appeared ready to call out the provincial legions to ensure an ample supply of electrical energy. He was an equally determined advocate of the use of Alberta coal to fuel the furnaces of Ontario. Again and again he deplored the millions of dollars which annually flowed south to purchase American coal, arguing that higher transportation costs would be a small price to pay for a policy which would put thousands of Canadians to work and help heal the divisions between east and west which were so pronounced in the 1920s. Similarly, he pointed to the huge deposits in Ontario of iron ore of a grade which had hitherto proved uneconomical to work and, deploring again the country's almost total dependence on an American resource which might be cut off at any time, he foresaw the possibility of linking east and west with an iron ore industry centred in the rock stretches above Lake Superior.[2]

He was full of great schemes to harness the country's natural resources and bind Canadians together. To a 'Good Roads' convention he proclaimed that a substantial reduction of railway rates was the primary remedy for the ills that beset Canada. Let Canadians, he insisted, pay a subsidy if that was necessary to increase the volume of traffic, thereby bringing the country together and reducing the flow of dollars south. Among his earliest policy moves was the establishment of committees to develop new programs for agriculture and highways, while in each department his ministers approached their tasks in the belief that major overhauls were in order and new programs urgently required. 'The time has come to wake up,' Ferguson asserted.[3] Ontario, he proclaimed in 1923, would establish a scientific bureau which would carry on medical and scientific research on such a scale as to benefit every commercial undertaking in the province. Although much of this was puffery, Ferguson undoubtedly intended to bend every effort, in the words of another age, 'to get the province moving again.' Himself a unique combination of the practical man of wide experience and the restless visionary, in a revealing remark he once explained to a protégé that he liked to see things done 'in a big way.' His intimate association with such business magnates as Flavelle, Kemp, Stanley Maclean, R.S. McLaughlin, and J.P. Bickell and with the leading Tory politicos on the national scene gave him an overweening confidence in his own ability to see large projects through to fruition.

The Ferguson government's economic policies were pursued within a framework of clearly defined assumptions and against a backdrop of prosperity and
industrial expansion. Ontario, like the nation as a whole, was slow in emerging
from the recession of the early 1920s and serious unemployment persisted into
the winter of 1925-6. Nonetheless from 1925 the economic curve was consistently up and all sectors, including agriculture, felt the benefits of prosperity.
Ontario was particularly fortunate and the government at Queen's Park reaped
political rewards for a situation to which it contributed relatively little. The
province held a position of pre-eminence in the nation's economy and its business community in the late 1920s attained unexampled heights of wealth and
achievement. As the *Canada Year Book* noted in 1930, 'except in forestry and
fisheries, Ontario led the other provinces and divisions in the productiveness of
the main branches of industry. The province yielded preference in forestry operations to Quebec alone. ... About 50 per cent of the net manufacturing output
of the country was contributed by Ontario, and 25.5 per cent of the agricultural
income.' Despite the rapid growth of industry in British Columbia, Manitoba,
and Quebec, Ontario maintained 'a manufacturing production more than equal
to that of the remainder of the Dominion,' with 51 per cent of the gross value of
production compared to 28 per cent for Quebec, its nearest competitor.[4] Yet for
the most part the industrial and financial communities operating on the national
level seem to have had little interest in provincial government and politics.
Ferguson's correspondence contains scant evidence that the captains of industry
and the magnates of finance paid more than sporadic attention to Queen's Park
and its affairs.

In a sense this was surprising. There were many points of contact at which the
interests of industrialists and financiers might have been affected by provincial
policies. The competition between Ontario and Ottawa to regulate insurance, the
struggle for control of power development, and the dispute over the right to
incorporate companies were all of more than passing concern to businessmen
and generated a degree of involvement with the Toronto government. For example, the great chartered banks which had been displeased when the Drury government had established the provincial savings offices made their views known to
Ferguson. 'The original set-up was four per cent for deposits...,' George Henry
later informed R.B. Bennett. 'After we came into office, and under pressure
from the Banks, we reduced the rate of interest to three per cent...'[5] The
province's assessment legislation was another source of business concern while
the expanded interest in technical education and the foundation later in the
decade of the Ontario Research Foundation owed much to the frequently
expressed desires of the CMA. There was also a considerable body of regulatory
legislation, including minimum wage and factory laws and a Workmen's Compensation Act, which affected the conditions of business. Yet there were no major
initiatives of that type in the later part of the decade, and perhaps for that

reason there was little occasion for pressure to be applied by interested parties. Naturally, economic groups would be affected by the province's fiscal policies. Corporation taxes and succession duties had been levied since the turn of the century and the resource industries were also subject to provincial taxation. Still, the level of these imposts was hardly burdensome and businessmen were rightly confident that under Tory rule there would be no threatening increases.

About all that was expected of the government in Toronto was economy in expenditures, some assurance of fiscal stability, and a 'fair' treatment of the resource industries which, after all, received much of their financial backing from the chartered banks. That this would be forthcoming from the Ferguson administration went without saying. There had been much satisfaction in the board rooms of Ontario when the Tories returned to office in 1923 but there seems to have been little direct assistance to either Conservatives or Liberals in that campaign; such involvement as there was in the provincial political scene continued to be individual and intermittent.

Of course there were exceptions but these were largely traditional and limited in nature. If the Premier's correspondence is any gauge, the principal concerns of Queen's Park in the 1920s remained power development, mining, lumbering, and pulp and paper and the policies of the provincially owned T&NO RR. Of course highway construction loomed increasingly large and the Ferguson government was particularly alert to the interests of the agricultural community. But over all, little had changed from the days of Cochrane and Whitney. Demands had increased, markets had grown, expansion had created new needs, and the frontier was being pushed north, west, and even east to Quebec, creating thereby a major clash with the Taschereau administration. In Ferguson's mind, northern development remained critical to the province's future and many of his policies were geared to that fact.

Equally in the spirit of Ontario's recent past was the nationalist posture within which the Tories developed their economic program. Ever since the manufacturing condition had been imposed at the turn of the century on pulpwood and timber cut from Crown land, efforts had been made to ensure that Ontario derived the maximum benefit from its natural resources. This was no easy task, as the long struggle to force International Nickel to erect a Canadian refinery had demonstrated. The mutual interdependence of the Canadian and American economies provided many pitfalls for the would-be nationalist. More than any previous premier, Ferguson was determined to lessen dependence on the United States and to ensure that to the maximum degree possible Canadian resources were developed by Canadian workers. The intensity of his imperial feelings and his instinctive distrust of dealings with the Americans were deepened by his resentment over the Chicago water steal and by the province's inability to reclaim electrical energy exported to the United States under old contracts. Profoundly suspicious of the implications of continentalist resource policies, he feared that federal negotiators might betray the national and more particularly the provincial interest in bargaining with the Americans over the St Lawrence development and he fought all suggestions that private enterprise or the federal government might allow additional amounts of electricity to be sent south. As well, he deplored Canadian dependence on American iron and coal and was equally adamant that it was a matter of urgency to free Canadian industry from its debilitating reliance on the American research capacity.

These ideas fitted well into his party's traditional adherence to the banner of the National Policy. Ferguson's program was not merely Ontario first, but represented a genuine concern for an integrated national economic structure which could take full advantage of the country's reserves of manpower, transportation networks, and natural resources. Of course, fundamentally, he was preaching the old Tory policy of high tariffs from which, some believed, Ontario had always benefitted most. In that tradition, he argued that it would be necessary to force American capital and technology north of the border and for a while at least he looked benevolently on the branch plant as one means to achieve nationalist goals. In the event, some of Ferguson's schemes succeeded, others failed, and, ironically, he himself was forced to spend an inordinate amount of time tending the needs of a pulp and paper industry controlled largely by American money and geared almost entirely to the needs of the American market. Then as now, Ontario, despite its Premier's nationalist rhetoric, was ambivalent about its battle against the forces of economic continentalism.

The political overtones of Tory economic policy were never more to the fore than in February 1924, when W.H. Price delivered his budget. Although the Treasurer announced an unprecedented deficit of over $15 million, he placed the blame for this on the previous administration. Claiming that Drury had charged innumerable items to capital account that belonged in ordinary and had juggled the books to claim surpluses in 1921 and 1922, Price asserted that in reality the Farmers had run up a deficit each year which averaged out at the then astounding figure of more than $6 million a year. Excoriating the late government's borrowing practices and many of its other procedures, he exclaimed that 'the deficit of $15,000,000 this year is as much as the Hearst administration spent on ordinary expenditure at the beginning of the war. It is three times the amount the Whitney government spent on ordinary expenditure at the time they came in.' The Drury government, he announced, was the 'most expensive experiment Ontario ever made.'[6]

As for his own policy, he called for the strictest economy, stating that he hoped to cut expenditures that year by $5 million and increase receipts by $4 million, despite the fact that 1922-3 receipts had actually decreased by $6 million. There would be no new taxes but revenue increases would be achieved through improved administrative procedures and collection methods. The financial condition of the province, he cautioned, was in such sorry shape that it might be some time before there could be a return to balanced budgets.

The initial reaction of the Farmer members to Price's figures was disbelief and the Liberals were equally sceptical. Yet in each of his next two budgets Price used the same ploy. Deficits of eight and a half million dollars in the 1924 fiscal year and slightly over five million in 1925 were presented as victories on the road back from the years of mismanagement. Price missed no opportunity to claim that the Tory record reflected ruthless economy and administrative efficiency. Book-keeping reforms, new collection methods, and the establishment in 1925 of a statistical branch in the treasury were lauded as evidence of Tory managerial skills. On every possible occasion, the Treasurer drew attention to his Department's business acumen in negotiating new loans at rates of interest lower than paid by the Farmers, while every economy, such as an alleged 50 per cent reduction in the cost of highway building alluded to in the 1925 budget, was cleverly exploited. In 1925 Price revealed that he was considering the introduction of a sinking fund aimed at controlling and reducing the provincial debt and in 1926, after a debt retirement committee had brought down its report, details were announced, amid great fanfare, of a plan by which some $1,500,000 a year would be used from current revenue together with contributions from the Hydro and other sources to effect major reductions in the province's debt over a forty-year period. The Tories calculated that the princely sum of $240 million would be saved by this plan.

When new taxes were introduced in 1925 — a gas tax of three cents a gallon which drew cries of outrage from the Ontario Motor League and a beverage tax designed principally to exploit the new 4.4 beer — they were accompanied by careful rationalizations boasting of the province's low level of taxation. Ferguson frequently asserted that only a small portion of the province's revenues were raised through taxation levied on the people as a whole. 'The policy of this government,' read a typical statement, 'is to secure revenues from or for services rendered. Those who enjoy the benefits of provincial services, special privileges, or the use of natural resources, should be the ones to contribute to the cost of the provincial service.'[7] Thus fees, fines, the dominion subsidy, revenue from the public domain, the gas tax, because it was paid by those who used the public highways, amusement taxes, paid presumably by those who chose to be amused, were all considered to be in return for 'services rendered.'

The opposition parties viewed things differently and argued that almost 70 per cent of the province's revenues came from taxes of one kind or another. There was criticism too of the well-publicized claim that Ferguson's pledge of economy was being fulfilled, with ordinary expenditures increasing from a 1923 level of $41,361,439.92 to a 1926 level of only $41,797,098. The Liberals accused the administration of the same kind of fiscal legerdemain which

Tories attributed to the Farmers. Pointing out that the expenditure level of 1923 had been unprecedented, they charged that Price at that time had invited all who did business with the government to send in their bills and generally had laboured mightily to build up a deficit which could be attributed to the Farmers. From that point forward, the Ferguson administration adopted as its habitual standard 'the horrible year 1923, when the Drury Government did the spending and the Ferguson Government did the bookkeeping.'[8] Despite these manipulations, the Ferguson government in each of 1924, 1925, and 1926 proved unable even in a period of prosperity to balance its books. According to Liberal calculations, the Tories in 1925 actually spent $2,500,000 more than in 'the horrible year' of 1923.

Then, in 1926, Price resorted to a new trick. He segregated interest charges and claimed that apart from such charges, the province had a $2 million surplus. Many Tory papers printed headlines similar to that of the Ottawa *Journal*: 'NO NEW TAX: OLD DEFICIT CUT: SURPLUS $2,000,000.' Yet despite the new gas and beverage taxes of 1925, a substantial deficit remained in ordinary expenditure; on capital account the provincial debt increased from over $240 million at the end of 1922 to almost $325 million at the end of 1925, notwithstanding the Tory claim in the 1926 election campaign that they had reduced capital expenditures from $25 million in 1923 to $15 million in 1925.[9] As for the debt retirement scheme, the Liberals pointed out that Price had neglected to mention that the Committee which had investigated the project had argued that it would be worse than useless to attempt any such effort until the province was able to balance its ordinary accounts.[10]

In truth, while the Tories had improved administrative procedures and reduced the rate of growth in provincial expenditures, they were helpless in the face of the rising demand for social and other services which all governments encountered in this period. More revealing than Price's dubious claims were what the budgets of the period left unsaid. Their only discernible fiscal philosophy was an unrestrained belief in the virtues of economy and of restricting taxes to those who benefitted from specific services. The opposition parties responded in the same terms and called for more restraint and even lower taxes. Occasionally there might be an element of disagreement over who should pay the taxes. The Toronto *Star*, for example, in an editorial entitled 'Making the Little Fellow Pay,' criticized the Tories for raising revenues through gas and beverage taxes which would hit 'the average citizen' and contrasted this with Drury who, it asserted, had increased succession duties payable on large estates, raised corporation taxes, doubled the rates of timber dues, and taxed racetrack bets.[11] The Ferguson government continued to tax lightly rather than risk raising the cost of production, and public domain levies and corporation taxes remained low.[12] There was in all this little awareness of the possibility of fiscal policy serving as a tool of economic management or as a social instrument for redistributing incomes, beyond the stock suggestion that business would be stimulated and unemployment relieved through strict economy and a program of public works.

The fiscal policy which was most characteristic and which provides the best insight into the beliefs of the day may be gleaned by comparing provincial and municipal expenditure statistics. Provincial government expenditures relative to personal incomes were below the national average but municipal expenditures were greater than in all other provinces. Combined government expenditures were equal to 12.2 per cent of personal income in Ontario compared to the national average of 12.5 per cent. Provincial and municipal expenditures together ranged in the 1926-30 period from $79 per capita in British Columbia to $18 in Prince Edward Island and $64 in Ontario, 15 per cent above the Canadian average of $55. Yet per capita income in Ontario was 18.3 per cent above that average. The Ontario expenditure figures resulted from municipal expenditures, which were well above, and provincial, which were well below the national average. In the same period, 'Ontario municipal expenditures per capita were higher than those of all other provinces individually and 26 per cent above the national average.'[13]

Because of its strong system of local government and its willingness to exploit the local tax base and to allow municipalities to levy different types of taxes, Ontario was able to rely on its municipal structure for a wide variety of services and functions. By mid-decade, however, the strains were beginning to tell. In March 1926 the representatives of Ontario municipalities told Ferguson that they were 'beginning to feel severely the burden of hospital and other welfare expenditure.' They pointed as well to spiralling road costs. Interestingly, their proposed solution was not a provincial assumption of more of these costly services; instead the municipalities asked for a share of the revenue from amusement and race track taxes and motor vehicle permits.[14] The Ferguson government, however, proved in no hurry either to lighten the municipal load or to share further its tax base with the local governments.

Another economic issue with political implications was the question of the extension of the T&NO RR. At first Ferguson's policy was determined by his commitment to economy and retrenchment. Believing that 'the Dominion of Canada is today suffering from the tremendous burden of debt incurred by building railways far in advance of the country's need,' he decided not to fall into that trap himself. Although a contract had been let in 1922 to build north from Cochrane for 70 miles, Ferguson was convinced that Ontario's interests would be served not by pushing on to James Bay but by the construction of branch lines as needed to serve the expanding mining and pulp and paper interests. Thus in January 1926 he cautioned one enthusiast that 'our experience with the T&NO has taught us that construction of a railway does not always bring about the development and return that is anticipated. We have some branches of our railway that in the light of experience should never have been built. We have delayed the construction through to James Bay simply because it is premature, and we would only be locking up capital for many years to come.'[15]

As well, Ferguson was aggressively on the alert to protect the investment already made. When he heard reports that the mining companies in South Lorraine were giving a lot of their business to the CPR, he angrily told T&NO chairman George Lee that 'we have spent half a million dollars building a railway and quarter of a million building a highway to serve these people, and it is rather remarkable if it is true that they should send their business in some other direction.'[16] Although there were several minor extensions northward over the next few years, the decision to build to the Bay was taken only near the end of Ferguson's tenure and by that time it reflected in some measure the deepening unemployment crisis and the need to create jobs.

The decision to focus on branch lines emphasized again the relationship between the T&NO and the great mining and pulp and paper interests. It led as well to a clash between Ontario and Quebec at a time when Ferguson was trying to form a common front with Taschereau on the hydro power question. The incident represented a new stage in the old commercial rivalry between Toronto and Montreal. Ontario mining interests played a prominent role in the Rouyn-Noranda gold rush of 1922-3 and out of this developed pressure for Ontario to provide transportation facilities. In early January 1925, Ferguson announced that the T&NO's subsidiary, the Nipissing Central, which held a federal charter and presumably possessed the right to proceed into the neighbouring province, would build a line to serve the Rouyn fields. Taschereau responded immediately by pressing the CNR to serve the area and CN president Sir Henry Thornton agreed to do so.[17] Ferguson for his part issued orders through Lee for the Nipissing Central to proceed 'with all possible speed.'[18]

Unfortunately for Ontario's aspirations, the federal government, sensitive to the position of its Liberal counterpart in Quebec, refused to issue the necessary order pursuant to the Railway Act to permit the Nipissing Central to proceed over Crown land in Quebec until the matter was heard before the Supreme Court. The case finally went to the Judicial Committee and although the Ontario position was upheld, the delay had allowed the CN to beat the Ontario line to Rouyn.[19]

Ferguson's position was frustrated even more thoroughly in another significant economic clash with Thorton and the CN, this time over energy policy and transportation rates. In the 1920s, people and industries relied on coal to an extent now difficult to imagine and a strike which occurred in 1922 in the American coal fields on which Ontario depended had far-reaching implications. Although Canadian coal reserves were estimated at 1234 billion tons, Canadians paid almost $89 million in 1921 to import American coal and Canadian mines were working below capacity with Canadian miners idle for long periods every year.[20] When the Drury government during the 1922 strike arranged for a small amount of Alberta coal to be sent to Ontario on an emergency basis, it whetted the appetite of the consumer for more. Unfortunately, Sir Henry Thornton 'after careful deliberation' informed Drury that the rate for coal moved during the period when freight cars were not tied up with the grain shipment would average nine dollars per ton. Such a rate, Drury replied, 'will, I fear, make the traffic in Alberta coal an impossibility except as an emergency measure ... I can quite understand, however, the wisdom of your decision from the railway point of view.'[21]

Howard Ferguson was not the man to let the matter drop after a word from Sir Henry. Soon after coming into office he spoke with the CN president and as a result the railroad agreed to ship up to 10,000 tons up to 31 October at the special seven-dollar rate which had been in effect during the emergency.[22] This was the beginning of a long and complicated struggle in which Ontario co-operated with Alberta in an effort to convince the federal government and the national rail lines to carry coal at a rate which would enable it to compete with the American product. After years of effort, many hearings before the Board of Railway Commissioners, many angry exchanges with Mackenzie King, and much frustration, Ferguson was forced to conclude that all his efforts had come to naught. The matter, he finally told the lawyer who had acted for the province, had received 'more political consideration than judicial consideration' and Ontario would pursue it no further.[23]

Yet if lack of federal support together with the high quality and lower cost of Pennsylvania coal had defeated Ferguson's effort to stimulate use of the domestic product, the episode nonetheless revealed a good deal about Ferguson's goals and aspirations in the field of national development. Ferguson feared the uncertainty of dependence on a foreign supplier for such an important energy source and he believed that higher transportation costs would be a small price to pay for a policy which would contribute to national unity by helping to tie east and west together in a mutually beneficial economic program. But if the economic goals were not attained, the political consequences more than repaid Ferguson for his efforts. Once again he was able to place federal politicians in the role of procrastinators and spoilers while he exuberantly presented himself to the public as the far-sighted defender of Canadian national interests. Canada, he told the Ontario legislature in March 1925, should work to form the scattered provinces into a more closely-knit nation by developing an interprovincial trade which would redound to the prosperity of all. 'As a matter of fact we are bound, if we live up to our Confederation obligation, to do that because these outlying provinces came into Confederation with a distinct understanding that ways and means of transporting their products to the centre would be provided.'[24] Once again, playing the role of statesman of national unity, Ferguson was laying down policy lines which his successors would utilize brilliantly in the maintenance of the Tory dynasty.

Certainly Mackenzie King was left in little doubt about the political potency of the coal question. Thus in a telegram to King, a copy of which he handed to the press, Ferguson in August 1925 exploited the nationalist cry. Ontario, he proclaimed, believed it 'vital that we should not be dependent on foreign nation for coal supply.' It was, he urged, 'extremely important for both East and West that facilities should be provided to make Alberta coal available in Ontario. Moreover feel strongly important we retain large amount of money involved in purchase of coal in circulation in Canada for benefit of Canadian commerce and Canadian people.'[25] With Mackenzie King's friends warning him that Ferguson would receive all the credit for the amounts of Alberta coal that did move east, the Ontario premier could console himself with the knowledge that politically at least his efforts had paid off.[26] Fighting the good fight to establish a national coal policy, he had once again seized the initiative and the federal record suffered by comparison.

The Rouyn extension and the Alberta coal policy were the economic questions with which Ferguson concerned himself most directly during his first term in office, but he continued to dabble in the affairs of all departments. The ministers who dealt with economic policy seemed largely cast from the same mould. Price, Henry, Lyons, McCrea, and John Martin, by no calculation spectacularly brilliant, were all solid, hard-working men, careful managers who could be counted on to do good work and at times to demonstrate a measure of imagination.

Perhaps Martin in Agriculture left the least imprint. Presented to the public as a man of outstanding abilities, a poultry farmer who, the Tory propagandists often pointed out, had won 'all the leading prizes at the New York State Fair for 20 consecutive years,' he lacked political flair and was dogged by indifferent health. The government was fortunate, however, that agricultural prices which had fallen to disastrous lows in 1922 and 1923, began a persistent trend upwards and, perhaps as a result, the old problem of rural depopulation was at least stabilized.[27] Ferguson was determined not to make the mistakes in agricultural policy which had cost the Drury government so dearly. One sign of his attitude was the decision to pay out of provincial funds the substantial sums formerly contributed by Ottawa to rural educational and demonstration work. Although unhappy about the federal decision to discontinue its agricultural grants, the Ferguson government ostentatiously carried on the work itself. Ferguson remained as solicitous about rural wishes as he had been in opposition and he was always anxious to listen to the views of farm leaders, including those of that old Tory, J.J. Morrison, now an occasional visitor to his office.[28]

As for policies, these did not differ fundamentally from those followed by Manning Doherty, although they were carried out with a more deft political touch; somehow it seemed more natural for a Tory than a Farmer government to claim to be applying 'sound business principles' to the problems of the farm. The department worked to promote efficient marketing procedures, even intervening directly on occasion, for example to dispose of 25,000 barrels of apples in the British market. Much attention was paid to marketing exhibits at international shows and this drove home the need for improved methods of quality control and grading. Although a good deal was achieved, much remained to be done. Hundreds of small cheese producers, to cite one obvious area in which improved regulation was sorely needed, continued to offer a product whose quality varied enormously and marketing efforts suffered from the stubborn resistance on the part of the small producer to inspection and control.[29] The 1924 and 1925 reports of the Agricultural Enquiry Committee focused on marketing problems and permeating their work 'was the conviction that marketing was the key to agricultural prosperity.'[30]

The department in the latter part of the 1920s engaged in extensive educational efforts and incentives were offered to producers willing to adhere to provincial standards. A Markets and Cooperation Branch was established in 1924 but the unwillingness of the Tory administration to move too far ahead of farm opinion meant that matters progressed slowly. The department did prove sympathetic to co-operative schemes in the marketing of honey and wool through producers' organizations. More funds were made available for research and an effort was made to give an agricultural bent to education in rural communities.[31] Occasionally legislation was resorted to, as in the Dairy Products Act of 1926, which provided new regulatory measures such as a provision for grading cream and pasteurizing cream for butter-making purposes and required new creameries and cheese factories to be certified. Progress, perhaps, was slower than it might have been under Manning Doherty; changes were seldom forced in the face of persistent rural opposition. In 1929 the department accelerated its efforts to persuade farmers to improve standards on their own and that year the Markets and Cooperation Branch expanded to include a Crops Division. Not until 1931, however, was the Ontario Marketing Board created as a full-fledged agency.[32] Gradualism, of course, could only produce results gradually yet, for the Ferguson Tories, it had the distinct advantage of contributing to a political image which would firmly entrench the party in much of rural Ontario.

The other policy initiative which won a large measure of rural support was an expanded program of rural electrification. The decision by Drury to pay half the cost of primary transmission lines had left the vast majority of farmers unable to afford the installation of electricity and Ferguson provided substantial financial assistance for secondary lines. The pace of rural electrification was thereby greatly accelerated. By 1928 Ontario Hydro was 'operating in 122 rural districts comprising 211 townships, and the aggregate peak load had reached 16,890-hp, as against 3514-hp in 1923.' According to Chairman Magrath, 'the endeavour of the Commission is not the concentration of industry at a few large power sites, but rather the broader policy of making as widespread distribution of electrical energy as is economically possible.'[33] Although certain sections and groups were still served less effectively than others, considering the other enormous demands on provincial funds, particularly for highway construction, the achievement in this area was creditable to both government and Commission.

The philosophy which informed Magrath's statement accorded well with the other social and economic policies of the Ferguson government. Although performance often fell short of the proclaimed goals of decentralization and extension of social and economic opportunity, and the concentration of wealth and power in the cities, particularly Toronto, was not checked let alone reversed, no administration could hope to challenge the forces which were contributing to that result. The intelligent concern which the government showed for the people of the hinterlands acted as a buffer and perhaps made the irresistible trend less painful to those affected most adversely.

The same concern appeared in highways policy. No major study exists of this vital area of provincial endeavour and the precise economic effects of the building boom of these years have yet to be gauged. Equally obscure are the political consequences. One suspects that in this period the construction men and the Tories perfected their alliance of convenience. However that may be, Ferguson appears to have had relatively little to do with the department. There was no minister he trusted more than the hardworking, knowledgeable George Henry and Highways and Public Works were entirely the bailiwick of the man from East York. Although the Public Works part of Henry's portfolio was far from insignificant and the new East Block of the Parliament buildings was one monument to his organizational capabilities, Highways demanded most of his attention. Given the scope of the work and the pioneering nature of many road-building problems, occasional mistakes were bound to occur; given the political morality of the day, it would be surprising if kickbacks had not found their way to the Tory campaign fund. It was no mean achievement, then, that the department under 'Honest George Henry' remained relatively untouched by scandal. Certainly Henry's careful administration kept it clear of the major embarrassments which had developed during the day of Frank Biggs.

As for policy, the provincial government was fully seized of the economic significance of highway development. Because of the importance of the automobile manufacturing industry and the effect of the car and truck on almost all aspects of social and economic life, Ontarians of this era developed a sense of living through a new industrial revolution. In 1918 there were 100,000 cars in Ontario; ten years later there were well over 400,000. By the mid-twenties, the province was building over 200 miles of highway a year at an average cost of

$25,000 a mile.[34] Apart from the commercial implications of the new trans-
portation system, Ontario in 1927 attracted over two million tourists who
entered for a period not exceeding 24 hours and 400,000 for a period not
exceeding two months.[35] According to federal estimates of that year, the tourist
traffic in Canada was valued at $275,000,000, second in total value only to
wheat exports. Ontario's highway system was a major attraction and a
memorandum prepared for the Premier pointed out that 'there are sheaves of
letters in the Highways Department testifying to that effect.'[36]

Despite the perceived value of the provincial trunk system, the goals of
provincial policy as enunciated by Ferguson in a February 1924 address to a
Good Roads Convention were to pay greater attention to secondary systems and
to deal more generously with local county roads. Although the province would
continue to spend substantial sums on maintenance of the trunk system, 'not a
single mile' would be added to it for some time.[37] In furtherance of this, the
Ferguson government provided substantially increased aid to counties and townships for roadbuilding purposes and resisted pressure to increase the province's
contribution to the cost of provincial highways from 80 to 100 per cent. 'As
long as I am Premier,' Ferguson informed the Good Roads Convention, 'we are
not going to do it.'

Privately he told Arthur Ford that the movement underfoot to have the
province assume the total cost of provincial highways had been inspired by
Frank Biggs and some of his friends. Ferguson believed this an impossible
proposition partly because counties which had already contributed through long-
term debenture schemes would demand provincial relief and much resentment
and jealousy would result. 'Just fancy what a flood of deputations and other
methods of pressure would be brought into being if we were to give free roads to
the public...' In any case, Ferguson intended to hold firm to the system already
in existence. 'I think when one takes into consideration the convenience to the
local people and the increased value of the property in the county, that this is
not an unfair charge. Besides this, I think it is a good principle to have local
people to contribute something towards the general highway programme. They
feel then that they have an interest in it.'[38] Decentralization and municipal
support in highways policy as in other activities remained a fundamental
principle of government in Ontario.

The Tories boasted a great deal about their efficiency in the Highways
Department; if the statistics of their campaign literature are to be believed, their
record was impressive. They had little success, however, in efforts to pry funds
loose from the dominion government. In October 1925 S.L. Squire, Deputy
Minister of Highways, pointed to the heavy financial burden on municipalities as
well as on the province and argued that since Ottawa derived enormous tax
revenues – in 1924 $94 million on auto parts alone – from the automobile
industry, and since roads had a vital economic significance, that some federal

contribution would be in order.[39] By late 1928 Ontario and other provinces, however, were still trying to convince Ottawa that it should provide assistance at least for roads that formed interprovincial links. The Canadian situation was in stark contrast to that in the United States where the federal government made enormous contributions to roadbuilding.

In the absence of federal assistance and despite its dubious constitutional validity, Ontario, following the example of several other provinces, decided to impose a gas tax. Rumours to this effect had been circulating for some time and a cry went up from interest groups including the Ontario Motor League that such a tax would make the automobile a luxury item far beyond the reach of the average man. Provincial officials had no sympathy with this attitude. Improved roads to be built by the larger provincial income which a tax would bring would save money for the motorist by improving his mileage. As well, the province still subscribed to the fiscal philosophy that the user must pay the cost and a gas tax conformed almost perfectly to this principle. When he met a deputation of several hundred Ontario Motor Leaguers in February 1925, Ferguson assured them that every penny of the revenue from a gas tax would be spent on road-building and maintenance.[40] He and Henry knew from their correspondence how great the pressure for more paved roads had become. Nonetheless, Ontario Motor Leaguers were stunned when Ferguson responded to their pressure by telling them the tax would be not two cents but three.

Despite the dire predictions, the new tax did nothing to slow down the onrushing automobile age. Ferguson sympathized with farmers and others when they wrote to complain about noise, dirt, and frightened horses. One rural resident, noting the proposed increase in the highway speed limit to 35 miles an hour, complained that this was class legislation and demanded that farmers be allowed in return to drive their horse vehicles on city streets at 20 miles an hour and 'swish around the trolleys on Yonge Street and make the autos take to the gutters...'[41] Ferguson, who had driven horses all his life and never owned a car, could appreciate that point of view. Asked to say a few words at a church picnic one afternoon, he lamented the impact the auto was having on Ontario's quiet countryside and described it as a curse on civilization. He was surprised the next day to discover that his remarks had been widely quoted in the Detroit press and that the Ford Motor Company was threatening a law suit.[42]

If Ferguson's intervention in Highways was sporadic, his concern with all matters relating to northern Ontario was direct and continuous. His special interest was the development of the province's forest industries. In mining matters he relied implicitly on Charles McCrea, one of Ontario's great ministers of Mines. There were, of course, exceptions to this rule and he took a personal interest in efforts to develop an Ontario iron-mining industry. A committee appointed by the Drury government to make recommendations on the possibility of utilizing local iron ore deposits in the iron and steel industry reported in

1923 that 'most thoughtful people' were apprehensive about the province's reliance on the United States for iron ore and recommended a bounty of one cent per unit on each ton. Ferguson supported the nationalist stance of the Iron Ore Committee which argued that it was 'better that this money should stay in our province and be used to build up and develop the industrial life of Ontario.'[43] His government in 1924 passed the Iron Ore Bounty Act, which attempted to stimulate the use of low grade ore by offering one half a cent per metallic unit 'in the long ton of beneficiated iron product, regardless of whether such ore were smelted in Ontario or not, also a similar bounty on natural ore, or ore not requiring beneficiation, mined and smelted in the province.' Speaking to the measure in the House, McCrea raised the possibility that with American sources nearing exhaustion, the United States might place an embargo on further exports. Unfortunately the provincial move was contingent upon an equivalent contribution from Ottawa and the federal government failed to act. Even if it had, it seems unlikely that the combined bounty could have had the desired effect.

Apparently Ferguson recognized this and he seems to have considered offering further aid to the Algoma Steel Company, believing it would play a leading part in any development of a process which would permit the economic utilization of Ontario ores. Early in 1925 he asked Edward Fitzgerald, formerly a Hudson's Bay Company executive, to analyze a 1924 report on the resources and capacity of Algoma, telling him he was 'extremely anxious to give some impetus to the development of our iron ores. I am convinced that therein lies the foundation of the greatest and most widespread industrial activity possible in this Province.'[44] But just as economic realities had prevented the success of efforts to replace American with Canadian coal, so too his efforts to encourage the mining of domestic iron ore floundered on the continued availability of a cheaper imported resource.

The Premier also demonstrated an active concern with the great new gold discovery at the Red Lake camp in the far northwest of the province. When promoter Jack Hammell asked to use government aircraft to freight supplies into the remote camp, he was surprised when Ferguson granted on-the-spot approval and provided four Provincial Air Service flying boats. Chartered at commercial rates, they allowed material to be brought in before the autumn freeze-up. A departmental publication later boasted that January 1926 saw 'the beginning of a gold rush that within the next few weeks lured well over a thousand prospectors into that remote and rugged land. It was, perhaps, the biggest rush since the Klondike...'[45]

Red Lake symbolized the return of prosperity to the Ontario mining fields. In the early postwar years, the production of nickel had slumped drastically and the annual production of minerals during the Drury administration averaged $65,600,000. For the rest of the decade, the figures showed a gradual but significant expansion. A 1923 output of just under $27,160,000 passed $85 million by 1926.[46] At mid-decade the province was approaching the stage of deep mining and McCrea undertook substantial research in methods applied in other countries where mining was carried on below three thousand feet. Yet despite changes in some of the conditions under which mining was carried on, the policies of the department under McCrea were similar in essentials to those established by his Tory predecessors, Ferguson and Cochrane.

Thus geological parties continued to be sent out to investigate particular regions and such a party contributed largely to the Red Lake discoveries. Prospectors were assisted in a variety of ways, including a limited number of free assays while the Temiskaming Testing Laboratory provided various services. The Ferguson government was particularly active in holding special classes for prospectors in mining centres and in another reform of some significance raised the status of the mining commissioner, an official responsible for adjudicating disputes, to the level of judge. Legislation also allowed the government, in McCrea's words, 'to promptly withdraw lands required for public purposes at strategic points, such as those required for townsites, etc., thus eliminating speculation and preventing complications.'[47] A start was made in the fight against the dread disease of silicosis, with research being carried on in conjunction with the Department of Health and legislation sponsored by the Attorney General bringing the disease under the list of those to which Workmen's Compensation applied. In this period, the provincial mine inspector was aided by four assistants and was responsible for overseeing safety and health precautions.[48]

Doubtless the increase in output during these years was due primarily to general economic circumstances; naturally, however, the Tories boasted that their policies had contributed to the increased prosperity. The Tory line was clear enough. They offered the operator stability, freedom from harassment, and a moderate level of taxation. The mine, McCrea boasted in 1926, 'pays no tax until it is making a profit of $10,000. When it is making its profit of $10,000, everything over that up to $1,000,000 is taxed to the extent of three per cent. Over $1,000,000 and up to $5,000,000 the tax is increased to five per cent, and for every million over that the tax increases one per cent.'[49] The Ferguson government also quietly removed the special levy which had been placed on nickel mines, and put that metal on the same basis as all others.[50] If the potentates of International Nickel had ever disliked Ferguson, they now had ample reason to change their minds.

The government argued vigorously that the speculative nature of the industry and the need to attract risk capital justified this low level of taxation. This, however, begged the question whether the great established mines of the province could not bear a heavier burden, thus returning vastly increased sums to the public treasury. McCrea's figures in his 1926 statement to the House are suggestive of the fortunes made by some mining men. The minister noted that in 1910-11 the level of gold production had not reached $150,000; in 1925 it was $30 million. Ontario, he pointed out, collected from its mining tax $287,000 but there was also a tax paid to the municipalities and one to the federal government. In addition, the province received some revenue from sale of mining lands, licenses, recording fees, and incidentals. McCrea estimated that the total 1925 tax paid by the mining companies to all levels of government was between $1,250,000 and $1,500,000. Total receipts for his department were $613,411 and expenditures were $285,863. Clearly the surplus of $327,000 representing the total amount the Ontario treasury received in that buoyant year from the vast mineral wealth of the province was a paltry sum.[51]

Was the public interest being served or were the owners robber barons denuding the province of its mineral wealth for their personal gain? There is no doubt that the government had the confidence of the operators and the *Northern Miner* was ecstatic in its support of Ferguson and McCrea. No wonder! Up to the end of 1925 the value of minerals taken from the Ontario northland exceeded $800,000,000; out of the silver camp had come over $200,000,000, out of the gold $480,000,000, 'and we have only scraped the fringe or edge of this gigantic area,' proclaimed the exuberant Mines minister. 'You can understand that perhaps some of us who are accused from time to time of being a little over-optimistic are not so far out in our judgement when we realize what has already been accomplished and when the best experts here tell us that whole area is of the kind where you are likely to have other Porcupines, other Kirkland Lakes, other Sudbury's and great metal wealth producing fields which are the property of the people of this province.'[52] Somehow the property of the people had become the profit of the owners. The Tories, however, argued convincingly that 'a widespread and prosperous mining industry is worth more to the province at large than any unduly heavy impost on production.' Although a slower and more controlled development might have been more in the long-run interest not only of the north but of the province at large, provincial policies contributed greatly to the prosperity of the people and excited little criticism from the men of the day.

The establishment of new camps, the creation of jobs, and the development of wealth seemed more important to decision makers than a higher immediate return from a more progressive tax scale — particularly since a slower rate of development might have wiped out those tax gains in any case. Certainly the boom psychology was hard to resist. The economic gains for Toronto and New York in the 1920s were not slight, and during the depression the continued high level of production in Ontario mining camps was a boon to the province. Still, the pace and kind of development left in its wake a social cost to be paid by later generations. Although the north supported and benefitted by extensive and rapid growth, many of the region's subsequent problems may be traced in some measure to the province's failure to shape more effectively the largely individualistic development of mining and also of pulp and paper. The only serious criticism offered in the twenties came from the hapless Farmer government, which so totally misunderstood the needs of the north and the mood of the day that the alternative it offered was swept away without serious consideration.

The failings of the developmental philosophy were most starkly revealed in the unchecked expansion of the forest industries, but there too the Ferguson administration at first seemed to go from triumph to triumph. After 1913 Canadian newsprint and pulp had unlimited free access to the American market and between that year and 1920 Canadian production of pulp and paper tripled to 867,000 tons. Throughout the 1920s as American demand grew, Canadian production expanded at a phenomenal rate and reached 2,725,000 tons in 1929. The statistics were impressive. By 1929 Canada accounted for 65 per cent of world newsprint exports. Of its 1929 production, '90 per cent was exported, and 90 per cent of this was exported to the United States.' Nine-tenths of this production came from Ontario and Quebec. This single industry was utilizing more than a quarter of the nation's water power capacity and about half that of Ontario and Quebec. In gross value of manufactured products, pulp and paper at $174 million in 1931 was far ahead of every other product; domestic export figures for 1932 showed wheat leading at $115 million and newsprint paper second at $103 million.[53] The impact of the industry on the Ontario economy was immense. Not one of the province's three million citizens was unaffected by the rise in its fortunes in the early twenties or its astounding collapse in the later years of the decade.

No other politician and few entrepreneurs possessed Howard Ferguson's intimate familiarity with the industry. Looking back from the depths of the depression, Ferguson told F.J. Sensenbrenner of Spruce Falls Pulp and Paper Company that 'I have always been keenly interested in the development of the northern portion of the province, and have given special personal attention to our forestry industries. ... I have had much to do from the very beginning with the initiation of almost all the newsprint undertakings in Ontario and I have sought to lend what assistance I might, consistent with the protection of the province, to the placing upon a permanent basis these great industrial establishments. It has been my good fortune to have enjoyed the co-operation and the confidence of the men in charge of the various plants manufacturing newsprint.'[54]

This boast betrayed the strengths and weaknesses of the Ferguson approach. Undoubtedly it was well that the administration should be headed by someone intimately familiar with the problems of pulp and paper development. The premier was in a position to expedite negotiations and carry through large projects to the advantage of the province. The year in which Ferguson assumed office saw 'the largest cut since the wartime high of 1915.'[55] Great new pulp mills were on the drawing boards while existing firms looked anxiously for assured supplies of timber. In these circumstances, the Ferguson Tories were busy devising new policies. Chastened perhaps by the Timber Commission and aware of the deficiencies of earlier timber administration in which the field force had received little supervision, Ferguson at an early stage created the position of Inspector of Crown Timber Agents and Supervisor of Operations and appointed to it Major J.I. Hartt, a hard-headed and competent public servant.[56] By late 1925 the government was ready with the most drastic changes in provincial policy since the days of the White-Cochrane reforms two decades earlier. They owed as much to Ferguson himself as to Lyons, the minister. Somehow, in a way which is not clear, the government had decided that American demands would continue to grow rapidly and a massive expansion was in order. Ferguson believed, somewhat recklessly perhaps, that 'in a few years we will practically have control of the United States market. ... If Ontario is to maintain her place she must keep up her production. This means the enlargement and stabilizing of our plants.'[57] Surely such inflated expectations explain much about what happened later.

The details of the new policy were announced on 13 January 1926.[58] The province had several objectives in view. Most important was expansion. The government, the press release stated, has 'concluded that the output of newsprint ... now amounting to approximately 2600 tons per day, should be increased to approximately 4500 tons per day...' To make this possible, timber sales had been offered in 1925 and tenders accepted from the Nipigon Corporation, the Spruce Falls Company, and several other companies. The construction of the necessary plant and water power facilities would require 'approximately 80 million dollars, and will give employment to about 14,000 employees.'

Secondly, the release emphasized, the companies had agreed to a new form of pulpwood contract. 'In the past pulp and paper companies have generally secured the areas allotted to them ... without due regard for the quantity of wood on such areas, but under the present agreements the companies only secure the right to cut a certain quantity of wood, which is estimated to be sufficient, by applying proper methods of cutting, and protection, to maintain their plants in continuous operation in perpetuity.' The new agreements bristled with clauses obliging the companies to contribute to fire protection, to specify how and when they would spend funds on their plant units and to carry out conservation measures. The government retained the right to deal with the lands and the timber, excepting pulp growing thereon, 'for settlement, mining, manufacturing, reforestation, or any other purpose whatsoever...' In return, the province promised to ensure that the company at all times had enough wood to produce the agreed upon volume of pulp. Each company had to deposit with the government $50,000 in cash and a $200,000 performance bond.

Thirdly, the new policy extended the nationalist creed of the manufacturing condition. Formerly, 'partial manufacture into pulp and paper was the basis of contract,' noted a 1926 campaign tract. The new policy, however, 'insures the exportation of the finished product rather than the raw material. In other words, the "development of home industry to the limit" is the new slogan.'[59] Speaking in the House in March 1924, James Lyons had cited statistics to show that by permitting the bulk of manufacturing to be done in the United States, Canadian industry had lost untold millions of dollars.[60] The new agreements required full manufacture into newsprint or the equivalent. Claiming itself unable to legislate to that effect, the province boasted that it had 'undertaken to do by agreement that which the Dominion Government should do through legislation.'[61]

The reforms of 1925 and 1926 largely achieved what White and Cochrane had attempted prematurely. Clearly the administration was responding to what it regarded as the interests of the province and its people and only secondarily to the wishes of the operators. And now the department had more of the machinery to ensure that its wishes were carried out. Under Major Hartt's leadership, annual conferences of outside timber agents were held while more effective enforcement, together with a 75 per cent increase in dues on spruce and balsam, meant a substantial growth in Crown revenues.[62] When complaints were made, they were as likely as not to reach the Premier's desk. Occasionally the big companies dragged their feet about buying pulpwood from the settlers. This was a serious matter to northerners and one man suggested to Ferguson that the province should take the timber off their hands. To do this, Ferguson replied, would require a huge staff of officials and 'would swamp the province.' Unable to act officially, he promised that 'if you have pulpwood for sale and cannot market it ... I will see that you get a sale for it.'[63]

Of course the Tories expected their northern policies to pay political dividends. With the 1926 election campaign in full swing, Ferguson was delighted when Abitibi agreed to establish a paper factory in Cochrane. Ferguson, who had carried out long negotiations with the company president, relayed the news to his Minister of Lands and Forests; so there would be no mistake he enclosed a copy of the correspondence, 'which of course you are at liberty to disclose to the people of Cochrane.'[64]

In fact the reforms announced in 1926 had been the result of arduous negotiations with the pulp and paper companies in which the Premier played a large role. Spruce Falls, with its operations centred at Kapuskasing, had been particularly nervous about the requirements of the new pulpwood contracts. In 1926 the *New York Times* purchased a major interest in Spruce Falls and apparently it was the *Times* which objected most strenuously. Ferguson's old friend, Strachan Johnston of the Tilley firm, was Spruce Falls' legal adviser and he wrote the Premier that the Company was having difficulty marketing its securities because of the stringency of the agreement.[65]

Ferguson responded with some heat. 'I was greatly astonished to read your letter,' he told Johnston, 'and frankly, I am still at a loss to understand why you should have found it necessary to write me on this subject.' The Crown, he reminded the corporation lawyer, 'has always retained to itself enabling power by which it might promptly and effectively protect itself. A clause in some such form as the one quoted is practically a standard clause ... but I know of no case in which it has ever been invoked...'

What the Crown expects is reasonable compliance with the covenants and obligations, and is always ready and willing to give consideration to difficulties that may arise to prevent the strict observance of the letter of a contract. Personally I think your clients are shying at a shadow. The Crown expects to receive a large income from timber cut by such companies as yours, and is of course deeply interested in their maintenance. One of the very purposes of the recent timber sale was to enable your company and others of a similar character to enlarge their capacity and put themselves on a sound financial basis, so that they may become perpetual industries. ... In a sense we are just as deeply interested in the success of your company as its shareholders. In fact, we are in a way the largest shareholders, because we contributed the power and the timber at a very reasonable price, that will undoubtedly enable your organization to flourish.[66]

The partnership Ferguson was postulating between government and private industry was a logical consequence of the Crown's ownership of the natural resource. The province retained every legal power to protect itself. Pulp and paper, however, was an international industry and the hollowness of Ferguson's boast that within a few years Canada would 'have control of the United States market' would soon be obvious to all. No one in the provincial government could begin to scrutinize the operations of the great international corporations, while the American publishers' lobby remained an independent force of enormous power. When the province agreed to expand the amount of pulpwood produced for export, there appears to have been little effort to assess the limits of the American market or the motives of the corporations which so readily agreed to build new plants. If difficulties did occur, how could the protective clauses of the pulpwood agreements provide a shield against economic realities? This was a risk that the conditions of the market imposed and against which government no more than private enterprise could ever be adequately shielded. One day there would be a price to pay.

But in 1925 and 1926, the balmy days continued. The pulp and paper industry reached undreamed-of levels of production and the booming mining camps created a golden age for the Ontario northland. The T&NO RR pushed ahead with its branch lines and the Ontario Hydro, determined that mining development would not again face the power shortage which had crippled production in some areas in the early part of the decade, engaged in an intensive effort to harness the northern rivers. In many instances, the companies themselves purchased power rights under strictly defined agreements, as Spruce Falls, for example, did at Smokey Falls; as well, the Hydro began to play a vital role in the north. One of its earliest operations was the Cameron Falls development on the Nipigon River. Above all, the north was losing its remoteness before the exploitive will and new technology of the day. The availability of surplus war planes and of men who could fly them gave Ontario a daring new breed, the bush pilots, who emulated the exploits of the voyageurs of old. There were also, of course, the brilliant young Hydro engineers who pioneered their technology as they went, the provincial geologists, the prospectors who flocked to each new camp and the mining engineers who were adapting the techniques of deep mining to the needs of Ontario. Taken together this wedding of technology and human daring contributed to the sense that a new age of discovery and adventure was unfolding in Ontario.

The Ferguson government was well tuned to this spirit. Beck had always exemplified it and now McCrea, Magrath, Lyons, and above all Ferguson himself brought imagination and a measure of daring to the once stodgy halls of government. The promoters, the speculators, the engineers, the prospectors, good men and bad, were familiar figures in the corridors of Queen's Park and the inner sanctums of the ministers. In 1923 the discontent of the north had yielded occasional calls for secession; the appointment of Frank Keefer, the member for Port Arthur, to the new position of Legislative Secretary for Northern Ontario was Ferguson's response to such mutterings. Perhaps this was merely a political gesture; Keefer was an able man but his appointment was less than a success. In a report dated 24 November 1924, he dilated on the benefits of the work he had done and claimed that 'the talk of separation which at one time had become very prevalent and endorsed by Boards of Trade locally, had completely died out.'[67] When he left his position in 1926, he was not replaced.

A more significant force in the life of the average settler than the Legislative Secretary was the Supervisor of Settlement, an official first appointed in 1924. The job went to an experienced northerner, Colonel W.R. Smyth, whose activities did much to bring pioneers' needs to the attention of Queen's Park. Under Smyth's influence, the inroads of spurious settlers whose real interest lay in denuding the land of timber were checked, while the pulp and paper companies were encouraged to buy wood wherever possible from the settlers. The average amount of land granted to a settler was reduced to a realistic quarter section or 80 acres. In general, Smyth was able, in the words of the annual report for 1925, to provide 'the hitherto missing link between the Government and the settler.'[68]

Certainly the province's faith in the agricultural possibilities of the Great Clay Belt remained undiminished and the same report asserted that 'the vast acreage in the Great Clay Plains ... some day must play a large part in feeding the teeming millions of Europe.' In an attack on Ottawa, it claimed that in the absence of 'a pronounced clear-cut immigration policy ... little hope can be held out for much beyond a very gradual development...' Yet the province, under Frank Keefer's leadership, did encourage several experiments in group settlement, most notably in the township of Sibley, near Port Arthur, in which a tract of land was reserved for Danes who received assistance from the province. In Keefer's mind at least, there was some advantage to bringing in Danes, Scandinavians, Hollanders, and other European Protestants, for these, he told Ferguson, 'will offset the steady inflow we are having of the French-Canadian, resulting from the Roman Catholic immigration policy.'[69]

The most significant change in policy at the administrative level was the creation in 1926 of a separate Department of Northern Development which took over the duties of several other departments, including that of Public Works for road and drainage work, and generally assumed responsibility for administering the funds provided under the Northern Ontario Development Act. The period was one of change as well in the Department of Lands and Forests. Largely through the enthusiasm of Jim Lyons, the Ontario Air Service was inaugurated in 1924 with a fleet of 16 flying boats and headquarters at the Sault. The Air Service soon proved of enormous value in the task of mapping and surveying and in fire prevention work, particularly in remote regions where no lookout tower organization existed.[70]

Finally, in another change of some moment, Dr Zavitz was elevated from head of the Forestry Branch to the new position of Deputy Minister of Forestry. For some time he had chafed under the unimaginative supervision of the Department's deputy minister, Walter Cain, whom the Farmers had appointed to replace Albert Grigg. When he had grumbled to some of his associates, the advice he received was 'Get to know your minister better.' Fortunately for Zavitz, his old friend Ferguson became Acting Minister of Lands and Forests for a few months at this time. Zavitz, so the story goes, decided to invite his chief on a fishing trip but took the precaution of preparing his ground in advance by stocking the stream at every likely overhang with several bottles of cold beer – presumably not the 4.4 variety. 'The best damn stream I ever fished,' was the Premier's response and within weeks Zavitz became a deputy minister.[71]

The assumptions which motivated the Ferguson administration's economic policies differed little from those of most other North American governments in the 1920s. Frugal administration and an uncritical commitment to the prevailing philosophy of development were the twin pillars on which Ferguson's several programs stood. Yet within the limits of those assumptions, Ferguson and his colleagues demonstrated an impressive managerial competence. They proved able to pursue large undertakings with skill and integrity. The developmental projects of the period — the highways built, the electrical power harnessed, the expansion in industrial capacity — were no mean achievements. And they were carried through without the breath of major scandal.

In a 1923 statement to *Maclean's Magazine*, the Premier revealed another side as he expressed some sense of the rapidly developing conservationist ethic and coupled the apparently contradictory goals of development and conservation of natural resources. 'I do not consider,' he asserted 'that the mere exploitation of these resources, regardless of the future, will tend to insure the lasting welfare and prosperity of the province. What we require is an intelligent and consistent policy in the management of our heritage...'[72] Yet if the work of the foresters and others proved that the conservationist ethic was not absent from provincial policies, the emphasis undeniably was on development. Nonetheless, if the return to the province through taxation was small, and if the evils of patronage had not been banished from the land, the Ferguson government did put an end to many of the depredations of an earlier day. Its policies in no sense represented a craven surrender to timber pirates, wildcat promoters, or Bay Street brokers. They were deliberately and responsibly arrived at and honestly and shrewdly administered. There is every reason to believe that they faithfully reflected the views of most Ontarians. The province's resources would benefit no one in their undeveloped state. Ontario was a great, raw province and whatever it might offer its people would only be made available when bold and imaginative men moved aggressively to make it so. Ferguson and his colleagues decided, rightly or wrongly, that Ontarians would benefit more by policies which would attract investment, create jobs, and develop those resources than by the deceptively attractive hope of a larger immediate return through higher taxes and dues.

Much of this development was made possible by American investment and American enterprise. Ferguson was aware of the threat to the provincial economy posed by continentalist trends of development and he directed much attention to policies designed to lessen Ontario's dependence on American raw materials. He attempted, with mixed success, to enunciate strategies, including the iron bounty, the Alberta coal policy, opposition to the export of electrical energy, and the extension of the manufacturing condition, which would benefit not only the provincial but the national economic interest. Whatever the deficiencies of those policies, they were pursued by men with a sincere concern for the public interest and a determination to assist in the creation of a healthy and balanced provincial economy. Many of the same challenges would remain to be taken up by the Ferguson administration during its second term.

The Limited State

For decades Ontarians boasted about the virtues of their school system; they believed as well, in the words of a minister in the Ferguson cabinet, that 'Ontario stands admittedly in the forefront of the provinces in regard to social legislation.'[1]

Once, no doubt, this had been true. As early as 1859 a board of inspectors in the United Canadas was established which provided creative leadership in the administration of hospitals, jails, and asylums; and a body of law concerned itself with the rights of children, mental illness, the protection of the poor, and community health. By 1867 almost a quarter of the provincial budget was spent on society's various welfare needs.[2] After Confederation, Ontario possessed buoyant revenues and the pace accelerated. The Charity Aid Act of 1874 provided for the inspection of private as well as public institutions in receipt of provincial funds, the grant structure was rationalized, and additional provincial institutions founded for the mentally ill, the deaf and dumb, and the blind. Under Mowat new legislative enactments were passed to protect the working-man, notably the Workmen's Compensation Act of 1886 and the Factory Act of the same year. A permanent Board of Health established in 1882 received authority to regulate local bodies and the Children's Act of 1893 provided support for the formation of children's aid societies. Typical of much Ontario legislation, the Children's Act mixed a measure of provincial funding and inspection with a reliance on private charitable initiative through volunteer workers, and the whole system was organized around the local government unit which retained primary financial and organizational responsibility.

The achievements of nineteenth-century social legislation need not obscure its true nature. In Oliver Mowat's Ontario, society remained small and intimate. Friends, neighbours, and above all the extended family would minister to the unfortunate. Legislative action when required was intended in most cases only for the unfortunate few. It was natural that such protection was usually provided by the municipality, for communities were still small and the Victorian sense of social and religious responsibility reinforced the close texture of familial relationships. Social legislation was an extension of the role of home and church. Attempts to regulate class and economic relationships were directed not at the entire population but at special circumstances. The factory laws, for example, were protective in nature. Theoretically they represented a significant interference by the state with the economy; in reality they affected a small portion of the population and cost little to administer. Massive, open-ended programs of government spending and extensive provincial regulation and intervention were unknown.

The simple, rural Ontario of Mowat's day was slow to change. Although the 1911 census showed that more than half the people of the province lived in incorporated communities, old habits and attitudes persisted. Not even the legislative record of Whitney progressivism portended any fundamental shift in social attitudes and the new Workmen's Compensation Act of 1914 excited a wildly exaggerated opposition. The recession of 1913-14 gave the province its first experience of mass unemployment while the dislocations caused by World War I – inflation, fuel and housing shortages, and social unrest – brought new needs to the fore. The Hearst government established a child welfare bureau and government employment offices, created a Department of Labour, provided limited funds to stimulate housing, and prepared but did not pass legislation to establish mothers' allowances and a minimum wage for women. Attacked by the rural press for making 'huge concessions to socialism' and by many old-time Tories who believed their party had been captured by Methodist do-gooders, the Hearst administration went down to resounding defeat. Although the Farmer-Labour government talked grandiosely about social reform and did implement the minimum wage and mothers' allowance legislation prepared by Hearst, its own record was as conventional as yesterday. Drury's Adoption Act, an Unmarried Parents Act, which placed financial responsibility for an illegitimate child on the father, and a Dependent Parents Act, which made children responsible for the care of indigent parents, were examples of sound Victorian legislation. They involved no new financial commitments and used the power of the state to define and enforce individual responsibility.

Howard Ferguson was in the same tradition. He was thirty years of age when the twentieth century began. The system of social relationships he understood had been shaped well prior to World War I. He was, of course, capable of adapting to change but it would take some nearly cataclysmic occurrence to shake his traditional beliefs and cause him to question his inherited value system. In the early 1920s even the Great War was regarded only as a tragic incident and in provincial affairs at least it was assumed that 'normalcy' would return and things would continue much as they always had.

These tendencies deepened when the 1923 election success of Ferguson's attack on the Drury administration's extravagance acquired almost symbolic significance. Ferguson was well aware of the growing demands on municipal and provincial governments but, like other politicians of the day, he believed that economy, balanced budgets, and tax reductions were the height of statesmanship. Under his leadership, there were occasional hints that attitudes were changing and that Queen's Park realized that the existing structure was inadequate to the needs of urban, industrial Ontario. Yet the only major breach in the prewar approach, old age pensions legislation, was a response to special political circumstances and was itself hedged with restrictions.

The attitudes of the 1920s were accurately delineated by A.E. Grauer, writing for the Rowell-Sirois Commission in the late 1930s, when he pointed out that governments still believed that the worker could best be assisted by the creation of a climate conducive to economic expansion and that wages were high enough to allow the individual to look after his own needs. 'The optimistic faith of a new country with vast natural resources in its future plus the stimulus of individualistic thought from the United States tended to keep political and business thought in Canada away from social insurance.'[3] To this must be added the conviction of most of the leaders of Ferguson's generation that there already existed an adequate system for coping with the needs of the 'unfortunate few'; in Ontario at least a fairly general prosperity served to sustain this faith until the end of the decade.

Certainly these considerations suggest the essence of Ferguson's beliefs. The Ontario premier, for example, seldom lost an opportunity to denounce the British dole system for undermining what he held to be the traditional self-reliance of Englishmen. So convinced was he on this score that even in the midst of the Great Depression he wrote from England to warn his successor against adopting any such scheme. Ontario, he insisted with monotonous frequency, could best be served by governmental economy and economic growth. A generous and progressive structure was already in place; it had developed organically over the years and he viewed it as elaborate and advanced. Its genius was the balance it struck between local initiative and provincial supervision, and with its day-to-day operation the province had little direct concern.

Thus when he received letters soliciting his support on behalf of a particular applicant before the Mothers' Allowance Commission, the Workmen's Compensation Board, or some other provincial agency, a standard response would go out under his signature. Carefully he would point out that 'the Government has no control over the Workmen's Compensation Board. ... We have no more right to interfere than we have in the affairs of the ordinary Court of Justice...' Sometimes he would add that 'we do not even contribute to the maintenance of the Board. The employers pay for the whole organization.' When applicants did not come within the strict terms which entitled them to assistance, they might receive a letter from the Premier telling them that 'there is a law on the Statute Book that says the Mothers' Allowance Board can give assistance to mothers with two children under 16 years of age. They cannot possibly go beyond that. ... I want you to understand that it is not any fault of the Mothers' Allowances Board – it is because they cannot go beyond the limit of the authority given them by the law.' Of course this was less than frank; Ferguson did not point out that with his majority he could have changed the law any time he saw fit to do so. Yet in a variety of ways by no means restricted to the welfare field he found it convenient to point to the limitations which the existence of provincial agencies and boards placed on his own powers. 'Of course you know that the Government does not control the Hydro-Electric Power Commission in any sense' was a frequent and disingenuous response to letters received. When flooded with complaints about lax enforcement of the OTA he would point out that 'you apparently have the impression ... that the Ontario Government is expected to police the Province and look after law enforcement in every locality. This, of course, is an erroneous idea.'[4]

If there had been any considerable discontent with the system as it existed, Ferguson's acute political sense would have reacted more positively, but neither he nor the leaders of the other Ontario political groups presented a significant program of social reform. Perhaps the old structures, the family, the church, the local community, could still respond adequately to the needs of the unfortunate; or perhaps politicians thinking too exclusively of economy and economic growth were deliberately turning a blind eye. The underprivileged, after all, remained powerless and inarticulate; they lacked the forums to make their presence felt. But that they were there, even in the 1920s, is not to be doubted. Ferguson's correspondence testified to that. The letters he received, usually semi-literate and scrawled in pencil on cheap paper, pointed to another Ontario, a province of lost and helpless people by-passed by the vaunted prosperity and technical proficiency of the age. Only the depression would fully reveal the extent to which the old Ontario of small communities and the extended family had passed into history; only the sufferings of that terrible decade would begin to elicit new solutions to the problems of poverty and despair.

Between 1921 and 1930 Ontario's expenditures on public welfare programs, excluding relief, grew from $3,491,000 to $10,557,000 while municipal expenditures went from $9,475,000 to $13,660,000.[5] Major responsibility for welfare administration during the Ferguson years rested with Provincial Secretary Lincoln Goldie, whose department included the Bureau of Municipal Affairs, the Neglected and Dependent Children's Branch (in which J.J. Kelso still laboured as supervisor), and the Hospitals and Prisons Branch. That such duties should devolve on the Provincial Secretary suggests that supervision and administration were held to be more significant than broader and more creative considerations. Goldie himself, a businessman with little experience in the welfare field, seems to have given little thought to policy review. Provincial aid for most of the institutions under his supervision was fixed by statute and about the only change of note during these years was a slight increase in amount.

The first line of responsibility for administering hospitals, orphanages, and houses of refuge normally lay with boards of trustees acting under provincial charters. As well, provincial statutes thrust a variety of responsibilities on the units of local government. Cities and counties were required to establish Houses of Refuge for the indigent-aged and these same bodies also often provided outdoor relief for the needy; the Mothers' Allowances legislation required substantial municipal contributions; the Children's Aid legislation directed municipalities to establish shelters or temporary homes. General hospitals were neither owned nor controlled by the province but were operated under trustees and financed by payments from patients and municipal grants with a minimum of provincial assistance. The major exceptions to this system of private initiative and municipal support were the Ontario Hospitals for the Insane. They were owned and directly controlled by the province – although local governments were responsible for the destitute insane. The province also ran institutions for the deaf and the blind.

The Ferguson government effected no fundamental changes in this structure. As a general rule, all who could afford to pay the full cost of any service provided were expected to do so and the law made careful provision for the collection of sums owing from the families or estates of any of those cared for. In the case of indigents, the responsibility was regarded as primarily municipal. The province assisted general hospitals by contributing 50 cents per day per patient for the first ten years of the hospital's existence but thereafter contribution was made only in the case of needy patients and 'in all cases the limit is 120 days, and if the patients remain in the hospital longer than that period the refuge rate of ten cents per day is allowed.'[6] Since the average daily cost was $3.12 per day, the provincial contribution was of marginal significance. Some of the other provinces did not restrict their grants merely to indigents but it is unclear whether this reflected greater generosity and a more highly developed sense of social responsibility on their part or weaker systems of municipal government. To sanatoria for consumptives, the province contributed seventy-five cents a day for the maintenance of indigents; grants to Houses of Refuge were ten cents a day and to orphanages five cents.

Obviously private philanthropy and municipal support played a major role in financing provincial health care and charitable institutions. Officially at least, the municipality still was considered an extension of the family and was expected to marshall its own resources in support of its people. Equally obvious, many families of small means lived in constant fear of being ruined financially by illness or other mishap. In return for its small financial contribution, the province assumed the responsibility of regulation and inspection; yet diversity remained the rule, with enormous variations across the province in standards and costs. More uniform standards and substantial increases in provincial funding were glaring needs but these reforms were precluded by the tenacious endurance of the older ethic of self-help and local control.

If the government refused to recognize the need for reform, those forced to work under the existing system understood its deficiencies well enough. Thus the 1926 submission of the Ontario Hospital Association to the province was a heart-felt request for increased financial support. Pointing to the 1924 report of the Inspector of Hospitals to Hospital Boards which emphasized the 'need for accommodation for the great number of people who cannot afford to pay the rates charged for private patients' rooms and yet who do not wish to be classed among the indigents,' the Association argued that the chief reason for this was that the municipalities and the province did not pay the hospitals 'anything like the actual cost of the maintenance of public ward or indigent patients.' As a result, the paying patient was forced to pay a portion of the cost of indigent care in his own bill.

The state, the association pointed out, paid the cost of educating the young; 'why should it not pay 100 per cent of the cost of the care of its indigent sick?' Every province in the dominion, except Quebec, paid more towards this cost than did Ontario. 'Holding down the revenue (from whatever source) of a hospital to an amount barely sufficient to enable it to function as a going concern makes it impossible to provide all those facilities and equipment that are now regarded as essential to proper diagnosis and treatment of disease. The small- and moderate-sized hospitals at many points throughout the Province and away from the large centres are absolutely essential,' the submission continued, and the Inspector's office in the Provincial Secretary's Department was well aware of how many of these institutions lacked adequate facilities 'simply because they require every dollar of revenue under existing conditions to pay the cost of running from day to day.'[7] In this area at least, ruthless economy and the philosophy of self-help were beginning to exact a price in the form of rapidly deteriorating standards of health care and a terrible burden of costs on thousands of citizens of moderate means.

In the early 1920s the functioning of the provincial inspectorate itself left much to be desired. In 1925 the report of an investigation into aspects of the Provincial Secretary's Department carried out by Colonel Lockhart Gordon and police officials at Ferguson's request revealed shocking conditions of laxity and criminality in the Inspectorate.[8] Although changes were effected in response to the Gordon report, the department continued to mark time until a Royal Commission investigation in 1930 emphasized again the need for fundamental reform.

There was, nonetheless, a growing recognition on the Premier's part that some at least of the province's social services demanded attention and reform. Early in 1924 he asked J.J. Kelso to give some thought to the state of child welfare work in Ontario. Kelso had grown old in the provincial service and, perhaps because he was so much a part of the existing system, he had little to offer beyond the suggestion that there should be 'better organization and coordination' among existing agencies and departments. Ferguson agreed that a thorough reorganization 'of all the welfare work that is to be done by the Government' was in order. He too may have been thinking largely of an administrative reordering and even here little seems to have been done.[9] In one area, however, he planned to strike out in an apparently new direction.

Yet the Premier's scheme as it unfolded only served to confirm the prevailing governmental approach to charitable and welfare work. It was no accident, perhaps, that it was modelled to a considerable extent on a similar scheme in Shawville, Quebec, the province in which welfare functions were most firmly in the hands of private and religious organizations. The new project, a Boys' Training School at Bowmanville, was, according to Ferguson, one phase of 'a policy of a comprehensive character that will more meet the needs of a proper child welfare programme for the whole Province.'[10] Undoubtedly the idea on which Bowmanville was based was liberal and reformist. Organized around a cottage system, the school received 'wayward' boys on the recommendation of the courts, service clubs, and other organizations whenever it was felt they might benefit from the available facilities. In many cases there was no offence involved and the expectation was that a change in environment and the application of professional guidance would be a useful social corrective. All boys were 'admitted' rather than 'committed' and as soon as appropriate were placed in private homes. Older boys were assisted to find employment and supervised through an innovative follow-up system under which they remained a ward of the home until they reached legal maturity.

It was Bowmanville's organizational structure which placed it firmly in an older tradition of social service. Wherever the original idea came from, Ferguson was the guiding force which saw the scheme through its formative stages. In January 1924 he told Judge J.F. McKinley of the Ottawa Juvenile Court that 'if we could organize an independent Board upon which the Government, of course, would have representation, but which would be largely made up of public-spirited people interested in the reformation of wayward lads, it would do infinitely better work than if operated directly as a Department of the Government. Organizations of this kind, when controlled exclusively by the Government, are apt to be regarded as penal rather than corrective, and they do not receive as wide-spread and generous support from the public as they should.' Ferguson's expectation was that Judge McKinley and others like him would canvass those interested in boys' work in the hope of securing 'practical aid in carrying out our plans. I am confident ... that if we can be assured of the active support in a financial way of a number of our friends, we could establish the best institution of this character anywhere on the continent.'[11]

Ferguson's plans went ahead rapidly. Able to draw on his vast circle of acquaintances and knowledgeable in all the techniques of fund-raising, he propagandized widely on behalf of Bowmanville. Of course it helped to be premier and his campaign was a practical demonstration of that mix of politics and pulpitry which was the style of his premiership. 'Let me thank you,' wrote the president of Rotary of Toronto, 'for the excellent presentation which you made ... of your proposal with respect to Boys' Work. ... As a direct result of your sincere and frank statement of your desire that this institution should be removed from the regular Government Institution, the Rotary Club have heartily endorsed the farm at Bowmanville.'[12] Rotary's provincial organization offered its support and from across the province Rotary clubs provided financial support, the Toronto Club, for example, promising up to $10,000.

With the original land donated by a public-spirited farmer and other service clubs and private citizens also offering assistance, Bowmanville was well launched. The province did its part by passing legislation and providing organizational assistance and leadership. 'No new departure in work for the benefit of children has ever proceeded with such phenomenal results' boasted the Tory 1926 election literature. Ferguson took enormous pride in Bowmanville and seldom failed to point out that 'it is not to be undertaken as a Government enterprise, because I am afraid that organizations of this kind, when they are entirely under the direction of the Government, do not always attract the support of public-spirited people as they should.'[13] The service clubs continued to offer assistance as Bowmanville became a functioning institution. Writing in 1929 to thank the president of Rotary of Hamilton for a contribution, Ferguson suggested that 'if we can carry on the Bowmanville undertaking on the basis of a public service supported by voluntary effort ... we will be able to rejoice in the fulfillment of a great work. The Bowmanville School will always be a monument to the spirit and effort and practical support of the various Service Clubs.'[14] Equally it was a monument to an older and not ignoble tradition of self-help in social service, one which would soon be found wanting as the province experienced the yet undreamed-of conditions of the Great Depression.

The other governmental body concerned with health and welfare needs was the Department of Health and Labour. The Department of Health, established in 1924, received responsibility for many of the duties of the earlier Board of Health and generally provided a thrust and direction previously lacking in the public health activities of the province. Ferguson gave the new portfolio to his old friend, Forbes Godfrey, who also retained Labour. Godfrey's record in the Health field was largely devoid of legislative achievements. As in other departments, such as Agriculture, conditions across the province warranted, perhaps demanded, that major emphasis be placed on practical efforts in the field.

'Education rather than legislation' has been the guide of the department, proclaimed the Tory campaign literature. That the new department did not take over responsibility for hospitals and related institutions from the Provincial

Secretary would indicate that at first it was regarded largely as a glorified Board of Health. It included under its wing an Industrial Hygiene Division, a Sanitary Engineering Branch, and a Division of Public Health Education.

The various units took as their first task the development of the field work and practical assistance which was so sorely needed across the province. In a sense this reflected again the Tory determination to achieve a fairer and more democratic dissemination of services and skills. An early effort started in September 1923 was the provision of free insulin to needy diabetics.[15] In 1925 Godfrey established a Division of Dental Services which during the first year of its existence provided dental examinations to 200,000 children about Ontario. This work was conducted with the co-operation of the Oral Hygiene Committee of the Ontario Dental Association. In a letter to Ferguson, the chairman of that group congratulated him on the efficiency with which Godfrey and the Department had carried on their work. Many municipalities, he noted, 'are organizing School Dental Services. Hospital Departments and Factory Clinics have also been established,' and he urged the province on to even greater efforts.[16] A Travelling Diagnostic Clinic with x-ray apparatus established in 1923 toured the province in an attempt to arrest the development of tuberculosis through early detection and to combat silicosis in miners. The Public Health Education Division embarked on a series of public health campaigns in the schools and in the community at large. By 1926, for example, three physicians and 15 public health nurses were employed to carry out a program of demonstrations and instructions designed to reduce the rate of infant mortality. Utilizing the press, radio, moving pictures, school fairs, and the Public Health Section of the CNE, the Division reached into the schools and homes of the province with an enormous variety of literature on nutrition, hygiene, child care, and other health matters.

Politically this approach had the advantage of being relatively inexpensive and not offending vested interests who would have been suspicious of any full-scale assault on old ways and habits. The Tories were also able to claim that the Department's activities were carrying health care and education to the remote parts of the province and distributing to rural communities advantages which formerly had been enjoyed only by those in the cities. Undoubtedly the effect of their propaganda helped obscure the deficiencies of their programs, yet while a more forceful provincial presence and an infusion of public funds on a more substantial scale would have achieved results more quickly, there was an undeniable need for the educational and practical campaign the Department was waging. Although the deficiencies of the province's health care system would soon become glaringly obvious, the very different approach of later years which stressed legislation and open-ended spending programs to some degree was built upon the more mundane achievements of the Department under Forbes Godfrey.

Godfrey's major interest lay in the health care field and it is not surprising that under his leadership the Department of Labour should be less active. As well, the Independent Labour party remained largely moribund and the trade unions themselves were in no position to apply pressure to the government. Union membership in Ontario declined from 87,105 in 1919 to 63,251 in 1925 and problems caused by unemployment, an open shop campaign among employers, and fear of federal immigration programs helped make the movement all but irrelevant politically.[17] In the absence of political pressure and under a minister whose real concerns were elsewhere, the Department was neither aggressive nor progressive. Legislation already on the books such as the Factory Act was enforced and several amendments widened and improved the application of the Workmen's Compensation Act. Silicosis and other diseases were added to those which qualified a workman for compensation and in 1924 a measure known as the Rehabilitation Act provided for the Board to assist workmen in re-establishing themselves in employment and learning new trades. Interestingly, the most important challenge the government faced in the labour field during its first term, the continuing crisis of unemployment, was handled not by Dr Godfrey but by the two strong men of the administration, Nickle and Ferguson.

The economic recovery underway in late 1923 had tapered off and the fall and early winter of 1924-5 saw the government beleaguered with requests for aid from individuals and municipalities. Shocked at the extent of the distress evident in a delegation of unemployed men from Hamilton, Ferguson in December fired off a telegram asking the Minister of Militia for permission to use the barracks in Hamilton as a temporary shelter. For several weeks he received a run-around and finally in early January the officer in charge returned a blunt refusal.[18] Telegrams and petitions continued to be received from city councils representing London, Hamilton, Kitchener, Kingston, and other municipalities, leaving no doubt of the seriousness of the situation. Typical was a message from the Welland City Council expressing its 'wish to impress upon you the urgent need of some method of relief for this district as the unemployment situation is increasing daily...'[19]

Once again the federal and provincial governments engaged in their depressingly familiar charade of attempting to pass responsibility on to the other. In 1921 the Meighen government had emphasized that 'unemployment relief always has been, and must necessarily continue to be, primarily a municipal responsibility, and in the second instance the responsibility of the province.' Similarly the King government in 1922 asserted that 'unemployment relief is fundamentally a municipal and provincial responsibility' and insisted that 'the abnormal economic and industrial conditions now existing and arising in a measure out of the late war alone afford justification for action on the part of the federal authorities.'[20] Gradually the King Liberals withdrew their financial support. Municipalities in Ontario received unemployment relief grants of

$162,000 in 1921-2, increasing to $520,000 in 1922-3 but dropping to $1300 in 1923-4.[21] In 1924-5, despite extensive unemployment and much distress, no federal money was received. Mackenzie King now saw fit to argue that as unemployment was a local matter, federal intervention would violate the constitution. In reply, W.F. Nickle defied King to point to anything in the BNA Act to prevent Ottawa from assuming part of the burden.[22]

Early in February 1925, Ferguson announced his program. At an estimated cost of $200,000, his government would share with the municipalities the expenditure upon unemployment relief incurred between 1 February and 15 April 1925, by paying one-third of the excess over the normal labour cost incurred by any municipality in work undertaken for the purpose of relieving unemployment; and, secondly, one-third of the excess expenditure incurred in respect of 'other unemployment relief measures.' Three aspects of this program were particularly revealing. Most obviously, the province was not relieving the municipalities of the major burden. Each co-operating municipality was to appoint an appropriate relief organization. Secondly, although the giving of food, fuel, and clothing were all declared eligible, 'cash doles' were explicitly rejected. Finally, as in everything the Ferguson government did, the political element was not lost to view. Ferguson's press release declaimed that

the view of the provincial government is that the responsibility for the care of its citizens rests primarily with the municipality. This has already been pointed out by the Prime Minister in a letter addressed to the Mayor of Toronto some months ago. ... The responsibility rests secondarily with the Dominion Government which has control of and encourages immigration, and not always with due care to proper selection. Moreover, from the broad national view of citizenship, the Dominion Government certainly owes it to all Canadian citizens to help maintain their position in the country under normal conditions.

It would appear, however, that the Dominion Government has declined to lend assistance in the present critical condition. The alleged reason given, I understand, is that under the British North America Act the Dominion Government is precluded from giving aid under such circumstances. I am sure that this will be a surprisingly novel interpretation of our constitution to our people. *Parliament surely is supreme and can vote public moneys for any purpose it may deem proper.*[23]

The province, Ferguson continued, had no direct responsibility but 'the condition has reached such a serious point that this is no time to cavil about the question of responsibility. Many of our people are in dire distress and must be provided with the means of sustenance.' If federal Liberal penny-pinching was to deny the province the sums it had formerly received in support of such work, Ferguson was determined to make King pay a political price. In the months ahead in his private correspondence he frequently informed petitioners that Ottawa, with control over immigration policy, was primarily responsible for the condition of things. Still, it took considerable gall for the provincial rights champion to argue so forthrightly in favour of the supremacy of Parliament and of the federal spending power.

Ferguson soon found himself attacked for even the sorely limited assistance the province deemed fit to offer the unemployed. Interestingly, most of the objections came largely from those who were far down the ladder of literacy. 'It is too bad,' wrote a disgusted taxpayer from RR 3, Havelock, 'for the honest tax payer to have to keep those lasey lofers it is time something was done to stop this foul play.'[24] Ferguson himself could only suggest that the government should try to speed up industry and support the development of such Canadian resources as Alberta coal, but he admitted that in the final analysis he was at a loss to know what else any government could do to 'meet the awful depression that existed today.'[25]

This line of argument was unacceptable to Peter Heenan, the Labour member for Kenora. When Heenan introduced a motion regretting the government's failure to establish an unemployment insurance scheme, Ferguson ordered the Deputy Minister of Labour, J.H. Ballantyne, to report on the situation. Ballantyne's views, entirely conventional, confirmed the Premier's own preconceptions and presented a useful statement of the current wisdom.[26] Although Ballantyne recognized that the development of modern industry had caused governments to attempt to alleviate the resulting social problems, he pointed to the grave financial difficulties faced by British unemployment schemes and claimed that 'the granting of cash doles or donations to unemployed persons is beyond question harmful and demoralizing to many of them...' In any case, he added, 'conditions are hardly comparable between Europe and America.' 'Countries that have adopted Unemployment Insurance Schemes have not the same opportunities for economic expansion and development as exist in this country.' In the United States the idea was taking root that each employer had an obligation to make provision for his own unemployed but in Europe there was 'a decided tendency ... for industry and labour to place their burdens upon the Government concerned.' This tradition was 'clearly reflected in the minds of many persons who migrate from Europe to this country'; much of the demand for the dole and other schemes came, he suggested, from radicalized immigrants and 'a considerable number of those who apply to Ontario Municipalities for relief during the winter seasons are new arrivals...'

Furthermore, according to the Deputy Minister, there was a growing belief that compulsory schemes covering all employees were unsatisfactory because they promoted 'an organized demand for ever increasing benefits and decreasing restrictions.' Employees might be encouraged to 'insist upon standards of employment and pay when economic conditions do not warrant' and, more serious still, 'it is inevitable that new forms of employment will not be sought so eagerly.' Above all, Ballantyne warned, such a scheme 'contributes to political unrest and retards the progressive trend of business movements.' Clearly, men of influence in both government and business were still not only using but even believing the hoary argument that, so far as human resources were concerned, the marketplace must not be interfered with – all the while offering and accepting a variety of favours and bonuses on their own behalf. Then the Deputy alluded to a consideration of special significance for the province where unemployment, restricted largely to the urban centres, was aggravated by 'an unwillingness or a physical unfitness on the part of some workers to engage in the kind of work offered by the essential industries of this Province, namely farming, mining, lumbering, building and constructing.'

Also of moment in Ballantyne's mind was the CMA's claim that unemployment insurance had failed everywhere attempted, caused enormous burdens to governments, and contributed to the pauperizing of the workers. Ballantyne left no doubt that he was in sympathy with the CMA rather than with the T&LC, which had asked Ottawa to enact such a scheme. Ontario, he concluded, was already doing its part through its public works programs, highway building, hydro development, its twenty-five employment offices, and the new initiatives announced that February. His only recommendation, therefore, was that additional steps be taken to ensure that orders for provincial and municipal supplies and government works projects were executed as far as practical during periods of business depression and 'allocated to Districts where unemployment is most acute.'

The 1925 debates in the House indicated that the views of Ballantyne rather than Heenan best represented most shades of opinion there. M.M. MacBride, the renegade Labour member, held that the dole might be necessary in a densely populated country like Britain but would be calamitous for Canada. Sam Clarke of the Liberals also decried the dole and insisted that Canada offered such opportunities that anyone with ordinary ability and intelligence could easily make his way. To Labour Minister Forbes Godfrey a higher tariff and public works were the answer. 'Is it not better,' he asked, 'to ... give a decent and industrious citizen a job rather than force him into the humiliating position of accepting a dole?' After warning against the dangers of 'an immigration composed of the polyglot races of Europe,' he concluded by asserting that 'I do not think any member of this house wants to see unemployment insurance applied to this province.'

Heenan, speaking to his motion, argued eloquently that conditions in which there were 30,000 unemployed in Toronto and 12,000 in Hamilton proved that new economic circumstances had created a perpetual unemployment problem which could be solved only through a government insurance plan. The British plan was not demoralizing, 'it is unemployment that is demoralizing.' But

Heenan did not have the sympathy of the House. Ferguson spoke for many when he claimed that unemployment insurance was not easily adaptable to Canada and argued that immigrants should be prepared to work in the mines, in the bush, and on the farms. He assured Heenan that the province was working with other levels of government to find a solution and emphasized that prospective immigrants should be given a clear understanding of labour conditions they would face. Reluctantly, Heenan withdrew his resolution.[27]

Thus unemployment relief continued to be regarded as an emergency function of government. The Minister of Labour's report for 1925 stated that slightly over $100,000 was expended by the province at this time on relief, including works schemes and direct relief, while the municipalities contributed $550,000. As in other fields of social endeavour in which the province leaned on the municipality as the body with the major responsibility, so too the same pattern existed, with less justification, with respect to relief from unemployment. These largely negative policies had little adverse political impact, for public opinion was not generally ready to accept or demand more. Ferguson even received a scroll from a group of workmen, dated 16 April 1925, which thanked him for 'the prompt manner in which you bestowed "the helping hand to those in distress" without the stigma of charity; so markedly in contrast to the callous indifference ... exhibited on the part of the Federal Government...'[28]

Obviously there was no prospect that Ontario would accept an insurance scheme itself or press such a project on Ottawa. The 1925 debate was significant, however, because it clearly delineated the nature of existing opinions and demonstrated how widely they were accepted by the province's several political groups. There is no doubt, too, that the Department of Labour was greatly concerned lest some step be taken which would inflate the cost of production through increases in the wages paid to workers. This attitude came to the fore again the following year in another memorandum prepared by Ballantyne. The problem arose after the Judicial Committee of the Privy Council in the famous Toronto Electric Commissioners v Snider case found the Industrial Disputes Investigation Act *ultra vires*. The King government responded with legislation which gave the provinces the right to place industrial disputes within federal jurisdiction and a private member's bill was introduced in the Ontario House by Karl Homuth (Labour, Waterloo North) to take advantage of this clause.

The desires of organized labour were clear. There had been disappointment when the IDIA had been ruled *ultra vires*, the executive of the T&LC holding that the decision would lead to confusion and lack of uniformity in the field of labour legislation and also that it 'would leave the door open for the enactment of legislation that would not be to the benefit of the workers.' Ballantyne placed his own views in opposition to those of labour. He pointed out that although the IDIA had been enacted in 1907, the province 'did not intend to have abrogated or limited their powers to deal with industrial disputes' and in 1914 had passed its own Trade Disputes Act. He noted that Ottawa's 1925 legislation was sweeping in its implications and that Homuth's bill therefore had widespread implications. The Ontario government, its commissions, and the subordinate municipal governments 'are becoming more and more large employers of labour and as every legislative power exercised by such bodies is or has to be granted by the Provincial Legislature it is a matter of serious question as to whether the power of dealing with industrial disputes which may arise in such undertakings should be handed over to the Dominion Authority.'[29]

The Ferguson government did not support the principle of the Homuth bill and in the years ahead provincial responsibilities in the whole field of labour legislation expanded dramatically. The inactivity of Dr Godfrey in the Labour portion of his dual portfolio meant that Ballantyne's influence became paramount. That Ferguson's own instincts did not depart significantly from the line laid down by the Deputy Minister was reflected in the policies followed by his administration. The same outlook reappeared by mid-decade in the vigorous debate conducted over old age pensions.

The federal Liberal party's need after the 1925 election for the votes of the Labour members resulted in its support for old age pensions legislation. Rejected by the Senate, it was reintroduced and approved in 1927. The question, however had come intermittently before the House over the years and parliamentary committees in 1924 and 1925 had suggested that the pensions question be discussed with the provinces. When provincial views were solicited in 1925, only BC showed much interest, Taschereau proclaimed his opposition, and Ferguson replied tersely, 'I will consider the matter.'[30]

Ferguson seems to have felt that public opinion was less than vocal in support of such a measure. Although the T&LC consistently petitioned in favour of pensions, the *Industrial Banner*, preoccupied with other matters, paid little attention to the issue and the church press, concerned with prohibition and missionary work, had little to say.[31] Ferguson's own correspondence included a number of letters from the needy aged but in volume they did not begin to compare with those received on an issue such as prohibition.

Perhaps some of them touched the heart strings of provincial bureaucrats. One old lady in Harcourt wrote pathetically to 'Mr fargesant' to see 'if thire is the old age pencion i heard thire was i am an old woman 73 and my husband is dead and he allways woarked for your side and i have helped to do the woark in the post office ... But I can do no more i go from place to place.' 'Dear Madam,' came the stiffly formal reply from a secretary, '...I am directed to advise you that there is no provision for an old age pension...'[32] In October the Premier received a letter which described a situation which remained all too typical. 'The years roll on,' began Magistrate Browne of Toronto, 'without the Police Magistrates being relieved of the depressing duty of committing friendless, penniless, offenceless and homeless old men – to Gaol.'[33]

Throughout 1926, Ferguson showed no enthusiasm for a pensions program. 'I am doubtful,' he remarked in March, 'if our finances would permit of any new ventures involving considerable expenditures. We want to balance our budget before we undertake any new commitments.'[34] No doubt too he was less than enthralled by the political motivation of King's 1926 legislation, particularly since it was generally conceded that pensions legislation was within provincial jurisdiction. Despite earlier overtures to the provinces, Ottawa now acted unilaterally. According to the shared costs arrangements of its scheme, 50 per cent of the cost of pensions would be paid by the federal government to any province choosing to enact enabling legislation which conformed to certain standards. The maximum pension was to be $20 a month to applicants 70 years of age or older whose other income did not exceed $125 per annum. Of course the taxpayers of provinces which stayed out would be contributing to the pensions in those which entered and the administrative costs would be borne entirely by the province. Such political blackmail did not endear the legislation to Ontario's Tory Premier. Fortunately, from Ferguson's point of view, tragically from that of the needy aged, the Senate veto postponed any need for a decision by the provincial government until at least 1927.

All in all, the record in the health and welfare field during Ferguson's first term in office, despite occasional spurts of imagination and enterprise, was a reflection in equal parts of traditionalism and parsimony. Although Howard Ferguson was not as active in this field as in others, undeniably it was a record which faithfully reflected his own ideas and opinions.

Minister of Education

A long-time interest in educational affairs and an acute awareness of the political dimensions of the portfolio accounted for Howard Ferguson's decision to retain Education for himself. He took the position seriously and at times the double burden began to tell. In December 1923 Sir John Willison told him he looked tired and overworked but Ferguson replied that for the present at least he could not relinquish Education because 'there are too many critical situations to take the chance.' More than that, however, he told Willison he had views he hoped to see 'firmly established as a basis of the future policy of the Department.'[1]

He had no intention, however, of becoming a political minister; he worked hard to stay on top of his portfolio and when he stepped down Judge Scott of Perth told him he had been assured 'time and time again, by the chief officials of the department that its business has never been so satisfactorily administered as under your direction.'[2] Ferguson believed education the very cornerstone of provincial affairs. Deeply imbued with the faith of the day that it held the key to progress and prosperity, he intended to leave his mark on the system.

The policies he followed were a typical mix of traditionalism and innovation. He presided over the Department in a period of economic growth and social flux which greatly affected the province's educational development but beneath the flurry of change there endured a solid substratum of conservatism. This was well suited to Ferguson's own style and talents. No one was more responsive than he to new situations or more receptive to innovative techniques, but at heart he was a bedrock Tory, devoted to the familiar goals of the pre-war generation. None-theless in Education he proved imaginative, open, responsive to new needs, and willing to take on large tasks.

The system benefitted from the enthusiasms of its powerful minister. New thrusts came quickly to the fore as Ferguson and his officials pressed to extend the reach of educational opportunity to the countryside, to the remoter parts of the province, and to previously neglected groups and classes. The goals, however, and even the framework, were largely conventional and the rhetoric often loomed larger than the achievements. The province in general and the different branches of industry in particular demanded better trained workers, while the health of the state required a citizenry which would be patriotic, of sound opinions and good character. These, even more than the training of intelligence, were the ends of education as defined by Ferguson and his advisers in the 1920s, thus lending an essential continuity to the province's educational policy which endured from the late nineteenth century to Ferguson's day and beyond.

It was possible for Ferguson to carry on his other duties without neglecting Education because of his confidence in his departmental deputies. Although he once noted privately that his deputy minister, A.H.U. Colquhoun, possessed a well-developed capacity for shirking work and avoiding responsibility, he retained a large measure of respect for the veteran civil servant's political acumen. Unfortunately Colquhoun was more politician than educator, a circumstance which combined with Ferguson's frequent absences from the Department to create a leadership gap at the top. In some measure this was filled by Dr F.W. Merchant, a strong-willed bureaucrat most knowledgeable in the fields of technical and French-language education. In 1923 Merchant became Chief Director of Education, a position vacant since the death in 1919 of Superintendent of Education John Seath. But Merchant although able was no Seath and at this point was in the later stages of his career. Deficiencies of leadership may account partially for the failure to carry through more effectively some of the projects which Ferguson hoped to accomplish during his tenure. Ferguson's eyes and ears in the Department were provided by Reta Saunderson, his personal secretary, a good friend devoted to the interests of her chief. Of course Merchant and Colquhoun had been close to Ferguson for years and because of the mutual understanding that existed, they accepted and Ferguson freely gave wide latitude in administrative and even policy matters.

The prominence of Ferguson, Merchant, and Colquhoun gave the Department in the 1920s a sense of déjà vu. Most of its goals extended back to Seath and beyond and the same three had worked together with Seath during the war to achieve those ends. The province had endeavoured to expand its technical education program since the appearance of John Seath's 1911 report, *Education for Industrial Purposes*. In the latter stages of Dr Pyne's long tenure in Education and then during the war, the Department had stagnated somewhat, but Harry Cody's brief period as minister had been marked by an ambitious reform program which included a conscious effort to elevate the teaching profession, an expanded commitment to technical education, and new school attendance legislation which by 1924-5 had helped double the number of students in the system The two friends, Ferguson and Cody, must have conferred frequently on this program and during Cody's absence because of illness, Ferguson in March 1919 marshalled much of it through the House. Thus it was Ferguson who had introduced a plan of dental and medical inspection aimed especially at rural areas and, significant in view of his later role, he also presented legislation which permitted local school districts to vote on the question of consolidation.[3] Unfortunately, Harry Cody's tenure of the Department was soon over and R.H. Grant, Drury's Minister of Education, lacked the self-confidence or perhaps the desire to sustain the pace set by his Tory predecessor. When Ferguson assumed control, the Department's policy lines and general inclinations were well established but the period of prewar and wartime inertia had not been entirely overcome and a strong hand was needed at the top.

Ferguson possessed the commitment to change and when time allowed he gave the department the leadership it needed. Just as he was bubbling over with enthusiastic schemes in the field of economic development, similarly in education he was quick to take up ideas and strike out in new directions. In his first months in office he spoke often of his educational goals to service clubs, educational conferences, and other public gatherings. They must have seemed to many a veritable educational smorgasbord. To a CNE directors' meeting in August 1923, he suggested that the child not the subject should be the nodal point of the classroom experience and criticized the schools for 'cramming knowledge into the young head instead of developing the youngster.' A new curriculum was being prepared, he announced, which would reduce the number of subjects while also providing more of a challenge for bright children 'so that they need not be held back by the backward child. We must also emphasize the individuality of the children by giving them more individual attention.' That November he pointed to the startling statistic that over 85 per cent of the children left school at or before the high school entrance year. Their training, he suggested, was utterly inadequate in areas essential to both their own welfare and that of the state, yet already they were over-tutored in some subjects 'which had deteriorated the mind rather than prepared it for intelligent citizenship.' The public school, Ferguson proclaimed, must be made more practical and useful; vast improvements were needed in rural education, particularly in the area of secondary schools, which should include technical as well as cultural instruction; the industrial schools and similar institutions needed upgrading, for so-called incorrigibles had as much right to education as others. In several speeches he made it clear that he deplored the subject-oriented approach of some educators; in fulfillment of a long-standing pledge he was 'out to get' homework. The chief aim of the educational system, he told the Orillia Canadian Club in May 1924, should be training and development, not knowledge. The latter would follow when the first was emphasized. As for the university field, he regretted that a minimal amount of research was being carried on. Research facilities needed to be developed with more attention to graduate education, perhaps centralized at Toronto with other institutions focusing on preparatory work. Much additional study would be needed, Ferguson admitted, before provincial legislation would be possible.[4]

Few ministers of education were in a position at the beginning of their tenure to adumbrate such a diversity of schemes and projects. Ferguson, of course, was drawing not only on his own earlier experiences but on a pot-pourri of ideas then current in the Department. Fully aware of it or not, he was articulating an educational philosophy long current in Ontario circles. In his emphasis on the inculcation of patriotism, largely through the vehicles of history and literature, in his conviction that the development of character took precedence over the provision of a smattering of knowledge of a great many subjects, and in his reaction against educational institutions that treated students as products rather than individuals, he was giving his own emphasis to the ideas of two German educators of the nineteenth century, Johann Friedrich Herbart and Friedrich Froebel, themselves indebted to the child-centred approach of Pestalozzi's institute in Switzerland. Although Herbartian thought first influenced Ontario educators in the 1860s, its impact was particularly strong in the years before World War I when, according to one educational historian, 'the Herbartian wave swept over the Canadian scene.'[5]

In Herbart's scheme, the purpose of education was to develop an individual able to make sound moral choices. History and literature were the subjects ideally suited to this task. The impact of the war strengthened his influence and the department's 1918 report is filled with Herbartian dicta. This accorded well with the desire of leaders of the imperialist school such as Cody and Ferguson to inculcate in the younger generation the proper imperial vision. To these men the war confirmed the virtues of what had become the Ontario approach. 'The German educationalists,' commented the 1918 report, 'thought of civilization in terms of the intellect, the British in terms of character. Which ideal is the safer and worthier, history has already pronounced...'

The influence of Herbart in the Department of Education was reinforced in the 1920s by Dr Samuel B. Sinclair, a highly regarded psychologist, who in 1920 became inspector of Auxiliary Classes. Sinclair taught that 'the formation of character was the highest aim of all education' and argued in his *Introductory Educational Psychology* that 'the child is not a receptacle to be filled with unassimilated knowledge...'[6] Ferguson in his curricular reforms and focus on character development was an obvious but probably unconscious Herbartian.

Froebel's impact was perhaps even more important. His belief that education must be child-centred and his focus upon activity and development rather than subject matter appear linked with some of the liberal influences brought to bear on the Ontario system in the 1920s. In an attempt to break away from the purely academic course of studies and to de-emphasize exams, Ontario students for a time were allowed, on the basis of teachers' recommendations, to avoid many of the rigorous testing procedures so firmly embedded in the provincial structure. Many of these ideas were advanced in the famous 1925 study of the British Columbia system undertaken by Dr G.M. Weir of UBC and J.H. Putman, a prominent Ottawa school inspector. As early as 1920 Putman had recommended such an approach in his own province.[7]

Another significant influence was E.L. Thorndike, an American psychologist whose claim that learning developed from stimulus-response situations helped break down the emphasis on a traditional subject-oriented curriculum and open the door for new approaches and subjects. But Thorndike, whose ideas came to Ontario largely through the influence of Peter Sandiford, a prominent figure in educational research at the University of Toronto, also placed great reliance on testing techniques and quantification and although this was 'for diagnostic rather than pupil evaluation purposes,' it may indirectly have helped to reinforce the Ontario department's traditional emphasis on examinations and have prevented enduring reform.[8] E.G. Savage, a British educator who spent six months in 1926 in the Ontario system, found the centralization, the emphasis on examinations, and the enforced uniformity all but stultifying.[9] The winds of change in Ontario blew out prematurely. What remained was greatly expanded, to be sure, and offered much variety of educational experience, but it was a system which, like the Canadian constitution, retained its original watertight compartments and many of its nineteenth-century characteristics.

That this should be so may be attributed largely to the traditionalism not only of the educational community but of the province at large. Yet if the goals which motivated the Department of Education were familiar and conventional, the physical and structural developments which took place under Ferguson's leadership were a forceful and imaginative response to the rapid changes in the province's social and economic system. The major trends became clear during Ferguson's first administration. In September 1924, he announced the first major curricular revision in years. Although a core of compulsory subjects was retained, local communities with the approval of the inspector would be free to supplement this by the choice of options suited to local needs. The minister believed this would be most helpful to the teacher in the small country school where the need for one person to teach too many subjects provided 'not a training but a smattering of knowledge.' As part of his effort to reduce the burden of homework, in each school day of five and a half hours there would be a non-teaching period of an hour and a half devoted to independent study under the teacher's supervision. The reformed structure, the 1924 report noted, was designed to allow 'the influence and personality of the teacher' to find 'their true place in the training of the child' as opposed to the mere cramming of knowledge. Other curricular changes followed, with an increased emphasis given to the teaching of history and literature and new teaching manuals introduced for each in 1926. And in an overture to rural opinion, instruction in agriculture was introduced wherever possible, often in co-operation with officials from the Department of Agriculture.[10]

Although even city children were given a taste of instruction with a rural flavour, a more important consequence for urban Ontario of the assault on the tyranny of the rigidly academic curriculum was the rapid advance in vocational and technical education. In 1923, Ontario had sixteen vocational schools with 7000 full-time and 1000 part-time students; by 1928, there were forty-two vocational schools with a full-time enrolment of over 20,000.[11] While this rapid expansion primarily reflected the need for skilled workers, the practical bent to Ferguson's mind caused him to press forward with enthusiasm. Vocational education developed in close conjunction with the needs of individual employers as the department established a program which allowed workers to attend classes part-time during the day while holding down a full-time job. Gradually a system of apprenticeship classes developed in the larger centres and mining and agriculture were prominent among subjects which received attention in appropriate parts of the province.[12] The structure was capped by the creation in 1925 of the Ontario Training College for Technical Teachers at Hamilton.

Another effort to reach children whose interests had been largely ignored by the department's traditional structure could be seen in the more active encouragement given part-time instruction. The 1923 report, noting the difficulties in attracting rural children into the secondary education system, argued that 'we must frankly admit, therefore, that full-time schools for such pupils, under present conditions ... are impossible.' Ferguson revived and extended an earlier experiment in part-time winter courses to serve farm children whose parents refused to send them to school on a full-time basis. And in 1925 the decision was taken to offer the elementary school program by correspondence, as done earlier in BC. By 1930 Ontario was paying the full cost, including the provision of books, for a thousand children who otherwise might have received no instruction at all.[13]

One program which received international publicity as an example of daring innovation was the famous railway school car project. In the 1920s about two-thirds of northern Ontario remained unorganized, populated by a shifting body of railway employees, workmen, trappers and, in the language of one departmental report, 'bushmen.' One veteran northern Ontario inspector conceived the idea of providing schooling for the area through the utilization of railway cars which could follow the settler from point to point but the Drury government proved unresponsive.[14] This was precisely the sort of scheme that appealed to Ferguson, who was undaunted by the prospect of twisting a few arms, if necessary, to elicit the co-operation of the railways. The 1925 report noted that plans were underway and pontificated that 'the history of this Province, during its early years of settlement and development, when schools were few and many had to go without an education, conveys a lesson which should not be ignored by the present generation.'[15] There were, however, problems to be surmounted and although the first school car went into operation in the fall of 1926, the idea came to fruition only during Ferguson's second administration.

Ferguson's most important endeavour as minister involved a bitter struggle fraught with enormous political dangers, whose consequences he avoided only by neat footwork and a tactical withdrawal. Indeed the incident provides a nice illustration of his political technique. There was no reform to which he was more deeply committed than the consolidation of the province's thousands of small local boards of education into larger township units. Few local sections had taken advantage of the 1919 legislation encouraging the formation of larger units, yet the need for township boards was real and pressing. The vast majority of rural children dropped out at or before the end of their elementary education and indeed the absence of a high school in their neighbourhood often all but precluded their continuing in school. School sections lacked sufficient students or could not themselves afford a secondary school and co-operation with neighbouring sections was notoriously difficult to achieve. As well, the system promoted great inequalities in school tax assessment. Ferguson's 1923 report noted the existence of 117 schools with 1 to 5 pupils, 365 with 6 to 9 and 824 where the average attendance was 10 to 14. Fifty-five per cent of the rural schools had an average attendance of less than 20 and 'the financial loss in maintaining many of these schools is startling.'

The arguments in favour of consolidation were overwhelming. In 1925 Ferguson introduced a bill to establish township boards. His intention, he explained, was to stimulate discussion; hence the legislation would be withdrawn after second reading. The reason for this caution soon became apparent. The Premier made the case for township boards on 14 April 1925 in a speech to the Ontario Educational Association and suffered the humiliation the next day of seeing the rural trustees section vote almost unanimously against his plan. The opposition came as no surprise although the depth of the feeling that existed would have caused a less stouthearted politician to head for cover. Ferguson pressed on – although he had no intention of forcing his bill through over the heads of the rural trustees. To him such a move would be unthinkable. Instead, in June he circulated a copy of the bill and an explanation of the government's viewpoint to many municipalities and all rural boards.[16] This was always his way; if he believed his position was right, he would begin an educational campaign to sell it to the people. In different cases, the tactics would vary and now he realized that patience would be required. Ontario's rural trustees did not intend to be pushed around by anyone.

His argument was carefully phrased to appeal to the rural mind. Beginning with the assertion that 'the country pupil is not getting as good a chance educationally as the city pupil,' he asked for constructive criticism and not 'merely an expression of your disapproval...' 'May I suggest,' he continued, 'that in considering this problem you keep uppermost in your mind the welfare of your children.' The response from trustee groups and municipal councils made it clear that no change was desired. 'If the rulers of our fair province disregard the almost unanimous wish of the rural electors,' one man told Ferguson, 'they are doomed...'[17] To R.H. Grant, his predecessor in Education, he wrote that the township proposal 'has so much to recommend it, and practically nothing against it except the resentment at interference with what is known as "local autonomy." I have always felt however, that since the ratepayers pay for and must actually operate the school system, the Department should not arbitrarily impose new conditions.' He had a duty to make the case, he told Grant, but 'if the local trustee board chooses to continue unnecessary expenditure, and the ratepayers approve of it, I suppose they have that right.'[18]

By February 1926 Ferguson thought public opinion was swinging towards him but that April he again addressed the OEA and saw his scheme rejected as overwhelmingly as before.[19] Soon it became a ritual; each year he would present his bill to the House and then withdraw it. Affection for the little red school house, a distaste for transporting children to a central school, dislike of a meddling bureaucracy and, no doubt, a fear on the part of some that a high school education might lose them their sons to the city were combining to block all possibility of change. Yet Ferguson, as stubborn as his opposition, refused to abandon his efforts. In the meantime, the Department encouraged the formation of continuation schools, which gave many rural children at least a taste of a secondary education.

Thus, as his role in the consolidation campaign testified, Ferguson as Minister of Education was reformist and conservative, anxious to extend educational opportunities to new areas and new classes, yet committed to a traditional philosophy to which Pyne, Ross, and even Ryerson could have subscribed. Like his predecessors, he was alert to that balance between local rights and central authority which was the genius of the Ontario system. Although frustrated by what he regarded as a stubborn resistance to change, it was something more than his sense of the political danger involved which made him hesitate to impose his will by provincial legislation or executive decree. He knew that the schools belonged to the people.

Certainly they were more dependent by far on local financial support in the 1920s than would later be the case. 'The people,' he noted approvingly in a 1925 speech, 'voluntarily tax themselves in the various Municipalities to the amount of $37,698,722, and in addition to this, the Province spent last year $9,259,464 for education.'[20] As was true in almost every area of endeavour, the provincial contribution remained significantly less than the municipal. Ferguson did note in a December 1925 letter that he believed it vital that 'the growing generation should have the benefit of the most modern and efficient educational facilities. It is for that reason,' he continued, 'that I have broken all precedent and departed from the rule that the Government should not contribute to capital expenditures for local institutions. Education is so essential, that there is more justification for contributing for this purpose than for any other service.'[21] But if the minister was willing to bend the established rules, he refused to break them. When William Finlayson (Conservative, Simcoe East) a few months later relayed the request of a school section in his constituency for financial assistance,

Ferguson responded that 'there is no provision under the law whereby grants are made towards the construction of schools in organized Ontario. I am constantly having such applications made but the law never has permitted it; I think the reason is obvious. If such a thing were undertaken the Provincial Treasurer would be swamped with applications.'[22]

Although Ferguson believed that major changes in the educational structure were needed to meet the requirements of postwar Ontario, and although he gave substantial encouragement to physical and organizational changes which increased the ability of the system to offer a diversity of educational experience, he never considered himself the master of the system. As had Ryerson, he recognized that change must proceed at a pace which public opinion could support and the treasury could afford.

This was a maxim which applied as well to his conduct of university affairs. There, however, the temptation to impose the department's wishes was in some ways greater, for the provincial financial contribution placed the post-secondary institutions in an increasingly dependent position. On one occasion, only partly in jest, Ferguson proclaimed publicly that 'I am the boss of the Toronto University.' Yet the reforms effected by the Whitney administration in 1906 were generally regarded as having had as a major objective the removal of the University of Toronto from improper political influence and after that date the politicians, including Ferguson, were careful to adhere to the spirit of non-interference. As well, the absence of institutional machinery in the post-1906 period to regularize governmental-university relations and define the provincial role meant that the University of Toronto under its new president, Robert Falconer, had been able to a remarkable extent to go its own way. And, of course, Queen's and Western as private institutions were also free as a general rule of provincial interference or regulation.

Yet this situation was more the result of the relative absence of controversial issues affecting university life, of the substantial financial independence of Queen's and Western and, perhaps, of the existence of a strong Board of Governors at Toronto, than of any theoretical or institutional commitment to academic freedom and university independence. In the late war period and during the early 1920s, several developments revealed how tenuous the so-called independence of Ontario's universities actually was. During the war, the regional universities, Queen's and Western, received for the first time significant public funding, although such support came through 'supplementary estimates' and was regarded as temporary. This new funding arrangement was a response to the growing financial needs of the universities and it expanded to such an extent that by 1922 they were receiving provincial funds in excess of that given to elementary and secondary education combined.[23] Although E.C. Drury had increased the level of support, he recognized as well the need for a systematic investigation of the province's financial role and appointed a royal commission chaired by Canon Cody to make recommendations.

The Commission, which included a number of members with close university connections, emphasized the value of the university to the community and suggested that funds might be raised through a property tax levy. Equally interesting, it recommended that 'in any University aided by State funds, no new faculty be established and no new building ... be erected' without cabinet consent and that 'a University Day be provided for in the Legislature on which the heads of the various Universities shall appear to report on their work.' While decrying any suggestion of political interference, the Cody Commission made it clear that 'the state, which gives the financial support, has the right (a) to determine how this education may be most effectively and economically carried on and, (b) to exercise supervision over projected developments involving financial outlay.'[24] That such recommendations should flow from a Commission sympathetic to the universities suggests that most Ontarians regarded it as axiomatic that the province which paid the bills must have a major voice in determining how its funds should be spent. Although most of the recommendations were effectively ignored, when the report was debated in the House Hartley Dewart offered his approval and demanded more direct provincial control. Significantly, Ferguson demurred. Pointing to the Whitney policy of 1906, which he interpreted as freeing higher education from political interference, he urged that the universities be treated generously.[25]

Nonetheless, Ferguson's approach to university affairs was in marked contrast to that of Drury. There were no more references of university business to committees of the House and no more than scattered debates about subjects of concern to academe. Ferguson marshalled his university estimates through the legislature with despatch; he appears to have handled university matters himself in spare moments. The trend towards involvement of the legislature which began in Drury's day was effectively reversed and Ferguson set the personal style which endured until at least the late 1940s. In 1923 he appointed Harry Cody to the chairmanship of the Board of Governors and one suspects that many decisions were made during private lunches by Ferguson, Cody, and such other old friends as Flavelle and T.A. Russell, who held positions on the Board. Yet the workings of this coterie did not mar Ferguson's relationship with President Falconer which, while formal, was cordial. When Ferguson hesitated in 1924 to accept the honorary degree which the Senate had unanimously offered because he doubted the propriety as 'the Head of the Government that finances the University' of accepting such an honour, Falconer unsuccessfully asked him to reconsider, assuring him that his attitude to the university had 'been uniformly favourable in the highest degree...'[26] Ferguson's sympathetic approach reflected the important place the university held in the esteem of Ontario's Tory establishment.

From the point of view of the universities, however, the expansion of the Premier's role and the downgrading of that of the legislature had dangers as well as advantages. Because formal machinery remained slight, a great deal depended on the good will of Ferguson and the universities were forced to go hat in hand to Queen's Park each year. Western and Queen's would both submit requests for funds accompanied by financial statements. The procedure for Toronto differed somewhat. As the provincial university, its Board would set an annual budget indicating levels of income and expenditure, including statutory grants, and if a deficit appeared, a submission to cabinet would follow.[27]

Although the province in the 1920s chose to be generous, W.H. Price in his 1924 budget noted that the University of Toronto was in receipt of grants totalling $2,696,217 and indicated that 'no matter what it is for, we are going too fast'; Ferguson himself occasionally grumbled about costs, but there were no major cutbacks. Operating grants moved from a 1920-1 level of $200,000 and $210,000 for Queen's and Western respectively to a peak of $350,000 for each in 1930-1.[28] Not until after World War II did the level of support for Queen's and Western, and for the University of Toronto as well, again reach that attained under Ferguson. Nonetheless, the Premier and his advisers kept a close eye on university financial operations. In 1925, for example, when the University of Toronto decided to sell some property, he quickly pointed out to the Chairman of the Board that some of the money realized should be used to reduce the amount of the institution's budget.[29]

Ferguson's desire for economy manifested itself principally in his desire to return the province's relation with Queen's and Western to its prewar status. In 1926 he told the House that the sums then being voted – still in supplementary estimates – represented the last of the amounts recommended by the Cody Commission in 1921. The previous year he had informed the two regional institutions that they could not expect continued support from the province. 'I give them notice that they should look around for some money.'[30] He did not believe the government should support three provincial universities; once again he argued that responsibility lay not with the province but with the community at large.

Interestingly, this viewpoint was not entirely unacceptable even to the institutions affected. 'While this shortening of the arm of the Ontario Government is inconvenient,' Principal R.B. Taylor of Queen's told Arthur Meighen, 'I know as a citizen it is right.'[31] In the 1920s most Ontarians took it for granted that the province's social role was limited and that they as private citizens had a financial and moral responsibility which must not be shirked. There was another consideration. Once substantial government funds were made available to the private universities, the government which undertook to withdraw them would run the risk of alienating important interests in the regions they served. A.T. Little, Chairman of Western's Board of Governors, stated publicly that although the province had reduced Western's grant from $350,000 to $250,000, the university would probably be able to carry on without being 'crippled'; but other members of the Board and university officials were pessimistic about Western's future. They argued that it was unfair for the province to concentrate its support so largely on Toronto, for although Varsity pretended to be the 'provincial' university, a full half of the students attending it resided in Toronto and another thirty per cent within a radius of thirty miles.[32] Clearly, Ferguson's desire to have Queen's and Western stand on their own feet clashed with his oft-stated purpose of decentralization and with his desire to help people in the regions achieve the same standards as those in the capital.

Another dimension of university-government relations loomed equally large. If it was generally accepted that the province which paid the bills must have a say in policy matters internal to the universities, it was also agreed that this included a substantial degree of control over the professoriat. The modern notion of academic freedom did not effectively exist in the Ontario of Howard Ferguson. In an address entitled 'Academic Freedom' delivered at Convocation Hall in February 1922, President Falconer expressed a widely held view when he argued that a professor at an institution supported by state funds should accept, as did the civil servant, certain limitations on his rights as a citizen.[33] The university, Falconer asserted, must serve the people as a whole and 'it is therefore expedient that a professor in a State university should take no active share in party-politics'; should he desire to play such a part, 'he should ask himself whether he ought not to abandon the secure seat which he holds as a professor.' The academic, Falconer maintained, is a member of the university community, the welfare of which depends upon the good will of the government and of the people as a whole. 'When he makes public utterances therefore, he does not involve himself alone. The public is prone to assume that he has some backing in the University for what he says...'

Falconer believed that the thoughtless section of the public would find 'only too good grounds for an attack upon the whole university in the political utterances of the indiscreet or thoughtless professor.' In his view, full academic freedom and the right to pronounce on controversial political issues were mutually exclusive principles. Falconer feared that the state would interfere with a variety of curricular and other matters internal to the university if members of the university community should exploit their protected positions to engage in partisan politics. Although his exposition did not lack a certain logic, it did not represent the path of future development and rings foreign to the modern ear. Nonetheless it may be taken as representative of the attitude of many fairminded citizens who were friends of the university and it is in that context that the relations between the university and the province must be viewed in the 1920s.

Certainly Falconer's position was also that of the Premier. In 1925 when the *Financial Post* interpreted some remarks by Professor Fay as sympathetic to

Communism, Ferguson fired off a warning to Cody that 'if it is true that he holds these views, and gives expression to them, I do not think he is the sort of man who should be on the staff.'[34] In the years ahead such incidents would multiply to the extent that Ferguson's attitude may have stifled the free expression of opinion in university circles. The universities, aware of the Premier's views and perhaps intimidated by his vigorous personality and his massive majority, probably trod gently so as not to awaken the slumbering beast.

A less serious kind of Prime Ministerial intervention appeared in Ferguson's habit of stepping in when students ran afoul of regulations and sought political support. Ferguson was conscious of the damage that could be done if the university developed a reputation for élitism or for the harsh and arbitrary exercise of power and he believed that as a provincial institution it should go out of its way to meet the wishes of its constituency. He did not lightly dismiss complaints when they were conveyed to him by concerned parents or through the local member. After one such case he told Falconer that 'we are constantly driving students out of the Province on account of the regulations or methods pursued by the University. ... I think you will agree that the sons and daughters of the people of Ontario, who maintain the Institution, should not be made to feel that while they support a University of their own they must send their children elsewhere...'[35] When a student was debarred and forced to sit out a year because of a deficiency of a few marks, he was concerned lest the regulations fall 'most heavily on those who can least afford it. ... Regulations of this kind might not worry those who have ample means. That is the sort of thing that is being said about the University today.'[36]

He took a harder line when such incidents became matters of public controversy. In 1925 a Tory backbencher complained in the House that his son, who had failed, was being refused readmission and Ferguson responded that he found it inconceivable that 'an act so arbitrary had occurred.' If so, he would 'see that no University authorities would carry out activities in that form.'[37] His usual response, however, was to write Falconer to set out the details of specific cases and to suggest that reconsideration was in order. There is no evidence that strong-arm methods were brought to bear and he believed Falconer was sincere in assuring him that every effort was being made 'to devise some method whereby all question will be removed as to possible injustice...'[38] When the university authorities believed their original decision was appropriate, they did not hesitate to tell him so; he for his part usually replied to complaints along the lines used when people wrote to him about the Hydro or one of the many provincial boards. 'I am unable to be of any service in the matter,' he told one supplicant, 'for the reason that the University organization is distinct from the Department of Education. They have their own standards and make their own regulations, without the Department having a voice or any control in the matter. I have sometimes been able to get things done by making representations. ... I would be glad to do this in your case, but I don't think they will waive the rule.'[39] Obviously, university autonomy had its uses.

In 1926, Ferguson embarked on his most far-reaching effort to impose provincial standards on the universities and succeeded only in eliciting a truly impressive display of institutional self-interest. C.B. Sissons, in his history of Victoria University, described Ferguson's initiative as the first 'serious intrusion on the part of the government in matters of curriculum' since the 1906 legislation.[40] In a February 1926 letter, the Premier told Falconer that 'after due consideration, the Department of Education reached the conclusion that the first year work now done by the University could well be done in the various local centres throughout the Province. My view is that it will inure to the advantage of the student himself; will cost the Province and the parent less money; and will mean that the expensive sorting process that takes place in Toronto will now be done locally...'[41] After pointing out that the plan would involve changes in the university's teaching program, Ferguson asked the President to take the matter up with his colleagues so that the scheme could be 'put into operation at the earliest possible date.'

Ferguson's letter fell like a bombshell; its peremptory wording spoke volumes about his assumption that the University was at the province's bidding. He took for granted too that Queen's and Western would readily fall into line. Still, the project should not have taken the universities unaware. As early as March 1916 when the University of Toronto had changed some of its requirements, an internal Department of Education memorandum had taken note of President Falconer's view that many high schools, with smaller classes and longer sessions, could handle the work of the first-year general course better than the university. This document argued that the schools undeniably were competent to undertake such work and the department therefore should offer no objections to Toronto's altered standards.[42]

There were others who also thought along this line. The 1921 report of the Cody Commission advised that 'if the future increase of candidates seeking admission to the Universities should be so great as to make still further increase of staff and buildings necessary, the Department of Education and the Universities of the Province be asked to consider the transfer of the present First-year University work to the Collegiate Institutes and High Schools.' This became more explicit when a 1923 legislative committee on the University of Toronto appointed by Drury recommended 'that the Department of Education provide throughout the Province convenient facilities for taking First-Year University work through the High Schools and Collegiate Institutes.'

The idea appealed to Ferguson. It would further his efforts to make educational opportunities more equally available and it would check the tendency of the provincial university to become big and impersonal. From time to time he spoke out in public along these lines. In Sarnia in January 1925, he referred to congestion in the U of T and suggested that 'unless we developed some scheme ... of extending courses at Collegiate Institutes to cover the first couple of years University work, we would be forced to further heavy capital expenditure' to expand an institution which was already so large it was becoming impossible to give students much personal attention. He was shocked the next day to discover the press had reported him as saying that 'Sir Robert Falconer was at the head of a big industry turning out a half-baked product.' He hastened to apologize to the President, who responded that he had 'been long in sympathy with your general purpose of putting in the leading schools of the province all the University work that they can carry,' but he added that 'I am afraid that the influences against it are pretty strong.'[43]

It was reassuring to know he could count on Falconer's support. As well, the reaction from some high schools and local boards, particularly those some distance from Toronto, indicated the scheme was addressed to a strongly felt need. From Lindsay, Windsor, Port Arthur, Fort William, and elsewhere, he received letters requesting such an extension of upper school work. In response he cautioned that 'there is no thought of undertaking at one sweep to take two years work away from the Universities and give it to the local Institutions. That involves so many complications that it is practically impossible.'[44] But still the demand grew and he was encouraged by letters such as that from Horace Brittain, the Director of the Citizens' Research Institute of Canada, that the proposal was 'likely to cause a realignment of educational forces ... which will certainly tend to revitalize the life of this Province...'[45]

One goal of the proposed reform was to reverse the tendency of recent years for the universities to take on work formerly done by high schools which in turn were doing more elementary school work. Ferguson hoped to achieve an upgrading of the system all along the line. The universities would be encouraged to improve their graduate facilities and conduct more research while the elementary schools in turn would offer more advanced work, responding thereby to the needs of rural Ontario. The changes, he emphasized, represented an 'interrelated' program for reform of the province's whole educational system, from grade school through to university.[46]

The key, of course, was the proposed junior college or extended high school structure. Dr Merchant was the strongest advocate of the reformed structure and it was he who provided Ferguson with a detailed rationale emphasizing the growing élitism of Toronto and the need to serve less favoured parts of the province. Noting that at least fifty per cent of the students at Varsity came from the city, Merchant insisted that 'students from the other large centres of population should, as far as practicable, share in the financial and other advantages of obtaining as great a portion as possible of their instruction at home or at schools where the expense is not as great as at Toronto.'[47] The high schools were being staffed with graduates of the university's highly regarded honours courses who would be well equipped to offer junior college courses. Since senior matriculants were already admitted to the second year of the four-year pass degree, why not extend the principle further? The local schools, Merchant believed, could offer better teaching and more personal contact than the large first-year university courses. Developing the concept of a community college, he pointed to other parts of the Empire and to the United States where such colleges were playing a large role and suggested that in Ontario too there were 'a large number of students who desire a college, rather than a university education...' Any municipality desiring to participate would be assisted financially. As outlined by Merchant, the plan was part of 'a comprehensive scheme covering the whole Province' whose purpose was to contribute to the reform and democratization of education in Ontario.

The universities reacted as though Ferguson had declared war. Although the idea had been on the drawing boards for years, Ferguson's remark in a letter to Falconer that he was 'delighted to see from some public utterances of yours that you concur in the view of the Department' suggested that liaison with the universities had been less than close.[48] Falconer seems to have been about the only university official in the province who had even a degree of sympathy. The Premier's remarks to the legislature on 30 March did not allay academic fears. When the Liberal leader voiced doubt that the collegiates would be able to give as good training in the first-year work as the universities, Ferguson returned to his refrain that the university had become an impersonal institution 'turning out more or less a product'; when it was suggested that Western and Queen's might not comply, he remarked, somewhat ominously, that they had always seen fit to do so in the past. Interestingly, Ferguson emphasized that economy was not the purpose of the change, pointing out that the new system might prove costlier than the old.

By this time Falconer had passed on Ferguson's 'request' to the colleges for discussion and the matter was also being debated in faculty councils, at the departmental level, and in the Senate. The university community marshalled every possible argument in defence of the integrity of the academy. It made little effort to hide its frankly self-interested fear of the material consequences of a substantial reduction in the number of fee-paying students, but the university men also provided a ringing defence of the unique value of their honours programs which, it was asserted, could never be duplicated by secondary institutions. Each of the federated colleges made clear the unanimity of its opposition. Victoria and Trinity demonstrated a determination to stand on their chartered rights and carry on first-year teaching whatever the university might decide. The Faculty of Arts at its fullest meeting in years adopted the sharply critical report of a special committee struck to investigate the Premier's proposal and the faculty decision in turn was endorsed unanimously by the Senate at its 14 May meeting. The various departments, in documents which apparently were not passed on to the Premier, added their objections and many individual faculty members wrote Falconer and Cody to vent their wrath. Generally, the unique nature of the honours programs and the distinction between the university experience and that of the schools were stressed. As well, it was frequently suggested that students who graduated from Ontario's vaunted schools system were so ill prepared for university work that it would be disastrous to extend the influence of the schools any further.[49]

Some of the more thoughtful responses came from individual faculty. Professor W.S. Milner told Falconer that 'the government and people of Ontario gravely overvalue their primary and secondary system ... and are almost equally ignorant of the real worth of this University...' Milner resented the university's lack of power to keep out weak students who 'are thrust upon us by a vicious and wooden examination, so mechanical and preposterous that it is impossible to describe...' and he warned that 'if this great University — and it is a great University — submits to this last invasion of its proper field it does itself a mortal injury. I believe I thoroughly know the feeling of the academic body. There is only one voice. Men recognize that we have come to a decisive moment.'[50] John Satterly of the Physics Department wrote Cody that there was 'not a teacher in the Province who could give anything like' his first-year course and he expressed his anger that those in power in the University — he meant Cody and Falconer — should 'allow themselves to be browbeaten by the ignoramuses in the Education Department.'[51]

Sadly, perhaps, the University response was a 'knee-jerk' defence of its own vested interests with little evidence of any effort to respond creatively or with insight — and this despite the fact that two major and recent provincial committees had seen fit to advocate such a change as a reform which might serve many Ontarians whose needs were not being met by the University. Of course the academics were performing a valuable service in defending the university against departmental officials and a Premier who were clearly in need of enlightenment and they were taking an important stand on behalf of the autonomy of their community. Yet despite President Falconer's belief that the University could offer a perfectly good degree after three years, as many European universities were doing, and despite the Education Department's commitment to a junior college system as in the interest of the province as a whole, there was little indication of any effort by the academics to understand the circumstances which had caused the Department to make its proposal. Indeed the Faculty of Arts council could only suggest that before embarking on such a 'costly experiment,' the province might test out its ideas 'in the northern part of the Province.' Principal Taylor of Queen's was equally negative in his May 1926 report to his Board of Trustees.[52] Interestingly, student opinion, according at least to *The Varsity*, found much good in the proposal. Doubtless many students had first-hand familiarity with the financial and other problems caused by an attendance of four years at the University of Toronto and they may also have agreed with some of the Department's criticism of the large first-year classes which the university offered.

By this time the opinions of university people were being reported in the press. The Toronto *Star* printed a list of objections offered by Principal Hutton of University College and stories appeared quoting Chancellor Bowles of Victoria, who argued that 'the right of a university to decide its own courses and not be dictated to by the Department of Education is the very life of a university.'[53] A few days later a thoroughly angered Premier told the Principal of Harbord Collegiate that 'there appears to be some attempt at a campaign against the suggestion of the Department. I notice Professor Alexander is actively inter-esting himself.'[54] To Ferguson such behaviour was almost intolerable, coming as it did from someone he regarded as virtually on the public payroll. 'I may be wrong but I have always held the view that it is the function of the Department of Education to determine questions of policy in connection with the general education of the people of the Province. It is the duty of the staff to give efficient service for the salary they receive in whatever duties may be assigned to them. I am always willing to discuss these matters ... but public controversy is a different matter.'[55]

Conveniently, the Premier had forgotten his earlier opinion that 'the uni-versity organization is distinct from the Department of Education.' But the indignant professors seemed equally oblivious of the Department's responsibility for the educational welfare of the province as a whole. They ignored the inter-relationships between the different levels of the system and the effect their inflexible reaction might have on secondary education and on communities beyond the gates of the ivory tower. Although many professors were quick to complain about the dismal 'products' sent them from the schools, their concern remained almost entirely with their own interests. To them the Department was an external threat to be resisted and in an impressive display of united action the university community banded together to destroy a proposal which threatened its cherished interests.

Falconer himself continued to see merit in the idea but when he forwarded the reaction of the federated colleges to the Premier in April, he could only observe that 'these replies are all of the same tenor, though I know that they have given independent consideration to the matter, and I am convinced also have dealt with it as sympathetically as possible...'[56] Ferguson had expected opposition but he also believed that Cody and Falconer would be listened to with some deference. He may have miscalculated because he had expected university opinion to judge the proposal on its merits and here too he was wrong. Now he was angered and he pressed stubbornly ahead. Clearly, the intelligentsia lacked the political leverage of the rural trustees.

On 22 December, Falconer received a peremptory note. 'I am exceedingly anxious,' Ferguson began, 'that this scheme should be put into effect at the beginning of the term of 1927. I would like to know what, if any, steps have been taken by the University to meet this suggestion. The Government has decided on this as a matter of policy and it is desirable that it be expedited in every way.'[57] The embattled Falconer again pointed out to Ferguson the extent of the opposition. 'Very serious difficulties have emerged especially in connection with the transfer of the honour courses ... moreover the Federated Universities have expressed strong opposition even to the transfer of the pass work.'[58] Thus, as his first administration drew to a close, Ferguson was dug in and apparently prepared to invite an all-out test of strength with the province's universities. Neither side was likely to yield and a donnybrook of unprecedented proportions between the powerful Premier and a determined university community seemed in store for the province.

If two relatively new problems, school board consolidation and the proposed transfer of a portion of the work of the universities to the high schools, caused Ferguson many anxious moments, two older difficulties were handled with relative ease. When those tired but dangerous perennials, the separate school question and the controversy about the role of the French language in the province's schools, came again to the fore, Ferguson, in a virtuoso performance, managed to satisfy the French community and to prevent the separate school problem from becoming a major political issue.

In 1921 and 1922, the Roman Catholic authorities had conducted an extensive campaign to influence the public and press the province to grant new school concessions. There was much justice in their cause. According to Catholic figures, the average annual cost of tax-supported schools between 1917 and 1922 had increased from $8.32 to $15.66 per head of population.[59] Separate school boards were incurring large deficits and needed frequent private subsidization. Although corporations since 1886 had been allowed to contribute to the support of separate schools an amount of their assessment proportionate to the holdings owned by Catholics, the complexity of the large corporations had rendered this provision largely nugatory and, in any case, separate schools received nothing from public service corporations. In this period, separate schools were also doing more work at the high school level, either by carrying on continuation work at the upper levels of the elementary system or through private Catholic high schools. Catholic leaders were determined to expand the amount of their high school work and to find the funds which would make the expansion possible.

On both counts the Catholic community encountered the province's fear that a fully developed Catholic system would threaten its structure of common schools. By World War I, departmental officials were concerned that the Catholic authorities were taking advantage of the right to establish continuation schools to make major extensions of their system into the secondary school level. In 1915, the Department angered Catholics by forbidding further extensions beyond the work of the fifth form and Bishop O'Brien of Peterborough told Ferguson, then Acting Minister of Education, that he was 'astonished' that a right which was unchallenged since Confederation was now being questioned. Ferguson bluntly responded that the bishops had 'an entire misconception of the position that Separate Schools occupy in the educational system of the Province.' The Department, he insisted, 'never has, and I venture to think, never will change the well defined, clear-cut and well understood line of demarcation between the work of our Public and Separate School and that of our Secondary or High School.' The high school field, he assured the bishop, was 'fully occupied and the work most efficiently done under a State System.'[60]

In the war period, however, Hearst and Ferguson agreed to a compromise by which the whole question was left pending until peace returned, at which time it would be submitted to the courts for settlement. During the early Drury years, as the costs of the Separate School system grew and the sense of crisis mounted, there remained those like Archbishop Neil McNeil who preferred to attempt to reach a settlement by private political negotiation.[61] Such methods did not attain the desired end. Unhappily for the Catholics, the public agitation they embarked upon to win public support alerted their historic enemies and separate schools emerged once again as a divisive issue. As a result, in spite of a number of meetings between Drury and church officials, the Farmer government failed to act.

Thus, when he came to power Ferguson faced a situation in which Catholic frustration was mounting and Protestant determination to resist concessions was increasingly vocal. The Drury government had decided to proceed with a stated court case but the Orange Order preferred that a Separate School Board be forced to sue as plaintiff. One of Ferguson's first moves was to ask Merchant to determine how many separate schools were doing middle school work and in January 1924 he was told that seventeen schools with 475 pupils were so engaged.[62] Finally, after discussions between the Premier and the Catholic authorities, it was agreed that 'a friendly action' would be preferable to a stated case as less likely to lead to unpleasant confrontations. With that decided, Ferguson told the House he would be well satisfied with his tenure as Education Minister if he could succeed in settling the various separate school difficulties.

At this point, Michael O'Brien of the Catholic Educational Council explained to Archbishop McNeil that the schools question had not been raised in the legislature because the government 'though seemingly well disposed was not prepared to deal with it during the first session of their incumbency...'[63] Nonetheless Bishop Fallon, the most vocal defender of separate schools, told Ferguson he believed the premier would 'treat our branch of the public education of the Province with justice and fairness' and assured him that 'their Lordships were much impressed by the reasons set forth ... for a change from a Stated Case to a Petition of Right...' Ferguson told the fiery cleric that he 'always thought to remove from the field of controversy all our educational problems. The judicial determination is, to my mind, the one way of bringing this about.'[64] The Premier even suggested through Charles McCrea that Thomas Battle would be a solicitor for their cause to whom he could speak frankly. The bishops proved accommodating and briefed Battle to argue their case.[65]

Fallon soon lost confidence in the Ferguson government. An undated and unsigned memorandum in his papers accuses Dr Merchant in May 1924 of breaking the 1917 agreement under which separate schools already doing secondary work would be allowed to continue to do so 'until the question was finally adjudicated' by notifying them that grants would no longer be paid for such work. An enraged Fallon charged that 'without legislation, without Order-in-Council, and in spite of such orders and legislation as exist, this letter by a single stroke of the pen of departmental officialdom relegates all those classes to the status of private schools. This is altogether the most arbitrary act against the welfare of the separate schools which their history reveals.'[66]

Other Catholic officials either did not share Fallon's sense of outrage or did not feel it politic to speak their minds. In any case, there was little point in carrying on an agitation while the matter was before the courts. Whether because they believed their case to be weak or because they thought the matter too vital to be left to judicial determination, the question of a fairer division of corporation taxes was not placed before the courts. The case was restricted to the question of the right to do advanced work and a dispute over the division of the legislative grant and these were dealt with together under the same principle. As Battle explained the case to Fallon, the Petition of Right 'treated Continuation Schools, High Schools and Collegiate Institutes as Common Schools within the meaning of the Common School Act of 1859 and Separate School Act of 1863 and by claiming a share on the average attendance basis of the monies granted these Schools we have opened the way wide for a complete argument as to whether or not these are Common Schools and if so we are exempted from taxation for them and we are also entitled to conduct the same courses of study and grades of education.'[67]

As usual in schools litigation, Norman Tilley and McGregor Young acted for the province. Battle was satisfied on the basis of assurances from Young that 'both sides would endeavour to raise fairly and equally all the points involved so that there would be no question of the case being decided ... on any technicality.'[68] The Petition of Right was brought between the Board of Trustees of the Roman Catholic Separate School for a school section in the Township of Tiny, on behalf of itself and all other boards of trustees of Roman Catholic separate schools in Ontario and His Majesty, the King. In May 1926, Mr Justice Rose pronounced against the separate school position throughout, but Battle believed the judgement a weak one which would present no obstacles on appeal.[69] Urgency was added the following month when the Separate School

Board of Toronto was unable to provide its teachers with either raise or bonus and the Teachers' Association asked the church to provide financial aid.[70] Separate School teachers had already suffered financial privations, including salary reductions in 1924, and Catholics were in no mood for further temporizing. Then, in October 1926, the Ontario Appeal Court unanimously found against the separate school position. Once again Battle and his colleague, I.F. Hellmuth, gave the bishops cause to hope that a final appeal to London might be favourable.[71] In public at least, there was no disposition to blame the government. Ferguson's tactics had succeeded in removing the issue from the political arena; little was heard of separate schools during the 1926 election.

More remarkably, this was also true of the bitterly contested French-language schools dispute. In the period after the war, the French Canadian Educational Association continued to resist the hated Regulation 17 and organized a remarkable structure of extra-legal schools in the province's centres of French-speaking population.[72] But the financial strain was great and ACFEO, desperate to effect a permanent solution, worked hard among the English-speaking population to enlist sympathy for its cause. Although many Franco-Ontarian leaders were apprehensive when their old enemy Ferguson came into power, Senator Belcourt believed that Ferguson must know that the Regulation was a terrible mistake and that by repealing it 'he can render Canada the greatest service since Confederation.' With his big majority, he could do whatever he liked. 'He practically has it in his own hands to say whether we shall have a national sentiment or ... the reverse.' In Belcourt's view, the repeal of Regulation 17 would be the best means for the Tories to break into Liberal Quebec. 'If he has vision,' the Senator concluded, 'he will see that this is the opportunity of his life both for himself and his party.'[73]

Ferguson must have been convinced. During the 1925 session of the legislature, he told the members he was not 'wedded to Regulation 17' and he announced the appointment of a commission headed by Dr Merchant and including Louis Côté, a Franco-Ontarian from Ottawa, and Judge Scott, well known as a leading Orangeman, to make 'a careful comprehensive survey of the whole situation.' The problem, of course, was far from solved and Ferguson would require his most deft political touch in the period after the election when the Commissioners reported and action could no longer be postponed.

13

Parties and Elections

One important feature of the first Ferguson administration was the growth in the Premier's own reputation. Even after the 1923 election, many Ontarians feared that the old political brawler, the man who was reputed to have bragged that patronage and the hope of patronage were what held the party together, would run a machine-ridden and disreputable administration. To this element, the crude, swaggering Ferguson of Timber Scandal notoriety, the champion of Orange extremism and gutter politics, was not fit to be Premier of Ontario. Although those who knew him recognized that this represented only one side of the Grenville man's complex character, undeniably Ferguson understood the seamy side of politics better than most of his contemporaries; if his many successes won him the applause of those who said he had the Macdonald touch, it was equally true that he never hesitated to use the Macdonald tools.

Yet, like Macdonald, Ferguson knew that the methods of the machine need not determine the quality of the administration. There were things one did to get into power; there were other things one had to do to stay in power. A responsible conservatism demanded honesty of purpose, administrative integrity, and a sure and resolute sense of the public interest. All these Ferguson by 1926 had demonstrated he possessed in full measure. Above all, his characteristic style was to focus public attention on what he conceived to be the large issues of public life. Although he possessed an extraordinary knowledge of the details of the administration of each department, his greatest strength lay in his ability to keep in mind the broader ends and to be able to communicate to his fellow Ontarians the sense that his government was pursuing great purposes and goals.

Gradually the image of the ruthless partisan was blurred by that of the constructive statesman. At times his closest associates hardly knew what to make of the mix of idealism and partisanship which composed his character. Mark Irish, one of his oldest friends, was flabbergasted after an intimate dinner party at Joseph Flavelle's in February 1926. 'I wonder if there came out of last night, midst all its delights,' Irish asked Flavelle, 'a surprise to you, or was I alone in my previous ignorance? The side of his character which Ferguson revealed was a positive astonishment to me: I had no previous inkling of it. If the trait was not assumed for the occasion, then he deserves to go far and greatly benefit his fellow citizens by the service he renders. My qualification is not meant unkindly, but will rather indicate that my awakening was as startling as it was sudden, and I am sorry for the injustice that I have apparently done him in the past.'[1]

Whether enthusing about Ontario's munificent heritage of natural resources, expounding upon the need for applied research to facilitate the intelligent use of those resources, or pointing to the value of educational structures which could better serve all of the people, the Premier's rhetoric was beginning to seem almost self-consciously high-minded. More than ever his speeches offered often pompous platitudes on such great themes as Canada's imperial heritage, the value of the National Policy as a source of national unity, and the perils of economic continentalism. By so behaving he was not denigrating provincial concerns but placing them in their national and international contexts. For a nationalist-imperialist this was logical behaviour but many drew the conclusion that Ferguson was preaching for a call. Those who remembered his role in the period before he entered the Hearst cabinet when he had propounded his vision of Canadian nationalism and insisted that 'Ontario must lead the way' realized that this was not necessarily the case. He had always believed that Ontario's political spokesmen had national responsibilities. Of course this concern offered tangible political benefits. People assumed that this was a new Ferguson. His calls for national unity, economic nationalism, and closer French-English relations, because they were accompanied by policies and programs to attain those objectives, won applause from those who once had regarded him with contempt.

There was another dimension to the regard which was growing for him across the province. Ferguson loved Ontario in a very personal way and was able to communicate this feeling to his fellow Ontarians. Invariably a capable stump orator, it was when he was extolling his province that he moved his audiences most deeply. To him Ontario was the garden of Eden, its resources the envy of North America, its people the salt of the earth. He himself epitomized its virtues and its shortcomings. It is less trite than is usually the case to say that Ferguson was the average Ontarian writ large. To one journalist, Ferguson, with his square-toed shoes, his conservatively-cut business suits, his flourishing yet ordinary appearance and the friendly sparkle from behind his steel-rimmed spectacles, looked more like 'a prosperous manufacturer's agent ... than a Prime Minister.'[2] He never stood out in a crowd until he opened his mouth and then, invariably, his witticisms and repartee made him the centre of attention.

Yet the transformation was gradual and he did not at once win the affection of those who considered themselves the leaders of Toronto society. Not only did old suspicions remain but his aura of a small-town lawyer for a while caused some Torontonians to turn up their noses. Slowly this changed and finally he received the full measure of affection and confidence of the sceptics and became the darling of Tory Toronto, the man who could do no wrong. Toryism under Ferguson by mid-decade assumed some of the characteristics of a religious revival. To live in Toronto, J.C. McRuer has recalled, and not to be a Tory, was to be beyond the pale.[3] Many Liberals, with Norman Tilley as a prominent example, remedied this by becoming Howard Ferguson Conservatives in provincial elections. Others remained a part of the Liberal rump and suffered a sense of exclusion from the establishment which ran affairs provincially and municipally in Toronto and in scores of other municipalities about the province.

Thus by 1926 or 1927 he basked in an adulation which contrasted curiously with the attitudes to which he had become accustomed. He had become the politician's politician and the people's choice. The chroniclers of that era described him in glowing terms. Sir John Willison believed that 'more than any other man in public life in Canada he represents the outlook of Sir John Macdonald and is more than anyone else the natural leader of the Conservative Party.' To the journalist Leslie Roberts, he was 'the Sage of Kemptville, perhaps the best working politician in our Tory ranks.' Hector Charlesworth, who had known all the Ontario premiers except Sandfield Macdonald, believed none to be 'more deeply imbued with wisdom, humour, energy and the spirit of progress than Mr Ferguson...' Those who worked most closely with him admired him the most. To T.L. Kennedy, he was 'the most astute politician that this country has ever seen. ... he taught me more about politics than anyone else.' To Thomas Crawford, who had sat in the House under seven premiers, Ferguson for knowledge of provincial affairs and departmental management topped them all. Almost to a man, the party was devoted to its leader and even those who differed with him over policy would defer to his sense of timing and judgement of the public mood. Arthur Ford, in the early twenties one of the most persistent sceptics, finally concluded that 'Howard Ferguson was the most human, the most personable, the wisest and the shrewdest politician of all the public men I have known.'[4]

Why had so many of the detractors been won over? Of course politicians love a winner and after 1926 there was no longer any doubt that Ferguson had the winning touch. But more was involved than this. Although he never doffed entirely the methods of the backroom politician and indeed, in his free-wheeling ways and offhand manner came to exemplify in some ways the spirit of the twenties in Canada, he also convinced many that he was still good, solid Ontario to the core and that he retained all the essential virtues of the day. There was little of the demagogue and no touch of the populist about him. However convivial and easy-going he might appear, he was undeniably an establishment figure, a lawyer, a Tory, an Anglican, an imperialist, one who moved easily in the seats of the mighty and was, eventually, accepted totally by the society of his day. Despite his reputation, those who mattered finally realized that beneath the surface Ferguson was a diligent, hard-working, and thoroughly reliable spokesman for the things that were important to them. That he was also a democratic politician who had the common touch and understood the psychology of mass leadership made him all the more effective as a spokesman for Ontario's ordered, conservative society.

The most important cause of the changed attitude was the record of his first administration. It appeared competent, businesslike, and efficient. The different interest groups and classes of the Ontario community found those who ruled at Queen's Park ready to listen and act. The cabinet provided able service and several of its members were of the first rank. In particular, W.F. Nickle helped provide a sense of firm purpose and steady respectability. The breath of scandal in a decade notorious for loose practices did not touch the government. It came closest when it was learned that the fuel supply firm, formerly headed by James Lyons, continued to do a certain amount of business with the province after Lyons became a minister, although he was no longer actively associated with it. Lyons's resignation was demanded forthwith by the Premier, who announced that he was determined 'not only that there shall be no wrong-doing, but that nothing can be permitted that can be so construed as to create suspicion or shake public confidence in the integrity of the Government or any of its members.' When remarks Lyons made in his own defence became a source of controversy, Ferguson dictated a statement and ordered the former minister to read it in the House.[5]

It was Ferguson's ready mastery of provincial affairs which allowed him the time to dabble in national politics. As early as November 1923, with much of the press convinced that he had federal ambitions, he responded that he was content to remain in Ontario and head the government of the province which had always dominated Canada. Said in jest, this nonetheless was an expression of Ferguson's real feeling about his position; on this occasion Meighen had to write to inform him that Ernest Lapointe was exploiting the statement in Quebec and to ask him to make some reference to the spirit in which the remark had been made.[6] Whatever the reason for the Ontario Premier's pronouncements on federal affairs, he was becoming a figure of national prominence. Meighen was pleased, then, when Ferguson responded to requests from various sources and agreed to accompany him for part of his western tour in December 1923. 'His presence,' Meighen told Arthur Ford, 'will attract a great deal of attention and I think will do a lot of good.' 'I don't know what the devil is taking me out West,' Ferguson wrote Meighen, 'but I have had so many messages urging me to go, and I feel that if there is any good service to be achieved I will be glad to make the trip.'[7]

Of course he was enjoying all this to the hilt. After the dark months of the Timber Scandal, it was exhilarating to be firmly in command of a successful provincial administration and to be a sought-after figure on the national scene. Another cloud which was beginning to disappear was the $27,000 personal debt he had accumulated during the 1923 election. As early as August of 1923, R.C. Matthews told Meighen he was 'thinking of heading a movement to supply a house in Toronto for the Premier of Ontario, or at least to gather a substantial sum to help him buy one.'[8] In time, wealthy Tories presented him with a fund, apparently in the neighbourhood of $250,000. The first thing he did was pay his debts and eventually plans were under way to build a Toronto home. Ferguson always proclaimed his ignorance of the source of the funds, saying only that 'one man assured me it was made up of small contributors, from people who had no political axes to grind.' According to Arthur Ford and to Douglas Oliver, a reporter who knew him well, it was decided that only the interest on the sum raised would be made available.[9] His friends knew that Ferguson was incurably extravagant. He lived well, sometimes paid little attention to where his money was going, liked to hand out boxes of dollar cigars to his friends. Although it soon became public knowledge that money had been so raised, and although he made no effort to conceal it, there was little criticism. People knew he had made great sacrifices to remain in politics; furthermore, the practice was in accord with the custom of the day and other prominent politicians received similar assistance. A few years later, he accepted another gift on similar terms. Somewhat more questionable was Ferguson's willingness while premier to let some of his wealthy friends, particularly the mining promoter J.P. Bickell, invest on his behalf in the stock market.[10] This period saw the beginnings of a very substantial fortune; in their later days Howard and Ella would have no financial worries.

One way in which the Fergusons spent their money gave them particular pleasure. They were delighted to be able to pay the medical bills and tend to other wants of needy children who came to their attention. Early in 1926, for example, a school principal from Dundas County told Howard of a young boy, nearly deaf and dumb, who came from a large, poor family and desperately needed medical attention. Telling the principal to buy the boy clothes and see that his medical needs were attended to, he later arranged to send him to Toronto's Sick Children's Hospital where apparently he was kept for many months at the Premier's expense.[11] Perhaps by this and other similar actions, Howard and Ella were filling a void in their lives left by the absence of children of their own.

Politically, the party under Ferguson maintained its close working relationship with the federal Conservatives. The victory of 1923 gave new confidence to both sections of the party and in October of that year Meighen asserted that Conservatism was 'stronger than ever in its history in the Province of Ontario.'[12]

Contact between the two leaders while not frequent was cordial and occasionally they met to tend to organizational matters. One problem was the Western Ontario organization, which had done such good service in the provincial election. Local funds were becoming exhausted but Arthur Ford hoped the federal and provincial parties would contribute equally to a fund which would allow the organizer to continue his work.[13] Ferguson, always in favour of the principle of regional organizations, strongly favoured this solution and to Ford's pleasure was able to arrange with E.B. Ryckman and other wealthy Tories to provide the wherewithal.

Although Gordon Reid, who was confirmed as organizer, began to take hold of affairs in the Western constituencies, finances remained a problem and the federal people had difficulties paying their fair share. Meighen seems to have been hesitant about over-committing himself to organizational work in Ontario and Ferguson pointedly agreed that it would be unwise for either wing of Conservatism to appear to be interfering with the organizational efforts of the other. A hint of contempt appeared in a January 1924 note to Jack Reid in which he reported that a successful meeting in London had 'proved to Meighen and his friends who wanted to discard my London organization, that it was the biggest thing in the province as a successful piece of machinery. Ontario to-day,' he continued, 'is ripe for a tremendous sweep in favour of the Party. It does not matter who is the leader.'[14]

The provincial party, of course, since the Massey Hall Convention, possessed its own structure and Ferguson was confident that with the assistance of Price, McCrea, and Bill Clysdale, it would remain in good fighting trim. The Ontario Liberal-Conservative Association was no longer as distinctly a provincial body as it once had been but there was no question where its ultimate loyalty lay. Bill Clysdale's salary was paid entirely by the Ontario party and a little later it even became necessary for the organizer to inform Hugh Guthrie, then Tory leader in the Commons, that it seemed only fair that his expenses in federal by-elections should come from Ottawa.[15]

But in 1924 and 1925, Ferguson was not inclined to quibble. He was aware of Meighen's difficulties in raising funds and although the provincial party itself was never well off, he was willing to make allowances. In return, Meighen was standing by him loyally in his efforts to prevent a political explosion over the OTA. The Tories experienced a major setback in November 1924 in an unexpected federal by-election loss in Hastings. Ferguson had assured Meighen that 'my reports indicate that the situation has improved very much for Porter in Hastings. There is no question now as to his election.'[16] Yet, days later, Porter fell and reports reaching Meighen confirmed what one provincial member told him, that 'the discontented government control chaps hit Ferguson through Porter...'[17] Meighen concluded that 'the numbers who voted against the Conservative Party on this ground were very large,' but he reacted to complaints about Ferguson's unpopularity by telling all his friends to 'stand loyally by Honourable Howard Ferguson at the present time. The opposition to him is not reasonable. He is capable and resourceful and will solve the difficulties that confront him.'[18]

It may have been the prohibition situation which induced Ferguson to advise Meighen in March 1925 to do whatever he could to avoid an early federal election. 'I have given the whole situation every consideration from every angle,' he told Meighen, 'and I am unreservedly of the opinion that you should accept any suggestion that will bring about the postponement of an election until after you have had another session. ... There are so many reasons to be advanced in favour of delay. ... Your stock is going up – King's going down.'[19] Meighen agreed, adding that 'I appreciate any suggestion from you as to strategy. There is no man in this country who knows more of that subject than you do ... If you are down this way, try and save a couple of hours for me.'[20]

Another consideration favouring delay was the federal party's financial difficulties. Party president John MacNicol told Meighen that according to Clysdale the federal party's Toronto office was 'at the end of its rope – away in arrears – may have to be closed.' As well, Gordon Reid, whose salary was supposed to have been shared by the federal and provincial parties, now was let go for lack of funds and given a position in the Treasurer's Department at Queen's Park. 'We have no organization,' Ford told Meighen, 'and have no one in Western Ontario to take hold of it...'[21] Yet if neither wing of the party was wealthy, Ferguson's position in Ontario presented other possibilities. From North Temiskaming, one candidate assured Meighen that 'with decent co-operation from the Toronto Government, particularly the Department of Lands and Forests ... I can almost guarantee you success. ... I hope to make in-roads upon the French-Canadian vote as a result of my attention to their needs in the matter of Provincial patronage...'[22]

Fortunately for the Tories, Mackenzie King delayed the election until October 1925. Then a new difficulty arose when the federal party tried to induce provincial members to run for the Commons. Although Meighen told Ferguson that 'we have sought to avoid wherever possible interfering with the present membership of the Conservative Party locally,' Ferguson replied that 'it broke Sir James Whitney's heart when some twelve members took Dominion nominations in 1911. We lost a number of the by-elections.' He reminded the federal leader that it was essential that the party's strength in Ontario be maintained. 'I don't want Liberal papers to start a story that local members are deserting the Ontario Government, nor do I want a lot of by-elections with the present disturbed state of public feeling.' Meighen had little choice but to respond that he was 'in complete agreement.'[23] When Earl Rowe decided to move into the federal arena, Ferguson did his best to convince him he had a great future in provincial politics but Rowe did not succumb to such blandishments.[24]

The Ferguson Conservatives nonetheless threw their full strength into the 1925 campaign. Ferguson viewed it as an opportunity to get the party machinery in condition for the subsequent provincial effort. He was also desperately anxious to see his own party in power nationally. Charles McCrea organized the north and W.H. Price supervised matters across the province, including Meighen's itinerary. Billy Price complained to Meighen that 'a great many of the factors were beyond my control and one had to do the best with the material at hand' and he had 'to do a great many things off my own bat, failing any directions from Ottawa,' but as Ferguson's political manager, he knew how to get all the machinery in motion.[25] Ferguson himself did not play an active platform role, feeling, perhaps, that with the OTA question still unsettled he might do more harm than good. His contribution was at the level of strategy, in throwing his lieutenants into the fray, and in deploying all the resources of the provincial machine.

At one stage Ferguson advised Meighen that there seemed to be some prospect of repeating the coup of 1911 in which the Liberal party had been split through the break of the 'noble 18.' On terms of intimacy with prominent Liberals who supported him provincially, he hoped with proper management to split the Liberal party wide open. Meighen was enthusiastic and informed Ryckman that 'Mr Ferguson says this time without the least difficulty there could be a break of the "noble 80." The name of R.A. Stapells of the Board of Trade has been suggested as the kind of man who could handle this well. ... This is well worth taking up and putting over...'[26] Although Home Smith, a Tory organizer, Meighen, and Ryckman devoted some effort to this ploy and Stapells secured a substantial number of Liberal signatures, the urgency of 1911 was lacking and the effort amounted to little.

Despite this misfire, optimism mounted as the campaign progressed, and towards the end Ferguson was predicting a sweep in Ontario. This was the province's first opportunity to see Ferguson's machine in action. For a variety of reasons, the federal Liberals suffered a major setback, taking only eleven Ontario seats, ten fewer than in 1921. 'Victory is yours,' a delighted Ferguson wired his friend. Mackenzie King, however, refused to resign and carried on with the support of the Progressives. The shaken Liberal chieftain rationalized his defeat by telling Premier Brownlee of Alberta that 'had the Tory Party not come into control in our province we would have carried in the province many more seats than we did in the recent campaign. Its whole force and power was directed against Liberals and Progressives alike...' And he assured J.E. Caron, a minister in the Taschereau cabinet, that 'we were bought out in constituency after constituency.'

These impressions seemed confirmed by the observations of others. A supporter in Little Current told King that 'the Ontario Government used its influence, in the way of bribing the electors with road jobs etc...' From Port

Arthur came the lament that 'we found it very difficult to combat the Ontario Government agencies; two of the Provincial Ministers of the Crown, went all through this constituency, and every possible promise was made, and intimidation means used and threats exercised; and a vast amount of money was spent...' Confirmation was received from Manley Chew, defeated in Simcoe East, who informed King that 'the Ferguson Party did a great deal to hurt us. ... In fact the action of the Provincial Government during the Federal Election was very effective. They did a great deal of extra road work and the officials were able to and did canvass all the rural sections from house to house.'[27]

In this way the legend of Howard Ferguson's 'Tammany methods' began to grow. With Liberalism on the defensive in Ontario, it was reassuring for party stalwarts to attribute their sorry record to the ravages of the awesome Ferguson machine. Peter Heenan, who had moved to the House of Commons, now told the members that the Ontario government was using the funds provided by the Northern Development Fund, voted in a lump sum and dispensed at the government's discretion, to corrupt the electorate of northern Ontario, 'and when such corruption has failed it has been used in order to intimidate, to discriminate against, and even to persecute settlers in the north country.'[28] Claiming he had eighteen affidavits to document his case, he charged that civil servants, 'the hired thugs of the Provincial Government,' had spread across the north warning settlers they would get no assistance unless they elected Tory candidates. James Lyons had gone about 'promising roads, bridges and everything else...' He had raised similar complaints in the Ontario House on 18 February 1925, Heenan recalled, but Ferguson had refused to allow an investigation. Another member had referred to the Saskatchewan machine, Heenan concluded, but 'I have never seen anything in my life anywhere that could compete with the machine we have in Ontario...' Heenan neglected to mention, however, that when he had originally levied his charges, he had been challenged at once by Ferguson, who assured him that if he would give him 'the name of any Government employee who has been doing that sort of thing, I'll see that he isn't a Government employee any longer.'[29]

Such charges expanded with repetition. By the late twenties, Ferguson was accused as a matter of course by the Liberal press of using gangster methods which threatened to snuff the life out of Ontario democracy. These complaints had some substance. There was a Tory machine and, as Ferguson's control tightened, its methods became more blatantly efficient, until by 1929 and 1930 there was cause for concern. Yet its power was still much exaggerated by opposition politicians and certainly in mid-decade the various charges were more a product of Ferguson's reputation and of Grit rationalizations of failure than of concrete reality. Years later, for example, one politician recalled sitting in the gallery of the Ontario House when a member was berating the government for having dismissed all those who held provincial positions who were not known

Conservatives. Only one Liberal, the member claimed, had survived. As the story went, Ferguson rose, ostentatiously took pen from pocket, apologized for the oversight, and requested the name of the Grit who remained on the payroll.[30] Such an incident may well have happened, but whether it did or not, these were the stories friend and foe alike loved to tell of Howard Ferguson.

Certainly the Ferguson government never hesitated to use the resources at its command. The Premier admitted that lower level positions in the service normally would go to Conservatives but denied that political considerations had any effect at all on the senior appointments.[31] He carefully guarded against suggestions that the government's power over the service was being exploited for political reasons. On several occasions, orders went out to members of his cabinet to ensure that no grounds be given to provide the shadow of justification for such charges. When Sinclair in 1927 claimed that civil servants were working for the Tories, mentioning even the names of individuals involved, Ferguson warned his ministers that 'it is entirely improper for members of the Public Service to be actively interested in party politics. Resolutions of the House have been unanimously passed declaring emphatically against this practice. ... You should at once make it known in your Department that the policy of this government is to adhere to the principle approved of by the whole Legislature.' Of course, this was a convenient pose, but the anger in the Premier's letter was sincere enough and he insisted that civil servants who behaved in such a fashion were 'placing the government in a position which will incur public censure' and that they were jeopardizing their own positions by following practices for which 'there is absolutely no defence.'[32]

Other practices Ferguson was less hasty to condemn. He placed Carroll Hele, his secretary who doubled as political fixer, in charge of ensuring that only friendly papers received government advertising. And in a minor effort to manage the press, Hele, with the co-operation for a time of veteran newsman W.E. Elliott, then employed by Ford's *Free Press*, sent out to newspapers a 'weekly letter' in which events in the legislature were reported in a manner which did not cause the Tory viewpoint to suffer. But if the Ferguson government generally had a friendly press, this was largely because the Premier was a past master at the art of getting on with journalists. He stayed on good terms even with the representatives of Grit journals and although it was his habit to speak to newsmen with much frankness, he almost never had a confidence betrayed.[33]

From time to time opposition members complained about the extent of patronage at the constituency level. Raney, for example, objected in 1925 that Tory candidates defeated in the 1923 election were controlling patronage in their constituencies. Such charges received the invariable response that 'all appointments are made either by the ministers in charge of the departments concerned or by the government on their recommendation, and are not otherwise controlled by anyone. The influence, special or otherwise, of any representation made to ministers depends on the value of the representations from the standpoint of the public interest.'[34] The Civil Service Commission, although it continued to exist, played a limited advisory role and offered no threat to ministerial patronage.

At the same time, there is little sign that the Tories under Ferguson commanded vast financial resources. Undeniably, they were well organized and used patronage to good effect, but the Liberals who controlled the federal government were not lacking in that respect. In the 1926 federal election, Ontario Liberals improvised creatively and led by wealthy businessman Percy Parker and by W.H. Moore put together an ad hoc organization which performed excellently. Once again, Price and McCrea and other provincial people did their best for the federal Tories. On 1 September, with the campaign in full swing, Meighen assured Ferguson that McCrea 'has done wonderful work' and that he could 'never forget or reward the work Price has done in Toronto. He is a real master.' Yet Meighen had misgivings and in an appeal to Ferguson told him he 'could do excellent work in the Northern Counties. ... We have the election won if you can give us a big swing in Ontario the last two weeks. I would certainly appreciate your help.'[35] Ferguson, however, was seen and heard infrequently, playing a far less active role than in the previous year's election.

Meighen's apprehensions were justified. The Liberals increased their seats in Ontario from eleven to twenty-six and Mackenzie King formed a majority government. There were, no doubt, many reasons for Tory losses; the Liberal sunshine budget and the party's ability to pick up support which had previously gone to the waning Progressive movement were important. But so too was the fact that the former easy co-operation between Meighen and Ferguson had collapsed many months before the election took place. By July 1926, Ferguson was increasingly angered by the federal party's failure to pull its organizational weight. In a blunt letter to Arthur Ford, he conveyed his displeasure in no uncertain terms, telling him that while he was 'not disposed to "split hairs" over the financial situation or the question of control over the Western Organization' yet it was true nonetheless that 'the Dominion people abandoned it, and we have undertaken it and are maintaining it ourselves.'[36] Reid's office had been revived at considerable cost to the provincial party for its own purposes and Ferguson was much concerned that provincial matters be attended to over the summer. 'I do not think,' he continued, 'the Organization should be taking directions from two or three people. If they desire our Organizations to take hold of the situation, they should at least communicate with us here. ... it would be advisable for you to write and point this out...'[37]

Ford did so, reminding Meighen that 'Gordon Reid's salary as organizer is paid , through Hon. Howard Ferguson and likewise any expenses re the office. ... Mr Ferguson has told me to go ahead and put Mr Reid and our organization at your disposal. At the same time, I think it would be good business for you to communicate with Mr Ferguson and his cabinet thanking them for their cooperation and possibly asking them for their advice in organization. I have good reason to believe that they are a little sore, feeling that they have not been consulted enough and were not given any thanks for their tremendous efforts on our behalf in the last Dominion Election.'[38]

The coldness which had caused Ferguson to communicate with Meighen through Ford could not be attributed entirely to disputes over organization. The previous November, Ferguson and Meighen had been scheduled to speak together at a banquet in Hamilton. Meighen told the Premier he would like to consult with him before the meeting and the two men conferred together at Ferguson's Toronto residence. Ferguson was horrified to learn that the federal leader intended to tell his audience that it would be his policy in the event of another war that there should be a general election before troops should leave Canadian shores. Clearly this was an effort to appeal to the French-Canadian community in Bagot County, Quebec, in a by-election which was to take place shortly. By raising again the old problems of war and conscription, it seemed to Ferguson like a bolt from the blue. He at once told Meighen he doubted that the French electorate could be won by such a transparent gesture and that in any case the place for such a speech was not Hamilton but Bagot. More important, Ontario had given the Tories all but fourteen of its seats and Meighen's stock was high; to disturb that situation, in Ferguson's opinion, was not only inopportune but dangerous. Sensitive to all the Ontario currents in a way that Meighen could never be, he warned that such a move was unneccessary and therefore unwise. Beyond that, of course, it was an affront to Ferguson's imperial vision. National unity, he argued, would not be promoted by having 'a battle of ballots with all the bitterness you will have before you have a battle of bayonets.'[39] Bluntly he told Meighen that if he proposed to make such a speech, he would not be accompanied on the platform by the Premier of Ontario. And if he were ever faced with the issue in the future, he would have no choice but to take issue with the national leader's policy.

Meighen had not consulted widely within the party. He had talked to Guthrie, Borden, Drayton, Kemp, and a few others and, according to his own account, only Ferguson had objected. He decided, therefore, to go ahead. 'I had no conception there would be anything like the opposition that was raised,' he later wrote.[40] During the 1926 election the disillusionment may have been reflected in an enormous drop in the popular vote in Tory, imperialist Toronto. Despite this, the Conservatives retained all the Toronto and York seats, and it may be true, as Meighen's biographer has argued, that 'Hamilton did less damage to the Conservative cause than has often been supposed.'[41] Certainly, despite Hamilton, Ferguson remained anxious, as he told Ford, 'to do what we can to ensure the success of the Party in the Dominion Election' and he did nothing to restrain McCrea, Price, and other provincial men when they lent assistance to the federal cause.[42] Still, undeniably, the enthusiasm was not what it had been in 1925. Ferguson believed Hamilton had cost the party twenty seats and that, if his advice had been followed, Meighen would have been confirmed in power by the 1926 election.[43]

There was agreement that the federal rebuff would not affect the party's provincial fortunes if Ferguson should decide on an early test of strength. 'In this Province, there were no Provincial issues to encompass our defeat,' Price told Meighen. 'The OTA is not popular but it did not account for our slump because we lost mostly in dry ridings. In this Province, we could tomorrow carry every seat in Northern Ontario. We could carry all the French seats which we lost.'[44] Ferguson's decision to stand back from the federal campaign undoubtedly redounded to the benefit of the provincial party. In any case, one issue was still crowding out everything else as a subject of discussion in the provincial arena.

For Ferguson, prohibition was dangerous ground. On no other issue did Ontarians feel so strongly and for that reason it was the one thing which could split the Conservative party down the middle. Ferguson knew from the figures of the 1924 plebiscite that 69 of the province's 111 constituencies had returned dry majorities and 45 of those dry ridings were held in the provincial House by his party. Many Tories prominent as constituency officers across the province were fervent drys and many of his rural members believed their cause would be hopeless should the party adopt a wet platform. From western Ontario, Arthur Ford played his usual role. 'I am convinced,' he warned, 'that if Ferguson goes to the country on government control, it would be disastrous as far as Western Ontario is concerned, outside of a few ridings. The Progressives would run as prohibitionists and recapture their lost ground in the rural ridings.'[45] With the election about to be announced, Ira Fallis of Peterborough, one of the party's most experienced workers in eastern Ontario, viewed the outcome as uncertain. 'It will be a hard fight and a very bitter one, and especially hard to work among the women as the United Church is going to campaign against us from the pulpit. I really scarcely have the courage to undertake it but it's no time to leave the ship when it is in danger.'[46] Ferguson knew he would face a sustained campaign of abuse from many of the Protestant churches and that if he accepted assistance from the liquor interests he would be vilified across the province. Yet the wets were equally importunate, threatening dire consequences unless he succumbed to their wishes. Not only the party but the cabinet threatened to split and his Grenville constituency was as dry as any in the province. His own record on the issue made him terribly vulnerable. He had boxed the compass and the twists and turns of more than a decade had made him suspect to both sides.

Fortunately for Tory prospects, another issue with potential for political damage was handled flawlessly when W.F. Nickle during the 1925 session steered through a committee of the House a bill relating to the property rights of those Presbyterians who chose to remain out of the new United Church. The government also avoided the worst excesses of criticism that session when it passed legislation increasing cabinet salaries from $6000 to $8000 and the sessional indemnity from $1400 to $2000. And a useful piece of legislation the following year abolished the need for new ministers to return to their constituencies to seek re-election. All in all, Ferguson had reason for confidence. Still, he had never forgotten how the prohibition issue had destroyed Hearst and he faced many a bad moment as he and his lieutenants felt the pulse of the party and the province and debated strategy.

Yet there was always the state of the opposition parties to reassure worried Tories. On one occasion, Ferguson told the House that 'when I look across the hall and see the two leaders of those once-great parties, those bedraggled, battered remnants of former greatness, I can look forward to a long public service.'[47] Following the 1923 election, there had been expectations that Liberals and Farmers by working together might mount a formidable opposition but hopes for post-electoral co-operation proved illusory. Liberals such as W.E.N. Sinclair, who in August 1923 was chosen by caucus as temporary and House leader of his party, regarded the Farmers as a dying force and Sinclair had readily accepted Ferguson's offer that his party become the official opposition. Most of the elected Farmer members were determined to achieve Drury's dream of a People's Progressive party and steps in this direction were taken shortly after the election. A disappointed Hay reported to King that he 'had thought better of Mr Drury, but I am afraid if he pursues the course apparently he now has in view, he will continue to injure the Liberal Party and not help himself.'[48] When the Farmer members named Manning Doherty as leader and held the founding convention in 1924 of the new Progressive party, the Morrison wing reacted with less than enthusiasm. Several Farmers continued to sit under the UFO label and the *Farmers' Sun* pronounced emphatically that the UFO and the Progressives were 'two separate organizations, separately administered and with distinct and separate aims and objectives.'[49] The Progressives were not helped when Doherty resigned in 1925 to become a Meighen Conservative and his successor, W.E. Raney, remained unpopular with many who should have been the party's strongest supporters. By the mid-1920s, there was no urgency left in a movement sustained only by memories and by the presence of a few elected members.

The state of the Liberals was equally pathetic. Federally and provincially the party was wracked by internal divisions and organizational weaknesses. The federal ministers failed to provide any leadership and Mackenzie King assumed as little responsibility as possible. The federal and provincial organizations were intertwined and it might have redounded to the benefit of the provincial group when the party pulled itself together for the 1926 federal election and ran an efficient campaign. It proved impossible, however, to sustain this enthusiasm for the approaching provincial contest. To some extent, this was because Ontario Liberals recognized that their cause was all but hopeless, but the party was not helped by the fumbling, timid leadership of W.E.N. Sinclair.

Committed to the traditional values of small town, Protestant Ontario and believing that the UFO were interlopers, Bill Sinclair was determined to regain the traditional Liberal power base in the largely rural areas. A staunch prohibitionist, he was bewildered and dismayed by the great social changes of the decade and in that sense, according to J.C. Anderson who practised law with him, he was himself a conservative. 'He was willing to make the changes, but only if they were conservative changes. ... He would never compromise his strong principles.'[50] Possessing none of the flamboyancy of a Ferguson, he was a throwback to the dour Presbyterian Grits of nineteenth-century Ontario. Sinclair stood for 'honesty and integrity in public life.' His social program had no attraction for anyone to the left of Howard Ferguson for, 'while he realized that Government help towards welfare was very important and necessary, he always felt that individuals could have done more for themselves than they did.' In his opinion 'private enterprise, personal effort without reliance on social support should be the main aim of everybody.'[51] In this sense, of course, he was a man of his time; Ferguson held the same views, as did most of the Farmer leaders. Yet in Sinclair this outlook seemed less a social philosophy tempered by experience than a rigid dogma. Although from time to time he took positions on social questions, such as the old age pension, which were more progressive than the Tory stance, the narrowly conservative aura which clung to him made it impossible to capitalize politically on such occasions. The federal Liberals under King paid lip service and sometimes more to new social ideals and benefitted thereby but Sinclair was incapable of making a comparable effort.

Nor was he a political tactician of any skill. Anderson suspected that while he opposed Ferguson, 'secretly he had some admiration for his political acumen. ... the two understood each other politically, and even if Mr Sinclair had an opportunity to hit below the belt, he would not have done so, because he secretly admired the courage of Howard Ferguson.'[52] He was also in awe of the Tory leader's power and of his political skills. In the late 1920s, J.C. McRuer was a member of a group of young Liberals who occasionally pressed for more progressive policies and he recalls drawing up a draft of a dependents' relief bill and showing it to Sinclair, whose only response was 'Oh, if I take that up, Ferguson will tear it to pieces.'[53] Two years later, a similar piece of legislation was introduced by Ferguson himself.

The most striking illustration of Sinclair's timidity and perhaps of his rigid adherence to his personal values was the stance he assumed on Regulation 17. Everyone knew that the Franco-Ontarian Liberals were out of sympathy with Sinclair's views on prohibition and also that they wanted more than anything else to win concessions on the schools question. A meeting was held on 30 December 1925, in Mackenzie King's office. Arranged largely by W.H. Moore, it included, as well, Sinclair, Belcourt, Senator Hardy, and several other federal and provincial politicians. According to King's diary, it was agreed that the Ontario party would continue to stand for prohibition in order to prevent the Progressives from reviving and detaching the support of the *Star*, the *Globe*, the United Church, and other uplifters. This strategy required a *quid pro quo* with the French members. All present agreed that the Liberal party should call for the abolition of Regulation 17. 'It was felt,' related King, 'French-Canadian constituencies tho' against prohibition would stand firm on this ground and that rural English-speaking constituencies would hold for prohibition. The two were to go together to be put forward as the policy of the party when Sinclair speaks on the address.'[54] At this time there were signs that Ferguson intended to grant major concessions and it was vital that Liberals not be left to follow in his wake.

Incredibly, Sinclair failed to live up to the agreement. 'You will readily understand,' Belcourt told C.B. Sissons, 'that since Sinclair did not accomplish his share of the bargain, the other side felt themselves at liberty to fully air their views and opposition to prohibition. You have no idea ... how little authority our present leader has over the French-Canadian representatives who compose nearly one half of his whole party' and who greatly preferred Ferguson to their own leader.[55] In 1932 Paul Leduc explained to Sinclair's successor, Mitchell Hepburn, the reason for the disastrous drop in the party's French-speaking following. 'I do not know if it was through lack of sympathy or through plain stupidity, but the result was that we could not point to a single word of our then leader to show that he also sympathized with us, and we lost thousands upon thousands of votes on that account.'[56]

If Ferguson was fortunate in his opposition, its weaknesses could not be laid entirely at its own door. The truth was that Ontario in the 1920s was naturally and pre-eminently a Tory province. In some ways this was its response to the solid Quebec Liberal bloc. But undoubtedly the Tories understood better and expressed more readily the province's social and political values. Taken as a whole, Ontario remained strongly Orange, Imperialist, and Conservative. No corrupt political machine was needed to get out the Conservative vote in most Ontario communities; the Tory farmers, small businessmen, workers, and artisans, election after election, turned out and voted for the old party of John A., of Whitney, and now of Ferguson.

This was a close-knit structure of social, economic, and political power. In centre after centre across the province, Conservatives occupied most of the positions of influence on school boards, in municipal government, in minor appointive offices, and in areas of community leadership and prestige generally. In one sense this was what a machine was all about, but it was equally true that Tory political hegemony was so firmly established, despite the accident of 1919, that a machine was almost superfluous. Being a Liberal in Toronto in the twenties, J.C. McRuer has recalled, was a little like being a Communist at a later date. If Mackenzie King refused to intervene actively in the affairs of the provincial party, it was to some degree because the cause was so utterly hopeless. This was driven home on a political tour in November 1924, when he was introduced at a function at Cochrane by the mayor who was, naturally, a Conservative: 'a Tory as usual,' King lamented, 'all the mayors of towns and cities seem Tory.'[57]

The suspense ended on 19 October. The election would be held on 1 December and Ferguson was offering government control. The same day came the news of W.F. Nickle's resignation. 'In my judgment,' began his published letter to the premier, 'the Ontario Temperance Act has contributed substantially to the well-being of the province.' Describing government control schemes in other provinces as 'alluring but deceptive,' he declared himself 'convinced that the wise course does not lie in the direction you intend to take.'[58]

The loss of the powerful Attorney-General whose appeal to the moral and reform vote of the province had been of inestimable value in 1923 was a serious blow. It was followed by defections of constituency officers, party workers, and several candidates and potential candidates. The president of the Gananoque Association, for example, called government control a terrible mistake; Aaron Sweet, the member for Dundas, anticipating a slaughter if he ran under the wet banner, denounced Ferguson, and withdrew; E.T. Essery, a leading London Tory, delivered a slashing attack on his leader which left western Ontario Conservatives gasping; in Guelph, the chairman of the Women's Conservative Association said that she greatly regretted that her principles left her no course but resignation; from Ottawa, Charlotte Whitton, a lifelong Tory and Executive Secretary of the Child Welfare Council of Canada, vowed she would devote all her free time to defeating Ferguson. As the party split gained momentum, it seemed that history might repeat itself; as Hearst had destroyed his party over prohibition, now Ferguson too had given the opposition groups the one issue on which they might hope for success. The uplift press touted Nickle as the leader of a dry coalition to save Ontario. On 17 November, huge headlines announced that his hat was in the ring as an independent in Kingston.

What the province saw in 1926, more than on any other occasion in its history, was a one-issue election. When Ferguson tried to talk about other subjects, he would lose the interest of his audiences. Nothing else seemed to matter and that was the danger. Again, as in 1923, the opposition focussed its attacks on him, recognizing that his destruction would ensure the victory of its cause. Soon rumours were circulating that he held extensive stock in Gooderham and Worts.[59] Federal Tory George Foster came to Ontario and raked him fore and aft as a breaker of pledges, a man without principle. Atkinson and his Toronto *Star* waged a holy war to rid the province of the man who would return Ontario to the dark ages. Each day the *Star* printed the slogan, 'Ferguson Government can't be trusted'; it ran stories based often on trumped-up evidence about the evils of alcohol and gave the Progressive party $5000 and the Ontario Temperance Federation a similar sum while Atkinson's personal contributions towards defeating Ferguson 'were considerable.'[60] The Protestant churches put up a furious battle against the anti-Christ Ferguson; the *Canadian Baptist* on 25 November expressed 'unequivocal opposition' to government sale and *The New Outlook*, the organ of the United Church, described Ferguson as a traitor to his party for abandoning, by his own fiat, the policy adopted at the 1920 Tory convention. 'Cleverness without character' the journal jibed and it decreed on 1 December that 'not in the lifetime of any of us ... has a public issue of greater or more critical importance been presented for decision.'[61]

Although through it all, he maintained his usual good temper, Ferguson deeply resented the nature of the attack and particularly the frequent imputation that he had been bought by the liquor interests or that he was moved purely by base political motives. All his life he had detested the Raneys, the Atkinsons, and the Ben Spences who claimed all virtue for themselves and made their way in public life by impugning the character of those who dared disagree with them. He was profoundly moved when one cleric charged that 'the dis-honourable Howard Ferguson' had assassinated Hearst in 1919 and his old chief, still a sincere temperance man, immediately came to his defence. Ferguson knew he would be subjected to the vilest of abuse and that he was running a grave risk; but for years he had seen the prohibition issue dominate political debate, much to the detriment of public life in Ontario. His opponents now charged that he must take the responsibility for bringing the question into politics, but the truth was that he was placing his political future on the line in an effort to remove the issue once and for all from the centre of the political stage.

That he was willing to take the risks involved testified again to the nature of his political beliefs. Of course he knew from the 1924 plebiscite, and from what was happening elsewhere in Canada, that the days of prohibition were numbered and he was relying as well on the weakness of the Liberal and Progressive parties to see him through. But most of all, perhaps, the decision to run on government control reflected his judgement that, with the time right and the goal good, he would be able to organize a rational appeal and lead public opinion to the desired objective. Of course he would be assisted in this task by all the resources of the Tory party, its newspapers, its campaign funds, and the position of prestige and authority it occupied in the public life of the province.

Even so, there would be thousands who would vote on this issue and none other. With great care, he placed his case before them. His views were stated most fully at Kemptville where he traced the long history of his party's efforts to reduce the evils of alcohol, from the Whitney policy of moderation and gradualism to the OTA, which he described as a product of the period of war and the spirit of sacrifice.[62] According to Ferguson, the drys had then lost sight of the abnormal circumstances in which prohibition had been attained and proceeded to take it for granted, believing 'there was nothing further to be done on behalf of the cause ... and from that date the education of the public upon the subject was practically abandoned.' He was equally accurate when he pointed to the cutting off of importation in 1921 as 'the beginning of the irritation' in which the movement lost ground most rapidly. 'Has the Act not lost public support,' he asked, 'because those interested in the cause of Temperance have practically abandoned their work during the past seven years? Since then we appear to have relied entirely on the force of the law. Our course has not been to advise and enlighten people, but to coerce them by penalties and prison terms.'

Ironically, Ferguson used the same arguments to which Nickle had appealed the previous year on behalf of 4.4 beer. Ontarians, he noted, were consuming vast quantities of alcohol, as attested to by the scandal of doctors' prescriptions, the booming government dispensaries, the prevalence of home brew and the ubiquitous bootlegger. 'Do you not think it would be better where the demand exists and there is a determination to secure liquor at any cost, that we should face the problems squarely and ... that the profits now enriching the dealers should be made available for public uses and the reduction of taxation in Ontario?' Interestingly, although the economic benefits of government control had a powerful appeal to a province suffering from substantial budget deficits, this argument was less prominent than might have been anticipated. Both sides preferred to focus on the effects of the OTA on the moral and social health of the province. In Belleville on 29 October, Ferguson noted that $402,536.52 had been spent in 1925 on the enforcement of the OTA and only $355,254.31 on all other laws combined. In short, the law had broken down. 'It is in the mouths of everyone that there is an almost universal spirit of law resistance and non-observance. To coerce people in an effort to compel obedience ... only aggravates dissension. ... I have been forced reluctantly to the conclusion that something must be done to stem the ever growing disposition to rebel against the laws of the Province.'

That was half his case. By itself it was convincing enough and Ferguson was unusually stern and serious as he presented it to audiences across the province. Equally important was the government control alternative. Here he was deliberately vague; even his erstwhile first lieutenant Nickle at the time of his resignation had complained he was in the dark as to the details. As always, Ferguson retained maximum flexibility and Ontario, the only province at this time to adopt government control at a general election rather than after a binding plebiscite, was thereby provided with an opportunity to shape the best possible system. All he promised was to establish a strong, independent commission of outstanding men who could command the respect of the province, and to give this body power to issue liquor permits to those over twenty-one. Each purchase would be recorded and if the privilege was abused the permit would be revoked. As well, beer by the glass might be established in areas which wanted it but there would be neither liquor stores nor beer outlets in those parts of the province under local option. A formal bill would be presented after the election. Above all, Ferguson emphasized that this was a temperance measure designed to improve on a law which had failed. Under government control the bootleggers would be combatted, the horrors of the bar room would not be restored, the clock of progress would not be set back. The goal was a truer temperance.

To Ferguson, these were not merely arguments for political consumption. Few who recalled the open bar in turn-of-the-century Ontario could countenance with equanimity a return to that order of things; even many who regarded prohibition as a failure were willing to admit that, in some respects, conditions had improved under the OTA. Ferguson was imbued with enough of the uplift spirit and with sufficient social responsibility to agree with much of what the more moderate churchmen were saying. Those who broke the rules, therefore, would be dealt with ruthlessly under the new dispensation. 'The man who is abusing the privilege or who misconducts himself will have the privilege taken away from him,' threatened the Premier. 'I state with all the force and emphasis I possess, that there will be no bars,' adding for good measure, that, 'all persons found with liquor for which they cannot produce their permit will go to jail.'

Understandably, Ferguson's opponents were furious at his arbitrary and high-handed treatment of the issue. Ferguson 'placed himself above the Legislature and the members of his own party,' spluttered Sinclair.[63] It was quite true that the Conservative party as a body had played no formal role in the enunciation of the new policy; the province itself was being asked to buy a pig in a poke. This, of course, was tactics and the wisdom of retaining freedom to manoeuvre was revealed a few weeks later as criticism of the 'beer by the glass' proposal built into a crescendo. Candidates such as T.L. Kennedy, running in overwhelmingly dry Peel, were at an enormous disadvantage but when Kennedy pointed out to the Premier the hopelessness of it all, he learned that Ferguson had no intention of writing off even the most dry of constituencies. Colonel Tom tells the story best:

"Mr Ferguson, the man doesn't live who can win on that platform in the County of Peel. We voted 86½ per cent for prohibition just last year and that's too great a handicap for me to overcome." And he looked at me for a moment, and said: "Tom, I think you're right. Now you run and don't say a word about anything. I have a card up my sleeve I haven't played yet."

About three weeks later, he called me into his office and told me: "Tom, I intend to hold a meeting at Orillia and at that meeting, I am going to withdraw beer by the glass. Now, I want you to go around to your temperance friends in Peel and tell them that you will not run unless I withdraw beer by the glass." I did as he suggested, and to this day some of the oldtimers believe I was responsible for getting beer withdrawn from the platform.[64]

Kennedy's memory served him well. This was why they called him 'Foxie Fergie.' On 1 November, at Orillia, 'beer by the glass' was withdrawn and Ferguson used the occasion to denounce the 'inflammatory demagogues' who were misrepresenting the Tory position. Stephen Leacock, on the platform with his old school chum, said he was doing a noble thing 'jeopardizing his whole career to come out on a principle which he believes to be right.'[65] Of course, withdrawal of 'beer by the glass' was an appeal to the women's vote and generally to all wavering drys. It should work, thought one Tory worker, 'if Ferguson doesn't adopt a new policy between now and Monday next.'[66] Although the hotel-keepers denounced the 'wobbler' who had 'doublecrossed' them, they could not throw their support to the totally dry Liberals and Progressives.

The strategy succeeded. Many lifelong prohibitionists were convinced. George B. Nicholson, who had chaired the Committee of One Hundred in 1916, agreed that the law could be enforced only when public opinion was behind it. Magistrate Emily Murphy (Howard's cousin) testified that she had opposed government control in Alberta, but subsequently her experience on the bench showed her that conditions had improved immensely under it. Most important of all, Joseph Flavelle, for years the staunchest pillar of the drys, initially an opponent of Ferguson because he abhorred the idea of the return of the beer halls, now endorsed the Ferguson policy. 'I dislike Government control as such,' he stated in a private letter, 'because I believe it will lead to the sale of more liquor, but I dislike unrebuked law-breaking more.' D.B. Harkness of the Social Service Council agreed, telling Flavelle that 'any condition which breeds disrespect for law is more greatly to be feared than a temporary relaxation of sumptuary laws.' Both men believed the dry forces should turn their energies to a serious educational effort with 'less of emotionalism and more of sound social judgment.'[67]

But temperance men who were able to view the issue in such dispassionate terms remained a minority. In a series of pamphlets, the Ontario Prohibition Union angrily stated its case. 'Every woman,' asserted one effort, '...must remember that she holds in her hand, a vote for childhood and youth, or for the gratification of a few drinkers and the liquor interests.' In another pamphlet, Reverend Murdoch McKinnon charged that Ferguson's policy was 'the boldest and most impudent challenge flung in the face of the Christian Church in a generation.'[68] The clerical intervention Laurier and the Rouges faced in nineteenth-century Quebec was as nothing to that encountered by Ferguson in 1926. Reverend Ben Spence in his pamphlet, *The Ferguson Liquor Policy*, blasted away with all his guns, piling argument on argument, statistic on statistic. Government control in the west had increased liquor sales and liquor related crimes and had not eliminated the bootlegger, he asserted – a claim the wets found difficult to counter. Although Spence made a strong argument on behalf of the beneficial impact of the OTA on Ontario society, he gave away his case in his attacks on 'the foreign element' and on the debauchery and corruption he alleged Ferguson had permitted during the 1924 plebiscite.

With many thoughtful drys reconsidering their position, the Tories capitalized on the rift in the prohibitionist camp and by a clever advertising effort appealed to Ontario's deferential value system. Long lists were published of the famous and prominent who were endorsing government control. 'I have been voting now for more than fifty years...,' Sir Allen Aylesworth, Laurier's minister of justice was quoted, 'and I have never given a Conservative vote but I am doing so this year...'[69] Prominent attorneys, businessmen, politicians, journalists, doctors, and even clerics echoed Sir Allen's judgment. Once again, good use was made of Sir John Willison, who wrote analyses of the state of affairs in the government control provinces, and of Canon Cody, who went on the radio and was credited with converting thousands.

Of Cody, Howard Ferguson used to say, 'Harry makes me look respectable. I benefit by the leavening of his holiness'; never did he benefit more than in 1926.[70] When the drys enlisted the support of young people in a 'Youth Refuses to Retreat' movement, Ferguson put to the test his theory that if the case was good, people would listen and sent out young Tories such as Maurice Cody, his old friend's only son, and David Walker, to the small towns and villages where they would engage in casual conversation and put forward the government position. 'You could change people at that time,' David Walker recalled. 'They started out by being cool and ended up quite receptive.'[71] One way the Tories reached people was through their imaginative use of radio and Ferguson took to the air waves on several occasions. Mark Irish, who managed the funds, later reported to R.B. Bennett that he spent 'I think for the first time in a Canadian election, more money on radio than I did on printers' ink.'[72]

Of course Ferguson had made certain that the party machinery was in a state of readiness before making his move and, as usual, he devoted lavish attention to enticing attractive candidates into the party. And on the day of Nickle's resignation, he brought new blood to the ministry. Price received the attorney-generalship, Dr J.D. Monteith of Stratford was given the Treasury, William Finlayson was elevated to Lands and Forests, and Dr David Jamieson became Minister without Portfolio. Despite the opposition press's dramatic headlining of defections from the Tory camp, there were, on the whole, remarkably few departures; possibly this was a tribute to Ferguson's elaborate preparatory work with the backbenchers and party workers.

On the other hand, the Liberals at a pre-election conference on 27 October managed to stifle anti-OTA sentiment only at the cost of driving it out of the party. At a counter-conference held later that same day, wet Liberals, including J.A. Pinard (Ottawa East), E.T. Tellier (Essex North), E. Proulx (Prescott), and Aurélien Belanger (Russell) pronounced in favour of government control and declared they would run as independents. Many Franco-Ontarian leaders were worried by the rising Ferguson tide. 'The main argument of the French-Canadian Conservatives who are supporting Ferguson,' Belcourt told Sissons, 'is that they, if elected, will be in a far better position to compel Ferguson to settle this [schools] question than Sinclair or Raney. ... I am amazed at the number of French-Canadian people who have swallowed the bait.'[73]

Liberal weakness was emphasized when the party nominated only 52 candidates. Such co-operation as existed between Liberals and Progressives was more a reflection of sheer desperation than of deliberate strategy. Nonetheless, the opposition groups should have benefitted as there were only 17 three-cornered contests and the *Farmers' Sun* and the UFO president called on farmers to support dry candidates under whatever label. In 10 constituencies the only opposition to the Tory was a Liberal-Progressive and in 28 a prohibitionist. But no opposition party nominated enough candidates to be regarded as an alternative to the Tories and the *Mail and Empire* poured scorn on 'the several little corporals' who could 'do nothing apart and ... nothing together. They are the most helpless bunch that ever attempted to present a front in a Canadian election.'[74]

Ferguson himself by election day was expecting 76 seats. The Tories swept back with 75, compared to 21 for the Liberals (including four elected as Independent Liberals), 13 Progressives, and 3 under the United Farmer label. All the cabinet except David Jamieson had been easily returned, Raney squeaked in by 44 votes and Sinclair, to Ferguson's pleasure, was a winner in Ontario South. Nickle lost convincingly. Every one of the new urban seats created by redistribution went Tory. Karl Homuth, who ran as a Labour candidate in Waterloo South, was unopposed by the Conservatives and his subsequent admission to the Tory caucus signalled the disappearance of independent labour representation from the House. The Tories also made significant inroads into the French vote. Although Pinard, Proulx, and Belanger survived in eastern Ontario as anti-prohibitionist Liberals and Théodore Légault turned back the Tories in Sturgeon Falls, Henry Morel retained Nipissing for the Conservatives, Cochrane North was won from the Liberals, and a second seat was gained when Paul Poisson was acclaimed in Essex North. One feature of the result was the drop of almost 110,000 votes in the 31 rural ridings that had supported the OTA in 1924. There was a decrease in the popular vote in every one of these constituencies. Yet across the province 63.6 per cent of the electorate turned out compared to 57 per cent in 1923. Once again, the Tories had taken more than half the popular vote, receiving 56 per cent, more than any party since Confederation.[75]

There was, of course, the bitter with the sweet. Ferguson knew that he had offended, perhaps irremediably, the deeply held feelings of a sizeable portion of the population. 'It is now 3 o'clock in the morning after your great victory,' went a typical letter. 'My only son has just been brought home to us drunk. ... May the judgment of God follow you, till you bitterly regret of the damned thing you have done this day.'[76] The churches had contributed most of all to the feeling that he should be held personally responsible for such occurrences. When a defeated Tory reported 'it was impossible for me to win against the organized efforts of the United and Baptist Churches,' it was with considerable feeling that Ferguson replied, 'the same unscrupulous tactics were used in every part of the Province...'[77]

Of course it is impossible to assess the results precisely; some believed that had government control not been at issue, the Tories would have lost only two or three seats.[78] Perhaps, although the Liberal and Progressive hold on some of the rural and semi-rural constituencies particularly of Western Ontario remained strong. Undoubtedly, however, despite the extent to which prohibition had dominated the campaign, the government's general record and Ferguson's years of careful political management had paid dividends. If the Ferguson record had been weaker or the opposition parties in finer fettle, prohibition would not have pushed all else off the political stage. Certainly Arthur Ford was right in his judgement that 'the election was a great personal triumph for Mr Ferguson,' but even more apt was the view of a correspondent of George Henry that 'the people always did like guts. The big feature of our recent campaign was not liquor at all but the fact that we now have in this province an outfit with courage enough to stand or fall on its policy...'[79]

Some pronounced it the death of Old Ontario. Prohibition was gone and with it, many feared, the values which had made Ontario such a moral, God-fearing, and successful community. Of course nothing of the sort had happened. Prohibition had been an experiment, perhaps a noble experiment. It had been achieved as part of a sweeping movement of moral and social reform in which the province had attempted to cope with the consequences of industrialization, urbanization, and immigration, partly as a result of the war situation. Now it had been pronounced a failure. Yet many of the values which had made it possible and which it expressed endured in other ways and other forms and lived on in the hearts and minds of the people.

Howard Ferguson recognized that; now it was his responsibility to frame legislation which reflected the enduring values of old Ontario but allowed as well for the changes of spirit in the new province of the 1920s. In that endeavour, he would succeed remarkably well.

14

The Second Administration

The 1926 Ontario election excited unprecedented interest across Canada and in many parts of the United States. One consequence was a great jump in brewery and distillery stocks and active trading in hotel and club properties. The Toronto stock exchange was a madhouse and shares worth millions were traded in the first half hour after the election. Obviously great things were expected in certain quarters. Once again, however, Ferguson proved that, if he expressed in some ways the freer spirit of the new day, he retained in full measure many of the values of the older society which had nurtured him.

When the smoke of battle cleared away, the leaders on both sides accepted the result with maturity. The Moderation Leaguers, although they had undoubtedly contributed much to the campaign, had wisely let Ferguson carry the principal burden of propounding the wet policy and now, with few exceptions, there was on their part a willingness to accept legislation which embodied many temperance ideals. Similarly the better side of the dry character now came to the fore. Ferguson was more than willing to take dry advice as he worked on the legislation which he would present to the House. The Reverend A.E. Armstrong, Secretary of the Board of Foreign Missions of the United Church, told him that all supporters of the OTA would be delighted to admit they had been wrong 'if the next two or three years demonstrate that Government Control really controls, and is not simply Government sale...'[1] Days after the election, Gilbert Agar of the Social Service Council assured him he would have full co-operation from the Council 'in cultivating respect for law and in ensuring to the new system the fair experiment it deserves.'[2] D.B. Harkness also reflected a fundamental shift in opinion on the Council when he told Flavelle in February that 'I find in myself a diminishing confidence in prohibitory legislation...'[3] The premier gave sympathetic consideration to the views put forward by Agar on 7 February. The Social Service group suggested that in the new legislation 'the element of private gain will be eliminated so far as possible...' and specifically they requested that advertising, canvassing, and soliciting be forbidden, that liquor be purchased only from the government board, and that imports be banned.[4]

Ferguson's meeting with the Social Service people was amiable and constructive, but while he may have appreciated their attitude he must have reflected that the Council's new posture with its emphasis on education instead of coercion, surely a long overdue change, had been adopted only after the dry campaign of vilification and character assassination had failed. Naturally he took advice as well from other sources. He continued to investigate the systems in operation in the west and Quebec and also drew on the experience of the Ontario government dispensaries. While Ferguson was studying, other Tories were lobbying as the competition for positions in the new government stores set up a scramble for patronage. Many of the quarrels, the press claimed, were resolved only in the Premier's office but at this stage the official position was that appointments would be under the control of the new Liquor Commission.[5]

On 8 February – before the legislation was presented to the House – Ferguson announced his Commission. Again he demonstrated his unerring ability to convince men of wide experience to enter the service of the province. D.B. Hanna, formerly the head of the CNR, became chairman and Robert Manion, a member of the House of Commons and Stewart McClenaghan, a former member, were commissioners. Perhaps to enhance the prestige of the new body, the Liquor Control Board of Ontario, the chairman was given the princely salary of $20,000 a year, more than the Premier or Chief Justice received. Another consequence of the new system which antedated the formal legislation was Dr Monteith's budget, in which he predicted, on the basis of revenues anticipated from the sale of alcoholic beverages, that Ontario would have its first surplus in many years.[6] Not coincidentally, W.E. Raney, rightly fearful of the implications of the apparent restoration of the Tory alliance with the trade, introduced another bill to control the raising of campaign funds.[7]

On 8 March the Tories held a long caucus. Presumably Ferguson used it to unveil his legislation but unlike the famous caucuses which had preceded the OTA a decade earlier, there was little of the spirit of disharmony. Two days later, the bill was introduced in the House; it followed predicted lines and contained no surprises. There would be no advertising and no beer parlours; the local option provision retained Whitney's three-fifths clause; hotels would be unable to supply wine or beer with meals, although guests could consume their LCBO liquor in their rooms. Generally speaking, the Ontario system was stricter than existed in other wet provinces. Speaking on second reading, Ferguson assumed his school-masterish pose: hands spread in front of him, fingers lightly touching his desk, he lectured the members: 'we are not here to push the sale of liquor. We are here to restrict it within reasonable bounds. We are here to eliminate all the abuses and excesses it is possible to eliminate. We are here to protect particularly the rising generation of this country from being poisoned ... with the methods that have been in vogue for the past number of years.' Quoting widely from dry papers to prove that the legislation incorporated many features desired by temperance leaders, he promised there would be no mercy for law-breakers, cancellation of the permit for those who abused it, jail without option of a fine for the bootlegger – and this on a first offence. 'We are determined to deal ruthlessly with the people who won't obey this law...'

Sure of his mandate and backed by his vast and now docile majority, he brushed aside criticism with a wave of his hand. Ben Spence expressed his views in a lengthy letter to the government and his new opinion that the open bar was preferable to the debauchery which would take place in private homes under the government's system was treated with the contempt it deserved.[8] For the Liberals, a subdued Sinclair refused to participate actively in the debate but read a prepared statement noting, in effect, that the people had spoken. Raney was more robust, attacking the great and often unspecified powers given to the Liquor Commission and denouncing the so-called patronage section which provided that all appointments by the Board were subject to the order of the government.[9] Of course his effort failed. From this date the new liquor store system to all appearances was an important cog in the Tory political machine.

Equally inevitable, Raney's bill banning contributions to any political party from any liquor interest was killed by Tory votes in the Privileges and Elections Committee. That April the manager of Gooderham and Worts told the federal customs probe that his company had contributed $25,000 to the last provincial campaign.[10] Ferguson, Clysdale, and other Conservatives denied, probably truthfully, any knowledge of this sum, and Ferguson added again that his party had not received a dollar from any liquor source. Apparently the money went to the Moderation League, and, considering the funds the drys had at their call and their exploitation of the power of the churches, it seems appropriate that such a contribution should have been made.

Ferguson kept a tight control over the liquor bill debate. He insisted, and the Speaker upheld him, that dry members not be allowed to reopen the whole problem of prohibition but be restricted to the merits of the particular legislation. And he strongly defended the wide powers given to the Commission, which would be able to cancel anyone's permit at its own discretion and even cancel the licence of any brewer or distiller without giving reason. This, he argued, would finally remove the liquor question from politics. Ferguson remembered with revulsion the debates in the House over the past decade when successive governments annually presented lists of OTA amendments. Now there would be no more of that, for a time at least, although he could not prevent private members from bringing forward motions of their own. When the vote was finally taken on second reading, the four French-speaking Liberals supported the government. Finally, and wisely, third reading passed without a division.

The new liquor stores were opened on 1 June 1927. At first there were six in Toronto and eighteen across the province. They did a booming business, reported a disgusted Ben Spence, who visited every Toronto store during its first day of operation. Many customers made their purchases with a reticence which would endure for decades. The era of the brown paper bag and the furtive glance had begun. Some claimed their purchases were for medical purposes. Although a later and uncomprehending generation would mock such attitudes and view the surviving structure of blue laws with disdain, most Ontarians of the day regarded the government control solution with satisfaction. Unlike its great southern neighbour, which in typically American fashion would abandon prohibition with ruthless thoroughness, Ontario did not opt at once, or for many years thereafter, for a totally open system. Instead, a progressive and conservative community again achieved its vaunted middle way. In some of the United States, total repeal would prove almost as unfortunate as total prohibition and to Ontarians each was unacceptable.

In fact Ferguson had come remarkably close to fulfilling his old vow to provide a system which would please every reasonable person. Not long after the new system was in operation, he was awakened in the middle of the night by a call from a Grit opponent suffering from a painful ulcer who needed instant relief. Equal to the occasion, Howard ordered a dispensary opened at once and his personal chauffeur delivered a bottle of champagne to the unfortunate sufferer. 'Government control,' said Ferguson, was 'for the good of everyone.'[11] That included the taxpayer. On 2 December 1927, the province's annual financial statement revealed that Ontario had achieved its first surplus in years. Two million dollars in liquor revenue had made the difference.

Now he was at the height of his power. With Arthur Meighen out of politics, he was Canada's best known and most popular Tory. Soon after his 1923 victory there had been suggestions that Lord Atholstan of the Montreal *Daily Star* and some others of the anti-Meighen persuasion looked to him as an early successor in the national leadership. There is no indication, however, that Ferguson himself at that time had any such ambitions. Now, in early 1927, with a leadership convention called for October in Winnipeg, he had but to nod and the position would be his. His resounding electoral successes, his administrative skills, his ability to attract men of high talent to the service of his administration, and generally the feeling that he was the true heir of the Macdonald tradition won him a growing yet unsolicited support from almost all elements in the party and from all regions of the country.

From the day the convention was announced, his was the name the press seized upon as the likeliest choice. Perhaps his earliest serious support continued to be from English-speaking Montrealers in close touch with the Quebec business community, who had never been satisfied with Meighen. In May, for example, C.H. Cahan, interested in the leadership himself, suggested to Ferguson that it seemed 'advisable that we should have a confidential chat ... over current political problems in the federal field' and the Premier agreed to see him.[12] But unsolicited advice arrived from all sides. The most flattering overture came in late June from F.D.L. Smith, a member of the central committee in charge of organizing the convention, who had travelled across the country on convention business. Now he told Ferguson that the most definite conclusion he had drawn from his survey was that,

all across Canada from Montreal and Windsor, through Ontario, Manitoba, Saskatchewan, Alberta and British Columbia, you are easily the favourite for the Federal leadership – the only man to beat the machine candidate, to win the next general election, to save the party and salvage Canada. This is the message I bring to you from Members of Parliament, defeated candidates and leading local politicians in Winnipeg, Regina, Saskatoon, Edmonton, Calgary, Vancouver and Victoria. This is the message I bring to you from Conservative editors in Montreal, Hamilton, London and Windsor and the West. Mr M.E. Nichol, Managing Director of the Winnipeg Tribune, asked me to convey to you personally his pledge that the Tribune will give you one hundred per cent support if you will come out. This is important, as you know that the Tribune has hitherto been very lukewarm in support of the Conservative cause. If you will allow your name to go to the Convention, you will have similar support from the other Conservative papers in the West. Mr Nichol thinks you should announce yourself without too much delay. Other editors want permission to start a Ferguson boom.

I do not put it too strongly when I say that you have caught the public imagination throughout the Dominion, and that the better elements in the party look to you to save it. The legend runs that you have the John A. Macdonald touch, that you have the genius for success, that you are a statesman as well as an astute politician, that you have a passion for real public service, that you are wise in the choice of your associates and agents, that you have the persuasive power to enlist influential men in support of your policies, and that if you allow your name to go to the Convention, all other contenders will fade into the dim distance.

Should you choose to become Federal leader, you will have brilliant lieutenants in the West to assist you. ... Once you are leader moreover, there will be plenty of money available in the East to establish a Conservative press in Saskatchewan and to assist the Western Conservatives in setting up more effective organizations.

I do not presume Mr Premier, to advise you what you should do. I merely set before you the personal conclusions to which my survey of the West has led me. You know how fearful prominent Conservatives are that the Convention will make a decision disastrous to the party. ... There is no general support for Mr Guthrie or for Mr Bennett even in the West ... you are the one man to save the situation.[13]

Smith's letter, labelled 'Very Confidential,' was part of a growing volume of evidence that the leadership was Ferguson's for the asking. On 28 July, Senator Smeaton White of the Montreal *Gazette* assured him that he and General McRae of Vancouver, a wealthy businessman prominent as an organizer of the Winnipeg convention, 'were both agreed if you could be persuaded to consider the leadership it would be a solution of one, at least, of a great many of our present difficulties.'[14] Senator White had even sounded out some of the leading Quebec Liberals as to which Tory might be most attractive to Quebec opinion and was told by 'one of the most influential members' of the Taschereau government that 'there was only one man who would be acceptable and have any chance in carrying this province, and that was your good self.' When White asked the Taschereau man to explain his reasoning, he pointed to Ferguson's success among the French element in New Ontario. 'He claimed his people were, perhaps, more clannish than the English-speaking and when ... the people of New Ontario speaking the French language, talked to their friends in Quebec ... they would, naturally, endorse the man they had voted for locally. He also claimed that already there had been a good deal of this sort of under-current existing amongst them.' White noted too that he had recently spoken with Premier Rhodes of Nova Scotia and Rhodes had learned 'in his casual conversation with leading men, that Ferguson was the only man who could recement and reorganize the party and he hoped it would be possible to obtain your consent.'[15]

If Ferguson had been angling for the leadership, he would surely have given the powerful Montreal newspaper lords a hint of encouragement. Instead he replied to White that because the matter had been pressed on him from so many circles, he had given it a great deal of consideration but 'the outlook hasn't any attraction for me, nor do I have any personal ambition or desire in the matter.'[16] He intended to make a public announcement to that effect shortly. Already he had refused to offer any encouragement to party friends in Ontario who had influence in the appointment of convention delegates and were seeking direction.[17]

Nonetheless some of his moves gave his admirers cause for hope. He talked federal affairs in several speeches in the early months of 1927, issuing a call for a 'New National Policy' which, on examination, involved little more than some tinkering with tariff policy and transportation rates along lines Meighen had advanced in the last campaign. Still, this was encouraging to some; and, as always, he was not reluctant in private correspondence with leading Tories to express his opinion on policy matters. The party must strike a higher note, 'not only along broad national lines,' he told White, 'but with a strong imperial spirit behind it. We will never get anywhere so long as we confine ourselves to discussing the cost of sawdust wharfs in any particular province ... there must be a strong note of national leadership that will grip the imagination of the public. We need vision based upon broad constructive principles. Canadian unity and imperial solidarity as a general policy will sweep this country.'[18] And he assured Atholstan that 'one cannot read the resolution presented by Sir John Macdonald, when he inaugurated the national policy, without being impressed by its comprehensive character and its inspiring tone. That, to my mind, is the kind of platform we need.'[19]

Ferguson always had a knack for mouthing Tory platitudes convincingly. The more he did so the more some elements boomed his name. His real concern, however, remained that of finding a policy and leader which could serve his party best and not promoting himself for the position. As well, he was giving increasing thought to ways and means of helping the party break into Liberal Quebec. 'Has the Tory party got any fellow,' he asked his old friend Senator Rufus Pope in May, 'that could be sure of making a successful inroad into the Quebec solid block?'[20] When Atholstan pressed him again in late September, telling him that indications were that 'an overwhelming number of the delegates' supported him, he cited as one reason for his reluctance the fact that 'somebody must do the work of consolidating the two provinces that have two-thirds of the people of the country, whose economic conditions and requirements are identical.' Interestingly, his concern with this work was not narrowly political; he regarded it as a matter of national reconstruction and he believed his own contribution would be greater if he stayed in Ontario. 'I have been bending my efforts along this line for a considerable time,' he told Atholstan, 'and I think it would be a mistake on my part to give up this work.'[21]

That the Ferguson-Taschereau alliance was creating concern in some quarters cannot be doubted. Writing in *Le Devoir* in early May during a Quebec provincial election campaign, Henri Bourassa blasted the Quebec premier as a tool of the Tory money power. 'On all that concerns Hydro-Electric development ... Mr Taschereau has allied himself with Mr Ferguson to back Mr King to the wall,' while on tariff and other matters he simply mouthed the Tory line. Bourassa was particularly outraged that 'on the problem of imperial relations ... Mr Taschereau has given the most potent proofs of that Toryism *à outrance* which wins him the most open or secret support of the most hopeless colonialists, the empire dervishes and all the other enemies of a free Canadian fatherland.'[22] Despite Bourassa's refusal to admit that there was diversity of opinion in Quebec on the imperial issue, there was no doubt that the power of the two premiers was sufficient to block the ending of judicial appeals to the British Privy Council which was so dear to those of Bourassa's persuasion. Yet at this time the alliance was not cemented; so long as Regulation 17 remained, there could be no hope of that.

Thus when *La Presse* of Montreal in March published a 'fraternal message' from the Ontario premier, *Le Devoir* used the occasion to warn him that until justice was done on the schools question, he could not hope for support at Winnipeg from French-Canadian delegates. *Le Droit* was blunter and told him *bonne entente* excursions, fine words, and the distribution of ice cream cones to Quebec urchins were not enough.[23] But Senator Belcourt remained sceptical that Ferguson's federal ambitions might induce him to do justice to the Franco-Ontarians; the ACFEO leader could not believe that a party which had just gotten rid of one leader whose reputation was black in Quebec would saddle itself with another albatross. 'I entertain no hope,' he told C.B. Sissons, 'of the repeal of the Regulation based upon the assumption that Ferguson is coming to Ottawa.'[24]

Nonetheless during the early months of 1927, with the Merchant-Scott-Côté Commission continuing its work, Ferguson gave assurances to Aurélien Belanger that he would do his best to see to it that the Ottawa Separate School Board was not 'molested by any legal action' arising out of its precarious financial position and that if such action did occur, he 'would help the trustees to defend the same.'[25] When the Commission Report appeared on 21 September, a few days before the opening of the Tory convention, Ferguson forthwith announced he was accepting its recommendations.

The commissioners, after visiting 843 classes in some 330 schools, had found the state of affairs far from satisfactory and in some ways worse than in 1912. Almost half the students were in 'the first and second grades where French was the sole language of instruction, and only one in ten was reaching grade eight.'[26] A total of 48.3 per cent of the teachers either held no Ontario teacher's certificate at all or one which was temporary or expired. While blame for this state of affairs could be variously assessed, no premier who professed to believe in equality of educational opportunity could allow it to continue; Ferguson knew that the policy of 1912 had failed and he seized on the commissioners' recommendations as the only possible solution. The report emphasized the great diversity of conditions which existed and suggested that 'no rule which prescribes the medium of instruction for different forms or grades of a system can be applied impartially to all schools within that system.' As a remedy, Merchant and his colleagues recommended that each case be examined on its own merits by inspectors who would then consult with a departmental committee to be composed of two new appointees, a director of English instruction and a director of French instruction and the province's chief inspector, who would also confer with the local inspector. Immediate changes would include the abolition of the hated double inspectorate, the recognition of the need to give the teaching of French the same importance as English, and a willingness to give less emphasis to some parts of the school program to leave more time for language training.

Publicly ACFEO expressed its pleasure, adding that much depended on how the new rules were applied; privately the Association's leaders gave vent to almost unrestrained enthusiasm. To a priest in Saskatchewan, ACFEO secretary Cloutier wrote that 'nous avons obtenu d'immenses concessions...' and he pointed out to another correspondent that provision was being made to overcome the special problems an English-language high school entrance examination posed for French-speaking students.[27] The surest proof of the Ferguson government's sincerity was its willingness to accept the University of Ottawa teaching training school into the provincial system without demanding any pedagogical changes. Cloutier triumphantly informed Omer Héroux, long a Quebec friend of ACFEO, that this would put 'virtuellement la formation de nos instituteurs entre nos mains. C'est là une concession encore plus grande que toutes celles qui sont contenues dans les recommendations du rapport.'[28]

If Belcourt and his associates were delighted, most other Canadians were also amazingly favourable. The history of the dispute suggested that recommendations which French Canadians regarded as a major victory would be viewed with dismay by other elements, particularly Orangemen and Irish Catholics. But the Irish leaders, anxious to work with the French to win concessions for the separate schools, had already reached an understanding with ACFEO and the prestige and wise policies of Archbishop Neil McNeil of Toronto ensured that there would be little dissent from that quarter, a fact of which Ferguson was aware.[29] More significant was Ferguson's own manipulation of the Orange Order. Orange spokesmen had been carefully sounded out and when Ferguson's decision was announced, prominent figures such as Horatio Hocken pronounced in the Orange *Sentinel* that Regulation 17 was an unlamented failure which Orangemen had always disliked.[30]

Across the country, Ferguson's move received overwhelming press endorsement. Many papers expressed their concern about the damage the dispute had done to national unity and some demonstrated a surprisingly sophisticated understanding of the significance of the language issue to the country's future. Senator Belcourt believed that the settlement and the response it elicited demonstrated that a new tolerance and a broader understanding of the nature of Canadian dualism existed in Ontario.[31] Another hopeful sign was the Ontario government's recent establishment in co-operation with Quebec of teacher exchanges whose purpose was to encourage more effective language training in the province's schools. Ferguson himself now told Taschereau that 'if ... you felt you could say that you recognize [the settlement] as an honest endeavour on the part of Ontario to meet a difficult situation, it would do more than anything else ... to allay inflammatory agitation.'[32] Taschereau relayed his congratulations and telegrams and letters from prominent Quebec figures revealed a growing friendliness from that quarter. By soliciting a public thank-you from Taschereau, Ferguson demonstrated that he considered it important in 1927 to appear in the public eye as a champion of national unity and, indeed, as a defender of the French fact in Canada. Much, it seemed, had changed in Ontario since 1912.

Nor was it possible for the sceptics to continue to argue that the Ferguson settlement was offered to further the Premier's personal political ambitions for by this time he had made it clear that his destiny did not lie in Ottawa. His first pronouncement which possessed the ring of finality came after an interview in mid-August with a *Globe* reporter. The *Globe* man, as Ferguson told William Hearst, had taken a casual conversation and turned it into an important announcement. 'He reported perhaps more of the conversation than I thought he would, but reported accurately and I have nothing to complain about.'[33] Ella seemed positively relieved and the next day told the reporters who appeared at the Ferguson door that 'it is nothing very new. His attitude for some time has been that he does not aspire to the federal leadership. ... He considers that his work is not yet done in Ontario and he prefers the provincial field.'[34] Interestingly, he himself pointed out that he was 57 years old and he hoped to be able to finish his Ontario work and retire by the time he was 60. Of course there were many who refused to take this pronouncement as final. *L'Evénement* proclaimed that he would be able to step into the position whenever he wanted it over the next few years and there was talk from some Tories, who saw Ferguson as their best chance for national power, of postponing the convention until 1928.[35]

His closest friends seemed genuinely pleased at his announcement. His Ontario colleagues recognized how much the provincial party relied on him. Hearst wrote 'as a personal friend' to 'express my satisfaction ... you have a great work yet to do in Ontario...' 'I have never had any thought of going to Ottawa' he told the former premier.[36] Even his particular enemy, the Toronto *Star* – he called it the paper with the largest circulation and the least influence in Canada – seemed relieved, noting editorially that 'the local political scene would be bereft of a cheering presence were Mr Howard Ferguson to leave it. ... His government could never be the same without him. He is a hearty, human and likeable man...'[37] It was Jack Reid, his oldest political associate, who, next to Ella, was most gratified. For some time he had been advising against the move and now he wrote that 'no man would be more pleased than I to see you Premier of Canada, but to take the chance you would make terrible sacrifices and I think you have made sacrifices enough and gone through too much to start fresh to build up the Dominion organization...'[38]

At once there was talk of a draft. 'The pressure on you is going to be too great for anyone to resist' wrote Harold Daly on 1 October.[39] Senator George Lynch-Staunton, however, warned that he should not allow himself to be swept into the leadership against his better judgement, pointing out that the Tories must expect ten years of opposition and 'I regard you as too valuable a man to be wasted...'[40] When suggestions were made that it was the prospect of this kind of a fight that made him hesitate, Sir Henry Drayton, who for months had been urging him to stand, scoffed that 'if there is a fighter amongst us, it is

Ferguson.'[41] On 6 October, R.B. Bennett again reaffirmed his support for the Ontario premier, saying 'I quite prefer him to Bennett,' and reports circulated that Bennett, Baxter, Rhodes and the other Tory chieftains had at last prevailed, telling him that he could not refuse a unanimous draft.[42] A few days before the convention was opened, Clifford Sifton assured Dafoe that 'everything indicates that Ferguson will be the choice...'[43]

There was also more pressure from Montreal from prominent English-speaking business figures including W.M. Birks, two Ogilvies, R.W. Reford, and J.M. Macdonnell of the National Trust. 'Most important of all,' they insisted, 'we feel that the recent concessions outlined in the Province of Ontario to French Canadian sentiment have put you in a stronger position than any other person to achieve that most essential of all things, a "rapprochement" between the two great Provinces of Ontario and Quebec.'[44] Taschereau himself was called on to deny reports that he intended to enter federal politics as the ally of Howard Ferguson. Then on 10 October, the day the convention opened, Ferguson addressed a letter to its chairman asking him to 'decline to accept any motion that would place my name before this Convention as a possible candidate...'[45] Ferguson's act of self-abnegation had already been confirmed at a press conference the previous day. After distributing a box of choice Havanas, he admonished, 'Don't be afraid boys, they aren't campaign cigars.' Then he lit up himself, blew smoke into the air, and nonchalantly cast aside the mantle of John A.

Although he often had referred to his preference for provincial affairs and cited his desire to complete the work he had started in Ontario, one is left to speculate as to the ultimate reason. His grandiose public statements notwithstanding, Ferguson always had a firm sense of his own strengths and limitations. His course had been run entirely on the provincial field; his mastery in Ontario was based on his intimate knowledge of the details of public administration and his unequalled understanding of the moods and ambitions of his native province. His transition to the federal arena would have been arduous and dangerous. Of course he loved a fight, but Senator Lynch-Staunton had expressed a view held by many when he had remarked that the Tories might expect to be in opposition a decade. At 57, Ferguson was feeling the strain of his years. The burden carried during the war in the Hearst administration had taken a great deal out of him and it had been followed immediately by the strenuous years of the Timber Scandal and the fight against the Drury administration. Nor had he slowed down since becoming Premier, keeping on top of the business of the various departments, overseeing party matters, and having his finger in almost every area of provincial endeavour.

Now it was beginning to tell. From time to time, particularly towards the end of session, his colleagues could not help but notice how worn out he looked. As well he was more susceptible than ever to a host of minor ailments, particularly an annoying bronchial condition and the flu. To start all over again, after what he had been through, was a great deal for his party to ask and Ella, who had said yes when he had hesitated in 1920, now was reluctant to see him risk his health in such an endeavour. Surely he was right to conclude that 'I can give better service both to the country and the party by continuing my activities in the provincial field. What we need is a lot of spade work in the way of organization, and I feel that I can get closer to the people and be much more effective along that line where I am at present.'[46] With the help he could offer as Premier of Ontario, the party could make a run at breaking the solid Quebec block; as well he hoped to be able to influence the new leader to adopt a broad platform along the lines of a 'new national policy' and appealing to imperial feeling. He saw no contradiction between that objective and his desire to win the French-Canadian voter.

Ferguson was certain that his influence on the new leader would be more substantial than it had ever been with Arthur Meighen. Although he had regarded Meighen as a close friend, there had always been a distance between the shrewd and pragmatic professional and the somewhat remote prairie lawyer. The new leader, Ferguson was convinced, would be R.B. Bennett. He had been dismayed when he had met with Bennett in Toronto on 23 August and the Calgary man had been emphatic that 'under no circumstances would he consider' the leadership.[47] But Ferguson was not impressed by the other possibilities, Drayton, Manion, Guthrie and Cahan, probably regarding them all as the lightweights they were, and doubtless he also saw the limitations of his old friend, Bob Rogers. Therefore he continued to press Bennett. Although he recognized that there would be problems of temperament to be overcome, he knew that Bennett towered above the others in ability.

Now he became virtually campaign manager for R.B., lining up the Ontario delegates, conferring with his Montreal friends, thrusting his views on delegates from the Maritimes and the west. Young David Walker, who went west with about 20 delegates representing the young Conservatives in the Macdonald-Cartier clubs of the universities – which Ferguson had been instrumental in organizing – recalls going to see the Premier in his hotel suite. 'He was surrounded by lieutenants from all the provinces planning how to get Bennett elected. And he said, now Davie while you are waiting ... go into that cupboard and pick out some reinforcements for your delegates. There was a cupboard, instead of clothes the closet was filled with all the whisky and gin. Marvellous. I picked out a fair supply for our delegation, but he said Davie who is your delegation voting for? I said, well we like Hugh Guthrie. ... Well, he said, that's all right Davie, that's fine, but who will you vote for on the second ballot. I said, hasn't he a chance of winning and he said no, he has no chance. ... And he said, well Davie, it isn't that I love him (this is the way he used to talk), what about Bennett...?' According to Walker, the Macdonald-Cartier club delegates all supported Bennett on the second ballot.[48]

Bennett stepped into the place Ferguson had vacated as the choice of the establishment and an easy second ballot victory was assured. The real excitement of the convention, a 24-hour sensation which plunged the gathering into turmoil, was a dramatic clash between the retiring leader and Ferguson. Meighen when invited to address the delegates had made it clear to convention organizers that he would talk about his Hamilton speech. This, surely, was a piece of unexampled egotism and arrogance. The Hamilton speech had been fiercely criticized by many Tories and had rent the party and contributed to its 1926 defeat. Evidently the criticism had rankled and now, oblivious to its effect on the party, Meighen intended to justify himself. Efforts to dissuade him failed and party leaders regarded his course with apprehension. Meighen seemed sincere in his determination to step down but there were some who believed he intended to use the occasion to deliver a stirring address and attempt to reclaim the leadership; others feared that some effort might be made to have the Hamilton doctrine incorporated into the party platform. Most likely his objective was personal vindication and the acclaim he received when he rose to speak was exceeded only by the tumultuous cheers which greeted his long defence of the Hamilton stance.

As he spoke, eliciting wave after wave of applause, the faces of the Tory sachems on the platform behind him were themselves a study. As P.D. Ross described the scene in the Ottawa *Journal*, 'Ferguson looked aggressive and proved so. Mr Bennett slumped back in his chair with an expression of hopeless disgust. Mr Guthrie looked bewildered. Mr Rhodes looked as though he were in the Speaker's chair in Parliament, with an angry row starting. Mr Rogers' expression would have justified tears in his eyes. Sir George Perley stroked his beard as if some bad catastrophe were threatening — as it was. Sir Robert Borden kept his eyes on the floor...'[49] There were whispered conversations between Baxter and Ferguson and Ferguson and Bennett.

With the roars of applause for the former leader still echoing forth, the Premier of Ontario pushed forward to the microphone. 'May I crave your indulgence for a very brief period,' he began, and breaking through the tumult he launched into an account of his meeting with Meighen two years before when the Hamilton speech was first broached. He had, he reported, told Meighen that it would be grossly unnecessary and therefore unwise to make such an address. This assertion only enraged some of the delegates — those who had been cheering Meighen to the hilt resented Ferguson's relation of the details of a private conversation. 'Sit down!' came cries from the floor. 'Three cheers for Arthur Meighen!' shouted others and many rose to their feet.

'I won't sit down,' came the flushed response from the stubborn, squat figure. 'If Mr Meighen can unnecessarily throw a wrench into the peace of this convention, I propose to make my position clear.' As if challenging the delegates to throw him out bodily, he advanced nearer the front of the platform. Boos, sprinkled with a few cheers, broke out again. By this point the great amphitheatre was a scene of pandemonium and for a while it seemed as though the convention which yesterday would have been willing to crown the Ontario man now intended to crucify him. 'I am not here to attack anyone,' Ferguson protested belligerently, 'I am here to justify a position. I don't care whether you approve it or not.' 'Rotten, shut up, sit down' came the retorts and many began to hiss. Angrily he continued, finally challenging the delegates that 'if the convention chooses to endorse Mr Meighen, I would dissociate myself entirely from the activities of this convention.'[50]

There can be no doubt that Meighen's determination to speak on Hamilton was selfish and short-sighted. Although he probably had no intention of exploiting the occasion to regain the leadership, he did tell his son before the convention that 'to secure it would be a very easy matter' and after his speech 'he was besieged by people wanting him to let his name stand and he believed that, had he given the word, he could have carried the convention and been reinstalled.' He also assured John Dafoe that 'he could have carried the convention if he had stood,' and Dafoe believed that 'this is the fact; but I judge that the party was as content to be rid of him; the circumstances of his open quarrel with Ferguson really put up the bars against his return to public life, at least in the near future.'[51]

The party managers must have suspected that some such purpose was in the back of Meighen's mind. Ferguson's intervention, supported so obviously by the party chieftains, ensured that such a move would be at the cost of a deeply divided party. More likely, the Tory leaders were concerned that Meighen's great oratorical effort would gain enormous publicity and might be formally adopted as party policy. The effect of Ferguson's intervention was that not Meighen's war policy but the sensational clash between the two men dominated the headlines. Although Ferguson had achieved this only at the cost of the humiliating experience of being howled down by a Tory convention, he had gained his purpose. The party would not be saddled with Meighen or with Hamilton.

In fact Ferguson had acted almost as the chosen agent of the party leaders, the man with the courage and force to stand against the popular tide. Sir Thomas White had argued that as he was out of politics and more neutral, he should be the one to reply. But Ferguson had insisted.[52] Soon wires and telegrams poured in from across the country commending him and proclaiming the value of the service he had performed. 'I never did anything more deliberately and did it exactly the way I intended,' he told 'Billy' Givens of the Kingston Whig-Standard. 'I realized that it was a case where headlines counted, and unless something of a sensational character was done, Meighen's speech would be the press headline. It had to be made Ferguson's row or somebody else's row. The more noise and confusion there was the better it suited my purpose.'[53] And to George E. Foster he affirmed that 'I was rather direct and emphatic in my language because I felt most indignant that one who had enjoyed all the honours that the Party could confer upon him should make use of the great Convention to re-affirm for personal reasons, the line of policy that had been sweepingly condemned at the polls. If it had not been for the Hamilton speech the Conservative Party would undoubtedly be in power today. ... I have every respect for any man's personal views, but I could not tolerate what appeared to me to be a glaring attempt to give to the public the impression that that view was approved of by the whole party. ... The Conservative Party hereafter would have had that mill-stone around its neck. ... It was no pleasure for me to do what I did. I, for years, have been a close personal friend of Mr Meighen's...'[54] Privately, to Arthur Ford and a few others, he admitted he had lost his temper and had done it badly, and Ella herself told him as much. Although opinion in the party was divided and Meighen's friends expressed outrage, the view that the former leader's own behaviour had provoked the incident gradually prevailed. That he should have attempted to exploit the gathering 'for purely selfish purposes' seemed to Joseph Flavelle 'about as evil a thing as a mean, selfish-spirited man could perform. The role played by Ferguson,' he told J.M. Macdonnell 'was unlovely. It was true to his blustering, impulsive way. ... I lay all the blame on Meighen, and at bottom am thankful to Ferguson for effectively dealing with a matter which needed rough usage...'[55]

In many ways, Bennett's elevation marked a new stage in Ferguson's political life. For some time he had been working to prepare conditions for a Tory incursion into Quebec; with Bennett in the leadership he believed it would be possible to make a determined run at 'the Mackenzie Kingdom.' A grateful Bennett recognized the role Ferguson played in his selection, and wanted the Premier's assistance for the long pull ahead. Ferguson for his part felt it his duty to offer fatherly advice to the new leader whom he regarded as somewhat rough around the political edges and he had the temerity to bring to his attention some of his political shortcomings. 'I pointed out to him ... that he has to overcome a certain prejudice that exists against him. He has been regarded as a bit over-bearing and impatient. His first big job is to ingratiate himself with the general public and start a current of public sentiment in his favour. I have always thought that in the field of public life the most important thing is the creation of an atmosphere.'[56]

When Bennett suggested he would like to come to Toronto often 'to discuss with me various public matters and lines of policy,' Ferguson advised against this. 'I told him I would be glad to talk with him at any time, but the important thing for him to do was to convince his followers in the House that they had his confidence and that he relied upon them for support. It would be disastrous if any of them got it into their heads that he was going outside for advice. Moreover, I do not propose to have any knowledge of Dominion affairs...'[57] The two men also talked from time to time about the Quebec situation and the division of the party there into factions. They agreed that the situation required much tactful handling. Ferguson promised to run down there 'if he and our friends in Quebec thought I could do even a little bit ... but that I thought the time was not yet opportune.' Bennett, he told Smeaton White, 'is experiencing a difficult transition process for himself. He has to overcome a lot of life habits and attitudes which naturally have become rather firmly fixed. We talked very freely upon this subject. ... He is prepared to listen and learn.'

Perhaps he listened, but the course of his subsequent career raised doubts about how much he learned. Possibly the High Tory Ontario Premier was the wrong man to be doing the teaching. In any case, the two men over the next few years operated together in close political alliance; for the best part of the next decade, their careers would be linked intimately and their fortunes rose and fell together. Dafoe's acute antennae picked this up. 'I am sure,' he told W.P.M. Kennedy, that 'Ferguson is the one man in Canada from whom he is taking advice.' Interestingly, Ferguson at Winnipeg had told Dafoe 'it would be a cinch to beat King and he would make it his own business to see that he was properly licked next election. His plan of campaign,' Dafoe informed Kennedy, 'is to get a solid Ontario. ... It will be accompanied by the usual anti-American outbursts...'[58]

In yet another way, Howard Ferguson made an impact on the Winnipeg convention. He had always believed that its explicit 1919 platform represented 'the greatest incubus the Liberal Party has had to struggle against.' Leaders, he knew, must have flexibility. 'In these days of rapidly changing conditions, platforms are dangerous things. ... The historic position of the Conservative Party,' he told Atholstan, 'and its constructive programme should be sufficiently attractive, if properly presented, without pronouncing upon individual problems.'[59]

An example of the approach he favoured was the convention's pronouncement upon the complicated St Lawrence seaway question:

This convention is of the opinion that the St Lawrence canal system as an all-Canadian project should be developed in the national interest, and as and when conditions warrant. In such an undertaking the sovereign rights of the respective provinces in the development of power shall be protected.

The precise origin of this ingenious resolution is unclear.[60] Obviously it placed the federal Tories firmly on the side of provincial rights and to that extent Ferguson's hand may be seen; its tacit anti-Americanism was equally in character. To Jack Reid he confided that 'the United States have never shown any good faith in any arrangement we have made with them. The Chicago steal is a most glaring example, and I am opposed to putting ourselves in their power.'[61]

Of course there were also the federal Liberals to confound and with the Tories' nationalist cry staring them in the face they would think twice about trying to get their hands on Ontario's water resources through some deal with the Americans. A furious Liberal opposition in Ontario pointed out that the Winnipeg resolution advocating all-Canadian construction would postpone indefinitely the construction of the Seaway and as such it constituted a radical change of front on the Premier's part. Many Ontario Conservatives were outraged, some spluttered about sabotage, and others wondered out loud whether the recent purchase of the party's major Toronto organ, the *Mail and Empire*, by the Montreal financier, I.W. Killam, the head of Royal Trust, had influenced the reversal. At any rate, the new stance put Ferguson squarely in line with the all-Canadian policy Taschereau had followed since 1921. Again there were mutterings about Ferguson's pandering to Quebec and some Tories began to wonder if the price to be paid for the breaking of the Quebec block might not be too high.

Although Ferguson does not seem to have explained in so many words the strategy behind the new departure, it had been obvious since the signing of the Gatineau contract in 1926 that the Ferguson-Taschereau axis might necessitate some unexpected turns. For the next four years, until he stepped out of office, the waterpower question remained at a high pitch of intensity and occupied an enormous amount of his time. Throughout this period, despite occasional differences, the alliance with Taschereau held firm and did yeoman service for both provinces. Although the federal government continued to stumble about, unclear how far it wanted or dared to move towards a national electrical energy policy, Ottawa fought a determined rearguard action against the two central provinces. The dispute went through so many phases and generated so much correspondence between King and Ferguson that it would be pointless to follow it down every path. It was complicated as well by the machinations of powerful private interests which fought each other desperately, attempting all the while to play off one level of government against the other. With Tory Ontario desperate for more energy and committed ideologically and emotionally to the public power movement, and Liberal, free enterprise Quebec equally anxious to protect its rights but less pressed to undertake new developments, the King Liberals proved unable to isolate the sister provinces or deflect them from their course.

The issue which cemented the Ferguson-Taschereau alliance was the struggle against the rights held on the Ottawa River by two competing companies, the Georgian Bay Canal Company and the National Hydro Electric Company, by this time a subsidiary of the powerful Shawinigan interests of Quebec. The Georgian Bay Canal Company had fallen into the hands of the sons of Sir Clifford Sifton who, it was believed, were far more interested in the energy than in the navigational rights granted by their charter. The National Hydro's federal lease to develop power at the Carillon was an equally formidable challenge to the provincial claim to control all water not needed for navigation. Although the rival entrepreneurs engaged in much sniping between themselves, the main engagement was the constitutional struggle between Ottawa and the central provinces.

By January 1927 Ontario was sceptical about buying power from the Carillon interests for fear of prejudicing its constitutional claim and the National Hydro in turn had become more aggressive. Magrath told Ferguson that the Company now took the position that by virtue of its licence from Ottawa it 'already possesses all rights essential to the development of power at Carillon, and that so far as any interest in the Province of Ontario is concerned, we are merely in the position that we have to consider whether we shall accept the Company's proposition and price but have substantially nothing else to consider.'[62] Magrath was still willing to negotiate but only if the company recognized 'that the proper scope of a Dominion license is limited to seeing that the needs of navigation are observed' and that it needed authority from the province before proceeding. 'The basis of any arrangement reached about Carillon will become a precedent...'[63]

The Georgian Bay Canal Company presented an even greater threat if only because its claims on the Ottawa were more extensive and it was controlled by the Siftons. Ferguson arranged with Tilley to oppose the Company's claims for a renewal of its charter before the private bills committee of the Commons and Magrath requested a joint protest of the two premiers on a principle which could be applied to both the Georgian Bay and Carillon positions. 'If you both fail to decide upon the amendment to be offered, the proponents of the Bill may drive a wedge between you.' He also suggested it would be useful for the provinces to request a legal opinion from Tilley and his Quebec counterpart. 'This seems to be the psychological time to get rid of the issue. If the issue is not settled now it means, I fear, Privy Council and very much delay.'[64]

Ferguson was taking no chances. On 17 February he promised Toronto Tories that when the Georgian Bay charter was up for renewal, he would wage one of the strongest provincial rights fights in the history of Canadian development. On 7 March the Ontario legislature strengthened his hand by passing unanimously a resolution condemning the charter and claiming the water in interprovincial streams as belonging to the provinces. Ferguson complained that the charter purported to give its owners 'an absolute blanket power to take possession of any power that may be developed on the Ottawa River.' He could recall 'nothing so alarming as the situation in which the province stands today with its property jeopardized at the hands of people whose history has not been entirely philanthropic.'[65] His appeal to the non-partisan public ownership sentiment on which Beck in his day had drawn so effectively succeeded admirably. The federal government was flooded with protests from Ontario municipalities, the press cried out against the would-be power barons, Magrath and the OMEA lobbied the federal members and Mackenzie King's correspondence relayed the message that 'the Georgian Bay Canal matter is being discussed by everyone and I never heard of any project which was more generally opposed.'[66] Asked for his alternative on the Ottawa, Ferguson responded that 'there's no question of alternative just now. It's just a question of "stop thief" before it's too late.'[67]

Taschereau while less aggressive was equally determined. The non-partisan front succeeded. Liberal papers such as the Toronto *Star* joined the hue and cry; in the Commons Tories such as Bennett were aided by Progressives such as Garland, who called the Sifton bid 'the worst example of commercial and political brigandage in my time' and by public ownership Liberals, including W.D. Euler, a cabinet member, who described it as 'unthinkable' that control of the Ottawa power should be in private hands.[68] To placate the Siftons, King allowed the charter renewal bill sponsored by a Liberal backbencher to proceed a certain way before bowing to the inevitable. Both the Georgian Bay charter and the Carillon lease were allowed to expire on 1 May. It had been a campaign worthy of Adam Beck himself.

Undoubtedly it was a great victory. The Georgian Bay Company's charter and National Hydro's lease through which Ottawa asserted its right to dispose of water powers on navigable streams had been dropped. Mackenzie King had retreated in disarray before the prospect of a provincial rights campaign which might well have defeated his government.[69] And Ontario had used the occasion to formulate a full statement of its theoretical position. With the legal statement suggested by Magrath still under preparation by Ontario and Quebec lawyers, the Hydro chairman had brought into his employ Loring C. Christie, a confidant of Sir Robert Borden who had served with distinction in the Department of External Affairs. Christie possessed a mind finely honed to the niceties of international negotiations and an ability to cut through a morass of detail to isolate and define broad principles.

Now he put his legal talents at the disposal of the Ontario Hydro. The Christie papers contain several brilliantly argued but unsigned memoranda on the water power dispute. In style and content these go beyond the sort of material which was being prepared on the question by A.W. Rogers of the Attorney-General's Department. This was precisely the kind of work which Magrath had in mind for Christie when he hired him and it may safely be assumed that he was their author.

In his first effort, dated 1 February 1927, Christie argued that the province should not proceed except 'with reference to some considered broad objective and scheme of action.'[70] He insisted that federal control over navigation gave Ottawa no right to delay indefinitely the production of power merely on the grounds that canalization was not at present required. And he pointed out that 'the idea has long been in the air in some quarters that you cannot treat power development apart from canalization, because canalization or navigation carried the ownership of what is called incidental water power. The popular expression of the idea is that by linking power with navigation you get navigation facilities free. It is an alluring mirage, but it is a vicious confusion of ideas and it ought to be swept away.'

Christie submitted a more formal and theoretical statement of the provincial position in a 24 February brief entitled 'Federal and Provincial Rights in Waterways.'[71] Arguing on three grounds, the Christie memorandum was a definitive statement of the provincial position. Firstly, it examined in detail the legal and constitutional basis of the federal claim. Only in one case, it noted, is water power specifically mentioned in the BNA Act and that is Section 108, the third schedule, which contains, as first among the items of public works and property conveyed at Confederation to the dominion, the following: 'Canals, with Lands and Water Power connected therewith.' Christie argued convincingly that this extremely limited conveyance had been expanded into 'a very considerable usurpation of provincial authority' by the Department of Railways and Canals which now interpreted it 'in a sense so wide as to sweep practically all the benefits of the whole Welland and Trent Rivers into the keeping of the Federal Government.' The real intent of the provision, he argued, was not to grant or define powers but to strike a balance sheet as to the division of assets and debts as they existed in 1867. In the succeeding years, the federal Department in administering navigation had 'assumed to grant power rights which were not theirs to grant.' 'It is the nature of great impersonal administrative organizations to conceive their authority at the widest stretch and to be intolerant of any others that may seem to overlap.'

Secondly, he insisted that 'the existing position is not in the public interest. To ignore the basic compacts of a federal system is to create "sectionalism." To confuse the jurisdictional question is to weaken the ability of all legislatures, governments and departments to negotiate with powerful special interests...' and with the United States as well. There was no adequate reason to allow such confusion to continue for both technically and financially it was a simple matter to separate power and navigation.

Finally, he provided the theoretical justification for the provincial stance, although here he was only spelling out more fully a position already assumed by Ferguson and others. 'Canada,' he asserted, 'was created by the act of the separate Provinces. They established a federal Union, yielding to the Union the rights and functions appropriate to a national endeavour, retaining to themselves what might be appropriate to local endeavours...' and he warned that 'it will not do to invoke here against this natural line between federal and provincial authority the various so-called doctrines of incidental powers, of ancillary legislation, of federal paramountcy and so on. Under these guises you could slowly convert Canada from a federal union into a legislative union...'

Of course Loring Christie was hardly a disinterested party. The opposite point of view was expressed by Sir Clifford Sifton and his journalistic associate, John

W. Dafoe, who for similar yet distinct reasons found themselves on common ground. Dafoe, of course, was an unabashed centralist. Commenting in July on the failure of the Georgian Bay charter to be renewed, he told Sifton that

The policy which the government might have declared, in my opinion, would have laid it down as a fundamental principle that all power developments must provide canalization for the stretches of the river affected, to be defrayed out of the power revenue. The claim – the impudent claim, as I cannot but think – was put forward last year, on behalf of Ontario and Quebec, that they were entitled to all power developed on the river without responsibility for any capital expenditure other than that necessary to produce the power itself. ... The implications of this claim are very extensive. I was astonished beyond measure that the Dominion Government did not challenge this dangerous doctrine and fight it out.[72]

Sifton, whose interest was not academic, replied that the cost of the St Lawrence Seaway would be appalling. 'There is only one basis upon which it can be built and that is that the power shall pay for the canal completely and entirely.'[73] Sifton did not know whether this was possible but as an influential member of the National Advisory Committee investigating Seaway prospects for the federal government, his views would not go unnoticed.

Clearly these two positions, that of Ontario as expressed by Christie and that of the Sifton-Dafoe group, evoked utterly contradictory conceptions of the future course of Canadian development. Those who accepted the Dafoe thesis feared excessive provincialism as the major threat to the Canadian nationality; those who spoke for Ontario and Quebec believed that any attempt to encroach upon provincial rights or to force the country into a too centralist mould would create a powerful reaction and lead to a truly destructive sectionalism.

Ferguson was under no illusions that the victory over the Siftons and the Shawinigan interests on the Ottawa had finally settled the question. The federal position remained as confused and unclear as ever. Ontario still lacked permission to proceed on the St Lawrence and complex negotiations lay ahead before development could advance on the Ottawa. On 13 April 1927, he told King that with the two leases expiring on 1 May he hoped there would be a fresh attempt to settle dominion-provincial disagreements 'and expedite the actual production of power whether at Carillon or elsewhere on the Ottawa River.' Again he pressed on King 'the practical urgency of getting this power into production. ... The interests of the public in the various uses of these waters are far too vast and important to have them tied up in any way through a possibly long drawn out controversy between the Provincial and Federal Governments.'[74] King replied that his government held 'if not all, practically all the rights at the Carillon Rapids controlling the water power development at that point' and that generally 'the consensus of legal opinion' was that Ottawa 'in the development

of water power through the construction of works for the purposes of navigation ... holds the rights to the water power so developed.' The dominion might,
however, be prepared if circumstances should so develop to sell to the province
waterpower generated 'at the point in question.' King seemed unaware of the
position taken by his own minister regarding ownership in April 1926, and of
the resolution of the House of Commons thereto or, if he was aware, he chose to
disregard it. Ferguson's response was to tell King that further consideration had
strengthened Ontario in its view as to its rights and that the whole subject was
being studied by Ontario counsel. He asked as well that the matter be included
on the agenda for the approaching Dominion-Provincial Conference. Some five
weeks later King replied that he would consider this possibility.[75]

Ferguson's anger and apprehension increased when he learned the Department of Railways and Canals was planning to produce electrical energy from the
new Welland Ship Canal. Immediately he pointed out to King that in 1914
Frank Cochrane on behalf of the federal government had formally agreed that all
surplus waters on the canal be reserved for the Ontario Hydro and he formally
protested 'against a departure from the well-established and recognized policy
followed up to the present time with regard to the use of Niagara Waters.'[76] He
was equally exercised over a new policy adopted by the Department of Railways
and Canals with regard to the St Mary's River. Although this was an international water connecting lakes Superior and Huron, the province had, as he told
Taschereau, 'always dealt with power development on the Canadian side.' Now,
when the Hydro routinely filed with the federal Department for an increased
water allowance, they received the reply that 'the Province has no right to
develop power except under lease from the Federal Crown.' Thoroughly
alarmed, he warned Taschereau that 'we are to have a determined stand on the
part of the Federal Government taking the position that they have the right to
control these waters even for the purpose of the development of power.'[77]
Taschereau responded that 'our Province will certainly resist to the utmost' and
Ferguson informed his Quebec associate that he was 'greatly gratified that the
two provinces are going to unite in their resistance to Ottawa's invasion of their
provincial rights. ... I intend to issue a public statement in the near future, giving
to the public a clear understanding of the aggressive anti-provincial course that
the Federal Government is pursuing.'[78]

Here, then, was the story behind the St Lawrence Seaway 'all-Canadian'
resolution at Winnipeg. Not Ferguson's personal ambition nor even his desire to
help the Tories break into Quebec could fully explain his dramatic shift in
position. Nor did it simply herald the beginnings of a Conservative effort to
appeal to the country on anti-American lines, although the American
ambassador, William Phillips, was rightly worried by this aspect.[79] The Ontario
Premier had been forced to his position by Ottawa's apparent determination to
begin its own electrical development program. If this challenge should continue,

it was essential that the alliance with Taschereau be maintained and strengthened. With Quebec willing to sell power to Ontario and Ontario willing to abandon for the foreseeable future its pro-Seaway policy, everything was ready for the provincial rights offensive. Old friends such as Frank Keefer, who, after all, had a watching brief from Ferguson to monitor St Lawrence developments, might grumble and charge that the *Mail and Empire* had sold its soul to the Montreal power trust. The *Globe* might run accusatory editorials and the *Star* could claim that Ontario Tories at the convention 'had something put over them and are disposed to blame their leaders.'[80] Ferguson, however, had concluded that the question of St Lawrence navigation was secondary to the battle with Ottawa over waterpower rights; his priorities had been settled and his alliances were firmly in place.

In this context the Dominion-Provincial Conference took place. It was described by King as the most important since Confederation. Ownership of waterpowers was not the only matter in dispute between Queen's Park and Ottawa. Ontario officials prepared for the Conference with great care; officers of several of the provincial departments, and no doubt their ministers as well, had for some time been harbouring a sense of grievance over the attitudes and policies of their dominion counterparts. The Ontario bureaucrats hoped to use the occasion to present their side of the case and to score points.

Attorney-General Price was in charge of supervising the preparation of position papers by the provincial departments.[81] The principal memoranda came from J.H.H. Ballantyne, the Deputy Minister of Labour, J.T. White, the solicitor to the Treasurer, F.V. Johns, the Deputy Provincial Secretary, and Leighton Foster, the Superintendent of Insurance. A.W. Rogers in Price's own department prepared material on the water power dispute and this was supplemented by a memorandum written in May by Loring Christie, obviously with the conference in mind. Much of this material went directly to Edward Bayly, a veteran civil servant who as Deputy Attorney-General co-ordinated the provincial preparations for his chief.

There was a remarkable similarity in the briefs prepared by the several departments. Edward Bayly, for example, noted that the 1925 decision of the JCPC in the Snider case had utterly annihilated the Industrial Disputes Investigation Act and that 'the Dominion, following its usual procedure where their departments are involved, treated the decision as a nullity, did not repeal the Act but added to it provisions ... which in my opinion are open to exactly the same objection to which the Judicial Committee gave effect in the original Act...'[82] Even if the province so desired, there was nothing it could do, in Bayly's opinion, to give the dominion jurisdiction and 'if the Provinces desire to enact legislation of that kind, there is no reason why their Governments should be hampered by any

Dominion arrangement.' There was, therefore, 'nothing to discuss.' As well, Bayly believed that with reference to the regulation of the sale of shares and securities of dominion companies, 'the question will be decided by the Courts in any case and is on its way now to be so decided by the Judicial Committee.'

Similarly F.V. Johns in a 31 October memorandum for Price on jurisdiction over company incorporation presented a variety of complaints over the practices of dominion officials. 'In the administration of the Companies Act in discussing with applicants the terms of petitions for incorporation we are at times told more or less bluntly that if the department is reluctant to grant the application in the terms asked that the application will be switched from Toronto to Ottawa.' Federal officials, it seemed, were more accommodating and Johns could not believe the public interest was being well served by this kind of trade-off.[83] Howard Ferguson was himself outraged, telling Norman Harris of the Toronto *Telegram* that 'we can control companies incorporated in Ontario, but the moment we attempt to interfere, they go to Ottawa and secure a Charter, and thus figuratively, snap their fingers at us.'[84]

Loring Christie was equally convinced that much of Ontario's difficulty could be laid at the door of self-serving, empire-building federal bureaucrats and he doubted for that reason that the province would ever be able to achieve its goals with respect to waterpower through negotiations:

The field is peculiarly one where departmental traditions are likely to prevail at Ottawa. Departmental practice there, in effect inimical to the Provincial interest, has attained a powerful momentum during the past quarter century, and the chances that this can be appreciably stemmed through any negotiation ... do not seem bright. The Federal Prime Minister's latest letter would seem to indicate that the Departmental thesis today holds the field in its most extreme form. In actual practice the political colour of the administration in control seems to have had an inconsiderable effect. Individual Ministers, whatever their views, are not likely to prevail against such a strong tradition and bureaucratic practice...

Christie suspected that only a general election fought on the provincial rights theme would succeed in countering such influences. A dominion-provincial conference would at best find a *modus vivendi*; it might 'disclose more precisely what the issue between the Federal and Provincial fields is' but ultimately a judicial decision would be called for.[85]

The same anger and frustration coupled with a belief that the Conference would achieve little of practical value appeared in documents prepared by Leighton Foster. Although the provincial position in the conflict over licensing and regulation of insurance companies had been vindicated by the Ontario Supreme Court in the insurance reference of 1926, Ottawa had ignored the decision. The dispute continued and in 1927 the interested provinces asked the federal government either to appeal the Ontario case or abide by it. Again there was no satisfaction. W.H. Price thereupon convinced members of the Quebec cabinet to co-operate with Ontario and license a group of American mutual companies not licensed at Ottawa and the two provinces undertook to intervene on their behalf if their rights were challenged by Ottawa. 'This action,' Foster pointed out in a memorandum prepared for the Conference, 'is calculated to provoke the Dominion into either prosecuting a test case to the Privy Council or abandoning its jurisdiction.'[86] Foster himself believed that only the Privy Council would give the provinces satisfaction. He noted that in April the Minister of Finance had been asked in the House of Commons what his government intended to do with the resolution relating to insurance regulation that Howard Ferguson as chairman of the interprovincial conference of June 1926 had forwarded to the government. The reply was that 'so far as the minister is aware none of the resolutions of the inter-provincial conference said to be held in June last has ever been submitted ... to the government.' During the 1927 session the dominion, intent on ignoring or bypassing the courts, had enacted more insurance legislation. Like his fellows in the Ontario service, Foster believed the public interest was negated by this situation. The dominion authorities, he argued, recognized that their jurisdiction 'was based largely on sufferance and hence appear to have deliberately favoured the insurance companies at the expense of the public.'[87]

In furtherance of this tradition, the Dominion government early in 1927 presented legislation requiring loan and trust companies to obtain an annual licence renewal from the Minister of Finance. On 2 March, Price formally protested to Mackenzie King but the Deputy Minister of Justice responded that the legislation was an entirely legitimate exercise of federal authority.[88] According to Foster, the constitutional question at issue followed the same general lines as in the case of regulation of insurance companies and the fundamental principles involved had been laid down as long ago as the Citizens Insurance Company v Parsons case of 1881:

The Ontario protest was inspired by the history of the conflict of jurisdiction over insurance legislation and a realization that a Dominion licensing system applied to Dominion loan and trust companies was no doubt the thin edge of the wedge. The Province of Ontario has registered and supervised the business of all loan and trust companies doing business in the province ... for 30 years. ... The invasion of the loan and trust company field is merely another example of the intention [sic] the Dominion to regulate business generally throughout Canada.[89]

Obviously, the provincial civil servants were exercised. Clearly, the bureaucracy had recovered from the state of near-demoralization which had existed in the early 1920s and now its leaders felt able to challenge the pretensions of their federal counterparts. There were other matters as well which they hoped their ministers would raise at the conference table. J.T. White, the Treasury Department solicitor, argued that the federal use of the income tax was an invasion of a provincial power and suggested that all revenue from the personal income tax be returned to the provinces.[90] And James Ballantyne vented his wrath on Ottawa's old age pension legislation, which required participating provinces to join on federal terms and pay not only half the cost of the pensions but all of the heavy administrative expenses as well.[91] In their views, however, the Conference would be useful largely as an occasion for showing the flag; their ultimate weapon, they readily conceded, was the JCPC.

Ferguson was aware of the views of the deputies and in full sympathy. Like them he placed his faith in the JCPC and expected little to be achieved at any conference chaired by Mackenzie King; he was too familiar with King's methods to be sanguine on that count. Nonetheless he considered that, with proper management, the Ferguson-Taschereau axis could be brought to bear and the other premiers might offer support if support were offered them. The *Mail and Empire* of 8 October printed the items Ferguson said he intended to raise and without exception they were the kind of hard, practical matters the civil servants had pointed to in their position papers.

In late September the Ontario Premier moved to ensure interprovincial co-operation by attempting to organize a meeting two days before the larger gathering at which the provinces would 'confer together and ascertain upon what questions they hold common views.' 'It will enable us,' he told James Gardiner of Saskatchewan, 'to present in an ordinary way the provincial point of view...'[92] Gardiner refused to attend such a gathering and forwarded his correspondence with Ferguson to Mackenzie King, telling his federal leader that 'Mr Ferguson appears to be putting forth every effort to organize any opposition that there may be to any attitude which your Government may decide to take...'[93]

At the Conference itself there was no overt indication that Ferguson was 'leader of the opposition.' Indeed he was all amiability and King for the most part was delighted with the progress made.[94] Yet little achievement was apparent in the proceedings of the first two sessions at which Justice Minister Lapointe raised two constitutional questions, that of Senate reform and of a procedure for the amendment of the BNA Act. Lapointe suggested that an age limit might be adopted for senators and that the system in effect in Great Britain whereby limitations had been placed on the veto of the House of Lords might be applied to Canada. Taschereau, however, could see no reason for constitutional change and feared that any tinkering with the Senate might 'open the door to further amendments of the agreements.' He was at once supported by Ferguson and backed by Baxter and Rhodes, the two other Tory premiers. The western premiers for their part wanted change but could not agree on the details.[95]

More significant but equally inconclusive was the discussion of Lapointe's proposal that Canada should assume the right to amend its own constitution without reference to Great Britain and that the federal Parliament should receive the right to act itself in those areas which did not refer to provincial or minority rights. King's diary records the reaction:

Ferguson strongly opposed on ground of leading to separation from Britain, gradually weakening of bonds, next to drop the appeal to Privy Council, then our own Govr. Genl., then nothing left, also that it means a "fundamental structural" change. ... Taschereau held that England was an "independent tribunal" & it was only fair to minorities & prov. to have an independent decision not a majority decision on matters of constitution. He sd he cld & wd get entire legislature of Quebec to vote against change in method. Ferguson asked Lapointe if his view was view of govt. L. asked me what to say. I said yes, but that we had no grievance, it was our position on a theoretical question. Ferguson's strong point was that there was no agitation for change, no declared opinion outside Winnipeg Free Press. – Baxter and Rhodes held with Ferguson & Taschereau. The Liberal and Progressive Premiers supported Lapointe.[96]

'It was,' concluded King, 'a discussion between East & West but even more between Liberal & Conservative opinion.'

King had no intention of pressing ahead on these abstract matters against strong opposition and, once his government's position was on record, he was glad to proceed to more practical questions. From Ferguson's perspective, however, both as imperialist and as provincialist, the points at issue were of profound significance. No doubt as an empire nationalist he was already fighting a losing battle, but his belief that imperial sentiment in Canada was threatened by the gradual erosion of both symbolic and institutional ties required that he take a stand. Nothing could be more natural than for an imperialist to fight every inch of the way, even if the 'little Canadians,' as Ferguson scornfully called them, were enabled thereby to paint a convincing picture of him and his ilk as died-in-the-wool reactionaries. In his view it was vital that such erosion be halted and that those who would turn Canada virtually into a unitary state with the provinces reduced to the level of glorified county councils be met and defeated. He believed that the British connection and through it the JCPC represented the best defence against such a disastrous eventuality.

When the conference moved on to financial matters and the perennial problem of the subsidy, the increases effected in payments to the Maritime provinces following the Duncan Commission and the claims of some of the western provinces for equal consideration came up for discussion, Ferguson made it clear, as the official précis noted, that 'his province contributed a higher per capita payment towards the burden of debt and toward the revenue of the Dominion' than did other provinces.[97] Yet in what he no doubt hoped would be interpreted as a gesture of sweeping generosity, he proclaimed that 'he did not intend ... to cavil about small things. He regarded it as supremely important to bring about a situation which would be satisfactory to all the provinces.' If the principle of the Duncan Report were correct, 'then there should be a similar investigation which would be Dominion wide.'[98] Ontario, which was not complaining, was spending substantial funds on development work which belonged to the dominion. A commission of outstanding financial men might be appointed to examine grievances, whether real or imaginary.

Ferguson's suggestion of a kind of commission on federal-provincial relations was not taken up by King, who doubtless feared it would lead to an all-out raid on the federal treasury. This impression was strengthened when Ferguson concluded by urging generosity toward provinces in need ₊and stated that 'the expenditure of a few hundred thousand dollars was nothing if optimism, harmony and industry could be inspired.' Taschereau followed in similar vein. Later there would be charges that Ferguson's support of higher subsidies and even of transfer payments to the 'have-not' provinces, as they subsequently were called, was all a political ploy whose purpose was transparently to win support on the waterways question. Such a conclusion underestimated the Ontario man's nationalism and did scant justice to his understanding of the problems of Confederation. In December 1926 when the Duncan Report on Maritime rights was being discussed, he had assured W.H. Dennis of the Halifax *Herald* that he had 'always felt that the Maritimes came into Confederation on the distinct understanding that provision would be made that would link them up with the rest of the Dominion and enable them to carry on exchange of products with the central markets. In that respect I do not think we have done all for the Maritimes that should have been done. I have always held this view and have not hesitated to express it in Ontario on a number of occasions.'[99] His attitude at the conference was no mere ploy but reflected a genuine and oft-repeated commitment to assist in the creation of a stronger transcontinental economy and to achieve a firmer national integration better able to resist the alluring pull of continentalism.

Yet the magnanimous attitude of Ontario and Quebec to the financial needs of the smaller provinces was not entirely lacking in ulterior motives. When it came time to discuss the waterpower issue, part of the reason for the generosity of the central provinces became apparent. Ontario and Quebec came to the conference armed with a legal opinion delivered by their solicitors on 24 October which, not surprisingly, strongly upheld their position in the dispute. Signed by E. Lafleur, A. Geoffrion, and W.N. Tilley, it held that 'the question of the ownership of navigable rivers and their beds was definitively settled in favour of the Provinces by the decision of the Privy Council in the Fisheries Case (1898) A.C.700. It follows that the potential waterpowers ... are also provincial property...'[100] Armed with this opinion, the two premiers were more confident over a reference of the question to the courts to clear up the jurisdictional dispute. Now Taschereau, who spoke to that effect, was followed by Ferguson, who told the gathering that if the dominion was prepared to do so, the matter might well be eliminated from the agenda. At this point Mackenzie King interjected that the other provinces might have something to say about the matter.

But the silence on their part was deafening. Presumably they either regarded the issue as none of their business or had decided that as the Ontario and Quebec premiers had supported their position in the subsidy question, the time had come to reciprocate. The following day Lapointe stated that the possibility of a reference to the courts would have to be decided by cabinet. Later, the decision was made to submit questions to the Supreme Court of Canada. Circumstances had left the King government little choice but to comply with the wishes of the two premiers.

This, perhaps, was the major achievement of the conference. On most other matters, the discussions were inconclusive. Most of the provinces spoke in favour of the resumption or continuation of various grants-in-aid which the Union Government had started but for which the Liberals had shown little sympathy. Ontario in fact suggested that such grants should not be temporary at all but placed on a permanent basis. Evidently the discussion had little impact on King, for his government continued its policy of withdrawing support from these programs. The dominion showed no sympathy for W.H. Price's suggestion that it vacate the personal income tax field.[101] Ferguson also ventilated several of his pet schemes, telling his fellow premiers that Canada 'should launch out into a new line in the matter of her fuel and steel, and [he] was not sure that a deficit on the Canadian National Railways should be regarded as a great calamity provided that it resulted in the development of the country.'[102] Such interchanges, however, had little impact.

Despite the pleasantries which prevailed, the growing number of disputes between Ottawa and the provinces could not be swept under the table entirely. Interestingly, Lapointe made the shrewd comment that such 'conflict' could not be avoided and should be settled in a spirit of compromise.[103] Certainly Ferguson recognized as did Lapointe that conflict had become part of the grit and gristle of Canadian federalism; time and again his government had faced such situations and there is little indication, except on the waterpower question, that he regarded these incidents as anything out of the ordinary. His experience, perhaps, was too great to expect anything else and while he might fire off furious letters in response to particular aggravations, he, like King, recognized that all this was part of the dynamic of Canadian federalism.

Thus much of the work of the Conference was shuffled off on subcommittees of civil servants. Lapointe did find it necessary to state in full session that there was no 'bureaucracy' in the federal civil service and that a harder working group of men imbued with a desire to serve their country never existed. The Ontario deputies saw things differently. Leighton Foster's notes taken during the sittings of the subcommittee dealing with insurance and loan and trust matters reveal their perspective.

Mr Finlayson [a federal official] introduced subject and spoke for 45 minutes with frequent interruptions by Mr Bayly ... his review of the decisions [legal decisions over regulation of insurance] was so ridiculous ... that Mr Bayly checked him severely.

When Finlayson concluded, Foster began to argue that the legislative power of the dominion,

as shown by the decisions was limited to the *incorporation* of insurance, loan and trust companies and rights incidental thereto and that the Dominion should withdraw from the field of *regulation*. ... Any attempt to delineate jurisdiction on some other basis could only result in continued dual supervision with its inevitable conflicts and embarrassment to the public and the business.

Mr Finlayson did not reply to my statement. He laughed, waved his hand, made a dirty remark about my looking for another job and said, by inference, that there was no use talking to me. I kept my mouth shut...[104]

After this fiasco, Price sent a note to Lucien Cannon, the responsible dominion minister, that 'if we are to make any progress the ministers will have to meet without the Deputies and decide what can reasonably be done.'[105] But no real progress proved possible and Cannon reported to the Conference that 'with respect to insurance, loan and trust companies a careful study would be made with a view to reaching a satisfactory basis of cooperation with the provinces.'[106]

The Ontario officials had been right from the beginning. Whether the politicians or the officials or the very structure of Canadian government was responsible, most of the issues in dispute would only be settled by the JCPC. On the insurance matter, for example, Ontario in 1929 again went to court to test the constitutionality of a new Dominion Insurance Act. Once more the case went to the Privy Council and a decision was rendered in 1931. 'The judgement,' Grant Dexter has recorded, 'reduced the Dominion Insurance Act to ruins. The provinces scored a knockout.'[107] But even this was not accepted as final and once again the dominion lawyers went to work and the whole mad process began anew.

Despite a sense of achievement felt by King, the 1927 conference was primarily a ceremonial event. Many matters were discussed; few were resolved. This no doubt was what the politicians had expected. Ferguson and Taschereau at least had cause to be pleased. After it was all over, Saunders of PEI wrote King that 'the big surprise to me, however, were Ferguson and Taschereau. ... I thought they would be political giants and would outshine anything around the council board. From the beginning to the end I thought that all the subject matters dealt with by Ferguson were of a most superficial nature. He is undoubtedly a politician and a great mixer, but I question whether he would really be fit for a federal appointment, much less a federal leader. I was greatly disappointed with Premier Taschereau ... he did not seem to take any stock in any of the Premiers save and except Premier Ferguson, and it seemed to me that his outstanding desire was to ... make himself popular in the esteem and estimation of Ferguson.'

Mackenzie King knew better. 'I should be inclined to credit both Ferguson and Taschereau with more in the way of ability, both political and otherwise, than you appear to be ready to accord them. Part of their aloofness was, I imagine, due to a desire to be seen and not heard, and for the most part, to use the conference to serve their own purpose rather than the purposes of others present.'[108] By that token, the gathering had achieved a measure of success.

15

'The Most Marked Contribution
We Have Made'

Despite Howard Ferguson's opinion that sound administration was the key to good government, his own record between 1926 and 1930 did not lack for legislative achievements and many of the measures passed were progressive and reformist. No facile attempt to place this Tory of Tories on some artificial political spectrum can do justice to the complexities of the Ontario situation or explain adequately the diversities of approach which his government applied to the governing of the province. Brokerage politics, the complex dynamics of federalism, the cool pragmatism of the political professional and, most of all, a reaction to the historic yet shifting needs of the Ontario region were all prominent components of the political process under his leadership.

Still, notwithstanding the passage of an impressive amount of significant legislation, there were few surprises during the final years of his political hegemony and few departures from established policy lines. The social and other legislation of the Ferguson years suggests the existence in Ontario of an intelligent establishment often sensitive to social currents and prepared on occasion to act creatively to meet perceived needs. It is equally true, however, that Ontarians in the 1920s were limited in their perceptions and slow to recognize the growing deficiencies of existing structures. This is only to say that Ferguson and his friends were men of their time. Given the relative prosperity of the period, it was natural that those in power should possess their share of the prevailing complacency; only the depression would reveal the bankruptcy of provincial social policy. Although mounting dissatisfactions on the part less of the poor themselves than of the professionals responsible for administering an increasingly defective system did become in the late 1920s a catalyst of change, many problems remained hidden in a veil of prosperity and the minority of unfortunates were too mute and too few to have much effect on the body politic.

Howard Ferguson sincerely believed that his government had made great strides in the welfare field. In 1929, for example, Sir Robert Borden told him that 'three notable events in your public career greatly impress me,' and Borden pointed to his 'undaunted' attitude when his political opponents had tried to destroy him through the Timber Commission; the courage with which he placed government control before the people in 1926; and the French-language school question which involved a 'deep-rooted prejudice that almost defied reason or argument. Undeterred by difficulties that would have daunted a less resolute spirit, you have added the solution of this question to your other triumphs.' Although Ferguson appreciated Borden's remarks, his response was interesting. His own view, he told Borden, was that his government's 'most lasting and beneficial accomplishment has been the complete revolution in the method of treatment of the unfortunate who are placed at a disadvantage either mentally, physically, or morally. I believe a new spirit and an improved attitude towards the whole question of reclamation will be of tremendous value in the development of higher standards of life. Our educational efforts with boys and youths who have slipped from the straight path, and the establishment of giving even the adult offender against the law a second chance, is, I believe, the most marked contribution we have made towards our national life.'[1]

Once again he was the son of Dr Charles, the heir of the rich family life of his Kemptville home. Always he had professed to believe that most politicians were there for the service they could offer and in his own case his record leaves little doubt that power for its own sake was not what kept him in public life. From his first day as head of the government he had tried to direct policy and guide the province along certain lines; prominent among his priorities was the ideal of social service to the community. If more was not achieved, it was not because he headed a party of wealthy Tories kept in power by reactionary business interests. His efforts could only be within the framework of his day and the limitations of his policies were also those of his age. His letter to Borden notwithstanding, there are signs that by 1929 he himself was beginning to recognize, albeit tentatively, the need to break out in new directions.

The policies he boasted of to Borden were described in his party's 1929 campaign literature as 'the most outstanding piece of social legislation Ontario has had for many years.'[2] By the Probation Act of 1929 magistrates were empowered to grant probation to adult offenders without first having to register a conviction against them. The same year the province also established in several cities domestic relations courts as part of an effort to separate such cases from the ordinary police court environment. A 1929 amendment to the Children's Protection Act allowed judges to give custody of a child to the mother or father in cases of mistreatment where previously there was only provision for a fine. The Magistrates Extended Jurisdiction Act gave the province the power to designate specific magistrates to deal with certain types of cases as part of an effort to segregate the various matters dealt with and to take advantage of the special skills of particular magistrates. Finally, the Dependents Relief Act of

1929 gave judges of Surrogate Court the power to make adequate provision for the families of those who in their wills had disposed of their estates to the detriment of their dependents. Perhaps the most significant advance in this body of legislation was the more extensive and rational use of the principle of probation for adult defenders.

Whatever these measures might suggest of the beginnings of a new enlightenment in legal and penal areas, they were of little benefit to the majority of the province's poor. A nicer indication of the province's role could be gained from another claim in the same 1929 Tory pamphlet which assessed the state of Ontario's 142 general hospitals and concluded proudly that 'the contribution of the Ontario Government to Hospitals and Charitable Institutions is in round numbers $1,500,000 per annum. What more noble contribution could be made than this contribution to assist those who ... are unable to assist themselves.'[3]

In this instance the social reality truly mocked the confident assertions of the campaign literature. In March 1927 Lincoln Goldie introduced legislation designed to save the province some $200,000 by cutting down the aid given to charity patients, leaving the slack to be taken up by the municipalities or the hospitals themselves. Since the provincial payment to hospitals in aid of charity patients already represented only a small portion of the total cost, medical authorities expressed outrage. Under the new law many struggling hospitals would face still larger deficits and the Toronto *Star* alleged that 'for months past interviews have been refused by the government to hospital representatives. They say that no practical hospital authorities were consulted in the framing of the bill. For three years the hospitals have been asking for more aid, and were led to believe it was coming. Now this bill comes like a bombshell.'[4]

After a wave of protest from hospitals and municipalities, the bill was hastily withdrawn. Apparently it had not even gone to committee and many Tory members expressed grave displeasure when they learned of its contents. While it is unclear whether this monumental blunder was Ferguson's or Goldie's, the general policy the bill expressed must have had cabinet approval. Typically, the measure had been given first reading late in the session, apparently as part of an effort to slip it through with little scrutiny. Most disturbing, it suggested that stern economy and municipal responsibility remained the predominant expression of the government's social philosophy. The session ended the following day.

This aborted effort caused some hospital administrators and medical men to conclude that the time had come to speak out. Major A.C. Galbraith, the Superintendent of Toronto Western Hospital and an official of the Ontario Hospital Association, used his address to the Association's annual meeting that year to attack the government's niggardly grants policy, particularly as it affected the care of sick indigents. 'This handicap,' Galbraith affirmed, 'is solely due to the lack of a properly balanced system of hospital finance...' Admitting that this was a problem across Canada, he believed nonetheless that Ontario 'has done practically the least of any province toward a constructive policy in this field.'[5] The Goldie bill he described as satisfactory to neither the Association, the hospitals, nor the municipalities and he deplored the fact that the existing governmental contribution for public ward patients was 'below the allowance made by any other province of Canada except Quebec and possibly PEI.' Galbraith argued that the Ontario system which placed these institutions under the provincial secretary made little sense but urged that more important than departmental arrangements was the need for the government to realize the necessity for the reform of funding arrangements.

One sign of progress was a 1928 decision to appoint a director of hospital services. There was no radical change, however, in the province's position that it was primarily the responsibility of private and municipal initiative to supply hospital services. In September 1929 Ferguson insisted that 'the Legislature could not undertake to provide for people in the General Hospitals further than the present per diem allowance enables us to do.'[6] By May 1930, however, when he received a letter pointing to the desperate straits in which medical costs left many families and suggesting a tax-supported insurance scheme, he was willing to admit that 'one of the most urgent needs is either cheaper hospital accommodation or some method of reducing the amount to be paid by the great bulk of our people. ... Indigents are well taken care of in the public wards. People of means are amply provided for in the special wards. Between these two extremes lies the man of moderate means who finds it difficult to secure reasonable accommodation.' He noted that the problem was having 'very careful consideration' and reported that he had 'threshed it out' with the General Hospital Board, which apparently promised to provide more moderately priced rooms.[7]

With professional opinion increasingly intent on change, the Department of Health under Dr Godfrey continued to devote its attention to educational activities and field services; however useful these peripheral efforts may have been, perhaps they were more logically the responsibility not of Queen's Park but of municipal groups, private agencies, and particularly of local boards of health. Thus the various divisions, Dental Services, Public Health, Industrial Hygiene and Sanitary Engineering, and the Travelling Diagnostic Clinic, still provided practical and educational services under the old motto, 'education not legislation.' Undeniably, however, in a province so newly urbanized and industrialized, such services were vitally needed as were the vaccines, the insulin, and the serums that the Department distributed free and 'on a more generous scale than does any other governmental department on the North American continent.'[8]

In his duties as Minister of Labour, Godfrey carried on in the same cautious manner, administering the Factory Act and other existing legislation but failing to look to larger needs. In 1929 there were 20 factory inspectors, 15 men and five women, and since 1924 they had carried out 107,443 inspections and made 40,000 recommendations for improvements. Certificates were issued to stationary engineers; the department supervised employment offices in 25 centres about the province; between 1926 when legislation was introduced and 1929, over $425,000 was 'assessed against the mine owners for silicosis work,' surely not an insignificant figure and yet the dread disease continued its path of destruction. In 1928 the department added an Industrial Safety Division and appointed an inspector as part of an effort to reduce the number of industrial accidents.[9]

All this was well-meaning and useful; much of it reflected the administration's goal of equalizing opportunity and bringing to the remotest communities services equivalent to those provided in Toronto. During the 1929 election, the party claimed that 'health instruction has been carried to the individual, to the home and to the community from the Great Lakes to the Hudson Bay by the Department's Public Health Nurses, and a determined effort is being made to secure to the rural and sparsely settled sections of the Province, public health advantages that before the operation of this educational campaign were enjoyed only by those in the larger cities.'[10] Unfortunately, perhaps because 'education' often was cheaper than 'legislation,' the Tories became the captive of their own slogans. Whether through a failure of imagination or, more likely, the lack of an organized demand and the unpropitious nature of the times, there was little sign of the development of any broader philosophy in either Health or Labour under Dr Godfrey. Industrial standards often remained abysmally low, there was little contact with or, if the deputy minister's views are indicative, sympathy for, the aspirations of organized labour and there was no minimum wage legislation for men which might have contributed to a fairer sharing of the growing prosperity of the day.

Ferguson himself was not entirely happy with the course of developments in Dr Godfrey's dual portfolio but his concern was probably restricted to administrative deficiencies. By this date personal problems appear to have diminished the minister's efficiency but the Premier hesitated to remove an old friend, one who in Ferguson's own time of troubles had offered robust support. As an alternative he delegated a respected confidant to drop into the department on occasion and keep his eye on things.[11] Meanwhile Goldie remained Provincial Secretary, a striking contrast to W.J. Hanna, who had made such a success of the same portfolio under Whitney. In such circumstances, some stagnation was to be expected; perhaps Ferguson allowed it because his expectations and demands were less in this field than in others.

In other areas as well, Ferguson proved unable to break free of his essentially nineteenth-century attitude towards the expenditure of public funds on social services. In January 1927 when the Neighbourhood Workers Association asked that the Mothers' Allowance Commission be given more discretion to grant allowances in exceptional cases, Ferguson replied that 'experience in permitting discretionary powers in legislation of this character is not encouraging.'[12] In 1928 the Ontario Dental Association together with social service groups applied considerable pressure in an attempt to convince the province it should 'assist municipalities and general hospitals to organize dental clinics for the treatment of the poor...'[13] The same year a number of the Children's Aid Societies pleaded for provincial assistance, pointing to the special grants provided to several societies by the Drury government. Ever the guardian of the treasury, Ferguson responded that the Drury precedent was an unfortunate mistake and 'we must refrain from complying with the great many requests that are meritorious and worthy...'[14]

The same fixation with costs and reluctance to break into new fields characterized Ferguson's treatment of the old age pension question. In the months after federal legislation was passed, and particularly after several of the western provinces entered the scheme, the Ontario Premier was questioned often about his intentions. He seemed to find it all very annoying. He was angry, and understandably so, to have had his hand forced by Ottawa and his priorities removed from his own control. Any number of times he insisted that pensions were a federal responsibility and he suggested that had been the view of most provinces at the Dominion-Provincial Conference. Almost as often he claimed that if Ontario adopted the scheme it would be flooded with indigents from other provinces.[15] Frequently he expressed apprehension about the costs of pensions to a province hard pressed to balance its budget; apparently his fear of raising taxes in rich Ontario was greater than his concern for the aged needy. Above all he remained firm in his belief that the family and, failing that, the community were best equipped to cope with the social problems of the day.

As a result, when his government finally acted it was more out of necessity than conviction. In 1928 the throne speech stated vaguely that 'one of the social problems engaging the earnest attention of my ministers is the better care of our dependent aged population.' In truth only days earlier had Horace Wallis, the deputy minister in the Prime Minister's department, been ordered to investigate existing company pension plans. One wonders why someone under Goldie or Godfrey was not given this chore. As well, J.A. Ellis of the Bureau of Municipal Affairs conducted a survey to determine the number eligible for a pension.[16] During the throne speech debate, the Liberals attacked government inaction and called such investigatory efforts a transparent attempt to stall. In his reply Ferguson showed for pensions all the enthusiasm of a man swallowing a distasteful medicine. He warned that new taxation would be required, suggested that Ottawa was avoiding its responsibilities, noted that the Parents' Maintenance Act already required children to support their aged parents, pointed to the responsibility of the municipalities and, finally, insisted that his government was in complete sympathy but could act only after full study.[17]

By this time the political dangers of inaction were more apparent than ever. Peter Heenan, now federal Minister of Labour, began to take potshots at his old adversary, insisting that the Ontario Tories were denying old people the necessities of life and hinting that Ferguson was trying to talk other provinces into staying out.[18] This was a possibility, of course, for Taschereau was violently opposed, but more likely Ferguson had recognized a *fait accompli* and was waiting for the right moment to act. In May he announced that legislation would be brought down in 1929. Many concluded he had decided on a 1929 election.

But if he had bowed to reality, he remained determined to make the legislation conform as closely as possible to his conception of what was appropriate for Ontario. To Ferguson this meant municipal financial participation. In the House when he announced the details of his legislation he was forced to defend the clause which required a 20 per cent local contribution. He did so firmly, insisting that 'the foundation of every move towards pensions should come from local sources, from the locality in which the applicant lives, where his circumstances are known, where they have all the machinery for investigating conditions...'[19] The municipalities, he reminded the members, paid half the cost of mothers' allowances, and there were no complaints about that.

His critics, however, charged that having been outmanoeuvred by Mackenzie King, he was determined to be as niggardly as possible. Although his statement that those who received the pension would do so 'as a matter of right' was applauded loudly, he went on to argue that many countries which had adopted non-contributory schemes were modifying them to allow at least a degree of contribution because experience proved non-contributory plans had 'a tendency to pauperize people.'[20] He was pleased therefore that with over half the employees of the province's 61 largest firms covered by company plans, only some 21,000 Ontarians would need the government pension. Of course the responsibility for the basic provisions of the Act rested not with Ontario but with Ottawa; under it pensions would be a maximum of $240 a year, and any income over $125 a year would be subtracted from that amount. Only Canadian citizens of twenty years and Ontario residents of five who were over seventy years of age would qualify. And in reaction to what had happened to so many other shared cost programs, the Ontario law provided that if Ottawa failed to live up to its financial obligations, the pensions would cease. Other legislation, including the Parents' Maintenance Act, would remain in effect and pensions would be paid only to those recommended by a local pensions board.

The legislation and what preceded it reflected the caution and the fears of the men of the 1920s. Although the well-worn argument of the effect of such schemes on the spirit of individual enterprise was much in evidence, Ferguson directed most of his efforts to setting at rest the minds of the taxpayer. In an age when salaries were small and money hard to come by for the average man, in a community which still cherished its rural traditions of economy and thrift, Ferguson set out to prove that the pensions scheme would be of limited application and limited cost. At length he reassured the members, calculating, for example, that the man who owned a $10,000 house in Fort William assessed at $5000 might expect to pay only 80 cents a year.[21] Although the province and its municipalities were together expected to contribute almost $2,500,000, no mean sum in terms of the total provincial budget, the thrust of his speech was that most old people would not qualify and that the average citizen's taxes would not be greatly affected. Again he repeated his well-worn argument that the majority of the province's revenue came not from taxes on the people but from services provided those who chose to receive them. In this way a conservative province backed into one of the first open-ended welfare programs in its history.

Possibly Ferguson was wrong. Ontario might have greeted the scheme with enthusiasm if he had presented it openly and fearlessly as a major innovation in the field of social justice. More than likely, he was right and many voters would have baulked. Nonetheless the ringing words in which he proclaimed 'What a difference it will make in the lives of many old people in the province of Ontario' seem in the circumstances hollow and even hypocritical.

Soon after the pensions legislation went on the books, the province faced the beginnings of an even greater social problem. Unemployment had been present in large pockets throughout the decade but during the last months of the Ferguson government, because of the onset of the Great Depression, it reached unprecedented proportions. During his first administration, Ferguson had developed a plan by which the province contributed a percentage to municipal relief and works schemes but he had never ceased to claim that Ottawa, with major responsibility for immigration, must also assume some of the burden of providing assistance in periods of unemployment.

During the winter of 1926-7 there was again pressure for Ontario to make the kind of contribution it had during previous periods of slackness. This time, however, Howard Ferguson himself, as Acting Minister of Labour in the absence of Dr Godfrey, put through an order-in-council which provided assistance on the same basis as previously, namely the payment to the municipality of a third of the labour cost over the normal labour cost on works carried out to relieve unemployment but now he added a rider: the words, 'conditional ... upon the participation on an equal basis by the Federal Government.'[22] No doubt he considered this no different than the kind of tactic used by Ottawa in its pensions legislation. A memorandum, apparently by the deputy minister of labour, dated 8 November 1927 and prepared for use at the Dominion-Provincial Conference, reminded the Ontario representatives that the province's action should be regarded as a declaration that unemployment relief costs were 'not exclusively a Provincial matter, and that the Federal Authority is likewise responsible.'[23]

Apparently the unemployed were now to join the ranks of the multitude who had suffered from the consequences of the protracted federal-provincial impasse. Ferguson furthered this trend the following year when he informed the authorities of York Township, in the course of refusing a grant in aid of unemployment relief, that 'unemployment is an entirely municipal affair ... it would not be just to use the money contributed by the whole province for purely local relief. The municipality derived the benefits from the workingmen in times of prosperity and should be prepared to bear the burden when times were not so bright.'[24] The responsibility, it seemed, rested everywhere but with the province.

During the winter of 1929-30 a new urgency and despair was reflected in growing bread lines and soup kitchens. The Premier's correspondence again contained pathetic appeals from the victims and demands from church, labour, and other bodies that the province play a larger role. Many blamed the immigrants and complained to Ferguson that they worked for unacceptably low wages, with the result that 'a good staunch Canadian can't get a job.'[25] Ferguson responded that little could be done 'so long as the Dominion pays no attention to our views...'[26] The province again paid its pittance of one-third the excess cost of public works carried out for relief purposes; as before Queen's Park placed orders for plant and machinery to help carry workers through the winter.[27]

More and more, Ferguson blamed federal policies. 'Thousands of men have been brought to this country as farm hands. ... I have talked with some of them myself who say they have no desire to farm,' he told one correspondent in March 1930. 'These men after brief employment in the west drift back east to the large centres...'[28] Whenever the possibility of unemployment insurance was raised, his patented response was to point out that it was, 'like the Old Age Pensions, a subject for federal jurisdiction.'[29] Although he professed to be deeply moved and insisted that 'no one feels more keenly than I do the unfortunate situation in which so many of our citizens find themselves,' he could only conclude lamely that 'with a climate that permits of only seasonal employment, I am afraid that it will always be difficult to avoid the present conditions.'[30]

There was irony in this admission of impotence. The eternal optimist and prophet of development had never before faltered in his faith in his ability to create jobs and wealth; now he could only throw up his hands, cry doom, and blame Ottawa.

Nor did he have the excuse that he did not know the dimensions of the problem. He had every reason to know that Ontario and Canada confronted a crisis which neither immigration methods nor seasonal unemployment could have caused. H.C. Hudson, the superintendent of employment services offices, regularly supplied him with reports surveying the provincial situation. 'The condition,' stated the report of 28 June 1930, 'is not confined to any one area but is general throughout the entire province. ... The significant feature of the present situation is not only the number of persons unemployed but the prevalence of part-time work in the factories of the Province. Ordinarily in June the manufacturing industries are working full-time or overtime, but this year at least 75 per cent are operating on a part-time basis or with greatly reduced staffs.'[31] Hudson also supplied statistics, compiled by the provincial offices, including aggregates and local breakdowns. At this time 11,788 had registered as unemployed compared to 5194 the previous year and Hudson estimated that in total there were 49,656 jobless. He also added a note on the economic effects of such a decline in purchasing power. 'The effect of this condition on the buying power of the various communities is serious and it is being felt to a great extent by retail merchants in every line.'[32]

Ontario, with its outmoded system of relief and welfare services, was tragically ill-equipped for the agonies of the depression years. Soon many of the province's municipalities were bankrupt or virtually so and the flimsy apparatus in which Ferguson had placed such pride collapsed around the ears of his political heirs. But even before the cataclysms of the 1930s, it was apparent that the province's vaunted social service structure direly needed overhaul or replacement. Ferguson himself admitted as much when in the midst of the 1929 election he abruptly appointed a Royal Commission on Public Welfare.

Chaired by stellar Tory P.D. Ross of the Ottawa *Journal* and including as commissioners J.M. McCutcheon, the chairman of the province's pliant civil service commission and D.M. Wright, a businessman, it was given broad terms of reference which enabled it to 'investigate and report upon' the whole range of hospital, penal, correctional, child care, and institutions for the elderly 'and any cognate subjects.' The potential existed for painstaking investigation. The Tory election pamphlet, *Plans and Projects for a Greater Ontario*, asserted that what was desired was a thorough investigation which would enquire into the methods used in other countries and would 'result in a great forward step being taken. ... The Commission will undoubtedly be able to lay before the Government a programme which should be an accurate guide to the Administration for many years to come.' The government, it continued, 'is thoroughly seized as to the need for increased assistance with respect to the portion of the population which temporarily or permanently required public aid.'[33] The phrasing suggested that the Tories were still thinking in terms only of those who could not pay their own way yet this tacit admission that all was not well was encouraging. The appointment of the Ross Commission signified that Ferguson's confidence in Lincoln Goldie and Dr Godfrey had been shaken and that he realized at last the need to look beyond the government for guidance and new ideas. The order-in-council formally establishing the Commission was not passed until 10 September 1929, after the election was safely out of the way.

Unlike some of their successors, Ross and his colleagues completed their work in less than a year while their expenses, totalling $5,116.98, would hardly pay the postage costs incurred by more recent royal commissions. But even if he had hoped for a report which would provide guidance for a major shake-up and perhaps ease his task of cabinet reconstruction, Ferguson never dreamed that Ross's findings could represent so sweeping an indictment of the status quo or that his recommendations would prove so far-reaching and expensive. The Toronto *Star* put it well when it commented that 'the complacency, not to say pride, with which the people of Ontario regard their social institutions has been rudely disturbed. ... The report shows that this province„while it may have been an example for other communities 20 years ago, is backward in its provisions for the sick, the feeble-minded and the delinquent and must spend large sums of money and make sweeping changes...'[34]

The commissioners had found little to praise. Almost without exception there was overcrowding, a need for new construction, a deficiency in modern equipment. There was a terrible lack of preventive work in the field of medicine and a need for periodic clinics where people could receive early advice and treatment. There was practically no such thing as follow-up work after the child, the patient, or the prisoner left institutional care with the result that 'we break the work off just when we may have got to the best point to make it effective.' One reason for this was the lack of a corps of trained social workers; the Social Science Department at the University of Toronto, which produced practically all personnel in the field, was too small and the commissioners believed each Ontario university should offer an equivalent program. It found that a couple of hundred social workers could be given positions at once and hundreds more would be needed shortly.

Ross and his colleagues were brutally frank in their assessment of conditions in jails and mental hospitals, the latter entirely a provincial responsibility. Idleness, lack of proper classification systems, and gross overcrowding were the rule, not the exception. Provisions for inspection were scandalously inadequate with one provincial officer and two assistants responsible for nearly 400 hospitals, charitable and corrective institutions. Among institutions of the same type there was little effort at co-ordinating programs or exchanging information. 'As regards the Corrective Institutions particularly, there is an unassorted, unstandardized, unstudied system of commitment, transfer and admission, which results in an overflow of delinquent population in these institutions, consisting of a mixture of normal, mentally deficient, light and very grave offenders, and unplaceables.' Turning to the nostrum of the day, the commissioners suggested that statistics indicated that much crime was due to heredity and unchanging mental deficiencies and recommended that Ontario consider following the practice of some provinces and American states and resort to sterilization.

What had gone wrong? Why had once progressive and still wealthy Ontario allowed such a state of affairs to develop? Clearly many Ontarians were surprised and shocked by this indictment. They had too easily assumed that their province still led the way in such matters, as perhaps it had in the days of Mowat and Whitney. Overconfidence and conceit had led to complacency and for too many years, perhaps since the day of W.J. Hanna, the province had marked time. Nor had its leaders really comprehended how the growth of the great cities and the development of new social and economic structures had rendered increasingly irrelevant the nineteenth-century way of doing things. Told by their leaders that all was well, Ontarians for too long had been willing to rely on private charities and on local governments to carry far too much of the burden.

Provincial inspectoral provisions had come to be treated too casually but even if made more rigorous could not have provided the vigorous central direction, the sensitivity to new methods and ideas and, above all, the more substantial financial contribution which conditions now demanded. Yet in no area was there more reliance on private initiative and local control than with respect to the Children's Aid Societies and these received high praise from the commissioners. Even so, they pointed out that the provincial contribution of $45,000 when compared to total disbursements of almost $600,000 did not 'indicate undue generosity on the part of the Provincial authority' and recommended as well that the societies' shelters be brought firmly under provincial inspection and the powers of the Provincial Superintendent of Neglected Children be increased. In other areas, they found even less justification for the lack of provincial assistance and superintendence.

In the final analysis, Ross regarded the problem as financial. Provincial politicians, particularly after the Drury débâcle, had been too fearful by far of increased expenditures. Now the Ross commission called for such increases and defended them on the grounds that they represented the course of true economy. A mental hospital for the north, completely reconstructed facilities at London, two new vocational schools, half the cost of a new sanatorium for treating tuberculosis, an expanded Bowmanville, and various other projects at a capital cost of between $20 and $25 million were described as 'absolutely and immediately desirable.' Other facilities were also needed, including a cancer hospital, a provincial psychiatric hospital, and a large expenditure to improve the equipment of practically all existing facilities. 'Let it be said, bluntly, too, that as to capital expenditure, the suggestions made in this Report should not be interpreted as calculated on the future needs of the province. They are not. They are assertions of present needs. If every new institution or construction spoken of were in existence tomorrow, all of the accommodation should be filled up next day.' Large increases in operating costs would also follow. Yet the commissioners calculated that the annual cost to the province of all matters dealt with in the report was then about $8 million and if the recommendations were carried out the increase would only be about 25 per cent. 'There may be real economy,' they pointed out astutely, 'in wise expenditure.' Comparisons with social expenditures in several American states were not in Ontario's favour. The investment on good roads, exclusive of the cities and the north, was $200 million since 1909, $350 million on the Hydro and, very recently, $50 million on railroad construction. Human resources had not received the same attention.

Indeed so far as the structure of expenditures was concerned, the recommendations were conservative. In a sense the commissioners, like Ferguson, proved unable to transcend the political culture in which they operated. Thus they did not suggest any very radical change in the balance of provincial-municipal functions or in the sharing of costs between the two governmental levels. In the area of general hospitals, for example, some provinces paid a grant for every patient but the Ontario contribution was still restricted to indigents. The commissioners noted that for the year ending 30 September 1929, total expenditure on general hospitals was $10,140,782.42; of this the Ontario grant covered $932,088, the municipalities contributed $1,565,942.81 and the paying patient paid most of the rest. Yet the only significant complaint the commissioners levied against this structure related to the failure to cover the full cost of indigent care and they suggested that in the future the burden should be relieved entirely from the hospitals, with the province paying a quarter of the cost and the municipality all the rest. And in recommending the construction of new sanatoria, the commissioners advised that this be done on the basis of province-county co-operation, with the province paying only half the cost. All this reflected the influence of the existing system. The only major change in the grant structure suggested was that infant care be included in grants paid by both province and municipality to the general hospitals. If the depression had started even months earlier, the commissioners would have been hard pressed to justify their failure to recommend a more radical reform of the provincial-municipal financial relationship in the welfare field.

Finally the report noted the organizational and administrative confusion then existing and pointed out that no fewer than 56 statutes dealt with the matters under review. Therefore, it suggested, some restructuring seemed in order and the government should consider the possibility of creating a Department of Public Welfare.

The Ontario press tended to accept this remarkable and courageous report at face value. Ferguson's reaction was a curious mixture of shocked surprise and of anger that the commissioners had dared to make such sweeping criticisms and suggest so many costly innovations. Finally he demonstrated an almost shame-faced admission that there was much sense in what was recommended. On 26 August he told Irving Robertson that 'there are a great many suggestions contained in it with which I would be very reluctant to agree. ... I am sure you will agree that there are a number of things that could not possibly be adopted at the present time, if indeed any Government can be found to face the expenditure and responsibility involved in carrying them out.'[35] Others were less fearful and Edward Reid, the managing director of the London Life Insurance Company, assured him that despite the cost, 'every right-thinking citizen will heartily support the Government in improving a situation which is by no means creditable to the leading Province in the Dominion...'[36]

The enthusiasm of those in the field was unrestrained. Dr E. Ryan of Rockwood Hospital, Kingston, described the Ross Report as one of the great state documents of recent years. 'The spirit of research manifested in this report, the wide range of subjects studied, the fearlessness with which the recommendations are made and the far-reaching effects of such recommendations cannot but impress every citizen...' Responding cautiously, Ferguson told Ryan he was greatly indebted to Ross for his efforts but 'it will take a long time to carry it out and many features are so distinctly matters of Government policy that they will have to have full consideration.'[37] Obviously, there would be no swift and comprehensive prime ministerial acceptance. Nonetheless, before leaving office weeks later, he would demonstrate that he had no intention of assigning the report to some convenient shelf and forgetting it existed.

In the field of education there was no shock to jolt the Ferguson government out of its complacency comparable to that offered by the Ross Commission. Perhaps there should have been, for the reforms of the day were far too much directed either to externals, such as bigger and better schools, or to achieving traditional goals in an age of turbulent growth. Significantly, Ferguson defined Education as 'the department that leads all others in importance to the State' and he meant that in no abstract sense. Still the dedicated 'Herbartian,' he did not allow his strong Empire nationalism to turn aside his commitment to Canadian studies and in 1928, in an effort to instil patriotism and promote citizenship, he substituted Canadian for British history in the third year of the high school curriculum. The move, which won immediate criticism for duplicating the courses of the first year and turning children out of secondary school bereft of British history, was resented by many parents and denounced by a number of Orange lodges.[38]

Another favorite project was the preparation of a new general history and of two books of biographical studies entitled *Great Men of Canada*. Inscribed with the label 'presented by Hon. G. Howard Ferguson, Minister of Education,' they contained an introduction in which the minister asserted that 'it is widely held, and I believe correctly, that the proper approach to more extended courses in history in the schools is through biography...'[39] Both the general history and the biographies, Ferguson told Robert Borden, were 'designedly written in simple story form, giving them a romantic tinge in the hope that they may interest public school pupils in the history of their country...' and also 'develop greater patriotism in the growing generation.'[40] By some strange oversight, the first volume dealt with not a single Liberal figure, causing considerable controversy, but when the second appeared in 1929 a full Grit panoply had won representation as fit subjects for patriotic consideration.

The conventional nature of Ferguson's goals, which included, of course, the desire to maintain a stable society and to provide workers able to cope with the needs of an industrial age, should not obscure the imagination and vigour of which the department was occasionally capable in the 1920s. There remained as well a significant commitment to social justice. Ferguson and Dr Merchant were still dedicated to the proposition that the day had come in Ontario education when the province must reach out to those beyond the great urban areas who were not in a position to benefit from the facilities and opportunities city children took for granted. Pointing out that only about six per cent of Ontario's children went beyond the public school, Ferguson insisted repeatedly that 'the great problem ... is to secure education for the out-lying sections of the province – as far as possible educational opportunities equally for every boy and girl....'[41]

Of course his first administration had contributed to the solution of this problem. Because rural schools posed the primary difficulty, they were encouraged to do continuation work wherever possible, other schools were allowed to offer courses for whatever part of the year their constituency might be willing to attend, and for those untouched by these measures the province had instituted and provided financial support for correspondence courses. 'The Department,' noted the 1930 report, 'receives grateful tributes from those who benefit by the courses and already a number of pupils have passed the high school entrance examinations.'

When the opposition of the universities delayed his plan to establish college-style academies across the province, the Premier turned to another avenue. His 1928 report raised the possibility of extending the program of instruction in the elementary schools, 'so that the pupils, especially those who reside outside of urban centres, may not be forced unnecessarily to leave home for the instruction to which they are entitled...' Whether the quality of work offered in the senior levels of the elementary and secondary schools improved very substantially as a result of those efforts is unclear, but certainly the desire was there on the part of the Department to effect a change for the better. In his 1929 report Ferguson pointed to his recent decision to require two years of normal school work for teachers who aspired to the highest certificate and he asserted that the purpose of this was to provide teachers better qualified to carry on this more senior work.

None of this reached to the root of the problem, however, and Ferguson pressed on with grim determination in his efforts to convince stubborn rural

Ontarians that significant progress could not be achieved without school district consolidation. For him this had become almost a crusade and each year he risked the displeasure of the rural voter by presenting legislation. In 1928 he told the House that he had reason to believe that the OEA was ready to endorse the proposed reform.[42] A few days later 600 rural trustees rose to the challenge by again condemning the plan unequivocally; only 12 offered support. 'The Premier may put this bill over,' one delegate pointed out, 'but he cannot stay long in power if he does.'[43] By this time he had tired of his annual humiliation and effected a change in tactics. The 1930 departmental report said little about township boards, but it did announce that the province had assumed control over the appointment of county school inspectors.

Piecemeal reform was all that the temper of rural trustees would allow. Ferguson had done everything possible and perhaps the way was eased somewhat for his successors by his extensive educational efforts. In 1938 the Hepburn administration would resort to special stimulation grants but even so the process remained slow and continued on into the 1950s and later. By that time departmental officials had become convinced that the township area itself was too small and that still more consolidation was needed.

It was well for Ferguson's peace of mind that other changes could be achieved more expeditiously. Technical and vocational education remained a high priority. When Ottawa, much to the Ontario premier's indignation, decided to withdraw the financial support offered since 1919, his 1928 report lamented the decision and announced that 'the failure of the Dominion to go on with its obligations will not be imitated by this Province.'[44] When the federal legislation expired in 1929, 'only Ontario had utilized much of the available monies.'[45] Vocational education in the province continued to be developed in the closest possible conjunction with actual employment situations. The Department worked closely with employers and many students attended classes part-time while holding down a job. Gradually a full system of apprenticeship classes developed in the province's largest centres and the movement culminated in the important Apprenticeship Act of 1928 which formalized and extended the developments of recent years. In this area at least, Ontario was in the van of North American progress.

Departmental officials were also able to take advantage of the technical education programs being offered to make major incursions into the field of adult education. Evening school instruction was carried on extensively and the 1928 report noted an attendance of 39,000 adults in 61 evening schools. Another worthwhile feature of the evening industrial classes was that by 1929, forty schools with an attendance of 3166 were providing English-language instruction for 'New Canadians.'[46] The inculcation of principles of citizenship was seldom absent from the purposes of the Ontario educational establishment.

Much of the progress in these areas was made possible by the prosperity of the decade, which permitted a new degree of innovation and experimentation. In these circumstances, more advantage was taken of the Auxiliary Classes Act of 1914 which allowed local boards to establish special classes for below average and handicapped children. In December 1920, only 26 such classes had been organized; by 1930 there were 283 in operation serving 5893 children and two or three boards were experimenting in the use of such classes for children with special aptitudes.[47] The province paid half the excess cost of such schools. To a degree, education had always been supported as a useful technique of socialization. That it continued to be so regarded despite the democratic impulses of the decade was clear from Ferguson's 1930 report where the boast was made that with the provision of non-academic, direct-learning types of classes under provincial legislation, 'the number of commitments for juvenile offences in Toronto has decidedly diminished. Records from these schools show that hundreds of girls and boys who under other conditions seemed inevitably doomed to social wastage are now self-supporting and self-respecting citizens.'

An even more direct attempt at social management was the province's well-publicized venture into the field of mobile education, the railway school car. By late 1926 two cars were in operation and two more were added in the course of the next few years so that by 1929 they covered a circuit of 600 miles in the Ontario northland. Part of each car served as a schoolroom and the rest was living quarters for the teacher and often his family. Occasionally a dental practitioner also came along to provide a much-needed service for northern communities and Ferguson took steps to extend this service to include medical facilities. In terms of publicity, the railway school cars were an unabashed success; they received extensive international attention and won wide acclaim for the Department of Education.

They were also a practical achievement of note. The cars would be left in one place long enough for the teacher to offer his lessons and to organize a full complement of work to be done before his next visit. The assistant chief inspector's 1927 report to Ferguson was lavish in praise of what had been achieved. The teachers, dedicated and imaginative men, were almost over-whelmed by the enthusiasm of children and parents. Inspector Gillies pointed to one Indian boy who 'came by canoe 32 miles up the river to the School Car with his hamper of food to last him a week.' Two other boys, David and Arthur Clement, came 40 miles in mid-winter, set up an old tent, thatched it with balsam boughs, and lived there week by week as the school car came along. The children appeared starved for education and one teacher reported that 'they want to work day and night.' The same was also true of some of their parents and the school car system turned education in the north into a family experience. When a mill closed or railway or other work shifted, the school cars did likewise, stopping at the most convenient points along the line. 'It is thus that station points vanish and rise as population shifts,' recorded a teacher, 'Rural population has moved to Mileage 58. We will stop there. Anstice has almost disappeared. Rapphoe is a new station. We will have 38 pupils still.'[48] What a boon these cars were to the pioneers hard at work on Ontario's last frontier!

In the north the Department's goal of promoting citizenship and patriotism seemed even more important than in other parts of the province. Eighty per cent of those served were of 'non-English' origin and the departmental reports noted proudly that 'through night school work in English and associated services, the communities are being wrought over into the fabric of loyal Canadian citizenship.' Library books were carefully selected, the most prominent feature of one of the cars was an immense Union Jack and the 1929 report noted happily that 'Bolshevik propaganda finds no place or acceptance wherever the school car operates.'[49]

The school cars caught the imagination of Ontarians and of many beyond the province and the Tories exploited their success for electoral purposes. The campaign literature of 1929 repeated the boast that the cars were 'exercising a wholesome Canadianizing influence all along the lines.'[50] One of the teachers was used to address service groups and educational gatherings and the school cars went on display at the CNE. Indeed many of the policies and programs of the Department were used for propaganda and Ferguson as minister was not averse to so using them. On scores of occasions he filled speaking commitments across Ontario by telling his audiences of his government's great achievements in the field of education; as usual, the Tories were successful in appealing to the province's pride in itself and its sense of accomplishment. Mowat and Whitney had used the same technique. Now, under Ferguson, Ontario and the Conservatives progressed together; the Tories were once again the governmental party.

The anti-communism which informed the school car strategy reflected the Premier's own strongly held beliefs. When he received a letter in March 1930 from a Swedish resident of Montreal who had lived in Russia, pointing to the existence of communist activities in Ontario and praising him as 'the first Premier in Canada who really sees the danger of letting this propaganda spread...' he responded that 'we are taking all possible steps to curb the activities of the communistic element in this Province. I think the situation is pretty well in hand.'[51] Although he still considered that 'the most insidious type of propaganda' was being spread among northern Ontario school children, he reported that 'with the agencies we now have established to combat this movement, I am advised that it is not making the progress it did some time ago.'[52] The deepening depression created considerable cause for alarm among the guardians of Ontario's political purity. A few weeks later he remarked again on the growth of communism and asserted that 'this Government has set its face against the movement and is constantly making efforts to suppress it.' The problem, he insisted, was the country's immigration methods and in August 1929 he suggested to King that the right of deportation should be extended 'to at least ten years.' The communists, he believed, were 'amply financed' and 'they adopt all sorts of ingenious methods to spread their vicious doctrines,' particularly among the children. 'We should have the arbitrary right of deportation for the sole reason that they are undesirable.'[53]

Such a willingness to use the coercive power of the state to enforce a narrow ideological conformity was disturbingly pervasive in provincial policies in the 1920s. Although education was first in line, it appeared as well in the area of immigration where Ferguson's goal was to protect the province's existing ethnic balance by attracting British immigrants. By 1928, convinced that 'we cannot secure sufficient agricultural settlers in the British Isles,' he was anxious that the province look elsewhere but only if the 'right type' of settler was available. Believing that large numbers of people had been brought to Canada 'whose ideas of citizenship and civil responsibilities are not only entirely removed, but in many cases absolutely antagonistic to the spirit of our institutions and life,' he satisfied himself during a European tour in the summer of 1928 that 'in Northern Europe there is a splendid type of people who could be readily assimilated.' As a result, the province began to make 'a special effort to secure Danes, Hollanders and Swedes.'[54]

When even this activity alarmed some of the more zealous defenders of a British Canada, Ferguson replied that 'I yield first place to nobody in the matter of maintaining British domination and ascendancy in this country.' Propounding once again the crude racial assumptions held by so many Canadians in the 1920s, he insisted that 'the Nordic races have proven, by our experiment where we have brought them here, that they do exceptionally well, and ... seem anxious to weave themselves into the general life of the Province.'[55] In the north such elements were particularly valuable for there 'one of our difficulties is that the British settler is not a bush man, generally speaking.' It would be many years before multiculturalism would become an official policy, adopted enthusiastically by Ferguson's political heirs.

He was equally ready to intervene when he received complaints about 'dirty books' in libraries and bookstores. Legislation passed in 1926 required the proprietors of private libraries to secure a permit and Ferguson told one bookseller that if there was a refusal to withdraw offending books after a warning 'his permit can be withdrawn from him and he will be subject to penalty on summary conviction.'[56] Ferguson believed the type of book in question to be 'obviously vicious and objectionable' and he offered assurances that 'there will be no attempt to restrict, regulate or supervise booksellers or libraries in any manner other than that which I have indicated, nor is it my intention to appoint a censor.'[57] If controversy arose, the matter would be referred to the deputy minister. Still, the new legislation, an amendment to the Public Libraries Act, seemed symptomatic of a growing tendency and was disturbing to many. It was opposed strenuously by the Toronto District Labour Council and heartily endorsed by the provincial executive of the IODE. The legislation was phrased in dangerously general terms. It gave the minister the power to withdraw the permit not only in cases 'where immoral or seditious literature has been loaned or offered for loan' but also in cases 'where conditions are deemed detrimental to the public interest.'[58] Such a law was capable of much abuse by a zealous or reactionary government.

Increasingly, too, in the late 1920s Ferguson found occasion to admonish officials of the provincial university. In May 1928 E.J. Urwick, the head of the Department of Political Economy, and H.A. Innis of the same department, incurred the Premier's wrath with comments about conditions in northern Ontario mining camps, including the assertion that the miners were prey to the evils of drink and gambling. Ferguson publicly rebuked the two professors, telling reporters that the duty of the staff of the university was 'to teach, not to interfere with matters that are in a sense political.'[59] The same year, when he received complaints that F.H. Underhill of the History Department had argued in a lecture that the British were as much if not more to blame for the outbreak of the war than the Germans, he wrote the chairman of the board. 'I should feel compelled, if I thought it was true, to take steps that might be thought drastic. I have always endeavoured to avoid interfering in University affairs, but I do think it is quite uncalled for that any member of the staff should be exploiting his own views to the students as to the cause of the war.'[60] Cody in turn asked Falconer to make a thorough investigation. The president reported that Underhill denied giving any such lecture and to mollify the premier he emphasized that 'in the War Professor Underhill had a most enviable record.'[61]

A final incident in 1929 revealed again the circumscribed nature of Ferguson's view of academic freedom. Objecting to an unsigned *Canadian Forum* article on rum-running, evidently written by Underhill, he angrily wrote Cody that 'this gentleman should be able to find opportunity for exploiting his talents on the job he is being paid for. It is getting rather monotonous to have my attention called at such frequent intervals to the activities of members of the University staff, which in my view are entirely outside their sphere. These articles are purely political. Some day when the estimates are brought over here I will be tempted to tick off a number of salaries of some men who seem to take more interest in interfering in matters of public policy and public controversy than they do in the work for which they are paid. I am writing you this personally as I think you should look into it.'[62]

There is no doubt that Ferguson's own concern was political in the sense that he was responding in some degree to that element of public opinion which resented the alleged élitism of the university. He added in the same letter that during the recent OEA meeting he 'had a talk with several fairly representative men ... and their comments were not very complimentary to the University or its staff.' But his efforts also reflected a still widely held opinion about the functions of the professoriat and the limitations that existed with respect to its participation in public affairs. Certainly Ferguson's attitude was not out of line with the views expressed by Falconer in 1922 in his pamphlet *Academic Freedom*. Falconer had not yet changed his mind about the possible dangers to the academy which might develop from involvement by faculty members in matters of political controversy; Ferguson's interventions seemed to offer justification for the president's cautious position.

Yet if such a viewpoint remained widely accepted, and if Ferguson's bark seems to have been worse than his bite, the whole position was potentially and perhaps actually debilitating. In Toronto in the 1920s the establishment exerted an occasionally suffocating influence and it would have taken a brave faculty member to dare to incur the wrath not only of Ferguson but probably also of such figures as Cody, Falconer, and Flavelle. Although the evidence is slight, it may well be that Ferguson's raw political power largely intimidated members of the University and stifled what could have been a creative participation in public affairs. If so, it was the province which suffered most and Ontario political life was a good deal duller because of it.

Perhaps this is to make too much of scattered incidents. On another issue, faculty and administration did not hesitate to oppose their will to the Premier's. When he learned of the extent of the faculty's resistance to his proposed transfer of the first- and second-year work of the universities to the high schools, Ferguson appears to have hoped that the University of Toronto Board of Governors would prove more co-operative. The day before a scheduled January 1927 meeting between the board and the president, he told Sir Joseph Flavelle that he could readily understand why university people 'should not be enthusiastic about the loss of a portion of their student body and the revenue that comes from them, but that is a college problem while mine is a province-wide problem.' As he went about the province, he assured Flavelle, he was impressed by the complaints people made about the cost of university; hoping to ensure the support of the influential industrialist, he reminded him that the purpose of the change was to disseminate educational facilities as widely as possible.[63]

Ferguson made it clear that the issue must be decided in private without recourse to public debate. In late February, Bowles of Victoria, McCorkell of St Michael's, and Maurice Hutton of University College were all quoted in the press as opposed to the Premier's scheme. 'In 50 years experience,' Hutton stated of a faculty gathering, 'I have never known a full academic meeting ... which was so amazingly close to unanimity.' A few days later the Liberals scored points in the House by criticizing the proposal. Forthwith Ferguson despatched a letter to

Falconer. 'I will be glad,' he began menacingly, 'to have your view as to the propriety of Principal Hutton ... giving interviews to the press upon this subject...'[64] Falconer meekly expressed his 'great regret' and assured Ferguson that Principal Hutton 'did not realize the impression that would be created...'[65]

By this time the matter had dragged on for almost a year; many faculty, Falconer told the Premier, were becoming restless over the uncertainty about the government's intentions. The delay, however, was the result not of any reconsideration on Ferguson's part but of the impasse which had developed. On 11 March, Dr Merchant provided Ferguson with a closely argued rationale which represented the Department's latest thoughts. The emphasis throughout was on the continuity between this and the Department's other reforms, which all aimed at the one objective – the equalization of educational opportunity. Merchant pointed to the extensive demand across the province for easier access to university level work. He noted too the declining percentage of students at the University from outside Toronto. Higher standards, a longer term and increased costs were barring the doors of the university to many deserving students. Schools and colleges, however well equipped, Merchant continued, 'have no direct influence upon the young people who are outside their doors.'[66]

There followed some additional forceful arguments. The honours graduates of the universities were well equipped to offer college level instruction in Ontario schools; the influence of the university would thereby extend to communities which would otherwise remain untouched. Similar programs in Britain had achieved great success and made it possible for British universities to offer three-year honours degrees. The universities need fear no lowering of standards for they would remain in control of admission to their second-year pass and honours programs. In a telling thrust, Dr Merchant suggested that because of the university emphasis on research, students might receive superior teaching in the proposed colleges. Many students would use the additional year at home and the experience offered to decide whether they wanted to continue in university level work, thus lessening the wastage of an expensive sorting-out year at a remote centre. But the overriding consideration, the memorandum urged, was 'whether the influence of university life be confined to a period of three years and extended to a greater proportion of the young people ... or continue to be spread over a period of four years and be confined very largely to students of the City of Toronto and from the homes of the rich outside.' The document concluded with an implied threat:

The University can continue to maintain its present provincial character only on the condition that it continues to serve the whole people and not a section or class. We have now reached a stage where this question cannot be regarded in the light of a mere academic discussion. No government can expect to secure from the legislature, from year to year, increased votes for the university when such a large proportion of the attendance is drawn from a limited area.

It is impossible to state with precision what motivated Ferguson and the Department to push ahead in the face of determined university opposition. One must assume that they were sincere in their stated purpose of equalizing opportunity. No doubt there were those who resented the élitism of Toronto's honours courses. The powerful democratic thrust of the 1920s did not see the universities in the van and there are many references in Ferguson's correspondence to the unpopularity of the university. In 1928 he may even have considered outflanking his academic opponents by passing legislation to allow the city to impose municipal taxation, but Falconer argued that Varsity's substantial contribution to the life of the city justified continued exemption.[67]

Yet there is little indication in his correspondence that Ferguson was responding to a popular movement or to any rising tide of anti-intellectualism, although these considerations were present. Of greater importance was the role of the Department of Education, which resented the semi-autonomous position of the universities, and of Dr Merchant, a vigorous reformer deeply committed to the democratic educational ideal. Ferguson supported his forceful assistant because he shared his philosophy. He believed the University of Toronto was quite large enough and that it would not serve the cause of education to allow the pace of expansion to continue. In his view, many of its departments, such as household science, were more fitted to the secondary level, allowing more of its resources to be devoted to the development of postgraduate work. 'In other words,' he told George Henry a little later, 'I would move the scale of the University activity a peg or two higher.' Finally, he had no doubt that 'the Department of Education who pays the bills should have a larger voice in University affairs' and he assured Henry that although many would protest, 'the fact is ... that you should have something more to say than merely approve of expenditures that have already been made and issue the Provincial cheque without question.'[68]

The province in the 1930s and 1940s would have benefitted greatly by an expansion in graduate school facilities and many communities about the province would also have gained much from some kind of junior college program. The trend towards more provincial intervention in university affairs was also the way of the future. Ferguson's stance should not be misunderstood. As the spokesman of the conservative establishment, he was a true friend of the university, and academe in the 1920s rested on foundations more secure than they would be again for many a year. Yet the Premier was also responsive to popular currents and for this reason was willing to do battle for fundamental reform. Unfortunately Ferguson's political talents did not extend to the campus and the matter was laid before the universities with a singular lack of skill. What finally emerged appears to have been a face-saving and unsatisfactory compromise. In 1931 the University of Toronto pass course was reduced to three years, the honours course remained at four, and senior matriculation was for the first time required of all applicants. A certain amount of the pass work henceforth was done in the collegiate institutes.[69]

Ferguson himself remained dissatisfied with the relationship between the province and the universities. He had reassessed his earlier opinion about the withdrawal of support from Queen's and Western and now recognized that they were doing work which the province must continue to finance. Apparently his nagging dissatisfaction with the size and some of the practices of the University of Toronto now made him look with greater favour on the regional institutions. He also knew that the whole procedure for determining university finance lacked system and was in dire need of rationalization. In 1927 he had told the House that the University of Toronto fiscal year might have to be changed to allow the members to scrutinize the institution's budget more effectively. In 1928 or '29 he tried to get former Dominions Secretary, L.S. Amery, to head a royal commission which would conduct a thorough investigation into both the financial and general administrative problems of Ontario's universities. Amery, however, was not then available; the commission was never appointed.[70]

Equally inconclusive was the drawn-out dispute over separate schools. With the adverse judgement of the courts, Roman Catholic frustration mounted and only by a rare combination of luck and good management did Ferguson avoid another explosive politico-religious crisis of the type which had bedevilled previous Ontario administrations. Early in 1927 he faced a serious disagreement with Catholic leaders who wished to carry their appeal to the Supreme Court of Canada. Ferguson bluntly told Thomas Battle, their legal representative, that 'the suggestion of an appeal to the Supreme Court came to me as a great surprise. It is rather a circuitous route to reach the final Court and I am not sure that I am justified in contributing to this unnecessary expense.'[71] Whether he was interested in saving time, as he indicated to Battle, or whether he simply wanted to avoid the Canadian court, is uncertain. Catholic leaders told the Premier they would be subject to censure if it could be argued that they had failed to take advantage of every possible appeal avenue. Battle warned Ferguson that, if he persisted, Catholic laymen might have to be told that the Supreme Court had not been used because the government declined to pay costs and 'our people would say that he was afraid to let our case be taken before the Supreme Court of Canada...'[72] Charles McCrea also made this argument and finally Ferguson agreed to pay costs of the case already heard in the Ontario Court of Appeal and of the Supreme Court reference if the matter could be expedited so as not to delay the government's desire to reform its general grants policy. 'Oh, well now,' Ferguson assured Battle, 'your people have always found me generous and you do what I am urging you to do and you will still find me generous.'[73]

On 10 October 1927, the Supreme Court divided almost equally with Chief Justice Anglin and Justice Rinfret supporting the Catholic claim in its entirety and Justice Mignault on most points; justices Duff, Newcombe, and Lamont rejected it on all points. The court was equally divided, so the appeal failed. The justices had split along religious lines. A sympathetic Chief Justice even offered to try to go to Toronto to discuss the decision with Archibishop McNeil.[74]

The JCPC on 12 June 1928 rejected the appeal on all counts. Viscount Haldane for the Board found that a separate school was only 'a special form of common school' and that 'the power of regulation must be interpreted in a wider sense than that given to it in the judgement of the Chief Justice of Canada.' Any appeal against a supposed injustice should be to the Governor-General in Council and through him to Parliament.[75] Of course since the Manitoba schools question that avenue was largely illusory and the Tiny Township judgement struck a harsh blow at Roman Catholic hopes. For a while, Catholic leaders were at a loss to know what course to pursue. McNeil and Senator Belcourt, now co-operating closely, agreed that little would be gained by appealing to Ottawa. Belcourt suggested that 'there is more hope of securing some measure of justice by putting our case openly and squarely before the present Prime Minister of Ontario.'[76]

The Catholic need was more pressing because with the grants and secondary school questions before the courts, private discussions had been ongoing with various corporations by which the Catholics attempted to win recognition of their rights under existing legislation. These negotiations had led nowhere and the province seemed unwilling to facilitate matters by a clarifying amendment. Many Catholics after the Privy Council decision believed that a show of force had become necessary. The decision, Franklin Walker has written, 'spurred Catholic leaders to action and there resulted an agitation supported by clerics and laymen which made the Charbonnel campaign of the 1850s look pale.'[77] Perhaps so, but with the Catholic vote so firmly tied to the Conservative party and with Ferguson so deeply entrenched in power, a political agitation was a dangerous course to pursue; many Catholics still believed with Belcourt that the man who had done justice to French-language education might also act on behalf of the separate schools. The bilingual schools question had demonstrated that he would act only during a political calm and that agitation would defeat the Catholic purpose.

It was likely, then, that continuing negotiations and the hope of concessions contributed to a caution which served to keep the issue largely out of the 1929 election. Although the Legislation Committee of the Grand Lodge of the Orange Order urged that every county master 'make sure that the candidate elected in the coming election is one who will oppose any further concessions to separate schools and especially resist the attempt to divide the school taxes of corporations,' the campaign did not degenerate into a Catholic-Protestant brawl.[78] The extent of Ferguson's political domination and his careful management helped ensure that.

In 1930 both sides became increasingly uneasy, the Catholics because they had no real assurance that Ferguson would act, and the enemies of separate schools because they feared he would. The pages of the Orange *Sentinel* leave no doubt that members of the Order were apprehensive. Judge Scott, who had played such an important role in settling the bilingual question, warned that any yielding to Catholic demands 'will arouse an agitation which cannot be controlled' and would damage the Ferguson government and detract from Bennett's hope of success in the approaching federal election. 'I ought to know, and I do know, the temper of the Orange Order in this Province as well as anyone. In the recent French language flurry I was convinced from the first that the rank and file could not be stampeded because they had no personal contact with the question and that the general public was not interested. This affair is, however, very different. There is a determination everywhere...'[79]

Ferguson regarded the mounting agitation with some dismay. On 30 January, he told the parish priest in Kemptville that the whole subject was 'a matter of wide-spread discussion and controversy' and that he had had many representations from both sides. 'Every aspect of the subject must be studied most thoroughly and carefully...'[80] That he had no intention of taking any initiative during the 1930 session became clear when he told a priest from Merrickville that he had not been 'advised' about any legislation being presented but that any measure would have 'the fullest consideration' from the government.[81] Meanwhile there were private discussions with the Premier and members of the House were approached by the Catholic authorities. In mid-January Bishop O'Brien of Kingston noted optimistically that 'I was in Toronto last week and the ground looks good.'[82] Father Burke, the chaplain of Newman Hall, also reported that discussions had been held with the Premier and his deputy minister and that 'as a result, Ferguson's mind is more receptive than at any previous time.'[83] Father Burke recognized that 'we have got to play politics and play them efficiently,' and advocated boring from within. And Ferguson's old friend, Tom McGarry, offered tactical hints, suggesting to Burke that one way to make progress would be through discussions with Harry Cody, 'Ferguson's alter ego.'[84]

Obviously Ferguson saw fit to hold out hopes; perhaps he would have found a way to manage important concessions. However, with his resignation later that year, the negotiations became the responsibility of his successor, George Henry, with results which were disastrous for the Ontario Conservative party.

If Ferguson by careful management had largely neutralized the separate school question and kept Orange and Green together in Tory ranks throughout his tenure as leader, his achievement in Ontario's other great schools problem was still more impressive. The schools concessions granted to Franco-Ontarians in 1927 had not yet stood the test of time and for a while he faced a determined opposition from some Orangemen convinced that he had thrown over principles sacred to the Order for the sake of political expediency. In November 1927, he appeared before the Orange Legislation Committee. Although much of the press painted a picture of an embattled Premier facing furious Orangemen in a critical turning point in his career and winning support for his policy by a brilliant oratorical display, his appearance in fact was carefully stage-managed and the Orange committee obliged by going on record as favouring a five-year trial period for the new policy.[85] In 1928 Ferguson defended his settlement before the annual conventions of the Grand Lodges for both Ontario West and Ontario East. The *Star* suggested hopefully that the Orange rank and file would make their displeasure known but Ferguson again won nearly unanimous backing. 'Support Ferguson and help win Quebec' was the cry used at the Ontario West meeting while one disgusted delegate complained that the Ontario East convention was run as though it was 'a political convention with all the Tory heelers from Ontario East packed in an 80 by 80 hall.'[86]

When Orange dissidents tried to excite a backlash in the 1929 election through the instrument of an 'English Language School League,' they failed so totally that the Ottawa *Journal* could assert that 'there is no longer a language issue in Ontario.'[87] That this was so owed more to the skill with which Ferguson had moved and to the unique relationship between Tories and Orangemen than to any sudden transformation of public opinion in a province which a decade earlier had been so totally committed to Regulation 17. Nonetheless Belcourt believed that the acceptance of the settlement proved his contention that when English-speaking Ontarians realized the full iniquity of Regulation 17 and its implications for national unity, they would do justice to the minority.[88] Perhaps so, but the Franco-Ontarians also owed their victory to their long and arduous resistance and to their shrewdness in substituting a willingness to negotiate for the earlier politics of confrontation which had inflamed the issue and prevented any compromise. For French-language schools in Ontario, still poor and under-privileged, the struggle was not over; yet a great victory had been won. The French community, accepting the implications of its minority status, had achieved more as a pressure group than it could ever have gained through the angry manipulation of the politics of race and religion.

All in all, Ferguson's record as Minister of Education was satisfactory and more. As anticipated, he had handled the position in its political dimensions in exemplary fashion, preventing educational issues from degenerating into cultural crises and contributing creatively to the permanent solution of at least one long-standing grievance which had disturbed the educational and political peace for a generation. Two of his major projects, it is true, met furious opposition, but refusing in each case to apply raw political power, he resorted instead to tactics of gradualism and pressed on without losing sight of the objective in view.

Always guiding his course was his overriding desire to extend the advantages of educational opportunity to groups, classes, and regions hitherto largely untouched. The 'concessions' he made to Franco-Ontarians owed much to this grand design. In a sense the expansion in numbers of students in attendance, particularly at the secondary school level, and the great school construction boom together represented sufficient monument to him and his associates. Yet despite the costs of expansion, the provincial contribution to educational costs remained remarkably small, with the grants for primary education increasing from $3,332,68.02 in 1923 to only $3,586,466.69 in 1928, and with support for secondary and technical education increasing at a somewhat higher rate.[89] Even in this field, which touched his interests most closely, he remained true to the ruling dictum that the principal burden must be borne by the municipality. It was because he still held to this traditional approach to the social functions of government that he never attempted to override the wishes of local trustees, who owned the schools and retained principal responsibility for their operation.

Just as important and characteristic was his refusal to accept the educational status quo as the last word in wisdom; virtually every year his departmental report contained some admonition to change and progress. In 1928, for example, the report proclaimed that 'the education system ... which rests upon its achievements and is content to mark time is really in a declining state, since changes to meet fresh situations are imperative.' The minister must be guided 'by the wisdom of progressive minds in education and not by honest reactionaries, well intentioned as their efforts may be.' This was an injunction from which his own government might have benefitted if applied more imaginatively to a broad range of social policies. Yet in the 1920s the pace of the day was slower and change for the sake of change and the worship of statistics of growth did not crowd out other considerations to the extent that they would in a later period. Under Ferguson and Merchant, growth occurred within the context of a firmly held educational philosophy and definite goals; and the most pronounced of these were the still firmly embedded Herbartian approach to curriculum and the democratic expansionism best expressed by the cliché, 'equal educational opportunity for all.'

If his predecessor in the portfolio, R.H. Grant, exaggerated when he stated in 1924 that there was no man in Ontario 'better able to grasp or be more seriously interested in educational questions' than Howard Ferguson, he had provided, nonetheless, a leadership which benefited many and served the province well.

The nationalism and commitment to ideals of citizenship which underlay Ferguson's educational philosophy also found expression in the persistence and quickening of his imperial vision. As his experience deepened, his wider understanding of Canadian political and economic realities served to increase his devotion to the imperial idea. In a 1924 letter to Stanley Baldwin he had informed the British Prime Minister that 'we in Canada, and particularly in this Province, are staunch imperialists, and are anxious that no opportunity be lost to disseminate and promote greater British sentiment in this country.'[90] The schools, of course, were one instrument of this purpose and each year that Ferguson was minister, an Empire Day volume full of patriotic sentiments was distributed. Immigration policy was another means and the province in the 1920s was a vigorous advocate of attracting more British settlers. The activities of Ontario House in London were expanded, extensive new quarters were provided in the Strand, and a propaganda sheet called the Ontario *Bulletin* was started which by 1930 was receiving wide circulation throughout Britain.

The ceremonial side was not neglected. When the Prince of Wales visited Canada in 1927, Ferguson and King jostled each other for precedence, with King lamenting at Niagara Falls that 'Ferguson was again put ahead of me. I felt deeply incensed. It looked like a deliberate plan...'[91] During the visit Ferguson placed his view of the imperial relationship before Baldwin, who accompanied the Prince. By this time Ferguson's acquaintanceship with British statesmen was extensive; from 1925 he made almost annual trips to Britain and the continent. As he watched the course of imperial events unfold and observed the growing focus in Canada on the concept of 'status' to which the 1926 Imperial Conference devoted so much attention, he was increasingly disturbed. Although he may have overestimated the extent to which Canadians were emotionally committed to the imperial idea, he was under no illusions about the weakness of economic and institutional ties. As the leader of a province whose economy was increasingly dependent on the United States, he greatly feared the inexorable drift of Canadian affairs. The Americans, he knew from experience, were hard and calculating bargainers with a firm sense of their own national interest; unless Canadians were eternally vigilant and possessed an equally calculated sense of purpose, the future looked bleak for the Canadian nationality.

In his view, the best hope lay in the strengthening of the traditional countervailing force. Because the formal ties that bound Canada to Britain were already so few, he indignantly resisted all efforts to cut those that remained. Ontarians became accustomed to speeches in which he trumpeted his opposition to the idea of a Canadian governor-general and to the suggestion that appeals to the JCPC should be abolished. The Canadian Supreme Court could not, he insisted, 'contribute to the binding together of the various sections of the Empire' as did the Privy Council 'sitting in London laying down the same judicial principles, expounding the same ideals all over the Empire...' Some day, he continued, 'somebody must rise up in this country and say we are going to change the course of the Canadian ship of state, we are going to turn toward the east instead of toward the south; and we are going to see that Canada not only leans upon the British Empire, but that she clings to the British Empire.'[92]

Those who spoke of the Empire in such terms were easily attacked as mossback Tories and Ferguson was particularly vulnerable to such ridicule. When, at a

1927 banquet in honour of retiring Lieutenant-Governor Cockshutt, he appealed for a return to titles, only half his audience bothered to applaud. But what made his imperialism a force of some significance was that it was of the head as well as of the heart. Certainly Taschereau and others who believed in the importance of provincial rights and were fervent supporters of the appeal to the JCPC would have agreed with the opinions he expressed in a Hart House debate in late November 1927 which considered the question of Canada assuming the right to amend its own constitution. 'We must look to the future,' he argued, and examine the effect of such a change on Canada's destiny. Noting with approval that Canada already had achieved a new status and the Empire had become the Commonwealth, he insisted that the question of amendment was different in kind and reached to the very vitals of the Confederation compact. 'Our constitution is the result of a pact signed between ourselves and placed in the hands of the British Government as referee.' And there it should stay. Ferguson could see only disintegration for Canada if the imperial tie was snapped. What kept the provinces together was the security of the British connection. There followed a pessimistic rendition of the state of a purely Canadian – little Canadian he usually called it – nationality. Canada, he asserted, had no more homogeneity than it had in 1867.

Our situation, our geography and topography are the same as in pre-Confederation days. Go to the Maritimes. They'll say that what holds Canada together is the British connection. If they thought only of their economic welfare they would leave Canada for the United States. Go to British Columbia. Their real interest is down the west coast.[93]

In 1928 Ontario's throne speech expressed the view that 'the compact of Confederation should be strictly observed in all respects and that the future of Canada can best be assured by maintaining the status of the provinces as established by the British North America Act.'

Unlike many imperialists, Ferguson did not take refuge in banal generalities when it became a question of a practical program. Although he believed in institutional ties and on occasion seemed to hint that he favoured some kind of imperial federation, this course he wisely never pursued. He never lost his faith in the importance of symbols and he won great applause from the imperialist camp when he decided in 1929 to call all the provincial highways, 'The King's Highways.' He believed it would serve as 'a constant reminder to our own people and visitors that we are part of the Empire' and was pleased when his action elicited an enthusiastic response, including a letter from Charles G.D. Roberts, who told him that 'a Canadian cannot be a sound Nationalist without being at the same time a thorough British Imperialist.'[94]

His real interest, however, lay in closer Empire economic relations. Regarding imperial free trade as 'an economic fallacy' which Canada's economic interests could never allow, he advocated closer trade relations and a return to the old alliance which in John A. Macdonald's day had contributed so greatly to the development of Canadian resources.[95] In the 1920s many Canadians still held this view, often with an increasing sense of urgency. Thus Charles Magrath, himself attracted for a while by the delusive notion of an imperial parliament, believed that economic ties would bind the empire most effectively. 'Mr King,' he told Ferguson, '...places too much reliance on the *Golden thread* idea, as a means of holding us all together. If I could only have any faith in that idea, I would feel fairly happy but like you, I consider the *material advantage* plan is essential.'[96]

In furtherance of this, Magrath in February 1928 prepared for Ferguson a confidential memorandum, full of anti-American bombast, looking to the possibility of a great Anglo-Canadian partnership in the construction of the St Lawrence Seaway.[97] The sceptics saw in Ferguson's opposition to a Canadian-American seaway only a desire to embarrass King and politics clearly were not absent from his motives; yet he was moved primarily by nationalist concern. 'I am opposed,' he assured Mr Justice Hodgins of the Ontario Supreme Court in January 1930, 'to giving sovereignty in any form to a foreign country over so vital a matter as transportation.'[98] While he admitted that the cost of the seaway would be substantial, if spread over 40 or 50 years, 'it is not going to be prohibitive. I would finance it by going to the British Government. They need food, and we are a great food producer. ... Why should we not have a partnership of some kind with them?'

Ferguson's suggestion overlooked the reality of American sovereign rights in the international section of the St Lawrence River and the limitations of British power and of British interest. Still, it was an expression of the Ontario Premier's abiding distrust of the American Empire and reflected his desire to call into play the partnership with Britain to redress the balance. Just as the CPR had been built as a great nationalist enterprise with British support, so too, he believed, the St Lawrence, Canada's historic river, might play a similar role in protecting the national heritage and reviving the old alliance. However unrealistic such opinions may seem in hindsight, Ferguson argued his case with considerable force. If more had shared his concern, the inroads of American economic power into Canada would not have proceeded at the pace they did.

Unfortunately, the influence of a provincial premier, even Ferguson of Ontario, was severely circumscribed. As well, his remedy, the power of the British Empire, was increasingly illusory. A day would soon come when he and his friends would have every opportunity to test their ideas. Then he would discover that in the world of power politics and international economics, Canadian nationalism was at once much more and much less than another form of imperialism.

16

Boss Ferguson

The prosperous twenties they were called and nowhere with more justification than in Ontario. The Ferguson government was the unblushing beneficiary of boom conditions in most sectors of the economy; lovingly and without shame, it regularly set before the province the statistics of development and progress. Each year, the Treasurer announced a surplus and as loudly as ever the claim went forth that of the province's ordinary revenue, which in 1928 amounted to $58,400,000, 'less than $2,000,000 are collected as taxes from all the people.' During the 1929 election, the Tories pointed with pride to a debt reduction program which had lowered provincial obligations by the then not inconsiderable amount of nearly $10,000,000. The Hydro, despite its great expansion program, contributed large sums to this cause under the Power Commission Act of 1926; similarly the T&NO RR's branch line construction program did not prevent its paying substantial amounts to the province out of surplus earnings. In clever but occasionally oppressive propaganda, the government claimed credit for all good things under the sun.

With taxes low and consumer demand great, industry prospered and tourism expanded as never before. The province's Publicity Bureau reached out for the tourist dollar, and in 1928 over 2,700,000 automobiles entered Ontario, an increase of 14 per cent over the previous year.[1] An administration conscious of the value of public relations expanded its Motion Picture Bureau until it became the country's largest film producer; its documentaries, shown widely by commercial operators, were not calculated to hurt the image of the Ferguson government.[2] In all areas, it seemed, the statistics told the same story. The number of customers served by Hydro increased from 348,028 in 1923 to 522,770 in 1928; generating capacity in the same period went from 756,982 HP to 1,141,887 HP.[3]

Prosperity and political management had stifled all but the tattered vestiges of agrarian protest. Rural depopulation, which had propelled the farmer into politics, apparently had been checked with assessed rural population increasing by over 35,000 between 1923 and 1928 and agricultural production growing by almost $78 million.[4] Similarly, the north continued to boom with public works and road construction much in evidence. The roads from Pembroke to the Sault and from Fort William to the American border were rebuilt and improved as were many others and the Ferguson Highway was widened and continued to Cochrane; the government's embarrassment was no more than momentary when the lead car in the procession which opened the new branch sank out of sight in a bog of muskeg, leaving the dignitaries to scramble to safety as best they might.[5] Those were the ordinary hazards of northern existence and no one seems to have been unkind enough to point an accusatory finger at the patronage practices of the provincial government. The Department of Northern Development continued to administer the funds voted under the Northern Development Act. In 1930, this was increased in amount from five to ten millions and a vision is conjured up of government agents, discreetly doubling as party workers, scurrying about the north in search of worthwhile projects for governmental largess. Despite scattered protests, the development funds were still allotted in a lump sum without scrutiny in departmental estimates. In the day of the boom, the opposition itself seemed disinclined to ask hard questions about even the most dubious practices.

Possibly the potential critics were intimidated by the burgeoning statistics of growth. Between 1923 and 1929, for example, mineral production increased by an annual average of 35 per cent over that attained during the Drury administration, reaching in 1929 the unprecedented level of $117,960,722.[6] There was in this period no change in mining tax policy; the Tories still insisted that 'a widespread and prosperous mining industry is worth more to the province at large than any unduly heavy impost on production.'[7] The circumstances of the day all but denied the critics of this approach a reasonable hearing for it seemed self-evident to most Ontarians that the prosperity of the mining camps, the payment of substantial dividends and still larger amounts 'in wages, for food, machinery, and supplies of all kinds, has had a wonderfully stimulating and vivifying effect on all kinds of business throughout the entire province.'[8] It was a simplistic claim, no doubt, but to many its truth seemed unimpeachable; in any case, there was no one to challenge it. There would come a day, and soon, when the Conservatives would no longer be as anxious to assume responsibility for the economic condition of the province. But that time was not yet.

Undoubtedly the most vivid symbol of the spirit of the age and of its practical accomplishments was the automobile. By 1928, over half a million motor vehicles, 'or nearly as many as the whole of the other provinces combined,' were registered in Ontario and almost 430,000 of these were passenger cars. By August 1929, the province had 1831 miles of paved road with no fewer than 1278 of these constructed by the Ferguson government. In 1928, the province devoted over $11 million to highway expenditures.[9] Ontario, in a variety of ways, was forced to recognize that the age of the car had arrived. One sign of the times was the appointment in 1929 of a royal commission to investigate car insurance rates; another was the increasing of the highway speed limit in 1927 to the reckless level of thirty-five miles an hour, coupled with the requirement that all buggies and other horse-drawn vehicles be equipped with tail lights for driving after dark. Another innovation was a 1927 order-in-council requiring drivers to acquire a licence and subjecting beginners to an examination.[10] By charging a fee of one dollar for its licences, the province provided itself with a significant new source of revenue.

Yet even with this, in addition to the $4,000,000 raised in 1927 from the gas tax and $5,900,000 from motor vehicle permits, provincial revenues did not match the massive costs incurred by the Department of Highways.[11] There followed, therefore, an increase in the gas tax from three to five cents a gallon in 1929. The costs of highway building remained a staggering burden for most provinces and pressure for still greater expenditure was intense. In February 1930 the city council of Port Arthur, for example, requested a road between the Sault and the Lakehead which would obviate the need for traffic to resort to American highways; similarly, the editor of *Maclean's* wrote Ferguson to press for provincial assistance in the completion of a continuous trans-Canada highway system. However appealing he found such prospects, Ferguson had little choice but to point out that the enormous expense necessitated a policy of gradualism.[12] Also he believed there was a national dimension to such work and hoped that some day the dominion would provide the assistance the provinces had repeatedly requested.

His concern with economy never prevented Ferguson from starting new programs if he believed a need existed. For years he had hoped to involve the province in the field of applied research and in 1928 he presented legislation to established the Ontario Research Foundation.[13] As well, the CMA had been pressing him to help provide research facilities for the hard-pressed small industrialist and his work in Education and Lands, Forests and Mines had long since convinced him that the need was there. Now in a move which proved enormously popular with a press and public imbued with the faith of the day that research would provide more wealth and better health for all, he helped direct a private fund-raising campaign and saw to it that the province matched the sum raised dollar for dollar.

Yet the capital so raised was not sufficient to cover the full cost of industrial research projects and Ferguson and the ORF's first chairman, Joseph Flavelle, devised the radical expedient of encouraging similar groups of industries to band together, bear the cost of the inquiry as a group, and enjoy in common the results secured. The group concept, however, gradually faded from view and as it did the role of government, to Ferguson's disappointment, increased commensurately. Ferguson had regarded the ORF as another example, somewhat like

Bowmanville in the social policy field, of government providing leadership and giving limited support to private individuals or groups anxious to carry on an endeavour of significance to the larger society. Although the ORF within its limitations of size proved a substantial success in its research service to government and industry, and although it set an example of aid to industry through research which Ferguson's Tory successors would one day proudly emulate, the new organization from the beginning owed its success primarily to the Premier's imagination and practical support. Just as the inadequacies of Ferguson's belief that the citizenry must bear the principal burden in the social welfare field had become glaringly apparent, so too the ORF's growing dependence on government demonstrated beyond cavil that here too practical realities were outpacing long-standing conventions.

If the ORF in some ways was the most interesting initiative in economic policy during Ferguson's second administration, it by no means stood alone. Because of his attitude towards Raney's 'Blue Sky' legislation, Ferguson's critics had assumed the government would take no effective action in the field of securities regulation. Yet in 1928, as the speculative fever mounted, he was ready with a really important Security Frauds Prevention Act coupled with a Companies Information Act, legislation which influenced almost every other province and demonstrated that Ontario, if it so desired, could by its example play a leading role in this field in Canada.[14] All this proved necessary, of course, because Ottawa had refused to be goaded by the Inter-provincial Conference of 1926 into taking adequate action on a national level. Equally interesting was the manner in which Ferguson's Tory government proved able to achieve major reform without exciting the kind of opposition which Raney's effort had encountered. Yet even so the legislation, which listed various practices as constituting fraud, required brokers and stock salesmen to register, and companies, whether incorporated by the province or not, to file information about their activities, could not eliminate all the dubious practices which characterized the crest of the speculative wave. The 1930 arrest and trial in a series of famous cases of Solloway, Mills and other prominent financial dealers proved embarrassing to the government and demonstrated the need for even more stringent regulatory measures.

The impression that the Ferguson government remained vigorous and innovative was also strengthened by a flurry of activity in Ferguson's old department, Lands & Forests, a field in which the Premier's strong hand was readily evident. The minister, William Finlayson, was also active and able, or so his legislative record indicated. His Forestry Act of 1927 provided an elaborate scheme for classifying land for purposes of promoting reforestation and gave the province, with safeguards, the power to transfer settlers off land deemed unsuited to agricultural uses, with three townships in Haliburton singled out for initial experiment.[15] Also of significance was the appointment of a five-member

Forestry Board to assist in research and planning in forest management. The Board included Dr Zavitz, C.D. Howe, the Dean of the Faculty of Forestry at the University of Toronto, and three representatives of lumbering companies. Described by one student of forestry in Ontario as 'an active and useful body,' it played an important role until its abolition in 1934 and contributed in some measure to Finlayson's other legislative innovations.[16] The Provincial Forests Act of 1929 extended provincial efforts in the field of land classification, designated several new Provincial Forest Reserves, and appointed a professional forester as overseer for 'the purpose of preserving them according to the best forestry practice and to gradually bring them under a sustained yield basis.'[17] The Pulp-wood Conservation Act of the same year took the province even further in its determination to apply forestry techniques to ensure its forest industries had a permanent supply of raw material. The Act required the pulp and paper companies to furnish the minister with extensive data about their operations and while based largely on an assumption of co-operation it nonetheless gave him 'the right and authority to direct and control the location, sequence or extent of cuttings and to limit the cutting from year to year, by any company, for the purpose of conserving the source of supply and placing Ontario on a sustained yield basis.' Finlayson's program was rounded out by amendments to existing legislation, including changes in the fire protection system of 1917, which imposed new controls over operators in provincial forests and required organized townships to develop a fire prevention system.[18]

While the depression and the upheavals following the Hepburn victory of 1934 prevented the systematic implementation of this extensive program, it remained a monument to progressive intentions and a tribute to the extent to which the influence of the professional forester had penetrated the Department at its highest levels. Dean Howe believed that 'from a forestry standpoint, the third session of the 17th legislature will go down in history as the beginning of an epoch. ... the recent legislation is a challenge to and an opportunity for the profession, such as it never had before in this Province.'[19] Although the future would bring disappointment, Finlayson deserved much credit; so did Ferguson, for the several measures could not have gone forward without his powerful backing and it seems likely that his contribution was not slight.

Legislation, however progressive, has little meaning unless it represents a measured response to particular circumstances and conditions. For years, since his days as a Hearst minister, Howard Ferguson had believed it to be to the mutual advantage of the people of Ontario and the pulp and paper producers that the industry be provided with an assured supply of raw material and that large units of production be encouraged in the interests of conservation, stability, and permanence. In furtherance of these aims, he placed an excessive faith in the business judgement and financial stability of such corporate giants as Abitibi, Spanish River, and Backus-Brooks. Yet because the foresters and the pulp and paper concerns shared an interest in ensuring the perpetuation of the forest, they were able for the moment to work together towards the magic goal of a sustained yield and the Department of Lands and Forests willingly formulated policies which embodied this objective.

In retrospect, it is obvious that the province should have questioned the developmental impulse and have directed its attention more to the general condition of the industry and the state of the market. With existing mills in 1924 and 1925 working at only 80 per cent capacity, the government should have regarded this as a sign of the disorders which lay ahead but, instead, between 1924 and 1929 capacity was increased by 102½ per cent and production by 96⅓ per cent.[20] With the industry's capitalization based largely on bonds, preferred stock, and debentures, and since production of at least 90 per cent capacity was generally required to meet fixed charges, the dangers should have been readily apparent.[21] The failure to apply any restraint may be variously explained. The province, lacking the expertise to assess market conditions, relied instead on the protection afforded by elaborate pulpwood contracts but the various penalty clauses could hardly be invoked until after the companies had called into being a large work force dependent on the continued success of their operations. The companies knew that in these circumstances the province would be most reluctant to exercise its undoubted authority and take punitive action. The pulpwood contracts, for all their imposing legal phraseology, proved of little value in the protection of the people's interest. The owners appear to have taken advantage of the fact that the provincial government was desperately anxious to further any economic expansion which would relieve the bothersome unemployment, which persisted intermittently throughout the decade. Thus the warning signs were ignored; Canadian pulp and paper exports continued to expand dramatically, despite the gradual decline of paper prices. Mesmerized by the statistics of growth, the Ontario and Quebec governments refused to look beyond the fact that they were helping create one of the country's truly great industries to examine in any very critical way the dangers in what they were doing.

The blame for what happened cannot be placed entirely on the shoulders of government. The evidence, while not conclusive, suggests that the dimensions of the impending crisis were not fully appreciated even within the industry itself until early 1928. The province, given Ferguson's preference for the large producer, probably viewed the consolidation movement, which by 1931 left six huge corporations in control of about eighty per cent of eastern Canadian production, as a useful stage in industrial rationalization. But neither the mergers nor the existence of interlocking directorates eliminated the vicious competition which was proving so damaging. A major attempt from within to promote co-operation led to the formation, in 1927, of the Canadian Newsprint Company composed of fourteen mills controlling fifty per cent of Canadian capacity. The Hearst interests, however, were able to negotiate contracts early in 1928 with two disenchanted members and the cartel collapsed in September. Further drops in the price per ton of paper followed and the disarray deepened.[22]

By early summer of 1928, with the Canadian Newsprint Company's failure impending, William Finlayson wrote Ferguson, who was vacationing in Europe, that officials of Abitibi had urged him to call a meeting of the industry to attempt to devise some plan to bring order to the situation. Finlayson's revealing response was that the companies should try to work something out themselves before approaching the government. But after a meeting of the producers led nowhere, Alexander Smith of Abitibi urged Ontario to appoint a controller and to follow with legislation. Finlayson regarded this as absurd. He doubted the province had such power, and told Smith that even if it did 'it would be extremely dangerous legislation.'[23]

Finlayson would not even call a meeting to consider the matter without seeking Taschereau's opinion. He met the Quebec premier in Montreal on 16 July and learned that Quebec was 'anxious to act in conjunction with the Ontario Government...' Finlayson told the Quebeckers that 'we would be opposed to attempting to control the industry in any way' and added that Howard Ferguson had cabled that 'it would be very dangerous to do anything that might antagonize the newspapers and look like an attempt to put up the price.' The most Finlayson thought should be attempted was a meeting attended by the industry and the provinces at which 'the question of over-production could be considered.' He was anxious that the companies cut down on production per mill rather than per company so there would be no danger of entire communities being stricken by companies closing down some mills entirely. And he believed that before any meeting the companies should file detailed statements of their capacities and commitments.[24]

The two provinces agreed to attempt this approach. Although Taschereau wanted an early meeting, the Ontario minister insisted that it be delayed until Ferguson's return. Still leery of provincial involvement, Finlayson continued to place responsibility for the situation largely on the companies themselves. Yet so much was at stake, he told Ferguson, that the province had little choice but to act. Already there was 'a very serious situation at Sturgeon Falls, Espanola and other points like that.'[25] Even so, he believed the province should merely suggest to the proprietors that 'they should appoint a committee who would ... try and find some remedy for the over-production, so that all the mills would be kept running to the greatest possible extent.' Regretting Ferguson's absence, he lamented that 'you are practically the only Member of the Cabinet who is familiar with the situation...'[26]

Taschereau, too, was not yet thinking of leaning heavily on the producers. He told his Ontario counterpart in late August that 'it is not our intention to take drastic measures, but there is a very strong feeling in the paper industry that if

Ontario and Quebec will join hands, a firm attitude will be useful.' Ferguson had reached the same conclusion. 'I do not think we should allow some of these people to make use of the provincial authority to pull their chestnuts out of the fire,' he assured Taschereau. 'At the same time, I realize that it is most important to the provinces that these industries should be stabilized and kept in operation. If they are unable to get together themselves in a very short time, this Government proposes to ask the companies who hold contracts from us, why the Government should not enforce some of the penalties provided in those contracts.'[27] Up to this point, there had been little opportunity for significant provincial intervention. Now the situation of the industry deteriorated rapidly. On the eve of the conference with the companies, finally held in late November, Ferguson in no uncertain terms made it clear that his patience had been exhausted.

In a letter addressed to the papermakers and released to the press, he pointed out that as part of its effort to settle and develop northern Ontario, the government had encouraged the establishment of newsprint mills and had worked to encourage financially strong industries which 'would be able to continue operations, maintain payrolls and markets, as well as protect the thousands of investors all over Ontario through periods of depression.' With this in mind, the government had revised and enlarged the scope of the pulpwood contracts and substantial urban communities had come into existence with supporting agricultural settlements which were 'practically dependent upon the forestry industries.'

Notwithstanding the assistance the Government has given to the paper business, as indicated above, the whole industry today finds itself in a very unfortunate condition. During the greater portion of the past year, this Government has hoped that the good sense of the people in charge of this great industry would bring about some arrangement that would stabilize conditions and enable everyone to carry on. It is apparent, however, that no serious effort along this line has been attempted. Methods have been pursued which have created what appears to be a condition of chaos.

This Government feels that it owes a duty to the people it represents. It does not intend to stand quietly by and see settlers and wage-earners suffer, and small investors all over the province have their savings jeopardized while those responsible for the efficient operation of this business spend their efforts in a keen competition for who can get the largest share of the market for his own particular mill, regardless of what becomes of the rest of the industry, or how the public interest generally may suffer.

It is with great regret that the Government finds it necessary to draw your attention to the fact that you are under contract with this province; that your contract contains a number of important covenants; that many of the companies are in arrears and default has occurred with respect to a number of the conditions and obligations provided in the contracts.

This condition cannot be allowed to continue. I am, therefore, writing you on behalf of the Government to say that, unless the people interested in the operation of this industry take some immediate steps to put the industry on a more satisfactory basis and improve the present situation, the Government will be compelled to give serious and immediate consideration to what action it should take under existing contracts to protect the interests of this province, its investors, its wage-earners, and its people generally.

May I request that you inform me promptly what immediate action is contemplated by your Company, and the others engaged in the industry, to rectify the present situation.[28]

Ferguson's blunt warning served notice that the province would not stand aside while selfish private interests trampled on the rights of the public; yet he had not really budged from the position that the industry had created the 'condition of chaos' and must now put its own house in order. When the premiers and the manufacturers met in Montreal on 23 November, much was at stake. Howard Ferguson took the position, then and later, that 'if the paper industry is to be preserved from a serious breakdown, if, indeed, not a total crash, it can only be done through the industry as a whole, sharing the burden on an equitable basis' and he urged as strongly as he could, 'a policy that would conform to this principle.'[29] On 27 November, he was 'still hoping that the attempt made to straighten out the newsprint situation will meet with success.' Much hinged on the attitude of A.R. Graustein of International, whose contract with the Hearst interests threatened to lead to further price-cutting and corporate bloodletting. Ferguson believed that 'if Mr Graustein is really in earnest, he can rearrange the Hearst contract.'[30] Back in Toronto before the negotiations concluded, he received a wire from Taschereau on 30 November proclaiming that a satisfactory agreement had been reached.

The solution conformed closely to the policy desired by the premiers. The Newspaper Institute, an unincorporated body composed of the major producers doing business in Ontario and Quebec, with the exception of International, Spruce Falls, and Ontario Paper, was established to bring a measure of control to the situation. The companies agreed to a set of rules and regulations for the conduct of the paper business which prorated tonnage among them according to rated capacity on the principle that the companies would run not only their most efficient mills but would afford employment to all mill communities by using as well their less efficient operations.[31] The meeting, occasionally stormy, had lasted the best part of a week before an agreement was hammered out. With the available business then unevenly distributed, those companies which would be reducing their production in the interest of a better distribution did so only after the premiers demonstrated they would brook no opposition.[32] As the new Institute's counsel described the settlement before a 1929 investigation by the United States Federal Trade Commission, the rules gave effect to the mandate of the premiers, who agreed to 'act as arbitrators in the event of any dispute arising.'[33]

Clearly, only pressure from the premiers allowed even that degree of accomplishment. The three firms which did not join cited the American anti-trust legislation, to which Taschereau responded testily that 'the Sherman anti-trust law does not apply in Canada.'[34] To the threat of American intervention was added the certainty of pressure from the powerful publishers' association. Ferguson's fear of this group was based on an appraisal of the extent of its power. In the past, it had demonstrated its ability to bring enormous influence to bear on American legislators and there was real danger that intervention on the part of the Ontario and Quebec governments, either to raise or maintain prices or to distribute orders within the industry, would result in vigorous retaliatory action. On 2 July 1930, the Federal Trade Commission charged that Ferguson and Taschereau were responsible for an increase of $5 a ton in the price of newsprint to Hearst newspapers and recommended to the Senate that Alaskan mills be developed to prevent a further raise. By this time, the Canadians had grown accustomed to threats from the south. The previous January, Ferguson learned that some of the large American publishers were thinking of looking to Norway and that Graustein was busily reopening antiquated American mills. 'The whole atmosphere,' he told Taschereau, 'indicates a combined determination to resist the claims of Ontario and Quebec for more generous consideration. I do not suppose there is anything we could do to frustrate such plans. I doubt if they will be carried through.' Taschereau was even more sanguine, believing talk of going to Norway to be 'mere bluff' and professing confidence that the old American mills could be operated only at a loss.[35]

Still, the threat refused to disappear. A few years later, Ontario directed G.T. Clarkson to attempt to determine to what extent American publishers could indeed obtain their paper supplies elsewhere than in Canada. His report asserted that 'they could cut down their Canadian imports of newsprint by upwards of 900,000 to 1,000,000 tons a year. ... Any such action ... would be disastrous to Canadian Newsprint Manufacturers and undoubtedly close up most of the Canadian mills.'[36]

The Sherman Act was not the only reason for the failure of the entire industry to join the Institute. Spruce Falls President F.J. Sensenbrenner and Vice-President J.H. Black explained to Ferguson that their company had 'spent almost $30,000,000 actual cash' on its Kapuskasing operation, which had not come into production until late 1928, 'about the time the seriousness of the situation of the industry was fully realized.'[37] Unlike other plants, Spruce Falls had had no opportunity to build up its capital reserves. As well, its product was 'practically all sold' yet the other manufacturers refused to take this into consideration when prorating ratios were being established or to make allowances for the fact that Spruce Falls was owned largely by the *New York Times* Company. Sensenbrenner also feared pressure from Institute members to raise prices, repeating again that this would alienate publishers and cause them to turn elsewhere and he suggested that 'the disastrous failure of the copper pool, the rubber pool, the nitrate pool, and ... the wheat pool, are noble illustrations of the disaster' which followed artificial efforts to maintain or increase prices.

No doubt the other companies stayed out for reasons which to them seemed equally compelling; International under Graustein was fighting to establish not only an expanded pulp and paper empire but to win incredibly wealthy power concessions in Quebec and was unlikely to surrender docilely. Still, the three dissenting firms in varying degrees did promise to adhere to the rules of the Institute. Sensenbrenner, Ferguson later reminded him, gave his personal undertaking that 'you would comply with the terms and conditions upon which that organization was established and authorized me to give my personal assurance on your behalf that you would do so. Knowing as I did from long and intimate dealings with you that I could absolutely rely on any promise you made me, I gladly undertook to induce the other members of the Institute to accept my assurance without your signature.'[38]

Spruce Falls and International together did most to destroy the Institute but the other companies were by no means blameless. For a short period, the intervention of the premiers did do some good. In the face of an agreement between Hearst and International Paper on a per ton price of $50, the price was raised after arduous negotiations conducted in the early months of 1929 and a general industry price of $55.20 was agreed to, with Canadian mills operating at 75 per cent capacity.[39] Abitibi, which had been most active in pressing for governmental intervention, seems to have benefitted most for it had been operating at only 50 per cent capacity. The company would have preferred to concentrate on its more efficient mills, but Ferguson insisted that its Espanola and Sault Ste Marie operations receive a fair share. Evidently Abitibi, having gained what it was after, then chose to disregard its part of the bargain; work at Espanola was confined to one of six machines and some two hundred men thrown out of work asked the Premier to intervene.[40] A few weeks later, Ferguson wrote J.H. Black of Spruce Falls that he was 'hearing disturbing rumblings about the paper situation. The rumor comes to me that you are not playing the game, and a gentleman prominent in Quebec has practically warned me that the Institute is likely to blow up and Spruce Falls will be responsible...' Presumably, it was Taschereau who had complained and Ferguson told Black that 'I do not like these disturbing rumours and it will be rather awkward if this arrangement should collapse and it be charged against one of our own Ontario operators.'[41]

But collapse it did. The prorating agreement could have no effect on American competitors and, in November, Sensenbrenner pointed out to Ferguson that the manufacturers of Ontario and Quebec, with the exception of International 'constitute only about 52% of the production capacity of the continent. All of the other manufacturers running full time, get the benefit of the advance without sharing the burdens of curtailment...'[42] International had always dragged its feet over prorating and continued to deal privately with Hearst in a way which jeopardized the Institute. When International's activities threatened a new price war, another conference took place with the premiers in attendance; the crisis was averted temporarily and A.R. Graustein vigorously denied that he was catering to American interests. 'We are Canadian,' he insisted, 'in our sympathies and our outlook...'[43]

As 1930 began, distrust was rampant on all sides. The diverse interests of the companies undermined all the efforts of the premiers and threatened the existence of the Institute. Abitibi, in particular, remained recalcitrant. In April, the City Council of Port Arthur protested that although the company had promised to operate its Thunder Bay mill at 70% capacity for March, there was 'no sign of opening of the mill' and families were being compelled 'to move from our City.'[44] With the companies on the verge of bankruptcy, threats from the premier would carry little weight.

When Ferguson learned that Spruce Falls intended to renege on its agreement with him and the Institute, he warned Sensenbrenner that a return to individualism would result in a total crash. 'Of course, I thoroughly appreciate the fact that you are entitled to do this if you so decide, but ... if you break away and begin cruising on your own account, it will be a signal for a campaign of piracy which will ultimately destroy the huge investment, as well as the commercial importance of this huge enterprise ... Candidly, Mr Sensenbrenner, I must tell you that it hurts me very deeply to think that Spruce Falls Mills, whose birth I attended, whose baptism I performed, and whose progress I have endeavoured to encourage, should be the one institution to initiate a course that inevitably, to my mind, means destruction.'[45] By this time no longer at the head of the government, he intervened because of his special knowledge of the situation and because, as he told Sensenbrenner, his impending departure 'makes me feel all the more keenly the prospect of a general breakdown at the very moment I leave.' And he assured George Henry that 'the one thing that has kept the industry alive and avoided the closing of a lot of mills ... is the fact that they have distributed the available tonnage on a proportionate basis...' Everything possible should be done, he told Henry, to convince Sensenbrenner of the need to maintain the Institute 'as the only method of preventing a war of prices, which would be disastrous.'[46]

Spruce Falls was not the only problem. Already Price Brothers and St Lawrence had broken away and new efforts, probably ill advised, on the part of the provinces and some of the companies to raise the price per ton caused further strains.[47] The Institute's formal collapse followed shortly and what Ferguson had feared now happened. In the early 1930s, Abitibi and Backus-Brooks went into receivership, Price Brothers went bankrupt, and other companies underwent radical reorganization. 'By the end of 1933, practically none of the newsprint companies was earning its bond interest.'[48] A great industry was in a shambles, thousands of innocent people were victimized, and the economy of eastern Canada suffered a staggering blow.

The blame may be variously assessed. A.R.M. Lower writes that 'the one agency which cannot be freed from responsibility is the provincial government.'[49] Undeniably hindsight dictates that a halt should have been called and expansion carefully controlled in mid-decade. Yet it is difficult to ascertain how and in what way the provincial governments could have acted to shape the course of events. In the early 1920s, Ontario officials believed they were presiding over the development of a great industry firmly based on an expanding demand; in the later period, when problems were perceived, provincial regulatory activities were rendered ineffective partly by the desire not to destroy existing jobs and partly by the manoeuvres of powerful foreign publishing interests and the desperate activities of overextended companies facing imminent bankruptcy. In the late 1920s the provinces acted vigorously but their efforts, which eased the blow temporarily, finally came to naught. Perhaps if Ontario had possessed in the early stages of the expansion a bureaucracy able to make a realistic assessment of the limitations of the market or if Ferguson and his advisers had been less fully imbued with the expansive spirit of the day, they would have been more cautious. Instead they succumbed to the mood of the times; they were defeated by the complexities of a situation they could not control and by the power of the international corporations whose first concern was the demands of an American market.

Even in England, Ferguson remained greatly concerned over the condition of the industry with which he had been so intimately connected. Writing to Henry in December 1932, he lamented that 'this was Canada's greatest industry' and suggested 'it still has a marvellous field, and the British people are tremendously interested.' Incredibly, at the depth of the depression, he could suggest that if reorganization could be effected, 'I feel sure that British capital will be available for further expansion...' But Ferguson still believed that only strong provincial action taken in co-operation with Taschereau could set matters right. Those who controlled the industry, he told Henry, 'have pursued a selfish, tragic policy of late. There has been no attempt at cooperation but each has been struggling on his own account by desperate means to survive.' Ferguson pointed out that tens of thousands of people had suffered and if matters were allowed to drift much longer, the credit of the province and its industries as investment opportunities would be grievously injured if not destroyed. 'I have not heard if you have taken any action to re-possess yourself of the rights under your agreements and power leases,' he noted pointedly, 'but I talked to a great many people in Canada while there amongst the bankers and investors, and they all agreed that drastic action must be taken to bring these people together.'[50]

The time for caution had passed, but Henry could only reply that G.T. Clarkson after his careful study of the industry, including an assessment of the availability of alternative American and foreign supplies, had advised against drastic action. Without buying from abroad, the United States, reported Clarkson, could take care of itself for all but about 600,000 tons. 'Conditions are very serious as it is,' Henry related 'and we think that if we did anything that would appear to be antagonistic or in any way a restraint of trade in relation to the United States, there might be a serious reaction and they would purchase from outside sources possibly their entire imports and we might be left in the lurch without any market at all.'[51]

Henry's fears prevailed. Little was done. Not until 1935 did Ontario and Quebec pass tough legislation which established and policed an effective pro-rating system and even this did not pull the industry out of its difficulties. Recovery was not achieved in the 1930s.

Significant in another way was the longstanding struggle to defend and exploit the province's water power resources. From 1928 to 1930 the dominion-provincial dispute over control of water power in navigable streams continued its dreary course as the principal actors remained determined to protect what they regarded as the rights of their respective domains. For a while, it seemed the pronouncement of the Supreme Court might lead to an easing of tensions and allow engineers and contractors to get to work. The reference had gotten off to a bad beginning when the federal government submitted the questions to the Court without inviting the provinces to participate in their phrasing. Ferguson was furious, believing this procedure to be in defiance of what had been agreed to. He was not far from the mark and King confided to Taschereau that it had been done deliberately to avoid having to confer with the unfriendly Ferguson administration.[52] W.N. Tilley was at once suspicious that the questions had been phrased to hinder any final appeal to the JCPC and Ferguson believed they were put so generally in order to make any definitive answer impossible and to cause more delay. He protested angrily and was backed by Quebec. Ottawa agreed to confer with the provincial lawyers and two additional questions were added.[53]

Unfortunately for Ontario power users, the situation was complicated by the enormously involved issue of the St Lawrence Seaway and negotiations with the United States. Ferguson had always insisted that power and navigation be dealt with separately; he continued to press Ottawa to approve the application filed so long ago for a power development at Morrisburg. And once again Charles Magrath was warning of an approaching crisis for Ontario users. The Gatineau purchase of 1926 had done little to relieve shortages in northern and eastern Ontario and pressure for more and cheaper power was mounting from those regions in particular. Now, in January 1928, the National Advisory Committee which King had appointed in 1924 to make recommendations on St Lawrence development brought down its report.

It would be difficult to imagine a more viciously anti-Ontario document. One may assume that the viewpoint of Sir Clifford Sifton, probably its most forceful member, and also of the private power interests of Quebec, well represented in the person of Wilfrid L. MacDougald, had prevented serious consideration being given the Ontario Hydro point of view. The Committee recommended that development first be undertaken in the national or Quebec section and suggested that the cost might be borne entirely by private agencies in return for the right to develop power. At a later date work might be carried out on the international section, the cost to be borne by the United States on the grounds that Canadian interests would already have incurred enormous expenses. Ontario, it suggested, in the period before the international section was developed, could buy whatever power it needed from private interests in Quebec.[54]

In January, Ferguson asked King for a copy of this astounding document but King, adding insult to injury, offered the excuse that the Committee asked that its recommendations remain private for the time being and refused to comply.[55] The report was made public in April 1928. C.P. Wright, the most careful student of St Lawrence development, has concluded that the Committee's purpose apparently was 'that of preventing the Hydro-Electric Power Commission of Ontario ... from securing an early development of its share of the power available at the international rapids, and of compelling it instead to meet its urgent and increasing needs for power by purchases from the private companies of the province of Quebec.'[56]

The whole affair was a disgrace. The Committee's membership was riddled with conflicts of interest and a minority report promptly challenged its conclusions. The Canadian minister at Washington submitted the gist of the recommendations to the United States government, cautioning that there were constitutional difficulties which remained to be resolved with the provinces; the American response, however, was that the Canadian proposal was a suitable basis for negotiation.[57] Ferguson, fearing that the province's position might easily be lost to sight in such negotiations, continued to sound the nationalist cry. 'The biggest asset we have,' he trumpeted, 'is the St Lawrence River and we should retain complete sovereignty of navigation to the sea. ... We have unhappy recollections of former international relationships with our neighbours to the South.'[58] In early May he told the Western Ontario Conservative Association he had been pressing King for five years to agree to a power development on the St Lawrence. In a fiery speech, he asserted his opposition 'to selling anything that belongs to Canadians to anyone outside of Canada. ... It would be a serious thing if we were to yield up one tittle of our sovereignty to foreign ownership.'[59]

The Americans, hoping for an agreement, pressed ahead. In July, King cautioned the American ambassador that the Canadian political situation was 'exceedingly delicate.' Premier Ferguson 'would be only too happy to start a row.'[60] King wanted time to prepare Canadian opinion and American Secretary of State Frank Kellogg told his minister that it would be wise 'not to press the matter so as to embarrass the Prime Minister at present.'[61] With Howard Ferguson marshalling the troops for a rerun of the 1911 election, this was the expedient decision.

The St Lawrence situation was political dynamite and King, unsure of his ground, decided to avoid any decision until after the next election.[62] In the meantime, however, he would have to deal with Ontario's persistent demands for more power. In April when he proposed a conference to discuss St Lawrence development with Ontario and Quebec, Ferguson reiterated that his province believed 'the power problem is the most pressing, and is quite separate and distinct' from the navigation project. Ontario needed 'immediate action to save her from a serious crisis so far as power supply is concerned, and industrial and commercial development that is dependent thereon.' Ontario, he pointed out, had been forced because of the long delay in considering its Morrisburg application to buy power outside the province but with $300 million dollars invested in the Hydro, it had too much at stake to permit further delay. He urged, therefore, that, with the questions before the court, power development be allowed to proceed without prejudice to the legal decision, thereby saving the province a great deal of time and 'many millions of dollars.' King waited several months before replying that power and navigation on the St Lawrence could not be separated and that no decision could be taken until the whole matter was dealt with in all its aspects.[63]

The judgement of the Supreme Court was not available until February 1929 and then initial opinion was that the answers were so vague that the reference had been an exercise in futility. King wrote in his diary that he 'could not make head or tail of it' but from an accompanying statement by Justice Duff he 'seemed to glean that the Dominion has no right to go into the navigation business for power purposes as such, that power belongs primarily to the provinces...'[64] There were signs that King now hoped to beat a retreat and stave off a provincial rights campaign in the election. If only the Ottawa development had been at stake, he might have used the decision as an opportunity to state unequivocally that power belonged to the provinces; but with the whole costly St Lawrence project to be considered, such a move would court disaster. Nonetheless King seemed to progress in that direction and a Hydro memorandum dated 26 March which Magrath forwarded to Ferguson noted that 'the judgment has indeed afforded a sufficient sanction ... to enable him in the course of several recent statements in Parliament to recognize that in the main the Provinces had the right of the matter...'[65]

Mackenzie King, however, had more to consider than the respective rights of the dominion and the provinces. With the United States pressing for an early seaway development, he recognized that 'it is the most important question which confronts us and I believe much of the future relations between the US and Canada depends on the skill with which it is handled.'[66] He might have added that with Ferguson and Bennett poised to embark on a nationalist campaign, the future of the Liberal party was also at stake. Therefore his response to the findings of the Supreme Court reflected his usual caution; he pointed out to Ferguson how inconclusive the reference had been and suggested 'the most satisfactory method of proceeding' would be a conference between Ontario, Quebec, and the dominion. Ferguson agreed and urged King to state in advance what his government's attitude would be at such a meeting. Of course King refused and, in any case, it proved impossible for the three governments to get together until early 1930.[67]

In the meantime Ontario's power needs remained as urgent as ever. The convention with the United States to allow Ontario to take more power from the Niagara was at last agreed to but failed to gain the consent of the American Senate. Fortunately an interim solution appeared which temporarily satisfied all three governments. Taschereau, at the behest of the Beauharnois Light, Heat and Power Co., supported that company's scheme to dam the St Lawrence in the national section. Still hoping to undercut pro-Seaway sentiment in Ontario, he agreed that Beauharnois should sell part of its power to the sister province. King, fearful of a political attack by Ferguson, was also pleased that more Quebec power would be made available to relieve the Ontario shortage. And since the Beauharnois purchase would further both the alliance with Quebec and the general political strategy adopted at the Winnipeg convention, Ferguson was also content. When Taschereau as a courtesy submitted the project to him, he replied that 'Beauharnois would seem to me to be a very convenient and favorable point' for Ontario to procure its power requirements.[68] The promoter of the scheme forwarded to King a copy of Ferguson's letter to Taschereau as proof that the Ontario premier would not attack it.

King had reason to fear that Ferguson would object to the speedy approval given Quebec's St Lawrence power development when Ontario's had been held up for years. Ferguson was soon subjected to attack by pro-Hydro and pro-Seaway elements in Ontario but Bennett came to his assistance and convinced Tommy Church and perhaps some others to hold their tongues.[69] Ferguson may also have been influenced to some extent by the impression that in approving Beauharnois by order-in-council on 8 March 1929, Ottawa was accepting some of the essentials of the provincial rights position.[70]

The provincial rights dispute and its dramatic confrontations tended to obscure other important issues involving the Hydro. The alliance with Quebec, so satisfactory in some respects, did not ensure easy agreement when it came to co-operation on the Ottawa. Additional power purchases were made from the sister province in 1929 in a contract signed with Beauharnois and in 1930 another major agreement was negotiated with Maclaren's. 'We must look away ahead, thirty, forty, fifty years,' Ferguson told Magrath, 'if we have confidence in the future of the Province. ... It behooves us, therefore, to secure every horse-power we can on proper terms, and conserve our own powers rather than wait until we exhaust the possibilities of our own property. ... Twenty-five years from now I venture to think we will pay a great deal higher price for any power we might require to buy.'[71] Yet only slow progress was made in negotiations with Quebec to allow development at the Chats and the Carillon, and agreement had not been finalized before Ferguson stepped out of office.

Other advances came more readily. The late twenties climaxed the efforts initiated by Sir Adam Beck to buy out the remaining major private producers and in 1929 the Hydro purchased at a price of $21 million the Dominion Power and Transmission Company serving Hamilton and other southern Ontario municipalities and the O'Brien interests on the Madawaska.[72] Even more significant was the decision to move into the north, long the domain of private corporations, and to undertake a massive program of northern electrical generation. The reasons for this decision are not entirely clear but many of the mine owners were delighted. Jack Hammell of the Howey Gold Mines in the Patricia District, for example, was able to utilize much of the power produced at Ear Falls. In an effusive letter Hammell assured Ferguson that 'you have done more towards the opening up of the north country by giving us cheap power than by any other move that has been made to date.'[73]

If Hydro served the interests of the businessmen, the farmer was not neglected. The enormous extension already in progress of services to rural consumers was carried further by the Rural Power District Loans Act of 1930 which eased the financial load for farmers wishing to take advantage of the new opportunities electrical power offered. The expansion of service and generating capacity was paralleled by administrative reforms which regularized the Commission's financial relations with the province and codified and reformed the body of law which had grown up over the years in definition of Hydro's rights and responsibilities.

Interestingly, the Commission which under Adam Beck's leadership had sometimes ridden roughshod over its opponents and had even defied the powers of the legislature was brought more effectively than ever before under the power of the provincial government and the new chairman made few if any important moves without obtaining the approval of the Premier. Although the Commission retained by statute considerable independence, the issue was now reduced to dimensions which could not compare in significance to the points in dispute in Beck's day.

Chairman Magrath, for example, felt that the Hydro as a commercial enter-prise would be harmed if compelled to answer all the questions posed by members of the legislature. 'There is not a working day of the year,' he pointed out, when government auditors were not at work in the Hydro offices to ensure that the organization was conforming precisely to the conditions of the law. In such circumstances, he believed it not unreasonable that Hydro, following the advice of auditors, 'must regard itself as bound by its status as trustee under existing legislation to exercise ... complete discretion as to whether it will answer the question...' Magrath believed that if the legislature persisted in its desire for an answer, its proper course was to pass a formal order or resolution which would supersede existing statutes. The responsibility for any commercial con-sequences to Hydro would then rest with the House.[74]

Ferguson responded that 'the Government will be prepared at all times to resist the asking of questions calling for disclosures which in the public interest should not be made' but reminded Magrath of 'the wide latitude enjoyed by members of a House whose rules entitle any Member to interrogate the Govern-ment on any public matter. ... The Legislature is the proper forum to elicit and receive information regarding the work of the Commission.' Although Magrath's concern was real and legitimate, the Premier had a firmer conception of the proper relationship between the Commission and the House. Under Ferguson not only was the Hydro tamed but the rights of the members were respected. The significance of the episode was clear to all who recalled the epic battles and irregular relationship which existed between the Commission and the province when Adam Beck had ruled supreme. The commission by 1929 retained little of the unchecked power of an earlier day.[75]

Two months after Ferguson left office, Magrath too stepped down. Together they had achieved much. 'Ontario Hydro,' concluded its official historian, 'was in a stronger position than it had ever been in its short but tumultuous history. ... Entering a depression which was to prove as unprecedented as the boom that preceded it, Hydro's position seemed as impregnable as human ability and integrity could make it.'[76]

In the midst of these events came the 1929 election. Truly it was less an election than a sweeping reaffirmation of Howard Ferguson's unprecedented political power. Ostensibly the issue once again was liquor. In an attempt to rid his party of the prohibition albatross, W.E.N. Sinclair, with the approval of the Liberal caucus, stated in June 1929 that the party was no longer bound by its 1922 temperance resolution; it accepted the Liquor Control Act but believed its administration by the Ferguson government left much to be desired. Sinclair made this announcement only after considerable soul searching and it was much resented by many of his supporters. During 1928 there had been some co-operation with the still aggressively dry Progressives but the new Liberal stance all but precluded success along this line.

Then, in mid-September, with the campaign almost under way, the Liberal leader announced that he favoured another plebiscite. At once the Tories, who had previously jibed that he had finally seen the wisdom of government control, began to mock him for his backtracking. There would be no more plebiscites, Ferguson promised, and the public was in no mood to see the issue reopened. As one correspondent put it to Mackenzie King, 'rather than let the Star and Globe force their program on him he [Sinclair] should have preferred to have lost their support...'[77]

In fact the Liberals were at their lowest ebb in Ontario. During the 1928 and 1929 sessions they were utterly ineffectual in the House. An alert opposition would have found much to criticize in the Ferguson record but Sinclair's major effort in 1928 was a farcical attempt to elevate into a major scandal a case in which a few ballots had been found in the streets of Ottawa after the 1926 election. A hastily appointed royal commission found the returning officer guilty of carelessness.

In 1929 a more serious incident occurred when the press uncovered letters sent by the Tories' 'Central' organization in Toronto to the liquor interests soliciting campaign funds. When Sinclair raised the matter in the House, Ferguson was ready. He pointed out that he had no authority over the Central but that he deplored such solicitation; he thereupon tabled a letter he had sent warning the Central's treasurer that 'surely appeals should not be made to people or organizations who have relations with the government. ... I think you should lay it down as a most inflexible rule that no funds should be solicited or accepted from either distillery, brewery or winery interests.'[78] Apparently the Toronto *Star* had sent wires to every winery in the province asking about Tory fund-raising methods but once again Ferguson was far ahead of Atkinson and his coterie. Now he told the members that he had already asked the Central to return any amounts received and he even won the plaudits of some of the drys for the purity of his intentions. To cap the affair, he induced the House to pass a motion of censure against the *Star* for inaccurately reporting the details of the incident. Similarly, when Sinclair on several occasions complained that the money passed under the Northern Ontario Development Act did not receive legislative scrutiny, he was able to offer no hard evidence of misuse of funds and he won no political yards for his party.

In fact the Liberal situation was hopeless. When one party official on 7 October approached King 'to beg money from the Federal fund for the Ontario campaign,' the Prime Minister reflected that the Ontario party might even emerge from the campaign worse off than before 'and it seems a shame to exhaust what resources we have.'[79] King steered clear of any involvement, informing Sinclair that 'it has seemed to me inadvisable that I should take any part,' but, even so, the greater part of what funds were available had to come from federal sources.[80] After it was all over, Sinclair lamented that 'in most of the ridings there was utter neglect of organization. ... In many ridings there were no chairmen of polls. ... the women were not made a part of the executive. Committee rooms were not opened in many towns. The only result was that voters were left to go to the polls if they chose. ... The party is dead in the ridings...'[81]

The Progressives were deader still. Raney had escaped to the Bench and J.G. Lethbridge, the new leader, inspired no one. There was nothing left to sustain them; only memory kept them alive. Many Progressives agreed with E.C. Drury that their only hope lay in close co-operation with the Liberals and after the 1929 débâcle, the ex-premier bitterly blamed Sinclair for the failure to achieve co-operation. The Liberal leader, Drury informed King, in both 1926 and 1929 had 'followed a policy of edging the Progressives out of the constituencies they held, wherever possible. This culminated in the recent election in seven three-cornered fights where Liberals were inserted into the contest in ridings held by the Progressives.'[82] In each case, the Tories won the seat. King himself lamented that 'Liberals lost, and Progressives lost, because they were fighting each other instead of fighting the common enemy.'[83] He was more honest when he admitted that Ontario had a premier 'in whom the people had confidence' and with whose record 'the province as a whole was fairly satisfied.'[84]

In the months before the election, Ferguson must have had little taste for the rigours a campaign would involve. Both Godfrey and Goldie were in poor health and of minimal assistance even when well, John Martin had been able to do little for months and, more seriously, Charles McCrea was also ill. To McCrea and Godfrey in Bermuda, he sent word to stay away as long as necessary. 'I have got this Health and Labour Department running so smoothly it will not need a minister for some time,' he told Godfrey and he assured McCrea that, except for a few minor amendments, there would be nothing of any significance from the Department of Mines when the House opened shortly.[85] Carrying an enormous burden, Ferguson was feeling its effects more than ever before. He was indisposed for some time before the session began and then in March, Mark Irish reported that 'Ferguson has again been laid away for a fortnight. ... They pulled all his teeth out, and I think removed his tonsils. ... After a few weeks of work in the House he began to suffer from fever, and they put him back to bed. They tell me he is pretty badly used up.'[86] Yet even with his government sadly in need of reconstruction, he hesitated to replace the old, familiar faces.

He could not afford to be idle for long. Believing a federal election would be fought in 1930, he desperately wanted to clear the decks for that eagerly awaited contest by winning a renewal of his own mandate. Thus although the

1929 session offered few indications of an impending election, and the noisy opposition to the increased gas tax indicated it might be wise to wait, Ferguson in reality was anxious to dissolve. W.E.N. Sinclair's ill advised pronouncements on the liquor question provided the opportunity; the province knew that the liquor issue had been finally decided in 1926 and the government's record was easily defended. Although the drys claimed that government control had failed and pointed to growing liquor sales as evidence, there was little enthusiasm. The Liberals, with their call for a plebiscite, and the Progressives who wanted to set back the clock, were placed in a thankless position.

Once again Price and Clysdale set to work, assisted this time by John R. MacNicol, the association president. A few months earlier MacNicol had assured Bennett that 'never in the history of the Province has there been any approach to the magnitude of Party organization as at present.'[87] Once more the regional organizations, particularly the Toronto Central under Garrett Tyrrell, Western Ontario under Gordon Reid, and Northern Ontario where McCrea took personal charge, worked in exemplary fashion. As in 1926, radio was put to effective use and in addition to the usual party messages the dulcet tones of Harry Cody reassured the electorate. What he feared most of all, Ferguson told Bennett, was that 'over-confidence may breed apathy' and he wrote each candidate, pointing out that 'a shortage of 2 or 3 votes in each sub-division very often spells the difference between victory and defeat. ... The one and only thing we fear is imperfect organization and lack of thorough canvass.'[88] Ferguson urged every candidate to 'work just as hard as if you had a very close contest' and J.R. MacNicol impressed on the workers that 'the desire of the Party is the largest popular majority in the history of the Province.'[89]

The only danger to the Tory cause was not the unimpressive opposition groups but a vague feeling that the Conservatives had become too strong. Ferguson, it was said, had assumed almost dictatorial powers and resorted to shocking machine tactics. Such complaints were made with increasing frequency during the later years of Ferguson rule and they did not lack justification. In September 1927, for example, Mrs Adam Shortt, the vice-chairman of the Mothers' Allowance Commission, resigned her position, charging that the Civil Service Commission was completely ignored and that she could not continue to act as long as political influence continued to determine appointments. The commissioner, Dr David Jamieson, admitted he was a strong Tory and said that appointments would continue to be given to Conservatives if they were as capable of handling them as persons who were not members of the party.[90] Then the advent of government control introduced a host of new patronage positions and some of Sinclair's most telling thrusts during the 1929 campaign were against Tory abuses of the Liquor Commission. Repeated attacks on the 'Tory machine' obviously nettled Ferguson and when the *Globe* in April 1929 suggested that the Department of Education was full of politics, he wrote Harry Anderson, the managing editor, more in sorrow than in anger.

His defence was not unconvincing. 'I resent the suggestion that political considerations are permitted to enter into the affairs of the Education Department,' he began. 'I could give you the names of a great number of Liberals whom I have taken into the Department, some of them with very prominent positions. ... I know many Liberals, not only in that Department, but in all parts of the service. ... Since this Government came into office, it has appointed more Liberals ... than was done in the fifteen years of Conservative administration before the Drury Government came in.' And he proceeded to point to important places held by strong Liberals. 'It is quite true,' he admitted, '...that where claims are equal, the Government gives preference to its supporters. That applies, however, only to minor positions in the service.'[91]

In truth it was his old reputation and his unprecedented success that gave rise to stories about 'Tammany methods.' The Tories did have a machine; often they paid their workers, although frequently they did not; they were reasonably well financed and highly efficient. Their opponents were inept. Rather than admit their own deficiencies, they conjured up the vision of the wicked Ferguson machine. The fact was that Tory patronage policies differed little from those of most governments of the day. As for members of the Civil Service engaging in political activities, Ferguson knew how damaging this might prove if exploited by the opposition; with the 1929 campaign in full force, George Henry warned one zealous bureaucrat not to do anything which could lead to the charge that he was taking part in politics. 'You know how strict the Prime Minister is with regard to this and I trust you will keep it constantly in mind.'[92]

One area in which the charges may have been justified was with respect to the Northern Development Fund and New Ontario. But the north, still a frontier, was susceptible to many abuses. Liberals as well as Tories benefitted from the system and in politics the region was a law unto itself. Still, his opponents lost no opportunity to raise the cry of machine politics and the Toronto *Star* pulled out all the stops, charging that 'the Ferguson government has created a political machine that operates ruthlessly in the legislature and throughout the province. ... Ontario is at the parting of the ways.' The Liberal leader, it accurately asserted, is not the kind of man to operate a ruthless political machine. 'Mr Sinclair has not the gangster mind...'[93]

Nothing could stem the Tory tide. 'Things look almost too good,' Arthur Ford reported to Bennett a few days before the voting, and Ferguson himself was said to feel it might be a good thing if a couple of Liberals managed to slip in in the Toronto area.[94] With about a week to go, his health gave out again; he had not spared himself and a severe attack of bronchitis forced him to take to bed. He was on his feet if not in top form for the 25 October rally at Massey

Hall, then to eastern Ontario for a series of meetings and back to Toronto for the result.

Now it was election night. 'With his gray fedora hat set at its characteristic angle and drawing with satisfaction on a cigar,' he addressed huge crowds from the balconies of the two Toronto Tory papers and spoke to the province from radio station CKCL. Even he was amazed at the extent of the sweep. The Conservatives went from 74 to 92 seats; the Liberals dropped from 21 to 13; the Progressives held only 4 and their leader lost his seat; Farquhar Oliver was the lone UFO member returned. Ontario to all intents and purposes had returned to a two-party system – or was it a one-party system? As usual, Toronto and the Yorks were solid Tory. The results ushered in what were then and remain the largest Conservative and smallest Liberal groups in the history of the province. 'The Liberal party in Ontario has ... practically ceased to exist,' a somewhat awed UK High Commissioner reported to his government in London.[95] Particularly striking were Tory gains in the rural dry belt of western Ontario and in the 'Gallic fringes' where once impregnable Liberal ridings fell with ease. The government gained no fewer than eight rural seats from the Progressives and eleven from the Liberals. Six Franco-Ontarians were elected, all Conservatives, as the Grit strong-holds of East Ottawa, Russell, and Prescott sold their souls to Howard Ferguson. To MacNicol, George Henry pointed out that such support for Ferguson 'will go far to break down the antagonism that has up to the present existed in Quebec. Mr Ferguson could well go into Quebec now ... on behalf of Mr Bennett, and have good results.'

In fact brokerage politics as practised by Ferguson with consummate skill had won to his cause the support of practically all classes, regions, and special interests in Ontario. Particularly successful was the appeal to the Catholic vote and McCrea reported to Bennett that about 90 per cent of the Catholic community had supported the Conservatives.[96] Grudgingly, the Toronto *Star*, which now more than ever considered itself the only effective opposition to entrenched Toryism, admitted that 'Premier Ferguson is the one and only politician who has learned the art of pleasing everybody.'[97] The popular vote told a somewhat different story. In an election in which the percentage of the electorate exercising the franchise dropped to 55.9% from 63.9% in 1926, the Liberals went from 284,873 to 329,248 votes and the Tories dropped by 68,000. One Conservative was elected for every 6000 votes, one Liberal for every 25,000. Still, the Tories took 56.9% of the votes cast, the largest total in the history of the province.[98]

The reaction in Ferguson's camp was mixed. Tories were delighted by what it portended for the federal campaign. ' "On to Ottawa" is the cry,' Arthur Ford exulted to Bennett, who at once asked Ferguson to encourage Price and McCrea to attend a federal organizational meeting.[99] But as for provincial affairs there was some regret that the opposition was so weak. 'We will, in a sense,' Henry admitted, 'need to be our own critics' and he told John Martin that 'possibly we have a surfeit of good things.'[100] He was right, of course. The peak had been reached; the decline, hardly perceptible at first, began at once.

Ferguson was in office for more than a year after the 1929 election. During this period his interests turned increasingly to national and imperial affairs. In particular, the still unsettled question of provincial rights in the power question became embroiled with federal politics. With Ontario able to satisfy its immediate needs through Quebec purchases, King believed that the Tories would be unable to make gains by accusing him of blocking the province on the Ottawa and St Lawrence rivers. He had not fully comprehended the extent to which Ferguson and Taschereau were determined to achieve recognition of the provincial position. In Ontario's case this was in part a desire to have its rights recognized in the abstract and partly a reflection of the Hydro's concern over what it still regarded as an impending power shortage. The two premiers were intent on using the conference with the federal government which was finally held on 24 January 1930 to win a final victory which would leave them unchallenged control over electrical energy sources.

At the conference the premiers believed they had finally succeeded. Charged with drafting a letter embodying the decision of the gathering, to be distributed under King's signature, they joyfully included the sentence: '...I am authorized to state that the Federal government recognizes the full proprietary rights of the Provinces in the beds and banks and waterpowers of all navigable rivers subject, of course, to the right of control of navigation by the Federal authority.' At this King baulked. He informed Ferguson that 'there has apparently been a mis-apprehension of our views.' Ottawa, while willing to attempt to find a practical solution which would allow development to begin, would not renounce its legal claims. The premiers were outraged. He and Taschereau, Ferguson bluntly informed King, had 'made use of the language which we both concurred accurately expresses the agreement reached, in the very words in which you, as Chairman, properly summed up the result of the day's deliberations.'[101]

King was not unmoved by this challenge to his competence and his veracity. Another formal conference was set for 8 March and Ferguson threatened to release his correspondence to the press after that date. 'Press and public persistently criticize and attack me for lack of action...' he wired King. 'Have no desire to embarrass you and trust you will understand my position no less difficult than your own.' At this King hastened to Toronto for a 3 March meeting in Ferguson's office but no progress was made either then or at the meeting of 8 March. On 28 April Ferguson informed King that provincial counsel were unanimous that 'to assent to your proposals would in effect mean the abandonment of the constitutional proprietary right of the Province in its water powers.'[102]

And there the dispute rested until injected into the federal election campaign later in the year. Undoubtedly Ferguson had guided the situation to allow himself freedom to exploit the issue politically. Yet he had worked tirelessly over the years not only to protect what he regarded as the province's rights but also to achieve a settlement which would enable the Hydro to begin to develop the power Ontario needed so urgently. The confusion, dilatoriness, and obfuscation he encountered at the hands of the federal government and its departments amply justified his unwavering position that the Hydro must control the development of Ontario's major energy resources. Yet Ferguson's efforts bore fruit and his successor, George Henry, was able in 1932 to reach a practical settlement with the Bennett Conservatives. The agreements between Ottawa and Queen's Park which were embodied in the abortive St Lawrence treaty of that year with the United States provided that ownership of all power developed by the Canadian part of the project in the international section would be vested in the province and the Ontario Hydro would own and pay for all power works it installed.[103] The victory, while not as complete as Ferguson would have liked, meant much to Ontario and the Hydro. When the Seaway was finally built some twenty years later, provincial rights were not seriously in jeopardy.

On a number of fronts during his years as Premier, Howard Ferguson had stubbornly and with skill defended the rights of Ontario against a sometimes encroaching and frequently vacillating federal administration. Some of the issues fought over remain unsettled today and must be regarded as part of the peculiar dynamic of Canadian federalism. There is no doubt that in the 1920s as in the 1960s such matters consumed an inordinate portion of governmental energies; disagreements were pursued relentlessly and at times with little apparent regard for the public interest.

Something of the frustration Ferguson felt appeared in a January 1930 letter to Wesley Gordon in which he pointed to the unfortunate consequences of Ottawa's withdrawal of responsibility in such fields as technical education, agriculture, and interprovincial transportation. In each of these the federal aid initiated by the Union Government had been cut off. Of course most of Ferguson's annoyance stemmed from the loss of federal grants-in-aid and he assured Gordon that 'since this Government came into power, we have been unable to secure any favorable consideration from the present government at Ottawa to the suggestion that we are entitled to more subsidy.' Ferguson's efforts ensured that Ontario was well equipped for future negotiations. By 1930 Ontario's alliance with Taschereau had become a formidable partnership, one he would bequeath intact to his successors; he believed as well that other provinces shared his views on dominion-provincial relations and he hoped that another full-scale conference with Ottawa would be held in 1930. He expected that the provinces would then 'formulate a united policy and put it vigorously up to the Dominion Government.'[104] Such a conference was never held.

But such was the way of the world and, if as his retirement approached many federal-provincial issues remained unresolved, this was equally true of many of the economic policies he had pursued with such vigour. His efforts to establish an Ontario iron mining industry, for example, seemed to have led nowhere and not a penny of the money the province had established in 1924 as a bounty had been touched. Ever an optimist, in January 1930 he told the Ontario division of the CMA that Ontario was on the verge of founding a marvellous new metal industry utilizing domestic iron ore.[105] Following discussions with Algoma Steel, he received assurances from the company that 'if the old Bill were changed to read 1¢ per unit, instead of ½¢ per unit, it would ... give the assurance that the ore properties would be developed as soon as we could consistently do so.'[106] Later that year the provincial bounty was increased to a full cent a unit. But not even this had much effect. Not until the Hepburn government in the late 1930s provided another bounty increase was the reorganized Algoma Steel Co. able to make significant strides in exploiting the iron ore deposits north of Lake Superior.

Eventually the development Ferguson had envisioned was carried out. In a limited way, the belated construction of the St Lawrence waterway on terms acceptable to the province and the later achievements of Algoma Steel fulfilled and gave meaning to Ferguson's economic goals. His persistent endeavour to formulate strategies to resist American encroachments and to effect a greater degree of national economic integration were, in the final analysis, beyond the power of any individual province to achieve. Of course his efforts reflected at once his sincere nationalism, his commitment to the traditions of the National Policy, and his conviction that Ontario as Canada's major industrial province must have a voice in determining national economic policies. In this he gained some success and his achievements helped his successors accomplish more. Yet, finally, he recognized the limitations of his provincial role. It was logical that increasingly he should turn to other means to achieve his political and nationalist purposes.

The federal Conservative party was one available instrument. In May, with the federal election at last underway, Ferguson threw himself into the fray. It was an open secret that he had vowed to help Bennett dispose of King. 'Mr King is the issue,' he announced, claiming that the Prime Minister's House of Commons statement that he would not contribute 'a five cent piece' to any Tory government to assist in unemployment relief had left him no choice but to enter the campaign. 'I have felt hurt today at Ferguson's endeavour to have the campaign made one of personal attack & bitterness towards myself,' King wrote the next day in his diary. 'I am through with Ferguson he is by nature a skunk.'[107] The truth, of course, was that King had more than met his match as a politician. Years later King told his assistant, J.W. Pickersgill, that after a meeting in Ottawa one day and a somewhat alcoholic lunch at the club, the two men had been driving back to the city and he had turned to the Ontario premier and said 'Now, Howard, you wouldn't expect me to give money to any of these Tory provincial governments so you could use it to put us out of office.' Ferguson had replied, 'I wouldn't give a five cent piece to any of them' and that conversation was in King's mind when he made his famous slip of the tongue in the Commons.[108] Now, ironically, Ferguson with his instinct for the jugular seized on the five-cent speech. King, he charged again and again, had degraded the office of Prime Minister.

This time Ferguson had little to do with the organization. His role was platform work and in that he did not stint. He spoke on the radio, at major rallies, and in constituencies across the province. Trying to fight back, the embattled Prime Minister on 18 June at Peterborough charged that the Ontario government was holding up the St Lawrence Seaway development. Again King had given Ferguson the excuse he needed. 'Such a statement is so entirely without foundation that it could be made with none other than a political motive' was Ferguson's response and he published all the recent correspondence between the two governments.[109] From that point, the election in Ontario degenerated into one great brawl between the King and Ferguson forces. Responsibility for the unemployed, the suspension of federal grants-in-aid, the Ferguson machine in the north, federal immigration policy, and the role of Ottawa and Queen's Park in the now suspect Beauharnois deal were all subjects of mutual recriminations. Ferguson vowed to throw all the resources of the provincial government into the fight and King fought back with the claim that the Tories were attempting to establish a Tammany-type monopoly across Canada. The Sifton interests wheeled to the attack, with Harry Sifton pointing to the 'horrible machine rule' and 'terrorism' which characterized Ferguson's methods, and the *Manitoba Free Press* denouncing the Ontario premier as 'a cheap, shallow, cunning politician of a type once familiar in the west...' John Dafoe discharged his choicest invective on the Tory he evidently hated and feared even more than he did Bennett. 'Mean, tricky, ungenerous, petty, malicious, malignant, unfair and untruthful – even these adjectives do not describe Mr Ferguson's nightly performance on the platform,' thundered the *Free Press*. In response Ferguson threatened the 'liars' of the *Free Press* and 'the Sifton gang' with legal action.[110]

On neither side was the spectacle edifying. Ferguson's boasts and braggadocio made him appear the bully and together with the efforts of his provincial machine may finally have reacted against his cause. In King's view the absence of three-cornered contests and the trade concessions to Britain made by the Dunning budget were also important elements.[111] For whatever reason, 'the whole weight' of the Ferguson government apparently failed to make much difference and in a contest in which the national tide was in favour of the Tories, they were able to gain only six seats in Ontario, taking 59 of 82 instead of the

70 the Ontario premier had promised. Ferguson, some Grits suggested hopefully, was the real loser and a still angry King was determined to make it so. 'I am sure you will agree,' he told Harry Anderson of the *Globe*, 'that from now on we should all make it a part of our existence to bring about the destruction of the Ferguson machine. If that is not done there will be little in the way of political liberty in Ontario.'[112]

Certainly many defeated Liberals blamed the activities of the Tory provincial machine for their downfall and while Bennett privately told King he had expected more, Ontario had given him not many less than half of his 137 elected members.[113] Ferguson himself was anything but disappointed. 'I had a real holiday during this election campaign and enjoyed it immensely,' he told Thomas Crawford. 'My job was to keep the pot boiling,' he told another correspondent and, undeniably, he had achieved his purpose. 'We had ten ministers tour Ontario and the Prime Minister spent the last week here,' he noted with some pride. Perhaps it was true, as one Tory assured him, that his active role 'permitted the Party to make substantial gains in other parts of Canada, as you drew Mr King's fire to yourself.' Ontario, Ferguson informed Borden, 'was the cockpit of the fight. I felt from the beginning that the budget was designed to capture this Province and realized that we had to make a desperate effort to combat the appeal to British sentiment. Unfortunately, in the early stages there did not seem to be any organization to look after the selection of candidates and we lost at least half a dozen seats that could easily have been won had some guidance been given the local people in making their selection.' He was content, then, with what had been achieved. Even Tommy Church, who was anything but a friend, wrote that 'without you victory would not have been possible.'[114]

There were those who said that he had made Bennett Prime Minister; it was a heavy burden to have to bear. Bennett himself on New Year's eve thanked him for 'all the service you have rendered our cause during the past year. I should like you also to understand how deep is my own sense of personal obligation.'[115] Bennett must have realized there would be a price to pay. 'We may now expect,' the Ontario premier wrote privately, 'good progress in the St Lawrence development and many others that have been a matter of controversy between the Provincial and Federal authorities.'[116]

Ferguson had made another contribution to the result. Finally, the solid Quebec block had been shattered and 24 Tories were elected in that province. There were many reasons for the breakthrough and Maurice Sauvé, a member of the Bennett cabinet, pointed to one that December when he stated that Howard Ferguson was a 'chief factor' in the Tory success in Quebec.[117]

King consoled himself with the belief that Ferguson's intervention and the methods used had cost him dearly in reputation. 'Many of our Liberals,' one supporter told King, 'in the past looked upon Ferguson as somewhat of a good fellow, but this election has removed the mask...'[118] In the weeks ahead, rumours surfaced about the lengths to which the Tories had gone in coercing the northern Ontario electorate. For the most part, all this was based on the flimsiest of evidence. King was delighted, therefore, when Dr Hurtubise, the new member for Nipissing, read several affidavits in the House of Commons 'which disclose that workers in Northern Ontario were obliged to swear before a Notary that they had voted Conservative before they were given pay cheques for work performed for the Ontario Government in Northern Ontario' and he suggested that with several provincial by-elections approaching such material could be used to destroy the Ferguson government.[119] Bill Sinclair was sceptical. He agreed that 'if we could get to the bottom of things there is plenty of material to upset any Government,' but he lamented to King that 'the Northern fellows are so linked up with this system, both Liberals and Conservatives, that they hesitate to give out any information for fear of results.'[120] The by-elections were held on 29 October with the Tories retaining three seats but losing Waterloo South to the Liberals.

In the meantime, weeks before resigning, Ferguson had reconstructed his government. That changes were long overdue had been brought home the previous March when Sinclair had produced in the House a letter written in 1929 by Forbes Godfrey in connection with the work of the Mothers' Allowance Commission to which was appended a PS in the minister's hand which hinted that one lady's pension might be continued *if* she supported the government in the pending election. A few days later Ferguson had startled the House by describing his minister's action as 'regrettable, inexcusable and highly improper.' When Godfrey's constituents sprang to his defence, Ferguson responded that 'it is certainly unthinkable that a minister of the Crown ... should make use of that position, and the organization which he directs under his department, to secure votes at an election.'[121] Once again, as in the case of James Lyons, Ferguson demonstrated a brutal touch when political necessity so dictated. This time the incident was particularly painful for it involved one of his oldest and closest friends. Perhaps that was why he now took his time before deciding on what action was required; for months he did nothing. Rumour had it that he told Godfrey that he could stay on a while and the two would leave public life together. Finally, as Ferguson's parting gesture, the long-awaited cabinet changes were announced in September.

They were timed to coincide with his decision with respect to action on the Ross Commission Report on Public Welfare; and they occasioned as well one final, stormy incident in his turbulent career in Ontario politics. For months Goldie, Godfrey, and John Martin had added no strength to the administration; Martin was a dying man while Goldie was described by Joseph Flavelle as 'quite incompetent.' Now, in a general departmental reorganization, the Labour portfolio was removed from the Department of Health and placed under Public Works with J.D. Monteith assuming the new combined ministry. Minister without Portfolio E.A. Dunlop moved into Monteith's former Treasury position with John M. Robb becoming Minister of Health, a portfolio which henceforth occupied the full time of a minister. The position of Provincial Secretary also achieved a new importance for it was given to one of the ablest and most progressive of the backbenchers, Leopold Macaulay. From the beginning Ferguson had been impressed by the young Toronto lawyer and had taken him under his wing; by giving him Goldie's old position he was opening the way for significant reforms in the many institutions for which the Secretary was responsible.[122] As well, he created, as Ross had recommended, a new ministry, that of Public Welfare, the first such department in Canada. The post went to William Martin, the member for Brantford. Finally, John Martin's replacement in Agriculture, Colonel T.L. Kennedy, for years would add strength to Conservative governments. Highways as well was given a separate minister, with Henry remaining at the post, testimony to the importance the portfolio had assumed in the 1920s.

Ferguson thus bequeathed to his successor a strengthened cabinet with the deadwood removed. There was sadness in the changes, for those who stayed as well as for those who departed. In a letter to Godfrey, Charles McCrea noted that 'it is only a matter of time until those of the original group of 1923 will in turn give way to others....' and 'Billy' Price in a note to Godfrey also referred not only to their association in the government but to 'the four years prior to that in opposition when we made such an outstanding fight to dislodge the Drury Administration.'[123] The proud little band which had fought with Ferguson in his time of troubles had now, finally and forever, been broken up. Ferguson had ensured that the new government would be well equipped to consider and, if it so desired, to act upon the other recommendations of the Ross Commission. And he himself on 23 September moved on another Ross recommendation when he announced that his government intended to establish in Toronto an institute for the treatment of cancer. Thus a beginning at least was made in rectifying the sorry situation which had developed over the decade through the province's failure to carry out or even to define adequately its social responsibilities in a rapidly changing province.

The only problem in all this developed when the Toronto *Star* broke a story claiming that Dr Godfrey had refused to resign and that Ferguson might have to 'ask the Crown' to eject him. The report, based on loud voices overheard at the Premier's keyhole, seems to have been almost entirely inaccurate. Foolishly, Ferguson overreacted and ordered his ministers to cease to supply *Star* reporters with news stories and press releases. This was denounced as a 'Mussolini-like edict' by newspapers of various political persuasion and before long even a few of his ministers, notably Leo Macaulay, were ignoring it. Ferguson, of course, had endured much from the inaccuracies and distortions of the *Star*, the most partisan sheet in Ontario, but his move revealed a growing insensitivity which was disturbing. Coupled with his intervention in the federal election and with other evidence of an increasingly short temper and an inclination to assume grand postures and to take himself too seriously, it suggested that the time had come to step down.

He had never intended to cling to political power. Now he did not. In 1927 he had announced that he would retire when he was sixty to give others a chance to see what they could do; and now he did so. But if he began thereby the great Tory tradition of internal rejuvenation, his choice of George Henry as a successor did little to allow that tradition to become established. He departed with a sense of relief and of regret. He told Colonel Kennedy, who warned that the party would be defeated at the next election if he left, that, 'Tom, I'm a slave. I have not got a moment to myself. I can't stand it any longer. ... Everybody's after you for something.' And he expressed similar sentiments to Forbes Godfrey. 'I confess to you,' he complained, 'that the burden of public office weighs upon me until I sometimes feel almost at the breaking point.'[124]

Of course he was not unaware of the impact his renunciation of his position when he seemed at the height of his influence would have on the public mind. But he was moving, of course, to the position which was regarded as the plum of Canada's young diplomatic service and he expected that under Bennett the Canadian High Commissioner in Great Britain would be at the centre of a major effort to realize the imperial ideals to which both he and the Prime Minister were so genuinely devoted. His friends believed, with Jospeh Flavelle, that he was making the move 'out of a deep sense of duty. I should be surprised,' Flavelle continued, 'if he does not suffer from loneliness and disappointment. He has been supreme in his position here. Whatever opposition or question might be raised, it was finally decided by the fiat of his determined purpose. I think it is fair to say he has been a brilliant, constructive leader, and the Province has reaped great advantage from his administration. In England, it is accepted that he will be the Dean of the representatives from overseas Dominions. ... But after you have said it all, he will find himself simply a counsellor. ... it will be a very different type of thing from the autocratic authority which he exercised in Queen's Park.'[125]

One thing was certain: he would be sorely missed by the party to which he owed so much and which owed so much to him. Ferguson was unique. Without him, public life in Ontario would not be the same again.

17

Saving the Empire

During and after the election it had been rumoured that Howard Ferguson would accept a position in any Bennett cabinet. The *Star* reminded the Prime Minister-elect of how Israel Tarte had tried to become master of the Laurier administration. Pointedly it asked, 'is he prepared to have the name of power and let the substance go? Will pomp and circumstance meet his need while Mr Ferguson rules?'[1]

Bennett may well have hesitated. Even the Governor-General assured Mackenzie King that if Ferguson came to Ottawa, 'there wd be real trouble between him and Bennett, they wd never work together in a Cabinet each would want to run everything.'[2] But with General McRae slated for the High Commissioner's office in London and Ferguson utterly unsuited for Washington, what, if anything, was to be done with him? Even if he merely remained master of all he surveyed in Ontario, there would be problems. 'There are only two absolute monarchs in the world Haile Selassie and Howard Ferguson,' quipped a young federal Liberal member named Mitch Hepburn in October. Bennett would with difficulty resist the grandiose claims of Ferguson on matters long in dispute between Ontario and Ottawa. Almost at once he faced the rumblings of a new constitutional offensive. When Ferguson told him of his fear that the approaching Imperial Conference of 1930, which would deal with the 1929 report of the Conference on the Operation of Dominion Legislation, would alter the existing constitutional balance without reference to the provinces, Bennett asked the Ontario premier to put his views in writing. Ferguson did so in his soon-to-be famous 10 September letter and memorandum in which he insisted that there be no changes 'until the matter has been submitted to the provinces.'[3] After releasing these documents to the press, Ferguson grandly announced that he too would be going to London. As the *Manitoba Free Press* remarked apprehensively, he would be attaching himself 'to Mr Bennett's entourage, no doubt for the purpose of tendering advice, instruction, and, if he deems it necessary, reproof.' Before leaving Canada, Ferguson told Herbert Bruce he intended to do his best to patch up differences which had developed between Bennett and Beaverbrook and Dr Bruce assured Beaverbrook that he would 'find Ferguson a tower of strength' in his campaign for intra-Empire trade.[4]

Howard and Ella sailed on the same ship and stayed at the same hotel as the Prime Minister and the suspicious *Free Press* charged that this portended a plot to upset the progress made at previous meetings.[5] Ferguson himself shyly admitted that 'while I am not a member of the Conference, I am deeply interested in the deliberations of the Conference because I have been battling to prevent the destruction of the whole fabric of the Canadian constitution.' His trip, he added, was a holiday and in London he would open the new Ontario government building in the Strand. Shipboard festivities with Bennett, Guthrie, Stevens, and Home Smith evidently effected a change in status, and in a pre-Conference interview with *The Times*, Bennett referred to the Ontario Premier as one of his chief advisers. By this time McRae had declined the High Commissioner's position and it must have been offered to Ferguson during if not just before the London trip.

In England Ferguson, knowing that his days as Premier were numbered, enjoyed himself immensely. Apart from attendance as an observer at some of the Conference meetings and the inclusion of Howard and Ella in many of the official entertainments, the highlight was an audience with George V at which the possibility of Ferguson's early return to Britain in an official capacity was a prominent subject of conversation. There was also a full complement of speeches, receptions, openings, and even a letter to *The Times* in which he alluded to the Loyalists as the source of Canadian attachment to the Empire and expressed his disappointment at Britain's apparent reluctance to enter more fully into a commercial partnership. At the opening of Ontario House, he continued this missionary endeavour, shamelessly informing platform guests Ramsay MacDonald, Britain's Labour Prime Minister, and Dominions Secretary J.H. Thomas that Canada wanted Britain to adopt tariffs. MacDonald replied neatly that it was his responsibility 'to listen to all kinds of opinions irrespective of their value' and John Stevenson relayed the news to Dafoe in Winnipeg that Ferguson had burned his fingers badly.[6]

But the irrepressible Ontarian pressed doggedly on with his imperial mission. At a luncheon in his honour at the Royal Empire Society, he warned of the extent of American influence in Canada, pointing to investments and the role of radio.[7] There were, he said, some 1500 branch industrial institutions established by American capital in Canada and fewer than 70 by British. 'Could anyone wonder that Canadians who were filled with devotion to the King and the Empire should ... say that they needed the cooperation of every portion of the Empire, if the Empire in its entirety was to be preserved?'

The Imperial Conference of 1930 thus was viewed by many Canadian Tories as a great opportunity. Little remained of the constitutional bonds, but

American tariff policy and the crisis of the depression together had given Canadian imperialists a chance to demonstrate the value of the Empire and to reconstitute the traditional countervailing force against growing American encroachments. The ties that bind must be more than pompous verbiage and high-minded sentiment. Only the flow of trade and of capital could serve the purpose and give new strength to the old alliance.

The work of the Conference was two-sided – constitutional and economic. On the constitutional side, Mackenzie King during the election had argued that the arch-imperialist Bennett if elected would turn back the clock and Ferguson had reversed the argument, insisting it was vital to Canada's future that the 'little Canadian' King not represent Canada at the forthcoming gathering. The Liberal nationalists feared not only the imperialism of the Tories but also the provincialism which Ferguson was propounding. 'With regard to Mr Ferguson and his monstrous claims to be a sort of liberum veto on the federal government,' Graham Spry, a leftward leaning intellectual informed Dafoe, 'it may be of interest to remark that Mr Bennett took with him a very carefully prepared, confidential memorandum answering Mr Ferguson's claim. Whether the Prime Minister accepts the position taken in that memorandum I do not know...'[8] In fact, Bennett also had access to an argument prepared in the Ontario Attorney-General's department which claimed that the report of the Conference on the Operation of Dominion Legislation 'seems to proceed upon the assumption that in the matter of legislative action by the Imperial Parliament affecting Canada, the only Canadian authority which is entitled to be heard or considered is the Dominion Parliament.'[9]

Yet if the Ontario man believed he was protecting the country against federal aggression, the nationalists saw him as a threat to the Canadian well-being. In a series of editorials, Dafoe's *Free Press*, mixing the imperialist and provincialist dangers to suit itself, thundered against Ferguson's presence in London as a menace to the national integrity. What was being attempted was 'to slow down the march of Canada towards nationhood to a snail-like progress that will not disturb the nerves of the antediluvians of Toronto.'[10] Norman Rogers expressed the feelings of many autonomists when he told Mackenzie King that because of Ferguson's protest, 'the normal growth of Canadian nationalism is threatened on one side by an exaggerated imperialism, and on the other by an exaggerated provincialism.'[11] In the *Canadian Forum*, Rogers argued that Ferguson's memorandum had urged 'by implication ... that all of the provinces must be consulted, and all become parties' to any amendment. To Rogers this doctrine of unanimous consent portended a dangerous constitutional rigidity. Another reason for Rogers's alarm emerged in a private letter to King. Ferguson's views would likely mean, Rogers asserted fearfully, that future constitutional change would come through judicial interpretation and this 'would be applied by the Privy Council which has always leaned towards the provinces...'[12]

The substance of Ferguson's claims hardly justified the Liberal nationalist hue and cry. For years, politicians had voiced motherhood sentiments about the compact theory and while Ferguson may have offended some by attempting to make these the basis for action, it seems more likely that what was under way in 1930 was less provincial aggression than the beginnings of a new federal counter-offensive. Significantly, the Ontario memorandum contained not the slightest objection to the conclusions of any of the imperial conferences so far as they related to Canadian autonomy. Nor did Ferguson make any overt claim that the constitution could not be amended without the unanimous consent of the provinces. What he did say was that Ontario held the view that the constitutional agreement 'should not be altered without the consent of the parties to it' and he protested 'against any steps being taken by the Dominion Government, or the Imperial Conference, to deal with the Provincial Treaty until the matter has been submitted to the provinces and they have had ample time to give the subject proper consideration.' This modest assertion hardly threatened the Dominion with constitutional bondage. Ernest Lapointe himself at the 1927 Dominion-Provincial Conference had suggested that 'the unanimous consent of the provinces should be obtained' for all amendments affecting provincial and minority rights. Ferguson, of course, recognized that the Dominion hitherto had often amended the BNA Act without reference to the provinces. The result of these precedents, his memorandum asserted, 'has been to undermine the constitutional right of the provinces to be consulted.' The time had come to call a halt.

But how did the upcoming Imperial Conference threaten provincial rights? Ferguson in his 10 September letter claimed that the course indicated by the 1929 Report on Dominion Legislation would prove dangerously disruptive. Yet the 1929 Committee had taken great pains not to upset in any way the balance of the Canadian constitution, recommending even that the proposed Statute of Westminster should contain a provision that 'Nothing in this Act shall be deemed to confer any power to repeal or alter the Constitution Acts of the Dominion of Canada, the Commonwealth of Australia, and the Dominion of New Zealand, otherwise than in accordance with the law and constitutional usage and practice heretofore exising.' But here was the rub. The Ontario lawyers feared that the words 'constitutional usage and practice heretofore existing' might give new status to the very precedents Ferguson found so distasteful whereby the Dominion had effected amendments unilaterally.

Ferguson knew that he had Bennett's support for his views. He also urged Taschereau to convey his attitude 'vigorously and promptly.' Taschereau complied; the Ontario-Quebec alliance had held firm. British Columbia and Saskatchewan also offered support.[13] Ferguson had won. Bennett agreed that before Canada signed the Statute of Westminster he would hold a Dominion-Provincial Conference to give the provinces an opportunity to examine the proposed changes. This took place in April 1931 and the result was what became Section 7 of the Statute of Westminster.[14] By it nothing in the Statute was 'deemed to apply to the repeal, amendment or alteration of the British North America Acts, 1867 to 1930...' The constitutional status quo had been preserved.

What had it all meant? The *Free Press*, following its customary line, mocked the April conference as 'quite out of order' and insisted that 'if amendments to the constitution are not at all subject to the consent of the provincial governments, what claim have they to consultation?'[15] A British official reported to his superior that 'the Provinces seem to have done well out of the discussion, and indeed to have made the Statute of Westminster an instrument for a certain amount of political blackmail' and a report from the office of Sir William Clark, Britain's High Commissioner in Canada, noted that the provinces 'with Quebec and Ontario in the lead, showed a strong disposition to insist on the last letter of their Provincial rights.'[16] In Dafoe's view, Bennett by agreeing to consult the provinces, 'for the saving of Ferguson's face I suppose,' had made 'a rod for his own back.' And he assured Brooke Claxton that 'Bennett's abandonment of the Dominion's right virtually to control the amendment of the constitution and his recognition of the right of each and every province, apparently, to exercise a veto may have consequences incalculably serious.'[17]

One can only speculate as to the consequences if the centralist viewpoint had remained unchallenged. During the depression, Ottawa would have been sorely tempted to take the shortcut of unilateral constitutional amendment to gain more powers to cope with the economic crisis. In this event, the damage to Canada's federal structure, so vital to her national survival, could have been severe. To Ferguson and Taschereau must go the credit or the blame for perceiving the threat and helping to block the dangerous path it opened.

Their achievement was noted by W.F. O'Connor, counsel to the Senate in its 1938 investigation of Canadian federalism. Commenting on the significance of Section 7 of the Statute of Westminster, the O'Connor Report asserted that 'it seems certain that the Imperial Government and Parliament will hold that Canada's Constitutional Acts will not be amended on request and consent of the Government of Canada alone.'[18]

All this, however important as a climax of Ferguson's years of effort, was but a sideshow in the London of 1930 where interest centred on Bennett's dramatic proposal for the establishment of a new Empire trading system. As Prime Minister, Bennett effected the sharpest increases in the Canadian tariff since John A.'s National Policy. In large measure this was in retaliation for the Smoot-Hawley tariff, which excluded so many Canadian goods from their traditional American markets. But high tariffs were not enough; trade was essential to Canada's existence and unless a market could be found for her newsprint, lumber, minerals, wheat, and other food supplies, economic recovery could never be achieved. Bennett's answer was a new imperialism, an Empire trading bloc in which Canada would receive a preference for her goods in the British market and in return provide Britain with concessions in Canada.

Yet as the Conference approached, Bennett failed to spell out how his program was to be effected or how it could be reconciled with the free trade views of the ruling Labour party.[19] From Ottawa Sir William Clark noted that Bennett's path at the Conference must then be a difficult one. 'Much is expected of him as a contribution to the speedy ending of the difficulties which at present beset Canada; but the electorate, and his supporters in particular, have but little understanding of the principles of give and take...' As an example, Clark pointed, rather inaccurately, to 'the peculiar mentality of such men as Mr Ferguson, the all powerful Conservative premier of Ontario, who refuse to see that inter-Empire Trade must be two-sided if it is to be placed on a preferential basis.'[20] Certainly the prospects for a major agreement with free-trade Britain seemed slight. For a while in 1929 and 1930, the Tory party seemed rent in twain by Lord Beaverbrook's spirited advocacy of Empire free trade, but in reality his efforts had little chance of success. Even if the British did prove willing to tax imports of raw materials from outside the Empire, the dominions would never expose their manufacturers to competition from highly developed British industry.

Like Bennett, Ferguson in his last days in Ontario was turning his thoughts to the new opportunities for Empire trade. He was under no illusions about Beaverbrook's crusade. Empire free trade was an impossible chimera and he agreed with William Noxon of Ontario House, who told him that no one 'imagines that an Empire Free Trade Policy, in its literal sense, can be brought about.' Noxon believed Beaverbrook's main goal was to make Britain a protectionist country which could offer preferences to the dominions, while Ferguson for his part appreciated that 'the great thing Beaverbrook has done is to focus public attention on this problem and make it a real live issue. People cannot live on sentiment,' he continued, and 'if our relations are to be based entirely on kind words and friendly gestures, we will not add much to the national fibre and strength.'[21] This had been his theme in a speech to the Empire Club of Canada in the spring of 1930. His remarks then had elicited praise from Beaverbrook, who told him they would 'be of the greatest value for the further-ance of the Empire policy we both have so much at heart.' He presented more of his ideas in an article in *The Empire Review*, hoping, he informed Beaverbrook, 'to disabuse the minds of any of our Old Country friends who may think that Canada is inspired by selfish motives. ... The first thing to do is to agree upon the broad principles of commercial cooperation.' Like Bennett, Ferguson believed the details must be left until later. He knew there would be resistance from the Labour government but the potential existed and 'the people of England would have to be shocked into the realization of their position.' Beaverbrook replied he was 'more than grateful to you for the splendid manner in which you are supporting our common cause in Canada.'[22]

Canadian 'shock tactics' were much in display at the Imperial Conference. From the beginning, Bennett, with his dramatic proposal that the Commonwealth countries stimulate trade among themselves by levying an increased tariff of ten per cent against the rest of the world, was the dominating figure. In a devastating thrust at Beaverbrook, he insisted this not be considered a step towards Empire free trade, which he described as 'neither desirable nor possible...' Beaverbrook and the Labour ministers were equally stunned. In cabinet, Foreign Secretary Arthur Henderson together with J.H. Thomas wanted to move part of the way towards the Bennett proposal but the uncompromising free trader, Phillip Snowden, insisted that 'to get an agreement ... we must give up something to people who had never given us anything...'[23] Nothing of substance was achieved and even Thomas in the Commons described Bennett's proposal as 'humbug.' Bennett replied with a statement pointing out that if the British government held to such an attitude, 'then I have little hope that any agreement which Canada may reach with the overseas Dominions will include the United Kingdom.' In his diary King described this sabre-rattling as 'a piece of Tory arrogance of the most unbounded nature. I could hardly believe my eyes'[24]

To many it seemed, incredibly, that Bennett's goal was the fall of the Labour government. And Ferguson was echoing the Bennett line. To London's Canada Club he took a strongly protectionist stance, warning that in its literal sense Empire free trade was a shibboleth which if applied could destroy industrial development in the Dominions. Evidently this did not discourage Beaverbrook, who told Dafoe on 4 October that 'Ferguson has spoken on the subject of Empire Free Trade. I hope that he is Saint John the Baptist and I have reason to think he is playing that role.'[25] Beaverbrook still hoped to exploit the protectionist views of the Canadian Tories for purposes of his own and with Ferguson in London he set out to cultivate him. There were several meetings between them and a weekend at Cherkley, Beaverbrook's country residence. What Beaverbrook wanted was for Ferguson to convince Bennett that he should explain away his attack on Empire free trade. A reconciliation was achieved on 30 October, although it is unclear if Ferguson played any role in bringing it about. The contact with Beaverbrook would prove invaluable to Ferguson when he returned to Britain in an official capacity.[26]

Ferguson sailed for Canada shortly ahead of Bennett. In a 21 November interview aboard ship he told reporters that he had been offered the position of High Commissioner and was considering acceptance. The *Globe* suggested that Ferguson would give the job 'new meaning. Mere routine duties will not hold him. ... He will decide that his place is with the public among the people, acquainting them with the potentialities of the overseas Dominions. ... At no time has it been so important that Canada be represented in Britain by a man burning with zeal for the welfare of the Empire...'[27] This reaction reflected the feeling in some circles that a new era was opening up in imperial relations and that Ferguson, the high priest of Canadian Toryism, would play no ordinary role in his new position. That, of course, was Ferguson's own view, too.

Unfortunately Ferguson had jumped the gun on the official announcement. An angry Governor-General complained to Acting Prime Minister Perley that 'surely it is unusual, to say the least, for an individual to divulge such matters in such a way!' and Perley wired Bennett that 'this unwise statement has made unfortunate impression and there is much strong criticism of his indiscretion.'[28] Bennett's only response was to order Perley to pass the necessary order-in-council and see to the official announcement.

In Britain the appointment was well received. *The Observer*, for example, seemed flattered that Bennett had appointed as his representative the 'most prominent figure in Conservatism in Canada' and the *Manchester Guardian* expected Ferguson to be 'a vital force' in pushing Bennett's program of imperial economic unity.[29] In Canada, Ferguson's enemies had a field day. 'You are about to lose your greatest asset,' Dafoe wrote Harry Sifton, 'who is going to carry his vulgar incompetence and his cheap smart-aleckism into a position in which he will reflect discredit upon the whole country...'[30] In his diary, Mackenzie King reported a conversation with Willingdon who told him 'he felt sure Ferguson wd make breaks in London. Said Meighen had told him he thought this & that Bennett and Ferguson were sure to have rows. He thought he wd be a very bitter partisan and very crude in many ways.'[31] King proceeded to warn Lloyd George, Sir John Simon, and Ramsay MacDonald that Bennett and the British Tories were conspiring together to destroy the Labour government and 'before Mr Ferguson has been very long in London, he will be espousing in public, as well as in secret, the cause of the Conservative Party in Britain.'[32]

Meanwhile Ferguson began to cut the old ties. On 28 November he informed his caucus. Apparently, this took an extraordinary turn. Grant Dexter of *The Free Press* wrote Dafoe that 'if his address to the Tory caucus ever gets out, there will be a really dreadful row.'

Ferguson said Bennett had offered him the job while in England. He declined. Subsequently, the King sent for him, said he knew of the offer and Ferguson's refusal and then, according to Ferguson, made a pathetic personal appeal. His Majesty, according to Ferguson's story to the caucus, said the Motherland was going to pot, the socialist government was ruining the country, destroying the morale of the people. Unless something was done, and that quickly, England's greatness would be but a memory.

It was a time, His Majesty continued, when big men ... were needed to bring Britain back to her senses, awaken the dormant, drugged, genius of the people. Ferguson was such a man, in His Majesty's estimation, and he pleaded with him to reconsider and accept.

Ferguson told the caucus that when he listened to his Sovereign, when His Majesty's wishes were laid upon him so strongly, there could be no refusal. And so he accepted, meant to go to London and do his best to revive the ancient vigor of the Empire.

This story, Dexter added, 'is going the rounds from lip to lip all over Ontario. It is too incredible, almost, for belief, and yet Ferguson must have said it.'[33]

As for the Canadian press, Conservative journals were effusive in their farewells and opposition organs mostly generous. 'Ontario politics,' said the *Globe*, 'will lack strife, snap and verve, and the Legislature may be expected to drop in public interest.' The *Star*, still under Ferguson's ban, contrasted his private person – kindly, generous, and a pleasure to meet – with his public role – a machine politician, every department of government passed under his control, the Cabinet ministers sat at his feet, private members scarcely dared venture an opinion, a facetious, cynical man who established an iron discipline and used it to reverse the traditional policies of his party.[34]

Then, abruptly, in several outbursts of oratory Ferguson demonstrated that perhaps he really was suffering from delusions of grandeur. In a 23 November interview he predicted an early election and the defeat of free trade views in England. This prediction did not go unnoticed and Thomas hastened to tell Bennett that he thought he would see Ferguson on his arrival and 'might give him a strong hint to be careful to refrain from anything which could be interpreted as intervention in the politics of the United Kingdom.'[35] Ferguson soon exceeded even this outburst when on 4 December he told a Toronto gathering that he was not going over there to sell wheat. 'I am going to London with the hope that I may be able to do something to remould, or revise, the contemporary spirit of the British people.' He did not mince words about the sad state of affairs in Britain. British persistence and traditions to a large extent had broken down, largely because of the payment of the 'dole' to children fifteen and up; a new school bill demonstrated 'how far the drift to extreme socialistic doctrine' had gone; the rate of death duties was destructive of the greatest institutions of England. 'The old Empire, I am afraid, has not struck bottom yet.'

British press reaction was restrained; political leaders and officials, both Canadian and British, were less so. On *The Times* report of the speech, a Foreign Office official minuted, 'This is most amazing behaviour' and an outraged Clark reported to Thomas that 'in thinly veiled language' Ferguson had 'hinted at an early repudiation by the electorate' of the Labour government and, he added, Perley and the Cabinet were 'much worried' over Ferguson's ebullition. 'Of course you are aware,' Clark asserted 'of the peculiarities of Ferguson's temperament which arise partly from the environment in which his political career has hitherto been conducted and that these indiscretions do not mean as much as if a more responsible statesman had uttered them.'[36] King reflected that Ferguson 'has destroyed in large part and is continuing to destroy himself' and concluded reassuringly, 'I believe he will come to a bad end.' Willingdon told King that

Ferguson's speech 'was terrible, it had made him furious... He intended to speak plainly to Ferguson first in bringing in the King's conversation in talking with his members (this is evidently true) ... I told His Ex. Ferguson would go for him in England and perhaps here if he did. His Ex. said he "didn't give a damn" ... Perley, he thought was ashamed of Ferguson, they all were, said he was drunk...'[37] Dexter too reported to Dafoe that 'Ferguson, it is said, by his friends, has been drinking heavily. Events of the past two months have gone to his head and he was half drunk when he spoke in Toronto.' Dafoe told Harry Sifton that 'the scales have fallen from the eyes of the people and they see Ferguson for the boor and the boob he is...' and he assured John Stevenson that 'he was always without character or ability or intellectual capacity or manners: just a glorified village cut-up. ... He is, of course, now hopelessly sunk.'[38]

The best commentary, a comic sketch in *The Free Press* brilliantly illustrated by Arch Dale, made the rounds in Britain. 'Greater love has no man than this, that he leave Toronto for his Empire's sake. ... The Hour has struck. Behold the Man appears...! But can we spare this Man? What of Canada, hard pressed and stricken? ... There can be only one answer. England must take him. Generously we tear this treasure from our heart...'[39] Of course, drunk or sober, the most important thing about these 'indiscretions' was that Ferguson meant every word; he really believed that going to London as Bennett's right-hand man he would be in a position to help 'save the Empire.'

The official rebuke was mild enough. The Dominions Secretary told Clark 'it might be well if Bennett himself ... could find an opportunity of warning Ferguson before his departure that it is undesirable and wholly contrary to accepted practice that a High Commissioner should appear to take part in the domestic politics of the country in which he is stationed and that further utterances of this nature could not fail to create an unfortunate impression here; already strong feeling exists in Cabinet.' When Clark presented these views, Bennett 'confessed himself wholly unable to understand how Mr Ferguson had come to be guilty of so indiscreet an utterance.'[40] One explanation offered by friends was that he had requested that his remarks be regarded as off the record but reporters present had breached his confidence. The British were somewhat placated a few days later when he claimed his remarks had been misinterpreted. He was not going over 'to sing patriotic songs or whistle imperial tunes' and recognized that it was not his place to interfere in British politics. 'This speech,' Clark told Thomas, 'was clearly intended as the *amende honorable*, and ... shows that Mr Ferguson has now a juster appreciation of his new position...'[41]

Meanwhile the last weeks in Canada were a flurry of dinners and parties, including a massive gathering of 1700 at Toronto's Royal York hotel. Time also had to be found to sit for the Kenneth Forbes portrait which today hangs in Queen's Park. On 13 December the 'fourteen-day book' appeared, a biography of Ferguson, seven days in writing and seven days printing and publishing, described by King as 'a sickening sort of business – full of bombast and puffery.'[42] In Toronto, London, Kemptville, and elsewhere Tories threw great dinners at which the faithful said their farewells to the man who had raised their party to such heights. Most revealing was an Albany Club dinner on 19 January at which a smiling Bennett remarked that some of Ferguson's speeches were diplomatically terrible and that diplomats had been recalled for similar breaches. Ferguson retorted that he was not selling his house, just turning a key, and would take only a suitcase with him.[43]

As the day for departure drew near, his greatest regret was that Ella, who had lived for so long in Toronto without a home of her own, would be forced to leave the comfortable Avenue Road residence into which they had moved so recently. The Fergusons were deeply touched by the warmth and friendship offered by so many. Sir William Mulock added something else, a stunning diamond brooch, his personal gift to Ella. Before many months had passed, many of these same people would be lamenting the change in Ontario's political climate and imploring the old leader to return home and save the party from evil days.

One of Ferguson's last acts before relinquishing the Premier's chair was to recommend to the Lieutenant-Governor that his successor be his old friend and companion, George S. Henry. In later days Ontario Tories would say that this decision was his greatest mistake. Yet Henry, whose selection was later con-firmed by a convention, was the logical choice. Price, who dearly wanted the job, always retained the aura of the ward politician and fixer. McCrea, who would have been ideal, was a Roman Catholic and therefore considered by many to be a dubious asset as leader. Henry, stolid, sensible, hard-working, possessed a knowledge of the work of government which rivalled even that of Ferguson. Time would prove that he lacked the flair and sensitivity required in such diffi-cult days. He did not grow with the job.

A few who wrote to congratulate Henry on his new position contrasted his attainments and character with those of his predecessor. A United Church clergy-man, for example, told him he was pleased that the premiership was now held by a man of quiet, steady, and unobtrusive Christian life because 'I have always found it impossible to trust your famous predecessor. ... I know that in this I speak for thousands of good citizens.' Henry replied that after seventeen years of the closest association with Ferguson, he remained convinced that he was 'carrying on the affairs of the Province on a very high plane...'[44] The embittered wife of Lincoln Goldie did not agree. 'If one half is true that is told about him, he is a disgrace to the Party no matter how clever a profession [sic] politician he is ... I was told the other day it was a crime the amount of money Mr Ferguson took out of the country. ... A prominent lawyer told me that if one Broker could be made to tell what he knows, Mr Bennett would have to recall him. It is passed from one to another that Conservatives are taking bets he will be back before two years.'[45]

As for formal briefing in his new duties, this was deplorably slight. He had some discussion with the Prime Minister on 18 December when he was sworn in and a few hours were spent going over the staffing of Canada House and other matters on 12 and 14 January. The Fergusons left Kemptville by rail on 22 January and Doug Oliver, Howard's old friend on *The Globe*, ran another story in the folksy tradition of the 'Old Fred' series. Fred, the old horse once owned by Dr Charles, now well into his thirties, was Howard's special companion, an equine wise in the ways and byways of Kemptville politics who insisted on being harnessed up one last time to take the Fergusons to the station. 'I can't take you with me, Fred,' Howard was heard to whisper in the horse's ear, 'but I've given Alf [the hired man] instructions to give you everything you want while I'm away.' As the train pulled away, Old Fred 'was to be seen streaking it down the road, the old red cutter swaying from side to side...'

In England there were more festivities. 'As time goes on,' he wrote Miss Saunderson in March, 'the riot of hospitality and entertainment seems to continue, but I am hopeful that after Easter there will be a respite.'[46] On arrival in London, the Fergusons went directly to a flat which Noxon had rented where they stayed for several months while Ella went house-hunting. Shocked by the cost of accommodation, they delayed a decision until Howard returned from a trip to Geneva and in the meantime occupied rooms in the Mayfair Hotel. Not until February 1932 did they move to No. 7 Cleveland House, St James Square. Among their neighbours there were the Beaverbrooks and Canada House at Trafalgar Square was within easy walking distance. With Canada House located in the very heart of London, the Fergusons soon became well acquainted with the city and its delights.

Howard Ferguson found the official welcome exhilarating. It appealed to his vanity and he enjoyed the bantering exchanges of the diplomatic circuit. At a Canada Club dinner in his honour Jimmy Thomas twitted him on the relative silence imposed by his new role and he responded that 'the moment I have to keep silent about the British Empire ... my resignation will be received by the Canadian Government.'[47] Not yet chastened, he 'broke out' again in late March and enraged many Canadians by attacking those who favoured abolition of the right of appeal to the Privy Council. In his next effusion he told British business-men they were paying all too little attention to Canada and unless they mended their ways they would soon be outdistanced in the race for prosperity.[48] From Canada, friends and enemies alike were beginning to wonder if he had taken leave of his senses. 'He regards himself not only as the Pope of the Tory Party, but his Eminence the Pope of all Europe,' sneered Tommy Church, and the *Manitoba Free Press* upbraided his 'invincible ignorance and incredible manners.'[49] But still he persisted. To an audience of Leeds businessmen he spoke of the extent of American investment in Canada, 'replete with American executives and American methods.' This time it was the Toronto *Star* which scoffed, insisting that Ferguson's estimate that American capital in Canada amounted to four times that of British was of little significance because 'there is less pro-United States sentiment in Canada today than ... when the amount of capital from the republic was but a fraction of what it is today.'[50]

After this series of speeches, Ferguson's oratory became more restrained. Perhaps Bennett had delivered another rebuke. It seems more likely, however, that both men had naïvely expected that Ferguson would be able to pay a quasi-political role in Britain as a missionary of Empire. When Bennett had dismissed Vincent Massey from the High Commissioner's position, he had argued that the post was in some measure political and that it should be held by someone in sympathy with Tory views. Ferguson obviously drew the conclusion that he would be able to continue in Britain the kind of pulpit punditry which had become his trademark in Ontario and he conceived of his 'mission' largely in those terms. There were some, such as Harry Anderson of the *Globe,* who assured him that members of both parties were 'rather enjoying the fact that Canada has at last a High Commissioner who is on the job and is heard from occasionally', but it is apparent that his efforts, if inspired by a considered political purpose, had little positive result.[51]

His first attempts at international conferencing were equally discouraging. Representing Canada in Rome at a gathering of forty-eight countries held in March whose purpose was to discuss the disastrous disorganization of the wheat trade, he recognized that there was little possibility for practical achievements. According to one observer, Ferguson 'was wise enough to make only a very short speech, in which he said that he could not agree to any compulsory limitation of acreage in Canada.' Later he reported to Bennett that the gathering was 'largely a talk feast.'[52] More stimulating was an audience with the Pope, even if it did earn him the denunciation of several Orange lodges in Canada. But the Conference did provide an illustration of the methods of the neophyte diplomat and of the nature of his relationship with Bennett. Somehow Ferguson while at Rome decided it would be a good idea to hold a follow-up conference which would include only the exporting countries. Although he doubted that much would be achieved, he 'wanted Canada to give leadership in an earnest endeavour' and he suggested his London offices as the location for such a gathering.[53] According to Sir William Clark's report to his government,

the invitation was issued with little or no prior consideration of the wide issues involved. Following an "en clair" telegram from Mr Ferguson which read "European preference killed. Everything famous," a further telegram arrived from the same source, asking for authority to invite wheat exporting countries to a conference but formulating no precise terms of reference. Departmental officials in Ottawa were somewhat horrified to find that the Prime Minister had replied within two days authorizing the issue of invitations, but making no stipulations as to the terms of reference. It was subsequently discovered that the conference was to be invited to organize on an international basis the exportation of the crop of 1931-32, and the Prime Minister, who is uncompromisingly opposed to international selling agreements of any kind, was faced with the task of formulating instructions...[54]

At this point it was of some importance that the Americans agree to attend and Ferguson, after discussions with General Charles Dawes, the United States ambassador to the Court of St James, learned that they would do so. The Canadian believed that if the affair 'proves abortive, they can very properly be blamed for its failure.'[55] As anticipated, the Americans opposed any cartel proposals and Ferguson, as Clark put it, was 'relieved of the odium of having to initiate opposition from the chair.' Despite the collapse of the London meeting, Ferguson believed it had achieved something merely by bringing together for discussions the Americans, the Russians, and representatives of the other exporting countries. In any case, the failure did nothing to restrain Ferguson's repartee. When the Soviet delegate began one speech by apologizing for his English, the chairman interrupted, 'Don't apologize for your English, apologize for your policy.'[56]

Meanwhile he was broadening his acquaintanceship with British politicians. During a weekend with Ramsay MacDonald at Chequers in late February, he 'had a long talk with him over the whole national outlook. He is greatly depressed and discouraged.'[57] Howard's more customary companions were the Tories. After lunching with Chamberlain and other Conservative leaders on 25 February, he told Henry that their hope was to force an appeal to the country and 'they are very confident of success when an appeal does come.' Yet, he noted glumly, there remained three years in Labour's term of office. 'It is this condition which is depressing people here more than anything else.'[58]

That May a prolonged stay in Geneva at International Labour Organization meetings took his mind off the bleak British political scene. Back in London, he gave much thought to means of improving the organization of Canadian business in the United Kingdom. From the beginning he was struck by the lack of Canadian news in the British press, but although Canada House stepped up its public relations efforts and Ferguson did his best to 'keep the Dominions' case in the forefront of discussion here,' he had to admit that progress was slow.[59]

More within the High Commissioner's control was Canada House itself and its relationship with the representatives of Canadian government departments. At the time of Ferguson's appointment, there had been speculation that he would not be content with the organization of Canada House as it then existed. Throughout the 1920s King had given his High Commissioner little scope for action and Larkin himself remarked at one point that 'the people of Canada think the High Commissioner ... is a person of some importance in London. He is not.'[60] An official 1931 document listed eight major functions of the office, including advising the government on developments in Britain, representing Canada at international conferences and on imperial bodies, the conveying of information to the British public, providing facilities for visiting Canadians, and supervising other Canadian governmental agencies in Britain. In particular the High Commissioner was 'to serve as a channel of communication between the Canadian and the British Governments.'[61]

The reality was very different. The Canadian government often communicated directly with the Dominions Office and even with other British departments, and many official communications did not pass through the High Commissioner's office. The British High Commissioner in Ottawa provided still another channel. One reason for this was King's determination during the 1920s that the power and prestige of the position should not be allowed to expand lest the High Commissioner be encouraged thereby to take undesired initiatives. If Ferguson hoped for early changes, he was soon disappointed. Although able to have the salary and allowances attached to the office increased, he found himself strapped for funds to carry on as he had hoped and engaged in a humiliating correspondence with Bennett over the cost of a car for his official duties. More serious, the office remained habitually understaffed. The High Commissioner's principal assistant was the Secretary and, shortly after Ferguson took office, Colonel Georges P. Vanier assumed this position. The officers next in rank were an Assistant Secretary and an accountant. Other staff members were at the clerical level. An External Affairs assessment reported there were not enough Canadians on staff and, most serious of all, there was not 'adequate provision, beyond the post of Secretary, for assistance with other than routine questions ... provision is not made for assistance in the questions of general policy...'[62]

The question, of course, is why Bennett did not expand and improve the Office now that it was occupied by his old friend. Perhaps the need to economize during the depression was to blame; or perhaps Bennett, advised by Skelton, did not see matters any differently than had King. Still, things had changed. Bennett had great hopes for his imperial policy, while his close relationship with Ferguson, who had his own grandiose expectations, added another dimension. Because Bennett on occasion gave Ferguson considerable latitude, this made the continued lack of high level assistance all the more serious.

British and Canadian officials were aware of the deficiencies of Canada House. In 1930, while Larkin was still alive, Dr Skelton hoped to rectify some of these by the appointment to London of Lester Pearson. An official in the British High Commissioner's Office in Ottawa reported in January 1930 that Skelton expected thereby to obtain 'regular and reliable information from London.' Although the official believed this might 'forge a new and valuable link in the rather weak chain between the Canadian representatives in London and our departments,' Pearson had to wait another five years before escaping from official Ottawa.[63] About the only assistance Ferguson received on policy matters came from Vanier, who although eager to succeed was himself somewhat lacking in experience. Ferguson hesitated to rely on him for too much.[64] Yet the Secretary entered into his duties diligently and at the end of 1931 reported to Bennett that he was 'extremely happy with my work at Canada House. My relations with Mr Ferguson are excellent in every way and he is the most considerate of chiefs.'[65]

The British early in Ferguson's term were not reluctant to take advantage of the inexperience and of the imperialist leanings of the High Commissioner and his principal assistant. Within days of Ferguson's arrival, Sir Edward Harding of the Dominions Office had engaged him in a discussion of the duties and opportunities of his new office. Carefully Harding explained that 'under present arrangements, the High Commissioner is expected personally to keep in touch with what is going on in relation to foreign affairs,' a fact of which Ferguson, according to Harding, had 'been previously quite unaware...'[66] When he informed the Canadian of the system of communicating information on foreign affairs to the high commissioners, Ferguson said he had been considering the possibility of having someone on his staff who could serve as 'liaison officer' and report to him so he could convey information to his government.

The idea of formalizing the system appealed to Harding, particularly since Australia and South Africa had officers charged with such work. He immediately assured Ferguson that if the Canadian government 'wished to develop a system of liaison on similar lines, the government here would welcome the idea...' For the Foreign Secretary to hold regular collective meetings with secretaries from the offices of the several dominion high commissioners seems to have been viewed by British officials as one means of achieving regular consultation on foreign policy and of moving in some measure towards co-ordinating that policy. Harding hesitated to push too hard, however, and told Clark that he had not raised the question of Canadian representation on the Committee of Imperial Defence as he 'felt that to do so would be inadvisable.'[67]

Vanier himself, anxious to undertake larger diplomatic duties, informed Batterbee of the Dominions Office on 3 July that he was gravely concerned that there was no imperial secretariat along the lines of the Secretariat of the League of Nations. When Batterbee explained some of the difficulties, Vanier responded that it would probably be necessary to proceed 'little by little.' Then in mid-July Sir Maurice Hankey, the powerful secretary to both the Cabinet and the Committee of Imperial Defence, returned to the attack. Hankey explained the duties performed by the Australian and South African liaison officers and told Vanier 'that our position would be very much more definite if we could get him established on a somewhat similar footing.' Vanier expressed great interest 'and undertook to tackle the High Commissioner on the subject' before Ferguson left for Canada in August. Hankey then told Vanier the story of the dominions' association with the Committee of Imperial Defence. The Secretary was particularly interested in this and said 'that the High Commissioner was also, and that he thought the High Commissioner's view was very similar to my own.' Hankey in his report to Batterbee emphasized that he had been cautious and had impressed on Vanier that 'of course we were not trying to force the door in any way, but merely to explain the situation...'[68]

Surely this effort was doomed from the beginning. If Ferguson ever broached with Bennett the possibility of an imperial secretariat, of regular foreign policy meetings, and of an active Canadian role on the Committee of Imperial Defence, the officials of External Affairs must have been aghast. Bennett's own interest in external affairs was notoriously sporadic and increasingly he relied on Under-Secretary Skelton, who would have given short shrift to such proposals. Ferguson and Vanier, it seemed, had been swept into the very vortex of British imperialism.

Ferguson's other 1931 initiative was more realistic and more successful. Uncertain at first whether he enjoyed his new position because it was 'so radically different in character from my work at home,' he once complained to a friend that 'when I find something to do, I like to do it immediately and get it over, but over here most things either come from Ottawa or have to be submitted to Ottawa.'[69] This much, however, he could accept and he even mocked his lack of real power by referring to himself as 'the office boy.' More infuriating was that he lacked even the authority to shape and direct the routine activities of Canadian government agencies in Britain. His experiences in Ontario gave him a good deal of confidence in his ability to deal with business questions and from the beginning he assumed he would have a considerable impact on all those trade matters which loomed so large in his eyes and in Bennett's. If he was going to be 'a glorified trade commissioner,' he was determined to be effective in that role and soon he was dismayed to discover how greatly he was hampered in this work by the existing organization of Canadian business in Britain.

Struck by the lack of co-ordination among the representatives of the government departments and by his own lack of effective authority, he summoned the chief officers of the dominion service from across the British Isles to an informal dinner. There the position of the various branches was frankly discussed. He ordered each to write a memorandum on his work together with suggestions for improvement and to send these to the Secretary of Canada House, at the time Lucien Pacaud. Pacaud collated these and sent them to Ferguson with suggestions of his own. Vanier when he replaced Pacaud entered into the task enthusiastically. Pacaud had pointed out that of the twelve divisions of government service in Britain, most of which were affiliated with one of the departments of Agriculture, Trade and Commerce, Immigration, and National Revenue, some worked closely with Canada House and others carried

on a distinct operation. He advised that the dangers of duplication and of working at cross-purposes were particularly severe in the areas of immigration and
publicity.[70]

Back in Canada in August 1931, Ferguson forwarded the Pacaud memorandum to Bennett and, on the High Commissioner's instructions, Vanier sent his
own views to External Affairs. The Secretary argued vigorously that 'there is
very great uncertainty in regard to authority, and very wasteful dispersion of
efforts and of forces.' He emphasized that it was the system which was at fault
and that the representatives of the departments would be anxious to collaborate
under the High Commissioner. There was, he argued, 'only one solution to the
state of uncertainty in authority and of dispersion in forces, which exists – the
coordination under the High Commissioner of all Canadian Government
activities in Great Britain. No organization should be without a head. ... At the
present time there is no General Manager in London.'[71]

While in Canada, Ferguson discussed the situation with Skelton, who acknowledged that the problems pointed to by Ferguson and Vanier were very real. 'The
various Canadian services in the United Kingdom and in other countries as well,
have grown up somewhat haphazardly and without much coordination. The
system of watertight compartments has drawbacks at Ottawa; it has still greater
drawbacks abroad.'[72] Skelton agreed that more centralization was needed to
prevent conflicting policies and he supported Ferguson on the understanding
that what he sought was not absolute control but improved supervision and
co-ordination.

Bennett moved quickly. A previous attempt to achieve co-ordination had
resulted in a 1922 order-in-council which provided that 'all the official activities
of the various agencies of the Canadian Government in the United Kingdom
should be placed under the supervision of the High Commissioner.' According to
Skelton, some steps had been taken to this end, 'but for reasons unnecessary to
go into ... no very great change appears to have been made.'[73] All Bennett
needed to do, therefore, was to write to the departments involved, remind them
of the legal situation and urge them to advise their representatives in Britain that
the High Commissioner was 'the boss.' On 7 October he informed his ministers
that 'matters to be brought to the attention of the various departments should be
directed to the High Commissioner's office. ... In my judgement,' the prime
minister continued, 'it will be quite in order for you to communicate direct with
the High Commissioner in respect of any matter of public business not involving
questions of policy, which should be properly communicated to him through the
Secretary of State for External Affairs.'[74] To tidy matters up, an order-in-council
was passed on 14 October, prior to Ferguson's departure for Britain.

The reorganization was at best a partial success. When Vincent Massey took
over the position in 1935, he complained that overlapping still existed and
pointed to the need for adjustments. In any case what was achieved related only

to internal organization and Lester Pearson, who began duties in Canada House the same year, lamented that 'important messages pass between Ottawa and London; and important decisions are made without this Office knowing about them at all...' Although Pearson found this situation 'humiliating,' the truth was that a radically altered attitude on the part of Ottawa to the status and functions of Canada House was required before any fully effective measure of reform could be brought about.[75]

In perhaps his most useful work in London, his representation of Canadian trading interests, Ferguson was aided considerably by his inclination to see the political dimensions of every task. He knew that more than diplomatic representations were necessary when great economic and political concerns were at stake and one of his first endeavours was to establish in Britain a network of contacts who could be relied on to support the Canadian position. These included backbenchers who could ask useful questions in the House, newspapermen of influence, business leaders, men prominent in municipal life and, of course, the whole clique of Tory imperialists. Such contacts on occasion proved invaluable, particularly after Ferguson learned how meaningless imperial sentiments actually were when they conflicted with hard material interests.

In his first year in London, he faced no more important or difficult problem than the search for an expanded British market for Canadian timber products. The American tariff had dealt a devastating blow to this great Canadian industry and Ferguson and Bennett believed that salvation might be found in the British market. Unfortunately the British already had a satisfactory source of supply in the Baltic countries, while higher Canadian transportation costs posed a perhaps insuperable barrier. Still, pressure from Canadian lobbyists dictated that a special effort be made.

The High Commissioner, however, was unable to induce any of the big British railway companies to buy Douglas fir, and the director of the London and North Eastern informed him that higher Canadian prices 'leave us no option' but to continue to use Baltic supplies. The attitude of the railway interests, Ferguson told Bennett, 'indicates that they regard it entirely from the selfish point of view.'[76] Ferguson should have regarded this as a lesson in international economics but the conclusion he seemed to draw was that Canadian timber was suffering from unfair competition. In the early 1930s the Soviet Union made a spirited return to world export markets. The principal Soviet concern was to earn credits, through the sale principally of wheat, timber, salmon, and furs, to be able to purchase machinery and other capital products; in pursuit of this end they were willing, if necessary, to sell their goods at prices which led such countries as Australia and Canada to accuse them of large-scale dumping. Such practices were made simpler for the Soviets because their trade was organized as a state monopoly. Investigations carried out by different sources, including the British government, revealed that some Soviet products, particularly timber, were produced by workers in Soviet prison camps under 'slave labour conditions.'[77]

Ferguson and Bennett were greatly exercised that Britain would encourage trade with a nation whose principles they found repugnant and would allow products produced under what they regarded as unfair competition to exclude Canadian goods from the British market. Ferguson indignantly voiced all these objections in a February 1931 letter to Bennett informing him that 'from all I can learn of the activities of the Russian authorities they are going to destroy the whole economic structure of the world before they get through. I am convinced that the only way to meet this situation is to refuse to have any commercial intercourse with them.'[78] He called for Canada to provide leadership 'in this matter in a voice that would resound all over the world.' But the Prime Minister had already acted. By order-in-council on 27 February, Canada banned the importation of seven major Soviet products. The Canadian example did not move the British to reciprocate. 'That we should not succeed in getting orders in fair competition does not give me cause for complaint,' Bennett lamented to Ferguson, 'but when the competition is of the character furnished by Russia I wonder just what the end will be.'[79] Thus encouraged, Ferguson remained alert to the Russian menace, warning Trade Minister Harry Stevens that some Canadian firms were seeking to buy quantities of Russian salmon for sale in Canada. This, Stevens responded, 'would indeed be a disastrous thing' and he recommended that canned salmon be added to the prohibited list.[80]

As for timber, it is difficult to judge whether the prices of the Soviet product did in reality represent dumping. The unsuitability of the Canadian product for the British market, the greater cost of transportation, and the high quality of Soviet timber, seem sufficient to account for Canadian difficulties. Yet Bennett complained to Ferguson that the Soviets had also ruined the British Columbia salmon industry, the Australians lived in fear of Russian wheat producers, and the British themselves were only too happy that the Canadian ban on Soviet anthracite freed them from competition with Soviet coal producers. Professor Ian Drummond, a leading authority on the subject, has argued that Bennett and his advisers had an exaggerated fear of Soviet competition based on ignorance of the purposes of the Five-Year Plan, but it is hard to avoid the conclusion that there was some very real basis for Canadian concern.[81]

Before World War I, for example, the Russians had held a considerable proportion of world trade in a number of items produced in Canada and Canadians had benefitted greatly from their withdrawal from world markets in the 1920s. At the London wheat conference presided over by Ferguson, the Soviets pointed out that if they were to accept an export quota it would have to be based on their prewar share of the market. In 1931 the Board of Trade figures for wheat imports to the United Kingdom showed Russia in first place with an increase from nothing in 1929 to 321,912 cwts in the first three months of 1930, and to 5,788,947 cwts in the corresponding period for 1931. 'It is not surprising,' Clark reported to Thomas, 'that proposals for an import quota system in the United Kingdom seem more welcome than ever to the hard-pressed Canadian producer.'[82] While one may attribute some of the resentment felt by Ferguson and Bennett to Tory prejudice and more to the proprietary way in which they viewed the British market, their fear of both the nature and the extent of the Soviet export capacity was well justified.

Ferguson tirelessly expended his energies and his ingenuity on behalf of Canadian timber. He told Bennett in March 1932 it was clear that he would have to

start some sort of campaign against the Russian invasion of timber sold at sacrifice prices. I have secured a number of timber men who sympathize with the Empire idea to write letters to the "Times." I succeeded in having the subject brought up many times on the floor of the House of Commons and in the Lords. ... We have been able to secure a great deal of publicity in the provincial Press that has helped to stir up opinion.

According to Ferguson, all this succeeded in staying the action of the Softwoods Association, 'who were about to complete a contract for 450,000,000 standards of Russian timber.' The Russians were manoeuvering to bring about the same result through the organization of a British company but he did not 'think that will go very well.'[83]

He was wrong. In the period after the Ottawa Agreements, the organization which was formed to market Russian timber, a consortium of over 170 British firms, was his major headache. In the meantime, he continued his efforts, soliciting from each Canadian province information about its timber resources, winning the co-operation of the editor of the *Timber Trades Journal*, supplying witnesses and material to a House of Commons Committee on the effects of Russian trade, and encouraging the organization of a Canadian lobby. Interestingly, there had been opposition in the British Cabinet in February 1931 to the establishment of a parliamentary committee of inquiry precisely on the grounds that 'there was little doubt that an investigation would show that Russian timber was handled by forced labour and was imported at prices with which the United Kingdom industry could not compete.'[84] Clearly the British did not want to jeopardize the lucrative Russian trade. Ferguson's efforts at least ensured that the Canadian case would not go unnoticed. To Bennett he boasted that 'we can claim to have had some part in pressing this Russian problem to the point where the government will have to take some stand...'[85] More would be heard about 'the Russian problem' at the Ottawa Conference and after.

As high commissioner, Ferguson made it a practice to try to arrange each year a long late-summer trip back to Canada. For some reason his first such visit, which began in August 1931, spun out into October, suggesting a remarkably casual attitude towards his duties. Even then he left only after embarrassing questions were asked in Parliament about the reasons for his prolonged stay. Part of his time was spent in Kemptville tending to family affairs and there was also the Ontario political situation to size up for George Henry. The truth was that on these frequent trips home he was recharging his political batteries, for he hated to be out of touch with the Ontario scene. There were always lunches, speeches, old contacts to look up, and a busy round of meetings with Henry and other Tories. On these occasions Ella enjoyed being restored to her Avenue Road home while Howard would hole up in his old Department of Education office. An extensive correspondence with Canadian friends could never replace being on the spot and only revealed how deeply he missed Canada. Imperialist he may have been, but unlike Bennett he never hankered after Britain as a permanent home.

No record seems to have survived of his discussions with Bennett and Skelton during his 1931 visit home but Grant Dexter sent one account to Dafoe.

Howard Ferguson has been here a good deal in the past few weeks. Bennett has been giving him Hell, in fact I suspect they are friends no longer. A curious incident is going the gossip rounds. Charlie Murphy went to see Bennett a few days ago and was ushered into his office only to find Ferguson there. He said, "Oh, I'm sorry. I thought the High Commissioner was through. I'll wait outside."

"Come right in Murphy," said Mr Bennett. "Howard has been through for 15 minutes, but doesn't realize it yet."

Ferguson got up, very red in the face, and beat it.[86]

John Stevenson offered another story of a farewell party at Government House in Ferguson's honour, 'before leaving these shores to complete the salvation of my native isle. ... He arrived,' the newspaperman related, 'quite well "ginned up" and under the influence of the generous hospitality which flows at the board at Rideau Hall' he demanded that the Countess of Bessborough produce her infant son, 'in order that he might breathe whiskey over him and be able to tell the King that he had seen his godson in the flesh.'[87]

Yet whatever his indiscretions, he remained on a 'Dear Dick' basis with the Prime Minister, something few others could claim. Undeniably their relationship had changed greatly since the days when they had worked together to defeat Mackenzie King. Whatever power Ferguson continued to possess now derived from Bennett. Undoubtedly Ferguson's style had placed strains on their relationship. Still, 1931 was the low point, and even then there was no open break. In the years ahead, their association and friendship remained firm and they continued to share a common imperial vision.

Because of his prolonged absence in Canada, Ferguson missed the most exciting crisis in British public life since the fall of Asquith. Economic difficulties brought a run on the pound leading to the defeat of Labour and to the formation on 24 August of a National government headed by Ramsay MacDonald charged with developing new economic policies to save the nation. This was the break the Canadian Tories had been waiting for. Many of the Conservatives who supported the new administration regarded a tariff as part of the answer to Britain's problems as did elements of the Labour and Liberal parties. Protectionist leaders pressed for an election and when it was held on 17 October, the Tory group won a stunning 473 seats, compared to 35 for the Liberals and 13 for Labour. The Labour wing outside the National government was reduced to 52 seats. Once again Ferguson landed in trouble when a jocular private telegram to George Henry – 'When us Britishers has a job to do, we does it' – fell into the hands of the press, leading to a renewed attack on him for interfering in British affairs.

With the free traders in retreat, the prospects for the kind of Empire trade agreements desired by Bennett and Ferguson seemed excellent. During these months Ferguson was able to supply his government with full despatches, often including the latest details of Cabinet discussions. In gathering information he drew on his many contacts in the House of Commons, especially on Neville Chamberlain, leader of the Tory protectionist wing who after the election replaced the freetrader Snowden as Chancellor of the Exchequer, and on Lord Hailsham, the Secretary for War. But most of all he relied on Beaverbrook. Ferguson never entirely trusted or, according to one intimate, even liked the aggressive press lord. Still, Beaverbrook had his uses. Little in British politics escaped him and some of his insider's view found its way into Ferguson's despatches.

Thus on 30 October Ferguson was able to tell Bennett that at the previous day's Cabinet meeting Ramsay MacDonald and some others favoured delaying the proposed imperial conference until at least March 1932, with Chamberlain desiring an earlier meeting and Stanley Baldwin indecisive. Ferguson warned that such a postponement would allow the enthusiasm generated during the British election to be dissipated and he reported that Chamberlain hoped that some forceful action on Bennett's part might force the issue. Ferguson was delighted when Bennett renewed his call for an early meeting in Ottawa and he reported that this had created 'widespread and intense enthusiasm' in Britain. At every opportunity he urged Bennett to visit Britain to pin down the details of the conference.[88]

These were months of excitement and of occasional doubt. Ferguson still feared the influence of the Labourites in the government and on 11 November, after Bennett had decided to make the trip to London, he cautioned that Ramsay MacDonald was proving evasive about the tariff, 'which was outstanding issue in election.'[89] With Bennett on the spot, Ferguson's time was taken up accompanying his chief on whirlwind visits to government departments and arranging entertainments. 'We have been working out all kinds of schemes,' he confided to Miss Saunderson, 'to bring pressure on the Government to lay down a policy that will lead to the goal we have in mind.' Evidently some of Bennett's cabinet colleagues believed the Prime Minister badly in need of a rest but Ferguson thought 'it was all nonsense to talk about Bennett being put into a deck chair on a steamer to sail around the Mediterranean. ... He would jump overboard in about two days.'[90] Ferguson believed the Bennett visit did much good. Private discussions with Dawson of *The Times* resulted in a more favourable attitude on its part to the forthcoming conference and Bennett himself through 'many quiet personal talks' gained 'an accurate knowledge of the situation over here that he certainly could not have had in any other way.' More specifically, Ferguson believed Bennett was largely responsible for the British decision to establish a quota system for wheat imports. He regarded this as 'not at all satisfactory, or the ultimate aim' but at least it did represent a commitment.[91]

Meanwhile, with protection on the march, the British government faced the serious problem posed by large-scale dumping of products on the domestic market before the anticipated protective structure could be established. The Abnormal Imports Act of November 1931, checked this flood but exempted the dominions on the grounds that they had not been among the offenders, and 'more particularly,' the Cabinet minute stated, 'because the Canadian Government had recently varied their anti-dumping legislation to meet our requirements.'[92] As the new Cabinet moved towards its historic decision, Ferguson remained in close touch with Chamberlain, who assured him that 'before many months we may be engaged in the hopeful task of consolidating the Empire by means of trade preferences.'[93] Not even these exciting events, however, could stem his occasional longing to be back in his old role of political chieftain. 'I am as busy as any indolent fellow wants to be,' he told George Henry in December 1931, 'but with it all I am constantly mentally harking back to conditions at home, and will be glad when I reach the point where I feel I have discharged my duty in coming here, and can get back to my favorite haunts.'

With the Cabinet moving ever closer to abandonment of free trade, Ferguson kept his Prime Minister fully informed. 'Matters have been sizzling for some time,' he reported on 22 January, 'All kinds of rumours of a break up are abroad.'[94] From Beaverbrook he learned that 'Cabinet is irreconcilable at the moment.' As these events unfolded, there was much uncertainty about how the proposed duties would be applied to the Commonwealth countries. Ferguson's initial concern was over the general tariff rate. He made it clear to J.H. Thomas that a 'ten per cent tariff with 33 per cent preference was useless and in my opinion would destroy prospect of success of Imperial Conference.'[95] Thomas replied that published figures were only tentative, but Ferguson warned that unless a more reasonable position emerged, the Conference would fail and 'they must take responsibility for Empire disintegration.' In an emotional outburst, he warned the Dominions Secretary that 'unless they display more reasonable spirit I was prepared to resign my position and take up matter here on platform because I felt that coming conference our last chance for Empire.'[96]

In the weeks ahead, Ferguson continued to be alarmed by the attitude of Thomas, who as Dominions Secretary was in line to head the UK's delegation to Ottawa. Hoping to undercut Thomas's position, he held discussions with Chamberlain

and one or two others I knew I could trust, and they are all agreed that it is most unfortunate that he should be sent out there heading the British Delegation. He goes about everywhere spreading reports that the Canadians are out to get everything they can regardless of the interests of Great Britain. He is constantly exhorting industry and the public generally towards the idea that they must drive a hard bargain...[97]

Ferguson was outraged by the Dominions Secretary's habit of telling everyone that Canada had 'been nurtured under British protection, with naval defence, the benefit of trustee securities and the prestige of Britain's position...' He was 'fed up,' he told Bennett and he had started a quiet campaign to get rid of Thomas and have Chamberlain named delegation head. An ugly confrontation occurred after a dinner party at the House. Stanley Baldwin's biographers relate that,

Thomas exceeded the bounds of the latitude which his good humour normally gained him. Baldwin had already left but Lord Camrose gave him an account. "Several guests stayed on, among them Thomas and Ferguson. ... Jem was pretty skin full and he got across with Ferguson and he said exceedingly rude things about Canada and at last Ferguson said he would report him to his government. Austen [Chamberlain] then apparently did the heavy father, told Jem to remember he was a minister of the Crown and reminded Ferguson that such unofficial talks are never repeated. But it was all very unfortunate and bodes none too well for Ottawa."[98]

Ferguson's version, relayed to Bennett, was that he had been waiting for an opportunity to respond and this was it. 'I did not hesitate to tell him that his attitude would ruin the possibility of achieving anything at this Conference. I added that if this Conference fails disintegration of the Empire would begin, and his would be the responsibility. Everybody took a hand in the discussion. ... I told him as well that his position was not any too strong in the Dominions. ... I think it opened the eyes of the others present...'[99] Chamberlain himself finally took the position that the easiest course would be to name Baldwin, as a former prime minister, to head the British delegation. Hearing this, Ferguson believed his anti-Thomas campaign had succeeded, but 'I do not relish this as much of an improvement,' he told Bennett, 'and I doubt if you will.'[100]

Meanwhile in the weeks preceding his clash with Thomas he made the dreary rounds of government offices, meeting with civil servants, lunching with Cabinet ministers, always talking up Ottawa. In December 1931, he was still worried and informed George Henry that the British Cabinet had

been told very frankly that there is no object in holding the Conference unless it is known in advance what the policy of this Government is in matters of trade with its Dominions. The problem here is to keep this subject in the foreground of public discussion ... there is a danger the Inter-Empire subject may be allowed to drift into the background. I think, however, the hesitation, or more or less drift of the Government, up to the present has been a real advantage in that it has impressed our friends with the necessity of constant agitation and pressure. In the end that is bound to succeed.[101]

A few weeks later he told Bennett that he had just had a long talk with Beaverbrook and an extensive organization was being created 'to force improved attitude towards Dominions.'[102]

At this stage Ferguson's greatest concern was that the tariff regulations which the British were establishing before the Conference would apply to the dominions as well as to foreign countries. On 25 January 1932, he wrote Thomas to urge that the dominions be exempt as under the Abnormal Imports Regulations until the Conference could discuss the matter.[103] A few days later he reported in alarm that it seemed likely there would be a general revenue tariff of ten per cent 'on all imports from every country' except on wheat (for which a quota system had been established earlier), meats, and a few other raw materials. Ferguson fought hard to secure an exemption for Empire commodities. At meetings with Thomas and Agriculture Secretary Gilmour he pressed that the dominions receive a general exemption until Ottawa. Although he was able to extract the promise that his case would receive Cabinet attention at its next meeting, he was 'not hopeful.'

He had been in politics long enough to know that more pressure would have to be applied and in a different place. Thomas had set his mind on applying the tariff to all countries in the belief that this would improve his bargaining position at Ottawa and Ferguson knew he would be unyielding. Therefore, he asked for Bennett's permission to approach the Chancellor of the Exchequer about 'putting our case before the Cabinet through him.'[104] This did the trick. In several meetings with Chamberlain, he conveyed the views he had extracted from

Bennett, who warned that discussions were under way to arrange a Canadian-American reciprocity agreement. The British move, Bennett intimated, might give the continentalists the opening they wanted. 'You have no idea,' he wired on 2 February, 'how closely neighbours are watching proceedings and if the British tariff legislation applies to Dominions generally, confidentially I am afraid the Conference will never meet.' He added that if the British persisted this would 'necessitate our taking drastic action...'[105] With this in hand, Ferguson wired back that very day, 'confident we have succeeded.' Chamberlain, committed to the success of Ottawa, was 'entirely of our view and told me he would go utmost he possibly could.'[106] Beaverbrook was also at work, advising Ferguson, pulling wires on his own.

True to his word, Chamberlain on 3 February raised the issue in Cabinet 'as a matter of urgency.' He told Cabinet he had misgivings about the effect of the new duties on the atmosphere at Ottawa and that Howard Ferguson 'had confirmed his worst fears. The High Commissioner was being bombarded by Chambers of Commerce, etc. He had also received a telephone message from the Prime Minister of the Dominion, who was much perturbed and had gone so far as to suggest that ... it would be no use to hold a Conference at Ottawa at all.' This convinced the Cabinet, which was determined 'to avoid anything calculated to destroy the atmosphere of the Ottawa Conference, and that in the circumstances it would be advisable to adopt the proposal which was understood to commend itself to the Prime Minister of Canada, that is to say, to announce the application of the tariff generally to all countries, including the Dominions but, pending the Ottawa Conference, to exempt the Dominions and India.'[107]

In the next few days Ferguson had discussions with Cabinet members over the details of the arrangement. He found the British, not surprisingly, somewhat at sea about the intricacies of tariff matters. 'I think,' he told Miss Saunderson, 'I have been able to help in a small degree. ... The question of tariffs is entirely new in this country, and they have no knowledge whatever of either the structure of a tariff or its applications. ... I had a number of interesting talks ... and furnished them with the Canadian legislation and regulations. Their whole organization is set up on the same lines as ours.'[108]

Finally it was agreed. By the Import Duties Bill of February 1932, there would be no duties against the dominions until 15 November or such later date as the House of Commons might fix. The victory had been won and it was only somewhat tempered by the discovery that newsprint and pulp products were to be on the free list. Ferguson believed that a ten per cent preference on these could give Canada and Newfoundland the whole British market. He at once asked Bennett to wire him emphasizing the bad impression created in Canada by this action and he was able to enlist Beaverbrook's support in a remedial campaign. But this detail, no matter how important, could not disguise what had been achieved.

Ferguson's role had been critical in winning the exemption for all the dominions. A delighted Beaverbrook wired Bennett that 'the remission of duty in favour of Dominions entirely due to Ferguson's intervention. His influence here is bigger than any High Commissioner of any Dominion at any time.' F.D.L. Smith, who saw Bennett in Ottawa that week, wrote Ferguson the Prime Minister was 'loud in praise of the service which you are rendering. ... He said "Canada has never had a High Commissioner in London before..." He added: "where would we have been if Mr Vincent Massey had been over there?" '[109]

During this pre-Ottawa period Ferguson remained in close touch not only with friendly Cabinet ministers but with leading civil servants such as Sir Horace Wilson, Chief Industrial Adviser to the government, who was chairing an inter-departmental committee on the conference. Despite these efforts, he was not briefed to engage in detailed preparatory discussions as were carried on between the UK and one or two of the other dominions. This reflected not any lack of confidence in him but rather the dilatoriness of official Ottawa. In these circumstances, he could do little more than to emphasize to his British contacts that most would be gained if all involved forsook hard bargaining in favour of a generous attitude. He pressed the same theme during a brief Canadian visit in April 1932, telling the Empire Club of Toronto that while Empire trade presented glowing opportunities, everything could not be settled at one conference, and cautioning as well that foreign trade must also be maintained. His whole purpose, he told F.D.L. Smith, was to impress upon the British cabinet that

nothing so important has happened for a century within the Empire. We cannot sit still as we are. We will either get closer together on a basis of mutual trade or failing that a process of disintegration will set in. ... I sincerely hope that Canada will meet the representatives of this country and of the other Dominions in a very generous attitude. Let us start off well. If we make any sort of progress, this will not be the last Conference, and from time to time we can extend the sphere of reciprocal trade. ... If we try, however, to create in our first effort a perfect working arrangement dealing with the whole category and variety of products we will make a mess of it.[110]

This particular trip to Canada had a special purpose. In March 1932 Senator Andrew Haydon testified before a Senate Committee constituted 'to consider the report of the House of Commons Committee on Beauharnois to the extent that it related to members of the Senate' that Beauharnois president R.O. Sweezey had told him that Ferguson when Premier had refused to allow a contract to be signed between his company and Ontario Hydro until he, Ferguson, was paid $200,000. Ferguson immediately returned to Canada and heatedly denied this before the Committee. Sweezey also denied it, although he did claim to have paid $125,000 to John Aird, Jr, a Toronto businessman whom he believed to be representing the Ontario Tories. Aird in turn testified that the money was a payment to him personally for advising Sweezey in his negotiations with the Hydro. There was no proof and the Committee concluded that 'it is impossible to find otherwise than that Senator Haydon's evidence in this regard was not correct.'[111] Why had Ferguson bothered to make a transoceanic journey for the sake of half an hour's evidence given before a committee? Would not a deposition have served as well? While the Haydon charge had created a good deal of interest in the Toronto press, and while Ferguson since the days of the Timber Scandal had jealously guarded his personal reputation, one wonders why he reacted so strongly. Those with suspicious minds might have believed there were matters in Ontario which only Ferguson could 'fix.'

The incident did nothing to dispel the aura of political boss which still clung to him. The story circulated that before Bennett had progressed very far with his government's investigation of Beauharnois, he took the precaution of phoning London to check with Ferguson. The salty reply was 'they can dig to China and back, they'll never find anything on me.'[112] However, Ferguson's evidence before the Senate Committee was substantiated to some extent by a confidential letter to George Henry in December 1931. 'So far as Beauharnois is concerned,' he told Henry, 'you know the story. I never had anything to do with Aird in the remotest way, nor indeed with Sweezey, except to be present in Montreal when the contract was finally consummated.' If evidence to the contrary ever existed, Ferguson probably made certain it would never see the light of day. And it may never have existed. Yet the gossip continued and Haydon himself quipped to Charlie Murphy, 'poor old Fergie will soon be returning to his lair after having helped to fix up or put chinks into some of the fences that innocents like Henry have allowed to become a bit rickety.'[113]

Back in England, he returned to his usual refrain. Possibly discussions with Bennett had disturbed him, for he cautioned Trade Minister Harry Stevens that 'it would be a great pity' if efforts at imperial construction 'were to get a set back because of our bargaining too closely, but I am sure you will understand what I mean.'[114] Naturally he hoped to be in Ottawa himself, at Bennett's right hand, basking in the limelight of a great imperial gathering. But as time passed there came no word and in May he wrote that he had 'rather been going on the assumption' he would be wanted in Ottawa. Bennett replied he had discussed the matter with his colleagues very fully and 'the opinion now is that we should have some person in London on whom we could absolutely rely in view of the fact that it will be constantly necessary for the British delegation to refer to England, and a suggestion from you at the right time might have incalculable value.'[115] Disappointed, obliged to represent Canada for several weeks in June at the Lausanne Disarmament Conference, Ferguson was reduced to writing Beaverbrook to ask 'what is going on at Ottawa.'[116]

In the event, the Conference proved a near disaster. Although Empire trade received some stimulation, the hard bargaining on all sides coupled with British outrage at Bennett's objectionable performance left a residue of bitterness. Yet, interestingly enough, Baldwin emphasized to the British cabinet that the agreements 'had removed the imminent danger of the absorption of Canada into the economic orbit of the United States of America...'[117] Today, of course, it is obvious how impotent Ottawa was to alter permanently world trading alignments; then it was less clear. Canada's agreement with Britain included new or increased preferences on a wide range of natural products. While Bennett did not get a hoped-for ban on Anglo-Soviet trade, Article 21 did provide that if either government felt its preferential rights were being frustrated 'through State action on the part of any foreign country,' the government would then 'prohibit the entry from such foreign country directly or indirectly of such commodities into its country...' In return, Canada increased and guaranteed for five years the preference on some 223 items and also agreed that Canadian customs administration would be liberalized.

Although on the whole the British ministers were forced to agree that Canada in the short run would profit most from the agreements, only time would determine whether any country had really benefitted. For the next three years, Howard Ferguson was busily engaged in the tedious and often thankless task of making the Ottawa agreements work. It was a role which offered no glory and much heartache.

18

The Dream Denied

The work of academic economists has emphasized the futility of the Ottawa agreements. As early as 1936 K.W. Taylor argued that statistics revealed 'little evidence of any general diversion of trade into Empire channels,' while Professor J.F. Parkinson suggested in 1939 that Ottawa had a minimal impact on the Canadian trade patterns of those years. More recently, Ian Drummond of the University of Toronto concluded that 'for the Empire countries, preferential British tariffs meant higher prices and outputs only when Empire consumption exceeded Empire output' and that the shifts which did take place reflected 'the peculiar and transitory events of the thirties.' Even D.R. Annett, who claimed that Canadian export industries were 'strongly aided' by the agreements, was finally sceptical and asserted that by the end of the decade the vision of an imperial zollverein had faded, perhaps forever.[1]

Despite the mystical element present in the devotion to the Empire of men like Bennett and Ferguson, they were not blind to the limits of the possible and neither was ever so foolish as to believe that preferences could lead to some form of Empire autarchy. As early as February 1932, Bennett told Ferguson that 'strong efforts are being made to arrange Reciprocity Agreement with us' and that the prospect of increased trade with the United States through such an agreement would 'command tremendous support throughout the country.'[2] Although the sentimental preference of most Tories was with the Empire, it was only the harsh realities of American and European tariffs which caused them to turn so sharply in that direction and even in those circumstances they usually recognized that the Ottawa agreements could be little more than a palliative.

Yet even a marginally increased market in Britain for Canadian natural resources would provide desperately needed jobs for thousands of Canadians. For Ferguson at least there was another dimension to his commitment to Empire trade. More deeply suspicious than ever of 'entanglements with our Republican friends,' he recounted that 'experience has taught me that we invariably get the worst of it in our dealings with them.' His years in Ontario had impressed upon him the extent of American power and he now wrote that his purpose was 'to get our roots so deeply embedded in this country that regardless of what the United States tariff or trade policy may be in the future our people will prefer the continued stable market connection with this country rather than be subject to the vagaries of the American political intrigues and manoeuvres.'[3] Apart from that, the British market remained highly inviting. Britain was still the world's greatest importer of food and raw materials and, despite the extent of industrialization in Canada, her economy and that of Britain to a considerable degree were complementary.

Still, Ferguson knew that a shift in American tariff policy might destroy all his hopes. In his daily work he learned how reluctant many British businessmen were to abandon established trading patterns in favour of Canada for fear that the American pull would again prove too strong for Canadians to resist. Because his constant concern was with the working out of the Ottawa agreements, Ferguson had little reason to be complacent on that score. The haggling began almost at once and had not ceased when he left office in 1935. If Ferguson's mood before Ottawa had been one of excitement and optimism, little of that now remained. To a friend he wrote of a meeting with several British cabinet ministers at which the Ottawa Conference was discussed. 'I dare not put on paper what they said,' he recounted, 'but some day there will be a bit of revelation...'[4] Nonetheless not even the problems involved in working out the less than satisfactory Ottawa agreements could shake his faith that in the British alliance lay Canada's best hope. Equally his dislike for the United States remained as strong as ever. 'Everybody is rather tired of listening to the Americans prating that they are not going to be mixed up in international affairs...' he told Flavelle in January 1933. 'I doubt if in the world's history any nation was so universally disliked...'[5]

From such carping, Geneva provided relief. During the Bennett years, Ferguson often headed the Canadian delegation at the League when a minister could not be present. Although his first trip there, as a delegate to an ILO conference in 1931, was purely routine, it did provide an opportunity to renew acquaintances with Dr W.A. Riddell, the Canadian Advisory Officer at Geneva, a former Deputy Minister of Labour in Ontario. On other trips it was Ferguson's responsibility to present the Canadian position in discussions of reparations, war debts, and disarmament. He found many of the discussions rather boring and the general situation often depressing. He expected little from the League Disarmament Conference which opened in 1932, noting that while most nations professed not to want war, 'they are all getting ready for it more and more.'[6] In particular, in 1933 he thought the Hitler movement would 'keep up an active agitation...'[7]

Ferguson was especially critical of the kind of instructions Ottawa was accustomed to send its delegates. 'Words, words,' he complained to Riddell, 'it gives

403 The Dream Denied

you no help as to how to vote or speak in a meeting of this kind.'[8] Ferguson
tried without success to get Dr Skelton to upgrade Riddell's status, or at least his
salary, and he also confided in Riddell that in his opinion Skelton, too much
influenced by his academic training, often failed to grasp the political side of
matters discussed at Geneva. When he and Skelton worked together in 1933, he
tried to get Skelton to stay on a while longer, in order to familiarize himself on
the spot with the nature of the work.[9]

His principal task remained in London. By this date he had learned the ropes
and was functioning to good effect. Following his 1933 stay at Canada House,
Skelton reported to Bennett that Ferguson 'keeps busy and seems to know
everyone who counts in London. ... He has been extremely helpful in my work
here and in every other way.'[10] Still regarding himself primarily as a salesman,
Ferguson continued to speak frequently to businessmen across the British Isles,
peddling Canadian merchandise at every opportunity. More important, perhaps,
was his role as intermediary between Ottawa and Whitehall. In this post-Ottawa
period British policy, strongly influenced by Walter Elliot, the aggressive
Minister of Agriculture and Fisheries, aimed at protecting the British farmer and
ensuring him a fair price for his produce. In a period of expansion for British
agriculture but also of falling prices and large imports, mostly under treaty,
Elliot's policies experienced grave difficulties and occasioned a variety of
expedients. In late 1932, for example, the British, in the hope of raising prices,
negotiated an arrangement by which foreign countries agreed to reduce their
meat exports to Britain by 20 per cent for a limited length of time. When the
dominions were requested to effect a 10 per cent reduction for two months,
Ferguson suggested that Canada comply by reducing pig exports by that level.
Bennett's response was that 'it would involve serious reflection on the Conference if this reduction of 10 per cent were to be its first fruits, and that it would
do this government great injury.' Ferguson, however, conveyed Elliot's view that
such a reduction was 'vital in order to prevent the complete breakdown of
agriculture here'; rather than see Canada isolated on the issue, as Ferguson
warned would happen, Bennett agreed to recommend to exporters that the
reduction be effected.[11]

The restrictions of 1932 were the first of a series of British moves whose
purpose was to assist British agriculture while maintaining an assured supply of
quality meats from the dominions and foreign countries. British policy went
through several phases, including a drastic restriction of foreign imports in 1933
under a recently passed Agricultural Marketing Act, subsidization of the
domestic producer, and pressure on Canada to improve the quality of its
exports. The need for better grading standards and quality control became
Ferguson's constant refrain in correspondence with official Ottawa and in public
addresses made on his annual visits to Canada. In December 1933 the two
governments agreed on a standstill in volume of Canadian meat exports but in

January 1934 Ferguson approached British officials to request modification of the agreement. This was achieved and the British were pleased when an estimate of the increase in the rate of expansion of Canadian pig meat shipments conveyed through Ferguson proved 'far more reasonable' than anticipated.[12]

In some of this, Ferguson's role was that of a mere conduit but often he was given some latitude in delicate policy discussions and he did earn a pat on the back from members of the government, conveyed through Bennett, for his efforts to convince the War Office that they were mistaken to rely so heavily on foreign bacon supplies.[13] Yet, serving an administration committed to imperial preference but stubbornly protectionist, and running an office deficient in experienced personnel, Ferguson's task was formidable. It was not rendered easier by the bouts of ill health, usually influenza or bronchitis, which attacked him frequently and sometimes laid him up for weeks at a time. The hard slogging of his daily routine would have worn down anyone unaccustomed to long hours, constant meetings, and mountains of paperwork. It had its effect on Ferguson.

There was no respite. Another problem arose in 1933 when British millers' organizations, alleging that Canada was shipping Canadian wheat and flour into the UK at a price below that which it received in Canada, took steps to prevent British factors from buying the Canadian product. Watching the situation with some alarm, Ferguson told Thomas that 'the course pursued is a direct and open violation of the spirit of the Ottawa Agreements' and suggested that the British government take remedial action. On this matter Stanley Bruce of Australia joined him in his efforts but the British, increasingly resentful at how Canadian customs administration and dumping duties were working to frustrate the preferences they had received at Ottawa, were in no mood to comply. Whiskard of the Dominions Office informed Harding that he had 'not the smallest sympathy with the complaint made by Canada and, in more moderate terms, by Australia. This is merely a case – and the first case I have yet had the pleasure of seeing – of an industry in this country adopting the kind of self-protective measure which is common ... in Canada and Australia...'[14] Despite a protracted correspondence, Ferguson received no satisfaction.

Although not without hitches, negotiations on milk, oats, meat, lead and zinc duties, and leather goods proceeded more smoothly. This was fortunate, for Ferguson's energies were now fully engaged by almost continuous and often discouraging sparring sessions with Thomas, Sir Horace Wilson, and Walter Runciman of the Board of Trade over the timber question. Following Ottawa, a delegation representing a majority of the timber interests of British Columbia visited Britain in an unsuccessful attempt to secure a bulk contract. The Canadians soon discovered they could not compete with the prices offered by Soviet suppliers and issued a public statement to that effect.[15] Even as the negotiations with the British Columbians were in progress, the Soviets were holding discussions with Timber Distributors Ltd, the consortium of 170 British firms which handled their product, over the terms of a contract for 1933. Such contracts had been negotiated between British and Soviet interests for several years but in this instance the Canadian government, through Ferguson, informed Thomas that the Timber Distributors' contract about to be struck appeared to be at a price which contravened Article 21 of the Canadian-British agreement. This had little effect, and a contract was signed providing for the import of 395,000 standards of Soviet timber. In close touch with many timber merchants, Ferguson made it clear to both Ottawa and Whitehall that in his view Timber Distributors' strategy was to sign up as many British timber dealers as possible 'in the hope that widespread distribution will enable maximum of pressure to be brought upon the Government to prevent interference.' He believed that Timber Distributors had become so powerful that many independent operators were left little choice but to buy through them. He suspected, too, that the Board of Trade, 'while not actually approving, knew agreement was to be signed and winked at it.'[16]

In the months ahead neither Ferguson nor Bennett made any headway in negotiations with Thomas and Wilson. In the summer of 1933 the British decided to refer the Canadian request for action under Article 21 to the Import Duties Advisory Committee for investigation, despite Bennett's view that delay in making the Article effective would render it nugatory by allowing the market to be saturated with Russian timber. At this point discussions between Wilson and Ferguson took place over procedure. Ferguson agreed that the hearings would be expedited if the Canadian case could be shown to the Soviets for comment. When newspapermen later asked him about this reference to Russia, Ferguson for some reason denied that he knew anything about the matter. When Wilson proceeded to show him documents which made it clear that he had been consulted and had agreed, he shifted his ground and insisted that his understanding had been that the matter would be sent merely to Soviet representatives in London.[17]

From the beginning Ferguson had been concerned about the delay. His denial to the press of prior knowledge may have merely reflected his annoyance that the Board of Trade without consultation had issued a press release stating that the Canadian case had been sent to the Soviet government 'with the approval of His Majesty's Government in Canada.' Harding himself regarded the release as unwise and believed that it would have been better to have referred to the 'concurrence' rather than the 'approval' of the Canadian government.[18] Still it seems strange that Ferguson should have continued to pursue such an argument when it was apparent that the documents had gone to the Soviets with his knowledge. Could he have forgotten what had been decided on such an important point? His health had taken a turn for the worse at precisely this time. He had contracted flu at an Armistice Day ceremony, had developed a touch of pneumonia, and had been forced to spend the best part of two months in bed.

'Mr Ferguson,' Vanier recorded on 5 January, 'has been ill for some time...'[19] Possibly he was merely embarrassed that a public announcement should be made on such a delicate point before he informed his government but this seems unlikely. Some time earlier in a cable to Ottawa he had supported the idea of showing the Canadian position to the Soviets on the grounds that 'it would be to our advantage to have Russian answer before enquiry so that we would know exactly their explanation...'[20]

Whatever the reason for this strange performance, on the whole he was a shrewd and active defender of Canadian timber interests against a powerful and well-organized opposition. The superior quality of the Russian timber and its lower prices coincided with the British national interest in trading with a nation which was its debtor. The combination was unbeatable and the only Canadian advantages were Article 21 and ties of sentiment. This last factor was not negligible. It was the London County Council's policy of Empire buying, Ferguson told Bennett in 1934,

that led the way for us particularly in our timber campaign. You know that they control, build and maintain nearly all the public institutions within the Metropolitan area so that they are huge purchasers of all kinds of supplies. The adoption of this policy by the LCC has enabled us to secure the same favourable position in Manchester, Birmingham, Liverpool and a great long list of other corporations both great and small. Moreover, it assisted us greatly in inducing the various Departments of the Government to adopt the same course.[21]

This itself was no small triumph. Its impact on the Canadian producer must have been considerable.

On the main issue, however, victory was unattainable. When the reference to the Import Duties Advisory Committee proved abortive and the British still faced the awkward Canadian request that Article 21 be invoked, they decided on a compromise which would be weighted in favour of the Soviets but which would also provide some openings for Canada. Horace Wilson conferred with Ferguson in early January 1934. The High Commissioner found that 'the atmosphere was entirely changed from former occasions and ... spirit of conciliation and compromise had completely changed to an attitude of determined resistance.' Wilson 'was very emphatic that he would not ask Russians to reduce supply below 350,000 standard nor would he ask them to eliminate either bulk sales or fall clause...' Ferguson told Bennett that he found the suggested arrangement 'utterly unsatisfactory.' Subsequent negotiations did succeed in extracting a few minor concessions, including elimination of the 'fall clause,' a pricing procedure which Canada believed worked to its disadvantage, and an assurance from the Soviets that they would not attempt to increase the amount they shipped to Britain 'by indirect purchase through Finland or otherwise.'[22]

Since the 350,000 maximum did represent a drop over the 550,000 standards maximum which might otherwise have been agreed to, the arrangement was as much as Canada could have hoped for. Bennett professed himself satisfied but Ferguson, in a private assessment, concluded:

Once or twice I have been rather hopeful that I might pull something favourable out of it, but I have reached the conclusion now that we are not going to get anything. ... Of course, we have done wonderfully well, particularly in the last year, with Canadian timber, and I think the market here will continue to grow, but it will only grow in spite of the Russian invasion, and prices will be ruinous ... it may ruin a lot of Canadian lumbermen. At any rate there will be no profit in the business.[23]

In the months ahead he continued to monitor the situation but it did little good. When he complained that the Russians by indirect imports through Scandinavia were frustrating the agreement and that Soviet practices kept prices so low that another case existed for action under Article 21, he was able to get nowhere with British officialdom.

Trade matters did not take all this time. As High Commissioner, Ferguson was called upon to play some role in several major financial crises of the 1930s. One urgent development arose in February 1933 when he learned that the Canadian dollar in what looked like an organized raid was being badly hammered on the London money market. On 2 February Beaverbrook had warned that rumours that Canada was about to go to sterling were 'precipitating a good deal of selling of Canadian securities.'[24] This crisis passed but the following month when Bennett was alarmed by what appeared to be British manipulation of the Canadian dollar, Ferguson upon inquiry was able to report that all that was happening was British buying of American dollars to maintain their own exchange rate.[25] Later the same month, Ferguson had to report that a proposal introduced into the Canadian budget that interest on dividends payable to non-residents would be taxed five per cent at source was creating great resentment in London. He kept in close touch with the City and on 31 March told Bennett that he had 'just learned from Chairman of the Stock Exchange that all quotations on Canadian securities have been omitted from today's lists and dealings suspended and this will continue until situation has been clarified...' Ferguson and Skelton, then in London for the Imperial Economic Committee's meetings, put their heads together and recommended to Bennett that a statement be issued at once. In a veiled threat, Sir Archibald Campbell, chairman of the Stock Exchange, told Ferguson that there was a strong feeling 'that tax will mean severe blow to Canadian credit...' Despite the protests, the tax does not appear to have been dropped.[26]

Different in character from these emergency situations were meetings with Montagu Norman, the brilliant and eccentric Governor of the Bank of England.

Norman, no particular friend of the dominions, had no belief in the efficacy of Ottawa and imperial preference. He and Ferguson were on good terms personally and saw something of each other in 1932 because of their mutual concern over the newsprint industry. There were also discussions about the advisability of founding a Canadian central bank and Norman offered advice based on his own great experience. In 1933 however, Norman's determination, as his biographer puts it, 'that the Dominions should not lean indefinitely on the City and the Bank in times of trouble' threw the two into conflict.[27] Norman, concerned over pressure on the London money market, believed funds sent to Canada usually flowed to New York. To rectify this he opposed loans negotiated in the London market directly with Canadian provinces and possessed the power to see that his wishes were respected.

Some sort of arrangement to this effect had been set up with Bennett in 1932, but despite this agreement New Brunswick in the spring of 1933 hoped to borrow about two and a half million dollars in London. When the Premier of New Brunswick told Ferguson the province was negotiating a loan with a private institution on the understanding it had the Governor's approval, Ferguson learned that such was not the case and apprised Bennett of the situation. Bennett, however, approved the purposes of the loan and Ferguson discussed the matter at length with Norman several times and also with Chamberlain. 'I have argued to the best of my ability for hours without effect and pointed out that Provinces own natural resources and must finance their own operations.' Ferguson believed it would 'have a very serious effect in Canada if it got abroad that Provinces and Municipalities cannot borrow in this market, particularly in view of Chancellor's statement that money was available for Dominions so long as spent within the Empire.' He tried to explain to the Governor that in Canada development was largely carried on within provincial jurisdiction and that if he persisted this would be retarded. 'As I expected, his answer was that we should establish a Central Bank in Canada which would cure all difficulties.' Norman insisted that 'Canada depends on New York and in that respect is in a different position from the other Dominions...' The Governor was backed by Chamberlain. New Brunswick's deal fell through.[28]

A similar matter involving James Dunn in an effort to use British funds to renegotiate Montreal Treasury bills also ran into Norman's opposition but in this instance the matter was a *fait accompli* before the Governor learned of it. Norman was outraged and Bennett and Ferguson went to considerable lengths to appease the powerful banker. When Norman insisted that Bennett take steps to prevent private Canadian loan transactions in London, Ferguson was able to have him amend an iron-clad formula he had prepared for Bennett's signature by inserting the words 'take such steps as he can to' between the word 'will' and the word 'prevent.' Norman maintained his tight control over Canadian operations on the London market into 1935 at least. In the face of a personal request from

Bennett he relayed, through Ferguson, a message refusing to consider a CPR refinancing proposal to be 'an exception to understanding that under present conditions there should be no borrowing of fresh funds on Canadian account except by the Dominion.'[29] In banking circles, it seemed, Canada and the Empire meant a good deal less in 1935 than in the 1880s when the CPR had received a friendly reception when it turned to London as a source of funds.

All the while, of course, Ferguson continued to keep his weather eye cocked on the Ontario political scene. In 1933 Mitchell Hepburn's scattergun attacks on the Henry administration were extremely damaging and Howard's friends began increasingly to look to London for salvation. 'For heavens sakes, bring Ferguson back from London to lead the Ontario Tories,' pleaded a correspondent of Bennett. 'He is popular and strong. If you do not it will be a regular landslide.' From the office of the President of the University of Toronto, Dr Cody lamented, 'if you were here, the whole situation would change over night...' Chafing to be back, Ferguson wondered 'why somebody does not give Arthur Slaght a punch in the "solar plexus" that would put him out of business.' He knew that if the Henry administration continued to sit back while Slaght and Hepburn's other lieutenants saturated Ontario 'with a lot of reckless and extravagant statements,' they would be in the fatal position of being placed on the defensive. As for Harry Nixon's boast that he would make the House interesting when it opened, 'I would choke him off in the first week. It is so easy to do it...' All this in a letter to Miss Saunderson which concluded with a moan audible almost to Queen's Park:

since I am not running the House there is no object in my telling you all these things. One gets a bit restless when you see the trend of events, and know it would be so easy to turn the tide. My job is now to think and not to act. ... I am hopeful though that the antics of Hepburn has sufficiently disgusted the public...

Over the next several weeks better news reached Canada House about Henry's chances. 'He is such a sound, straightforward, honest chap...' Ferguson confided to Cody, and reassuringly he told Henry that he had 'always felt that there would be a reaction from the campaign of vilification. ... They began their campaign too early; they are bound to run out of material and the thing grows stale...'[30]

The situation, however, did not improve, as Ferguson discovered himself on his late summer visit in 1933. At Henry's request, he flew trial balloons with reporters on such matters as the liquor question and a possible 1933 election and drew on his wide circle of contacts to feel the Ontario political pulse. On 24 October he reported that

...I spent a good deal of time around the Toronto Fair, and felt the pulse of hundreds of people. I went to Hamilton, London and to Ottawa and saw a great many people and followed the same policy of enquiry in order to secure a consensus of opinion. I was at a good many smaller places as well such as Coburg [sic], Kingston, Brockville and Smith's Falls. I did all my travelling by motor and saw quite a large number of people on the farms and in the intervening small villages...

He also arranged with Arthur Ford to 'have a little dinner at the Country Club at London and get all the Western members in.' Some 17 or 18 members attended and he was struck by the extent of the apathy which existed. The depression in party spirit could be overcome, in his view, by a concerted showing 'of active political organization and effort.' Henry, he urged, should hire Tom Magladery to organize the north and Earl Rowe and Bill Ireland the south and pay them about $5000 each plus expenses for working full-time until the summer tending to the constituencies. Moving to sensitive ground, he told his old friend that he 'should do something that can only be regarded as an assertion of your personal determination to give distinctive, courageous leadership, and dominate the Government and the Party.' The only successful organizations, he assured him, 'are the ones that are controlled and directed in the last analysis by one man.' As for a platform, what better than beer by the glass on a local option basis. But he should be careful, Ferguson emphasized, not to reveal his policy until he was ready to appeal to the country.

It was the school question, Ferguson suggested, which would give Henry his 'most delicate and difficult problem...' The Roman Catholics were under the impression that the Premier had made definite promises to them and were ready to strike if he did not act soon. 'As you know, they have thoroughly organized further effort...' The only way to avoid being caught in a blind squeeze was to send the matter to the courts but first it should be discussed with Colquhoun and Tilley, both good tacticians. If they concurred, it might be best to establish a commission which would bring down a report recommending that the matter be dealt with judicially. After discussing it with them, 'put it up to McCrea. In the meantime, I would keep the matter entirely to myself. While you are reaching a conclusion in your own mind, I would not even talk to my colleagues.' As for tactics, Ferguson suggested that there be no legislative program and a short session to stifle opposition in the Public Accounts Committee; 'distinct, vigorous, aggressive action' would best enthuse the party and capture the public imagination.[31] Ironically, after delivering this homily on elementary tactics, he told Henry that he had stayed away from his office as much as possible, 'as I have heard on a number of occasions that there was a good deal of resentment in some quarters at what was termed "my desire or attempt to run the Government of the Province".' Ferguson doubted that his advice would be followed or that Henry appreciated the gravity of the situation.[32]

Although he never again tendered such detailed advice, he continued to fret. Reports in late 1933 and early 1934 were uniformly bad and he regretted that 'more active organization work, and a really definite attempt at shaking things up at the inside, has not been undertaken...' He was pleased when Earl Rowe was taken on as an organizer. When Henry during the 1934 session succeeded in splitting the Liberal party with his Liquor Control Act amendments, Ferguson pressed him to go to the country 'at the earliest possible date.' But there was no early election. Not until the last day of the 1934 session did Henry announce that the school question would be submitted to the courts. This temporizing was puzzling and Ferguson feared that the enthusiasm evident at the end of the session would be dissipated. It allowed 'the opposition to get away from the main issue which the Government carried so successfully through the House...' To succeed, Henry would have to ensure that there was 'one dominant issue. That is the way you create and move public sentiment.' He was equally disturbed by the extent to which his Ontario friends seemed to be counting on divisions in the ranks of the opposition to pull them through.

Still, his view in January was that the party ought to be able to squeak through, 'even with only a narrow majority.' When Henry finally named 19 June as election day, Ferguson, in a secret code used during the Timber Commission, wired from London 'everybody should concentrate on major issue which wound up Session so enthusiastically. ... Never mind side winds. ... You cannot win rear guard battle action.'[33] He himself might have been able to keep the focus on the liquor question but people in the depression had other things on their minds. The student of elections must forever regret that the 1934 campaign was not fought between Ferguson and Hepburn. As it was, Henry was no match for the ebullient young onion farmer from Elgin County. Hepburn swept to power, partly on the basis of a solid Catholic vote. The Tories, wiped out north and west of Toronto, were reduced to a rump of 17 seats.[34]

Despite the time devoted to a few major problems such as wheat and timber, Ferguson had to be a jack-of-all trades. When Canada and Australia embarrassed the British in an unsuccessful attempt to extend the purview of Article 21 beyond the Soviets in order to block what they regarded as German and French dumping of wheat into Britain, it was the High Commissioner's duty to present the Canadian case.[35] Other matters were more routine in nature. Always conscious of the need to publicize Canadian products, Ferguson gave close supervision to the dispensing of funds for advertising and encouraged all expedients to win free space in the British press. 'I think the steps that you have taken to bring the position of Canada ... to the attention of the English reading public are most admirable,' Bennett told him.[36] When British customs officials proved overly meticulous in their application of regulations, Bennett felt this was a matter best settled through official correspondence as a 'matter of government policy.'

Ferguson preferred direct action and despite Bennett's orders he went ahead and arranged meetings between Canadian and British officials. 'You will agree...' he told Skelton, 'that more can be done in ten minutes' conversation where cordial personal relations have been established than by reams of correspondence.' In this instance, the Ferguson method worked wonders. A pleased Deputy Minister of Trade and Commerce told his Minister that 'through Mr Ferguson's persistent and diplomatic way of handling the situation, we have been able to favourably dispose of a large number of the disputes' and Harry Stevens wrote Bennett 'to convey to you my very high appreciation' of Ferguson's work. Ferguson, the Prime Minister told Stevens, had been given instructions to deal with the matter in another manner. 'I, however, accepted his views as being better than my own in connection with the British officials.'[37]

It was useful to have a High Commissioner who would speak up when he disagreed with the Prime Minister. From his years of political effort he had become a self-starter who made excellent use of his many contacts and he was always on the alert for useful initiatives. When, for example, he learned from the South African High Commissioner that no Canadian company had tendered on a large order from South Africa for steel rails, he wired Bennett that he was at a loss to understand why this should be and told the Prime Minister that he probably would be able to arrange matters so that Canadian firms could be given consideration. A return wire came from Bennett the same day: 'Do not let contract be closed until you hear further from me.' As a result, the South African government a few months later placed an order with Dominion Steel Company for 50 track miles or approximately 7542 tons of rails.[38] He was equally alert to rectify complaints about Canadian products. When broken glass was found in Canadian cheese, Ferguson helped arranged a swift out-of-court settlement to prevent adverse publicity.

In a busy office, each day brought its full complement of problems. Negotiations with BBC officials to enable Gladstone Murray to take a position with Bennett's new CRBC; efforts to facilitate the interchange of personnel between Britain and Canada for the Hudson's Bay Company; advice to Bennett, following discussions with officials of Harrods, that the quality of Canadian cheese would always be suspect in Britain 'so long as we maintain such a large number of small, uneconomical, unsanitary factories'; an infuriating correspondence with British officials in an attempt to gain permission to impose the Crown upon the Maple Leaf for use as a distinctive national mark for Canadian products; meetings with the Polish ambassador to urge the importance of early action in ongoing commercial negotiations; efforts to promote a visit to Canada of the Lord Mayor of London as 'a splendid stroke to stir Imperial feeling'; urgent supplications to Ottawa on behalf of British merchants who were actively interested in Canadian trade but who were being thwarted by some of the harsher aspects of Bennett's customs administration; the promotion in 1934 of a

Canadian tour by a large party of British merchants – these were the routine functions of Canada House. And Howard and Ella derived great pleasure from being able to bring Canadian students in London together for afternoon gatherings.

Probably his role in promoting trade gave Ferguson his greatest satisfaction. He was boyishly delighted by Bennett's amazement when he took him around to some of the British stores and showed him their extensive stocks of Canadian products. He was also pleased when his efforts began to receive recognition in Canada. A glowing 1934 article in the *Globe* praised him as 'more than a Commissioner in the accepted sense; he has been his country's commerical traveller, its best salesman.'[39] Whatever the statistics might prove, whatever may have been his personal feelings after experiencing the rigidities of some British officials and the unbending pursuit of national self-interest which characterized both Canadian and British attitudes, he remained stubbornly convinced even into the later 1930s that 'Empire cooperation means economic salvation.'[40] This was less than realistic. In the period after 1935, Britain and the dominions negotiated increasing numbers of trade agreements with foreign countries and the distinction between treaties without and those within the Empire became almost meaningless. In the long run, there was little of substance to show for the great hopes of 1932.

Apart from trade questions, the most distinctive feature of Ferguson's tenure was his special relationship with the Prime Minister. Bennett retained a high regard for his work and Ferguson for his part had no compunctions about offering political advice to his old comrade-in-arms. Thus from the London office there came a steady flow of homespun hints on political strategy, including suggestions on how to embarrass Mackenzie King in the Commons and even a copy of a report by William Beveridge which Ferguson believed would be useful in the preparation of Bennett's own Unemployment Insurance Act. Occasionally he would prepare long memoranda for the Prime Minister which revealed his thoughts on everything from schemes for British immigration, which he hoped would be revived at the earliest possible date, to his belief that the breakup of the World Economic Conference of 1933 and the declaration of the Empire countries which followed would redound to the imperial cause.[41]

There were, of course, annoyances. When Ferguson on a protracted Canadian visit in 1933 showed no signs of returning to his duties, he was speeded on his way by a peremptory Bennett order but even on that occasion the Prime Minister all but apologized for his intervention. On Bennett's frequent trips to London, Ferguson arranged entertainments and accompanied him on his whirlwind visits with ministers and officials. Although the British appear to have regarded these encounters with some apprehension, there is no indication that Ferguson was other than happy to have the Prime Minister on the spot. He admired Bennett's 'direct methods' and believed the British could use a little shaking up.

Any assessment of Ferguson's performance in London must in the final analysis remain highly subjective. On his appointment many had anticipated the worst. 'I squirm when I think of what they say in England about Ferguson,' John Dafoe had told W.L. Grant of Upper Canada College—'the amused contempt, the resolve to treat him with mock politeness as an oaf, a freak from the outer marches.'[42] Sir William Clark's reports to the Dominions Secretary leave no doubt that he too held Ferguson in less than the highest regard. As for J.H. Thomas, he and Ferguson were scrapping from the day they met. On one occasion Ferguson was arguing Canada's case rather untactfully. 'What you are apt to forget, Mr High Commissioner,' the Dominions Secretary interrupted, 'is that under the Statute of Westminster ... we have Dominion status too.'[43]

Despite Thomas's jibe, Ferguson had always recognized that trade was a two-way street. He was delighted when Canadian purchases in Britain increased substantially in 1934 because 'it is good business for us to spend money here and increase the purchasing power in this country.'[44] Still, he was undeniably aggressive, usually his arguments lacked subtlety, and not even the blandness of official documents entirely disguises the resentment which British officials occasionally felt when dealing with him. Yet Thomas himself encouraged Bennett, who had doubts about Ferguson's capacity to deal with certain economic issues, to agree that he chair the Imperial Economic Committee and Ferguson served in this capacity from 1933 to 1935.[45] Other evidence of official British opinion of Canada House and of Ferguson emerged during a new skirmish in an old dispute over channels of communication and consultation. In April 1935, External Affairs reacted with some anger to a press report to the effect that Canada had been consulted and concurred in British policy during the Disarmament Conference. When the familiar Canadian note about the distinction between consultation and information was despatched, a Foreign Office official expressed surprise that Canada should rely on 'garbled press accounts' for information rather than on a report from Canada House. The Dominions Office realized, however, that 'Canada House as at present organized is not really equipped for sending to Ottawa accounts of the kind suggested by the Foreign Office.'[46] This surely was a damning commentary on Canada House understaffing, for the despatching of such reports could hardly have been regarded as an extraordinary or onerous duty.

Equally revealing was a comment made a few months after Ferguson left office by an official in the office of the British High Commissioner in Ottawa to Batterbee of the Dominions Office. Commenting on the desire of Canadian ministers to minimize the role of their High Commissioner in London so as to lessen the possibility of undesirable commitments, the official noted that 'as regards the personal factor, it appears that if the High Commissioner is generally regarded as capable and intelligent, as in the case of Massey, or if he is thought to be rather uninformed, as in the case of Ferguson, the effect in each case is to minimize his importance; in the first place because he might aspire to direct Canadian foreign policy from London, and, in the latter, lest he should be unwittingly led into some commitment by the more capable and astute British Ministers.' That a British diplomat should prefer the cultured Massey to a bumptious provincial politician is not surprising; more interesting was his conclusion that 'the Canadian High Commissionership in London certainly seems to be rather a thankless task for a capable man!'[47]

Ferguson had often presented Canada's position virtually on his own in confrontation sometimes with several ministers backed by a highly skilled civil service. Doubtless he did appear uninformed at times and if so the fault lay more with his government and with the structure of Canada House than with him. Not until Canada House was radically reformed would such situations be eliminated. On the whole, Ferguson in London avoided the worst excesses his critics had anticipated. Despite occasional gaffes and a style which left conventional diplomats gasping, he served Canada energetically and imaginatively. Although he achieved several triumphs which would have been beyond the reach of a less political representative, his greatest contribution lay in the hard, daily labour of speeches and meetings in which he worked to protect the Canadian interest and to sell Canadian products to his British hosts.

Ferguson experienced mixed feelings as the October federal election approached which would surely end his tenure of office. Those schemes of imperial reorganization of which he had sometimes dreamed remained unattained. When he passed on to Bennett in 1935 a federationist project which had been brought to his attention, it was dismissed by the Prime Minister with the comment that until there was a complete change of public opinion it was not feasible and in fact already had been rejected.[48] He recognized the truth of this but he still wanted to believe that in some respects the ties of Empire could be drawn closer. His hope that Canada might begin to play a role on the Committee of Imperial Defence also came to nothing; in a later article in *Maclean's* he compared his country unfavourably to South Africa, New Zealand, and Australia in this respect.[49] Of course, he was delighted that Anglo-Canadian trade had increased so substantially. Canadian imports from the UK rose from $94,000,000 in 1932 to $117,000,000 in 1934 while exports went from $178,000,000 in 1932 to $304,000,000 in 1935.[50] Ferguson believed not unnaturally that his own tireless efforts in Whitehall and across the British Isles had contributed to that result. At least there were no economists on hand to tell him that what had transpired had been inevitable on the one hand and would prove ephemeral on the other.

Even so, in letters to Canadian correspondents in 1934 and 1935 he had to admit that the British remained fearful that their exports to Canada would be 'greatly, if not entirely shattered if the Americans knock down their tariff wall. ... They feel very strongly,' he told Charles Magrath, 'that if they neglect their foreign markets for the benefit of Canadian trade that we may someday switch to America and they will lose our business and will in the meantime have lost their foreign trade...'[51] The clearest illustration of this possibility was the difficulty he had in trying to convince London port authorities to install the equipment necessary for the handling of Canadian livestock. To Harry Stevens he wrote that 'their fear is that the United States tariff may be reduced, and turn the tide of the Canadian cattle trade to the South...'[52] A year later the problem remained unsolved. The cost of the port improvements, Ferguson informed Bennett, would be ten thousand pounds and 'the Port authorities were unable to undertake it unless they had some assurance of continued business, and, of course, that was a condition that could not be fulfilled.'[53]

In a sense, it had all come to this. How slight by 1935 were the remaining fragments of the great dream; yet he clung to those fragments for they expressed not only his past hopes but they continued to represent the values he held dear and to give meaning to his life. Disappointment after Ottawa he knew in full measure but the total disillusionment of the realists he could never share. He had been an imperialist all the years of his life and his faith in the Empire would not die. Before returning home, however, one last stormy episode remained in his overseas career.

In his *Memoirs*, Lester Pearson has described the Italo-Ethiopian dispute of 1935 as 'the most important international crisis between the wars.'[54] Mussolini's invasion of Abyssinia put to the test the efficacy of collective security and the inability of the League of Nations to respond effectively dealt a crippling blow to its credibility. Canada's own position was particularly sensitive and difficult. Pressures existed for her to follow whatever lead the United Kingdom might take, while in Quebec considerable sympathy existed for Catholic Italy. The Department of External Affairs was still dominated by O.D. Skelton, always suspicious of collective security; while R.B. Bennett's own intermittent interest in foreign policy added an unsettling element. As the storm clouds gathered in 1935, Bennett again despatched Ferguson to Geneva as delegation head. He also forwarded Lester Pearson from External Affairs to lend professional expertise.

Because of the famous 'Riddell incident' in which the government of Mackenzie King disavowed the initiative taken by its representative to add oil to the list of sanctions imposed against Italy, Canada's role in the events at Geneva has been a source of great controversy. The crisis came at the height of the 1935 federal election; thus confusion developed over the line to be followed by Canada's representatives, and it has been argued with much force that the men on the spot took advantage of this state of affairs to follow a course they knew did not have the approval of External Affairs. It is further suggested that it was the success the Canadian delegation experienced between 7 and 14 October, when it was headed by Ferguson, in reacting to events in Geneva rather than following the wishes of Ottawa, that 'inspired and virtually guaranteed Riddell's later boldness' with respect to oil sanctions.[55] These are serious charges that merit careful consideration.

On 29 July, British Foreign Secretary Sir Samuel Hoare briefed the Dominion High Commissioners on the unfolding situation. As both Hoare and Anthony Eden, the British cabinet minister responsible for League affairs, later noted, the attitude of the Dominions at this stage was uncertain. Ferguson merely remarked at this gathering that it seemed likely that 'the use of collective security would find no advocate except within the Empire, and it was not certain what the attitude of the Dominion Governments on that point might be.'[56] On 3 September the Canadian government forwarded to Whitehall a full statement of views which followed the traditionally cautious line on sanctions. At this stage, however, Britain took a hard position in favour of collective security at the General Assembly and Ferguson received permisssion from Skelton to say that 'Canada will join with the other members of the League in considering how by unanimous action peace can be enforced.'

As the sense of crisis mounted, there were frequent meetings of the Commonwealth delegates during the rest of September. At one such gathering, Ferguson asked the object of an explanation the British ambassador had made to Mussolini which emphasized that the British fleet in the Mediterranean had no aggressive intent. Ferguson, it has been suggested, had become a 'hard-liner'; this seems far-fetched and his question in all likelihood was meant to elicit information.[57] Then the following day Eden explained that 'if Italy went to war in defiance of the judgement given under Article 15, and that if that judgement was accepted by Abyssinia, then the application of Article 16 of the League convenant which provided for automatic sanctions against an aggressor became automatic.' It has been argued that because Ferguson did not dissent from Eden's statement, 'as Ottawa would most certainly have done,' that his 'consent by silence implied that Canada believed sanctions were automatic once an aggressor was identified as such by the League.'[58] This is misleading. Skelton so far from dissenting from this interpretation was shortly to use precisely the same argument about Article 16 to support his own views. In any case such meetings, as Ottawa had made perfectly clear, were merely a sounding board and to argue that Eden reached firm conclusions about Canada's attitude because of Ferguson's silence strains the evidence.

On 3 October news reached London that Italian bombers had struck Adowa. In Eden's view, 'the League was certainly now on trial before the world' and if it stumbled again as it had during the Manchurian crisis, the whole idea of collective security might be forever discredited. Swift action was essential. On 6 October a special committee reported that Italy had resorted to war in disregard of the Covenant and the Council unanimously, except for Italy, accepted the report of its committee. The member nations now confronted Article 16, which required all other members of the League to sever 'all trade or financial relations' with any member so condemned.

On 7 October Riddell cabled Ottawa that delegations would soon be called on to state their position on the Council's decision and requested 'explicit instructions' and Ferguson, still in London, also asked for 'full instructions ... relating to sanctions...' Riddell the same day 'asked whether Canada should accept membership on any committee created ... to draw up plans for the collective imposition of sanctions.' He received no reply and tried again the following day, 'emphasizing that Canada's abstention through lack of instructions would be most unfortunate as the country would be grouped with others which abstained because of instructions.' That same day the delegation sent a third request for instructions.[59]

Finally, on 8 October, Skelton was in touch with Bennett who was campaigning in Cornwall, Ontario, and two telegrams were despatched to Geneva. The first instructed the Canadian delegation 'not actively to seek membership on any assembly committee involved with sanctions, but not to refuse membership if offered.' The second instructed Ferguson to tell the Assembly that Canada would refrain from voting because Parliament had been dissolved and 'it is not considered advisable to anticipate in any way the action of the new Parliament.'[60] This message fell like a bombshell. Pearson recalls that he 'could hardly eat my continental breakfast at the Hotel de la Paix before rushing off to see Mr Ferguson.'[61] The Canadian delegates were rightly appalled at a decision which would isolate Canada by placing her in the same camp as one or two countries which sympathized with the fascist cause.

At once Ferguson despatched a telegram to Ottawa in blunt language which suggested that all his influence with Bennett was being placed on the line. After emphasizing that only Hungary and perhaps Austria would abstain from voting to declare Italy the aggressor, it pointed out that 'our acceptance today of the fact of Italian aggression would of course be without prejudice to our attitude towards any scheme of sanctions which might be later proposed.'[62] The trouble was that there was little chance of getting a reply from Ottawa before the Assembly opened that afternoon. Pearson later recounted that when he asked Ferguson what he was going to do, 'in his forthright way, he replied, "Rather than abstain as instructed and join that minority of one or two, I'll not go to the Assembly at all. We'll go and play golf." The Geneva golf course,' Pearson continued, 'was a nice easy one and I enjoyed playing on it, but not in these circumstances; the thought of disobeying such important instructions from Ottawa would make my slice even worse than usual. So I suggested that we try to get Mr Bennett on the transatlantic telephone and have our instructions changed.' Never before had there been a telephone call from Geneva to the Canadian government and 'we had never before conducted business this way with a prime minister, especially one on an election tour. But Mr Ferguson was not one to worry about unconventional procedures...'[63]

Ferguson proceeded to tell Bennett that on arrival in Geneva he found the telegram of 9 October waiting him. He felt that the telegram was based on a misconception of the situation for the vote in the Assembly was merely to confirm the unanimous decision of the Council declaring Italy the aggressor. A co-ordinating committee would be set up later to deal with the question of sanctions and that morning he had refused to have Canada represented on it because he considered it advisable not to do or say anything at the moment. Only later would the question of sanctions be decided. Ferguson then read the telegram sent that morning to Ottawa. At this Bennett agreed to cancel the original instructions and told Ferguson to use his own judgement along the proposed lines. According to Pearson's account, the Prime Minister added that Ferguson for the time being should keep clear of membership on the proposed sanctions committee.

On hearing Bennett's decision, Pearson has recalled, he uttered 'a great sigh of relief and satisfaction, which no doubt was audible across the ocean in Lindsay.' The High Commissioner then asked 'R.B.' how the election was going. 'Fine, Fergy, we have them licked,' was the reply. Pearson later commented, 'Optimism could go no further.'

Much relieved, we went off to the Palais des Nations and were just in time to join all the members of the League of Nations, except Italy, Austria and Hungary, in declaring that the fascist government of Italy had violated the Covenant of the League of Nations. ... It was a narrow escape from making Canada look ridiculous on an issue of far-reaching importance.[64]

At least two officials in External were less pleased at this 'narrow escape.' According to one account, Loring Christie, who had rejoined the Department short weeks before and whose view of the League closely coincided with Skelton's, 'reportedly "all but choked with rage" as Bennett tauntingly informed him of his decision.'[65] And when Skelton discussed these events over the phone with the Prime minister, who was then in Toronto, the Under-Secretary did not bother to disguise his fury:

R.B.B. Any further word from Geneva? Understood further telegram was to come.
O.D.S. Only telegram today refers to procedure in voting...
R.B.B. Have talked with Ferguson ... agree with him that can decide only one question at a time ... that question now before League is whether Italy is guilty and that only one answer can be made to that: so we will give our verdict of "guilty."

420 G. Howard Ferguson

O.D.S. Certainly no question as to Italy's guilt, and we should say so; but to say
so without explanation or qualification under circumstances involves
commitment to apply sanctions. Ferguson's statement emphatically not
a correct or honest picture.

R.B.B. No commitment as to kind of sanctions, and if it did require such
commitment, cannot evade that. No doubt we signed Covenant; no
doubt of Italy's guilt; we must take the consequences. Talk about
honesty! Can you deny we gave our pledge in the covenant?

O.D.S. No. But I also insist we repeatedly and publicly declared our opposition
to sanctions, and that whole League development since then re
sanctions, disarmament, etc., must be considered, not change our
position without fullest consideration, merely because Britain has
changed...[66]

Was Ferguson's assurance that the statement of Italian guilt and the call for
sanctions were two separate issues incorrect and dishonest, as Skelton charged?
Certainly there was no question as to Italy's guilt. To seek to evade the consequences of that was, as Bennett indicated, less than honest and Article 16
followed all but automatically from that fact. Yet even in his *Memoirs*, Pearson
has continued to assert that 'the specific question of sanctions was not involved
in this vote' to declare Italy an aggressor.[67] By this he meant that sanctions
followed automatically but their form and extent did not.

Shortly after these events, Pearson and Skelton debated the matter in private
correspondence. The Under-Secretary told Pearson he could not agree that a
declaration that Italy was the aggressor 'left a country free to determine the
form of sanctions. With the smooth-working Tammany machine that has
developed at Geneva, it is not even true, and if true, it would be of minimum
importance. The vital fact was that declaring Italy an aggressor ... committed
Canada ... to any and all sanctions that might be applied under Article 16.'
Pearson rebutted that 'all the discussions at Geneva were conducted with the
assumption that no such literal interpretation of Article 16 was even under
consideration. ... Your reply to that view is that with the smooth-working
Tammany machine that has developed at Geneva our technical freedom from
responsibility would not matter. Personally I do not think that however smooth
working that machine may be it could drag us into any commitment which we
do not ourselves desire to take.'[68]

An equally serious disagreement developed over Canada's membership on the
proposed 'sanctions committee.' Bennett's order that for the time being Canada
was not to accept membership was clear enough. In fact two committees were
set up, the co-ordinating committee and a smaller working committee, later
called the Committee of Eighteen. It has been argued recently that Riddell, and
by implication Ferguson and Pearson, engaged in a dishonest intrigue to commit

Ottawa to membership on the Committee of Eighteen without Ottawa even being aware of its existence. Membership on that Committee, according to this analysis, 'was formally accepted without instruction' and with the knowledge, in the opinion at least of a Dominions Office official, that all nations who sat on the working committee would 'at any rate be committed.' The Canadian delegation, it is suggested, 'was turning the tables on External Affairs; sensing that the Department would disapprove of its actions and attitudes, it took advantage of the confusion caused by the election and couched its reports in ambiguous terms, omitting significant information.'[69]

These charges raise doubts about the integrity not only of Ferguson and Riddell but of Pearson, whose own version is that the initial instructions not to sit on any sanctions committee, even a committee of the whole, 'were changed, however, on an appeal from Geneva and the Canadian delegate was authorized to serve.' Pearson has added that Skelton's desire to 'put a brake on any possible initiative from the delegation' had been checked by Mr Bennett, whose position was, 'simply, that we should discharge our obligations under the Covenant. ... So Canada became a member not only of the full committee, but also of the smaller Committee of Eighteen set up to do the effective work of organizing and directing sanctions.' Pearson also points out that Skelton felt that Bennett's decision to allow Canada to sit on the Co-ordinating Committee 'did not cover membership on the Committee of Eighteen' but that Riddell 'took exception to this criticism, and rightly so. He pointed out that throughout the crisis he had kept the department fully and swiftly informed of developments but had great difficulty in getting any instructions from Ottawa in time to be of help...'[70] Although he did not say so specifically, Pearson seemed to be of the view that permission to sit on the full sanctions committee 'covered' the question of membership on its subcommittees.

This, however, seems a large assumption. Ottawa's response on 10 October to Riddell's 8 October request for instructions was that 'Prime Minister's view regarding membership on Sanctions Committee is that we should not seek place, but in certain contingencies should not refuse if requested to serve. If Canadian membership proposed, advise us immediately.' In response, on 10 October Ferguson wired that the Assembly had adopted a Council report recommending a sanctions committee composed of all members of the Assembly and that he would provisionally accept membership on that committee subject to instructions. 'Please wire instructions at once.' The reply sent the same day stated that permission was granted 'as the committee is to consist of all Members of the Assembly' and added that 'as practically all Ministers are out of town it will however be impossible to send instructions until the beginning of the week, and no definite attitude should be taken until further communication is sent.'[71] The Co-ordinating Committee set to work next day and created the working Committee of Eighteen, which itself had several subcommittees. Ferguson accepted membership on the Committee of Eighteen, possibly, as Pearson hints in his *Memoirs*, because the Canadian delegation believed that permission to serve on a committee – the Co-ordinating Committee – naturally included permission to serve on other bodies the parent committee might deem fit to establish.

This was not the defence offered by Riddell on 7 December in his response to a reprimand received from Skelton on 1 November. Riddell informed Skelton that the first sitting of the Co-ordinating Committee had taken place on 11 October, within two hours of the telegram (sent 10 October, decoded 11 October) authorizing Canada to sit on it. 'Immediately after this meeting you were informed by cable No. 158 of the constitution and terms of reference of the Committee of Sixteen (now the Committee of Eighteen) and that the Canadian delegation had been invited to be represented. You were further advised that the Committee of Sixteen would meet in the afternoon to propose the adoption of certain measures of embargo to the plenary Committee convened for the same evening.' In view of these circumstances, Riddell continued, the delegation considered that 'it should provisionally accept membership on the Committee of Sixteen.' Riddell argued that the delegation felt it had acted in accordance with the instructions of 9 October that it should not seek a place on any sanctions committee 'but in certain contingencies should not refuse if requested to serve.' The delegation, he continued, 'did not seek a place; it was requested to serve without previous soundings or advance notice.' In Riddell's view, 'that the delegation did not act with undue haste in accepting membership is evident from the fact that only on the 12th October, two days after my telegram of the 10th asking for general instructions, did the delegation respond to a request from the chairman of the Co-ordination Committee by informing him in writing that Canada would be represented on both the Co-ordination Committee and the Committee of Eighteen.'[72] And cable No. 158 does indeed state perfectly clearly that 'At the opening of meeting this morning Sanctions Co-ordinating Committee ... set up a small Co-ordinating Committee of Sixteen,' including Canada, and that 'it will meet for the first time this afternoon...'[73]

Clearly, then, the delegation had been at pains to inform Skelton at the earliest possible opportunity of the Co-ordinating Committee's decision to form a smaller working committee. Certainly the speed of events at Geneva made it difficult to send information to and receive instructions from Canada in good time and there was room for resentment to develop in Ottawa. Still, membership on the smaller committee, an offspring of the full committee on which the Canadians were authorized to serve, was accepted only *provisionally*; Ottawa was informed *immediately* that the smaller committee was being established; and the Canadian delegates finally accepted membership only two days after Riddell's telegram of 10 October. In all of this, it is difficult to see how Ferguson and his colleagues consciously sought to mislead Ottawa by withholding or distorting information. In any case, Ferguson knew he had Bennett's confidence and there was no possible motive for him to try to mislead the Prime Minister.

Another point remains unexplained. Eden had informed a meeting of Commonwealth delegates on 7 October, immediately after the Council report condemning Italy, that a committee of the whole and a subcommittee would be set up to study means of implementing sanctions. Riddell reported this meeting to External on 7 October, but did not distinguish between the full and the subcommittee. Then, on 8 October, the Commonwealth delegates discussed which of their number should be represented on the proposed 'sanctions committee.' Although Eden suggested South Africa and India, Riddell pressed hard for Canada. Again it has been argued that this was extraordinary behaviour, particularly since te Water of South Africa 'objected that the Commonwealth was overstocking the Committee, but Riddell was unmoved.'[74] Riddell telegraphed his government for permission for Canada to serve, but in the meantime received on 10 October the cable instructing Canada not to seek a place on the sanctions committee; however, 'these instructions came too late' as Canadian membership had already been proposed by the Canadian delegate himself.

This account, however, neglects to mention that at the meeting of Commonwealth delegates on 9 October, Howard Ferguson reported that no reply had yet been received from his government to a telegram sent the preceding night asking whether they wished to be represented on the Co-ordinating Committee. At that meeting Ferguson expressed the view that Ottawa probably would not have any strong feelings on the matter and that Canada would be prepared to step down in favour of South Africa. Riddell, it should be noted, was present at this meeting.[75] This suggests that at this very early stage the Commonwealth delegates, or at least the Canadians, were not making any distinction between the two sanctions committees – and perhaps this was because they had not yet been established and no information could be very definite. Ferguson, so far from pressing for Canadian membership, was entirely willing to see South Africa rather than Canada serve.

There is no doubt that a sense of urgency gripped Geneva in these days and decisions were being made in haste. If the Committee of Eighteen was established with some speed, it was because it was expected to report at once to the Assembly. Every hour the League delayed, the possibilities of success diminished. As Canada's representative on the Committee of Eighteen, Ferguson shared the view of Eden and others that swift action was imperative. But he also knew he had been instructed on 10 October that 'no definite attitude should be taken until further communication is sent...' Despite this, he declined to play a passive role. At the opening of the Committee of Eighteen when the Argentine delegate raised technicalities which threatened delay, Ferguson reminded committee members that 'the sole problem before the Committee was to decide what sanctions the delegations could all agree upon that afternoon and put into application immediately. Let them show the world that the League was no longer to be scoffed at or laughed at, but that it meant business...'[76] Otherwise, he concluded, the League might as well dissolve. Riddell has recorded that Ferguson's bold words were greeted with applause and 'the feeling of the meeting was overwhelmingly in accord' with him.[77]

Two facts need emphasis here. First, Ferguson by arguing that it was up to the delegates to agree upon what sanctions should be put into effect thereby confirmed the assurances given his government that the actual form of sanctions had not been predetermined by the vote to declare Italy an aggressor.[78] Secondly, the point Ferguson was making was essentially procedural. Soon he would be accused of having recommended an immediate arms embargo against Italy and this charge would be echoed by later historians.[79] Ferguson's point, however, was simply that within hours the Committee was expected to recommend measures to be taken against the aggressor and it should get down to its business, the discussion of a possible arms embargo. Riddell himself in response to a reprimand from Skelton was at pains to emphasize that Ferguson merely 'spoke when a protracted and irrelevant discussion was delaying the work of the Committee. ... He called attention to the purpose for which the meeting had been called and in saying that action, rather than debate, was the duty of the Committee, he was naturally led to refer to the measures which had already been taken by the Government of the United States, and to ask if similar action could not be considered by the Committee. Beyond this he did not go.'[80] That this was the case must be apparent to anyone who has read the official record. The Committee was sitting for one purpose and one purpose only: to recommend what form sanctions should take. Ferguson merely recommended that the Committee attend to the business at hand. The Committee minutes record that 'he suggested that the Committee could perhaps deal at once with the question of the arms embargo, upon which all members might be able to agree. As time went on there would perhaps have to be some method of adopting progressive sanctions from time to time, but surely there was something – perhaps with regard to a financial sanction or arms embargo – that could be announced to the world tonight in order that it might be known that the League was taking some action.'[81] Skelton preferred to put his own gloss on the facts. The record also shows that Eden 'emphatically endorsed' what Ferguson had said and that it was Eden who proposed an arms embargo. This then was unanimously endorsed by the Committee and that same evening the Co-ordinating Committee adopted a general embargo on the export of arms to Italy.

At the fourth meeting of the Committee, Ferguson again played a prominent role. The Argentine delegate had intimated that any action his country might take would have to await the action of the Argentine Congress, which was not then in session, or alternatively be taken to the Supreme Court. 'The import of this speech,' Riddell states, 'was not clear to the Committee. It exploded in their midst, causing consternation and dismay. ... Again, Mr Ferguson intervened in the debate with good effect...' telling the Committee that 'Canada had joined the League ... with a full knowledge of her undertakings, and fully appreciating the obligations imposed upon her and the risks she was running.' If one country after another was now going to discover 'difficulties so great that they thought they could not face them, then let the delegations go home.'[82] Ferguson's intervention, Riddell recorded, 'cleared the air and elicited from the Argentine delegate a more satisfactory statement...'[83] A Canadian on the League Secretariat reported to Dafoe that 'Ferguson has been very useful in the Co-ordination Committee. He has twice cut across rambling apologies and withdrawings, and has made it clear to everyone that the Canadians are determined to see the collective system put in motion in this case.'[84]

Of course he had also exceeded his 10 October instructions. Of his 11 October intervention, James Eayrs noted, 'Geneva had never heard a stronger plea in support of collective security from a Canadian delegate; by the same token it had never heard a speech less typically Canadian.'[85] On the other hand Ferguson knew that Ottawa, in the final throes of an election, had been unable to react to requests for instructions; and he knew too that the Committee of Eighteen had been given a task of urgency with orders to present its recommendations at once. Nor were his remarks made to 'Geneva,' as Professor Eayrs suggests, but to a closed meeting of a working committee.[86] Of the nature of that Committee's work, Hertzog, the prime minister of South Africa, commenting on his delegate's role asserted that 'Mr te Water spoke as a member of the Committee of Eighteen; Members of this Committee do not in their discussions speak on behalf of their Governments.'[87] Hertzog's position sounds strained but undeniably it was an attitude which existed at the time and reflected the emergency conditions in which the Committee did its work. In any case, Ferguson's interventions, it must be repeated, were procedural in nature.

O.D. Skelton refused to accept this position. In his reprimand to Riddell he insisted that 'in spite of instructions that no definite attitude should be taken until a further communication was received, the Canadian delegation actually took the initiative in making the first proposal for the application of sanctions.'[88] Of course Ferguson's words as recorded in the Committee minutes are open to this interpretation, although both the context in which they were spoken and the words themselves strongly suggest otherwise. Skelton, however, refused either to accept this or to make any allowances for the unique circumstances which prevailed in both Ottawa and Geneva. The problem perhaps arose from Skelton's expectation that Ferguson, in the absence of any positive instructions, would simply remain mute and take no active part in the work of the Committee. No doubt the Under-Secretary had every right to be confident that an official such as Riddell would have no choice but to play such a role. Ferguson, however, was no 'External Affairs' man but a friend and colleague of the Prime Minister, an old politician accustomed to speak his mind within limits finally determined not by Skelton but by Bennett.

It seems likely that Skelton miscalculated the politics of the situation. Bennett, he knew, was a sometime supporter of collective security, an anglophile with a tendency to follow the British lead in European affairs. But the Prime Minister, preoccupied with domestic affairs, relied heavily on Skelton, whose views had usually prevailed. The problem in this case was that Ferguson had 'gotten to' the prime minister by phone and had been given a degree of latitude which enraged both Skelton and Loring Christie. Skelton also knew that in a few days Bennett, Ferguson, and all their works would be swept away by the Canadian electorate. It has been suggested that the Canadian delegation was taking advantage of the 'confusion' caused by the election to relay incomplete and ambiguous information to Ottawa as part of a plan to 'turn the tables on External Affairs.'[89] The evidence for this is slight and it seems more likely that the Under-Secretary, knowing that Bennett temporarily at least had been swayed by Ferguson, was himself turning the tables and acting improperly. Taking advantage of the state of affairs in Ottawa, it may be that he deliberately left the Canadian delegation without instructions beyond those of 10 October. In a few days, Skelton knew, a Prime Minister more to his liking would be in office. Could this fact, rather than 'confusion' caused by the election, account for Ottawa's failure, despite repeated requests by the delegates, to transmit adequate instructions at such a vital moment in the history of the League? It seems incredible that Skelton could not have reached Bennett if he had really wanted to formulate further instructions. Probably he preferred to wait. The return to office of a Liberal government on 15 October gave Skelton the power to act on behalf of those views he held so tenaciously throughout his Ottawa career. Soon he was back in the saddle. On 6 November he was able to tell Pearson that, 'as regards Geneva, matters seem to be going along swimmingly.'[90]

The day after the Canadian election, Ferguson left for London. He remained there as High Commissioner until the Bennett government's resignation and, at the request of Mackenzie King, for a short time thereafter. Of all his activities as a Canadian representative abroad, his role at Geneva remains the most controversial. That Riddell, who stepped into Ferguson's position as delegation head, soon encountered his own difficulties with the Liberal government has been attributed in some measure to the bad habits he developed while serving under Ferguson. Yet Ferguson must have experienced some satisfaction when one of the first moves of the new Liberal administration was to express its support in a press release of 29 October for 'the effective application of the economic sanctions against Italy proposed by the Co-ordination Committee.' Something at least had been achieved during those exciting few days at Geneva. It was Riddell, unfortunately, who had to face the wrath of the Liberal chieftains. Riddell's account of a January 1936 meeting with King and Lapointe reveals the extent to which they blamed Ferguson for Canada's unwelcome commitment to a sanctions policy:

...Lapointe at once asked me what Ferguson had to do with sanctions over there and why he had proposed them. I told Lapointe that Ferguson never proposed sanctions. This rather annoyed Lapointe as he seemed to have his knife in for Ferguson. I told him that all that Ferguson did was to try to keep the discussion within the limits that had been set for it, which was to consider the question of sanctions, as the subcommittee had to report to the meeting at 6 o'clock that afternoon ... to consider definite action. Mr King also seemed to be annoyed that I had tried to defend Ferguson...[91]

Of Ferguson's qualifications to represent Canada at Geneva it has been stated that he 'considered foreign affairs to be an extension of eternal verities. He prized the virtues of integrity and "steadiness" which he found were lacking in non-British stock.'[92] It is easy enough to sneer at the figure cut at Geneva by the old politico who was, in truth, no very close student of international affairs. Some of Ferguson's prejudices were caught in a 1936 assessment by the American Consul-General in Toronto, who wrote that 'it used to give [Ferguson] an awful pain at Geneva to hear some little fellow, representing some little nation, and speaking some language other than English get up and talk for an hour or so, and to know that the little fellow had the same right as he did to cast a vote.'[93] This was accurate enough. Ferguson himself had earlier expressed the view that 'there must be a very strong feeling everywhere with the fact that the overwhelming majority of representatives at these various conferences come from small countries of little importance, and greatly retard the possibility of the important Powers reaching some sort of agreement.' This was not an uncommon attitude, it was one which he shared with no less a personage than Mackenzie King.[94]

Yet Ferguson, while not unaddicted to 'the eternal verities,' retained the skills which had taken him so far in Ontario. He recognized that the rivalries which existed in provincial politics operated as well on the vastly expanded canvas of international affairs. Unawed by important decisions, able to express his views cogently and effectively, well schooled in the psychology of deliberative bodies, he brought qualities to Geneva that to a very considerable extent made up for his obvious defects. For those defects, the trained diplomats, Pearson and Riddell, were more than able to compensate and, as a result, Ferguson's positive attributes came into play at a critical moment in the League's history.

Riddell, no unbiased observer but one of unrivalled experience, has written that too few of the national representatives at Geneva possessed the qualities required of a good delegate. Howard Ferguson, he asserted, was one who did. If on the whole stage his contribution remained small, nonetheless it was perhaps fortunate that Canada's influence at this critical juncture was used for a brief moment on behalf of a strong League and collective security. Failure followed. Of that failure, Riddell concluded that 'the last chance of averting World War II had gone forever.'[95]

Conclusion

Before leaving for Canada, Howard Ferguson reflected on the events at Geneva. The previous summer he had told reporters in New York that he had 'never been keen on the League of Nations'; in retrospect he was convinced that the part it had played 'was more than I was inclined to give them credit for before I went over there.' The League, he believed, had helped develop a world public opinion 'that had the effect not only of restraining the Italians but it confined the war area to Abyssinia and the conflict to the Italians and Abyssinians. This itself was a great achievement.' Yet now it appeared that 'Mussolini is getting ready to kill off a few more black people and then settle the war...'[1]

Bennett himself quipped to Ferguson the day after the federal election that 'the operations of the Italian Ethiopian campaign were extended yesterday along the Quebec Front with heavy casualties...'[2] Of course the Tory defeat had been no surprise. Although King's majority was larger than Ferguson had anticipated, he was pleased that stable government was assured and that the electorate had rejected 'all these quack nostrums that are going to cure all our political ills.'[3] His British years had not lessened his distaste for leftist views and third parties. Also in character was his comment to Beaverbrook that King appeared to have constructed a fairly strong cabinet that would 'restore confidence in the business interests.'[4]

In the months before the election, while recognizing that 'Bennett may get smashed,' he had believed that collapse might be averted 'if the situation is tactfully handled.'[5] When Harry Stevens's Price Spreads Commission was causing friction with Bennett, he had warned him that the Trade Minister had much public sympathy and that 'to turn the tide of public opinion would require careful and tactful handling. I urged upon him,' he related to Colquhoun, 'that it would be disastrous to follow the course he had in mind of immediately and peremptorily dispensing with Stevens.' Public opinion should be manipulated and Stevens placed unequivocally in the wrong before the coup was administered. But Bennett was in no mood to listen and Ferguson regretfully concluded 'it seems pretty difficult to convince the Chief that the public do not care a hoot about all the things he has achieved in the past...' What the times demanded was 'some spectacular or emotional appeal. It is entirely a question of moving the mob rather than appealing to the intelligence of the public.'

With all the cynicism of the weary professional again to the fore, he dispensed advice on the less pleasant aspects of public life in the style which had won him the sobriquet 'foxie Fergie.' In a series of letters written in response to the Hepburn victory and the Bennett defeat, he dilated upon the manipulative side of politics. His apparently jaundiced attitude towards democracy reflected opinions which were fairly widespread in some circles, but few of his Canadian contemporaries would have so readily committed such views to paper. After confiding in Colquhoun that Bennett would have to make some grand gesture, he told his old friend that 'as a matter of fact, the public has no intelligence. No election was ever won by logic or arguments. Educated intelligent people ... are in a hopeless minority. With our Utopian wide-open franchise the mob rules. The problem is to capture the imagination of the mob.' Asserting that 'hungry, workless and resentful' people were highly susceptible to demagogic appeals, he believed that when conditions returned to normal, 'we will settle down to a saner situation.'

He pointed to Mitch Hepburn as typical of Depression demagogues. 'Our little friend in Ontario has caught the idea,' he told Colquhoun. 'I think it comes natural to him because he is of that tribe himself. ... It is simply a sort of psychological response to the clamour of the noisy crowd. It will ride this crest for a time but it is never long lived and the reaction will be disastrous for him.'[6]

With Victor Sinclair, a civil servant on whom the Hepburn hatchet had fallen, he commiserated that 'this can only continue for a limited time. Under our vaunted system of democracy, intelligence plays a small part; the mob rules and the mob's activities are always destructive. It will go for a short time until the saner elements of the crowd realize the dangers ahead...'[7] To Ferguson the remedy was leadership. 'Every government must essentially be a one-man Government,' he informed Beaverbrook's secretary. 'You cannot run a Church nor a football team, nor even the Sunday Express!!! without one dominating voice dictating the policy. Of course, I agree that such dictation should be based upon a broad knowledge of public opinion and conditions as an outcome of enquiry and consultation.'[8] In Ontario he had always run a one-man government, but then the élitism of his outlook had been softened by the warmth of his personality and by his careful cultivation of public opinion. Possibly five years of appointive office together with his associations in Britain had hardened and narrowed his Toryism.

Ferguson had demanded something spectacular and Bennett's New Deal delighted him. It was, he wrote approvingly, 'a programme with outlook and vision.' His distaste for the dole was now forgotten as he pronounced the proposed social reforms impressive and sound, if not really new. What was most exciting of course, almost all that mattered, were the political implications. 'Bennett has so long been regarded as a capitalist allied with big interests ... that his declaration comes as an unusually spectacular and unexpected move.' He had gained centre stage and, Ferguson conjectured, perhaps placed King in a bit of a hole. Politics, he pontificated, 'is pure psychology and nothing else. Once you start the trend of public opinion you can guide it and direct it and develop it just as the shepherd's dog rounds up and directs the course of the flock.'[9]

By August some of this optimism had dissipated and privately he was discussing the advantages of some kind of a National government. He himself had received unofficial overtures in 1933 and his impression of the work of the National government in the United Kingdom made it appear in his mind as a real possibility. He should have known better. With victory within their grasp, leading Liberals would never consider such a proposal and an analogy Ferguson drew to 1917 was remarkably far-fetched.[10] In October came the massive Tory defeat. When its dimensions were known he was left to pay off an election wager with Beaverbrook and to provide him with some analysis of what had happened. He attributed the Liberal sweep to the Depression, Tory neglect of organization after 1930, and the formation of Harry Stevens's Reconstruction party.[11]

Before he left the United Kingdom, he experienced one disappointment. In May, Bennett had considered recommending him for a knighthood but action was postponed because the honours list at that time was a long one. Now, on the day before he left office, the prime minister formally made the recommendation and on 23 October received word that 'the King will be pleased to approve of your recommendation...' By this time, however, Mackenzie King was in office and King opposed the appointment. While Bennett expressed regret that 'the faithful and efficient services of a great public servant should not receive merited recognition,' he concurred that 'His Majesty must not be involved in any controversy...' The matter was quietly dropped.[12]

Now it was time to go home. Ferguson received a generous send-off from his hosts and *The Times* in a 6 December editorial warmly praised his work in England. Some hint of his thinking on his future employment was provided by an interview in the same paper in which he remarked that he might well be returning to political life in his native land. That he should yearn for the bustle and excitement of politics after five years as High Commissioner is not surprising. On his arrival in Toronto there were frequent press queries about his intentions. Usually his only reply was a smile. Ella was more definite. 'We're out of politics,' she pronounced. Despite this, for a year or two occasional reports appeared that he might be taking up the cudgels again. Yet in 1936 and 1937 he and Ella spent much of their time abroad with trips to Africa, China, and Japan. He was back in London in 1937 at the time of the Imperial Conference. Clearly the years of unremitting effort had taken their toll and Mackenzie King, who met him at one of the official parties, noted in his diary that 'he looks very frail. He tells me his wife has suffered terribly from shingles. They are pathetic figures on the stage which they left a year or two ago, and to which they would have been just as wise not to return.'

When home he was in demand as a public speaker. Some who heard him felt that he had lost nothing of his old form. George Doucett, later a member of the Drew cabinet, was at Smiths Falls one day when Howard Ferguson came to town and Doucett recalls how vigorously he argued that only through re-armament would the western democracies have much chance in the coming world crisis.[13] This Churchillian refrain was repeated often. He turned to it again in a 1937 article in *Maclean's* entitled 'Canada Must Arm':

We are not arguing the question of war or peace. ... There is in Canada no war party. In our zeal for Imperial connection, our desire to maintain the senti-mental ties that bind us so firmly to the motherland, we are not needlessly risking our future. In the present state of world opinion, it is obvious to most people that a strong Empire working for a common goal of peace, but fully prepared for any emergency, is the best insurance against attack. The League of Nations has failed. ... The Empire affords for us a league of nations so strategically situated that, banded together and properly equipped, it can be the dominating force for world peace.[14]

Although his prejudices against unnamed little European nations who 'are only impressed by strength' were undiminished, he was critical too of the extent to which Britain had dis..rmed. This, he claimed, had accounted for much of Italy's boldness in the Abyssinian crisis.

Still, the old attachments had not waned. In a December 1935 address to the Empire Club, which greeted him with cheers and prolonged applause, he did little more than tell stories, admittedly entertaining ones, about the royal family. Mysticism is the greatest influence in the world, he told his listeners, 'and the mysticism that surrounds monarchy and all the old traditional institutions creates an atmosphere that has a wonderful effect. I confess I am inoculated with it.'[15] This kind of sentimental monarchism Ferguson shared with other Canadians of his day. For most English Canadians at least, it served as a unifying force whose vigour the royal tour of 1939 would once again demonstrate.

In a more serious vein, he told the Montreal branch of the University of Toronto Alumni Federation that 'my conception of Canada isn't nationalistic at all; my conception is that we ought to play a large part in world affairs.' Equating nationalism with the isolationism preached by so many of its advocates, he insisted that Canada could best play this wider role in association with Great Britain. In an October 1936 address to the Canadian Club of Toronto, he spoke about the threat to world peace. 'There is no doubt in my

mind that Germany is awaiting the opportune time to acquire some territory ... the German hive must swarm some day.' In his opinion German action
would be taken only in conjunction with Italy. That being so, he argued that it
was essential that the Empire should be prepared for joint action. He related
how impressed he had been at Geneva by the deference paid by other nations to
a united Empire and how carefully unfriendly powers searched for evidence of
disharmony.[16]

In language made familiar by generations of Canadian imperialists, he insisted
that '...we shall get much greater prestige as part of a great world organization,
dominating and directing civilization, than we shall as a small unit of ten million
people. The prestige of being part of the Empire is something that is one of the
wonders of foreign countries.' Almost half a century had gone by since Ferguson
had been present in a Toronto hall to hear John A. Macdonald make his famous
'British subject I will die' speech. Since that day much had changed, but for
Ferguson and other English Canadians of his generation, the sun would never set
on the British Empire and their faith in its glories and its virtues would never
waver.

During these years was he hoping for some kind of call? In 1936 the field of
federal politics was hardly an attractive option for an elderly Ontario Tory.
Perhaps he was looking to Queen's Park, where George Henry after his
ignominious defeat was about to be replaced. Who was better qualified to rally
the disgruntled provincial Tories than the old leader returned to his happy
hunting ground? For a while in 1936 a Ferguson boomlet developed. In early
May, Garrett Tyrrell suggested there was 'quite a strong build-up' for Ferguson
to be a candidate in the party's convention that month. Possibly this was a
balloon sent up to test the prevailing currents; possibly some of the old pros
were trying to press him into standing.

In 1936 Elmer Bell, afterward Ontario party president, was an unknown
young Conservative lawyer from Exeter. Concerned by the state into which
Conservatism had fallen, he wrote the former premier to tell him that his party
needed him if it were to be restored to its former greatness and to implore him
to throw his hat into the ring.[17] But Ferguson was noncommittal. He may
merely have concluded that for the moment Mitch Hepburn was unbeatable. Of
course his own re-entry into public life would be the occasion for the Grits to
unleash a host of charges against his former administration and he knew how
damaging politically it would be to be placed on the defensive.

In November 1934, for example, Carroll Hele had warned that Hepburn and
Roebuck were looking hard for dirt and were attacking him in the House. Then
he had told Hele 'that does not worry me at all. In fact I have been surprised
that they have not tried to drag me into the limelight long ago.'[18] But Hepburn's
friends were determined to find something to pin on their old enemy. Thus one
man told Hepburn that Ferguson's sister was one of the Liquor Board

toll-holders. And in June 1934 Senator Hardy had breathlessly informed 'Mitch' that 'yesterday I got information that will blow up H. Ferguson...'[19] What it was remained unclear, but Ferguson may well have hesitated to tempt fate by a re-entry into public life and be labelled 'one of the old gang.'

Nonetheless Bell and some others of the rank and file still believed that the old magic could be called forth again. At the Convention in May they decided that since their choice remained silent they would have to act themselves. They hastened to a printing shop and got out a little pamphlet to the effect that it was time for Ferguson and victory. That night this was distributed under the hotel doors of delegates, the press picked up the story, and soon the impression had been created that a well-organized campaign was being waged for Ferguson. There was a stir of excitement next day as the delegates assembled.[20] Of course the whole thing led nowhere but if Ferguson had given the sign the job might have been his.

Instead he had been applying pressure on Earl Rowe, then a federal member, to take the position. His decision not to return was a wise one. In the tradition of his refusal of 1927 and his retirement in 1930, it reflected his ability to assess accurately his personal situation; his age, his uncertain health, and perhaps Ella's opposition bore most strongly. Earl Rowe won a first-ballot victory. Henceforth Ferguson more than ever was content to enjoy the role of senior statesman and to settle easily into a life of leisure.

Not that he was totally idle. And what better suited to a Tory ex-premier of Ontario than to be president of an insurance company? He had been elected a director of the Crown Life Insurance Company shortly after his return from the United Kingdom on the recommendation of its president, Sir Robert Borden. There had long existed a friendship, though not an intimate one, between the two men and when Ferguson had stepped down in 1935 Borden had been kind enough to write that 'it is universally acknowledged that you have discharged with great ability and distinction ... your duties as High Commissioner.'[21] Now, perhaps because he himself had known what it was like to move from a position of authority to one of relative obscurity, Borden offered the Crown Life directorship and Ferguson, fearing that he would be at loose ends, was delighted to accept. On Borden's death in 1937, he was elected to the company's presidency, a post he held for nine years.

The Crown Life was good to him and he was able to make some contribution to it. At that time the position of president was analogous to that of chairman of the board today and he played no real role in the daily administration of the Company. Nonetheless he was delighted with the position and most days spent the morning at the Company offices at the foot of Yonge Street. H.R. Stevenson, who was General Manager throughout Ferguson's years there, found him most helpful in the public relations end of the business.[22] He got to know all the agents and was a stimulating force with the field personnel, at conventions, and in campaigns for new business. In the investment area his contribution was minimal.

Although much of the old vigour had departed, he was blessed with fair health during these early years of semi-retirement. Perhaps the absence of the pressures of public life had lessened his susceptibility to the ailments which had afflicted him since the 1920s. Now he and Ella had an opportunity to grow even closer. The only time he ever felt sorry for himself was over the continued deterioration of his eyesight. More than ever Ella spent enjoyable hours reading to him from his substantial library, weighted heavily towards British political history. Despite their large house, the Fergusons did not keep a maid, though someone came in to assist with the housework. They did not often give large parties. Ella liked to have friends in to tea and there were many intimate dinner groups. When close friends such as the David Walkers came to call, he would show their children the miniature paintings that the Queen had given him of Princess Elizabeth and Princess Margaret Rose and tell charming stories of the little princesses and of how much they had enjoyed a Banbury Cross ride on his knee.

His routine allowed several hours each day simply to chat with old friends and new. His office at the Crown Life was a level above the executive floor but he would be found a good deal of the time on the lower floor conversing happily with colleagues and acquaintances. Without the Crown Life and the downtown facilities it provided, to say nothing of the salary he received, life would have been a good deal less pleasant. Most days too he would wander off to one of his clubs for lunch, often the Albany on whose board he served, sometimes the York, to spend a few enjoyable hours before wending his way back to Avenue Road. Many Saturdays a group would meet for lunch at the York Club and this usually included Mark Irish, R.A. Stapells, Tommy Russell, J.J. Gibbons, and others. Every summer, of course, he would return to Kemptville. He had sold his home and farm there in 1935 and each year fewer of his old friends remained. Now he would joke that he was going back 'to see my horse. Well, I'll have to see some of the boys too. That's not so pleasant.'

He never changed his early view of the Hepburnites as the barbarians at the gates, yet through occasional contact with the Premier he developed a grudging admiration for him. They shared, after all, that jaunty, devil-may-care nature though Ferguson had always kept his own reckless streak within bounds. Shortly after returning to Canada he decided to pay a duty call on the new ruler of Queen's Park. During a relaxed conversation, Hepburn told of his revenue problems and of his fear of raising the gas tax by a penny. Ferguson, drawing on his own experience, advised that it be raised two cents; after all people could not yell much louder over the higher figure than over the lower.[23] Apparently Hepburn, who respected the old Tory's political 'savvy,' now was won over completely.

Occasionally Hepburn would drop into the Crown Life to chat and from time to time turned up at the Ferguson home. Once at least he brought Maurice Duplessis along with him; another time Ella conscripted him to serve tea. 'If I didn't know he was such a horrid man I'd like him,' she confided to an intimate.[24] Ferguson did his best to convince the Premier how wrong he had been when Ontario repudiated its pledged word and denounced the Quebec power contracts. Perhaps Hepburn's decision to renegotiate them owed a little to his urging. Something of their relationship is caught in a 1939 note Ferguson addressed to the Premier:

I am enclosing you herewith a letter addressed to me, evidently intended for you. At any rate –
There ain't no Premier Ferguson any more!
I understand there ain't no Government House any more!![25]

On the other hand, Ferguson's opinion of some of his own party's leaders was less than flattering. When Bennett decided in 1938 to retire, he was unimpressed by the alternatives available. The leading candidate was Manion, whom he liked but regarded as a lightweight. In late May, Bennett wrote that he was 'very anxious' to arrange a meeting in Toronto because 'there are so many matters I wish to speak to you about'; the Tory leadership was undoubtedly high on the agenda.[26] Ferguson was one of the old guard who urged Bennett to be a candidate to succeed himself, but the former prime minister refused. Manion's performance after assuming the mantle gave Ferguson no cause to alter his opinion. During the 1940 federal election he urged the new leader to announce that those elected under the national government banner would be given an opportunity to choose their own leader after the balloting. Manion who had already announced that he favoured a national government believed this proposal was simply an effort to get rid of him. He reacted with anger, telling Ferguson that if he permitted such a thing it would appear 'that I was to be bought out immediately after ... to allow Bennett or Meighen or some other to do things I had promised I should not do.'[27]

The old man's opinion of the Ontario party's leadership was equally unenthusiastic. Addressing the 1938 convention called to choose a successor to Rowe, he stated that he could never approve of the way in which Colonel George Drew had deserted the party during the 1937 election. In a pithy speech salted with humour, he warned that whoever was chosen must not take himself too seriously but advised that the task before the party was well within its powers. He himself, he reminded the delegates, had started out in 1920 'without friends, without money, nothing but a shotgun and a few loads in it,' yet it had been like potting rabbits and 'the fence was full of their hides.' His fighting remarks elicited round after round of applause.[28]

After Mackenzie King's landslide victory in 1940, R.B. Hanson stepped up as the federal party's House leader. Ferguson had no respect for Hanson. At a private 1941 dinner at the Toronto Club for Hanson given by J.M. Macdonnell, Howard interrupted the speakers so loudly and so frequently that Macdonnell had to ask him to quieten down. At this he left in a huff and David Walker recalls that 'he rumbled all the way home in criticism of the people at that dinner.' Although he felt that the sooner the party got rid of Hanson the better, he was less than thrilled to learn that Arthur Meighen, after his own ill-fated restoration, was attempting to promote John Bracken, the Progressive Premier of Manitoba. Here was someone else Ferguson thought the Conservative party could do without. As a result he helped write the speech David Walker delivered at the Winnipeg Convention nominating John Diefenbaker.[29] The leader, Walker intoned 'should be a Conservative, not an outsider. We don't want someone who is going to sell our birthright for a mess of pottage...' As the young Toronto lawyer delivered the words Ferguson had drafted, he was greeted with prolonged booing from Bracken's Winnipeg supporters and from many of the delegates.

Ferguson was equally frank about George Drew. Not that he doubted Drew's abilities or objected to his policies; the problem was the man himself. One evening when Drew was leader of the opposition in Ontario a friend of his, Norman Perry, a prominent industrialist, held a dinner at the York Club at which Tory problems and prospects were to be discussed. When Perry turned to Ferguson, who had been unusually quiet, and asked what he thought Drew could do to become a good leader, the reply, which came without hesitation, was 'he should be born again.'[30] Indiscretion remained a way of life for Ferguson. When this got back to Drew, relations were on the chilly side for some time.

Still, he seldom hesitated to offer advice and after the Tories were restored to office in 1943 he would drop in from time to time to exchange gossip with members of the Cabinet. With George Doucett, for example, the eastern Ontario man who held the Highways portfolio, he liked to discuss the state of patronage and how it compared with the situation in his day. Doucett recalls one occasion when he, Drew, and Ferguson travelled together to attend the funeral of a prominent party member. In the car Ferguson said, 'George, you are a great speaker,' and Drew's chest swelled; but then he continued, 'George, I hope you don't mind my giving you a piece of advice. You sometimes talk above your audience. You should always avoid this. You can easily talk at too high a level but you can never talk at too low a level.'[31]

In the period before the 1945 election, Ferguson shared the fear of many at the inroads the CCF was making. In his 1943 report to the Crown Life, he denounced the socialist bogey and declaimed against the 'ignorance, misunderstanding or sinister motive of a zealous group of fanatics who seek to get control of all personal activities...' through the creation of what he described as 'the most gigantic monopoly that can be conceived.' Doubtless the impassioned anti-socialist campaign which swept George Drew to his landslide victory in 1945 had his full approval. One day he went to see Drew, told him that the weak spot for the Tories was northern Ontario and suggested that Doucett be sent up as organizer. When the election came Drew remembered this advice; Doucett went north and performed a good effect.[32]

These, then, were generally happy and satisfying autumn years. Surrounded by new friends and old, Ferguson was enjoying life to the full. The honours and positions he accepted included membership on the Board of the Royal Ontario Museum, director of Toronto General Trusts Corporation, the British American Insurance Company, the Western Assurance Company, and Brazilian Traction. Still interested in charitable and welfare work, he gave freely of his time and talents to a number of organizations and in 1941 acted as chairman of the Health League of Canada fund drive. And he and Ella donated a mobile canteen as their contribution to the war effort. An appointment he particularly appreciated came when Mitch Hepburn named the man he once had been determined to 'get' to the Board of Governors of the University of Toronto.

This led to an unpleasant incident. Ferguson, very much of the old school, still believed professors should not use their protected positions to engage in political controversy. He had never forgotten how Frank Underhill in the 1920s had apparently promulgated what he regarded as almost treasonous doctrines about the origins of World War I. Now Underhill was at it again. With Canada at war and the United States neutral, he was quoted by the press in September 1940 as saying that Canada had two loyalties, one to North America, and the other to Britain, that many Canadians doubted British policy and that 'the relative importance of Britain is going to sink now no matter what happens.' Many Canadians found Underhill's remarks offensive; and in the superheated atmosphere of wartime some believed he should be interned as Camilien Houde had been.

Interestingly, in the early months of 1939 in a similar incident involving Underhill, Ferguson had played a very different role. At that time George Drew had taken strong exception to some isolationist sentiments of the Toronto professor which appeared in the 1938 volume by R.A. MacKay and E.B. Rogers, *Canada Looks Abroad*. When Drew raised the matter in the House he was supported by Hepburn, who blustered and threatened penalties, thereby causing alarm in the office of the President and among the Board of Governors. In this earlier instance, however, Ferguson's principal concern seems to have been to help Harry Cody out of a tight spot. Underhill himself reported that 'Howard Ferguson, of all people, was operating with his usual smoothness to prevent any trouble. He of course was assisting Cody' and together they 'prevented things from becoming hot.'[33]

But now, in 1940, Ferguson's position had hardened in the emotional climate of wartime. The Board of Governors, including Ferguson and Chancellor

Mulock, determined on dismissal and Cody himself, taking the position that what was at issue was less the particular incident than the accumulation of thirteen years of outrageous indiscretions damaging to the University, asked for Underhill's resignation.[34] Yet final decision was deferred over several Board meetings and in the interval there was furious activity on all sides. Many students and faculty took the opportunity to organize and protest. Even at this point, there are indications that despite his sense of outrage at Underhill's remarks, Ferguson's primary purpose was still to assist the President through a difficult situation. In early January 1941, Underhill believed that 'the pressure really comes from Hepburn who has been seen in vain by both Howard Ferguson and the President.'[35] After the matter was postponed at the January Board meeting until June, Ferguson himself, on the 26th of that month, in the face of student and faculty opinion, presented a motion for dismissal. At this time Cody argued against firing Underhill and Mulock pointed out that only the President could dismiss a faculty member.[36] Although the Ferguson motion carried, Ferguson's position had been undercut. It would have been unthinkable for him to mount an attack on Harry Cody and no action was ever taken to implement the motion. Ferguson felt betrayed and was furious. David Walker, in whom he confided, later recalled that while he resented Cody's action, he got over that but he never did forgive Mulock. The two men became bitter enemies.[37]

The events of the war, of course, remained the absorbing topic of interest throughout these years. It made little practical difference to Ferguson's way of life, although he did decide to abandon Atlantic City for his holidays because he could no longer stand to listen to the Americans boast of how they were single-handedly winning the war for the Allies. By this time his health was failing and more than ever Ella became his eyes, telling him when people he knew were approaching.

In October 1942 he was hit by a car in front of his home. His injuries did not appear serious but he failed to bounce back. About a year before his death, he was noticed, 'standing alone in the centre of the Union Station at Ottawa. He had been guest at a banquet earlier in the evening, but somehow his younger hosts had broken off to gather in hotel rooms and had forgotten him. Unrecognizing crowds bustled past him. A redcap with a truck full of luggage swerved quickly to avoid knocking him down. He was a vague, frail old man searching dazedly in his pocket for a lost ticket. A tolerant young railway employee finally took him in tow and ushered him to his train.'[38]

He was feeling dejected and forgotten, Arthur Ford recounts, when in May 1945 he was appointed Chancellor of the University of Western Ontario. This gesture gave him a good deal of pleasure but of course the ravages of old age continued. For a time he seemed to rally and to the very end he maintained his two lifetime interests, people and politics. Wanting to keep in touch with some of the younger Tories, he invited David Walker, Roland Michener, Gordon

Graydon, and Donald Fleming and their wives to a small dinner party. In fine fettle that night, he greatly enjoyed bantering with Fleming about his prohibitionist views. The talk, as always, was of politics, of what could be done to improve the party's dismal prospects at Ottawa.[39] He died two days later, suddenly, after a heart attack, at 2 AM on 21 February 1946. He was 76 years old.

The funeral was conducted by Harry Cody. Some years earlier he and Harry had been together at the rites of a mutual friend and he had turned and said, 'Some day you will be laying me away. Remember, I don't want any long-winded eulogy like that.' His wish was respected. The service consisted of scripture readings and, appropriately, the singing of his favourite hymn, 'Fight the Good Fight.' Interment was in Toronto's Mount Pleasant Cemetery.

Notes

CHAPTER 1: THE FERGUSONS OF KEMPTVILLE

1 Details of Dr Ferguson's life are from his obituary notice, Kemptville *Advance*, 30 September 1909.

2 For a brief history of the village see the booklet, *Historical Review of Kempt-ville and District* (Kemptville 1957), Kemptville Centennial Committee.

3 *Ibid.* 12

4 *Ibid.* 13

5 *Ibid.* 22

6 John Henderson, *Howard Ferguson* (Toronto 1930) 7

7 Obituary notice

8 Interview, Miss Margaret Storey, Mrs John Stephenson, Kemptville, 11 May 1967

9 Obituary notice

10 This story was related by Ferguson himself on several occasions to close friends. See also Toronto *Star Weekly*, 23 November 1929.

11 In 1924 Gregory Clark interviewed Howard's sister, Mrs Storey, and talked to other Kemptville residents. Several of the stories related here come from Mr Clark's account, Toronto *Star Weekly*, 4 October 1924.

12 Toronto *Daily Star,* obituary notice, 21 February 1946

13 Forbes Godfrey, cited in Toronto *Star*, 26 February 1927

14 Greg Clark, *Star Weekly*, 4 October 1924

15 Toronto *Star*, March 12 1927, 'In the Days of Temperance Badges'

16 *Ibid.*

17 Greg Clark, *Star Weekly*, 4 October 1924

18 Toronto *Globe*, 8 December 1930. Ferguson himself, about to leave Ontario politics, told the story of the enduring influence of 'the tramp,' Keane.

19 FP, Ferguson to W.D. Gregory, 12 October 1925; Kemptville Centennial Booklet 40

20 W.E. Elliott, 'Master of Arts Political,' unpublished manuscript. Mr Elliott, a reporter with the Toronto *News*, the *Mail & Empire*, and several other papers, knew Ferguson well.
21 Ralph L. Curry, *Stephen Leacock* (New York 1959) 50, 54. According to Curry, Leacock and Ferguson were roommates again by Leacock's senior year.
22 Elliott, 'Master of Arts Political'
23 Surviving University of Toronto records cover only Ferguson's third and fourth years there.
24 The reference to Ferguson as class president is in Curry, *Leacock*. My own search of the *Varsity* failed to get him beyond vice-president, but it is not unlikely that he later stepped up.
25 David Walker, interview, 4 June 1970. The story seems confirmed by the Toronto *Varsity*, 25 November & 2 December 1890.
26 See R.E. Knowles, Toronto *Star*, 12 January 1931.
27 Curry, *Leacock* 54; Bruce Murphy, 'Stephen Leacock – the Greatest Living Humourist,' *Ontario Library Review* XII (February 1928)
28 The story, with a minor variation, was confirmed by Miss Margaret Higginson, interview, 18 May 1967.
29 Stephen Leacock, *My University Days* (Toronto 1923)

CHAPTER 2: 'THE CHEEKY SHALL GET THERE'
1 Kemptville *Advance*, 28 April 1898
2 Interview, Miss Margaret Higginson, 18 May 1967. Other details of Mrs Ferguson's early life are in 'Canada's Most Envied Hostess,' *Chatelaine* (Feb. 1931).
3 *Ibid.*
4 Kemptville *Advance*, 20 January 1898
5 He was defeated by the Tory, Robert Joynt, by 611 votes.
6 Kemptville *Advance*, 24 February 1898
7 *Ibid.*, 15 December 1898
8 *Ibid.*, 29 December 1898
9 Kemptville Centennial Booklet 48
10 Interview, Miss Storey and Mrs Stephenson, 11 May 1967
11 Kemptville *Advance*, 2 November 1899
12 1 February 1901.
13 *Kemptville Telegram*, 2 January 1901.
14 For many years the Kemptville *Advance*, founded in 1880, was the town's only paper, the earlier *Progressionist* being long defunct. Although Ruth Mackenzie's *Leeds and Grenville* (Toronto 1967) describes the paper as Liberal, it was not aggressively so. The *Telegram*, however, was decidedly Tory. Founded in 1900, it was soon purchased by a company owned by Mr

& Mrs Howard Ferguson and Mr & Mrs T.A. Craig. In 1913 the two papers amalgamated and the *Telegram* disappeared. Ferguson sold his interest about the time he left Ontario politics.

15 *Kemptville Telegram*, 23 May 1901
16 *Ibid.*, 25 July 1901
17 *Kemptville Telegram*, 30 May 1901
18 Toronto *Telegram*, cited in *Kemptville Telegram*, 11 July 1901
19 Kemptville *Advance*, 8 May 1902
20 Roderick Lewis, *A Statistical History of All the Electoral Districts of the Province of Ontario since 1867* (Toronto, nd) 68
21 This point remains unclear. The above is derived largely from Joynt's own circular letters describing the affair, copies of which are in the Ferguson Papers.
22 FP, affidavits from Smith, Albert Whitney, and John Mundle
23 *Ibid.*
24 The convention is described in the Kemptville *Advance* and in FP, Joynt 'To the Electors of Grenville Riding,' 9 January 1905.
25 *Ibid.*
26 Kemptville *Advance*, 10 December 1903
27 Whitney Papers, Carmichael to Whitney, 27 January 1904
28 *Ibid.*
29 Kemptville *Advance*, 2 November 1904
30 *Ibid.*, 4, 11 January 1905
31 FP, Joynt circular letter, 'To the Electors of Grenville Riding,' 9 January 1905
32 FP, Ferguson to Joynt, 11 January 1905
33 FP, William Stafford to Ferguson, 10 January 1905
34 For the nature of the Tory campaign see C.W. Humphries, 'The Political Career of James P. Whitney,' Ph D thesis (University of Toronto 1966) ch. 5.

CHAPTER 3: 'ONTARIO MUST TAKE THE LEAD'

1 See letter of Colonel Pratt in Toronto *Globe*, 18 June 1923.
2 *CAR* (1905) 271. I owe much of my understanding of these years to Professor C.W. Humphries's sensitive study of Whitney cited *supra*.
3 See Whitney Papers, Ferguson to Whitney 26 June and reply, 27 June 1906; also Whitney Papers (collection owned by C.W. Humphries), Ferguson to Whitney, 29 June and reply, 3 July 1906.
4 FP, Ferguson to the Rev. J.B. Robinson, March 1908. See also several other letters, 1906-8, in same file as above.
5 *Kemptville Telegram*, 2 May 1907
6 Hamilton *Spectator*, cited in *Kemptville Telegram*, 2 April 1908
7 *Kemptville Telegram*, 21 June 1908

8 *Ibid.*, 4 June 1908
9 Whitney Papers, Ferguson to Whitney, 3 April 1911
10 *Kemptville Telegram*, 21 May 1908
11 Whitney Papers, Whitney to F.C. Milligan, 14 May 1908
12 *Kemptville Telegram*, 4 June 1908
13 I.W.C. Solloway, *Speculators and Politicians* (Westmount 1932) 196
14 Whitney Papers, Dr Richard Preston to Whitney, 29 January 1909
15 Whitney Papers, Whitney to Ferguson, 19 March 1910
16 Toronto *Mail*, 24 November 1886, cited in Franklin Walker, *Catholic Education and Politics in Ontario* (Toronto 1964) 129
17 See Province of Ontario, *Report of the Royal Commission on Education in Ontario, 1950* (Hope Commission) (Toronto 1950) 402.
18 See Walker, *Catholic Education,* 264.
19 See Congrès d'Education des Canadiens-Français d'Ontario, *Rapport Officiel* (Ottawa: Association Canadienne-Français d'Education 1910).
20 Henri Lemay, 'The Future of the French Canadian Race,' *The Canadian Magazine* (May 1911)
21 Whitney Papers, J.A.C. Evans to Whitney, 29 January 1910; Toronto *World*, 10 March 1910
22 University of Toronto Archives, 'Correspondence between the Ontario Department of Education and the Roman Catholic Authorities Concerning the Bi-lingual School Issue,' Whitney to Archibishop McEvay, 9 March 1910
23 ACFEO Papers, President and Secretary of General Committee to Father A. Charbonneau, 18 November 1909; *Rapport du Comité de la Statistique au Congrès d'Education* (nd). For a different emphasis, see Marilyn Barber, 'The Ontario Bilingual Schools Issue: Sources of Conflict,' *CHR* (September 1966) 239.
24 Whitney Papers, Whitney to Belcourt, 12 August 1910
25 Kemptville *Advance*, 8 December 1910
26 Toronto *Globe*, 8 December 1910
27 ACFEO Papers, Délégués Apostoliques, l'Hon. G. Howard Ferguson et la Règlement XVII; Toronto *News*, 17 November 1911
28 Toronto *Globe*, 23 March 1911; *Evening Telegram*, cited in Walker 258
29 Kemptville *Advance*, 2 February 1911; telephone interview with P.M. Dewan, March 1976
30 Toronto *Globe*, 23 March 1911
31 Kemptville *Advance*, 2 February, 30 March 1911
32 Kingston *Standard*, 3 November 1910
33 Kemptville *Advance*, 2 November 1911
34 *Ibid.*, 13 July 1911
35 *Ibid.*, 28 September 1911
36 KP, King to Violet Markham, 15 December 1911

37 Kemptville *Advance*, 7 December 1911
38 Toronto *Globe*, 21 November 1911; Walker 261
39 Toronto *Evening Telegram*, cited in Kemptville *Advance*, 7 December 1911
40 C.B. Sissons, *Bilingual Schools in Canada* (Toronto 1917) 98
41 FP, Ferguson to Ernie McQuatt, 1 February 1928

CHAPTER 4: TORY HATCHET MAN
1 O.D. Skelton, *Life and Letters of Sir Wilfrid Laurier* (Toronto 1921) II, 256
2 *Mail & Empire*, 16 February 1914
3 Kemptville *Advance*, 18 June 1914
4 This account is taken largely from *The Globe* and the *Mail & Empire*.
5 Toronto *Globe*, 26 April 1913
6 *Ibid.*, 1 May 1913
7 *Ibid.*, 2 May 1913
8 *CAR* (1913) 406-7
9 Kemptville *Advance*, 21 March 1911
10 *CAR* (1914) 372
11 *Mail & Empire*, 26 February 1914
12 *Ibid.*, 29 April 1914
13 Kemptville *Advance*, 5 March 1914
14 Canada, House of Commons, *Debates*, 6 June 1914, 4990; *Mail & Empire*, 10 March 1914
15 *Mail & Empire*, 12 March 1915
16 Toronto *Globe*, 18, 19 March 1914
17 Kemptville *Advance*, 26 March 1914
18 House of Commons, *Debates*, 6 June 1914, 4987.
19 FP, Ferguson to Beck 15 January 1912 and reply, 25 January; Ferguson to Gaby, 5 December 1913
20 W.R. Plewman, *Adam Beck and the Ontario Hydro* (Toronto 1947) 147
21 See Walker, *Catholic Education* 281.
22 Kemptville *Advance*, 18 June 1914

CHAPTER 5: THE HEARST ADMINISTRATION
1 Toronto *Globe*, 23 December 1914. For fuller accounts of the Hearst administration, see B.D. Tennyson, 'The Political Career of Sir William H. Hearst,' MA thesis (University of Toronto 1963) and Peter Oliver, *Public & Private Persons: The Ontario Political Culture, 1914-1934* (Toronto 1975) ch. 2.
2 Richard S. Lambert with P. Pross, *Renewing Nature's Wealth: A Centennial History of the Public Management of Lands, Forests and Wildlife in Ontario, 1763-1967* (Ontario Department of Lands & Forests 1967) 258
3 Evidence given before the Timber Commission of the early 1920s makes this

perfectly obvious. The departmental history, however, argues somewhat mis-
leadingly that it was only with Aubrey White's death early in the war period
that Ferguson was 'deprived of the capable, powerful administrator so essential to the smooth running of the Department.' See Lambert & Pross 263.
4 A.P. Pross, 'The Development of a Forest Policy: A Study of the Ontario
Department of Lands and Forests,' Ph D thesis (University of Toronto 1967)
211-13
5 For statistical evidence, see Oliver, *Public & Private Persons* 43.
6 Interview, E.J. Zavitz, August 1967
7 See 'The Government and its Chief Critic,' UFO election pamphlet (1923)
11-12.
8 *AR*, Department of Lands and Forests (1916)
9 *CAR* (1914) 542; *CAR* (1916) 484-5; *CAR* (1918) 626
10 *AR* (1917)
11 Toronto *Globe*, 13 August 1915
12 A.R.M. Lower and H.A. Innis, *Settlement and the Forest and Mining
Frontiers* (Toronto 1936) 143
13 J.C. Hopkins, *The Province of Ontario in the War* (Toronto 1919) 40
14 Lambert and Pross 210
15 *Ibid.* 211-12
16 *Ibid.* 213
17 *CAR* (1916) 527
18 FP, selections from Legislature debates, 14 April 1916
19 Lomer Gouin Papers, J.A. Myrand to the editor, Ottawa *Citizen*, 15 March
1916
20 U of T Archives, 'Correspondence ... Concerning the Bilingual Schools Issue,'
Folder G, 'Contents of the Report on English-French Schools' (1915) 85
21 Department of Education, 'Memorandum re Regulation 17 (Private) for the
Hon. G.H. Ferguson,' 25 March 1916
22 FP, Borden to Ferguson, 23 February 1916, and reply, 25 February
23 Borden Diary, 8 April 1916
24 Borden Papers, Ferguson to Borden, 10 April 1916
25 FP, W.J. Brown to Ferguson, 18 February 1916, and reply, 25 February
26 FP, Ferguson to Borden, 25 February 1916
27 FP, *Debates*, 14 April 1916
28 FP, Ferguson to Patenaude, 14 September 1916
29 Laurier Papers, Laurier to Stewart Lyon, 9 March 1916
30 Toronto *Globe*, 15 April 1916
31 Laurier Papers, Rowell to Laurier, 15 April 1916
32 *Robert Laird Borden, His Memoirs* (New York 1938) II, 588-9
33 ACFEO Papers, bishops File, Bruchési: 'Pourparlers de sa Grandeur

Monseigneur Bruchési avec MM les Curés, MM les Commissaires d'Ecoles et les Officiers de l'Association d'Education, 1915'

34 *Ibid.*

35 *Ibid.* For more on the compromise effort of 1915, see FP, McGregor Young to P. Charbonneau, 28 September 1915.

36 Ottawa *Journal*, 21 June 1916; Ottawa *Citizen*, 26 June; FP, 'Fair Play' to Ferguson (np, nd)

37 Ottawa *Journal*, 17 September 1916

38 C.B. Sissons, *Church and State in Canadian Education* (Toronto 1959) 91-2; *CAR* (1916) 531-2

39 Belcourt Papers, Belcourt to Dewart, 26 March 1917

40 Neil McNeil Papers, Belcourt to W.H. Moore, 27 July 1921

41 Borden Diary, 31 August 1916

42 See Plewman, *Beck* 189-90.

43 *Ibid.* 193-5

44 Toronto *Globe*, 29 October 1916; Laurier Papers, Atkinson to Goddard, 26 August 1916

45 Toronto *Globe*, 11 October 1915

46 Toronto *Evening Telegram*, 21 October 1929

47 Borden Papers, Ferguson to Borden, 27 January 1916

48 *CAR* (1916) 535-9

49 *Ibid.*

50 Borden Papers, Ferguson to Borden, 27 January 1916

51 Toronto *World*, 14 July 1916

52 Borden Papers, E.F. Wood to Borden, 20 July 1916

53 *CAR* (1917) 659. For a fuller discussion, see O.W. Main, *The Canadian Nickel Industry* (Toronto 1955).

54 *CAR* (1916) 501-2

55 Laurier Papers, Atkinson to Goddard, 26 August 1916

56 *CAR* (1916) 503

57 Laurier Papers, Atkinson to Goddard, 26 August 1916

58 W.L. Grant Papers, Skelton to Grant, 19 March 1917

59 Hearst Papers, Hearst to Lieutenant W.I. Hearst, 18 April 1917

60 Borden Papers, Ferguson to Borden, 3 July 1917

61 Borden Papers, Ferguson to Borden, nd

62 See Jean MacLeod, 'The United Farmer Movement in Ontario,' MA thesis (Queen's University 1958) 71. For a fuller account of the fall of the Hearst government, see Peter Oliver, *Public & Private Persons* (Clarke, Irwin 1975) ch. 2.

63 Rowell Papers, Rowell to Proudfoot, 2 July 1919

64 J.J. Morrison, *Memoirs* 60

65 Hearst Papers, unsigned letter to Ferguson, 25 September 1919
66 Borden Papers, Keefer to Borden, 22 October 1919
67 Borden Papers, Reid to Borden, 23 October 1919
68 Toronto *Globe*, 2 September 1919
69 Toronto *Star*, 8 October 1919

CHAPTER 6: HIDES ON THE FENCE
1 Interview, C.A. Morrison, 18 March 1971
2 See Jean MacLeod, 'The United Farmer Movement' 56-63, for a fuller discussion.
3 Toronto *Globe*, 30 October 1919
4 Morrison *Memoirs* 79-80
5 *Ibid.*
6 E.C. Drury, *Farmer Premier: The Memoirs of E.C. Drury* (Toronto 1966) 108
7 Toronto *Star*, 9 February 1922
8 See Martin Robin, *Radical Politics and Canadian Labour: 1880-1930*, ch. 14.
9 Interview, C.A. Morrison, 18 March 1971
10 Toronto *Star*, 17 March 1920
11 See Jean MacLeod, 'The United Farmer Movement' 86.
12 *Ibid.* 87
13 *CAR* (1920) 583
14 Toronto *Star*, 28 August 1920
15 Morrison *Memoirs*. Of course these give only one side of the story.
16 KP, Harding to King, 28 June 1920. See also Oliver, *Public & Private Persons*, ch. 3, for a fuller account of the Timber Scandal.
17 Toronto *Globe*, 30 April 1920
18 Cody Papers, Ontario Archives, Justice Ferguson to Cody, 20 July 1927
19 *Ibid.*
20 Timber Commission Hearings, typescript, 6396-6404
21 *Ibid.* 6423-44
22 *Ibid.*
23 Toronto *Star*, 3 November 1920
24 Toronto *Evening Telegram*, 26 November, 1 December 1920
25 Toronto *Globe*, 25 November 1920
26 Toronto *Star Weekly*, 4 October 1924
27 Toronto *Globe* 2 December 1920
28 Willison Papers, Meighen to Willison, 4 December 1920
29 Interview, Arthur Ford, 11 April 1967
30 Toronto *Evening Telegram*, 3 December; *Saturday Night*, 18 December 1920
31 Dafoe Papers, Sifton to Dafoe, 3 December 1920; cited in Ramsay Cook, ed., *The Dafoe-Sifton Correspondence, 1919-1927* (Manitoba Record Society 1966) 46-7

32 The correspondence appeared in the press of 4 December 1920.

33 Jennings Papers, Ferguson to Jennings, 5 May 1921

34 For this interview see Toronto *Star Weekly*, 11 December 1920. It was one of a series in which the reader was warned that the article contained 'what the speakers would be likely to say confessionally.'

35 The correspondence was published in the Toronto *Star*, 31 January 1921.

36 Sifton Papers, memorandum for Dafoe, 23 December 1920.

37 MP, Ford to Meighen, 3 August 1921

38 FP, transcript of speech at Pine Grove, 1921

39 Sifton Papers, Sifton to Dafoe, 3 October 1924; for the Kenora situation see Peter Heenan Papers, Mayor Toole of Kenora to Backus, 23 December 1920.

40 F.R. Latchford Papers, Latchford to Senator?, 30 May 1923; King Diary, 24 August 1921

41 Toronto *Star*, 16 January 1922

42 *Ibid.*, 30 March 1922

43 Exclusive of several special reports on particular companies, the Timber Commission Report was a remarkably brief 43 pages.

44 Toronto *Star*, 27 July and 11 August 1922. For very different conclusions, see H.V. Nelles, *The Politics of Development* (Toronto 1974), ch. 10, especially 385-94.

CHAPTER 7: THE OLD-TIME POLITICAL RELIGION

1 KP, Curry to King, 24 and 28 October 1919

2 MP, Ferguson to Meighen, 7 December 1922 and reply, 9 December

3 Throne speech debate, 21 January 1921

4 Jennings Papers, Ferguson to Jennings, 14 May 1921

5 OHSS, oral history interview, Elmer Bell, 1971

6 Jennings Papers, Ferguson to Jennings, 14 May 1921

7 See Druryite election pamphlet, *The Government and Its Chief Critic.*

8 *Ibid.*

9 W.C. Good Papers, Waldron to Good, 27 May 1922

10 Good Papers, Good to Drury, 22 April 1922

11 Toronto *Star*, 1 February 1922

12 Toronto *Globe*, 15 June 1923

13 Toronto *Star*, 7 April 1922

14 For a brief account of Price's early career see Attorney-General's Papers, clipping, Toronto *Globe*, 16 March 1933

15 Interview, David Walker, 4 June 1970

16 Manion Papers, Ferguson to Manion, 7 December 1921

17 W.F. Maclean Papers, Bristol to Maclean, 9 December 1921

18 MP, Meighen to Ferguson, 15 February 1922 and reply, 22 February; Meighen to Ferguson, 4 September, and reply 12 September 1922

19 MP, Meighen to Ferguson, 14 September 1922 and reply, 20 September; Meighen to Ferguson, 27 September
20 Toronto *Star*, 3 November 1921
21 MP, Ferguson to Meighen, 20 September 1922
22 *Ibid.*
23 MP, Ferguson to Meighen, 7 December 1922
24 MP, Anderson to Meighen, 31 January 1922
25 MP, Ford to Meighen, 7 October 1922
26 MP, Ford to Meighen, 20 February 1923; Willison Papers, Ford to Willison, 4 June 1923
27 MP, Ferguson to Meighen, 26 February 1923
28 MP, Ford to Meighen, 4 July 1923
29 *Ibid.*
30 MP, Ferguson to Meighen, 23 September 1922 and reply, 27 September
31 MP, Ferguson to Meighen, 21 October 1922 and reply, 30 October
32 *Mail and Empire*, cited in Lambert & Pross 268
33 *Northern Miner*, 27 December 1919; 5 February 1921
34 *Ibid.*, 26 February 1921
35 Toronto *Star*, 18 March, 1 April 1921
36 Toronto *Star*, 30 April 1921. The Ferguson line was supported by K.S. Stover, the Liberal member for Algoma.
37 Toronto *Star*, 12 February 1921
38 Toronto *Globe*, 31 January 1923
39 *Northern Miner*, 26 May 1923
40 W.H. Casselman Papers, undated speech
41 Toronto *Star*, 25 February 1921
42 M.S. Donnelly, *The Government of Manitoba* (Toronto 1963) 59
43 M. Robin, *Radical Politics* 244
44 *Ibid.* 244-5
45 *Ibid.* 247
46 Jean MacLeod, 'Agriculture and Politics in Ontario since 1867,' Ph D thesis (University of London 1961)
47 The W.C. Good papers contain many letters relating to this effort.
48 See W.H. Casselman Papers, undated speech on Dairy Standards Act.
49 Casselman Papers, speech to his constituents 1923
50 *CAR* (1921) 614-15
51 Casselman Papers, speech to his constituents 1923
52 Casselman Papers, Morrison to Casselman, 3 August 1921
53 Toronto *Star*, 12 March 1920
54 Toronto *Star*, 30 March 1920
55 Drury, *Farmer Premier* 94
56 Norman Lambert Papers, Morrison to Lambert, 1 December 1922

57 Drury, *Farmer Premier* 149
58 *CAR* (1921) 543
59 KP, P.C. Larkin to King, 8 December 1921. The information came from Hay.
60 HP, Sinclair to Ferguson, 3 January 1922
61 *Ibid.*, 21 January 1922
62 *CAR* (1922) 647-8
63 King Diary, 13 January 1923
64 KP, W.C. Kennedy to King, 30 December 1922
65 Toronto *Globe*, 12 April 1923
66 The W.C. Good Papers are full of correspondence on this issue.
67 Good Papers, Good to Raney, 29 April 1923
68 Good Papers, Good to Morrison, 1 February 1923
69 Good Papers, Staples to Good, 20 February 1923
70 Toronto *Telegram*, 28, 29, 30 July suggests the guarded attitude that journal maintained towards Ferguson; see Toronto *Globe*, 14 June 1923 for its comment and that of the *Citizen*.
71 Good Papers, Good to John Hamm, 9 May 1923
72 Willison Papers, Ford to Willison, 6 March 1923; Toronto *Globe*, 15 May 1923
73 MP, Matthews to Meighen, 27 June 1923
74 Toronto *Globe*, 18 June 1923
75 Arthur Ford, *As the World Wags On* (Toronto 1950) 155
76 Toronto *Star*, 24 February 1926
77 This statement was made to the House; Toronto *Star*, 2 March 1926.
78 MP, Meighen to Ferguson, 7 October 1922 and reply, 19 October
79 See Toronto *Star*, 2, 6, 8 January 1922.
80 *Mail and Empire*, 7 April 1922
81 *CAR* (1922) 638
82 Toronto *Star*, 6 July 1922
83 See Liberal campaign pamphlet, *The Liberal Handbook*. The remarks were made in Hamilton in February 1923.
84 Willison Papers, Ford to Willison, 6 March 1923; MP, Ford to Meighen, 11 May 1923 and reply, 14 May
85 Toronto *Globe*, 16 May 1923
86 Good Papers, Staples to Good, 29 May 1923
87 Jennings Papers, Price to Jennings, 6 June 1923
88 MP, Matthews to Meighen, 26 April 1923
89 MP, Meighen to Ferguson, 5 February 1923 and reply, 26 February; Meighen to Ferguson, 25 May 1923
90 KP, Hardy to King, 11 June 1923
91 Drury, *Farmer Premier* 157
92 Leslie M. Frost Papers (private), notes on speeches during 1923 campaign

93 ACFEO Papers, Bishop of Alexandria to Monsignor ? , 4 June 1923; Bishop Scollard to Rev. J. Richard, SJ, 25 May 1923
94 Belcourt Papers, Sissons to Belcourt, 16 July 1923
95 Flavelle Papers, Flavelle to W.E. Rundle, 25 June 1923
96 Flavelle Papers, Flavelle to Rundle, 27 June 1923

CHAPTER 8: THE RETURN OF THE OLD ORDER
1 Flavelle Papers, Willison to Flavelle, 25 June 1923
2 KP, King to Fred Johnson, 3 July 1923
3 W.M. Nickle to the author, 18 January 1968
4 KP, letter dated 16 October 1923, sent to Murphy and passed on to King
5 HP, Ferguson to Henry, 8 May 1931
6 MP, Meighen to Monty, 29 June 1923 and reply, 5 July
7 MP, Matthews to Meighen, 27 June 1923; Willison Papers, Irish to Willison, 26 June and Price to Willison, 16 July 1923; Flavelle Papers, Willison to Flavelle, 17 July 1923; Foster Diary, 9-15 July 1923
8 See, for example, his remarks reported in the *Globe* of 29 June and 17 October 1923.
9 Toronto *Star*, 25 July 1923
10 Civil Service Commission personnel statistics, as cited in Walter Brzozowicz, 'The Civil Service Commission of Ontario: A Management Body, 1918-1937,' undergraduate research paper (York University 1973)
11 FP, Ferguson to Beck, 23 November 1923
12 FP, Ferguson to H.R. Drummond-Hay, 16 May 1929
13 Plewman, *Beck* 358
14 *Ibid.* 367-8
15 Flavelle Papers, Ferguson to Flavelle, 3 January 1924
16 Toronto *Star*, 18 July 1923
17 Toronto *Globe*, 17 September 1923
18 Interview, J.C. McRuer, 27 May 1971
19 FP, Ferguson to Reid, 28 January 1924
20 *Ibid.*
21 Stenographic copy of legislative debates taken by W.E. Elliott, 18 February 1926. When Ferguson or some other minister gave the sign, Mr Elliott would make shorthand notes of particular debates. According to Elliott, the ministers often found it useful to have a precise record of what had been said, particularly by opposition members. The advantage of this to the party in power is clear and perhaps explains in part why Ontario was so slow in establishing an official Hansard record.
22 These figures were computed with aid of an almanac.
23 W.E. Elliott, note attached to letter of 5 March 1970 to the author
24 Telephone interview, Farquhar Oliver, 16 February 1970

25 There is a good deal of correspondence on the amendments of 1924 in the Attorney-General's Papers. See, for example, P.T. McGibbon to Nickle, 27 March 1924 and reply, 7 April; Bd of License Commissioners to Nickle, 15 February 1924; J.A. Ayearst, OTA Branch, OPP, to Nickle, 14 February 1924.
26 Toronto *Globe*, 2 October 1923
27 FP, transcript of House debates, 6 March 1924
28 Flavelle Papers, Flavelle to Spence, 8 February 1922
29 Ontario Plebiscite Committee, 1924, T.A. Moore to the Rev. S.F. Dixon, 29 September 1924 and reply 1 October
30 Ontario Plebiscite Committee, 1924, G.A. Warburton to Gundy, 20 July 1924
31 *Ibid.*
32 Ontario Plebiscite Committee, 1924, Secretary of Finance Committee to Messrs Childs Company, New York, 14 October 1924; unsigned letter (apparently Moore) to Wm A. Pearson, 24 September 1924; Summary of Receipts and Disbursements to 25 June 1925
33 Toronto *Globe*, 19 July 1924
34 Ontario Plebiscite Committee, 1924, Warburton to Gundy, 20 July 1924
35 Ontario Plebiscite Committee, 1924, Ferguson to Warburton, 25 September 1924
36 Ontario Plebiscite Committee, 1924, Organizer for York and Ontario Counties to P.W. Pearson, 8 October 1924; Addiction Research Foundation Archives, Dr John Linton Collection, Ferguson to Moore, 7 October 1924
37 Toronto *Telegram*, 24 October 1924
38 See FP, 'Comparative Statement of Returns of Plebiscite Votes (Ontario) 1919 and 1924'; Toronto *Star*, 20 March 1925.
39 Toronto *Telegram*, 24 October 1924
40 *Farmers' Sun*, cited in *Literary Digest*, 22 November 1924
41 FP, anonymous, 24 October 1924; Toronto *Telegram*, 25 October 1924
42 Toronto *Telegram*, 7 November 1924
43 Toronto *Telegram*, 19 November 1924
44 Toronto *Star*, 10, 13, 18 February 1925; FP, Spence to Ferguson, 7 April 1925; *Christian Guardian*, 25 February 1925
45 Toronto *Star*, 14 February 1925
46 See FP for a printed copy of Nickle's 17 February speech in the House.
47 Toronto *Star*, 5 March 1925. This address was also recorded verbatim by W.E. Elliott.
48 FP, Ferguson to Hilliard, 24 March 1925; Elizabeth Barnes to Ferguson, 25 March 1925; Anonymous to Ferguson, 13 August 1925
49 Toronto *Star*, 22 May 1925
50 *Ibid.*, 27 May 1925
51 HP, Henry to Mayor of Goderich, March 1925

52 HP, Henry to Dr Tolmie, 17 February 1932
53 Toronto *Star*, 11 April 1925
54 *Ibid.*
55 Toronto *Star*, 20 June 1925
56 Toronto *Star*, 3 September 1925
57 *Speech on the Budget*...by Harold Fisher, KC, 23 March 1926, Liberal pamphlet
58 Toronto *Star*, 15 May 1926

CHAPTER 9: POWER TO THE PROVINCES
 1 *Report of the Royal Commission on Dominion-Provincial Relations* (Ottawa 1940) Book I, ch. 5, 'The Post War Prosperity, 1921-30' 112-37 (popularly known as the Rowell-Sirois Report). For the several Judicial Committee decisions, see the *O'Connor Report to the Senate, 1939* Annex 3.
 2 Rowell-Sirois *Report,* Book I, 130
 3 Toronto *Star*, 9 February 1925
 4 KP, Fisher to Lapointe, 14 April 1924; F.R. Latchford Papers, Latchford to John S. Ewart, 29 March 1924
 5 FP, 'Re: Proposed Amendment to BNA Act,' July 5 1924
 6 FP, Nickle to Lapointe, 10 July 1924
 7 Toronto *Globe*, 12, 14 July 1924
 8 KP, Ferguson to King, 3 July 1924 and reply, 7 July
 9 KP, Ferguson to King, 22 July and reply 24 July; Ferguson to King, 29 July
10 KP, Nickle to King, 11 August 1924; *CAR* (1924-5) 604
11 Toronto *Globe*, 1 November 1923
12 Toronto *Star*, 5 November 1923
13 FP, Charles Magrath, 'Re Quebec Power Contracts,' 21 October 1935
14 FP, Beck to Ferguson, 9 January 1924
15 FP, Ferguson to A.G. Chisholm, 28 July 1924
16 W.R. Willoughby, *The St Lawrence Waterway: A Study in Politics and Diplomacy* (Madison 1961) 96
17 *Ibid.* 98
18 MP, Meighen to Frank Keefer, 7 July 1923
19 See Debates, House of Commons, 7 April 1926, remarks of T.L. Church.
20 This estimate was cited by Loring Christie in a document prepared when he was in the employ of the Hydro. See Christie Papers, 'Federal and Provincial Rights in Waterways,' 24 February 1927, 2-3.
21 See Christie Papers, 'Federal and Provincial Rights...' 24 February 1927.
22 MP, Ferguson to King, 7 September 1923
23 MP, Ferguson to King, 16 April 1925
24 *Ibid.*
25 KP, Lapointe to King, 1 June 1925; MP, King to Ferguson, 12 June 1925

26 HEPC Archives, Ferguson to Stewart, 9 February 1925 and reply 4 May
27 KP, Ferguson to Stewart, 30 November 1925 and reply, 4 December
28 KP, Graham to King, 3 December 1925
29 MP, Meighen to Ferguson, 6 February 1925 and reply, 9 February
30 KP, Ferguson to King, 24 December 1925 and reply 6 February 1926;
    Ferguson to King, 3 February
31 Toronto *Star*, 8 April 1926.
32 FP, Ferguson to Keefer, 23 July 1926
33 FP, Taschereau to Ferguson, 15 May and 7 October 1924
34 MP, Ferguson to Meighen, 10 March 1924
35 FP, Charles Magrath, 'Re Quebec Power Contracts,' 21 October 1925. The
    statement was made by Beck on 15 November 1923.
36 HEPC Archives, Beck to Ferguson, 8 January 1925
37 FP, Taschereau to Ferguson, 26 February 1925
38 Laurent Tremblay, *Entre Deux Livraisons, 1913-1963* (*Le Droit* 1963) 66
39 KP, Haydon to King, 26 October 1927
40 FP, Ferguson to R.W. Shannon, 16 May 1925
41 FP, Ferguson to editor, *La Presse*, 19 May 1925; *La Presse*, 13 May 1925
42 HEPC Archives, Taschereau to Ferguson, 18 December 1925
43 HEPC Archives, Magrath to Ferguson, 8 January 1926
44 FP, memorandum for Premier Ferguson, 14 January 1926
45 HEPC Archives, Magrath to Ferguson, 8 January 1926
46 HEPC Archives, Magrath to Ferguson, 1 March 1926
47 FP, Magrath, 'Re Quebec Power Contracts' 9
48 FP, '1926 Gatineau Contract'; Magrath, 'Re Quebec Power Contracts' 10
49 KP, Haydon to King, 26 October 1927
50 Debates, House of Commons, 7 April 1926
51 *CAR* (1925-6) 342
52 HEPC Archives, Magrath to Ferguson, 13 August 1926
53 FP, Ferguson to Taschereau, 29 September 1926
54 *Ibid*. Of course Ferguson recognized that navigation remained the function
    of the federal government but he believed that the provinces might do some-
    thing to facilitate such development and thereby outflank the private charter
    holders.
55 MP, telegram, Meighen to Drayton, 20 August 1926
56 Toronto *Star*, 17 August 1927, printed Drayton's letter
57 H.B. Neatby, *Mackenzie King: The Lonely Heights* (Toronto 1963) 225-6
58 FP, Ferguson to Taschereau, 4 October 1926 and reply, 5 October
59 Toronto *Star*, 7 July 1926, reported some of these negotiations.
60 KP, Haydon to King, 26 October 1927
61 KP, 'To Mr King, Proposed Provincial Conference,' 26 March 1926
62 KP, King to Taschereau, 26 March 1926

63 *Ibid.*
64 For the proceedings see *Dominion and Interprovincial Conferences from 1887 to 1926* (Ottawa 1951) 105-14.
65 FP, Ferguson to King, 15 June 1926 and reply, 17 June

CHAPTER 10: 'ON THE TIDE OF PROSPERITY'
1 Diamond Jubilee of Confederation, *Ontario: On the Tide of Prosperity* (Toronto, nd) 6, 30
2 Newspaper Hansard, 26 February 1924
3 Newspaper Hansard, 27 February 1925
4 *Canada Year Book, 1930* 187; 1927-8, 419
5 HP, Henry to Bennett, 9 March 1933
6 Newspaper Hansard, 20 February 1924
7 Provincial Treasurer's Department, 'Surpluses-Deficits, 1914-1927'
8 Harold Fisher, Speech on the Budget, 23 March 1926, Liberal pamphlet
9 Ontario Conservative party, *Business Methods in Public Administration* (1926) 12-19
10 Fisher, Budget Address, 1926
11 Toronto *Star*, 26 March 1925
12 C.E. Wood, 'A Study of Provincial Government Finance in Ontario, 1926-1960,' MA thesis (Queen's University 1962) 151, offers a fuller exposition.
13 Wood, 'Provincial Government Finance' 24
14 FP, Memorandum, 26 March 1926, City Clerk's Office, Toronto
15 FP, Ferguson to T.G. Brigham, 7 January 1926
16 FP, Ferguson to Lee, 11 August 1926
17 *CAR* (1925-6) 180-2
18 FP, unsigned letter (Lee) to H.F. McLean & Co., 12 March 1925
19 See Toronto *Star*, 29 November 1927. The same issue gave the legal costs of the case. The Tilley law firm received $65,000 in fees, according to the *Star*.
20 *CAR* (1922) 115-16
21 Drury Papers, Thornton to Drury, 5 May 1923 and reply, 17 May
22 *CAR* (1923) 584
23 FP, Ferguson to Earl Lawson, 2 June 1930
24 Toronto *Star*, 5 March 1925
25 Toronto *Star*, 31 August 1925; FP, Ferguson to Greenfield, 31 August containing text of telegram to King
26 KP, King to Howard Cane, 20 September 1923
27 Ontario Conservative party, *Business Methods* 26
28 Interview, C.A. Morrison, 18 March 1971
29 Much of my understanding of the agricultural policies of the Drury and Ferguson governments is derived from the fine theses by Jean MacLeod. The Tories' own view of their policies was presented in the 1926 pamphlet, *Splendid Agricultural Record of Ferguson Government.*

30 Marion Jean MacLeod, 'Agriculture and Politics in Ontario since 1867,' Ph D thesis (University of London 1961) 158
31 *Splendid Agricultural Record* 10-11, 18
32 *CAR* (1930-1) 141
33 Merrill Denison, *The People's Power* (Toronto 1960) 186.
34 FP, 'Memo for Prime Minister re Gas Tax and Road Finances,' office of minister of Public Works and Highways, 12 October 1928
35 *Ibid.* The figure is in terms of cars, not individuals.
36 *Ibid.*
37 Newspaper Hansard, 29 February 1924
38 Arthur Ford Papers, Ferguson to Ford, 28 January 1924
39 Newspaper Hansard, 26 February 1925; FP, memorandum of 12 October 1928
40 Newspaper Hansard, 24 February 1925
41 FP, W.O. Langs to Ferguson, 22 February 1926 and reply, 25 February
42 Arthur Ford, *As the World Wags On* 156-7
43 Province of Ontario, *Report of the Ontario Iron Ore Committee* (1923)
44 FP, Ferguson to Fitzgerald, 8 June 1925
45 L. Carson Brown, *The Red Lake Gold Field* (Ontario Department of Mines 1966) 9
46 Figures from *CAR* (1919-27) and from the Tory pamphlet, *Business Methods* 62-5
47 FP, speech in Legislature by Charles McCrea, 7 April 1926, 19
48 *Ibid.* 9-10
49 *Ibid.* 10-11
50 Ontario Conservative party, *Plans and Projects for a Greater Ontario*, 1929 election pamphlet, 75
51 Speech, 7 April 1926, 12, 15
52 *Ibid.* 17-18
53 A.E. Safarian, *The Canadian Economy in the Great Depression* (Carleton Library edition 1970) 43-5; C.P. Fell, 'The Newsprint Industry' in H.A. Innis and A.F.W. Plumptre, *The Canadian Economy and Its Problems* (Toronto 1934) 40-1
54 HP, Ferguson to Sensenbrenner, 10 January 1931
55 Lambert & Pross, *Renewing Nature's Wealth* 273
56 *Business Methods* 71
57 FP, Ferguson to F.A. Drake, 25 November 1925
58 FP, press release, 13 January 1926
59 *Business Methods* 70
60 Newspaper Hansard, 28 March 1924
61 Press release, 13 January 1926
62 *Business Methods* 70-1
63 FP, Ferguson to Lewis D. Greer, 17 May 1926

64 FP, Ferguson to Finlayson, 11 November 1926
65 FP, Strachan Johnston to Ferguson, 17 April 1926
66 FP, Ferguson to Johnston, 21 April 1926
67 FP, Keefer to Ferguson, 24 November 1924
68 DLF, *AR* (1925) Land Transactions
69 FP, Keefer to Ferguson, 16 November 1927
70 DLF, *AR* (1926) 11
71 Interview, R.N. Johnston (formerly of DLF), 11 April 1970
72 *Maclean's Magazine*, 1 October 1923

CHAPTER 11: THE LIMITED STATE
1 See Provincial Treasurer's Papers, 'Pre-Session Financial Statement by E.A. Dunlop, Provincial Treasurer,' nd (1931).
2 See Richard Splane, *Social Welfare in Ontario, 1791-1893* (Toronto 1965) 282.
3 A.E. Grauer, *Public Assistance and Social Insurance*, a study prepared for the Royal Commission on Dominion-Provincial Relations (Ottawa 1939) 55
4 FP, Ferguson to R. Rudd, 5 December 1928; to the Rev. A.C. Calder, 16 December 1926; to Mrs Ethel Begley, 5 November 1928; to J. Willoughby, 19 April 1928; to Mary Foy, 11 January 1926
5 Rowell-Sirois *Report*, III, 61
6 Ontario, Sessional Papers, *Fifty-Sixth Annual Report of the Inspector of Prisons and Public Charities* (1926) Part IV, 3, as cited in M.K. Strong, *Public Welfare Administration in Canada* (Chicago 1930) 123. For the more generous grants system of other provinces see Grauer, *op. cit.*, Appendix IV, Statutory Payments to the General Hospitals.
7 FP, The Ontario Hospital Association, Requests of the Hospitals of Ontario to the Government, 25 February 1926
8 Provincial Treasurer's Papers, Condensed Report to the Prime Minister, Clarkson, Gordon & Dilworth, 3 September 1925
9 FP, J.J. Kelso to Ferguson, 1 May 1924 and reply, 2 May
10 FP, Ferguson to C.H. Anderson, 7 May 1924
11 FP, Ferguson to Judge McKinley, 21 January 1924
12 FP, Norman Sommerville to Ferguson, 11 October 1924
13 *CAR* (1924-5) 278
14 FP, Ferguson to F.K. Hamilton, 20 June 1929
15 Ontario Conservative party, *Business Methods in Public Administration* 78-9
16 FP, Arthur Ellis to Ferguson, 14 December 1925
17 The figures are from Ronald Sinclair, 'The Attitudes of the Ontario Labour Movement, 1919-1929,' undergraduate research paper (York University 1972) 21, 28; Ottawa, Department of Labour, *The Annual Report on Labour Organizations in Canada*, 1921, 1922, 1929.

18 FP, Col. Borden to Ferguson, 8 January 1925
19 FP, City Council, Welland, to Ferguson, 4 February 1925
20 A.E. Grauer, *op. cit.* 17
21 Wilfrid Eggleston & C.T. Kraft, *Dominion-Provincial Subsidies and Grants* (Ottawa 1939) 129
22 Toronto *Star*, 3 February 1925
23 Toronto *Star*, 9 February 1925. Emphasis mine
24 FP, J. Seabrook to Ferguson, 26 February 1925
25 Toronto *Star*, 5 March 1925
26 FP, 'Memorandum on Unemployment Insurance to Hon. G.H. Ferguson, Premier,' 18 March 1925
27 Toronto *Star*, 26 March 1925
28 Miss Margaret Storey, Premier Ferguson's niece, showed me this document.
29 FP, 'Memorandum to Hon. Dr Forbes Godfrey ... Re Industrial Disputes Investigation Act,' 29 March 1926, J.H.H. Ballantyne
30 Ottawa, King's Printer, *Old Age Pensions in Canada* (1929) 10
31 Duncan Greene, 'Old Age Pensions for Ontario,' undergraduate research paper (York University 1972) 13-15
32 FP, Sarah Maguire to Ferguson, 6 April 1926 and reply, 12 April
33 FP, Magistrate Browne to Ferguson, 5 October 1926
34 Hamilton *Spectator*, 24 March 1926

CHAPTER 12: MINISTER OF EDUCATION
1 FP, Willison to Ferguson, 29 December 1923 and reply, 3 January 1924
2 FP, Judge Scott to Ferguson, 10 December 1930
3 For an excellent analysis of the Cody school policies see Pat Oxley, 'Dr H.J. Cody, Minister of Education for the Province of Ontario, 1918-1919,' undergraduate research paper (York University 1969).
4 Ottawa *Journal*, 31 August 1923; Toronto *Globe*, 7 February 1924; Toronto *Telegram*, 24 September 1924; *CAR* (1923) 581: Department of Education, *AR* (1924)
5 R.M. Stamp, 'Education and the Economic and Social Milieu: The English-Canadian Scene from the 1870's to 1914,' 310, in J.D. Wilson, R.M. Stamp, L.-P. Audet, eds., *Canadian Education: A History* (Toronto 1970)
6 Dr Samuel Sinclair, as cited in M.C. Johnston, 'The Development of Special Education Class Programmes for Gifted Children in the Elementary Schools of Ontario from 1910-1962,' D. Ed. thesis (University of Toronto 1964) 25
7 See R.S. Patterson, 'Society and Education during the Wars and Their Inter-lude,' in Wilson, Stamp, and Audet, *op. cit.* 371-2.
8 Edison J. Quick, 'The Development of Geography and History Curricula in the Elementary Schools of Ontario, 1846-1966,' D.Ed. thesis (University of Toronto 1967) ch. 7. I wish to thank Professor Robert Stamp

for pointing out to me the diagnostic intent behind Sandiford's emphasis on testing techniques.

9 E.G. Savage, *Secondary Education in Ontario* (London 1928)
10 *AR* (1924)
11 *AR* (1928)
12 *Ibid.*
13 *AR* (1930)
14 Information from Professor Robert Stamp; and see R.M. Stamp, 'Schools on Wheels: The Railway Car Schools of Northern Ontario,' *Canada: An Historical Magazine* I, 3 (Spring 1974).
15 *AR* (1925)
16 FP, 'The Bill to Establish Township Boards of Trustees: A Letter from the Hon. G.H. Ferguson...' (Toronto 1925)
17 See Ferguson Papers.
18 FP, Ferguson to R.H. Grant, 10 February 1926
19 FP, Ferguson to R. Procter, 23 February 1926
20 FP, speeches, undated
21 FP, Ferguson to George Ecclestone, 8 December 1925
22 FP, Finlayson to Ferguson, 4 June 1926 and reply, 14 June
23 See E.E. Stewart, 'The Role of the Provincial Government in the Development of the Universities of Ontario, 1791-1964,' D. Ed. thesis (University of Toronto 1970) 353.
24 *CAR* (1921) 588-9
25 Toronto *Globe*, 22 April 1921
26 FP, Falconer to Ferguson, 26 April 1924, and reply, 6 May; Falconer Papers, Falconer to Ferguson, 8 May 1924
27 See Stewart, *op. cit.* 357-75.
28 *Ibid.* 357
29 FP, Ferguson to Cody, 17 April 1925
30 Toronto *Star*, 31 March 1926
31 MP, R.B. Taylor to Meighen, 12 February 1926
32 Toronto *Star*, 3 April 1926
33 Sir Robert Falconer, *Academic Freedom* (Toronto 1922)
34 FP, Ferguson to Cody, 8 December 1925
35 Falconer Papers, Ferguson to Falconer, 26 September 1924
36 *Ibid.*
37 Toronto *Globe*, 1 March 1924
38 Falconer Papers, Falconer to Ferguson, 29 September 1924
39 FP, Ferguson to R.J. Taber, 8 October 1926
40 C.B. Sissons, *A History of Victoria University* (Toronto 1952) 290-1
41 FP, Ferguson to Falconer, 17 February 1926
42 Department of Education, Memorandum for the Minister of Education, 17 March 1916

43 Falconer Papers, Ferguson to Falconer, 20 January 1925; FP, Falconer to Ferguson, 21 January.

44 FP, Ferguson to F.W. Wilson, 9 February 1925

45 FP, Brittain to Ferguson, 22 January 1925

46 Department of Education, *AR* (1928) vii

47 FP, memorandum, 6 April 1926

48 FP, Ferguson to Falconer, 17 February 1926

49 FP, 'The Council of the Faculty of Arts,' 5pp. document. The Falconer papers contain voluminous documentation on the response of the university community.

50 Falconer Papers, Milner to Falconer, 10 April 1926

51 Cody Papers, Ontario Archives, Satterly to Cody, 2 February 1927

52 Toronto *Star*, 17 May 1926

53 Toronto *Star*, 12, 17 April 1926

54 FP, Ferguson to E.W. Hagerty, 21 April 1926

55 *Ibid.*

56 FP, Falconer to Ferguson, 6 April 1926

57 Falconer Papers, Ferguson to Falconer, 22 December 1926

58 Falconer Papers, Falconer to Ferguson, 23 December 1926

59 Kingston Archdiocesan Archives, *School Taxes and Separate Schools*, The Catholic Truth Society (Toronto 1927) 3

60 F. Walker, *Catholic Education*, 334-5.

61 Toronto Archdiocesan Archives, Neil McNeil Papers, 'The Separate Schools, Notes on High School Work' (nd) 8

62 FP, Merchant to Ferguson, 4 January 1924

63 N. McNeil Papers, O'Brien to McNeil, 25 May 1924

64 FP, Fallon to Ferguson, 31 May 1924 and reply, 2 June

65 *Ibid.*

66 London Archdiocesan Archives, Fallon Papers, 'Issue: The Status of Separate Schools Doing Advanced Work' (nd)

67 Fallon Papers, Battle to Fallon, 30 December 1924

68 *Ibid.*

69 Neil McNeil Papers, Battle to McNeil, 21 May 1926

70 Neil McNeil Papers, Secretary of Separate School Teachers Association to McNeil, 8 June 1926

71 Neil McNeil Papers, Battle to McNeil, 29 December 1926

72 For a fuller discussion see Peter Oliver, *Public & Private Persons*, ch. 5.

73 Belcourt Papers, Belcourt to W.H. Moore, 5 July 1923

CHAPTER 13: PARTIES AND ELECTIONS

1 Flavelle Papers, Irish to Flavelle, 19 February 1926

2 Leslie Roberts, *These Be Your Gods* (Toronto 1929) 113

3 Interview, J.C. McRuer, 27 May 1971

4 Willison quoted in Colquhoun, *Press, Politics and People* 284; Roberts, *op. cit.* 111; Hector Charlesworth, *More Candid Chronicles* (Toronto 1928) 197; Ralph Hyman, *Tom Kennedy's Story* (Toronto 1960) 36; Toronto *Globe*, 1 November 1923; Arthur Ford, *As the World Wags On* 154

5 FP, Lyons to Ferguson, 1 March 1926 and reply, 1 March. For a detailed account of the Lyons's resignation see W.E. Elliott, *Politics is Funny* (Toronto 1952) 148-50. Ferguson invited Lyons back into the cabinet two months later but Lyons replied that the demands of his business prevented this.

6 MP, Meighen to Ferguson, 28 November 1923

7 MP, Meighen to Ford, 29 November 1923; Ferguson to Meighen, 3 December 1923

8 MP, Matthews to Meighen, 15 August 1923

9 Interviews, Arthur Ford, 19 April 1967; Douglas Oliver, 23 February 1967. The Toronto *Star* of 17 April 1930 also reported that Ferguson was to have only the interest until he retired from political life. The *Star* suggested that the decision to raise a sum for the Premier resulted from his remark in the House that he had spent all his personal property on the 1923 campaign and gone into debt. Apparently this resulted in a $100,000 gift while 'a further gift of $250,000, when he returned to Ontario from his European trip in the summer of 1928' was also made on the same condition. The *Star* did not give its source. Mackenzie King commented on the later gift in his diary.

10 Interview, David Walker, 4 June 1970

11 There is correspondence relating to this and several similar cases in the Ferguson Papers.

12 MP, Meighen to R.C. Matthews, 23 October 1923

13 MP, Ford to Meighen, 16 August 1923

14 FP, Ferguson to Reid, 28 January 1924

15 BP, Clysdale to Guthrie, 26 July 1927

16 MP, Ferguson to Meighen, 11 November 1924.

17 MP, W.G. Weichel to Meighen, 2 January 1925

18 MP, Meighen to Robert Templeton, 6 December 1924; Meighen to David Spence, 6 December 1924

19 MP, Ferguson to Meighen, 6 March 1925

20 MP, Meighen to Ferguson, 7 March 1925

21 MP, MacNicol to Meighen, 10 June 1925; Ford to Meighen, 11 May 1925

22 MP, Carill to Meighen, 10 June 1925. J.R. O'Neill was the official Tory in 1925.

23 MP, Meighen to Ferguson, 29 August 1925; Ferguson to Meighen, 3 September and reply, 5 September

24 Earl Rowe to the author, 16 August 1969

25 MP, Price to Meighen, 9 July 1926
26 MP, Meighen to Rykman, 5 September 1925
27 KP, King to Brownlee, 26 November 1925; King to Caron, 21 November; J. Carruthers to King, 23 November; I.L. Matthews to King, 21 November; Manley Chew to L.C. Moyer, (sec.) 30 November
28 Newspaper Hansard, 18, 19 February 1925; *Debates*, House of Commons, 11 May 1926, 3286-96
29 Newspaper Hansard, 19 February 1925
30 OHSS interview, Elmer Bell, 1972
31 FP, Ferguson to Harry Anderson, 5 April 1929
32 Provincial Treasurer's Papers, Ferguson to Monteith, 5 May 1927
33 Interview, Douglas Oliver, 23 February 1967
34 Newspaper Hansard, 21 March 1925
35 MP, Meighen to Ferguson, 1 September 1926
36 Ford Papers, Ferguson to Ford, 9 July 1926
37 *Ibid.*
38 MP, Ford to Meighen, 12 July 1926
39 This at least was the account given by Ferguson in his remarks at the Winnipeg Convention.
40 Graham, *Meighen* II, 356
41 *Ibid.* 471
42 Ford Papers, Ferguson to Ford, 9 July 1926
43 FP, Ferguson to M.T. Lester, 22 October 1927; Ferguson to Henry Cockshutt, 22 October 1927
44 MP, Price to Meighen, 16 September 1926
45 MP, Ford to Meighen, nd
46 MP, Mrs Fallis to Meighen, 5 October 1926
47 Transcript of debates prepared by W.E. Elliott, nd (March 1925)
48 KP, Hay to King, 14 July 1923
49 *Farmers' Sun*, 1 April 1926
50 Judge J.C. Anderson to author, 7 March 1972
51 *Ibid.*
52 *Ibid.*
53 Interview, J.C. McRuer, 27 May 1971
54 King Diary, 30 December 1925
55 Sissons Papers, Belcourt to Sissons, 9 November 1926
56 Hepburn Papers, Leduc to Hepburn, 9 December 1932
57 King Diary, 6 November 1924
58 Toronto *Star*, 19 October 1926
59 See FP, Carroll Hele to Almonte *Gazette*, 24 November 1926.
60 Ross Harkness, *J.E. Atkinson of the Star* (Toronto 1963) 226
61 *The New Outlook*, 1 December 1926

62 Speech of 22 October 1926, published as 'Hon. G. Howard Ferguson on the Leading Public Issues'
63 'The Liberal Manifesto,' The Ontario Liberal Committee, 1926
64 Col. T.L. Kennedy, with Ralph Hyman, *Tom Kennedy's Story* (Toronto 1960) 28
65 Toronto *Star*, 2 November 1926
66 *Ibid.*, 3 November 1926
67 Flavelle Papers, Flavelle to Mrs A.B. Cunningham, 19 November 1926; D.B. Harkness to Flavelle, 29 November 1926
68 An excellent pamphlet collection on prohibition is in the United Church Archives, Victoria University, Toronto.
69 Ontario Conservative Committee, advertisement, 'When People Like These Endorse Government Control,' 1926.
70 Interview, David Walker, 11 May 1970
71 *Ibid.* Senator Walker's diary, 14 July 1927, recounts a conversation with Ferguson in which he described his conviction that in the 1926 election he would be able to swing public opinion.
72 BP, Irish to Bennett, 7 November 1928
73 Sissons Papers, Belcourt to Sissons, 9 November 1926
74 *Mail and Empire*, 25 November 1926
75 Diary, David Walker, 14 July 1927. On this date Ferguson told Walker that he and his strategists were wrong on only six seats. Popular vote figures are from Howard A. Scarrow, *Canada Votes* (New Orleans 1961) 211, 213. For slightly different figures see J. Wilson and D. Hoffman, 'Ontario,' in M. Robin, ed., *Canadian Provincial Politics* (Scarborough 1972) 204-5.
76 FP, J.A. Austin to Ferguson, nd
77 FP, F.D. Bell to Ferguson, 2 December 1926 and reply 15 December
78 HP, H.A. Clark to Henry, nd
79 Willison Papers, Ford to Willison, 3 December 1926; HP, William Findlay to Henry, 3 December 1926

CHAPTER 14: THE SECOND ADMINISTRATION
1 FP, Armstrong to Ferguson, 2 December 1926
2 Flavelle Papers, Agar to Ferguson (copy), 15 December 1926
3 Flavelle Papers, Harkness to Flavelle, 8 February 1927
4 Attorney-General's Papers, Agar to Ferguson, 7 February 1927
5 See, for example, the many requests for positions in the R.B. Bennett Papers.
6 Toronto *Star*, 23 February 1927
7 Toronto *Star*, 1 March 1927
8 For more of Spence's views see Attorney-General's Papers, letter and memorandum from Spence, 23 March 1927.
9 Toronto *Star*, 16, 22 March 1927

10 The bill was defeated on 31 March by a 7 to 2 vote. See Toronto *Star*, 12 April 1927 for the charges about liquor interest campaign contributions. A 1929 'Act Respecting Political Contributions,' assented to on 29 March, appears to have been little more than a pious gesture.
11 Toronto *Star*, 26 October 1967
12 Graham, *Meighen* II, 254; FP, Cahan to Ferguson, 4 May 1927
13 FP, Smith to Ferguson, 20 June 1927
14 FP, White to Ferguson, 28 July 1927
15 *Ibid.*
16 FP, Ferguson to White, 2 August 1927
17 FP, Ferguson to Dr E.A. Mooney, 25 May 1927
18 FP, Ferguson to White, 19 July 1927
19 FP, Ferguson to Atholstan, 3 October 1927
20 FP, Ferguson to Pope, 13 May 1927
21 FP, Atholstan to Ferguson, 26 September 1927 and reply 3 October
22 Toronto *Star*, 14 May 1927
23 See Toronto *Star*, 14 May 1927.
24 Sissons Papers, Belcourt to Sissons, 10 December 1926
25 ACFEO Papers, Belanger to Ferguson, 28 March 1927
26 C.B. Sissons, *Church and State in Canadian Education* 93
27 ACFEO Papers, E. Cloutier to the Rev. Père U. Langlois, 12 October 1927
28 ACFEO Papers, Cloutier to Omer Héroux, 29 September 1927
29 See McNeil's statement, Toronto *Star*, 22 September 1927.
30 Orange *Sentinel*, 29 September 1927
31 Belcourt Papers, Belcourt to Henri Bourassa, 10 December 1927
32 FP, Ferguson to Taschereau, 21 September 1927
33 FP, Ferguson to Hearst, 23 August 1927
34 Toronto *Star*, 20 August 1927
35 *Ibid.*, 22 August 1927
36 FP, Hearst to Ferguson, nd, and reply, 23 August 1927
37 Toronto *Star*, 22 August 1927
38 FP, Reid to Ferguson, 20 August 1927
39 FP, Harold Daly to Ferguson, 1 October 1927
40 FP, Lynch-Staunton to Ferguson, 5 October 1927
41 Toronto *Star*, 8 October 1927
42 *Ibid.*, 7 October 1927
43 Dafoe Papers, Sifton to Dafoe, 6 October 1927
44 FP, letter of 3 October 1927
45 FP, Ferguson to 'Mr Chairman,' 10 October 1927
46 FP, Ferguson to Atholstan, 3 October 1927
47 FP, Ferguson to Emily Murphy, 23 August 1927
48 Interview, David Walker, 11 May 1970

49 FP, clipping, Ottawa *Journal*, nd
50 London *Advertiser*, 11 October; Toronto *Star*, 11 October 1927
51 Graham, *Meighen* II, 491, 497; Dafoe Papers, Dafoe to Sifton, 15 October 1927
52 Interview, Arthur Ford, 19 April 1967
53 FP, Ferguson to W.R. Givens, 30 November 1927
54 FP, Ferguson to Foster, 22 October 1927
55 Flavelle Papers, Flavelle to Macdonnell, 19 October 1927
56 FP, Ferguson to Smeaton White, 28 December 1927
57 *Ibid.*
58 Dafoe Papers, Dafoe to Kennedy, 18 November 1928
59 FP, Ferguson to Atholstan, 3 October 1927
60 For some enlightenment see FP, George B. Nicholson to Ferguson, 22 October 1927 and accompanying memorandum. Nicholson chaired the sub-committee which dealt with this question.
61 See KP and FP, 1927, 1928 for a voluminous correspondence.
62 HEPC Archives, Magrath to Ferguson, 25 January 1927
63 *Ibid.*
64 HEPC Archives, Magrath to Ferguson, 24 February 1927; Magrath to Ferguson, 4 April 1927
65 Toronto *Star*, 8 March 1927. A copy of the resolution is in the King Papers.
66 KP, H.J. Sims to King, 23 March 1927
67 Toronto *Star*, 4 March 1927
68 *Ibid.*, 29 March 1927
69 Neatby, *King* II, 227
70 Loring C. Christie Papers, 'Notes On Draft of Amendments. ... The Montreal, Ottawa and Georgian Bay Canal Company,' 1 February 1927
71 Christie Papers, 'Federal and Provincial Rights in Waterways,' 24 February 1927
72 Dafoe Papers, Dafoe to Sifton, 28 July 1927
73 Dafoe Papers, Sifton to Dafoe, 10 August 1927
74 KP, Ferguson to King, 13 April 1927
75 KP, King to Ferguson, 23 April 1927; Ferguson to King, 6 July; King to Ferguson, 16 August
76 KP, Ferguson to King, 2 August 1927
77 FP, Ferguson to Taschereau, 3 August 1927
78 FP, Taschereau to Ferguson, 4 August 1927 and reply 9 August
79 See W.R. Willoughby, *The St Lawrence Waterway* 114.
80 Toronto *Star*, 27 October 1927
81 Most of the preparatory material on the Ontario side may be found in the Attorney-General's Papers.
82 Attorney-General's Papers, memorandum, 26 October 1927, Edward Bayly

83 Attorney-General's Papers, memorandum, 31 October 1927, F.V. Johns
84 FP, Ferguson to Harris, 26 June 1926
85 Christie Papers, 'Considerations Concerning ... Water Rights,' 11 May
86 Attorney-General's Papers, 'Memorandum re Insurance,' November 1927
87 *Ibid.*
88 Attorney-General's Papers, Price to King, 2 March 1927 and see memorandum, 'Inter-provincial Conference, re Insurance,' November 1927
89 *Ibid.*
90 Attorney-General's Papers, 'Brief re Delimitation of Fields of Taxation...,' Controller of Revenue
91 Attorney-General's Papers, 'Memorandum re Old Age Pensions,' J.H.H. Ballantyne and covering letter, 8 November 1927
92 KP, Ferguson to Gardiner, 23 September 1927
93 KP, Gardiner to King, 28 September and 1 October 1927
94 Neatby, *King* II, 242
95 *Ibid.* 235
96 King Diary, 4 November 1927; official précis of 1927 conference
97 *Dominion-Provincial Conferences* (Ottawa 1951) 25
98 *Ibid.*
99 FP, Ferguson to Dennis, 15 December 1926
100 A copy is in the Ferguson Papers. Shortly after the conference in December 1927, an opinion from British counsel, Sir John Simon, confirmed this view.
101 *Dominion-Provincial Conferences* (1927) 25-6, 35-6
102 *Ibid .* 37
103 *Ibid.* 27
104 Attorney-General's Papers, minutes of subcommittee meeting by Leighton Foster, handwritten
105 Attorney-General's Papers, Price to Cannon, nd
106 *Dominion-Provincial Conferences* (1927) 37
107 Grant Dexter, 'Commerce and the Canadian Constitution,' *Queen's Quarterly* XXXIX (1932)
108 KP, Saunders to King, 4 April 1928 and reply, 14 July

CHAPTER 15: 'THE MOST MARKED CONTRIBUTION WE HAVE MADE'
1 Borden Papers, Borden to Ferguson, 31 October 1929 and reply, 15 November
2 Ontario Conservative party, 1929, *Plans And Projects for a Greater Ontario* 6
3 *Ibid.* 92
4 Toronto *Star*, 31 March 1927
5 *Ibid.*, 20 October 1927

6 FP, Ferguson to Dr J.C. Connell, 3 April 1928; Ferguson to G. Greenway, 28 September 1929
7 FP, W. Wheelans to Ferguson, 3 May 1930 and reply, 6 May
8 *Plans and Projects* 24
9 *Ibid.* 31-3
10 *Ibid.* 23
11 OHSS interview, Harry Price, 31 May 1973
12 FP, F.N. Stapleford to Ferguson, 11 January 1927 and reply, 14 January
13 FP, letter and petition, 1 March 1928
14 FP, Ferguson to Mrs C.C. McCullough, 5 November 1928
15 See Toronto *Star*, 15 February, 1 March 1928.
16 FP, F.A. Ellis to Ferguson, 22 March 1929 for Ellis's final report
17 Toronto *Star*, 15 February, 1 March 1928
18 *Ibid.*, 8 March 1928
19 FP, speech in House, 21 March 1929
20 *Ibid.*
21 *Ibid.* See also *CAR*(1928-9) 349.
22 Attorney-General's Papers, copy of an order-in-council, 12 April 1927
23 Attorney-General's Papers, 'Memorandum re Unemployment Relief' and covering letter, 8 November 1927
24 Toronto *Star*, 26 July 1930
25 FP, A.J. Moore to Ferguson, nd
26 FP, Ferguson to Moore, 6 January 1930
27 FP, Letter of 22 March 1930 on unemployment
28 *Ibid.*
29 *Ibid.*
30 *Ibid.*
31 FP, H.C. Hudson to Ferguson, 28 June 1930
32 *Ibid.*
33 *Plans and Projects* 83-4
34 Toronto *Star*, 26 August 1930
35 FP, Ferguson to Irving Robertson, 26 August 1930; *The Royal Commission on Public Welfare, Report to the Lieutenant-Governor in Council* (Toronto 1930)
36 FP, Reid to Ferguson, 8 September 1930
37 FP, Ryan to Ferguson, 25 August 1930 and reply, 27 August
38 W.E. Elliott, transcript of debate, 18 February 1926; Toronto *Star*, 12 September 1928
39 John Henderson, *Great Men of Canada* (published for the Government of Ontario by Southam Press, Toronto)
40 FP, Ferguson to Borden, 3 January 1929
41 W.E. Elliott, transcript of debates, 18 February 1926

42 Toronto *Star*, 30 March 1928
43 Toronto *Star*, 11 April 1928
44 Department of Education, *AR* (1928)
45 R.S. Patterson, 'Society and Education during the Wars and Their Interlude: 1914-1945,' in Wilson, Stamp, and Audet, eds., *Canadian Education* 362
46 Department of Education, *AR* (1929)
47 See M.C. Johnson, 'The Development of Special Class Programmes for Gifted Children in the Elementary Schools of Ontario from 1910-1962.' D. Ed. thesis (University of Toronto 1964) ch. 4.
48 FP, Report of J.B. MacDougall, Assistant Chief Inspector, 6 May 1927
49 Department of Education *AR* (1929). See also R. Stamp, 'Schools on Wheels,' *Canada: An Historical Magazine* (Spring 1974).
50 Stamp, *op. cit.* 38
51 FP, Carl Ruckman to Ferguson, 19 March 1930 and reply, 21 March
52 *Ibid.*
53 FP, Ferguson to Secretary of Toronto Board of Trade, 10 May 1930
54 FP, Ferguson to Bishop George E. Lloyd, Prince Albert, Sask., 12 December 1928
55 *Ibid.*
56 FP, Ferguson to W. Doreen, 25 February 1926
57 *Ibid.*
58 See FP, 'An Act to Amend the Public Libraries Act, 1926.'
59 Toronto *Star*, 19 May 1928
60 Falconer Papers, Ferguson to Cody, 17 October 1928
61 Falconer Papers, Falconer to Ferguson, 23 October 1928
62 Public Archives of Ontario, Cody Papers, Ferguson to Cody, 6 April 1929
63 FP, Ferguson to Flavelle, 12 January 1927
64 Toronto *Star*, 26, 28 February 1927; Falconer Papers, Ferguson to Falconer, 1 March 1927
65 Falconer Papers, Falconer to Ferguson, 2 March 1927
66 FP, Merchant to Ferguson, 11 March 1927
67 Falconer Papers, Falconer to Ferguson, 20 September 1928, 'Memorandum Regarding the University and the City'
68 HP, Ferguson to Henry, 2 March 1932
69 For Falconer's continued support of the transfer of first-year pass work to the high schools see Ontario, Sessional Papers, Misc., *Report of the University of Toronto for 1929*. In his history of Victoria University, C.B. Sissons attributed the curricular changes adopted in 1931 to Ferguson's earlier campaign.
70 HP, Ferguson to Henry, 15 February 1932. For the budget proposals see E.E. Stewart, *The Role of the Provincial Government in the Development of the Universities of Ontario* 362.

71 N. McNeil Papers, Ferguson to Battle, 26 January 1927
72 N. McNeil Papers, Battle to McNeil, 31 January 1927
73 *Ibid.*, Battle to McNeil, 2 February 1927
74 *Ibid.*, Chief Justice Anglin to McNeil, 5 November 1927
75 F.G. Carter, *Judicial Decisions on Denominational Schools* (Toronto 1962) 99
76 N. McNeil Papers, Belcourt to McNeil, 18 and 27 June 1928
77 Walker, *Catholic Education* 349
78 For more on the Orange campaign see Walker 350-1.
79 FP, Scott to Ferguson, 19 February 1930
80 Kingston Archdiocesan Archives, O'Brien Papers, Ferguson to the priest at Church of the Holy Cross, Kemptville
81 O'Brien Papers, Ferguson to parish priest, Merrickville, 28 January 1930
82 O'Brien Papers, Bishop O'Brien to Father P. McKieran, 15 January 1930
83 O'Brien Papers, Burke to O'Brien, 30 January 1930
84 *Ibid.*
85 See FP, Judge Scott to Ferguson, 25 November 1927.
86 Toronto *Star*, 16, 23 March 1928
87 Ottawa *Journal*, 31 October 1929
88 ACFEO Papers, Belcourt statement on the Merchant-Scott-Coté Report, 1927
89 *Plans and Projects* 102
90 FP, Ferguson to Baldwin, 21 May 1924
91 King Diary, 6 August 1927
92 Toronto *Star*, 18 February 1927
93 Toronto *Star*, 1 December 1927
94 FP, Roberts to Ferguson, 9 July 1929 and reply, 10 July
95 Toronto *Star*, 14 January 1930
96 Magrath Papers, Magrath to Ferguson, 14 July 1927
97 Magrath Papers, memorandum, 22 February 1928
98 FP, Ferguson to Hodgins, 11 January 1930

CHAPTER 16: BOSS FERGUSON
1 *Plans and Projects* 81
2 Toronto *Star*, 11 December 1971
3 *Plans and Projects* 16-22
4 *Ibid.* 8
5 This story has several sources and its truth was confirmed by Kelso Roberts in an interview, September 1969. The date of the incident remains elusive, however.
6 *CAR* (1930-1) 129
7 *Plans and Projects* 75
8 *Ibid.* 76

9 *Ibid.* 38-40
10 Toronto *Star*, 27 May 1927
11 See FP, 'Memo for Prime Minister re Gas Tax and Road Finances,' 12 October 1928.
12 FP, City Clerk of Port Arthur to Ferguson, 12 February 1930; Ferguson to editor of *Maclean's*, 17 January 1930
13 For a fuller discussion of the ORF, see Oliver, *Public & Private Persons*, ch. 7.
14 See J.P. Williamson, *Securities Regulation in Canada* (Toronto 1960) 21-2; and E.P. Neufeld, *The Financial System of Canada* (Toronto 1972) 536-7.
15 *CAR* (1926-7) 329
16 Paul Pross, 'The Development of Professions in the Public Service: The Foresters in Ontario,' *Canadian Public Administration* X (1967) 395
17 Department of Lands and Forests, *AR* (1929), as cited in Pross, *op. cit.* 393
18 *Ibid.* 392
19 J.W.B. Sisam, *Forestry Education at Toronto* (Toronto 1961) 40. Dean Howe was referring particularly to the 1929 Pulpwood Act.
20 Eugene Forsey, 'The Pulp And Paper Industry,' *CJEPS* I (1935) 502
21 For more on the rigid financial structure of the industry, see Forsey, *op. cit.* 502-3.
22 *Ibid.* 504; L. Ethan Ellis, *Newsprint Producers, Publishers, Political Pressures* (including the text of *Print Paper Pendulum*) (New Brunswick, NJ 1960) 134.
23 FP, Finlayson to Ferguson, 19 July 1928
24 *Ibid.*
25 *Ibid.*
26 *Ibid.*
27 FP, Taschereau to Ferguson, 20 August 1928 and reply 28 August
28 FP, Ferguson to pulp and paper companies, 19 November 1928
29 HP, Ferguson to Sensenbrenner, 10 January 1931
30 FP, Ferguson to E.A. Wallberg, 27 November 1928
31 FP, 'Rules and Regulations for the Conduct of the Newsprint Industry,' nd
32 For an example of the tough position Ferguson was taking at this time with Graustein see FP, Ferguson to Graustein, 12 December 1928.
33 V.W. Bladen, *An Introduction to Political Economy* (Toronto 1956) 195-6
34 Toronto *Star*, 23 January 1929
35 Toronto *Star*, 3 July 1930; FP, Ferguson to Taschereau, 11 January 1930 and reply, 16 January
36 HP, Clarkson to Henry, 21 February 1933
37 HP, Sensenbrenner to Ferguson, 13 January 1931; J.H. Black to Ferguson, 19 February 1929
38 HP, Ferguson to Sensenbrenner, 10 January 1931
39 Toronto *Star*, 26 February 1929
40 Toronto *Star*, 28 March 1929

41 FP, Ferguson to Black, 6 May 1929
42 HP, Sensenbrenner to Ferguson, 9 November 1929
43 Toronto *Star*, 28 November 1929
44 FP, City Clerk, Port Arthur, to Ferguson, 9 April 1930
45 HP, Ferguson to Sensenbrenner, 10 January 1931
46 HP, Ferguson to Henry, 12 January 1931
47 Bladen, *Political Economy* 197
48 Forsey, 'Pulp and Paper' 505
49 A.R.M. Lower, *Settlement and the Forest Frontier in Eastern Canada* (Toronto 1936) 129
50 HP, Ferguson to Henry, 24 December 1932
51 HP, Henry to Ferguson, 24 February 1933
52 KP, King to Taschereau, 20 February 1928
53 FP, Ferguson to Lapointe, 2 February 1928
54 See C.P. Wright, *The St Lawrence Deep Waterway* (Toronto 1935) ch. 4.
55 KP, King to Ferguson, 28 January 1928
56 Wright, *The St Lawrence* 129
57 Willoughby, *The St Lawrence Waterway* 117-18
58 Toronto *Star*, 17 April 1928
59 Toronto *Star*, 12 May 1928
60 Willoughby, *The St Lawrence* 119
61 *Ibid.*
62 King Diary, 26 February 1929
63 FP, Ferguson to King, 3 May 1929 and reply, 14 August
64 King Diary, 5 February 1929
65 HEPC Archives, Magrath to Ferguson, 26 March 1929 and memorandum, 27 March
66 King Diary, 24 February 1929
67 FP, King to Ferguson, 25 February 1929; Ferguson to King, 22 March 1929
68 KP, Ferguson to Taschereau, 19 November 1928 (copy)
69 Wright, *The St Lawrence* 228
70 *Ibid.* 218-20; see also FP, Magrath to Ferguson, 26 March and memorandum, 27 March 1929.
71 HEPC Archives, Ferguson to Magrath, 3 May 1930
72 See Merrill Denison, *The People's Power* 179.
73 FP, Hammell to Ferguson, 15 April 1929
74 HEPC Archives, Magrath to Ferguson, 9 February, 25 February 1929
75 HEPC Archives, Ferguson to Magrath, 14 February 1929. For a different viewpoint, see Nelles, *The Politics of Development* 423-5.
76 Merrill Denison, *The People's Power* 188
77 KP, J. Day to King, 9 December 1929
78 Toronto *Star*, 14, 15 February 1929

79 King Diary, 7 October 1929
80 KP, King to Sinclair, 30 September 1929; Sen. James Spence to King, 28 November 1929
81 KP, Sinclair to King, 26 December 1929
82 KP, Drury to King, 12 December 1929
83 KP, King to James Day, 13 January 1930
84 *Ibid.*
85 FP, Ferguson to McCrea, 14 January 1929; Ferguson to Godfrey, 14 January 1929
86 Flavelle Papers, Irish to Flavelle, 13 March 1929
87 BP, MacNicol to Bennett, 21 March 1929
88 BP, Ferguson to Bennett, 27 September 1929; HP, Ferguson to Henry, 26 September 1929
89 HP, MacNicol to Henry, 26 October 1929
90 Toronto *Star*, 29 September 1927. But Mrs Shortt in a 30 March 1930 letter to Ferguson blamed Dr Godfrey for this state of affairs and told the premier: 'it is a good thing for the public that there is a man at the helm in Ontario who has the courage to publicly repudiate crookedness in the administration of any Department...' Another interesting incident occurred in 1928 in a by-election in North Renfrew in which Paul Martin, then a young student, opposed E.A. Dunlop. According to an interview Escott Reid had with Mr Martin in 1932, Martin stated that a Tory organizer offered him a bribe of $10,000 to step out of the contest. Senator Martin later told the author that he knew nothing of this incident and it seems incredible that it should slip his mind. Interview, 12 May 1970; PAC, 'Canadian Politics, Notes on Interviews, 1930-1932,' interview, 22-3 June 1932 with Paul Martin by Escott Reid
91 FP, Ferguson to Anderson, 5 April 1929
92 HP, Henry to M.M. McBride, 17 September 1929
93 Toronto *Star*, 29 October 1929
94 BP, Ford to Bennett, 18 October 1929
95 DO/35/68/D15560, Sir William Clark to Secretary of State for Dominions, 4 December 1929
96 HP, Henry to MacNicol, 4 November 1929; BP, McCrea to Bennett, 31 March 1930
97 Toronto *Star*, 31 October 1929
98 Scarrow, *Canada Votes* 213
99 BP, Ford to Bennett, 7 November 1929; Bennett to Ferguson, 29 October 1929
100 HP, Henry to Martin, 31 October 1929
101 FP, unsigned document dated 4 February 1930; King to Ferguson, 15 February 1930; Ferguson to King, 24 February 1930

102 FP, Ferguson to King, 27 February and 28 April 1930; King Diary, 3 March 1930
103 See Willoughby, *The St Lawrence* 144-5.
104 FP, Ferguson to W.A. Gordon, 13 January 1930
105 Toronto *Star*, 22 January 1930
106 FP, J.D. Jones, vice-president, to Ferguson, 26 February 1930
107 King Diary, 17 May 1930
108 J.W. Pickersgill to author, 27 January 1970; for confirmation see *One Canada: Memoirs of The Rt. Hon. John G. Diefenbaker* (Toronto 1975) I, 171-2.
109 Toronto *Star*, 30 June 1930
110 Toronto *Star*, 19, 23 July 1930
111 King Diary, 23 July 1930; T.M. Mulligan to King, 31 July 1930
112 KP, King to Anderson, 20 August 1930; Geo. A. MacLean to King, 21 August 1930
113 King Diary, 29 July 1930
114 FP, Ferguson to Crawford, 31 July, to J.E. Armstrong, 7 August, to J. Haig, 1 August, to R. Borden, 1 August; R. Morand to Ferguson, 1 August; Church to Ferguson, 6 August
115 FP, Bennett to Ferguson, 31 December 1930
116 FP, Ferguson to C. Mitchell, 6 August 1930
117 Toronto *Telegram*, 12 December 1930
118 KP, T.M. McCarron to King, 30 July 1930
119 KP, King to Sinclair, 13 September 1930
120 KP, Sinclair to King, 17 September 1930. See Debates, House of Commons, 11 and 12 September 1930 and also Peter Heenan's speech, 20 April 1931.
121 Toronto *Star*, 26 March 1930; FP, Ferguson to New Toronto Conservative Association, 1 April 1930
122 Flavelle Papers, Flavelle to Rundle, 3 December 1930; interview, Leopold Macaulay, 8 May 1967
123 Forbes Godfrey Papers, McCrea to Godfrey, 23 September 1930; Price to Godfrey, 16 September 1930
124 T.L. Kennedy, *Tom Kennedy's Story* 28; FP, Ferguson to Godfrey, 15 September 1930
125 Flavelle Papers, Flavelle to Rundle, 3 December 1930

CHAPTER 17: SAVING THE EMPIRE

1 Toronto *Star*, 31 July 1930
2 King Diary, 31 July 1930
3 FP, Ferguson to Bennett, 10 September 1930 and 'Memorandum re Amendments to the British North America Act...'
4 *Manitoba Free Press*, 1 October 1930; Herbert Bruce Papers, Bruce to Beaverbrook, 23 September 1930

5 *Ibid.*
6 Dafoe Papers, Stevenson to Dafoe, 22 October 1930
7 *The Times*, 25 October 1930
8 Dafoe Papers, Spry to Dafoe, 6 October 1930
9 Department of External Affairs Papers, Under-Secretary of State, 'Representations of the Ontario Government on the Conference of 1929 on the Operation of Dominion Legislation' and 'Memorandum on the Objections Set Out in Ontario's Memorandum, to the Proposals of the ODL Report, 1929'
10 *Manitoba Free Press*, 1 October and 3 October 1930
11 KP, Rogers to King, 23 November 1930
12 *Ibid.*
13 See Ottawa *Journal*, 2 October, *Manitoba Free Press*, 3 October and Montreal *Gazette*, 4 October 1930.
14 The proceedings of the Dominion-Provincial Conference of April 1931 were not included in the précis of discussions of such conferences published by the King's Printer. In a statement in the House of Commons on 16 April, Bennett made it clear that the minutes would not be presented to Parliament or made public. Informally, however, a member of the Department of External Affairs sent a copy to the Dominions Office. See DO35/92/4020/108 and 'Dominion-Provincial Conference, 1931,' DO35/92/XJ/1487.
15 *Manitoba Free Press*, 7 April 1931
16 D035/92/4020/108, despatch, P. Liesching to J.H. Thomas, 23 April 1931 and Sir Maurice Gwyer to Sir Edward Harding, 21 May 1931
17 Dafoe Papers, Dafoe to Brooke Claxton, 29 December; Dafoe to Stevenson, 29 December 1930
18 The Senate of Canada, Session of 1939, *O'Connor Report*, Annex 5, 24
19 For a full discussion of the Ottawa Conference and the events surrounding it, see Ian M. Drummond, *Imperial Economic Policy 1917-1939* (London 1974).
20 DO35/90/4011/243, Clark to Dominions Office
21 FP, Noxon to Ferguson, 4 March 1930 and reply, 13 March
22 Beaverbrook Papers, Ferguson to Beaverbrook, 11 May 1930 and reply, 5 June.
23 PRO, CAB 23/65, 29 October 1930
24 Bennett's statement was issued 1 December. See A.E. Morrison, 'R.B. Bennett and the Imperial Preference Trade Agreements, 1932,' MA thesis (University of New Brunswick 1966) 89-91; King Diary, 2 December 1930.
25 Dafoe Papers, Beaverbrook to Dafoe, 4 October 1930
26 See Beaverbrook Papers, Beaverbrook to Ferguson, 13 and 20 October 1930; Dafoe Papers, Beaverbrook to Dafoe, 8 October 1930.
27 Toronto *Globe*, 22 November 1930
28 BP, Willingdon to Perley, 21 November 1930

29 *The Observer*, 23 November 1930; *Manchester Guardian*, 5 December. Norman Hillmer brought these to my attention.
30 Dafoe Papers, Dafoe to Sifton, 26 November 1930
31 King Diary, 27 November
32 KP, letters to Lloyd George and MacDonald, 3 December; to Simon, 5 December
33 Dafoe Papers, Grant Dexter to Dafoe, 8 December 1930
34 Toronto *Globe*, 30 November; Toronto *Daily Star*, 29 November 1930
35 DO35/105/4145/8, Thomas to Clark, 9 December 1930
36 FO 627/25/4673, minuted by Speaight, 10/12, 1930; DO35/105/4145/8, Clark to Thomas, 6 December 1930.
37 King Diary, 16 December 1930
38 Dafoe Papers, Dexter to Dafoe, 8 December; Dafoe to Sifton, 23 December; Dafoe to Stevenson, 29 December 1930.
39 *Manitoba Free Press*, 8 December 1930. I wish to thank Norman Hillmer for bringing this editorial to my attention and for letting me use his research from the J.H. Thomas Papers. A copy is in those papers.
40 DO35/105/4145/8, Thomas to Clark, 9 December 1930; DO35/195, Clark to Thomas, 16 December 1930
41 DO35/195, Clark to Thomas, 17 December 1930
42 King Diary, 13 December 1930. For an insight into King's own techniques at biographic puffery see M. Moher, 'The "Biography" in Politics: Mackenzie King in 1935,' *CHR* (June 1974) 239-248.
43 *Manitoba Free Press*, 23 January 1931
44 HP, the Rev. J.W. Gordon to Henry, 17 July 1931 and reply, 20 July
45 HP, Mrs Lincoln Goldie to Henry, nd
46 FP, Ferguson to Saunderson, 20 March 1931
47 Ottawa *Citizen*, 11 February 1931
48 Toronto *Star*, 29 April 1931
49 Toronto *Star* editorial, 29 April 1931
50 Toronto *Star*, 30 April. See also the Montreal *Gazette*, 29 April 1931.
51 FP, Anderson to Ferguson, 11 May 1931
52 External Affairs, Ferguson to Bennett, 17 April 1931; for Ferguson's expectations, see BP, Ferguson to Bennett, 23 March 1931.
53 External Affairs, Ferguson to Bennett, 17 April 1931
54 DO35/235/8791/30, Report on Rome Wheat Conference to Foreign Secretary by R. Graham, HM Minister at Rome; DO35/235/8791/49, Conference of Wheat Exporting Countries, London 1931; DO35/196, despatch, Clark to Thomas, 29 May 1931
55 BP, Ferguson to Dawes, 22 April; Ferguson to Bennett, 23 April 1931
56 Mme Vanier to author, 7 December 1973. Mme Vanier was not certain when this incident occurred. In a 24 October 1935 letter, H. Mackie told

Mackenzie King that at a banquet in London Ferguson had 'deeply insulted the Soviet Ambassador' but this was doubtless a different incident. See KP for this.

57 HP, Ferguson to Henry, 26 February 1931
58 HP, Ferguson to Henry, 26 February, 9 March 1931
59 FP, Ferguson to Senator Rufus Pope, 23 December 1931
60 See Toronto *Star*, 3 January 1931.
61 External Affairs, Bennett to Stevens, 7 October 1931 and attached document
62 External Affairs, 'High Commissioner's Office: Staff,' nd
63 See *ibid.*, and also PRO, ADM.116/2717. Norman Hillmer brought this document to my attention.
64 Interview, Senator David Walker, 4 June 1970
65 BP, Vanier to Bennett, 15 December 1931
66 DO35/155/6094/12, Harding to Clark, 9 February 1931
67 *Ibid.*
68 DO35/155/6094/17, H. Batterbee to Harding, 28 July 1931: Maurice Hankey to Batterbee, 4 August; Hankey to Batterbee, 17 July; minute by Batterbee, 4 July; Ferguson to Thomas, 28 July
69 FP, Ferguson to Saunderson, 20 March 1931
70 See BP, Ferguson to Bennett, 31 August 1931, plus memorandum by Pacaud, nd.
71 External Affairs, Vanier to Skelton, 21 August 1931 (personal and official letters)
72 BP, 'Memorandum for the Prime Minister,' 4 September 1931. No signature but almost certainly by Skelton
73 *Ibid.*
74 BP, Bennett to Minister of Agriculture, 7 October 1931
75 L.B. Pearson papers, 'Canada House, Activities and Organization of the Political Section'
76 BP, Ferguson to Bennett, 23 February; W. Whitelaw to Ferguson, 20 February 1931
77 Aloysius Balawyder, *Canadian-Soviet Relations between the Wars* (Toronto 1972) 131-9
78 BP, Ferguson to Bennett, 23 February 1931
79 BP, Bennett to Ferguson, 11 March 1931
80 Stevens Papers, Stevens to Perley, 19 November 1931
81 See Drummond, 'Empire Trade and Russian Trade: Economic Diplomacy in the 1930's,' *Canadian Journal of Economics* (February 1972) 47.
82 DO35/196, Clark to Thomas, 29 May 1931
83 BP, Ferguson to Bennett, 4 March 1932
84 CAB23/66, 11 February 1931

85 BP, Ferguson to Bennett, 5 March 1932
86 Dafoe Papers, Dexter to Dafoe, 6 October 1931
87 Dafoe Papers, Stevenson to Dafoe, nd
88 BP, Ferguson to Bennett, 30 October and 4 November 1931
89 BP, Ferguson to Bennett, 11 November 1931
90 FP, Ferguson to Saunderson, 1 December; Ferguson to Rufus Pope, 23 December 1931
91 FP, Ferguson to Strachan Johnston, 18 December 1931
92 CAB23/69, 18 November 1931
93 BP, Chamberlain to Ferguson, 28 December 1931
94 BP, Ferguson to Bennett, 22 January 1932
95 External Affairs, Ferguson to Bennett, 25 January 1932
96 *Ibid.*
97 FP, Ferguson to Bennett, 3 March 1932
98 Keith Middlemas and John Barnes, *Baldwin* (London 1969) 671-2
99 FP, Ferguson to Bennett, 3 March 1932
100 See A.E. Morrison, *Bennett and the Trade Agreements* 114.
101 HP, Ferguson to Henry, 10 December 1931
102 External Affairs, Ferguson to Bennett, 25 January 1932
103 *Ibid.*
104 External Affairs, Ferguson to Bennett, 29 January 1932
105 FP, Bennett to Ferguson, 2 February 1932
106 BP, Ferguson to Bennett, 2 February 1932
107 CAB23/70, 3 February 1932
108 FP, Ferguson to Saunderson, 13 February 1932
109 Beaverbrook Papers, Beaverbrook to Bennett, 4 February 1932; FP, Smith to Ferguson, 16 February 1932
110 FP, Ferguson to Smith, 3 March 1932
111 The Senate of Canada, *Report and Proceedings of the Special Committee* (Ottawa 1932) xxviii
112 See *The Beauharnois Inquiry* (nd, Toronto *Telegram*).
113 HP, Ferguson to Henry, 10 December 1931; Murphy Papers, Haydon to Murphy, 24 April 1932
114 FP, Ferguson to Stevens, 5 March 1932
115 BP, Ferguson to Bennett, 13 May and reply, 28 June 1932
116 FP, Ferguson to Beaverbrook, 13 June 1932
117 CAB23/72, 27 August, 28 September 1932

CHAPTER 18: THE DREAM DENIED

1 See K.W. Taylor, 'The Effect of the Ottawa Agreements on Canadian Trade,' CIIA (Toronto 1936); J.F. Parkinson, *Memorandum on the Bases of Canadian Commercial Policy 1926-1938,* CIIA (1939) 223; Ian M.

Drummond, *British Economic Policy and the Empire, 1919-1939* (London 1927) 23, 34, and *Imperial Economic Policy 1917-1939* (London 1974); D.R. Annett, *British Preference in Canadian Commercial Policy* (Toronto 1948) 79.

2 FP, Bennett to Ferguson, 2 February 1932
3 FP, Ferguson to Magrath, 18 June 1934
4 FP, Ferguson to Saunderson, 11 November 1932
5 FP, Ferguson to Flavelle, 18 January 1933
6 FP, Ferguson to Saunderson, 11 December 1931
7 FP, Ferguson to Cody, 22 March 1933
8 York University Archives, W.A. Riddell Diaries, 15 March 1933
9 Riddell Diaries, 13 March 1933
10 BP, Skelton to Bennett, 21 February 1933
11 See BP, letters of 14, 15, 17 November 1932.
12 DO35/315/9503/83, 9 January 1934, Ministry of Agriculture official to W.B. Amery
13 BP, Bennett to Ferguson, 2 March 1934
14 BP, Ferguson to Thomas, 13 January 1933; DO35/212, Whiskard to Harding, 10 February 1933
15 BP, Ferguson to Bennett, 26 November 1932; DO35/296/X/J/1571, 'Russian Timber,' 14-pg memo by Sir Horace Wilson
16 BP, Ferguson to Bennett, 5 January 1933
17 DO35/296/X/J/1571, Wilson to Harding, 18 October 1933. For this incident see also DO35/296/9313c.
18 DO35/270/9259/66, Harding to Sir William Clark, 3 November 1933
19 BP, Vanier to Bennett, 5 January 1934
20 BP, Ferguson to Bennett, 10 October 1933
21 BP, Ferguson to Bennett, 9 May 1934
22 BP, Ferguson to Bennett, 10 January 1934; DO114/61/X/J/1559, prints, correspondence between Ferguson and Walter Runciman, President of the Board of Trade
23 FP, Ferguson to Saunderson, 16 January 1934
24 BP, Ferguson to Bennett, 2 February 1933
25 BP, Ferguson to Bennett, 6 March 1933
26 BP, Ferguson to Bennett, 30 and 31 March 1933; *CAR* (1933) 61
27 Andrew Boyle, *Montagu Norman* (New York 1967) 284
28 BP, Ferguson to Bennett, 19 May and reply 23 May 1933
29 BP, Bennett to Ferguson, 19 June 1934 and reply June 21; Ferguson to Bennett, 25 June and reply 27 June, conveying message to Norman
30 BP, F. Wallis to Bennett, 25 March 1933; FP, Cody to Ferguson, 22 January 1933; Ferguson to Saunderson, 16 February 1933; Ferguson to Cody, 22 March 1933; HP, Ferguson to Henry, 27 March 1933
31 FP, Ferguson to Henry, 24 October 1933

32 FP, Ferguson to Saunderson, 31 October 1933
33 FP, Ferguson to Saunderson, 16 January 1934; HP, Ferguson to Henry, 13
    April 1934; FP, Ferguson to Saunderson, 16 May 1934; HP, Carroll Hele to
    Henry, 28 May 1934
34 See HP, Henry to Ferguson, 21 June 1934, for the Premier's own comments
    on his defeat.
35 See DO35/212/8324/182 and DO114/50, prints; BP, Ferguson to Bennett,
    13 January 1933, enclosing documents
36 BP, Bennett to Ferguson, 1 May 1934
37 BP, Bennett to Ferguson, 29 January 1934; Ferguson to Skelton, 15 March;
    Stevens to Bennett, 16 April; Deputy Minister to Stevens, 16 April; Bennett
    to Stevens, 17 April
38 BP, Ferguson to Bennett, 23 January 1934 and replies, 23, 24 January.
    Secretary to Bennett, 17 August 1934. There were later difficulties. See
    Perley to Ferguson for Bennett, 3 May 1935.
39 Toronto *Globe*, undated clipping in Ferguson Papers, evidently January
    1934
40 G.H. Ferguson, 'Canada Must Arm,' *Maclean's Magazine*, 15 April 1937
41 See for example, FP, Ferguson to Bennett, 11 August 1933.
42 W.L. Grant Papers, Dafoe to Grant, 27 December 1930
43 Gregory Blaxland, *J.H. Thomas: A Life for Unity* (Tonbridge, Kent 1964)
    263
44 FP, Ferguson to A.H.U. Colquhoun, 6 November 1934
45 DO114/36, Prints, Thomas to Clark, 6 March 1931; Thomas Papers, Clark to
    Thomas, 11 March
46 DO35/119, O.G. Sargent, FO to Batterbee, DO, 16 April 1935; DO to Sir
    Francis Floud, high commissioner, Ottawa, 3 May 1935
47 DO35/156/6109, N.E. Archer to Batterbee 1936
48 BP, Ferguson to Bennett, 27 May 1935
49 *Maclean's*, 15 April 1937
50 See K.W. Taylor, 'The Effect of the Ottawa Agreements' (Toronto 1936).
51 FP, Ferguson to Magrath, 18 June 1934
52 BP, Ferguson as cited in Stevens to Bennett, 23 March 1933
53 BP, Ferguson to Bennett, 14 June 1934
54 *Mike: The Memoirs of the Rt Hon. Lester B. Pearson* (Toronto 1972) I, 92
55 See Robert Bothwell and John English, ' "Dirty Work at the Crossroads":
    New Perspectives on the Riddell Incident,' *CHAAR* (1972) 281.
56 DO35/155/6109A/184 and 186, report on meetings of 29 July, 21 August
    1935 by Paul Mason
57 Bothwell and English 268
58 *Ibid.*
59 KP, Ferguson to Bennett, 7 October 1935; James Eayrs, *In Defence of
    Canada: Appeasement and Rearmament* (Toronto 1965) 12

60 For this series of telegrams, see the account of Eayrs 12. See also DO114/ 67/6109A/445, Floud to Dominions Secretary, 8 October 1935.
61 Pearson, *Memoirs* I, 94
62 Riddell Papers, Ferguson to Bennett, 9 October 1935
63 Pearson, *Memoirs* I, 94-5
64 Pearson, *Memoirs* 95
65 Bothwell and English 270
66 *DCER,* V, 391, notes by Skelton, 10 October 1935
67 Pearson, *Memoirs* 94
68 Pearson Papers, Skelton to Pearson, 6 November 1935 and reply, 22 November
69 Bothwell and English 270-1
70 Pearson, *Memoirs* 95-6
71 Riddell Papers, Ferguson to Bennett, 10 October and reply, External to Ferguson, 10 October 1935
72 Pearson Papers, Riddell to Skelton, 7 December 1935
73 KP, Riddell, to Bennett, 11 October 1935
74 Bothwell and English 270
75 DO114/66, print, 9 October 1935
76 League of Nations, dispute between Ethiopia and Italy, *Official Journal,* Special Supplement, No. 145, 30
77 Riddell, *World Security by Conference* (Toronto 1947) 106
78 For a different viewpoint, see Eayrs, *op. cit.* 15, note. But in fact there was no contradiction, for Ferguson's statement made it clear that the form, as opposed to the fact, of sanctions did indeed remain to be determined.
79 Bothwell and English 272
80 Pearson Papers, Riddell to Skelton, 7 December 1935
81 League of Nations, *Official Journal,* Special Supplement 31
82 *Ibid.* 53-4.
83 Riddell, *World Security* 107-8
84 Mary McGeachy to Dafoe, as cited in Eayrs, *op. cit.* 15
85 *Ibid.*
86 *Ibid.*
87 Gwendolyn Carter, *The British Commonwealth and International Security* (Toronto 1947) 199
88 Eayrs, *op. cit.* 15
89 Bothwell and English 271
90 Pearson Papers, Skelton to Pearson, 6 November 1935
91 Riddell Diaries, 29 January 1936
92 Bothwell and English 265
93 *Ibid.*
94 Riddell Papers, Ferguson to Riddell 29 December 1933. For an indication of King's attitude, see Eayrs, *op. cit.* 37

95 Riddell, *World Security* 145

CONCLUSION

1 FP, Ferguson to Noxon, 22 October 1935; S.M. Eastman, *Canada at Geneva* (Toronto 1949) 96
2 FP, Bennett to Ferguson, 16 October 1935
3 FP, Ferguson to Noxon, 22 October 1935
4 FP, Ferguson to Beaverbrook, 2 November 1935
5 FP, Ferguson to C. Doherty (private secretary to Beaverbrook), 12 December 1934
6 FP, Ferguson to Colquhoun, 6 November 1934
7 FP, Ferguson to Sinclair, 23 November 1934
8 FP, Ferguson to Doherty, 12 December 1934
9 FP, Ferguson to Colquhoun, 25 January 1935
10 FP, Ferguson to W.H. Ireland, 14 August 1935; Riddell Diaries, 15 March 1933
11 FP, Ferguson to Beaverbrook, 2 November 1935
12 BP, Private Secretary to HM, The King to Bennett, 23 October 1935; Bennett to A.F. Redfern, Secretary to Governor-General, 20 November 1935
13 Ontario Archives, OHSS, oral history interview, George Doucett, August 1972
14 *Maclean's Magazine*, 15 April 1937
15 Empire Club, *Speeches, 1935-6* 71
16 Montreal *Gazette*, 28 November 1936; *Proceedings of the Canadian Club of Toronto, 1936-37* 62-9
17 OHSS, oral history interview, Elmer Bell, 1972
18 FP, Ferguson to Hele, 14 November 1934
19 Hepburn Papers, memorandum, 27 July 1934, 'M.F.H.,' attached to letter, 16 November 1934, Hepburn to Arthur Slaght; Hardy to Hepburn, 28 June 1934
20 OHSS, oral history interview, Elmer Bell, 1972
21 Borden Papers, Borden to Ferguson, 23 November 1935
22 Interview, H.R. Stevenson, 22 April 1970
23 Interview, Douglas Oliver, 23 February 1967
24 Interview, Miss Margaret Higginson (Mrs Ferguson's niece), 18 May 1967
25 Hepburn Papers, Ferguson to Hepburn, 13 December 1939
26 FP, Bennett to Ferguson, 30 May 1938
27 J.L. Granatstein, *The Politics of Survival* (Toronto 1967) 46
28 Toronto *Globe*, 9 December 1938
29 Interview, David Walker, 4 June 1970
30 *Ibid.*, 11 May 1970
31 OHSS, oral history interview, George Doucett, August 1972
32 *Ibid.*

33 This quotation, from the Underhill Papers at the PAC, Underhill to George Ferguson, 21 April 1939, appears in chapter 6 of an uncompleted PhD thesis on Underhill by Douglas Francis at York University. I am indebted to Mr Francis for letting me see his material.

34 U of T Archives, Cody Papers, Cody to L.R. Thomson, 15 January 1941

35 U of T Archives, Minutes, Board of Governors, 19, 27 December 1940, 23 January 1941. See also Underhill Papers, Underhill to H.G. Keenleyside, 7 January 1941, cited in the uncompleted thesis by Mr Francis.

36 See Douglas Francis, uncompleted thesis.

37 Interview, David Walker, 4 June 1970; Diary, David Walker, 5 October 1942

38 Warren Baldwin, quoted by Victor Lauriston in *Chatham Daily News*, 15 November 1957. Dr James Band brought this to my attention.

39 Interview, David Walker, 4 June 1970

Bibliography

This study was based primarily on manuscript sources, contemporary news-papers, and interviews. The press accounts which proved most valuable are cited in the notes, as are government documents, theses, and secondary sources. What follows is a listing of manuscript materials.

PUBLIC ARCHIVES OF ONTARIO
Belcher, A.E.; Bristol, Edmund; Church, T.L.; Cody, H.J.; Drury, E.C.; Ferguson, G.H.; Hearst, W.H.; Heenan, Peter; Henry, George S.; Hepburn, M.F.; Lucas, I.B.; Whitney, J.P.

Departmental records: attorney-general; provincial secretary; education; provincial treasurer

PUBLIC ARCHIVES OF CANADA
Bennett, R.B.; Borden, Sir Henry; Bourassa, Henri; Christie, Loring C.; Dafoe, J.W.; Daly, Harold; Dewart, Hartley; Dunn, Sir James; Foster, Sir George E.; Good, W.C.; Gouin, Sir Lomer; Grant, W.L.; Hanson, R.B.; Kemp, Sir Edward; King, W.L.M.; Lapointe, Ernest; Latchford, F.R.; Laurier, Sir Wilfrid; Maclean, W.F.; Magrath, Charles; Manion, R.J.; Meighen, Arthur; Morrison, J.J.; Murphy, Charles; Pearson, L.B.; Rowell, N.W.; Sifton, Sir Clifford; Sissons, C.B.; Stevens, H.H.; Vanier, Georges S. & Pauline; Willison, Sir John S.; Dept of External Affairs

PUBLIC ARCHIVES OF QUEBEC
Lemieux, François

HYDRO-ELECTRIC POWER COMMISSION OF ONTARIO
Beck, Sir Adam, General No. 7, 1914-23; Beck, Sir Adam, General, 1916-19; Beck, Sir Adam, 'Outside,' 1916-20; Beck, Sir Adam, Miscellaneous; Premier

of Ontario, General, 1915-30; Premier of Ontario, Special Files; Robinson, C.C., 1916-27

UNIVERSITY ARCHIVES
Queen's
Bruce, Herbert; Crerar, T.A.; Flavelle, J.W.; Gregory, W.D.; Lambert, Norman; Macdonnell, J.M.; Rogers, Norman

New Brunswick
Hazen, J.D.

Ottawa
Centre de Recherche en Civilisation Canadienne-Française; Papers of the French Canadian Educational Association of Ontario

St Paul's University
Belcourt, N.A.; Landry, P.

Toronto
Cassidy, Harry; Cody, H.J.; Falconer, Robert; Walker, Sir Edmund; Wrong, George M.

Board of Governors, letter-books (microfilm), 1940; correspondence between the Ontario Department of Education and the Roman Catholic authorities concerning the bilingual school issue

Victoria University (Toronto), United Church Archives
Chown, S.D.; Moore, T.A.; Warburton, G.A.; Records of the Ontario Plebiscite Committee, 1924

York
Riddell, W.A.

ARCHDIOCESAN AND DIOCESAN ARCHIVES
Kingston
Archbishop Gauthier; Archbishop O'Brien

London
Bishop Fallon

Ottawa
Miscellaneous

Toronto
Archbishop Neil McNeil

TORONTO PUBLIC LIBRARY
Johnson, Main

DRUG AND ALCOHOLIC ADDICTION RESEARCH FOUNDATION,
TORONTO
Dr John Linton Collection, Prohibition

PRIVATE COLLECTIONS
Casselman, W.H.; Ford, Arthur (I understand that these papers were subse-
    quently destroyed), Godfrey, Dr Forbes; Morrison, J.J.

PUBLIC RECORD OFFICE, LONDON, ENGLAND
Dominions Office; Foreign Office; Cabinet

BEAVERBROOK LIBRARY, LONDON, ENGLAND
Lord Beaverbrook

Index

United Church of Canada 169, 265-70, 381
United Farmers' Cooperative Company 91, 92
United Farmers of Ontario 87-144, 169, 194-5, 266-7, 362
United Kingdom 132, 362, 375, 377-80, 388-400, 402-6, 411-16, 431-2, 434
United States 83-4, 88, 175-83, 191-4, 198, 205, 208-11, 214, 217, 277, 280, 292, 296, 348, 352-4, 364, 383-4, 389, 397, 400-2, 415-16, 424, 438
United States Federal Trades Commission 348
University of Ottawa, teacher training school 285
University of Toronto 13-14, 32, 235-47 passim, 318, 327-31, 401, 409, 432, 438, 439
University of Western Ontario 239, 241-2, 244, 246, 331, 439
Unmarried Parents Act (1921) 216
Urwick, E.J. 327

Vanier, Georges P. 385-8, 406
Varsity, Toronto 13, 247

Waldron, Gordon 97, 119
Walker, David 274, 288, 435, 437, 439
Walker, Franklin 332
Wallace, Thomas 38
Wallis, Horace 313
War Time Election Act (1917) 86
Warburton, George 82, 162
Waugh, J. 76
Weichel, W.G. 164
Weir, Dr G.M. 234
Welland Canal, 177, 180, 298
Whig-Standard, Kingston 290

Whiskard, Sir Geoffrey 404
White, Aubrey 34, 67-8, 113, 209-10
White, John T. 299, 302
White, Peter 109
White, Senator Smeaton 282-3, 292
Whitney, Albert 25
Whitney, Sir James P. 19, 24, 26, 29-59 passim, 64-6, 89, 90, 117-29 passim, 148, 152, 158, 190-4, 216, 239, 259, 268, 271, 278, 312, 319, 325
Whitson, J.F. 70
Whitton, Charlotte 269
Wilkie (Liberal party member) 134
Willingdon, Lord, Governor General 378
Willison, Sir John 80, 105, 123, 137, 139, 144, 148, 231, 255
Willoughby, W.A. 31
Wilson, Sir Daniel 13
Wilson, Frank W. 138, 159, 164-5, 168
Wilson, Sir Horace 398, 404-6
Winnipeg 280, 292, 355, 372
Wood, Henry Wise 91
Workmen's Compensation Act (1914) 52, 94, 192, 206, 213, 216, 224
Workmen's Compensation Board 217
World, Toronto 26
World Economic Conference (1933) 413
World War I 65-6, 77, 83, 86, 216, 249, 327, 390, 438
World War II 156, 428
Wright, C.P. 353
Wright, D.M. 317

Young, McGregor 76, 77, 251
Youth Refuses to Retreat (movement) 274

Zavitz, Dr E.J. 68, 71, 213, 343